SAP PRESS e-books

Print or e-book, Kindle or iPad, workplace or airplane: Choose where and how to read your SAP PRESS books! You can now get all our titles as e-books, too:

▶ By download and online access
▶ For all popular devices
▶ And, of course, DRM-free

Convinced? Then go to **www.sap-press.com** and get your e-book today.

SAP® BW 7.4 — Practical Guide

SAP PRESS is a joint initiative of SAP and Rheinwerk Publishing. The know-how offered by SAP specialists combined with the expertise of Rheinwerk Publishing offers the reader expert books in the field. SAP PRESS features first-hand information and expert advice, and provides useful skills for professional decision-making.

SAP PRESS offers a variety of books on technical and business-related topics for the SAP user. For further information, please visit our website: *www.sap-press.com*.

Merz, Hügens, Blum
Implementing SAP BW on SAP HANA
2015, 470 pages, hardcover
ISBN 978-1-4932-1003-9

Joe Darlak, Jesper Christensen
SAP BW: Administration and Performance Optimization
2014, 652 pages, hardcover
ISBN 978-1-59229-853-2

Christian Ah-Soon, Peter Snowdon
Getting Started with SAP Lumira
2014, 540 pages, hardcover
ISBN 978-1-4932-1033-6

Xavier Hacking, Jeroen van der A
Getting Started with SAP BusinessObjects Design Studio
2013, 468 pages, hardcover
ISBN 978-1-59229-895-2

Amol Palekar, Bharat Patel, Shreekant Shiralkar

SAP® BW 7.4 — Practical Guide

Bonn • Boston

Editor Laura Korslund
Acquisitions Editor Kelly Grace Weaver
Copyeditor Julie McNamee
Cover Design Graham Geary
Photo Credit Shutterstock.com: 207999058/© Lim Yong Hian, 11232937/
　　　　© Daniel Padavona, 132989363/© isak55
Layout Design Vera Brauner
Production Graham Geary
Typesetting III-satz, Husby (Germany)
Printed and bound in the United States of America, on paper from sustainable sources

ISBN 978-1-4932-1191-3
© 2015 by Rheinwerk Publishing, Inc., Boston (MA)
3rd edition 2015

Library of Congress Cataloging-in-Publication Data
Palekar, Amol, 1979-
SAP BW 7.4 : practical guide / Amol Palekar, Bharat Patel, Shreekant Shiralkar. -- 3rd edition.
pages cm
Based on: SAP NetWeaver BW 7.3 : practical guide / Amol Palekar, Bharat Patel, and Shreekant Shiralkar. 2nd edition. 2013.
Includes index.
ISBN 978-1-4932-1191-3 (print : alk. paper) -- ISBN 1-4932-1191-9 (print : alk. paper) -- ISBN 978-1-4932-1192-0 (ebook) --
ISBN 978-1-4932-1193-7 (print and ebook : alk. paper) 1. SAP Business information warehouse 2. Data warehousing.
3. Business intelligence--Data processing. I. Patel, Bharat, 1967- II. Shiralkar, Shreekant. III. Palekar, Amol, 1979- SAP
NetWeaver BW7.3. IV. Title.
QA76.9.D37P35 2015
005.74'5--dc23
2015000994

Contents at a Glance

Dear Reader,

As John C. Maxwell said, "Change is inevitable. Growth is optional." I'm sure that this quote reads only too true for you—any technology blog, article, or book (if not your evolving job requirements) constantly reminds you that change occurs faster than ever in this day and age. How do you keep up with all of these changes and grow your skill set with them, as life and career make never-ending demands on your time?

Expert authors Amol Palekar, Bharat Patel, and Shreekant Shiralkar make keeping up and staying ahead of the curve less complicated with this updated third edition. Whether you're new to SAP BW or have prior experience, you're sure to find helpful information that will make your job easier. These dedicated authors have poured their skills into constructing detailed steps and guiding screenshots for a truly practical experience with SAP BW. Featuring SAP BW information that will cement your knowledge and highlight new additions to the product and evolving topics, I'm confident that this book has everything you need.

What did you think about the third edition of *SAP BW 7.4—Practical Guide*? Your comments and suggestions are the most useful tools to help us make our books the best they can be. We encourage you to visit our website at *www.sap-press.com* and share your feedback.

Thank you for purchasing a book from SAP PRESS!

Laura Korslund
Editor, SAP PRESS

Rheinwerk Publishing
Boston, MA

laurak@rheinwerk-publishing.com
www.sap-press.com

Contents

5   InfoCubes 151

8 Data Extraction from Source Systems 393

9   Creating Queries Using BEx Query Designer 427

13   Reporting with the SAP BusinessObjects BI Suite 703

14   Administration and Monitoring 725

Acknowledgments

We would like to take this opportunity to acknowledge those who have significantly influenced us and the contents of this book.

We were privileged to be supported by the team at Rheinwerk Publishing, Inc., especially Laura Korslund as our editor, who patiently and—at appropriate times—forcefully ensured this book's timely journey, while also playing a crucial role in developing and structuring the contents. We'd also like to thank Graham Geary, our production editor, whose timely input helped us meet the publication schedule without a glitch.

Amol Palekar would like to thank his wife, Simple, and his son, Abir, who patiently gave up their time with him and yet remained understanding and supportive throughout this endeavor. He would also like to express his gratitude to his parents Dr. Purushottam P. Palekar and Indira P. Palekar for believing in him all these years. Amol would like to dedicate this book to his teachers and friends from Jawahar Navodaya Vidyalaya (Amravati), who influenced his character and his journey thus far, in so many ways.

Bharat Patel would like to thank his wife, Swati, and his son, Akshay, for doing without him almost without complaint for so many weekends and holidays and nevertheless actively supporting him in this book project. He also sincerely thanks his colleagues and senior management, particularly Mr. K. B. Narayanan, Mr. J. R. Akut, and Mr. M. S. Ramakrishnan of Bharat Petroleum Corporation Ltd. for motivating and supporting him in this project. He is also thankful to young BW professional Mr. Ramanender Singh of Bharat Petroleum Corporation Ltd, for help with the development of various images.

Shreekant Shiralkar expresses his gratitude to his sisters Asha A. Deshmukh and Suhasini D. Parulkar, and his brothers Dr. Mangesh and (late) Makarand W. Shiralkar, who supported and more than made up for lost parents, through his growing-up phase of life.

Introduction

Information technology has transformed the way business is managed today, and one of the most dramatic impacts of this transformation is the pace of change. Companies that possess a deep understanding of their business and the forces impacting it can better navigate the weather of this rapid change with ease and predictability. Although not all aspects of change can be intercepted and interpreted in the form of trends or projections, it is possible to analyze and manage some of them. By using the science of statistics, supported by modern *business intelligence* (BI) solutions, it becomes possible to analyze consumer spending behavior, key economic indicators, and much more. Analysts say that BI solutions are the most essential tools for managing businesses today.

SAP is the most significant and largest solution in enterprise resource planning (ERP), and one of its BI solutions is *SAP Business Warehouse (BW)*, currently in release 7.4. In this book, our goal is to facilitate your understanding of SAP BW. Because we believe that learning is greatly enhanced by applying knowledge to solve real-world problems, we've crafted the contents of this book as a testimony to that philosophy. In these pages, you'll find detailed explanations of SAP BW functionalities and features, discussions of their relevance and application to typical business requirements, and step-by-step instructions and detailed screenshots that walk you through it all. We've also provided some data files based on the example scenario discussed throughout the book, which are downloadable from the book's website at *www.sap-press.com/3733*. We urge you to re-create the sales analysis scenario presented in the book in your own system and use it to develop basic understanding first, and then expertise.

The purpose of this book is to explain SAP BW in a way that allows you to easily understand and use the system. Our explanations avoid overly technical details but still allow you to take full advantage of SAP BW as an effective BI solution.

Each chapter begins with a chapter introduction that establishes an overall context for the core content and outlines the scope of the subject covered in the chapter. We've structured the topics within chapters in a sequence that makes it easy for you to understand, moving from broad introductions to specific information.

Each of the individual topics within a section is explained using illustrations, screen captures, examples, and code.

- **Chapter 1** outlines the book's case study, based on a typical company (ABCD Corp.), which is used throughout the text as a way to explain the technical aspects of SAP BW as they relate to business requirements and sales analysis. We describe ABCD Corp.'s entities and business processes (specifically the sales and billing process), as well as what ABCD Corp. requires from a BI solution.

- **Chapter 2** provides an overview of SAP BW as a BI solution and includes a discussion of its benefits, technical architecture, and implementation options. The chapter introduces the system by exploring actual navigation through screens.

- **Chapter 3** engages you in step-by-step activities that will help you understand the business requirements mentioned in the first chapter. We explain the concept of the InfoObject, the basic building block of SAP BW, and how knowledge of InfoObjects is essential to building a strong and reliable solution that will be scalable and relevant for a long time.

- **Chapter 4**, **Chapter 5**, and **Chapter 6** cover the major building blocks of SAP BW as a data warehousing solution, discussing DataStore Objects (DSOs), InfoCubes, and other types of InfoProviders. We also introduce the most important aspects of InfoSet objects, with a brief mention of VirtualProviders, semantically partitioned object (SPOs), HybridProviders, and CompositeProviders. Chapter 6 also covers newly introduced InfoProviders such as the open ODS view (OOV).

- **Chapters 7** and **Chapter 8** cover extraction, transformation, and loading (ETL) concepts and their design in SAP BW. Chapter 7 explains the entire ETL process, beginning with data acquisition from source systems to its transformation to the desired format, and concluding with the process of loading to data targets. Chapter 8 explains the detailed process of data extraction from SAP source systems, the activation of SAP BW Business Content, and the extraction of data from an SAP system using a generic extractor. It also briefly covers data extraction from a non-SAP source system and the newly introduced methods using Operational Data Provisioning/Operational Delta Queue ODP/ODQ and SAP LT Replication Server (SLT).

- **Chapter 9** explains the creation of queries using BEx Query Designer, and introduces the various features and functionalities offered by SAP BW to build queries and present data for analysis.

- **Chapter 10** introduces you to the reporting and analysis tools in SAP BW. We briefly introduce the SAP Business Explorer (BEx) toolset, and then offer detailed explanations of BEx Analyzer and BEx Web Analyzer. We also explain some important features that enable self-service reporting: BW Workspaces and CompositeProviders.

- **Chapter 11** covers BEx Web Application Designer, which is used to build custom web applications in SAP BW. We describe a wide spectrum of ways to perform reporting and analysis in Excel, as well as in a web/portal environment.

- **Chapter 12** teaches you how to build planning applications in SAP BW, including a discussion of the SAP BW Integrated Planning component. We discuss this topic in the context of the planning requirements for ABCD Corp.

- **Chapter 13** provides a primer on SAP BusinessObjects BI and SAP BW integration. We explain the different SAP BusinessObjects BI reporting tools and their positioning based on various reporting needs.

- **Chapter 14** explains the administration and maintenance aspects of SAP BW, including the newly introduced functionality of Early Unload Concept for SAP BW on SAP HANA. In this chapter, we move from step-by-step explanations to a do-it-yourself approach.

- **Chapter 15** introduces you to the advanced features of SAP BW. The features we explain in this chapter are meant to get you started with an advanced understanding of SAP BW as a data warehousing, reporting, and analysis tool. This chapter also includes the newly introduced SAP HANA analysis process (HAP).

As we've mentioned, in addition to what we've presented in this text, please visit the book's website at *www.sap-press.com/3733* for ancillary material related to ABCD Corp.

We have years of experience with SAP's BI solutions as practitioners, trainers, and authors. Because BI is an ever-changing target, SAP continues to capitalize on its innovations in this area, for example, with SAP HANA and in-memory technology. As such, it's necessary for all practitioners to commit to continuous education on the topic of SAP and BI. This book is our contribution to this commitment. Our experience has helped us to develop a deep understanding of SAP BW, its components, and the aspects of its implementation, and we're thrilled to be able to share this knowledge with you. We sincerely hope that you enjoy reading this book as much as we've enjoyed writing it, and that you find it to be the most simple and effective way of learning SAP BW.

Amol Palekar
Bharat Patel
Shreekant W. Shiralkar

Clear and comprehensive business requirements lead to a better designed business intelligence solution. In this chapter, we present a basic sales process scenario for an example company, which will then be referred to in subsequent chapters.

1   The Business Scenario: ABCD Corp.

A good *business intelligence (BI)* solution improves the efficiency and transparency of operations, offers better control over the outcomes of decisions, and allows better exploration of all the options that are at a company's disposal. Business managers always prefer making informed decisions, which is a process that *BI* solutions enable. Further, it can also assist in the automation of managerial processes.

Sales analytics is the process of making decisions for sales growth based on quantitative information, which forms one of the most common requirements for BI solutions across different companies worldwide. For this reason, we've chosen to build a simple sales analytics example for a typical company, called ABCD Corp. ABCD Corp. is a company located in North America with headquarters in New York City. It sells different electronics and electrical appliances to customers spread all over the world (Figure 1.1).

In the process of building sales analytics for ABCD Corp., we explain all aspects of designing a BI solution based on SAP Business Warehouse (SAP BW) 7.4. This chapter first describes ABCD Corp. and then describes the entities involved in the typical selling processes. Each entity and the process will be referred to throughout the book as we build different components of an analytics solution using SAP BW 7.4.

> **Note**
>
> Data files for the ABCD Corp. example scenario are available on the book's website at *www.sap-press.com/3733*.

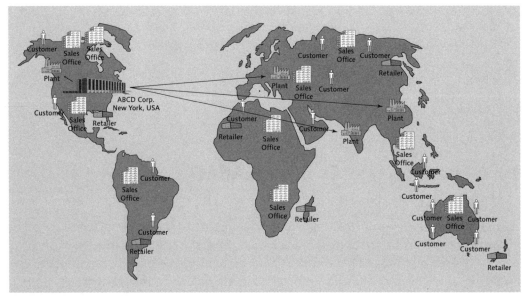

Figure 1.1 Overview of ABCD Corp.

1.1 Marketing Network

ABCD Corp. has more than 90 worldwide customers, which are either retail chains or independent stores (see Table A.3 in Appendix A). The company has three main markets—North America, Europe, and Asia-Pacific—and each market has one or more regional marketing offices. Within the United States, the customers are grouped by states; outside the United States, they are grouped under their respective country or city (e.g., London). ABCD Corp. has sales offices in most cities where customers are located, and the sales offices report to their corresponding regional marketing office. Figure 1.2 shows a hierarchy of the marketing network.

Each sales office has one or more salespeople, and a specific salesperson services each customer to maintain regular contact with his customers mainly for the purpose of taking *sales orders* from them. Whenever an order is placed, a *sales transaction* is created in the SAP system located at the sales office. The salesperson then contacts his sales office with the details of the order. If the regular sales office is closed, the salesman contacts a sales office in a nearby country to ensure on-time delivery to the customer. Salespeople are rotated from customer to customer after a certain period of time or after the achievement of set target sales.

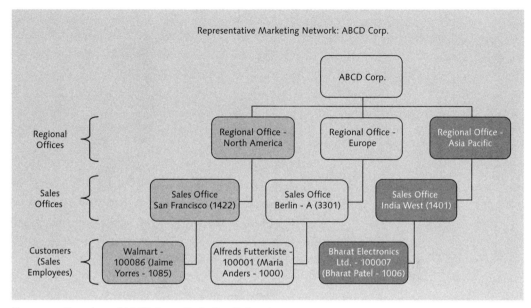

Figure 1.2 Overview of ABCD Corp. Marketing Network

ABCD Corp. has more than 30 products, which are logically grouped into three portfolios: consumer electronics, domestic appliances, and consumer lifestyle (see Table A.5 in Appendix A). The company has four manufacturing plants to supply these products (see Table A.2).

1.2   The Sales and Billing Process

ABCD Corp. sells its products through two different *selling channels*: either directly or through the Internet. Product sales happen via a *billing document*; a typical flow of information generated by the creation of a billing document is illustrated in Figure 1.3.

Each billing document is represented by a unique number. Within the billing document, one or more products is listed, each of which is identified with an *item number*. In addition to the item numbers, the billing document also lists the quantity sold and a selling price for each product. In most cases, ABCD Corp. receives payment for products sold when they are delivered to the customer; in some cases, larger customers are permitted to make delayed payments.

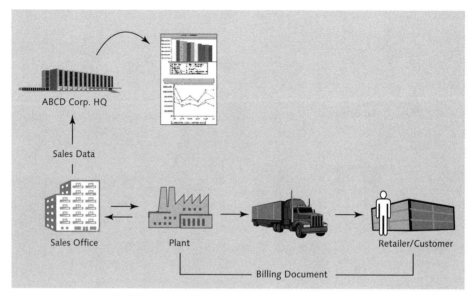

Figure 1.3 Overview of ABCD Corp. Selling Process

The *terms of payment* and *type of billing document* for transactions differ, based on the method by which the transaction has taken place. For example, a specific type of billing document is generated if the customer makes the payment using a credit card or any other mode of delayed payment, and a different type of billing document is generated for immediate payments (see Table A.9 in Appendix A).

If the product is sold to a customer outside the United States, the corresponding billing document is identified as an export; within the United States, it's treated as a domestic sale (see Table A.10).

Whenever the value of a record in the billing document is more than $10,000, the transaction is identified as a *high-value transaction,* and the billing document is marked with an indicator to differentiate it from those with lower transaction values.

Similarly, if the cost of any item in the bill is listed without a value (i.e., is a free item), the system is designed to identify such a record separately (see Table A.11 in Appendix A). Usually, most items require payment; however, for special occasions (the holiday season, clearing sales, etc.), some low-value products (e.g., cords or batteries) are provided free with a bigger purchase. Such items are listed with an item category of DC, whereas normal items are identified with an item category of NOR. The cost of items under item category DC is recorded on the billing document, but taxes or other costs aren't recorded.

Figure 1.4 shows a sample billing document for ABCD Corp.

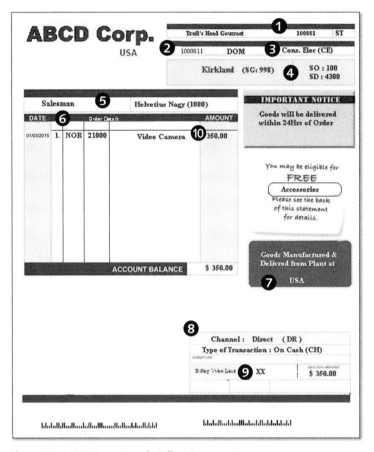

Figure 1.4 ABCD Corp. Sample Billing Document

The sample billing document shows how the business entities and processes are presented as shown in Figure 1.4 and listed here:

❶ Customer name, customer code, and customer group

❷ Billing document number and type of billing transaction

❸ Product group

❹ Sales office, sales district, and sales group that services the customer

❺ Name and code of the salesperson responsible for a specific sale

❻ Product, product code, type of item, and product description

❼ Plant that manufactured and dispatched the product

❽ Types of transaction and selling channel

❾ Types of billing value and gross billing amount

❿ Quantity, cost, and net value in USD

Returns
For product returns, a credit is issued to the customer. Each item in the return billing document has detailed information about the transaction, such as the quantity, cost, net value, and so on.

1.3 Business Intelligence Requirements

ABCD Corp. wants to have a global BI solution for sales analysis that accesses business transaction data from SAP (as the main data source) and Excel sheets, or *flat files* (as the secondary data source). The goal is to build a robust and scalable BI solution based on SAP BW that has reporting capabilities with the following guiding principles:

► Ease the management of the company at the corporate and local level through improved control and visibility.

► Move to a more digitalized company to support growth and enable quicker integration of new acquisitions.

► Increase return on investments by optimizing the cost and time spent on the design, deployment, and maintenance of the BI solution. Use SAP BW Business Content (also known as BI Content), which addresses a significant number of sales analysis requirements.

ABCD Corp. wants to analyze its sales process and find answers to the following types of questions:

► What products are selling in different sales organizations?

► Which product lines or specific products are selling highest or lowest?

► How does ABCD Corp.'s current year compare to the previous year?

► What are the top 10 best-selling products?

The *analysts* of ABCD Corp. require the solution to allow them to easily create their own reports when existing reports don't meet their reporting needs. The *auditors* of ABCD Corp. require the solution to provide traceability to specific billing documents for a customer when the need arises to analyze instances of variances; additionally, this investigation at the sales document level must be addressed in SAP BW, instead of in the transactional system. The *IT team* at ABCD Corp. requires the solution to be automated for most processes, including email alerts of successes or failures of systemic processes. They also require that the existing SAP ERP system work at optimal efficiency by removing old data related to business-critical transactions from the Online Transaction Processing (OLTP) system. The *head of planning* at ABCD Corp. requires the BI solution to compare actual and planned sales to ascertain and address the causes of variances or to correct plan figures.

In this book, the concept, design, and development of different SAP BW components are explained by using each of these requirements as examples.

1.4   The Business Planning Scenario

Within ABCD Corp., *sales planning* is an annual cycle for all three sales organizations: 1000 (APAC), 2000 (Europe), and 3000 (North America). Each sales organization projects sales figures according to three different divisions or product ranges: consumer electronics (CE), daily appliances (DA), and consumer lifestyle appliances (CL). This is a high-level plan for the organization, and high-level values for each of the product ranges are transferred to different products belonging to these product ranges.

Each sales organization has a product range manager who is responsible for planning the sales of each product under his assigned product range. The plan for a year (January to December) is divided into quarters; thus, there are four planning periods: Quarter 1 (Q1), Quarter 2 (Q2), Quarter 3 (Q3), and Quarter 4 (Q4). Figure 1.5 is a graphical representation of this scenario.

This business scenario description should provide you with an understanding of ABCD Corp. and its sales process. In Appendix A, we provide additional information in the form of tables, which have more details about the business scenario. These tables also include the specific SAP codes used to identify each element.

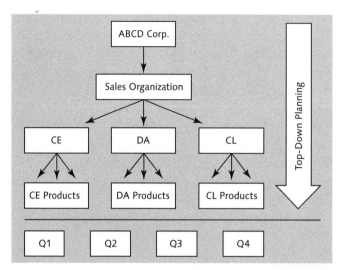

Figure 1.5 Overview of ABCD Corp. Sales Planning Process

1.5 Summary

In this chapter, we explained a very basic business scenario for a typical company. We also explained the BI needs for this company, specifically those related to analyzing its sales process. While creating the scenario, we've addressed some aspects with more detail than others; those explained in detail relate to the realization of the technical requirements we discussed in Section 1.3 and are dealt with in subsequent chapters of this book. In the next chapter, we provide a brief overview of SAP BW.

This chapter describes the fundamental benefits of SAP BW as a business intelligence solution, unique aspects of its technical architecture, and different implementation options.

2 Overview of SAP Business Warehouse

Companies employ BI solutions to have visibility and control across their entities, functions, and business processes. This chapter discusses the evolution of SAP Business Warehouse (SAP BW) and its architectural layers, and then explains the basics of navigation within screens. More specifically, it covers the Data Warehousing Workbench functions, activation of Business Content, and the implementation and architecture options of SAP BW. In its concluding section, the chapter lists additional resources for SAP BW.

2.1 Evolution of SAP BW

Up to 1997, SAP had maintained and developed its reporting and analysis offerings within the core SAP ERP solution, which included components such as Logistics Information System (LIS), Executive Information System (EIS), and Report Painter. In 1998, SAP launched the first version of the product focused specifically on data warehousing and reporting, Business Warehouse Information System. Although it experienced several name changes along the way, it's now called SAP BW. Figure 2.1 shows the evolution of SAP BW.

A variety of features and capabilities have been added to SAP BW since it was first launched; for example, it was integrated with SAP BusinessObjects, providing additional options of information delivery, and now it's available on SAP HANA. In general, business analytics solutions from SAP are on course to deliver deeper insights and real-time information. What this ultimately means is that these solutions will be applicable regardless of the DataSource a company is accessing (ERP data, data from social networking sites, etc.), the type of report that needs to be created (e.g., actual numbers, budget numbers, trends, or predictive analysis), and the device being used (e.g., laptops or mobile devices). This vision statement is predicated on delivering better integration across the business analytics portfolio, which includes data warehousing (DW), enterprise information management (EIM), business intelligence (BI), enterprise performance management (EPM), governance, risk, and compliance (GRC), and mobile clients that make content more universally accessible and customizable.

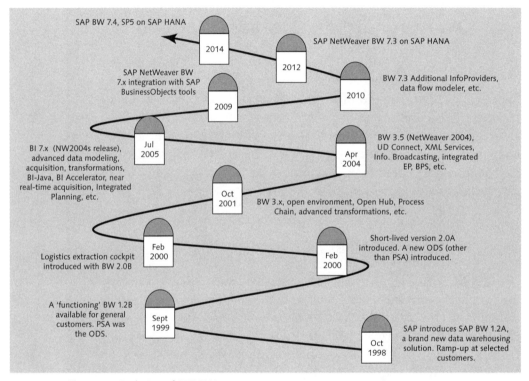

Figure 2.1 Evolution of SAP BW

Also, with the advent of SAP HANA, SAP BW can be used as a data warehousing solution with SAP HANA as the in-memory database. By moving information from multiple disparate sources into SAP HANA, companies are experiencing a dramatic improvement in their ability to view and explore information, enabling them to make faster decisions and enjoy a more efficient organization. Eventually, every part of the SAP business analytics portfolio will leverage and run on top of SAP HANA; business analytics and in-memory will be inseparable topics. The overall positioning of SAP BW powered by SAP HANA is illustrated in Figure 2.2.

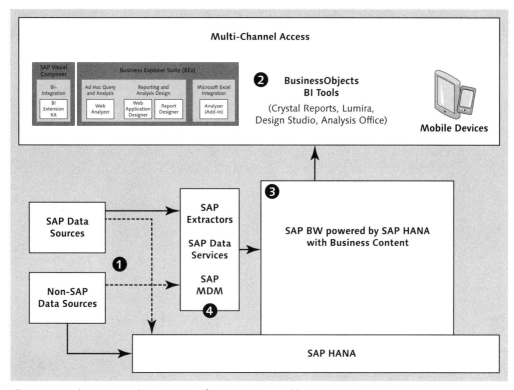

Figure 2.2 Architecture and Positioning of SAP BW Powered by SAP HANA

While the extraction and data acquisition interface remains tightly integrated (❶ and ❹ of Figure 2.2), reporting is more flexible and can also be performed directly on the data models from SAP HANA's database ❷.

SAP HANA, being an in-memory database, allows for enterprise data warehouse (EDW) data to be stored in-memory, making additional performance-enhancing components such as SAP BW Accelerator (BWA) unnecessary. SAP has also delivered some data models optimized for SAP HANA as a part of standard Business Content ❸.

As a portfolio of products, SAP BW is meant to provide a closed loop and tighter integration among strategy, execution, and the ability to respond to results in real time; it's a leading BI solution that provides data warehousing capabilities on a comprehensive platform. Combining a scalable and layered architecture with a rich set of predefined business content, SAP BW is one of the best-of-breed BI solutions and provides the following:

- Tightly integrated and reliable data acquisition from all applications and business processes in the SAP Business Suite, including the ability to acquire data from heterogeneous sources (❶ of Figure 2.2).

- A strong Online Analytical Processing (OLAP) capability, essential for a robust foundation for computing business data across dimensions and hierarchies. This also provides a strong framework for designing planning applications that are tightly integrated with the enterprise reporting.

- Business-driven models that help in rapid implementation through SAP Best Practices and rich predefined business content across most industry and business processes ❸.

- State-of-the-art lifecycle management functionality at three levels ❹:
  - System lifecycle management
  - Metadata lifecycle management
  - Information lifecycle management

- Advanced tools and functionalities for optimized operations of administration and maintenance tasks; active push of critical events and actionable recommendations for recovery.

SAP Business Content

With a view to accelerate solution deployment and to offer SAP Best Practices on industry-specific analytic scenarios, SAP delivers preconfigured end-to-end analytic solutions. All of the underlying components and objects necessary for preconfigured scenarios are also delivered as a collection. This collection of all of the preconfigured scenarios based on SAP Best Practices and their components is provided as part of SAP Business Content.

The advantages of SAP BW have led more and more customers to design their corporate data warehousing strategy using the product, citing the end-to-end conception of SAP BW. In comparison to fragmented technologies, the integrated metadata concept spanning from data integration through to analysis leads to lower total costs for most projects.

The following are some of the high-end and unique tools and functionalities that SAP BW offers:

- User-friendly modeling and development interfaces
- Tools for efficient maintenance of the solution, including process chains, re-modeling, Administration Cockpit, and so on

- Powerful ad hoc analysis tools, such as BEx Web Analyzer
- SAP BW Integrated Planning, which assists with a closed-loop planning process
- The ability to perform reporting and analysis from a portal as well as from an Excel interface
- Integration with SAP BusinessObjects tools

Now that you have an understanding of how SAP BW has evolved to provide more and better functionality over the years, let's get into the details of SAP BW architecture, navigation, and functionality.

2.2   SAP BW Layers

SAP BW has different layers that are responsible for reliable data acquisition and information processing, along with robust analytical capabilities (see Figure 2.3).

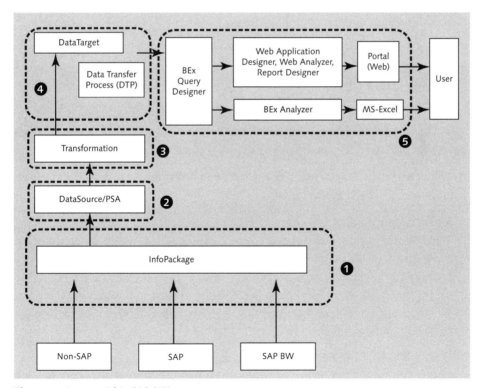

Figure 2.3 Layers within SAP BW

Based on the functions and applications in the solution, the different layers in SAP BW are listed here:

- Extraction layer
- Staging layer
- Transformation layer
- Loading layer
- Reporting and analysis layer
- Planning and advanced analytics layer

These layers are discussed next.

2.2.1 Extraction Layer

The extraction layer (❶ of Figure 2.3) is related to the *extraction process*, which is the collection of data from source systems. It aims to guarantee the integrity of data while eliminating reporting burdens on the source systems.

When data is being extracted into the data warehouse by actions triggered on the data warehouse, it's called *pull mode*; when data is being exported by the source system based on a trigger outside of the data warehouse, it's called *push mode*.

Data is acquired from SAP BW using pull mode, through objects called *InfoPackages*. Parameters for data acquisition can be set in the InfoPackage. The extraction process is discussed in more detail in Chapter 7 and Chapter 8.

As previously mentioned, SAP BW is capable of acquiring data from a wide spectrum of sources, such as the following:

- **Extraction from SAP systems**
  SAP BW offers predefined, customizable extractors for application data from the entire SAP Business Suite; you can also design extractors for customized SAP applications. Most extractors for SAP applications are delta-enabled, which means that these extractors have the capability to extract new and changed data sets since the last extraction from the source system (instead of extracting the entire set of data in every extraction).

- **Direct extraction from databases**
  These extractions are based on table or view definitions using the Database (DB) Connect and Universal Data (UD) Connect extraction interfaces:

- DB Connect permits the extraction from and direct access to data lying in tables or views of database management systems. This feature is available only for some specific databases.

- UD Connect permits the extraction from and direct access to both relational and multidimensional data.

- **ODP source systems**
  The Operational Data Provisioning (ODP) data replication interface provides transfer data from specific SAP repositories (especially from SAP HANA and SAP Business ByDesign) to SAP BW.

- **ODS views and SAP HANA SDA (SDA)**
  Open Operational DataStore (ODS) views] provide a flexible integration to non-SAP DataSources into SAP BW and enables access to external data from supported databases, such as SAP Sybase ASE, SAP Sybase IQ, Intel Distribution for Apache Hadoop, Teradata, and SAP HANA via Smart Data Access (SDA).

- **SAP Data Services**
  With the release of SAP BW 7.3, SAP Data Services was made available as a new source system: Data Services. This source system type provides access to SAP Data Services datastores and data flows. With this, the extraction, transformation, and loading (ETL) capabilities of SAP Data Services can be seamlessly integrated with SAP BW.

- **Flat file interface**
  This interface enables extraction from flat files in ASCII and CSV format.

- **Staging Business Application Programming Interfaces (BAPIs)**
  Staging BAPIs are open interfaces from which third-party tools can extract data from older systems. The data transfer can be triggered by a request from the SAP BW system or by a third-party tool.

- **Web Services**
  These services allow you to push data to the SAP BW system with external control.

2.2.2 Staging Layer

Extracted data is received and temporarily stored in the *staging layer* of SAP BW (❷ of Figure 2.3). The data staging layer primarily serves the following purposes:

▸ Stores source data from different operational sources. All needed transformations can then occur without interfering with the operations in the source systems.

▸ Preprocesses data for cleansing before calculation and/or aggregation based on business requirements.

This layer is mostly represented by the *Persistent Staging Area (PSA)*, where data is stored in SAP BW after it's extracted. The technical structure of a PSA depends on the structure of the DataSource. More details about PSA and staging are discussed in Chapter 7.

2.2.3 Transformation Layer

The transformation layer of SAP BW (❸ of Figure 2.3) facilitates the consolidation, cleaning, and integration of data to synchronize it technically and semantically. It converts data from the source data format into the desired destination data format. Data transformation can involve data mapping, the application of a custom transformation program, and formulas. We cover transformation in detail in Chapter 7.

2.2.4 Loading Layer

The process of adding transformed data to data targets is called the *loading process* (❹ of Figure 2.3). A data transfer process (DTP) transforms the data based on the parameters defined between the DataSource and the data target. For more details on DTPs and loading, see Chapter 7.

2.2.5 Reporting and Analysis Layer

The *reporting and analysis layer* (❺ of Figure 2.3) is where data is presented in different forms, such as reports and dashboards (Figure 2.4). This layer allows you to perform analysis on the data stored in SAP BW.

Various components that represent the reporting and analysis layer in SAP BW are grouped together as SAP Business Explorer (BEx) components. The reporting and analysis layer is discussed in more detail in Chapter 9 and Chapter 10.

Figure 2.4 Reporting and Analysis in SAP BW

2.2.6 Planning and Advanced Analytics Layer

The planning and advanced analytics layer consists of two different solutions that are integrated in SAP BW to perform planning activities and advanced analysis (see Figure 2.5):

❶ **Integrated Planning**

This component allows you to create planning applications that are integrated with reporting and analysis functions. The detail modeling and planning methods are designed to be multidimensional, so they are also very flexible. This topic is discussed in more detail in Chapter 12.

❷ **Analysis Process Designer (APD)**

This component allows you to perform advanced analysis, such as data mining.

Data Mining

Data mining is the process of automatically determining significant patterns and hidden associations in large amounts of data.

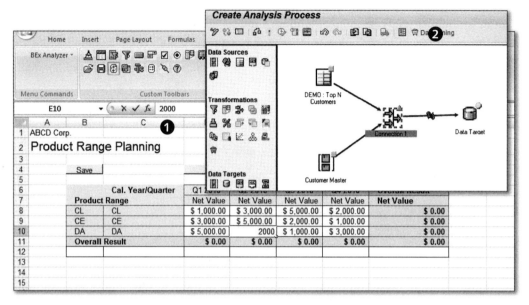

Figure 2.5 Planning and Advanced Analytics in SAP BW

APD offers the following data mining capabilities:

▶ **Decision trees**
Decision trees display data using (noncontinuous) category quantities. The display rules are determined in training using those sections of historic data where the assignment to categories is already known.

▶ **Clustering**
Clustering is used to split data into homogeneous groups. The model looks for a global structure for the data, with the aim of partitioning the data into clusters.

▶ **Association analysis**
Association analysis is the search for associations among objects with comparable information content. Statements are formulated about partial structures in the data, and they take the form of rules. In contrast to decision tree classification, clustering and association analysis determine the models using data itself. One of the uses of association analysis is to identify cross-selling opportunities.

▶ **Scoring and weighted score tables**
In scoring, data is displayed using continuous quantities, which allow you to split the data into classes (if needed). The scoring function can either be specified using weighted score tables or determined by using historic data.

▸ **ABC classification**
ABC classification displays data grouped into classes (A, B, C, etc.) using thresholds and classification rules. The classified results are displayed in the form of an ABC chart or list.

2.3 Basic Navigation

In this section, we explain how to navigate within SAP BW, including logging on to the system, screen elements, and basic navigation functions in the Data Warehousing Workbench. We also introduce some specific terms used in subsequent chapters of the book.

2.3.1 Logging On to SAP BW

To log on to an SAP BW system, you must have a valid user ID and password, along with the appropriate SAP GUI (graphical user interface) version loaded on your PC. The illustrations used in this book are based on SAP GUI for Windows. Follow these steps to log on to SAP BW.

1. From the Windows START menu, follow the path PROGRAMS • SAP FRONT END • SAP LOGON. You see the SAP logon pad, as shown in Figure 2.6.

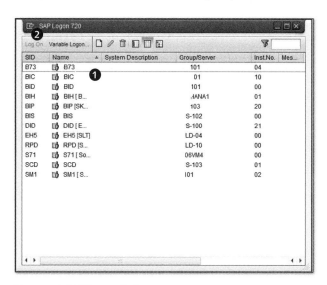

Figure 2.6 SAP Logon Pad

2. The SAP logon pad displays the SAP systems configured for access on your Windows system; select the SAP BW system you want to access (❶ of Figure 2.6).

3. Click on the Log On button ❷, and you'll get the SAP Logon screen, as shown in Figure 2.7.

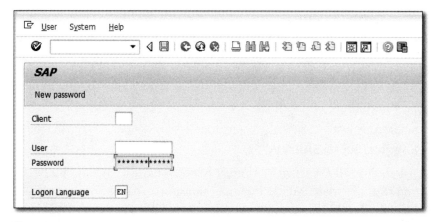

Figure 2.7 SAP Logon Screen

4. Enter the values for the Client field, User ID, Password, and Logon Language. All of these values are required and should be available from the administrator of your SAP BW system. Press Enter, or click on the Continue icon to log on. A successful logon brings you to Figure 2.8, shown in the next section.

Always log off when you've completed your work. To log off, follow the menu path System • Log off. You can also use Transaction /NEX.

2.3.2 Screen Elements

The initial screen displayed after logon is known as the SAP Easy Access screen (though this default screen can be changed and customized).

The SAP Easy Access screen can contain the following simple screen elements (see Figure 2.8):

❶ **Command field**
You can start applications directly by entering the specific transaction code in the Command field. Type the code, and press Enter.

❷ **Menu bar**

Different menu functions are available in the menu bar of the SAP screen. The menus shown can change depending on the application you're using. These menus may also contain cascading menus.

❸ **Standard toolbar**

The standard toolbar buttons are shown on every SAP screen. Not all of the buttons shown on a standard toolbar are available at all times; depending on the context, the button may be deactivated.

❹ **Title bar (dynamic menu bar)**

The title bar displays the function you're currently using.

❺ **Application toolbar**

The application toolbar shows the function buttons available in the current application.

Figure 2.8 SAP Easy Access Screen

❻ Status bar

The status bar provides general information on the SAP system and transaction or task you're working on. The left side of the bar contains warnings and errors; the right side contains status information. The status information on the status bar can be hidden or displayed using the COLLAPSE/EXPAND icon.

2.3.3   The Modeling View in the Database Warehousing Workbench

The Data Warehousing Workbench is the central tool for developers and administrators (Figure 2.9). You can create, maintain, monitor, and administer SAP BW objects using the DATA WAREHOUSING WORKBENCH screen.

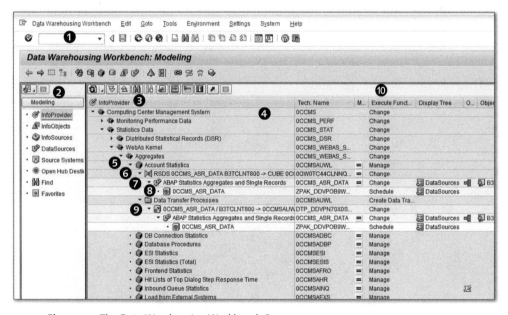

Figure 2.9 The Data Warehousing Workbench Screen

To start the Data Warehousing Workbench, enter Transaction RSA1 in the COMMAND field (❶ of Figure 2.9).

/N and /O in Transaction Codes

When you want to call a transaction while you're already working in a transaction, preface the transaction code with either "/N" or "/O". Using the former opens the new transaction in the same session (i.e., the same window); the latter opens the new transaction in a new session (i.e., a new window).

The screen is divided into two panels; the left panel ❷ is known as the *navigator section*, and the right panel is known as the *tree* section ❸.

The following options are available under the navigator:

- MODELING
- ADMINISTRATION
- TRANSPORT CONNECTION
- DOCUMENTS
- BI CONTENT
- TRANSLATION
- METADATA REPOSITORY

The tree on the right side of the screen is refreshed based on the option selected in the navigator.

By default, the DATA WAREHOUSING WORKBENCH screen opens in the MODELING option, which is the focus of this section. (The other options are discussed in Section 2.4.) Different suboptions are available under MODELING, which are different types of objects that can be modeled in the Data Warehousing Workbench. If you select the INFOPROVIDER option, the right side displays the INFOPROVIDER tree (❸ of Figure 2.9), which consists of different objects associated with InfoProviders. Each object has a description and a unique technical name. In SAP BW, different icons are used to represent different objects. Some of these icons are shown in Figure 2.10.

Figure 2.10 Icons for Various Objects in the Data Warehousing Workbench

The INFOPROVIDER tree illustrates the InfoProvider hierarchy. For example, the InfoArea with the description COMPUTING CENTER MANAGEMENT SYSTEM has the technical name 0CCMS (refer to ❹ of Figure 2.9). All of the objects related to this InfoArea are displayed under it in a hierarchical fashion, which is an arrangement known as *nesting InfoAreas*. InfoAreas can be nested at multiple levels; under the AGGREGATES InfoArea, for example, the ACCOUNT STATISTICS *InfoCube* (technical name: 0CCMSAUWL) is created as shown in ❺ of Figure 2.9. In other words, we can say that InfoCube 0CCMSAUWL is attached to the AGGREGATES InfoArea. This InfoCube is a part of the data flow in SAP BW, and all objects related to the Info-Cube are displayed under it. The objects marked with ❻, ❼, ❽, and ❾ show the visual data flow from a DataSource to an InfoCube.

Each object supports various functions that you can maintain and configure. To call the list of various functions available for an object, select the object, and call the context menu. The most common function for each object type is available under the EXECUTE FUNCT column in the tree section (❿ of Figure 2.9). You can see that MANAGE is the most common function available for InfoCubes, whereas CHANGE is the most common function for InfoAreas. By double-clicking on an object, you can start the default function available for that object.

When you double-click on InfoCube 0CCMSAUWL, a third panel opens up to the right of the tree section, as shown in Figure 2.11. This third panel shows you the object-specific settings and definitions.

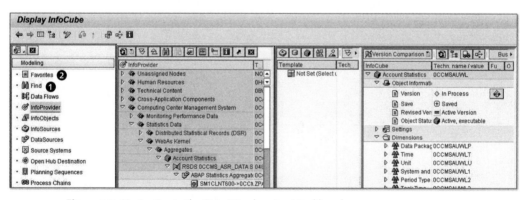

Figure 2.11 Navigation in the Data Warehousing Workbench

Now that you have a basic understanding of how to navigate in the MODELING view in the Data Warehousing Workbench, let's examine three specific functions it offers: hide/unhide, find/search, and favorites.

Hide/Unhide

You have the option of hiding or unhiding the navigator or tree. These settings are visible after clicking on the SETTING LIST icon ⊞ (Figure 2.12). Hiding the navigator or tree after navigation is useful if you want to free up some of the display space on the screen (Figure 2.12).

The other option is to hide the tree after navigation. When you double-click on an InfoCube, the tree panel is hidden, as shown in Figure 2.13.

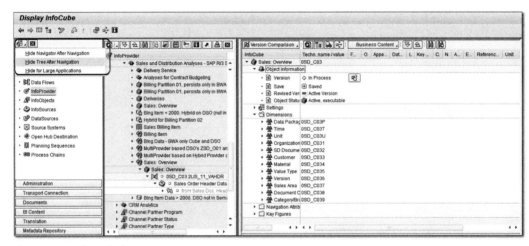

Figure 2.12 Hide/Unhide Navigator

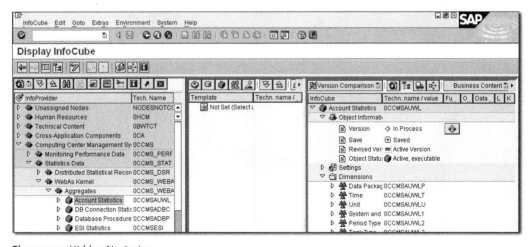

Figure 2.13 Hidden Navigator

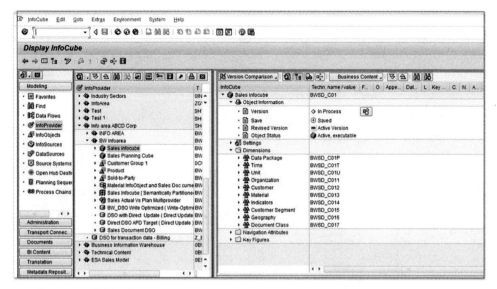

Figure 2.14 Hidden Tree

When you double-click on an InfoCube with both options selected, both the navigator and tree panel are hidden (Figure 2.15).

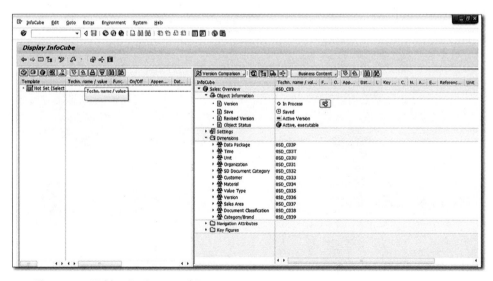

Figure 2.15 Hidden Navigator and Tree

The hide option selected is saved for you in the system.

Find/Search

You can find or search objects in the Data Warehousing Workbench by using their technical names or descriptions. Two different options are available for this purpose; the first (the search method) allows you to search for a selected object type from the navigator:

1. Click on the type of object you want to search, as shown in ❶ of Figure 2.16. In the example here, we're searching for InfoCube 0SD_C03, so we've selected INFOPROVIDER under MODELING.

2. Click on the SEARCH icon ❷. SAP BW displays the OBJECT SEARCH IN TREE box, as shown in Figure 2.16.

3. Type the technical name or description of the object you want to search for in the FIND box ❸, and indicate which object you're searching for ❹. If you want, restrict your search to an InfoProvider or InfoArea ❺.

4. Click on the SEARCH icon ❻.

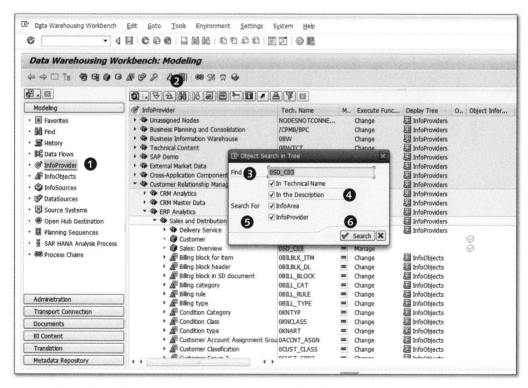

Figure 2.16 Searching Objects in the Data Warehousing Workbench

If an object is found, it's displayed in the DATA WAREHOUSING WORKBENCH screen; otherwise, an appropriate message is displayed in the status bar.

The second option (the find method) uses the FIND option under the MODELING section of the navigator. It allows you to search across all object types at once. To do so, follow these steps:

1. Click on FIND under the MODELING section of the navigator. SAP BW displays a GENERAL SEARCH IN THE DATA WAREHOUSING WORKBENCH pop-up box, as shown in Figure 2.17.

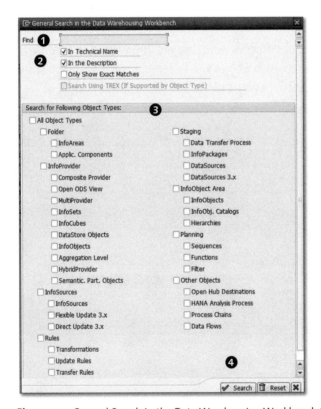

Figure 2.17 General Search in the Data Warehousing Workbench Screen

2. Type the technical name or description of the object you're trying to search in the FIND box (❶ of Figure 2.17).

3. Select the checkbox indicating whether you want to restrict your search to the technical name or description ❷.

4. If you don't know what kind of object you're searching for, select ALL OBJECT TYPES. If you do know the object type, tick the appropriate checkbox ❸.

5. Click on the SEARCH button ❹. SAP BW shows the result of this search, as shown in Figure 2.18.

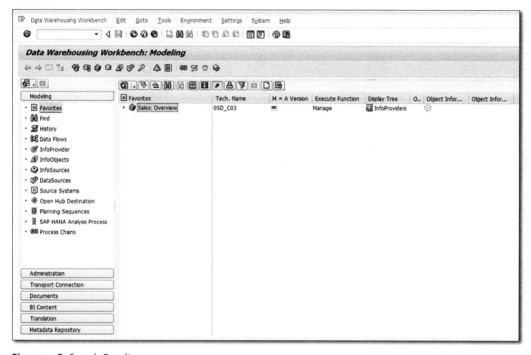

Figure 2.18 Search Results

Favorites

Many objects are available in the SAP BW system, but you'll probably only work with a few at a time. The favorites functionality helps you keep your most commonly used objects in one area. To use this functionality, follow these steps:

1. Select the object you want to mark as a favorite (❶ of Figure 2.19).

2. Click on ADD OBJECT TO FAVORITES ❷. SAP BW displays a message stating that the object has been added to the FAVORITES list.

To view the objects in this list, click on FAVORITES under MODELING (Figure 2.20). If required, you can also remove the objects by opening the context menu and selecting DELETE OBJECT FROM FAVORITES.

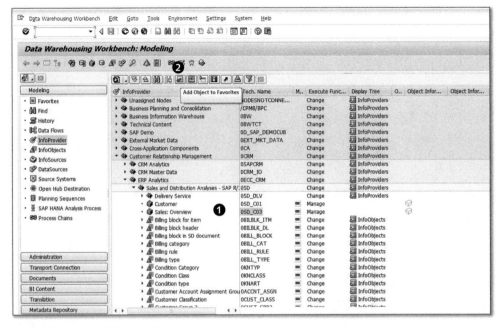

Figure 2.19 Adding an Object to Favorites

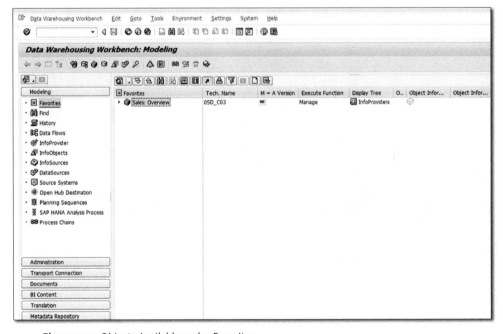

Figure 2.20 Objects Available under Favorites

2.4 The Data Warehousing Workbench Functions

As stated earlier, the Data Warehousing Workbench is the central tool for designers and administrators of SAP BW. In the previous section, we briefly covered the default view in the DATA WAREHOUSING WORKBENCH screen—MODELING. In this section, we explain the rest of the functionalities available in the DATA WAREHOUSING WORKBENCH screen.

As shown previously, the initial DATA WAREHOUSING WORKBENCH screen has the following sections, which are described in more detail here and called out in Figure 2.21 (Transaction RSA1):

❶ MODELING

Modeling is a very important section of the DATA WAREHOUSING WORKBENCH screen because it's used for the creation and modification of almost all SAP BW objects, including InfoObjects, InfoObject catalogs, InfoAreas, InfoCubes, DataStore objects (DSOs), MultiProviders, InfoSets, InfoSources, DataSources, transformations, data transfer processes (DTPs), source systems, Open Hub destinations, and so on.

Figure 2.21 Various Functionalities in the Data Warehousing Workbench

❷ ADMINISTRATION

All of the administrative activities related to SAP BW are combined under this section, including the ability to monitor the data loading process. Other functions, such as remodeling, repartitioning, and analyzing, are also available here. For complex loading and monitoring of data from multiple sources, SAP BW delivers a tool called *process chains*. Creating and monitoring process chains is done using the PROCESS CHAIN option under the ADMINISTRATION section.

❸ TRANSPORT CONNECTION

The design and creation of SAP BW objects is done in the SAP BW development system. After initial testing is complete, the objects are moved to the quality assurance (QA) system for integration testing. This process of moving objects from one system to another is known as *transport*. After integration testing is completed in the QA system, the objects are transported to the production system, which is accessed by end users. The transport connection functionality helps to collect required objects in a transport request, which is then transported to the target system using the Change and Transport Organizer (CTO) tool.

❹ DOCUMENTS

You may be required to attach comments to your query output (i.e., your report) that can be viewed by you and other users. This is accomplished by using the DOCUMENTS functionality (which also allows you to create different versions of the same document). The search functionality is available for retrieving attached documents.

❺ BI CONTENT

Preconfigured information models based on metadata are available under the BI CONTENT section (note: SAP sometimes refers to Business Content as BI Content), which helps shorten SAP BW project time lines by eliminating the need to create everything from scratch. These objects are marked with a D (for "delivered"); before using them, you must activate them using the activation process (see Section 2.5). Activated objects are available for use, as well as for building your own information models.

❻ TRANSLATION

Each object in SAP BW contains a technical name and description (short and long text), and the translation functionality helps to translate this text into multiple languages.

❼ METADATA REPOSITORY

All SAP BW objects (those delivered by Business Content as well as those already active in the system), their related objects, and links among these objects, are stored in the Metadata Repository. This is a good place to study Business Content (in delivered status) before activating them. The Metadata Repository also offers a search functionality that allows you to search for a particular object. Finally, you can exchange metadata between different systems and list metadata in HTML pages.

> **Metadata**
>
> *Metadata* is information about data. For example, the technical name and description of a table that contains data is known as the metadata for that table. Similarly, for a specific field in the table, information such as name, size, data type, and so on represents the metadata for that field.

2.5 Activation of SAP Business Content

SAP Business Content plays a crucial role in any SAP BW project. In this section, we explain the process of activating Business Content. Start the Data Warehousing Workbench using Transaction RSA1, and click on BI CONTENT, as shown in ❶ of Figure 2.22.

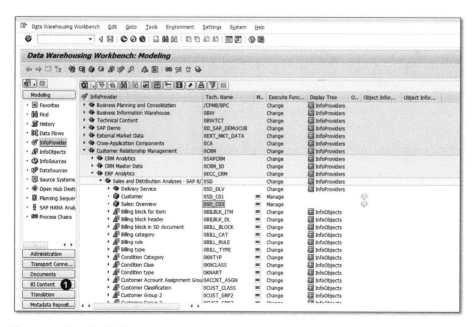

Figure 2.22 Starting BI Content

As shown in ❶ of Figure 2.23, various options are listed under BI CONTENT. The various options allow you to select objects in an effective manner. The right panel shows the screen for COLLECTED OBJECTS ❷.

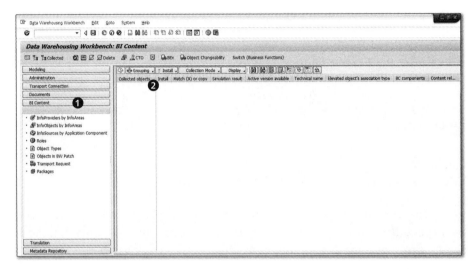

Figure 2.23 BI Content Initial Screen

When you click on INFOPROVIDERS BY INFOAREAS, the screen shown in Figure 2.24 appears.

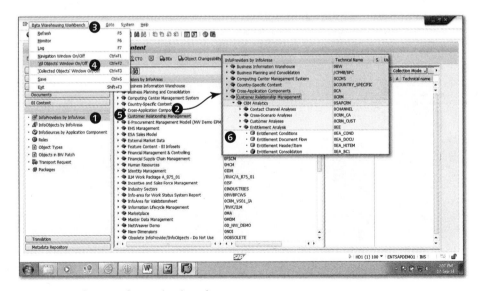

Figure 2.24 Selecting InfoProviders by InfoArea

As shown in ❶ of Figure 2.24, the selected option is now highlighted. On the right side, one more panel—INFOPROVIDER BY INFOAREAS—opens up ❷. If you're unable to view this panel, click on the DATA WAREHOUSING WORKBENCH menu, and select ALL OBJECTS WINDOW ON/OFF, as shown in ❸ and ❹.

All of the InfoAreas offered by Business Content are listed in this panel. Expand CUSTOMER RELATIONSHIP MANAGEMENT (0CRM) (❺ of Figure 2.24), and you can see an expanded tree structure displaying InfoAreas and data targets ❻. (Info-Areas and data targets are explained in more detail in subsequent chapters.)

Now click on ROLES, as shown in ❶ of Figure 2.25. The right panel shows a list of roles offered by Business Content ❷.

Figure 2.25 Business Content: Roles

SAP BW offers roles for different industries, such as apparel and footwear, automotive, banking, and so on. Within industries, various roles are classified for different jobs; for example, some banking industry roles ❸ are ACCOUNTANT, BRANCH MANAGER, and PROFIT CENTER MANAGER. When you activate a role, all of the relevant objects (DataSources, data targets, queries to web templates, etc.) are activated in the system. These activated objects can be used immediately in a productive system.

For demonstration purposes, we've activated a single InfoObject from Business Content, 0AD_AUTHID (Author ID). Click on OBJECT TYPES under BI CONTENT, as shown in ❶ of Figure 2.26. The panel on the right side now shows different available object types ❷.

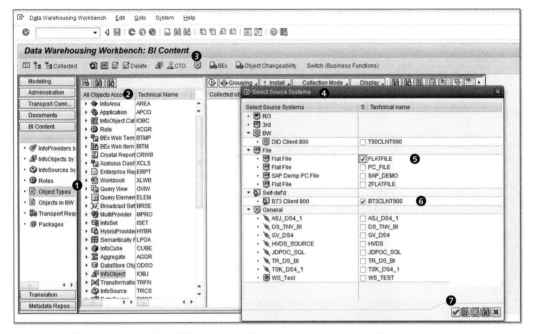

Figure 2.26 Selecting Object Type and Source System in Business Content

SAP BW can extract data from a number of systems, referred to as *source system s*. There may be many source systems connected to SAP BW, and a number of objects may be connected to particular source systems. When activating Business Content, you must inform the SAP BW system about the source system connection because the activation process activates objects related to that source system.

To do this, click on the SOURCE SYSTEM icon ⬚, as shown in ❸ of Figure 2.26. This action results in a pop-up window where you can select from the source systems ❹, which are classified into different categories (R/3, 3RD, BW, FILE, etc.). There are also different types of file source systems connected, as shown in ❺; we explain the process of creating file source systems in Chapter 7.

As shown in ❻, there is a source system called SELF-DEF'D, which stands for *self-defined*. This system is also known as a *myself connection* and is used when loading data from one data target to another data target in the same SAP BW system. For our demonstration, we need only the myself connection, which is set. (The FLAT-FILE source system isn't required for our demonstration purposes; it's configured just to show that multiple source system connections can be configured.) Click on the CONTINUE icon ☑ ❼.

Before selecting the object and starting the activation process, you need to configure a few more options as discussed in the following sections. After explaining the options, we explain the activation itself.

2.5.1 Grouping

The most important option, which can significantly affect the number of objects that can be activated by the system, is GROUPING. Open the GROUPING menu, as shown in ❶ of Figure 2.27, to see the four options available ❷:

▸ ONLY NECESSARY OBJECTS
This option activates the minimum number of objects required to activate the selected object. Thus, if you've selected one InfoObject A, and InfoObjects B and C are attributes of InfoObject A, the system activates all three objects. For this example, we've selected this option, as shown in ❷ of Figure 2.27.

▸ IN DATA FLOW BEFORE
This option activates all objects that are required to supply the data to the selected object. So, when you select InfoCube A for activation, and there are two different DataSources that give data to InfoCube A, the system activates all of the InfoObjects required to activate InfoCube A *and* the two DataSources.

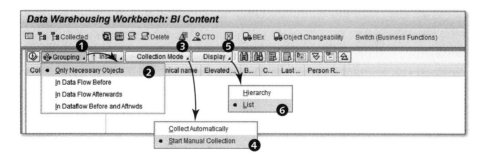

Figure 2.27 Configuring Various Options before Activating Business Content

▶ IN DATA FLOW AFTERWARDS
This option activates all of the objects that get data from the selected objects. So, if you've selected InfoCube A for activation, and there are two queries that are based on this InfoCube, the system activates all of the InfoObjects required to activate InfoCube A, the two queries, and all of the related objects required to activate these two queries. If these queries are associated with web templates, the system also activates the web templates.

▶ IN DATAFLOW BEFORE AND AFTRWDS
This option is a combination of the IN DATA FLOW BEFORE option and the IN DATA FLOW AFTERWARDS options.

2.5.2 Collection Mode

To activate any object, you must first select it from the list and drag and drop it over the COLLECTED OBJECTS area. There are two collection modes, as shown in ❸ and ❹ of Figure 2.27:

▶ COLLECT AUTOMATICALLY
This option starts the collection of other objects as soon as you drop the object in this area.

▶ START MANUAL COLLECTION
This option can be used to select multiple objects (one by one). Drag and drop required objects into the COLLECTED OBJECTS area, and click on the EXECUTE icon ⊕ to start the collection. Because we're selecting single objects in our example, either option will work. We've selected START MANUAL COLLECTION, as shown in ❹ of Figure 2.27.

2.5.3 Display

The DISPLAY option (❺ of Figure 2.27) shows the collected objects in two different ways: HIERARCHY, in which collected objects are shown in a hierarchical fashion; and LIST, in which collected objects are shown in list fashion. We've selected LIST ❻.

2.5.4 Activating the InfoObject

Now that the options are set, we can select InfoObject 0AD_AUTHID. Expand the INFOOBJECT tree, and double-click on SELECT OBJECTS, as shown in ❹ of Figure 2.28.

Thee DATA WAREHOUSING WORKBENCH BI CONTENT pop-up box appears ❺. This pop-up box lists all of the InfoObjects available in the system, both active and inactive. Find the InfoObject 0AD_AUTHID by using the scroll bar or FIND icon. Select it ❻, and click on the TRANSFER SELECTIONS button ❼.

Figure 2.28 Selecting InfoObject for Activation

InfoObject 0AD_AUTHID is now available under COLLECTED OBJECTS, as shown in ❶ of Figure 2.29. The I column (INSTALL) shows a tick for this InfoObject ❷. This tick isn't available for editing (in gray) and indicates that the InfoObject isn't active. Click on the EXECUTE icon ❸. The system now collects all of the necessary objects that are required to activate InfoObject 0AD_AUTHID and lists them ❹.

If the list shows an object that is already active, you can reactivate it from BI CONTENT. You can configure this by checking the MATCH (x) or COPY column, as shown in ❺ of Figure 2.29. There are multiple scenarios when you may need to execute reactivation; for example, you may have modified a BI CONTENT object and then want to revert to the original.

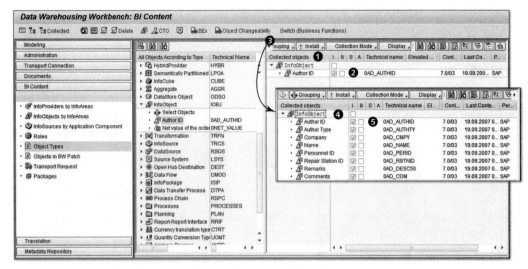

Figure 2.29 InfoObject Selected and Objects Collected

Now select the INSTALL dropdown menu, as shown in ❶ of Figure 2.30. Click on SIMULATE INSTALLATION ❷. Selecting this option simulates the installation of the selected objects and shows the simulation result ❸. Clicking on the OK icon shows that the simulation result is positive and that there won't be any errors when actually activating the selected objects in the system.

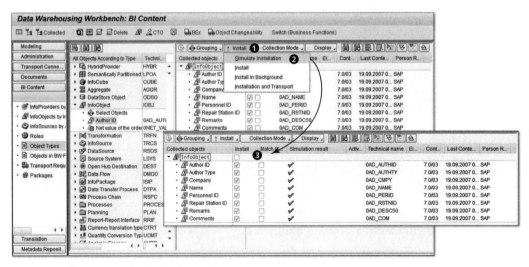

Figure 2.30 Simulating Activation

When the simulation result is positive, you can install the selected objects in the system. Select INSTALL from the INSTALL dropdown menu (❶ and ❷ of Figure 2.31).

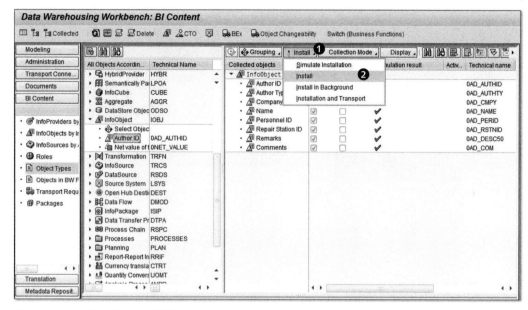

Figure 2.31 Installing Selected Objects

This action activates all of the selected objects in the system.

2.6 Implementation and Architecture Options

Large companies with many business entities or establishments across various countries operating in different time zones may have several SAP BW instances and possibly other data warehouse tools as well. The two landscape options for organizing SAP BW solutions for consistency and company-specific requirements are discussed next (core and peripheral).

2.6.1 Core Landscape

A *core landscape* uses SAP BW as the core information hub across the company (Figure 2.32). In this setup, a core SAP BW instance is implemented. It contains a data warehouse layer as well as data mart layer services and includes operative-level reporting.

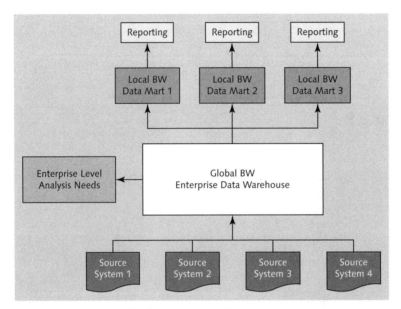

Figure 2.32 Landscape with Core SAP BW Instance

The core SAP BW instance aims to source all relevant information and relays relevant data to local SAP BW instances. The local analytical and reporting needs are serviced by the local SAP BW instances, whereas the enterprise-level analytical needs are met via the core instance, and it's possible to separate reporting and analysis services as the load increases. Implementing a core SAP BW instance is always the best option within a single division company with a strong headquarters.

That being said, certain conditions (e.g., a regional enterprise structure without process integration between the regions), coupled with technical and political factors, can cause an enterprise to use the alternative setup, a peripheral landscape.

2.6.2 Peripheral Landscape

A *peripheral landscape* is based on local instances of SAP BW within various units of a company that all provide and receive data to and from a higher-level global instance of SAP BW, possibly at the company's headquarters (Figure 2.33).

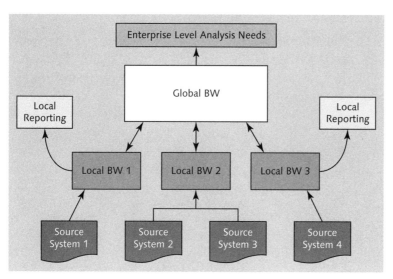

Figure 2.33 Landscape with Peripheral SAP BW Instance(s)

Each peripheral SAP BW instance operates like an EDW for its own area as it sources information from local source systems and meets all of the operative unit-level reporting locally. In this way, the sum of the local EDWs forms a quasi-virtual EDW. Having a peripheral landscape architecture means that for overarching reporting and analysis, at least one additional integration layer is required to consolidate the data from the local SAP BW instances; this is referred to as the *global SAP BW*.

The core EDW requires all corporate data to be integrated at a granular data level; although always preferable, this isn't necessary with peripheral SAP BW instances because each peripheral EDW necessarily ensures a peripheral granular data integration. A hybrid of both options is also possible and is sometimes used as a result of company mergers and acquisitions.

The implementation options just mentioned now have an additional deployment option of either on-premise or on SAP HANA Enterprise Cloud (HEC).

HEC is a secure and fully managed cloud environment offered by SAP. The HEC deployment option enables growth of the application at a pace that is aligned to its consumption and avoids any upfront capital expenditures and investments.

2.6.3   Layered Scalable Architecture (LSA)

Layered Scalable Architecture (LSA) is a reference architecture framework for modeling and designing that became part of the evolution of SAP BW. LSA is based on the industry's best practices for building an EDW. The architecture provided scalability by segregating the EDW architecture into various layers (Figure 2.34).

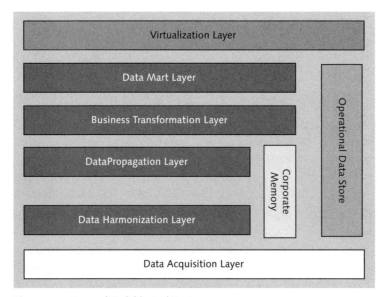

Figure 2.34 Layered Scalable Architecture

Each layer in the LSA architecture serves a specific purpose. The following list describes their specific functions:

▸ **Data acquisition layer**
The acquisition layer is the inbox for the EDW. It accepts the data from the source with the least processing, transformations, or checks. This layer is the primary storage layer for data in the source system format.

▸ **Data harmonization layer**
The quality checks and standardization of source data is performed in the data harmonization layer. This layer also is used to merge and harmonize the data from different source systems into a single data set. It must be noted that no business scenario-driven transformation is made in this layer to ensure reusability of the data in the propagation layer.

▶ **Data propagation layer**

Data is persistent and stored in DSOs in this layer after ensuring it's compliant with the defined quality, integration, and unification standards. This layer data conforms to the "extract once, deploy many" and "single version of truth" requirements (reusability) aspects.

▶ **Corporate memory**

Corporate memory contains the complete history of the loaded data by filing it independently of the update into the architected data marts. It eliminates dependence on the source system and the need to access the sources again for reconstruction.

▶ **Business transformation layer**

In this layer, the data transformations take place to serve the needs of the data mart layer. All business scenario-driven transformations are modeled in this layer. Dedicated DSOs in the business transformation layer may be necessary for join or merge data from various propagator layer DSOs. It's essential that only business transformation rules are applied on reusable propagation layer data targets.

▶ **Reporting layer**

As the name suggests, this layer contains the reporting-related InfoProviders (architected data marts). The reporting layer objects can be implemented as InfoCubes with or without the BWA or sometimes as DSOs.

▶ **Virtualization layer**

This layer has objects that don't have data stored in them such as MultiProviders and composite providers. To ensure greater flexibility, the queries are defined on logical InfoProviders such as MultiProviders or composite providers.

▶ **Operational datastore**

This layer provides for operational analysis and can have data extraction on a continual basis or shorter periodicity. This layer can also serve as a source of data to other layers within the data warehouse layer and can have the data stored in different levels of granularity. For example, whereas the operational datastore layer contains all the changes to the data, only the day-end status is stored in the data warehouse layer.

SAP provided a set of 10 data flow templates conforming to the LSA standards in the Business Content with SAP BW version 7.3, which makes it easier to define and document basic settings for reuse when creating data flows.

2.6.4 Enhanced Layered Scalable Architecture [LSA++]

The in-memory capabilities of SAP HANA enable a more open logical architecture with less persistence. LSA++ is the reference architecture for implementing an EDW with SAP BW powered by SAP HANA. While LSA was applicable for SAP BW on any RDBMS, LSA++ is applicable for SAP BW on SAP HANA and delivers more flexibility, scalability, and options covering business needs.

Figure 2.35 illustrates the LSA++ architectural layers.

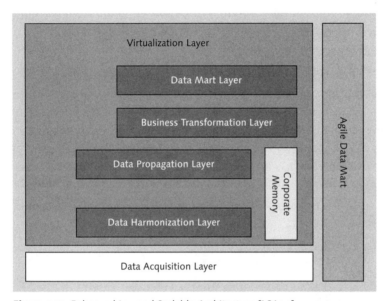

Figure 2.35 Enhanced Layered Scalable Architecture [LSA++]

LSA versus LSA++

Note the differences between the LSA++ architecture and the LSA. For example, the virtualization begins immediately from the data acquisition layer.

Each layer in the LSA++ architecture serves a specific purpose. The following list describes some of these layers in greater detail:

▶ **Data propagation layer**
This layer consists of SAP HANA-optimized DSOs to enable higher flexibility from faster activation and loading time, flexible modeling, visibility of all data in the data propagation, and queries directly on the data propagation layer.

▶ **Business transformation layer**
This layer has SAP HANA-optimized InfoCubes to enable faster data loading and simpler data modeling. There is also no dependency on conventional multidimensional modeling for better performance. Additional persistent data layers for data aggregation and creation of aggregated data sets and DB indexes aren't needed.

▶ **Virtualization layer**
The LSA+ architecture emphasizes more on the virtualization layer, which means the use of logical InfoProviders isn't limited to the report on the data residing in data mart layers alone.

The data stored in the most granular form in the bottom layers of LSA++ can also be directly used to report on through the virtualization later. As a result, LSA++ offers better flexibility to the architecture as the data models that don't contain any data can be changed more quickly and in a nondisruptive fashion. The virtualization layer creates parenthesis, which includes all persistency layers while maintaining flexibility.

▶ **Agile data mart layer**
Note that in LSA++ architecture, the data mart layer may not need InfoCubes (conventional multi-dimensional data targets) except some specific scenarios and business requirements.

2.7   Additional Resources

Many training guides, enhanced documentations, ASAP accelerators, and how-to guides are available that offer support to SAP BW users. These documents all focus on offering support with concrete challenges that arise during a project (Figure 2.36) and are detailed next.

▶ **Partner Academy**
SAP and some of its partners offer educational courses about SAP as part of Partner Academy. These are classroom trainings where the trainer uses structured courseware and SAP solutions to train participants.

▶ **SAP Help Portal**
SAP has a dedicated portal for details on its solutions and functionalities.

▶ **SAP Community Network**
A large number of technocrats practicing SAP and implementing SAP solutions

collaborate on the SAP Community Network (SCN) to exchange and grow knowledge. SAP runs and manages this portal.

▶ **Books and professional journals**

The growth of SAP has seen an explosion in books and periodicals on SAP and its solutions. We specifically recommend the following:

 ▸ *Supply Chain Analytics with SAP NetWeaver Business Warehouse* (Palekar and Shiralkar, Tata McGraw-Hill Education, 2012)

 ▸ *Performance Optimization for SAP BW* (Shiralkar and Sawant, *http://5102.espresso-tutorials.com,* 2015)

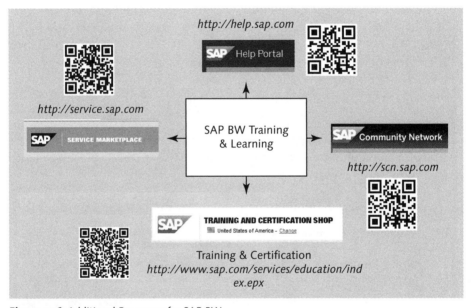

Figure 2.36 Additional Resources for SAP BW

2.8 Summary

In this chapter, we explained the aspects and components of SAP BW that make it a leading BI solution. We covered its components, unique architecture, various screen elements, terminology, and relevant navigation modes. We also explained how to activate Business Content, the most distinguishing feature of SAP BW, and the landscape architecture options for a company using SAP BW. Finally, we concluded with a brief list of the different resources available for SAP BW.

In this chapter, we explain the concept of the InfoObject, which is the basic building block of SAP BW. Understanding this building block and its configuration will help you create a robust, scalable data warehousing solution that remains relevant for a long time.

3   InfoObjects and Master Data

A typical business intelligence solution is comprised of many objects, each serving a specific purpose. For example, there are objects that source and store data (*data targets*), objects that make the data available for analytical purposes (*InfoProviders*), and objects that present data in the form of a report (*queries*). Together, these objects make up the infrastructure of a data warehouse that serves the following purposes:

▸ To receive and obtain information from its source

▸ To modify and arrange information in the required form

▸ To present and report information in the desired form

The basic and smallest building block used in building other objects is called the *InfoObject*.

The Smallest Building Block

In SAP BW, an InfoObject is the smallest building block. You need to use InfoObjects to design or configure other SAP BW objects such as InfoCubes, DataStore objects (DSOs), MultiProviders, queries, InfoSets, and so on.

Figure 3.1 represents how an InfoObject is used in creating all other objects.

We explain InfoCubes and DSOs in subsequent chapters of this book. In this chapter, we focus on creating and configuring custom InfoObjects. We discuss types of InfoObjects, different organizational entities, and how to create and configure different types of InfoObjects (e.g., the characteristic, key figure, and unit types).

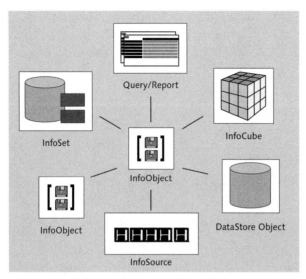

Figure 3.1 InfoObject: The Basic Building Block

3.1 Types of InfoObjects

There are five types of InfoObjects, each representing a type of business entity or establishing a relationship between entities. Figure 3.2 shows each type of Info-Object with examples of their relevant business entities or numeric measures.

The following are types of InfoObjects:

- **Characteristic**
  This type of InfoObject represents business entities that are the subjects of analysis, for example, product, customer, and marketing regions.

- **Key figure**
  This type of InfoObject represents numeric measures of business entities, for example, weight, number, quantity, and amount.

- **Time characteristic**
  This type of InfoObject represents the period of the transaction between entities, for example, date of billing, month of sale, and fiscal year. Time characteristics are delivered by SAP and aren't customizable.

- **Unit**
  This type of InfoObject represents the unit of measure for the numeric measures

of business entities, for example, the currency, unit of weight, unit of volume, and so on.

▸ **Technical characteristic**

This type of InfoObject represents entities that are internal to SAP BW and are technical in type, for example, a data load request ID. (The data load request ID helps in the maintenance and administration of the SAP BW system.) Technical characteristics are delivered by SAP and aren't customizable.

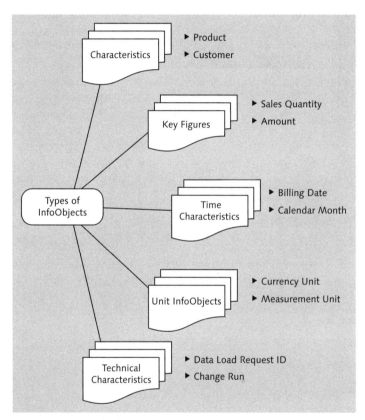

Figure 3.2 Types of InfoObjects

All types of InfoObjects are delivered by SAP as part of Business Content. If you can't find an appropriate InfoObject in the ones provided by SAP, you can create a custom one (except for time characteristic and technical characteristic InfoObjects). We explain the procedure for creating custom characteristic, key figure, and unit InfoObjects in Section 3.4.

3.2   Creating an InfoArea

A typical data warehouse has a large number of objects. To facilitate the task of managing these objects, they are organized in groups. *InfoAreas* represent the highest level of grouping; for example, all objects related to sales processes are grouped under one InfoArea, whereas all objects related to finance are grouped under another InfoArea.

This logical grouping in the form of InfoAreas is also used for managing the authorizations of data warehouse functions. For example, a developer working with sales analytics can't access or change any objects relevant for finance; similarly, another developer designing finance analytics can't access or change any objects relevant for sales. We explain more about authorizations in Chapter 14.

You can also create an InfoArea within an InfoArea, as shown in Figure 3.3, which represents a structure of InfoAreas: InfoArea 0ECC_CRM is a subset of InfoArea 0CRM; and InfoArea 0SD_DLV is a subset of InfoArea 0SD, which is a subset of InfoArea 0ECC_CRM. In this mode, you can logically organize and group InfoObjects or other objects.

Let's now explore the process of creating a custom InfoArea. In our example, we'll use the technical name BW_AREA.

1. Start the Data Warehousing Workbench using Transaction RSA1.

2. Click on MODELING to start the modeling tasks of the Data Warehousing Workbench (❶ of Figure 3.4).

3. Within the modeling tasks, click on INFOOBJECTS ❷. On the right panel of the screen, a tree structure displays existing InfoAreas arranged in a hierarchy (Figure 3.4).

4. Select the InfoArea under which you want to create your custom InfoArea ❸, and select CREATE INFOAREA from the context menu.

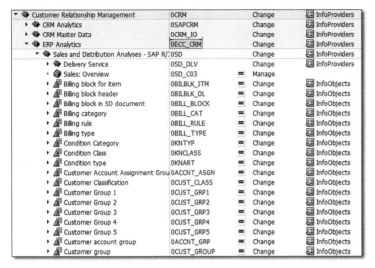

Figure 3.3 InfoArea Tree Structure

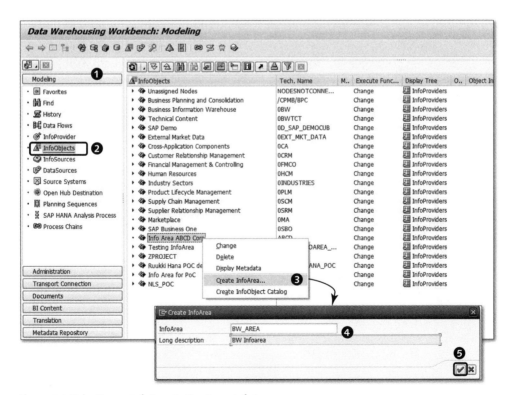

Figure 3.4 Selecting an InfoArea to Create an InfoArea

5. In the CREATE INFOAREA box, enter the technical name and description of the InfoArea ❹, and then click on the CONTINUE button ☑, or press ⌈Enter⌋ ❺.

As you can see in Figure 3.5, the structure of InfoArea ABCD is updated, and InfoArea BW INFOAREA is visible as a subset.

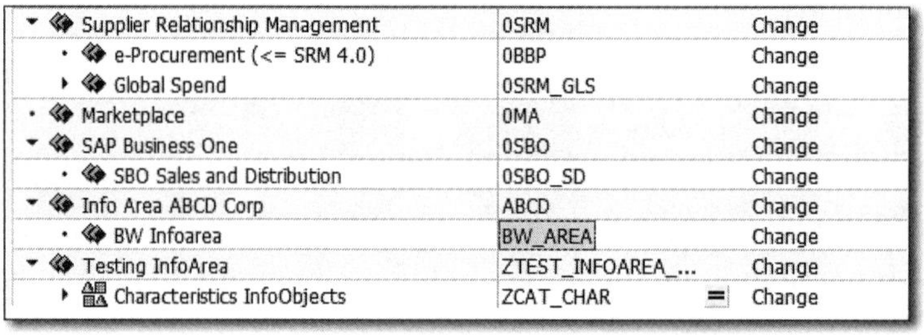

▼ ✦ Supplier Relationship Management	0SRM		Change
• ✦ e-Procurement (<= SRM 4.0)	0BBP		Change
▸ ✦ Global Spend	0SRM_GLS		Change
• ✦ Marketplace	0MA		Change
▼ ✦ SAP Business One	0SBO		Change
• ✦ SBO Sales and Distribution	0SBO_SD		Change
▼ ✦ Info Area ABCD Corp	ABCD		Change
• ✦ BW Infoarea	BW_AREA		Change
▼ ✦ Testing InfoArea	ZTEST_INFOAREA_...		Change
▸ ▦ Characteristics InfoObjects	ZCAT_CHAR	=	Change

Figure 3.5 Newly Created InfoArea BW_AREA under InfoArea ABCD

3.3   Creating an InfoObject Catalog

To arrange a vast number of InfoObjects within an InfoArea in a logical group, InfoObjects are grouped in an *InfoObject catalog*. To make a simple comparison, an InfoObject is like a file, and an InfoObject catalog is like a file folder. InfoObject catalogs are created under an InfoArea.

The two types of InfoObject catalogs are shown in Figure 3.6. One type groups the characteristic InfoObjects ▰, and the other groups key figure InfoObjects ▱.

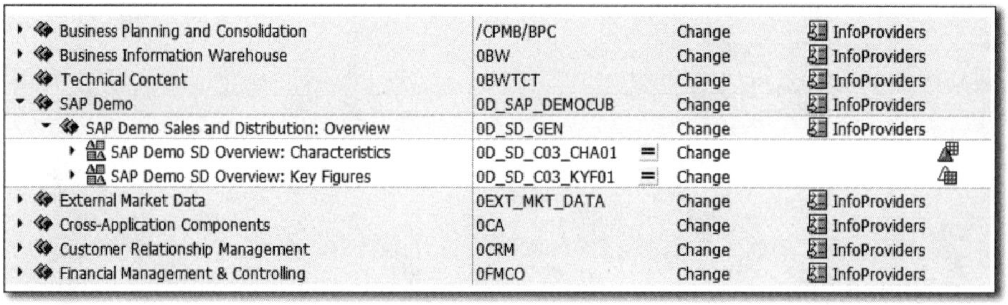

▸ ✦ Business Planning and Consolidation	/CPMB/BPC		Change	▦ InfoProviders
▸ ✦ Business Information Warehouse	0BW		Change	▦ InfoProviders
▸ ✦ Technical Content	0BWTCT		Change	▦ InfoProviders
▼ ✦ SAP Demo	0D_SAP_DEMOCUB		Change	▦ InfoProviders
▼ ✦ SAP Demo Sales and Distribution: Overview	0D_SD_GEN		Change	▦ InfoProviders
▸ ▦ SAP Demo SD Overview: Characteristics	0D_SD_C03_CHA01	=	Change	▰
▸ ▦ SAP Demo SD Overview: Key Figures	0D_SD_C03_KYF01	=	Change	▱
▸ ✦ External Market Data	0EXT_MKT_DATA		Change	▦ InfoProviders
▸ ✦ Cross-Application Components	0CA		Change	▦ InfoProviders
▸ ✦ Customer Relationship Management	0CRM		Change	▦ InfoProviders
▸ ✦ Financial Management & Controlling	0FMCO		Change	▦ InfoProviders

Figure 3.6 InfoObject Catalogs

We recommend that you maintain a naming convention that easily identifies the type of InfoObject catalog. In our example, the name for the characteristics catalog is 0D_SD_C03_CHA01 (SAP Demo SD Overview: Characteristics), and the name for the key figures catalog is 0D_SD_C03_KYF01 (SAP Demo SD Overview: Key Figures).

> **Note**
>
> It isn't mandatory to create an InfoObject catalog before creating an InfoObject. Info-Objects created without assignment to InfoObject catalogs are grouped under a pre-delivered InfoObject catalog called CHANOTASSIGNED.

Follow these steps to create an InfoObject catalog:

1. Start the Data Warehousing Workbench using Transaction RSA1.

2. Click on MODELING to start the modeling tasks of the Data Warehousing Workbench.

3. Within the modeling tasks, click on INFOOBJECTS. A tree structure appears on the right side of the screen (Figure 3.7). Click on any row, and the branch opens into the folders or the branches below it.

▸ ◈ Supply Chain Management	0SCM		Change
▸ ◈ Supplier Relationship Management	0SRM		Change
· ◈ Marketplace	0MA		Change
▸ ◈ SAP Business One	0SBO		Change
▾ ◈ Info Area ABCD Corp	ABCD		Change
· ◈ BW Infoarea	BW_AREA		Change
▾ ◈ Testing InfoAre Change	ZTEST_INFOAREA_...		Change
▸ 🔠 Characterist Delete	ZCAT_CHAR	=	Change
▸ 🔠 KeyFigure I Display Metadata	ZCAT_KFG	=	Change
▾ ◈ ZPROJECT Create InfoArea...	ZPROJECT		Change
▸ 🔠 ZPROJ_CHA Create InfoObject Catalog	ZPROJ_CHA	=	Change
▸ 🔠 ZPROJ_KFG	ZPROJ_KFG	=	Change
▸ ◈ Info Area for PoC	ZCOE_POC		Change

Figure 3.7 Create InfoObject Catalog

4. To create an InfoObject catalog, select the InfoArea where you want the catalog to be created. We chose InfoArea BW_AREA. Use the context menu to select CREATE INFOOBJECT CATALOG (Figure 3.7). The screen shown in Figure 3.8 appears.

5. Enter the technical name of the InfoObject catalog and its text description (❶ of Figure 3.8).

6. Because you're creating a characteristic InfoObject catalog, select the CHAR. radio button ❷.

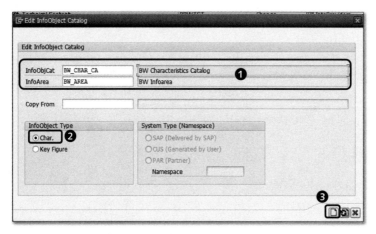

Figure 3.8 Edit InfoObject Catalog

7. Having defined the name for the InfoObject catalog, click on the CREATE icon ❸, or press F5 on the keyboard. The system creates the new InfoObject catalog, which is still inactive (Figure 3.9).

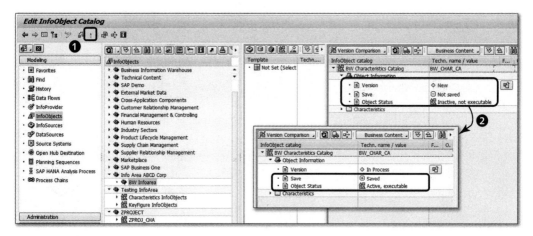

Figure 3.9 Activate InfoObject Catalog

8. Activate the InfoObject catalog using the ACTIVATE icon (❶ of Figure 3.9).

After you activate the InfoObject catalog, you'll see a message confirming activation in the status bar at the bottom of the screen. You can also view your newly created InfoObject catalog BW_CHAR_CA under InfoArea BW_AREA. As you can see in ❷ of Figure 3.9, the InfoObject catalog is listed as active.

3.4   Creating a Custom Characteristic InfoObject

In this section, we explain the procedure for creating a custom characteristic InfoObject within the newly created BW_CHAR_CA InfoObject catalog. The custom characteristic InfoObject will have the technical name BW_CUST and the text description SOLD-TO-PARTY.

Naming Convention Conditions

To distinguish custom objects from those delivered in Business Content, the following conditions apply to their naming convention:

▶ The technical name of a custom object can't begin with a zero.

▶ The technical name of a custom object can't have any special characters (such as * or $).

▶ The technical name of a custom object should have a minimum of three characters and a maximum of nine characters; it can include the letters a to z, special characters such as _ (underscore), and numbers zero to nine. You can't begin a name with a number or special character, however.

To create a custom characteristic InfoObject, follow these steps:

1. Start the DATA WAREHOUSING WORKBENCH using Transaction RSA1.

2. Click on MODELING to start the modeling tasks of the Data Warehousing Workbench.

3. Within the modeling tasks, click on INFOOBJECTS. A tree structure appears on the right of the screen. Click on INFOOBJECT CATALOG BW_CHAR_CA, and select CREATE INFOOBJECT from the context menu (Figure 3.10). A screen appears prompting you to enter the name of the characteristic InfoObject you want to create (❶ of Figure 3.11).

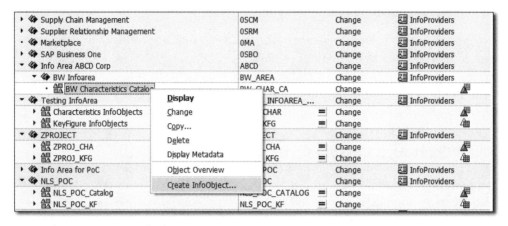

Figure 3.10 Create InfoObject: Context Menu

4. Enter the name of the InfoObject ("BW_CUST") and description ("Sold-to-Party"). From ❷ and ❸ of Figure 3.11, you can see that there are two additional fields: REFERENCE CHARACTERISTIC and TEMPLATE. For our example scenario requirements, we leave these blank.

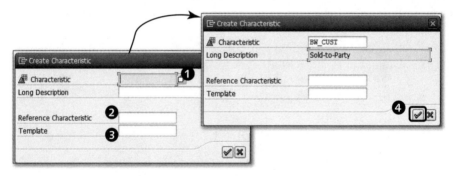

Figure 3.11 Creating Characteristic InfoObject

5. Click on the CONTINUE icon ❹.

It isn't always necessary to fill in the REFERENCE CHARACTERISTIC and TEMPLATE fields. However, it's important to know what they mean, so we briefly discuss them in the following sections.

3.4.1 Reference Characteristic Field

To understand how this field is used, assume you have an existing InfoObject (BW_CUST, Sold-to-Party) with master data. Whenever this InfoObject is used, its description is listed as SOLD-TO-PARTY. As the smallest building block, the InfoObject is likely to be used in many InfoCubes (or InfoProviders); because of this, its description as a SOLD-TO PARTY may not always be accurate. For example, a report for the department that collects payments would use customer data contained in InfoObject BW_CUST, but they wouldn't want customers to be referred to as sold-to parties; rather, they would want them to be referred to as payers. To solve this problem, you can create an identical InfoObject—comprised of the same definition (explained in detail in Section 3.5) and master data—with the only difference being the description (PAYER instead of SOLD-TO-PARTY). To do this, enter the technical name of the existing InfoObject into the REFERENCE CHARACTERISTIC field (refer to ❷ of Figure 3.11).

> **Note**
>
> You can't change the technical settings of an InfoObject created by reference to another InfoObject.

3.4.2 Template Field

To understand how this field is used, assume that you want to create a new InfoObject that is similar to an existing InfoObject. Enter the name of the new InfoObject in the field titled CHARACTERISTIC, and enter the name of the already-available InfoObject in the TEMPLATE field (❸ of Figure 3.11). Click on the CONTINUE icon ❹.

The system copies all of the definitions of the existing InfoObject (its data type, length, etc.), saving you the work of defining them individually; if necessary, you can change the copied definitions based on your requirements. Upon activation of the new InfoObject, the system automatically identifies it as separate from the one that was chosen for its template. The master data for this new InfoObject must be loaded separately (the process of loading master data is discussed in Chapter 7).

In our example, we don't use the TEMPLATE or REFERENCE CHARACTERISTIC field; we chose to click on the CONTINUE icon.

3.5   Configuring a Characteristic InfoObject

Creating a custom InfoObject (without using a template or reference to another InfoObject) involves configuring various settings for meeting specific requirements. When you click on the CONTINUE icon, the screen shown in Figure 3.12 appears.

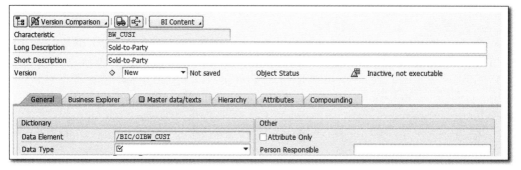

Figure 3.12 Characteristic InfoObjects: Tabs

Six different tabs are available when configuring characteristic InfoObjects: GEN-ERAL, BUSINESS EXPLORER, MASTER DATA/TEXTS, HIERARCHY, ATTRIBUTES, and COM-POUNDING. We explain each of these tabs next.

3.5.1   General Tab

Two of the three basic settings you must configure when creating a custom characteristic InfoObject are the *type* and *size* of the data it stores. Table 3.1 lists the four types of data.

Data Type	Explanation
CHAR	Used to store character strings of both numbers and letters, for example, customer numbers, material numbers, vendor numbers, and so on. Minimum length allowed is 1, and maximum is 250.
NUMC	Used to store character strings of only numbers, for example, item numbers for billing documents. Minimum length allowed is 1, and maximum is 69.
DATS	Used to store dates; for example, a field of eight characters would use the YYYYMMDD format.
TIMS	Used to store times; for example, a field of six characters would use the HHMMSS format.

Table 3.1 Data Types for Characteristic InfoObjects

In our example, the InfoObject stores characteristic customer IDs that are 10 characters in length. Using this information, configure the DATA TYPE and LENGTH fields shown in ❶ of Figure 3.13.

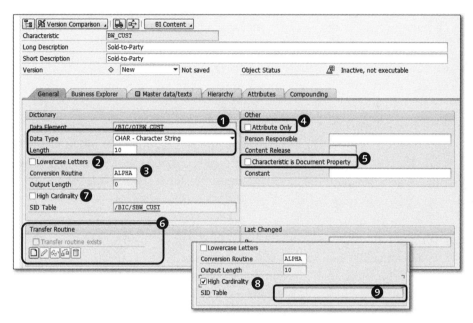

Figure 3.13 General Tab

The CONVERSION ROUTINE is defaulted by the system as ALPHA for the CHAR data type ❸. The conversion routine determines the following:

▶ That data is stored in a specific and acceptable format in the database

▶ The way data is stored in an internal format, as well as the way the data appears on screen

For example, if the length of BW_CUST is 10, and you have an ALPHA conversion routine, a BW_CUST value of 1 is stored as 0000000001; so is a BW_CUST value of 0001, 001, and so on. Without the conversion routine, the system would treat BW_CUST value = 1 and BW_CUST value = 0001 as two different customers. Let's briefly discuss the rest of the settings in the GENERAL tab, as shown in Figure 3.13:

▶ LOWERCASE LETTERS ❷
This setting determines whether the system converts the text value into upper-case letters. If you check this box, the system uses the value exactly as it's

entered. If you leave the box unchecked, the value entered is converted to upper-case letters in the screen template as, for example, a variable (see Chapter 9).

▶ ATTRIBUTE ONLY ❹
Checking this box means that the InfoObject can be assigned as an attribute of another InfoObject but can't be used as a navigational attribute. So, it can be a display attribute only. (See Section 3.5.3 for more information.)

▶ CHARACTERISTIC IS DOCUMENT PROPERTY ❺
Checking this box allows an analyst to record and document comments in the report, which is available for reference later.

▶ TRANSFER ROUTINE ❻
This setting is used to indicate the manipulation of incoming data by custom ABAP code. The ABAP code used here, also known as a *global transfer routine,* gets executed whenever the InfoObject is used in transfer rules or transformation.

▶ HIGH CARDINALITY ❼
When you define an InfoObject and activate it, the system creates a table called a surrogate ID (SID) table. For each CHARACTERISTICS value, the system generates a distinct SID value that is stored in this table. The system doesn't support scenarios for more than 2 billion values of SID, which is due to the technical implementation of the SID table (data type INT4).

In this case, you select the HIGH CARDINALITY flag. In this case, the system doesn't create a SID table (refer to ❽ and ❾ of Figure 3.13). SID values are created dynamically during reporting. This makes reporting slower. Select HIGH CARDINALITY only when necessary because the characteristics can't be used for the following:

- ▶ InfoCubes
- ▶ Compounding parents
- ▶ Navigation attributes
- ▶ Hierarchies
- ▶ SAP HANA analysis process

You can activate the custom InfoObject after filling in the three essential fields (LONG DESCRIPTION, DATA TYPE, and LENGTH) in the GENERAL tab.

> **Note**
>
> A long description isn't mandatory. The system activates the InfoObject without entering a long description, but it's recommended to have it.

3.5.2 Business Explorer Tab

The BUSINESS EXPLORER tab's settings (Figure 3.14) are divided into three main areas: GENERAL SETTINGS, QUERY FILTER VALUE SETTINGS, and BEX MAP.

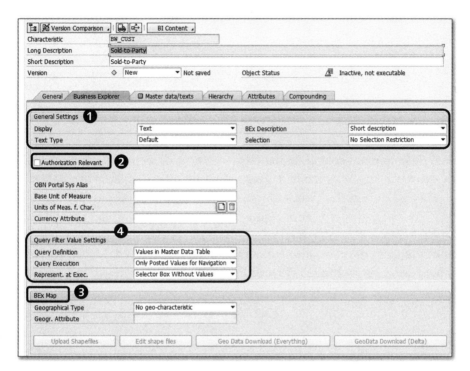

Figure 3.14 Business Explorer Tab

General Settings Area

The configuration settings in this area influence the presentation in a report that uses this InfoObject. By default, the DISPLAY field is filled with TEXT, which means when you execute a report that uses InfoObject BW_CUST, the report displays the customer text. On the other hand, if the field is filled with KEY, the report displays the customer key. You can select NO DISPLAY, KEY, TEXT, KEY AND TEXT, and TEXT AND KEY.

We explain this briefly using the sample data from BW_CUST in Table 3.2. A report with the setting DISPLAY = KEY would only show 100066, 100006, and 100017; it wouldn't show the text values (ROMERO Y TOMILLO, BEST BUY, and CONSUMER ELECTRONIC STORE).

85

BW_CUST_KEY	BW_CUST_TEXT
100066	Romero y tomillo
100006	Best Buy
100017	Consumer Electronic Store

Table 3.2 Sample Data for Customer Texts

> **Note**
>
> In subsequent chapters dealing with report design, we'll explain how you can change these default values that are set in the DISPLAY field of the InfoObject.

One of the important settings in the GENERAL SETTINGS section is the AUTHORIZA-TION RELEVANT flag. As the name suggests, this option is for managing administration and access control. If you want to show limited or no data relating to this InfoObject, check this box (❷ of Figure 3.14). Note, however, higher-level organizational objects (e.g., a marketing region, marketing office, or plant) generally control the authorizations; also, additional steps are required beyond checking this box. Our case study doesn't require any access restrictions, so we leave this unchecked.

BEx Map Area

The BEX MAP area (❸ of Figure 3.14) is relevant when you want to use geographical areas as part of your analysis. Such analysis requires that you provide geographic information about the objects of analysis; for customers, for example, you might be required to upload the longitude, latitude, and height above sea level for their physical addresses. Our case study doesn't require any edits to this area.

Query Filter Value Settings

As shown in ❹ of Figure 3.14, there are three settings available under this section. These settings define how the filter values are determined when you define/execute a query. These filter settings are discussed in Chapter 9 where we explain SAP Business Explorer (BEx). Our case study doesn't require any changes, so we go with default values.

3.5.3   Master Data/Texts Tab

Master data for a business entity, such as a customer or material, is usually stored in characteristic InfoObjects. In some exceptions, it's stored in a DSO; for example, master data coming from multiple sources is first received in a DSO for harmonization and consolidation before being moved to the InfoObject. However, our case study doesn't have such exceptions.

The other purpose of this tab is to configure the way text is stored in the system. Understandably, it's difficult for an analyst to memorize the codes of all products and customers. So, it's important to have text descriptions for the codes of the business entities included in a report. A report can provide text descriptions only if such information is stored in the SAP BW system, and the details of this storage are included in this tab.

Master Data

Master data is defined as a type of data that stores information about a business entity (such as a customer or a product), doesn't change over a long period of time, and is nontransactional.

For example, a customer's city is part of the master data for that customer because it provides information about the location of the customer and doesn't change over a long period of time (unlike the sales invoice value or quantity in sale, for example).

Next we discuss the two main areas of this tab, which are configured by selecting the WITH MASTER DATA flag and the WITH TEXTS flag.

With Texts Settings

BW_CUST is configured to store the names of customers, which is indicated in this tab by selecting the WITH TEXTS checkbox (❷ of Figure 3.15). There are additional steps related to the process of providing text information about business entities in a report, but we'll cover these steps in more detail in Chapter 9.

Let's explore some of the more important fields of the TEXT TABLE PROPERTIES area (Figure 3.16), which become editable when you check the WITH TEXTS box.

By default, the SAP BW system chooses the SHORT TEXT flag (❶ of Figure 3.16) and the LANGUAGE-DEP. TEXT flag ❷. This indicates, respectively, that the system receives and stores only short text for the InfoObject and that the text can be in different languages.

Figure 3.16 shows that you have three options for storing text information:

▶ SHORT TEXT
The system stores up to 20 characters.

▶ MEDIUM TEXT
The system stores up to 40 characters.

▶ LONG TEXT
The system stores up to 60 characters. On selecting this flag, you get additional option to select LONG TEXT IS XL flag. This allows you to store up to 1,333 characters.

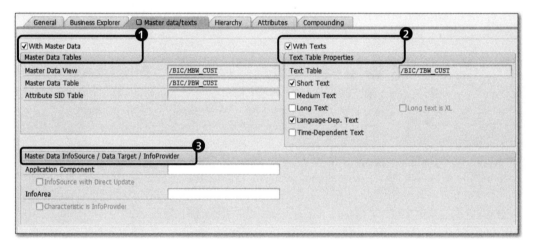

Figure 3.15 Master Data/Texts Tab

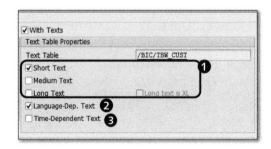

Figure 3.16 Configuring Texts for the InfoObject

You have the flexibility to select one or more of these options; your selection depends on how you're getting text information from the source system (the

DataSource) and what you require in the reports. Our case study requires that we select SHORT TEXT and LONG TEXT.

If you check the LANGUAGE-DEP. TEXT checkbox (❷ of Figure 3.16), the system creates the necessary infrastructure that allows you to load and store text data in different languages. After you load text data in different languages, SAP BW uses the language chosen when you log on to the system. (Note that checking this checkbox isn't sufficient to enable working in multiple languages; there are many more activities required, and discussion is beyond the scope of this book.)

Another important setting in this tab is the TIME-DEPENDENT TEXT checkbox (❸ of Figure 3.16). Imagine a scenario where a customer has changed his name, and the new name of the customer is valid from a particular date. Assume that you've already loaded master data for this customer (along with textual information). If this box isn't checked, and you load the same customer master data with the new name, the old name is overwritten by the new name. Our case study requires you to analyze sales data for both the new name and the former name based on the period of analysis (i.e., before the change and after the change). This requirement is met by selecting this checkbox.

To summarize, for the MASTER DATA/TEXTS tab, we chose the checkboxes shown in Figure 3.17.

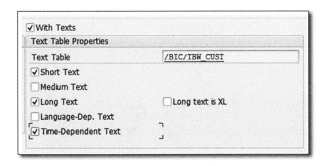

Figure 3.17 With Texts Settings

With Master Data Setting

Before we get into the details of this checkbox, we must explain some basic information regarding master data. When business analysts analyze customer sales data, they are often interested in relating this sales information to other data, such as the customer's marketing office or city. In SAP BW terminology, this type of information is known as an *attribute*. In other words, attributes provide additional information about characteristics (in this case, an InfoObject).

In the example given in Figure 3.18, the marketing office, city, and delivery plant are attributes of the characteristic InfoObject BW_CUST. Attributes themselves are also created (or delivered) as InfoObjects in the system.

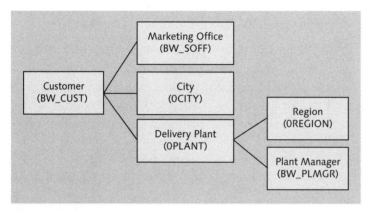

Figure 3.18 Attributes of InfoObjects

Figure 3.18 shows that the marketing office, city, and delivery plan provide information about the customer that is technically replicated in the system by assigning the following three attributes to InfoObject BW_CUST:

► BW_SOFF (marketing office)

► 0CITY (city of customer)

► 0PLANT (plant from which products are delivered to customer)

As mentioned earlier, these attributes are also InfoObjects. You can create custom InfoObjects and assign them as attributes (BW_SOFF is an attribute of BW_CUST), and also use SAP-delivered InfoObjects as attributes (0CITY and 0PLANT are SAP-delivered InfoObjects and assigned as attributes to your custom InfoObject).

It's important and interesting to note that attributes of InfoObjects (which are themselves InfoObjects) can have their own attributes, as shown in Figure 3.18. 0PLANT is an attribute of BW_CUST, while 0PLANT has its own attributes (i.e., 0REGION, which refers to the region where the plant is located; and BW_PLMGR, the plant manager). In this example, we've attached our own InfoObject (BW_PLMGR) to an SAP-delivered InfoObject (0PLANT).

To create InfoObject BW_CUST with the preceding definition, we need to create two of our own InfoObjects (BW_SOFF and BW_PLMGR) and also activate three predelivered InfoObjects (0CITY, 0REGION, 0PLANT) from Business Content. This brings us back to the subject at hand, which is the WITH MASTER DATA checkbox. To assign attributes to characteristic InfoObjects, you must check this box (Figure 3.19). After you check this box, the ATTRIBUTES tab appears. This tab is explained in Section 3.5.5.

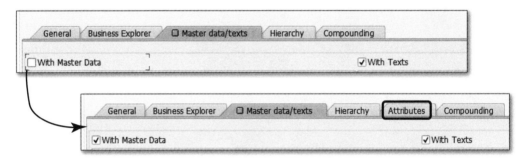

Figure 3.19 With Master Data Checkbox

3.5.4 Hierarchy Tab

Hierarchies are used to display data in tree structures and can have multiple levels with nodes and leaves arranged in parent-child relationships. The data based on a hierarchy is grouped according to the relationship defined in that hierarchy. On the HIERARCHY tab, you can define whether a characteristic can have hierarchies built on it, as well as the type and properties of hierarchies. You can create multiple hierarchies on the same characteristic InfoObject.

Consider an example of customer data where each customer (sold-to party) is assigned to a specific region. A hierarchy representing this relationship between customer and region can be built on the customer characteristic (Figure 3.20).

Check the WITH HIERARCHIES box (❶ of Figure 3.21) to enable hierarchies for a characteristic InfoObject.

You can either manually create a hierarchy or load it from the source system. Two types of parent nodes are available in a hierarchy: the text node and the characteristic node. Each hierarchy has a root node. You can add a text node (from our example, northern region, western region, eastern region, or southern region) and then add a leaf (which is a characteristic value, in this case, because the hierarchy is based on customers) below the text node, as shown in Figure 3.20.

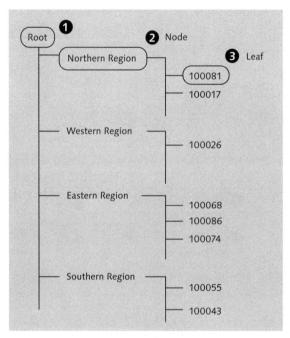

Figure 3.20 Customer: Regional Hierarchy

A hierarchy can have multiple levels, with a maximum of 98.

> **Other Ways to Maintain Hierarchies**
>
> When the hierarchy for master data objects is available in the SAP ERP system, the SAP ERP configuration menu offers a way to create a DataSource that will extract this hierarchical structure for loading into SAP BW. You can also load the hierarchy from a flat file.

To configure a hierarchy for this InfoObject (BW_CUST), check the WITH HIERARCHIES checkbox. SAP BW then allows you to configure the other options shown in Figure 3.21.

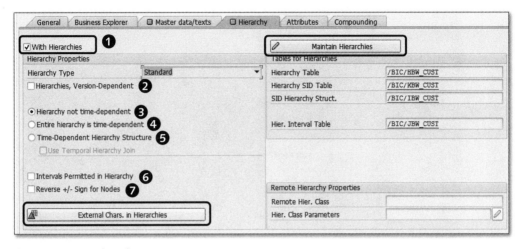

Figure 3.21 Hierarchy Tab

Next, we divide our discussion into four main topics: multiple hierarchies, time dependence, intervals, and reversing signs for nodes.

Multiple Hierarchies

To provide analysts the flexibility to analyze data in different ways, you can create multiple hierarchies for a characteristic, as well as multiple versions of the same hierarchy. For example, consider a situation where, due to re-organization, customer 100074 moves from the eastern region to the northern region.

If your business analyst doesn't want to lose data from the former relationship (i.e., customer 100074 as a part of the eastern region), you can create a new version of the hierarchy by defining the hierarchy as version-dependent. To do this, flag the HIERARCHIES, VERSION-DEPENDENT checkbox (❷ of Figure 3.21). You can now add a new version of the existing hierarchy where customer 100074 is assigned to the northern region (Figure 3.22).

When the analyst chooses hierarchy version 001, the sales for customer 100074 are aggregated under the eastern region node. When the analyst chooses version 002, the sales for customer 100074 are aggregated under the northern region node (Figure 3.22).

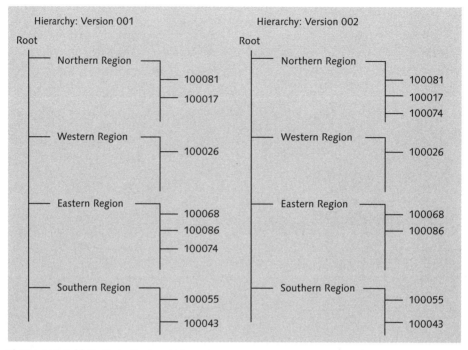

Figure 3.22 Sold-To Party: Regional Hierarchy

Time Dependency

The HIERARCHY tab has settings related to time dependency. By default, the hierarchy isn't time-dependent (refer to ❸ of Figure 3.21), which means that it's valid for all time periods. The other two time-dependent settings are ENTIRE HIERARCHY IS TIME-DEPENDENT and TIME-DEPENDENT HIERARCHY STRUCTURE. The key difference between these two options is that, with the former, you create a new hierarchy structure with a new validity period. With the latter, you have a single hierarchy with different nodes/leafs that have different validity periods.

To explain the implication of the time-dependency options, let's once again refer to the example in Figure 3.22, where customer 100074 changes from the eastern region to the northern region. Let's also assume that this change of region is applicable from a specific date: April 1, 2015. For this situation, you must enter the validity period, not the version, when creating a hierarchy with a new relationship. This can be done by choosing the ENTIRE HIERARCHY IS TIME-DEPENDENT radio button (refer to ❹ of Figure 3.21), which means that the time validity is applicable for the entire hierarchy. This option provides another type of flexibility to business analysts because they can now analyze region data based on a specific time period. To do this, the analyst must choose a specific date; based on this date, the system uses the appropriate hierarchy. In our example, if the date chosen by an analyst is before March 31, 2015, customer 100074 is shown as part of the eastern region; otherwise, the customer is shown as part of the northern region (Figure 3.23).

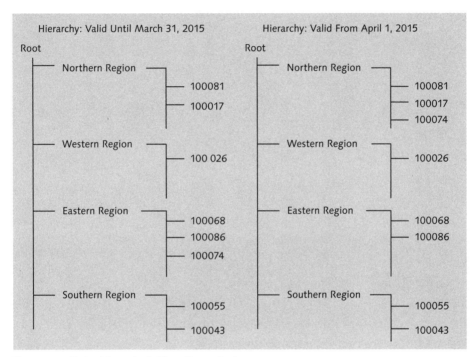

Figure 3.23 Entire Hierarchy Is Time-Dependent

For simplicity's sake, we've shown only two validity periods for the hierarchy. Customer 100074 is now part of the northern region (instead of the eastern region), which is valid from April 1, 2015. With this setting option, we create a new hierarchy valid from April 1, 2015, onward. We now have two hierarchies, each valid for different periods of time. The appropriate hierarchy to be used in a report depends on the selected date of the query at runtime.

The TIME-DEPENDENT HIERARCHY STRUCTURE option (refer to ❺ of Figure 3.21) is used when you want to use a single hierarchy, but when you also have leaf values (refer to ❸ of Figure 3.20) that change nodes (refer to ❷ of Figure 3.20) based on the time period. For example, assume customer 100074 was attached to the eastern region from April 1, 2006, to March 31, 2015, and from April 1, 2015, onward, is changed to the northern region. In this case, the system automatically maintains the end validity date as March 31, 2015. At runtime, SAP BW uses the date chosen in the query to construct the structure of the hierarchy. In Figure 3.24, you can see that customer 100074 is part of two nodes (eastern region as well as northern region) but with different validity periods.

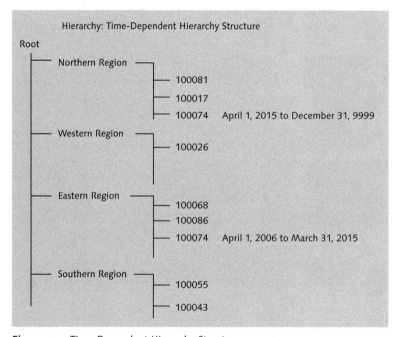

Figure 3.24 Time-Dependent Hierarchy Structure

> **Note**
>
> The HIERARCHIES, VERSION-DEPENDENT option is offered as a checkbox, meaning that you can check this checkbox *and* one of the radio buttons, allowing you to configure both versions of hierarchies and time-dependent hierarchies.

Intervals

In some cases, there are such a large number of customers that assigning each one to a node in a hierarchy and then maintaining this data when changes occur is too tedious. SAP BW solves this problem by using the INTERVALS PERMITTED IN HIERARCHY option (refer to ❻ of Figure 3.21). By checking this flag for a hierarchy on customers grouped under regions, you can assign customers to specific regions based on their customer key values. For example, assume you've created a hierarchy where customers 000 to 105,000 belong in the northern region, and customers 105,001 to 110,000 belong in the southern region. All of the customers falling within the range are automatically assigned to their respective nodes; additionally, when you gain a new customer, the customer is automatically assigned to the correct node. For example, customer 102000 is automatically assigned to the northern region without specific maintenance for the hierarchy.

In summary, the major advantage of this option is that it allows you to create a hierarchy quickly. Another advantage is that you don't need the entire customer list at the time of creating the hierarchy. Even if you have 2,000 customers, you can configure nodes for ranges that exceed 2,000; then, when new customers are added within these predefined ranges, they are automatically assigned to a node.

Reversing Signs for Nodes

When the REVERSE +/– SIGN FOR NODES checkbox (❼ of Figure 3.21) is checked, you can decide whether to reverse the sign of transaction data displayed in reports. This functionality only affects the display of data in the report, not the underlying actual data. For example, if you have a hierarchy on income and expense where income is displayed with minus signs and expenses are displayed with plus signs (according to accounting norms), this functionality allows you to display the income node with a negative sign.

3.5.5   Attribute Tab

> **Note**
>
> To see this tab, you must check the WITH MASTER DATA checkbox in the MASTER DATA/ TEXTS tab.

As stated earlier, attributes give additional information about characteristic Info-Objects. Assume that in our case study, we want to analyze sales data for a customer with additional information about that customer, for example, the marketing office of the customer, the group to which this customer belongs, and so on. To meet this requirement, you must add the appropriate InfoObjects (sales office, customer group, etc.) as attributes of BW_CUST. You can assign multiple attributes to BW_CUST (Figure 3.25).

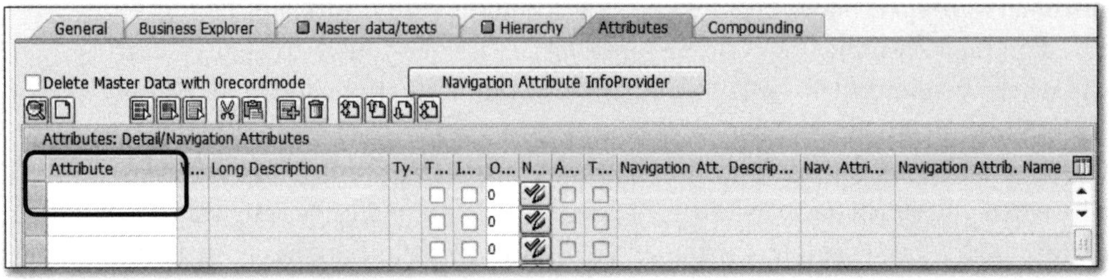

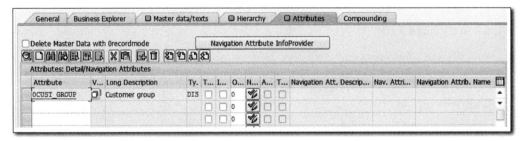

Figure 3.25 Attributes Tab

For our example, assign the following InfoObjects as attributes of BW_CUST:

- 0CUST_GROUP (Customer GRP2)

- 0CUST_GRP1 (Customer GRP)

- 0SALES_OFF (Sales Office)

- 0SALES_GRP (Sales Group)

- 0SALESEMPLY (Sales Employee)

- 0SALES_DIST (Sales District)

Assign each of these InfoObjects under the ATTRIBUTE column. As shown in Figure 3.26, enter "0CUST_GROUP" and press [Enter]. SAP BW automatically displays the rest of the column information, that is, LONG DESCRIPTION and TY. (type of attribute).

Figure 3.26 Entering Attributes

SAP BW offers two different types of attributes (displayed in the TY. column):

- **Display attribute** (DIS)
  By default, SAP BW marks attributes as display attributes so that when you analyze a report that contains the InfoObject in question (in this example, the cus-

tomer group InfoObject), you can get additional information displayed in the report. For example, if 0SALES_DIST (SALES DISTRICT) is the display attribute of BW_CUST, you can display the values of the sales district for the respective customer in your report.

► **Navigational attribute** (NAV)
Defining an attribute as a navigational attribute enables additional navigational capabilities (such as sorting and drilldown) when the report is executed. SAP BW queries don't differentiate between characteristics (which are part of InfoCubes) and navigational attributes (which aren't part of InfoCubes).

> **Note**
>
> The choice to define an InfoObject as a characteristic or a navigational attribute depends on your reporting requirements, business processes, and SAP BW modeling techniques, as well as SAP Best Practices.

When you enter your attributes, they are automatically defined as display attributes. To change this, click on the NAVIGATIONAL ATTRIBUTE ON/OFF icon (❶ of Figure 3.27) for the appropriate attribute.

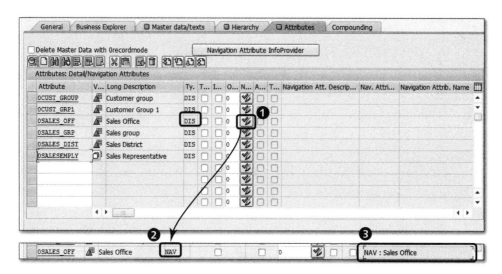

Figure 3.27 Defining Attributes

For our case study, we define 0SALES_OFF as a navigational attribute. When you assign this definition, SAP BW offers you a field for a description of the navigational attribute (❸ of Figure 3.27). You should always fill this out because it helps query designers distinguish whether the InfoObject is being used is a navigational attribute or a characteristic.

For each attribute, you can decide whether to make it time-dependent. You should use this if you want to keep track of specific data changes, for example, when the sales employees attached to certain customers change. If you don't want to keep track of this, leave this checkbox deselected. In this case, the information you load when you first load master data is what is used in reports; if the data is changed after master data is loaded, the old data is overwritten.

If you're interested in keeping track of these changes, you must define sales employee as a time-dependent attribute of BW_CUST (Figure 3.28). When any attribute is declared as time-dependent, the system internally uses two InfoObjects, 0DATEFROM (VALID FROM) and 0DATETO (VALID TO), to store the values of dates when changes in the attributes are made. So, when you attach a customer to a sales employee, you must specify the dates for which that attachment is valid.

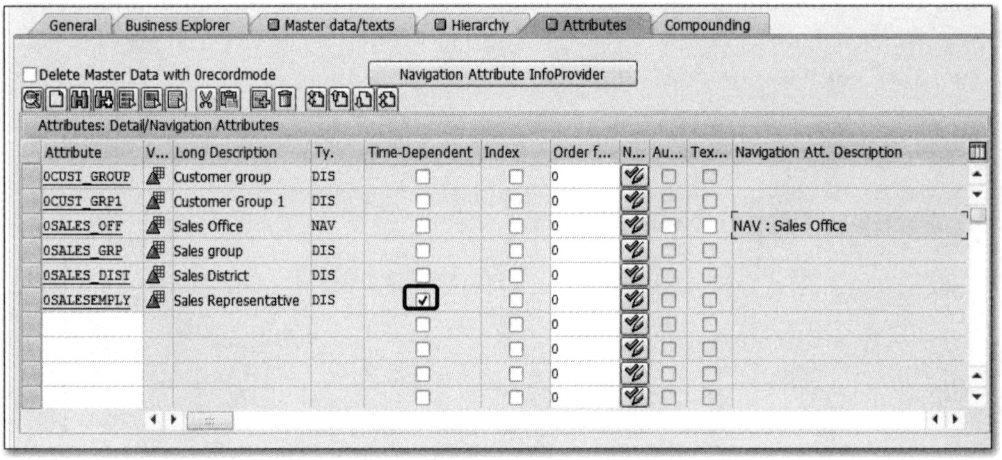

Figure 3.28 Switching Time Dependency

Let's consider a situation where the master data for a customer has the values listed in Table 3.3. (Note: The data here is in a simplified form for the purpose of explaining InfoObjects.)

BW_CUST	0SALESEMPLY	0DATEFROM
100086	12349999	01.01.2008

Table 3.3 Sample Data to Illustrate Time Dependency (A)

When loaded, it's stored as shown in Table 3.4.

Record Number	BW_CUST	0SALESEMPLY	0DATEFROM	0DATETO
1	100086	N/A	01.01.1000	12.31.2007
2	100086	12349999	01.01.2008	12.31.9999

Table 3.4 Sample Data to Illustrate Time Dependency (B)

As you can see from Table 3.4, one record becomes two records; due to the attribute's time dependency, an additional record is created for the time period starting from January 1, 1000 (i.e., the past) up to one day before the valid-from date. This is done to show that the customer was *not* attached to an employee before the valid-from date.

Now, assume that on March 15, 2009, the customer is assigned to a new sales employee. As a result, you would load the new master data shown in Table 3.5.

BW_CUST	0SALESEMPLY	0DATEFROM
100086	67679999	03.15.2009

Table 3.5 Sample Data to Illustrate Time Dependency (C)

The system stores the data as shown in Table 3.6.

Record Number	BW_CUST	0SALESEMPLY	0DATEFROM	0DATETO
1	100086	N/A	01.01.1000	12.31.2007
2	100086	12349999	01.01.2008	03.14.2009
3	100086	67679999	03.15.2009	12.31.9999

Table 3.6 Sample Data to Illustrate Time Dependency (D)

As you can see from Table 3.6:

▶ Record 1 isn't changed.

▶ For record 2, the value of 0DATETO is changed from 12.31.9999 to 03.14.2009.

▶ For record 3, the newly added 0SALESEMPLY is valid from 03.15.2009 to 12.31.9999 (i.e., the future).

3.5.6 Compounding Tab

In some situations, BW_CUST doesn't have a unique value of its own but always depends on some other InfoObject for uniqueness. This is true, for example, when you have multiple sales organizations (0SALESORG), and the BW_CUST value is repeated throughout them. Without the value of the sales organization in the report, there's no unique value for BW_CUST. As shown in Table 3.7, BW_CUST = 100086 in 0SALESORG 1000 and 2000; so without including 0SALESORG in the query, the data in the report would be incorrectly accumulated under 100086.

0SALESORG	BW_CUST	BW_CUST (Text)
1000	100086	Walmart
2000	100086	Electronic Shop

Table 3.7 Sample Data for Compounding

It's this type of situation where you need to use and configure the compounding function. To begin, enter "0SALESORG" in the SUPERIOR INFOOBJECT column (Figure 3.29). You do this because in the given situation, BW_CUST must be compounded by 0SALESORG. After this relationship is defined at the InfoObject definition level, SAP BW includes 0SALESORG whenever you use the BW_CUST InfoObject (for designing InfoCubes, queries, etc.). Please note that the preceding situation isn't part of the ABCD Corp. example scenario. Therefore, for the example requirement, you don't need compounding.

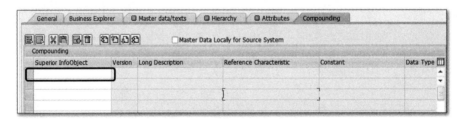

Figure 3.29 Compounding Tab

Multiple Superior InfoObjects

You can include multiple superior InfoObjects, if required.

> **Note**
>
> In a business scenario that requires compounding, we recommend configuring the settings in the COMPOUNDING tab first and then configuring the settings in the ATTRIBUTES tab.

Activate the InfoObject by using the ACTIVATE icon. An activated InfoObject can be used for creating other objects, such as InfoCubes, DSOs, and so on.

You've now completed all the activities required to create and configure a characteristic InfoObject.

3.6   Creating a Key Figure InfoObject

In earlier sections, we explained the creation and configuration of characteristic InfoObjects that relate to business entities such as customers and products. In this section, we explain *key figure InfoObjects*, which relate to numeric measures of business entities in the form of quantities, values, and so on.

Key figure InfoObjects are created and stored in a separate InfoObject catalog. Before we explain key figure InfoObjects in more detail, let's first create an Info-Object catalog for key figures; the procedure for creating an InfoObject catalog is explained in Section 3.3 of this chapter. Create an InfoObject catalog under InfoArea BW_AREA with the following information:

- InfoObject Catalog name: BW_KF_CA
- Description: BW KEY FIGURES CATALOG
- InfoObject type: KEY FIGURE

Activate the InfoObject catalog. Now you can create custom key figure InfoObjects under this InfoObject catalog.

Follow these steps to create a key figure InfoObject:

1. Start the Data Warehousing Workbench using Transaction RSA1.

2. Click on MODELING to start the modeling tasks of the Data Warehousing Workbench.

3. Within the modeling tasks, click on INFOOBJECTS. A tree structure appears.

4. Select InfoObject catalog BW_KF_CA, open the context menu, and click on CRE-ATE INFOOBJECT (Figure 3.30 ❶).

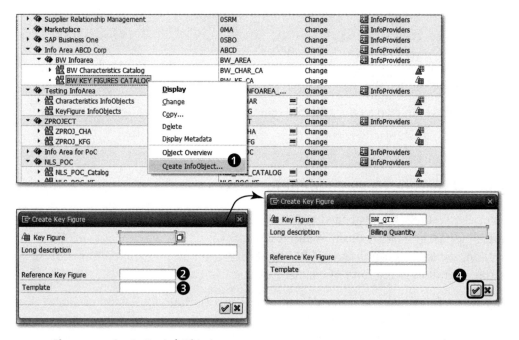

Figure 3.30 Create Key InfoObject

5. In the resulting screen, you're prompted for the technical name and long description of the InfoObject. Additionally, there are two input fields: REFER-ENCE KEY FIGURE ❷ and TEMPLATE ❸, as described here:

  ► REFERENCE KEY FIGURE

  You may want to create a key figure with a reference to eliminate internal business volume; for example, the value of service revenue from internal work must be eliminated when accounting for the service revenue at the company level. When creating a key figure with reference, you see an additional tab page, ELIMINATION. Enter one or more characteristic pairs in this tab regarding the key figure to be eliminated. In doing so, always choose a *sending characteristic* and a *receiving characteristic*. A typical example for such a pair of characteristics is SENDING COST CENTER and RECEIVING COST CENTER. The characteristics of such a pair must have the same reference characteristic.

▶ TEMPLATE
If you want to copy an existing key figure as a template for the new InfoObject, enter the name of the original key figure in the TEMPLATE field. This creates a new key figure, copying all of the settings and properties from the template (which you can then edit, if needed). The new key figure doesn't have any reference to the template key figure.

Our case study doesn't have any such requirement, so we leave both of these fields empty.

6. Next, enter the technical name and the long description for the key figure, and create the InfoObject with the following specifications:

   ▶ Key figure: BW_QTY

   ▶ Long description: BILLING QUANTITY

7. Click on the CONTINUE icon (❹ of Figure 3.30).

3.7 Configuring a Key Figure InfoObject

Creating a custom key figure InfoObject involves configuring various settings based on specific requirements. The configuration settings are segregated in the following tabs:

▶ TYPE/UNIT

▶ AGGREGATION

▶ ADDITIONAL PROPERTIES

Next, we discuss each of these tabs in detail.

3.7.1 Type/Unit Tab

In this tab (Figure 3.31), you choose the TYPE/DATA TYPE of the key figure InfoObject you're creating. Six types of key figures can be created: AMOUNT, QUANTITY, NUMBER, INTEGER, DATE, and TIME.

A couple of other relevant settings are also available on this tab:

▶ ATTRIBUTE ONLY
When you set this for a key figure, you can't use the key figure as a navigational attribute when configuring other characteristic InfoObjects. You only attach this key figure as a display attribute.

▶ PERSON RESPONSIBLE

This field is used to indicate the person responsible for maintaining this key figure. This is used only for documentation purposes.

Next we explain types of key figures in more detail.

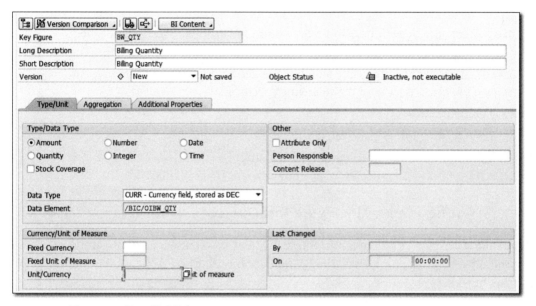

Figure 3.31 Type/Unit Tab

Amount Key Figure

Business measures associated with currency are created using amount key figure InfoObjects, for example, billing amounts, discounts, costs, and so on. Without a currency associated with this type of information, these numbers don't carry any significance.

The data type for a key figure is set by selecting from the DATA TYPE dropdown menu shown in Figure 3.32.

Two different data types are associated with an amount key figure InfoObject:

▶ CURR

The value is internally stored as a packed number with two decimal places and +/− sign.

▸ FLTP

The value is internally stored as a floating point number with no fixed number of digits before and after the decimal point.

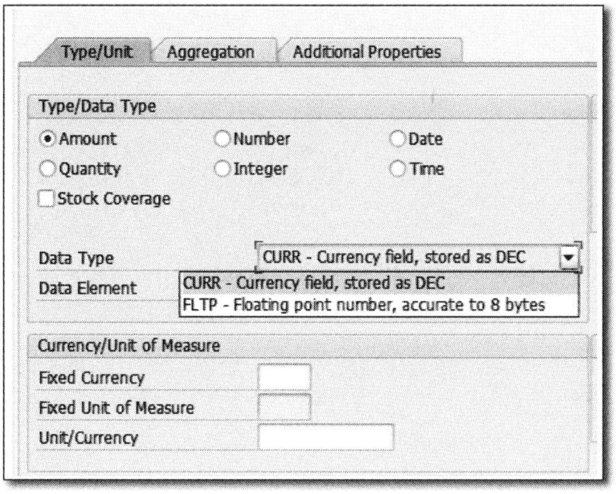

Figure 3.32 Create Key Figure: Data Type for Amount

The definition of an amount key figure InfoObject isn't complete until the currency information is maintained for the InfoObject. You have the flexibility to associate a key figure InfoObject with either a fixed currency (❶ of Figure 3.33) or a variable currency ❷.

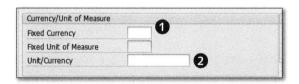

Figure 3.33 Fixed/Variable Currency

Your choice between a fixed and variable currency depends entirely on your business requirements. If all your business transactions are carried out in a single currency, a fixed currency is appropriate. On the other hand, if your business transactions occur in different currencies, you should fill in the Unit/Currency field ❷. A unit InfoObject (e.g., 0CURRENCY) should be maintained in this field. This unit InfoObject will store the currency information when the data is loaded for the key figure. (Unit InfoObjects are discussed in more detail in Section 3.8.)

Quantity Key Figure

Business measures such as billing quantity, net weight, and sales volume are always associated with a unit of measurement. By choosing the quantity key figure InfoObject, the key figure InfoObject is always linked to a unit. For a quantity key figure InfoObject, you can store data in one of the two options, as shown in Figure 3.34:

▸ QUAN
   Value internally stored as a packed number with three decimal places.

▸ FLTP
   Value internally stored as a floating point number.

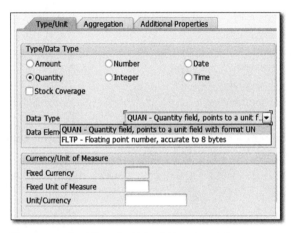

Figure 3.34 Data Type for Unit of Measurement

A quantity without a unit of measure has no meaning. In a scenario where all business transactions use only one unit of measure (meter, kilogram, etc.), you can enter a value in the FIXED UNIT OF MEASURE field (❶ of Figure 3.35). Otherwise, you use a unit InfoObject ❷, which can store varying units of measure for business transactions.

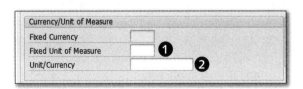

Figure 3.35 Fixed/Variable Unit of Measurement

Number Key Figure

Business scenarios always have some measures that don't have a unit or currency and, further, may not be a whole number (e.g., exchange rates and interest rates). In this situation, you use a number key figure InfoObject (Figure 3.36). When you select the NUMBER radio button, the CURRENCY/UNIT OF MEASURE area is grayed out and can't be edited.

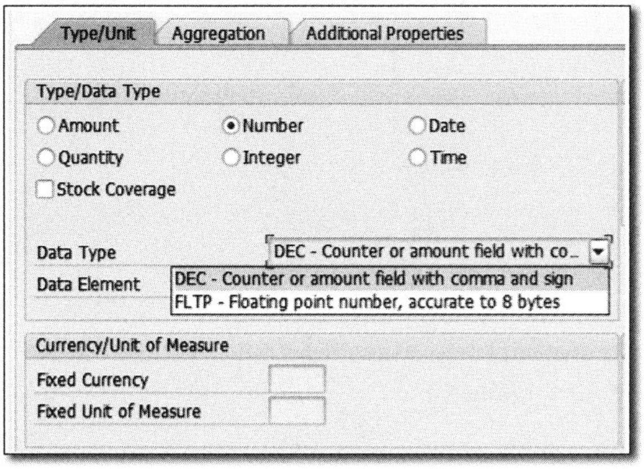

Figure 3.36 Number Key Figure

Your two options for this data type are the following:

▸ DEC
Value internally stored as a packed number with three decimal places.

▸ FLTP
Value internally stored as a floating point number.

Integer Key Figure

When a business scenario has a measure that is always a whole number (e.g., item positions), you can use the integer key figure InfoObject (Figure 3.37). Again, in this case, the key figure doesn't require reference to any currency or unit of measurement.

Internally, the system stores information in only one format, INT4: 4-byte integers without decimal places.

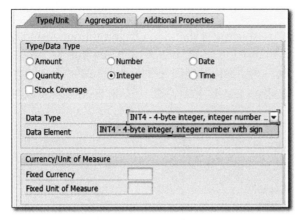

Figure 3.37 Integer Key Figure

Date Key Figure

When the business scenario has a measure that is always a date, use the date key figure InfoObject (shipment date, billing date, etc.).

Your two options for this data type (Figure 3.38) are the following:

▶ DEC
Value internally stored as a number of days, starting from 01.01.0001.

▶ DATS
Value internally stored as characters, length 8, in the format YYYYMMDD.

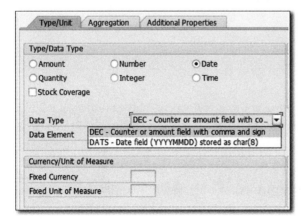

Figure 3.38 Date Key Figure

Time Key Figure

When the business scenario has a measure that is in time, you use the time key figure InfoObject. This is used to keep track of things such as the time a vehicle entered a plant, the time an employee entered the office, and so on.

Your two options for this data type (Figure 3.39) are the following:

▶ DEC
Value internally stored as number of seconds starting from zero o'clock. You can use this for calculation.

▶ TIMS
Value internally stored as characters, length 6, in the format HHMMSS.

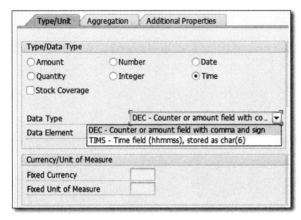

Figure 3.39 Time Key Figure

Stock Coverage

The STOCK COVERAGE checkbox is only available to key figure types Quantity, Number, and Integer. It calculates how long the stock will last. The calculation is based on REFERENCED STOCK KEY FIGURE, REFERENCED DEMAND KEY FIGURE, and MAX. NUMBER OF COVERED PERIODS.

When you select the STOCK COVERAGE checkbox for any key figure, the additional STOCK COVERAGE tab, as shown in ❶ of Figure 3.40, is available to you for defining values of REFERENCED STOCK KEY FIGURE, REFERENCED DEMAND KEY FIGURE, and MAX. NUMBER OF COVERED PERIODS ❷. You can also define the stock type as beginning of period or end of period as shown in ❸ of Figure 3.40.

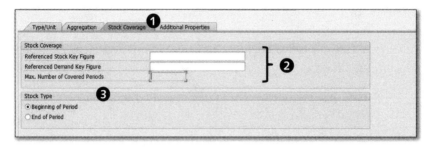

Figure 3.40 Stock Coverage Options

Our case study doesn't include stock coverage so we don't select that option.

Case Study

Our case study requires the key figure BW_QTY to be defined as a quantity key figure InfoObject (❶ of Figure 3.41) because the key figure corresponds to billing quantity ❷.

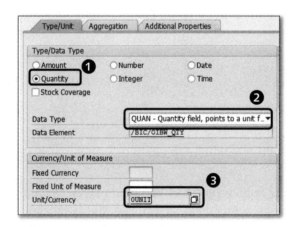

Figure 3.41 Create Key BW_QTY

Because this key figure could have many different units of measure, you should define 0UNIT as the unit of measure ❸.

3.7.2 Aggregation Tab

There are two areas in the AGGREGATION tab (Figure 3.42):

▶ AGGREGATION

▶ CUMULATIVE/NON-CUMULATIVE VALUES

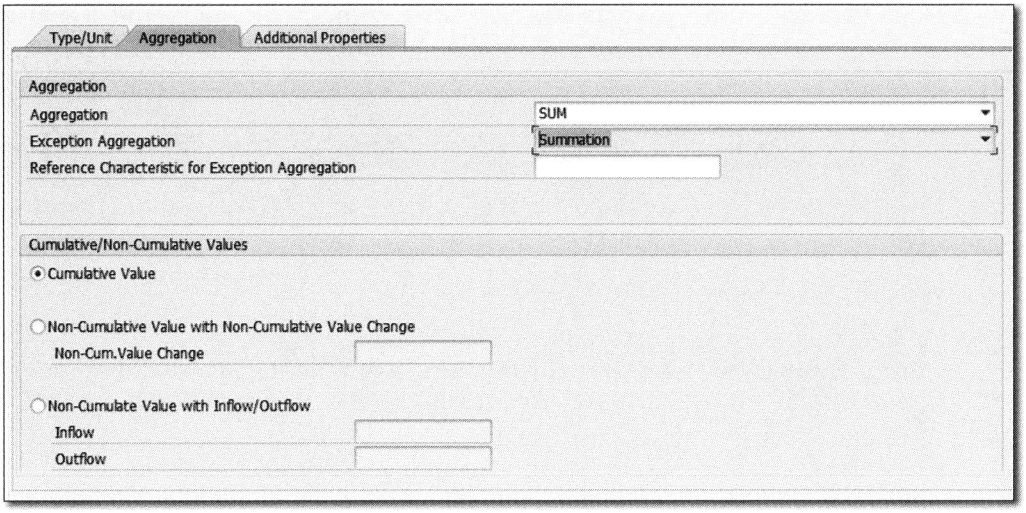

Figure 3.42 Create Key Figure: Aggregation

We discuss these areas next.

Aggregation Area

The settings and configuration in the AGGREGATION area define how values of a key figure are aggregated when evaluated using different characteristics. We explain the implication of the AGGREGATION field (Figure 3.42) using the sample data in Table 3.8.

BW_CUST	Material	Month	Billing Quantity (in SKU)
100086	38300	01.2015	100
100086	38300	02.2015	120
100086	38300	03.2015	110
100086	42000	01.2015	55
100086	42000	02.2015	58
100086	42000	03.2015	62

Table 3.8 Sample Data for Aggregation Behavior of Key Figure (Main)

In a report based on the data shown in Table 3.8, assume that you decide to remove the month characteristic, so you can focus just on billing quantity and material. Because the aggregation and exception aggregation settings for BW_QTY are defined as SUM (which is the default setting) in the AGGREGATION field of Figure 3.42, the system adds up the billing quantity for each material (Table 3.9) sold to a customer.

BW_CUST	Material	Billing Quantity (in SKU)
100086	38300	330
100086	42000	175

Table 3.9 Aggregation Behavior of Key Figure (A)

Now, assume that you remove characteristics material from the report to view the data only at the customer level. As a result, SAP BW adds the billing quantity for all of the materials sold to a customer (Table 3.10).

BW_CUST	Billing Quantity (in SKU)
100086	505

Table 3.10 Aggregation Behavior of Key Figure (B)

The aggregation settings for a key figure allow you to define aggregation options such as MINIMUM and MAXIMUM value from the range of stored values (Figure 3.43), depending on the scenario in consideration.

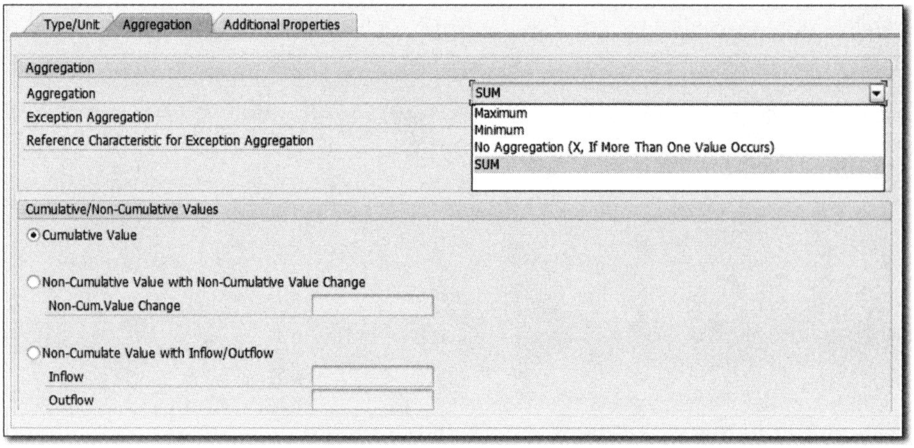

Figure 3.43 Create Key Figure: Aggregation

To explain the Exception Aggregation field, we use the sample data presented in Table 3.11.

Country	City	CalYear	Population (in Millions)
USA	New York	2013	10.5
USA	New York	2014	10.9
USA	New York	2015	11.0
USA	Detroit	2013	2.5
USA	Detroit	2014	2.6
USA	Detroit	2015	2.7

Table 3.11 Sample Data for Exception Aggregation of Key Figure (Main)

In this example, assume you decide to remove the CalYear column from the report. If SAP BW followed the same technique of summation as we discussed in the previous example, the resulting data would look like Table 3.12.

Country	City	Population (in Millions)
USA	New York	32.4
USA	Detroit	7.8

Table 3.12 Sample Data for Exception Aggregation of Key Figure (A)

Clearly, this is logically incorrect. This happened because the definition of the population key figure has SUM in both its Aggregation *and* Exception Aggregation fields. When you can't accumulate the value of key figures for different characteristics, you need to use the exception aggregation. Instead of SUM, Last Value (i.e., the most recent value) is a more appropriate selection (Figure 3.44).

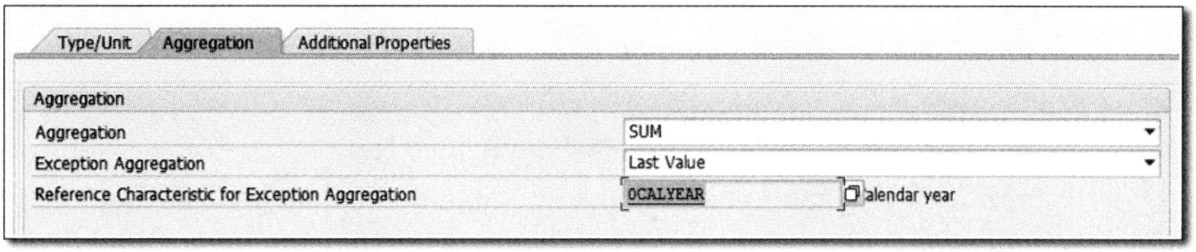

Figure 3.44 Create Key Figure: Exception Aggregation

Using the definition shown in Figure 3.44, SAP BW is instructed to perform the Last Value operation on the population key figure, using the Reference Characteristic for Exception Aggregation. In this example, the reference characteristic is 0CALYEAR. (In most cases, the aggregation reference characteristic is a time characteristic, but not always.)

Now when CalYear is removed from the report, it results in the data shown in Table 3.13.

Country	City	Population (in Millions)
USA	New York	11.0
USA	Detroit	2.7

Table 3.13 Sample Data for Exception Aggregation of Key Figure (B)

SAP BW offers a variety of functions for the Exception Aggregation field, some of which are shown in Figure 3.45.

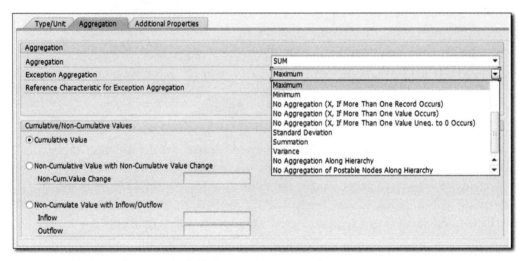

Figure 3.45 Functions Available for Exception Aggregation

Cumulative/Non-Cumulative Values Area

Cumulative key figures are those that can be meaningfully accumulated over a period of time. For example, the billing quantity for a customer over several months can be accumulated to get a total billing quantity for a customer for the quarter. *Non-cumulative key figures* are those that can't be accumulated meaningfully over a period of time; for example, the inventory of a certain material over three months of a quarter can't be added to get the total inventory at the end of the quarter. A key figure must be defined as cumulative or non-cumulative.

Cumulative Key Figures versus Exception Aggregation
The concept of cumulative versus non-cumulative key figures differs from the concept of exception aggregation because the latter only works at the report level (e.g., with BEx Analyzer output), while the former relates to data storage.

When you define a key figure as non-cumulative and use it in the definition of an InfoCube, it's known as a *non-cumulative InfoCube*. For non-cumulative Info-Cubes, SAP BW maintains a specific feature called a *marker*, which is normally a time pointer. For this marker, the system calculates the value of a non-cumulative key figure; for the rest of the time periods, values are calculated at runtime based on the value at the marker and the non-cumulative value changes. For example, assume the value of a non-cumulative key figure on its marker (January 1, 2014) is 1000. The value of this key figure on December 31, 2014, is calculated by taking 1000 as the baseline and then, at runtime, adding/subtracting the subsequent value changes that have occurred between its marker (January 1, 2014) and December 31, 2014.

Value changes are stored in two ways, depending on how your DataSource supplies the value. The first way uses non-cumulative values to calculate value changes. For example, for inventory balance (which is, as we discussed, a non-cumulative value), the source system sends only the value change of inventory, whether a reduction or an increase, from the base value. If your change value is supplied using only one key figure from your DataSource, define your non-cumulative key figure, as shown in ❷ of Figure 3.46. It's essential that the key figure used for the value change is cumulative.

The second way to define a non-cumulative key figure (❸ of Figure 3.46) is to have two cumulative key figures, one that will indicate the addition of value (INFLOW) and another that will indicate the reduction of value (OUTFLOW). If your DataSource supplies value changes using two different cumulative key figures, you can define your non-cumulative key figure using these settings.

Non-cumulative key figures add additional processing burden to the system because the values are calculated at runtime and therefore take a longer time to report. We strongly recommend that you don't define a non-cumulative key figure unless your business scenario demands it.

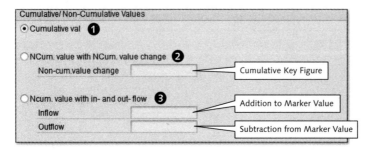

Figure 3.46 Non-Cumulative Key Figure

For our example scenario, we retain the AGGREGATION tab settings for BW_QTY shown earlier in Figure 3.42.

3.7.3 Additional Properties Tab

The ADDITIONAL PROPERTIES tab allows you to set the properties shown in Figure 3.47.

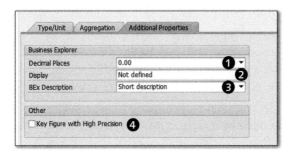

Figure 3.47 Additional Properties for Key Figures

The ADDITIONAL PROPERTIES tab is divided into two main areas, which we discuss next.

Business Explorer Area

The settings configured here are applied in the report only.

❶ DECIMAL PLACES

You can define how many decimal places key figures can have when displayed in query output. The user of the query can override this setting.

❷ DISPLAY

When the value of the key figure is large, it's difficult to read. You can solve this by defining the scaling factor in the DISPLAY field. For example, if you select THOUSAND, a key figure of 563412 is displayed as 563.412.

❸ BEx DESCRIPTION

This indicates whether the short or long description is displayed in query output.

Other Area

The only setting in the OTHER area is KEY FIGURE WITH HIGH PRECISION ❹. When you configure this setting for a key figure, SAP BW reduces the rounding issues for floating point numbers.

We don't need to change any settings for our example, so we keep those shown in Figure 3.47.

Use the ACTIVATE icon in the Dynamic menu bar to activate the key figure Info-Object. Figure 3.48 shows the active version of key figure InfoObject BW_QTY.

Figure 3.48 Key Figure: Active Status

Using the BACK icon to return to the main Data Warehousing Workbench screen, you can see that your newly created key figure InfoObject is now available under InfoObject catalog BW_KF_CA (Figure 3.49).

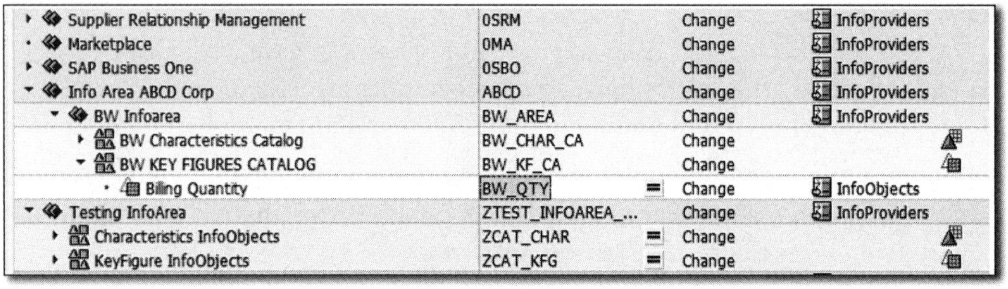

▸ ◈ Supplier Relationship Management	0SRM	Change	▤ InfoProviders	
· ◈ Marketplace	0MA	Change	▤ InfoProviders	
▸ ◈ SAP Business One	0SBO	Change	▤ InfoProviders	
▾ ◈ Info Area ABCD Corp	ABCD	Change	▤ InfoProviders	
▾ ◈ BW Infoarea	BW_AREA	Change	▤ InfoProviders	
▸ ▨ BW Characteristics Catalog	BW_CHAR_CA	Change		▤
▾ ▨ BW KEY FIGURES CATALOG	BW_KF_CA	Change		▤
· ▤ Billing Quantity	BW_QTY =	Change	▤ InfoObjects	
▾ ◈ Testing InfoArea	ZTEST_INFOAREA_...	Change	▤ InfoProviders	
▸ ▨ Characteristics InfoObjects	ZCAT_CHAR =	Change		▤
▸ ▨ KeyFigure InfoObjects	ZCAT_KFG =	Change		▤

Figure 3.49 BW_QTY under InfoObject Catalog BW_KF_CA

We've now completed the process of creating a key figure InfoObject in SAP BW. In subsequent chapters of this book, we'll use the characteristic InfoObject BW_CUST and the key figure InfoObject BW_QTY to build our example scenario for ABCD Corp.

3.8 Creating a Unit InfoObject

We've now shown you the step-by-step process for creating characteristic and key figure InfoObjects; however, as we've already mentioned, you can't create time and technical InfoObjects. In this section, we conclude our explanation of creating InfoObjects by briefly explaining how to create a unit InfoObject. (Note, however, that we don't require a specific unit InfoObject to be created or configured for our case study.)

To create a unit InfoObject, follow these steps:

1. Use Transaction RSD1 to open the EDIT INFOOBJECTS: START screen (Figure 3.50).

2. Select UNIT from the TYPE area (❶ of Figure 3.50).

3. Enter the technical name for the unit ❷.

4. Click on the CREATE icon ❸.

5. In the CREATE UNIT box, enter the LONG DESCRIPTION ❹.

6. Click on the CONTINUE button ❺. The next screen displays the InfoObject definition and the GENERAL tab (as shown in ❶ of Figure 3.51).

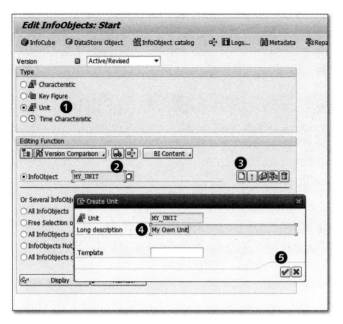

Figure 3.50 Creating a Custom Unit InfoObject: Part 1

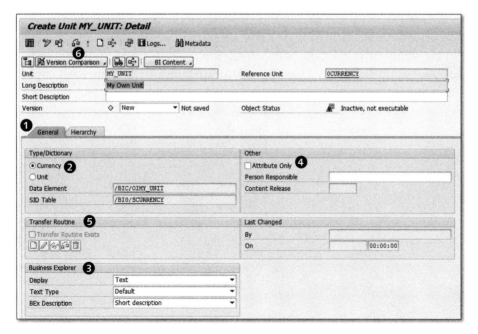

Figure 3.51 Creating a Custom Unit InfoObject: Part 2

7. Select either CURRENCY or UNIT, as shown in ❷ of. Figure 3.51. Unit InfoObjects are always created with reference to the SAP-delivered definition of unit/currency. So, if the data type is selected as CURRENCY, the reference unit is always 0CURRENCY. If UNIT is selected, the reference unit is always 0UNIT.

> **Note**
>
> Other settings are shown in ❸, ❹, and ❺ of Figure 3.51. These settings have the same meaning as those explained in Section 3.5.1 and Section 3.5.2.

8. Activate your unit InfoObject ❻.

We recommend creating the following three InfoObjects in your system: BW_PRICE, BW_PROD, and BW_VAL. (Refer to Appendix B for more information about their definitions.) These InfoObjects are based on our ABCD Corp. example scenario, and will be referenced throughout the book.

3.9   Summary

Because they are the smallest building block, InfoObjects are one of the most important objects in SAP BW. In this chapter, we explained the types of InfoObjects, how to create them, and how to configure them. You'll learn the relevance and use of different InfoObjects in subsequent chapters of the book. In the next chapter, we explain the DSO, its architecture, and the different types and application scenarios.

In this chapter, we explain the details of DSOs. DSOs play crucial roles in the overall design of data warehousing, so understanding how they work will help you design SAP BW solutions more effectively.

4   DataStore Objects

Storing operational data at the most detailed level is an integral function of a typical data warehouse. To this end, SAP BW's technical architecture includes the DataStore object (DSO), which stores data at a detailed level, tracks changes to data, and stores master data.

> **Note**
>
> DSOs were previously referred to as *operational DataStore objects* (ODS), but the title was changed to eliminate some common misinterpretations and assumptions related to the function and purpose of these objects.

In this chapter, we explain DSO types, architectures, configuration setting options, and usage scenarios.

4.1   Introduction to DSOs

In this section, we offer a brief introduction to the definition and purpose of DSOs, and then introduce the three types of DSOs offered by SAP BW.

4.1.1   Definition and Purpose

A *DSO* is an object that stores data at the most granular level; for example, storing records by business transactions such as billing documents (Figure 4.1).

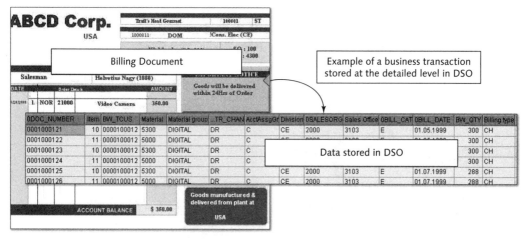

Figure 4.1 Detailed Storage of Business Transaction Data in a DSO

In SAP BW, data targets are objects that physically store data. InfoProviders, on the other hand, are objects you can use to create queries for reporting. Queries can also be created on most data targets, so a data target can be an InfoProvider, but not all InfoProviders are data targets. DSOs are data targets but not necessarily InfoProviders. The central data target in SAP BW is an *InfoCube*, which normally stores data at the aggregated level and is used for creating queries (see Chapter 5 for more details on InfoCubes). In any SAP BW design, it's a good practice to have DSOs as the staging layer that stores the transaction level data and/or stores data received from multiple sources, before relaying it onto InfoCubes or other data targets.

DSOs in SAP BW Powered by SAP HANA

With SAP BW 7.4 powered by SAP HANA, where data is stored in-memory, the DSO is also recommended as an InfoProvider. Prior to SAP HANA, the DSO was primarily used to store granular level data, and the InfoCube was used to store data at the aggregated level. In this way, the InfoCube was optimized for query execution. For SAP BW powered by SAP HANA, the DSO function is a lot more than the data staging layer. The Layered Scalable Architecture (LSA++) defined in Chapter 2 positions the DSO as the final layer of data storage to store the data at a detailed level. However, there are certain situations in which an InfoCube is required.

DSOs have two types of fields: key fields and data fields. While the *key fields* uniquely identify a record in a DSO, all other fields are the *data fields*, which can contain both characteristic and key figure InfoObjects. When a DSO is created for a billing document with multiple items, the key fields of the DSO are generally the billing document number and item number. However, if you reset billing document numbers every year (making it possible to have duplicate billing document numbers across different years), the DSO must have the billing document number, item number, and the year as the key fields.

One of the major benefits of DSOs are their overwrite capability. Unlike Info-Cubes, DSOs are transparent tables and can overwrite stored data for a defined key. In database parlance, a table's *key* uniquely identifies each record in the table. The key for a DSO is a unique combination of key field values. In addition to overwriting, DSOs can be configured to cumulate data for a defined key.

A DSO serves the following functions of data warehousing:

▶ Replication of business-critical data from the transactional source system into the data warehouse, which provides flexibility for archiving the data from the source system.

▶ Flexibility within data warehousing solutions to redesign other data targets, such as InfoCubes, that receive data from DSOs.

▶ A mechanism to identify changes in the original records for DataSources that send entire data sets every time a change is made. This feature helps in transmitting only relevant records or changes in the record to data targets that receive data from the DSO in the data flow of the data warehouse.

▶ A data staging layer within the data warehouse where data validation, data cleansing, and data synchronization can be managed.

Data can be loaded into DSOs from any source system, as shown in ❶ and ❺ of Figure 4.2. The data stored in a DSO is normally very detailed and is usually further sent to InfoCubes where it's summarized, as shown in ❷ of Figure 4.2. A DSO that is supplying data to an InfoCube can also be an InfoProvider; that is, queries can be created on this DSO ❸. That being said, it isn't *mandatory* to extract data from DSOs to InfoCubes; if you don't, the DSO is the end of the data flow, and queries can be created based on the DSO directly ❻. And you also create queries based on an InfoCube that stores data at a summarized level ❹. Finally, SAP BW offers a function called *report-to-report interface* (RRI), which you can use to jump from an InfoCube query to a DSO query ❼ to view detailed level data.

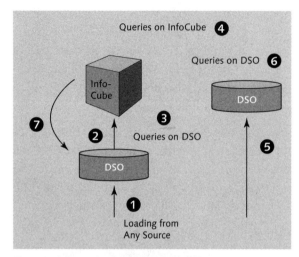

Figure 4.2 Position of a DSO in SAP BW

Report-to-Report Interface (RRI)

RRI is a function that allows a BEx query (defined as the sender) to interact with another query, a BEx web application, a transaction code, or an ABAP report. These are known as the jump targets (defined as the receiver) and can be either inside or outside of the SAP BW system. This feature is available in the query navigation context menu, under the Goto function.

4.1.2 Types of DSOs

There are three types of DSOs in SAP BW, as described next.

Standard DSOs

This type of DSO is used most often in the data staging layer and allows the data fields to be overwritten and the key figure values to be added. Data in this type of DSO can be loaded using the standard data staging processes (i.e., data extraction, transformation, and data transfer processes), which are discussed in more detail in Chapter 7. A standard DSO consists of three tables: the activation queue (new data) table, active data table, and change log table. The change log table keeps track of record changes for a record with the same key field values. (Tables will be discussed in more detail in Section 4.2.) Data from a standard DSO can be loaded to another DSO or to an InfoCube.

Write-Optimized DSOs

The architecture of this type of DSO is optimized for writing data into it and was introduced with SAP BW 7.0. It can load data more quickly than a standard DSO because it isn't necessary to process the activation of a newly loaded request (explained in more detail in Section 4.5). This type of DSO consists of only one table: the active data table. Data in this type of DSO can be loaded using the standard data staging process.

Direct-Update DSOs

The data in this type of DSO can't be loaded using the standard data staging process; instead, SAP BW supplies a few application programming interfaces (APIs). This type of DSO is used as a data target in the Analysis Process Designer (APD) process. As with the write-optimized DSO, this type consists of only the active data table.

DSO Type Comparison

Table 4.1 provides a brief comparison of the three types of DSOs. This table should help you understand the architecture and usage of each type.

Type of DSO	Activation Required?	Active Data Table	Activation Queue (New Data) Table	Change Log Table	Reporting Possible?	SID Generation
Standard	Yes	Yes	Yes	Yes	Yes	Yes
Write-Optimized	No	Yes	No	No	Yes	No
Direct-Update	No	Yes	No	No	Yes	No

Table 4.1 Comparison of Different Features of DSOs

4.2 Architecture of the Standard DSO

Because the standard DSO is the most widely used and is relevant to our ABCD Corp. example, this section focuses specifically on its architecture. In cases where the other types of DSOs differ from the standard, we make specific efforts to call it out.

In this section, we discuss the types of tables in a standard DSO and its activation process. We then conclude the section with a discussion of InfoObject 0RECORD-MODE, which plays a crucial role in the way data is updated in a standard DSO.

4.2.1 Types of Tables

As we've mentioned, the standard DSO consists of three tables: the activation queue (new data), active data, and change log tables (Figure 4.3). These are discussed in more detail next.

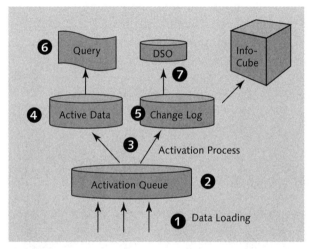

Figure 4.3 Architecture of a Standard DSO

Activation Queue (New Data) Table

The activation queue (new data) table is only relevant for standard DSOs. When data is loaded into a standard DSO (❶ in Figure 4.3), it's first stored in this table ❷. The key fields of this table are technical and consist of the *Request SID (surrogate ID)*, the data package ID (data package number), and the data record number. The Request SID is a number given to each new data loading, and each Request SID is divided into a number of data sets known as the *package ID*. Individual records in each package ID are assigned a number, starting from 1, and this is the record number. The data available in the activation queue (new data) table is neither available for reporting nor for sending to another data target because data in the activation queue (new data) table, by definition, hasn't yet been activated.

Active Data Table

The data from the active data table ❹ is generally used for reporting, as shown in ❻ of Figure 4.3. In some cases, this table also supplies the full data upload to another data target. The key field chosen while designing a DSO is the key of this table. This key is also known as the *semantic key* of the DSO. The activation process (only applicable to standard DSOs) moves the data from the activation queue (new data) table to the active data table and the change log table ❸.

Change Log Table

All of the changes to existing records (i.e., records with the same key field combination) are recorded in the change log table. The key fields of this table are technical, so they are comprised of a combination of the request's request ID, package ID, part number (partition value for the Persistent Staging Area [PSA] table), and record number. This key field combination isn't the same as that for the activation queue (new data) table.

The change log table is related to the other two tables in such a way that the activation process moves data from the activation queue (new data) table to the change log table (❺ of Figure 4.3) and active data table ❹. When data from a standard DSO is updated to other data targets, the delta load is supplied from the change log table ❼.

4.2.2 Activation Process for a Standard DSO

As we explained earlier, data in standard DSOs are contained within three tables. Data moves among these tables during the activation process. More specifically, the activation process moves data from the activation queue (new data) table to the active data and change log tables, deleting it from the activation queue (new data) table on successful activation.

> **Note**
>
> Write-optimized and direct-update DSOs have one table only: the active data table. As such, there is no movement among tables in these two types of DSOs. This discussion of data movement applies to the standard DSO only.

To explain this concept more thoroughly, let's use an example as shown in Figure 4.4. The key field for the DSO in Figure 4.4 is the DOCUMENT NUMBER field, and its two data fields are CUSTOMER and AMOUNT. The AMOUNT field is set to the overwrite mode. The process of configuring the overwrite mode is explained in Chapter 7.

When a request is loaded into a standard DSO, the loaded data gets stored in the activation queue (new data) table as shown in Figure 4.4. The key field combination of the activation queue (new data) table is technical, as stated earlier. At this moment, the active data table and change log table are both empty.

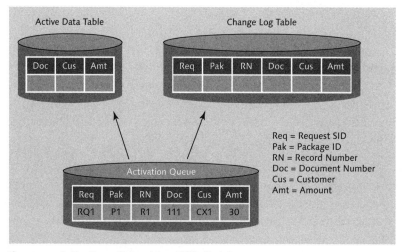

Figure 4.4 Activating a Request in a DSO: Part 1

When a request (let's call it request RQ1) is activated, the data is moved *from* the activation queue (new data) table *to* the active data and change log tables (Figure 4.5).

Because the active data and change log tables were empty, the records in request RQ1 are inserted into them. The key field combination of the active data table is semantic (developer configured), and the key field combination of the change log table is technical. The request ID in the activation queue (new data) table and the activated request in the change log table are different; in this case, we identify the request in the change log table as RX1.

Now assume that a second request, request RQ2, is loaded into the DSO (Figure 4.6). As you can see, RQ2 shows that document number 111 in the source system has been changed; the amount was 30 and is now 40. Because this request is still not activated, the data in the active data and change log tables remain unaffected.

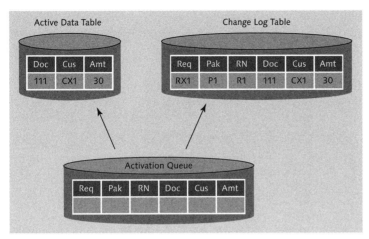

Figure 4.5 Activating a Request in a DSO: Part 2

During the activation process for RQ2, SAP BW checks the existence of the records in the active data table. If a record with the same semantic key is found, the values of the data fields are overwritten. To keep track of this change, SAP BW creates two records in the change log table. One record is known as the *before image*, which is a copy of the existing record with the key figures negated. The second record is known as the *after image*, which is the latest value in the record.

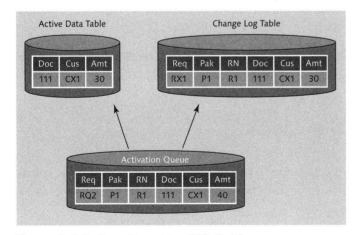

Figure 4.6 Activating a Request in a DSO: Part 3

As shown in Figure 4.7, the active data table still shows only one record because the former record was overwritten by the latest value of the amount key figure.

The change log table, on the other hand, has three records after activation. The first record is from the previous activation, and the next two records are from the current activation process.

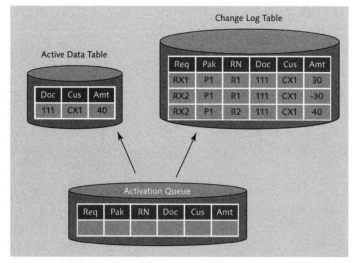

Figure 4.7 Activating a Request in a DSO: Part 4

In short, whenever any change happens to the existing record of a standard DSO, two records are inserted in the change log table, as shown in Table 4.2. The total change in value of the AMOUNT field is 10 (–30 + 40).

	Req	Pak	RN	Doc	Cus	Amt
Before Image	RX2	P1	R1	111	CX1	–30
After Image	RX2	P1	R2	111	CX1	40

Table 4.2 Before Image and After Image Generated in the Change Log Table

Field changes don't only happen to fields with numeric values (as was the case in this example) but can also happen to nonnumeric fields, such as DELIVERY DATE, STATUS OF RECORD, and so on.

4.2.3 InfoObject 0RECORDMODE

When a standard DSO is activated, SAP BW adds the InfoObject 0RECORDMODE to the definition of the standard DSO (in addition to the key fields and data fields)

and to all three tables of the standard DSO. This InfoObject is used internally by SAP BW. You can overwrite the existing record for the same semantic key field combination, in addition to adding key figure values for the record with the same semantic key field combination.

SAP Business Content offers DataSources for a number of standard business processes. The DATASOURCE ROCANCEL field, for example, is mapped to InfoObject 0RECORDMODE in SAP BW. The combination of the update mode (overwrite or add) set in the transformation and the value of InfoObject 0RECORDMODE helps SAP BW properly treat the incoming record in the active data and change log tables.

For example, consider a situation where you've created and loaded a SAP source system document in the DSO, and now you're forced to cancel this document in the SAP source system. The DataSource sends the reverse image of the document to SAP BW, which is communicated using ROCANCEL and 0RECORDMODE mapping. The treatment given to this record in the active data and change log tables depends on this value. Alternatively, another DataSource in this situation might send a delete signal using the ROCANCEL and 0RECORDMODE mapping. In this case, the treatment given to the record in the DSO is different. The following are the values for the ROCANCEL field and the meaning that they communicate about the record:

- BLANK: The record provides an after image.
- X: The record provides a before image.
- A: The record provides an additive image.
- D: The record must be deleted.
- R: The record provides a reverse image.
- N: The record provides a new image.

Note on Multiple Requests

When using standard DSOs, multiple requests can be loaded and activated in parallel. While doing so, SAP BW internally sorts the data—first using the technical key and then using the semantic key. This ensures that the records in the active data table are updated in the correct sequence. Sequence plays a very important role when multiple changes are made to the same document.

4.3 Designing a DSO

For the purposes of the case study we've been using throughout this book, let's assume that the auditors of ABCD Corp. require traceability to a specific billing document. This might be needed to analyze instances of variances or when aggregated results require investigation at the billing document level, and the information is contained in the data warehouse solution (as opposed to transactional systems, where records are archived over periods of time). This means that you must have a DSO that stores billing documents at the most detailed level.

With this scenario in mind, this section explains the process of creating a standard DSO and adding InfoObjects to the DSO. Although there are three types of DSOs, the processes of creating all three are similar. The process explained in this section applies to all three types of DSOs.

To begin, open the DATA WAREHOUSING WORKBENCH screen by using Transaction RSA1. Under MODELING in the NAVIGATION section, select INFOPROVIDER, as shown in ❶ of Figure 4.8. DSOs are created under InfoArea. From the tree section of the screen, select the InfoArea to which you want to attach your DSO ❷. In this example, the InfoArea BW_INFOAREA is selected.

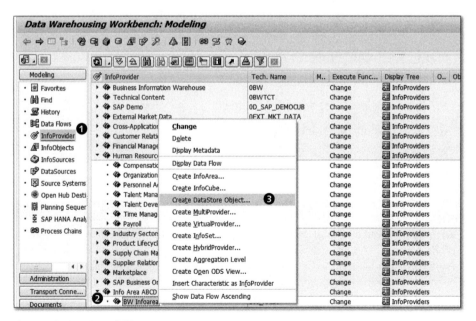

Figure 4.8 Creating a DSO

Using the BW_INFOAREA context menu, select the CREATE DATASTORE OBJECT option ❸. The CREATE DATASTORE OBJECT pop-up box appears (Figure 4.9).

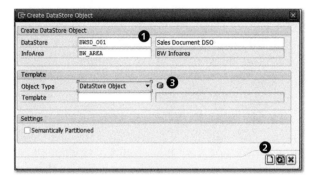

Figure 4.9 Creating a DSO: Entering the Name and Description

DSOs require a unique technical name and description. In this example, we use the technical name "BWSD_O01" and the description "Sales Document DSO", as shown in ❶ of Figure 4.9. If you're creating a DSO that is similar to another DSO in the SAP BW system, you can copy the structure of that DSO by entering its name in the TEMPLATE field shown in ❸. Click on the CREATE icon ▢ ❷. The resulting screen is shown in Figure 4.10.

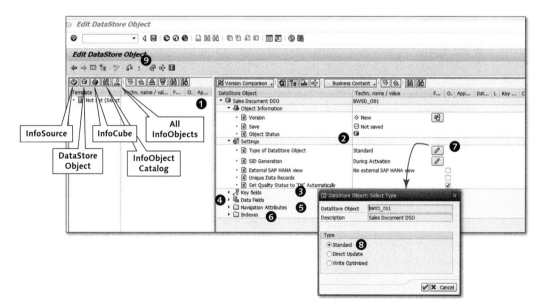

Figure 4.10 Key Settings in a DSO

The settings available when creating the DSO are shown in ❷ of Figure 4.10 and are explained in detail in Section 4.4.1. Different sections of a DSO definition are visible as key fields ❸, data fields ❹, navigation attributes ❺, and the index ❻.

By default, the DSO type is created as the standard type ❼. This can be changed by clicking on the CHANGE icon ⌐✎⌐. The resulting pop-up box ❽ allows you to change the type of the DSO by selecting the appropriate radio button.

4.4 Configuration of the Standard DSO

Although the process of designing a DSO (discussed in Section 4.3) is the same for all three types, some of the configuration settings for each one differ. In this section, we explain the configuration settings for a standard DSO.

4.4.1 Key Settings in a Standard DSO

There are a few key settings for a DSO that play a very important role in its overall design and functionality. Figure 4.10 shows the screen with the SETTINGS ❷ we discuss in this section. You can access this screen by selecting the DSO from the DATA WAREHOUSE WORKBENCH screen and choosing CHANGE from the context menu.

SID Generation

When checked (which occurs by default), the SID GENERATION box causes the system to generate an integer number known as the *surrogate ID* (SID) for each master data value. These SIDs are stored in separate tables called *SID tables*. For each characteristic InfoObject, SAP BW generates a separate SID table. When loading and activating data into a DSO, SAP BW checks for the existence of an SID value for each value of the InfoObject (if the InfoObject contains master data) in the SID table. The system then generates a new value of SID if an existing value isn't found. The SID value is used internally by SAP BW when a query is based on a DSO.

There may be a situation where you create and use a standard DSO for intermediate data staging; that is, you create a standard DSO that only keeps data that is sent to another DSO or InfoCube. This DSO may not be used for reporting purposes. In this situation, you select the NEVER CREATE SIDs option (shown later in ❻ of Figure 4.11) to save time spent on SID generation during DSO activation.

You may also choose to create the SIDs during reporting, which means the SIDs will be checked when a query is run on this DSO data. This option speeds up activation time but slows down reporting.

Because our case study requires that this DSO be used for reporting purposes, we didn't change this default setting.

External SAP HANA View

This setting is only available if you're using an SAP HANA database. This setting generates a corresponding SAP HANA data model (SAP HANA view) when the DSO is activated. Generally, the SAP HANA view is created using the SAP HANA Modeler perspective. Here, if you have a scenario where other reporting tools needs to read data, you can generate the SAP HANA view automatically, which gives access to SAP BW data by simply setting this flag. The SAP HANA view generated is similar to the DSO structure. Various SAP BusinessObjects reporting applications and SQL frontends can then access SAP BW data via these views directly. You can also enhance the view in SAP HANA Modeler for some additional modeling requirements and use it for reporting.

Unique Data Records

This setting is used when there's no chance that the data being loaded into a standard DSO will create a duplicate record, and it improves performance by eliminating some internal processes (such as sorting or creating a before image). If this box is checked, and it turns out that there *are* duplicate records, you'll receive an error message. Because of this, you should only select this box when you're sure that you won't have duplicate data. For example, when your source system doesn't have the ability to edit, change, or delete created documents, you can safely use this setting.

Set Quality Status to 'OK' Automatically

The SET QUALITY STATUS TO 'OK' AUTOMATICALLY flag results in the quality status of the data being set to OK after being loaded without any technical errors; the status must be set to OK to activate newly loaded data in a standard DSO. Only activated data can be passed to further data targets. This flag is checked by default, and we don't recommend changing this. After all of the key settings are configured, you must include InfoObjects in the DSO.

4.4.2   Including InfoObjects in the DSO

At this point, you must decide which InfoObjects you want to include in the DSO. The most important decision is to finalize its key fields because combinations of these uniquely identify each record in the DSO. Using the case study scenario we described at the beginning of this section, you design the DSO for storing billing records at the detail level. Billing records contain details such as the sold-to party, material, billing date, billed quantity, billed amount, and so on, and all of these details can be uniquely identified by the combination of a billing document number and its billing item number. In this case, the billing document number and billing item number can be designed as key fields of the DSO, and all other objects can be included as data fields.

The InfoObjects to be included in a DSO can be selected using two different methods—templates and direct-input—which we discuss in more detail next.

Using Templates

The left pane of Figure 4.11 allows you to select InfoObjects using the template function (refer to ❶ of Figure 4.10). Several types of templates are available for selecting InfoObjects: InfoSource, DataStore Object, InfoCube, InfoObject Catalog, and All InfoObjects.

In this example, we'll use the template called InfoObject Catalog. To do this, click on the INFOOBJECT CATALOG icon 🔲, as shown in ❶ of Figure 4.11. SAP BW opens the SELECT INFOOBJECT CATALOG pop-up screen. Click on the INFOAREA icon 🔲 ❷. The InfoObject catalog attached to the selected InfoArea is listed ❸. Double-click on InfoObject catalog BW_CHAR_CA. The TEMPLATE area ❹ on the screen now shows all of the InfoObjects available under the selected InfoObject catalog. You can select one or multiple InfoObjects by dragging and dropping over either KEY FIELDS or DATA FIELDS ❺. In the SETTINGS section, if you click on the CHANGE icon 🔲 for SID GENERATION, a CREATE SIDs pop-up box ❻ with three options appears:

- ▶ DURING REPORTING
  SIDs are generated when reporting is done on this DSO.

- ▶ DURING ACTIVATION
  SIDs are generated when activating requests in this DSO.

- ▶ NEVER CREATE SIDs
  No SIDs are generated.

Choose DURING ACTIVATION, and click on the CONTINUE button ❼.

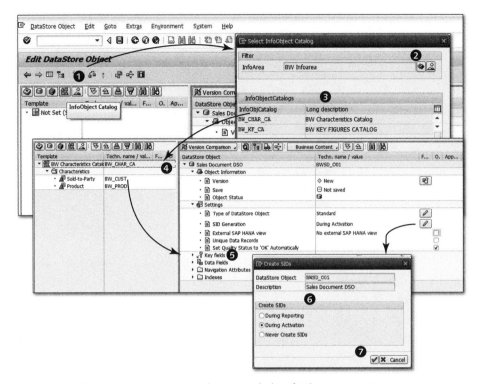

Figure 4.11 Editing the DSO: Using Templates to Include InfoObjects in a DSO

Direct Input

If you already know the technical names of the InfoObjects you want to include in the design of your DSO, you can use this method. Referring back to our case study scenario, the key fields of DSO BWSD_O01 are BILLING DOCUMENT NUMBER or SALES DOCUMENT NUMBER (InfoObject 0DOC_NUMBER) and BILLING ITEM NUMBER or SALES DOCUMENT ITEM (InfoObject 0S_ORD_ITEM). Because the names of these InfoObjects are already known, we can use the direct-input method. Select KEY FIELDS, as shown in ❶ of Figure 4.12. Using the context menu, select the INFO-OBJECT DIRECT INPUT option ❷.

Type the technical name of the InfoObjects you want to include as key fields of the DSO. Enter "0DOC_NUMBER" and "0S_ORD_ITEM" ❸, and press ⌨Enter. (SAP BW automatically checks the entered InfoObject names and shows the long description if they are validated correctly.) Now click on the CONTINUE icon ❹.

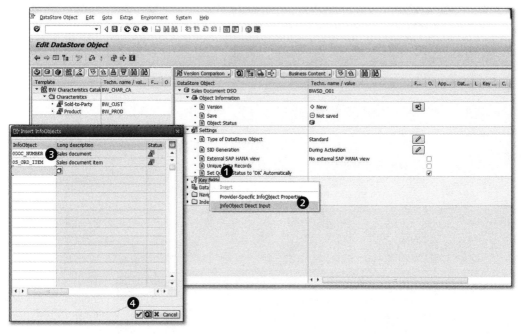

Figure 4.12 Editing the DSO: Direct Input

The result of this action is shown in ❶ of Figure 4.13. Both InfoObjects 0DOC_NUMBER and 0S_ORD_ITEM are now part of key fields.

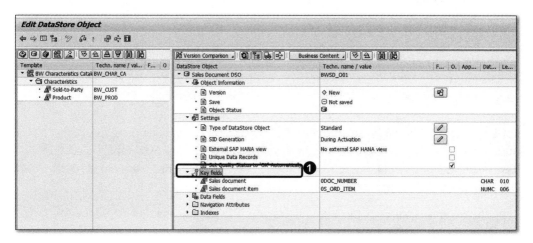

Figure 4.13 Edit DSO: Key Fields

4.4.3 Entering Data Fields

The next step in configuring a standard DSO is to enter the data fields. The data fields can have both characteristic and key figure InfoObjects.

> **Note**
>
> Including InfoObjects in data fields is accomplished by the exact same process as including InfoObjects in key fields (either by the template or direct-input method).

Navigation attributes defined for the included InfoObjects are available for viewing under the NAVIGATION ATTRIBUTES column. They are included automatically, and you need to confirm them by selection, as shown in ❶ of Figure 4.14.

The box in the ON/OFF column ❷ indicates whether the navigation attribute is switched on (included) or off (excluded). SAP BW follows a standard naming convention for navigation attributes: NAME_OF_CHARACTERISTICS__NAME_OF_ATTRIBUTE. So, for example, the name 0MATERIAL__0DIVISION indicates that 0DIVISION is the navigation attribute of the 0MATERIAL InfoObject ❸.

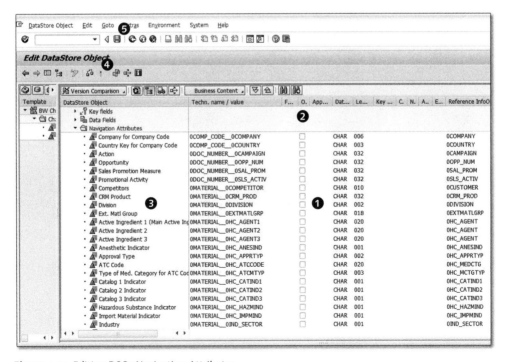

Figure 4.14 Editing DSO: Navigation Attributes

Note

Reporting performance on the DSO is improved by use of secondary indexes. You can create secondary indexes in all types of DSOs. At the same time, however, many secondary indexes impair the loading performance.

This completes the steps required to configure a standard DSO; the final design of DSO BWSD_O01 is shown in Table 4.3.

Type	InfoObject Name
Key Fields	0DOC_NUMBER
	0S_ORD_ITEM
Data Fields	0BILL_TYPE
	0ITEM_CATEG
	0BILL_CAT
	0BILL_DATE
	BW_CUST
	0VTYPE
	0CUST_GRP1
	0CUST_GROUP
	0MATERIAL
	0DIVISION
	0MATL_GROUP
	0PLANT
	0COMP_CODE
	0SALESORG
	0REGION
	0DISTR_CHAN
	0COUNTRY
	0SALES_OFF
	0SALES_GRP
	0SALES_DIST
	BW_QTY
	0NET_WGT_DL
	0GRS_WGT_DL
	0UNIT_OF_WT
	0UNIT
	0DOC_CATEG
	0COST

Table 4.3 Design of DSO BWSD_O01

Type	InfoObject Name
Data Fields	0LOC_CURRCY 0DOC_CURRCY 0ACCNT_ASGN 0CO_AREA 0NET_VALUE 0SUBTOTAL_1 0SUBTOTAL_2 0VALUE_LC

Table 4.3 Design of DSO BWSD_O01 (Cont.)

You can now activate the DSO using the ACTIVATE icon ⬛, as shown in ❹ of Figure 4.14. Activating the DSO creates the three tables we mentioned earlier: the activation queue (new data), active data, and change log tables.

Return to the initial DATA WAREHOUSING WORKBENCH screen by using the BACK icon (❺ of Figure 4.14). As you can see in ❶ of Figure 4.15, the newly created DSO BWSD_O01 is available under InfoArea BW_INFOAREA.

Figure 4.15 DSO BWSD_O01 under InfoArea BW_InfoArea

4.5 Configuration of Write-Optimized DSOs

In this section, we explain the configuration details of the second type of DSO, the write-optimized DSO. Write-optimized DSOs consist of only one table, the active data table. Because there is no activation queue (new data) table or change log table, there is no activation process; data is loaded directly into the active data table. This type of DSO is useful when you have a large amount of data, and complex transformations are involved. After data is loaded into this DSO, the transformed data can be loaded into other smaller InfoProviders using different filters. You can also use this type of DSO as your source system copy data; source system data is stored in this DSO without any transformation. This DSO can then be used as a source of data for other InfoProviders.

Compared to standard DSOs, the settings required while creating a write-optimized DSO are much less complex (Figure 4.16). To access this screen, select DSO from the DATA WAREHOUSING WORKBENCH screen. From the context menu, select CHANGE.

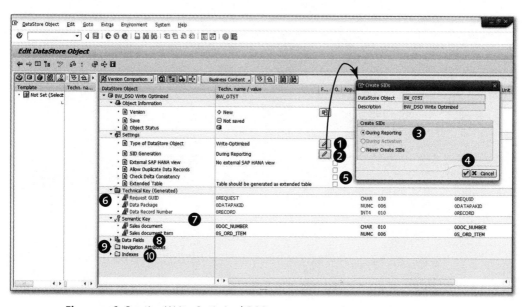

Figure 4.16 Creating Write-Optimized DSOs

The first thing to do when creating a write-optimized DSO is to change the TYPE OF DATASTORE OBJECT to WRITE-OPTIMIZED, as shown in ❶ of Figure 4.16. The system then generates the technical key, which consists of the following fields: REQUEST GUID, DATA PACKAGE, and DATA RECORD NUMBER ❻.

The ALLOW DUPLICATE DATA RECORDS indicator is only relevant for write-optimized DSOs. With these objects, the TECHNICAL KEY of the active tables always consists of the fields REQUEST, DATA PACKAGE, and DATA RECORD. The InfoObjects that appear in the maintenance dialog in the KEY FIELDS folder form the semantic key of the write-optimized DSO.

If you don't set this indicator, the uniqueness of the data is checked, and the system generates a unique index in the semantic key of the InfoObject. This index has the technical name KEY. If this indicator is set, the active table of the DSO can contain more than one record with the same key.

As shown in Figure 4.16, you need to maintain the SEMANTIC KEY ❼, DATA FIELDS ❽, NAVIGATION ATTRIBUTES ❾, and INDEXES ❿ areas of the screen. The SEMANTIC KEY on this screen is the same as the key fields of the standard DSO, as are the rest of the settings.

Data can be loaded into a write-optimized DSO using standard data staging, that is, using transformation and the data transfer process (DTP) (discussed in Chapter 7). Data from this DSO can be sent to other data targets using the details of the request.

Upon activation (accomplished by clicking on the ACTIVATE icon ⬚), a write-optimized DSO is available in the DATA WAREHOUSING WORKBENCH screen under InfoProvider, as shown in ❶ of Figure 4.17. As you can see, it's indicated with a special icon ⬚ that appears to the right of its technical name.

> **Early Unload Concept for SAP BW Powered by SAP HANA**
>
> This concept is applicable to the SAP HANA database only. SAP BW systems normally store large amounts of data. Out of this, large chunks of data may not be regularly accessed. For example, most inactive data is stored in BW in objects like Persistent Staging Area (PSA) and write-optimized DSOs. They store data in a particular fashion. Whenever new data is loaded in both of these objects, SAP BW creates a new partition and stores the data in this newly created partition, so the early unload concept enables the system to identify the data that can be offloaded from memory first when SAP HANA memory becomes bottlenecked.
>
> Here, the system identifies inactive data (i.e., data in the old partitions) and displaces it from memory. Data in the newest partition is not displaced during this process. In this way, the system optimizes the requirement of SAP HANA's memory.

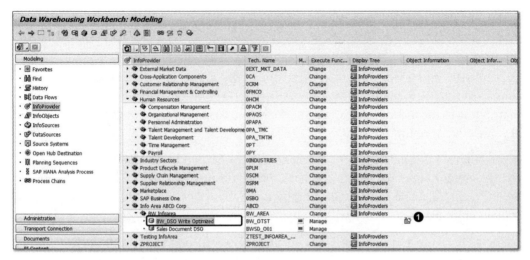

Figure 4.17 Write-Optimized DSO in the Data Warehousing Workbench

4.6 Configuration of Direct-Update DSOs

In earlier versions of SAP BW releases, the direct-update DSO was called the *transactional DSO*. Like the write-optimized DSO, it consists of only one table: the active data table. Data can't be loaded into this type of DSO using data staging, but there are special APIs available in SAP BW that can write into it (even from an external system). Additionally, multiple users can simultaneously write into this DSO, and the newly written data is immediately available for further usage.

This DSO is mainly used as a data target in the APD process. (The APD tool supports complex analysis tasks, including merging, manipulating, and transforming data from different sources. APD is explained in more detail in Chapter 15.)

When creating a direct-update DSO, first change TYPE OF DATASTORE OBJECT to DIRECT UPDATE, as shown in ❶ of Figure 4.18. This type of DSO contains a semantic key, which is defined while creating the DSO ❺. No other settings are available while creating a direct-update DSO. You must also select the DATA FIELDS ❻, NAVIGATION ATTRIBUTES ❼, and INDEXES ❽. Direct-update DSOs can be used in Integrated Planning scenarios. To do so, check the PLANNING MODE flag ❾.

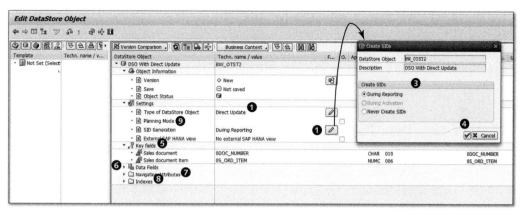

Figure 4.18 Creating a Direct-Update DSO

Once activated, the direct-update DSO is available in the DATA WAREHOUSING WORKBENCH screen under INFOPROVIDER, as shown in ❶ of Figure 4.19. As you can see, it's indicated with an icon ⧈ that appears to the right of its technical name.

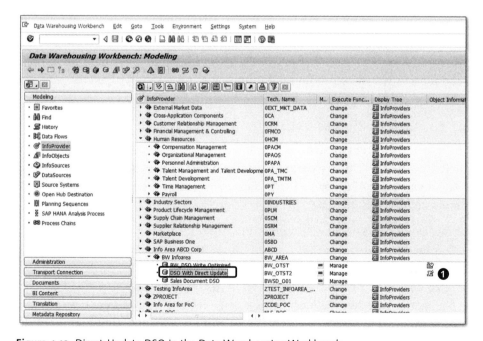

Figure 4.19 Direct-Update DSO in the Data Warehousing Workbench

4.7 Usage Scenarios for DSOs

The technical architecture of a DSO enables it to fulfill the requirements of data warehousing. In this section, we briefly explain some of the application scenarios for DSOs.

4.7.1 Data Staging

Some typical business processes require a DSO for storing data before transmitting it to an InfoCube and serving as the data staging layer. There are scenarios where data from multiple source systems is extracted and stored in a DSO, and a harmonized and synchronized set of data is transmitted to InfoCubes or other data targets as a delta load. For example, this is true of Business Content Data-Sources for Accounts Payable, Accounts Receivable, and SAP General Ledger in Financial Accounting, all of which need a DSO as a staging layer before data flows as a delta load to their respective InfoCubes.

4.7.2 Temporary Storage Area

Other business scenarios require dealing with extremely large sets of data. When executing complex transformations in such a scenario, use a write-optimized DSO because the system doesn't generate SIDs, and the request to the DSO doesn't need to be activated, which means you can save and further process data quickly.

4.7.3 Analysis Process Designer

There are certain requirements where you might want to perform calculations or analysis on SAP BW query output (or on other sources of data in SAP BW). SAP BW provides the APD for just this purpose. In this case, a direct-update DSO should be used to store data.

To give you a more practical example, let's say ABCD Corp. uses queries based on data from different systems to calculate organizational-level performance metrics. Because these metrics change every day, senior management wants to track how they change over a period of time. You need to persistently save the data from these queries together for future analysis. To do this, you can build an analysis process where you merge the results from all needed queries and then store the data in a direct-update DSO. The details of APD are explained in Chapter 15.

4.7.4 Pseudo-Delta

We explained the data activation process earlier in this chapter. The typical architecture of the standard DSO enables it to identify changes in original records for the DataSources that send entire data sets every time a change is made. This feature helps transmit only relevant records to the data targets above the DSO in the data flow of the data warehouse. To explain this further, let's take a very simple scenario in which SAP BW receives billing document 123456 with a quantity of 10, and then the quantity is changed to 12. The DSO transmits only delta for the changes in the data field value, which is +2 in this case (Table 4.4).

Sequence from Source	Data from Source		Net Result in DSO Tables		Net Transmission to InfoCube
	Key Field of DSO Billing Document No.	Data Field of DSO (Quantity)	Active Table in DSO	Change Log in DSO	
First Time Receipt	123456	10	10	10	10
Second Time Receipt	123456	12	12	+2	+2

Table 4.4 Illustration of Delta Functionality Using a DSO

These four application scenarios explain how the unique technical architecture of a DSO provides a variety of application options, besides its predominant use as a data staging component.

4.8 Summary

In this chapter, we introduced you to the basic concepts involved in DSOs. We began our discussion with some information about DSOs in general and then moved on to an explanation of their respective architectures. After that, we explained the process of setting up a DSO (which is common to all three types of DSOs) and then went into the individual configuration details for each type.

In the next chapter, we explain the InfoCube, the central object in SAP BW.

Understanding the InfoCube and its design is essential to creating a robust data warehousing solution based on SAP BW. This chapter gets you started on this path.

5   InfoCubes

As a data warehouse, SAP BW stores data from different sources, predominantly Online Transaction Processing (OLTP) systems and other data warehousing solutions (if required). However, it also has the capacity for running off of Online Analytical Processing (OLAP) systems. To do this, SAP BW uses the *extended star schema model*. The *InfoCube*, which is the subject of this chapter, is based on this model and is one of the data targets (objects that physically store data) in SAP BW; in fact, it's the central object of SAP BW. Because it's based on the extended star schema, InfoCubes can perform OLAP tasks more quickly than other objects, such as the DataStore object (DSO). As such, they play an integral role in addressing a majority of OLAP requirements in SAP BW.

In this chapter, we introduce you to InfoCubes by describing the high-level modeling process, a key element of which is the conversion of analysis requirements from common business language to technical requirements. We then cover the types of InfoCubes and the process of creating them in the system, as well as some of the finer aspects of their design.

InfoCubes and SAP HANA

With SAP HANA coming into the picture, InfoCube design and multidimensional modeling has little significance for query performance or for layered scalable architecture. Nevertheless, SAP BW systems that aren't based on SAP HANA still continue to benefit from InfoCube modeling. An overview of SAP HANA-optimized InfoCubes (in an SAP BW powered by SAP HANA system) is given in Section 5.2.2.

5.1 Modeling InfoCubes

To effectively model and design an InfoCube, it's essential to understand the way analytical requirements are expressed in business language; a clear understanding of business requirements and source data is an important precondition to ensure a scalable and maintainable design. When assessing analytical requirements, start with a high-level business model involving key entities, and then transform this into a high-level logical data model. After that, you can determine the scope of the business process and drill down the processes to build a detailed logical data model. This is an SAP Best Practice and has two advantages. First, because it starts with a high-level business model, the detailed logical model is designed with reference to a bigger picture involving business functions. Second, if the solution scope expands over time, scaling it up will be a lot easier and will require minimum rework.

The business intelligence (BI) requirements discussed in Chapter 1 were expressed in nontechnical terms. We now need to translate them into technical terms that will help you design a multidimensional model that meets analysis requirements. This process begins by evaluating each aspect of a business process and its representation in the technical model of a BI system. We can then use this information to generate reports in the form of tables, dashboards, charts, and so on, thereby providing the information needed to make intelligent business decisions.

In this section, we'll describe the process of designing an InfoCube for our example company, ABCD Corp. To start, we'll identify the key technical terms and their relation to business entities. Then we'll walk you through each of the following steps in the process of creating an InfoCube:

- ▶ Drawing assignment tables
- ▶ Creating bubble models
- ▶ Identifying dimensions
- ▶ Converting bubble models to classic star schemas
- ▶ Designing extended star schemas

Finally, we'll conclude with a few things to keep in mind about InfoCubes.

5.1.1 Key Terms

Before we begin our explanation of how to model an InfoCube, you should understand the following important terms:

▸ **Characteristic**

A characteristic defines a business entity that is being evaluated or measured by a key figure in SAP BW. Customers and companies, for example, are both characteristics.

▸ **Key figure**

Key figures are numeric values or quantities, such as per unit sales price, quantity sold, and sales revenue in SAP. Billing quantity and volume, for example, are both key figures.

▸ **Fact**

A fact represents data in the form of key figures or measures.

▸ **Dimension**

A dimension is a logical grouping of characteristics that belong together, for example, a product and product category or a customer and customer segment.

▸ **Attributes**

Attributes are features that define a specific aspect of a characteristic. For example, a product is a characteristic, and the color of the product is an attribute.

▸ **Granularity**

Granularity is the level of detailing; for example, the data available at a day level is more granular than that at a month level. Similarly, the more characteristics that define a key combination for identifying a fact record, the higher the granularity.

5.1.2 Drawing Assignment Tables for Characteristics and Key Figures

In a business process, all types of entities are related to each other. To visualize and understand their relationships, you draw an assignment table, which is a visual representation of these relationships (Figure 5.1).

Characteristics → / Key Figures ↓	Customer	Company	Sales Office	Sales Group	Division	Plant	Sales Organization	Distribution Channel	Controlling Area	Region	Sales District	Product	Product Group	Customer Group 1	Customer Group	Value Type	Assignment Group	Billing Type	Billing Category	Item Category
Billing Quantity	✔		✔		✔	✔	✔	✔				✔								
Net Weight												✔								
Gross Weight												✔								
Volume												✔								
Cost in Document Currency			✔																	
Net Value of Item in DC	✔		✔				✔	✔				✔								
Subtotal 1	✔		✔				✔	✔				✔								
Tax	✔		✔				✔	✔				✔								
Amount in Local Currency			✔																	

Figure 5.1 Assignment Table for Characteristics and Key Figures

As you can see, the assignment table has columns (❷ of Figure 5.1) that list the characteristics and rows ❸ that list the key figures. The relationships of all the characteristics and key figures are established by marking the cell where there is an association; these markings should be based on your individual business model. For example, if a billing document for a customer has a billing quantity, the cell at the intersection of these two entities should be checked ❹.

For the ABCD Corp. case study, we're studying the billing process and key figures in a billing document. All key figures are related to all of the characteristics, so all cells in the assignment table should be checked. This is, of course, unique to this particular case study; the assignment tables will change depending on individual business scenarios.

5.1.3 Creating Bubble Models

After the assignment table is developed, you can develop a *bubble model* that articulates the relationships of entities in visual form. To do this, you must group characteristics based on their relationship with each other. There are two types of possible relationships:

▸ **M:N relationship**
The relationship between two characteristics is many to many; for example, a customer can buy any of the products being sold, and the products can be sold to any customer.

▸ **1:N relationship**
The relationship between two characteristics is one to many; for example, a customer can belong to only one sales office, but each sales office can have multiple customers.

To simplify the model, characteristics that have M:N relationships are kept in different groups, whereas those that have 1:N relationships are grouped together. In our scenario, customers and products have an M:N relationship and are grouped separately. However, each material (or product) can have only one material group (or product group) and therefore has a 1:N relationship, so materials and material groups are grouped together.

Figure 5.2 shows a bubble model with all key figures in the center, surrounded by bubbles that represent grouped characteristics (i.e., characteristics with 1:N relationships). Bubble models are the basis for the extended star schema architectures on which InfoCubes are based.

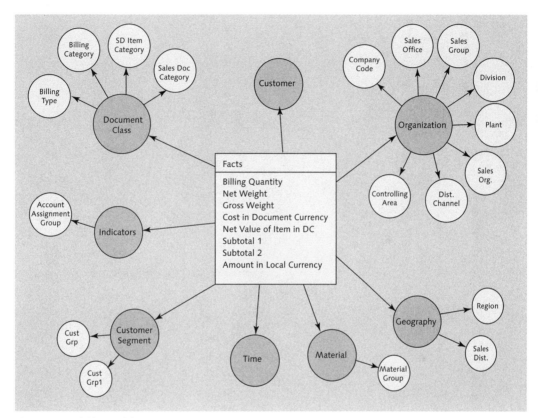

Figure 5.2 Bubble Model

5.1.4 Identifying Dimensions

The bubble model in Figure 5.3 has *facts* (i.e., the key figures in the center) surrounded by bubbles, which represent characteristics. As shown by the circles in Figure 5.3, these characteristics are separated into groups, which are identified as dimensions.

For the bubble model in Figure 5.3, the dimensions are shown as follows:

❶ Customer

❷ Organization

❸ Geography

❹ Material

❺ Time

❻ Customer Segment

❼ Indicators

❽ Document Class

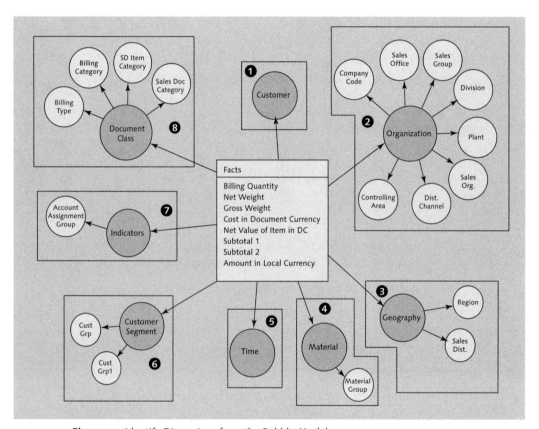

Figure 5.3 Identify Dimensions from the Bubble Model

5.1.5 Converting a Bubble Model to a Classic Star Schema

In this section, we explain how to convert a bubble model to a classic star schema model. The characteristics and their groups are identified from the bubble model, and the characteristics belonging to an identified group are assigned to that dimension in the InfoCube design. So, for example, it can be interpreted that the material and material group characteristics (0MATERIAL and 0MATL_GROUP, respectively) are assigned to the material dimension.

In technical terms, a dimension is a table in the database, referred to as a *dimension table*. Each dimension table has a unique key (i.e., a character string) to identify a unique record from the table. For example, the key for the material dimension is MATERIAL_DIM_ID.

Similarly, the key figures are part of the fact table and are linked to different dimensions using dimension IDs (DIM_IDs). The combination of DIM_IDs from all dimensions forms a unique key for the fact table.

Following these principles, the technical model is generated in Figure 5.4.

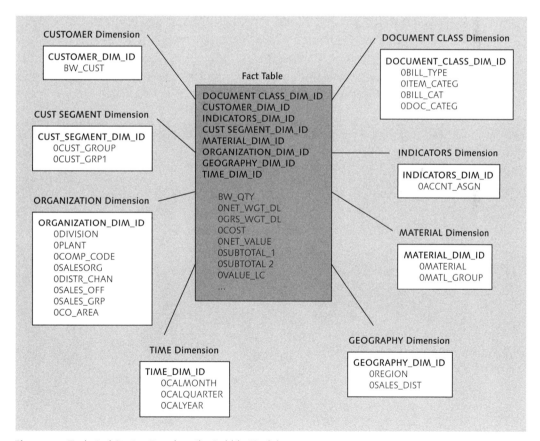

Figure 5.4 Technical Design Based on the Bubble Model

This classic star schema model has the actual value of the material and material group from the transaction data stored in the material dimension table.

5.1.6 Designing an Extended Star Schema

SAP BW's technical architecture is based on an improved version of the classic star schema, known as the *extended star schema*. The extended star schema stores a generated value known as the surrogate ID (SID) in the dimension table, instead of storing the actual values of the characteristics. SIDs are system-generated numeric values that are stored in the SID table of a characteristic InfoObject. The SID table is created for each InfoObject when the InfoObject definition is activated.

For example, the material dimension stores SIDs for the material (SID_0MATE-RIAL) and material group (SID_0MATL_GROUP) characteristics. InfoObject 0MATERIAL has its own SID values, which are stored separately in the SID table associated with InfoObject 0MATERIAL. In the same way, InfoObject 0MATL_GROUP has its own SID values, which are stored separately in SID tables associated with InfoObject 0MATL_GROUP (Figure 5.5).

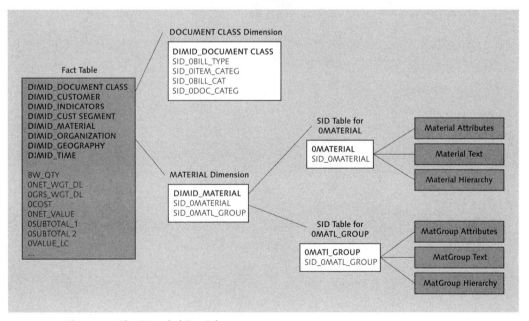

Figure 5.5 The Extended Star Schema

In the extended star schema, the dimension ID (DIM_ID) is also a system-generated numerical value, which is generated for each unique combination of SIDs in the dimension table. So, for the material dimension, SAP BW generates a unique DIM_ID for each unique combination of 0MATERIAL and 0MATL_GROUP (Figure 5.5).

The DIM_IDs generated for all different dimensions in this manner are combined to form the key of the fact table. The key figure values stored in the fact table are linked to the values in the dimension table through DIM_IDs.

To explain the way data is stored in the extended star schema, let's consider an example of a simple model that includes only three dimensions in an InfoCube:

- **Customer dimension**
  Has the customer (CUST) characteristic assigned to it.

- **Material dimension**
  Has the material (MAT) and material group (MGR) characteristics assigned to it.

- **Time dimension**
  Has the month (MONTH) characteristic assigned to it.

For the purpose of this example, make the following assumptions for the SIDs:

- The customer master data is loaded to the customer InfoObject, and the SIDs for the three customers (C1, C2, and C3) are 1, 2, and 3, respectively. This is shown in the SID table for CUST in Figure 5.6.

- The material master data is loaded to the material InfoObject, and the SIDs for the five materials (M1, M2, M3, M4, and M5) are 1, 2, 3, 4, and 5, respectively. This is shown in the SID table for MAT in Figure 5.6.

- The material group master data is loaded to the material group InfoObject, and the SIDs for the three material groups (MG1, MG2, and MG3) are 1, 2, and 3, respectively. This is shown in the SID table for MGR in Figure 5.6.

- The time granularity for this InfoCube is *month*. The time master data is generated by the system, and SIDs for all of the month values are generated and available. The SIDs for the three month values (08.2009, 09.2009, and 10.2009) are 11, 12, and 13, respectively. This is shown in the SID table for MONTH in Figure 5.6. (For high-level analysis, you can also assign the quarter and year characteristics to the time dimension. These are derived directly from the month characteristic.)

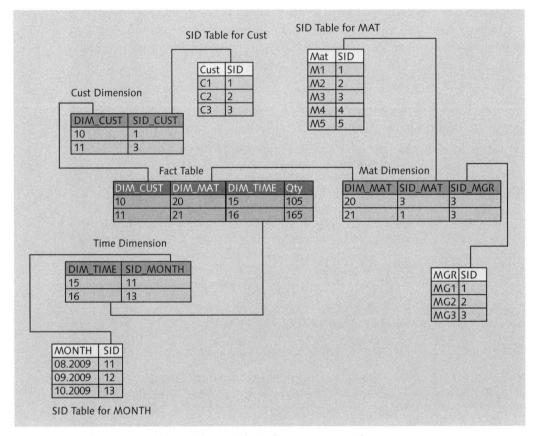

Figure 5.6 Extended Star Schema: Relation between DIMs and SIDs

Now let's assume that two transaction records, shown in Table 5.1, are to be loaded into this InfoCube.

Customer	Material	Material Group	Month	Quantity
C1	M3	MG3	08.2009	105
C3	M1	MG3	10.2009	165

Table 5.1 Sample Data for Illustrating DIM/SID Relationship

When this data is loaded, it's stored in the InfoCube model, as shown in Figure 5.6. Again, dimension tables save the data of the characteristics values shown in

Table 5.1, but instead of storing the actual characteristic values, the dimension tables store the SID values. For example, the first record in the transaction data has the customer value listed as C1, but the dimension table stores the SID. Because only one characteristic is assigned to the CUST dimension, for each unique value of the customer SID, the system creates a DIM_ID for it in the dimension table. In Figure 5.6, DIM_ID 10 is generated for SID_CUST = 1. The key of the customer dimension table is DIM_CUST.

In a similar fashion, the material dimension with two characteristics assigned to it forms a unique record from the combination of the material and material group SID values. A DIM_ID is generated for each unique combination of SIDs of the characteristics included in the dimension. The key of the material dimension table is DIM_MAT.

Finally, the fact table stores key figures associated with the InfoCube. For this example, the values for the quantity key figure (Qᴛʏ in Figure 5.6) are stored in the fact table, along with the DIM_IDs from all of the dimensions.

Summary

- The InfoCube design is based on the extended star schema.
- The key figure values are linked to different dimensions using DIM_IDs.
- The dimensions are linked to the actual values of characteristics through the SIDs stored in the dimension table.

5.1.7 Additional InfoCube Considerations

To conclude our discussion about modeling an InfoCube, we should review a few requirements that must be considered when designing an InfoCube in SAP BW:

- You can include a maximum of 233 key figures in an InfoCube. All InfoCubes must have at least 1 key figure.
- You can attach a maximum of 248 characteristics to one dimension.
- You can include a maximum of 16 dimensions in an InfoCube. The minimum is 4, with 3 systems defined and at least 1 customer defined.
- Out of these 16 dimensions, 3 are system-defined: time, unit, and data package.
- The time dimension is mandatory.

▶ The unit dimension stores units/currencies associated with the key figures within an InfoCube.

▶ The data package dimension is a technical requirement that SAP BW uses internally.

5.2 Types of InfoCubes

In this section, we explain the different types of InfoCubes that capitalize on the technical architecture of the extended star schema in different and unique ways.

5.2.1 Standard InfoCube

A *standard InfoCube* is the most commonly used InfoCube in SAP BW. This InfoCube physically stores data (using the extended star schema) and is classified as a data target. Data can be loaded to a standard InfoCube using the data staging process. This type of InfoCube is optimized for reading data from the fact table; in other words, it's used for reporting.

Note
With SAP BW powered by SAP HANA, all new developed InfoCubes are SAP HANA-optimized InfoCubes. If you've migrated your BW system from a non-SAP HANA database to SAP HANA, then there's a procedure to convert your previously defined non-SAP HANA-optimized standard InfoCube to a SAP HANA-optimized InfoCube. This is explained in the next section.

5.2.2 SAP HANA-Optimized InfoCube

With SAP BW on SAP HANA, you can only create an *SAP HANA-optimized InfoCube*, which is a standard InfoCube that has been optimized to use the power of SAP HANA. (The standard InfoCube is explained in Section 5.2.1).

An SAP HANA-optimized InfoCube is a simplified version of a standard InfoCube (see Figure 5.7).

As illustrated in Figure 5.7, the following differences are highlighted between an SAP HANA-optimized InfoCube and the InfoCube in SAP BW on a non-SAP HANA database:

▶ Dimension tables aren't created.

▶ SIDs (master data IDs) are directly written to the fact table.

▶ A separate E fact table for compressed data isn't created.

▶ The structural changes indicated in Figure 5.7 are done keeping in mind that the InfoCube data resides in SAP HANA in-memory. As dimension tables aren't created, DIM_IDs need not be generated, increasing the loading performance significantly.

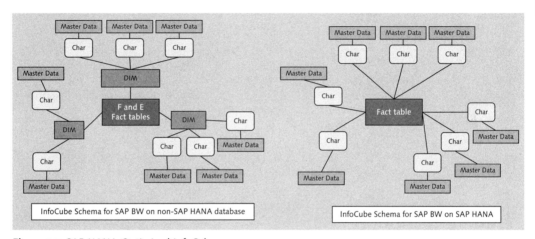

Figure 5.7 SAP HANA-Optimized InfoCube

Also, as shown in Figure 5.7, each characteristic included in the SAP HANA-optimized InfoCube is directly connected to the fact table using SIDs. This means the grouping of characteristics in dimensions has no significance on the InfoCube performance. Each characteristic included in the InfoCube behaves as a line item dimension in itself, irrespective of the way those are grouped in the dimensions.

Converting to an SAP HANA-Optimized InfoCube

This section is applicable to those who had an SAP BW system on a non-SAP HANA database and now have migrated onto an SAP HANA system. To take advantage of SAP HANA, there are two ways to convert the InfoCube/DSO: the first method allows you to convert a single InfoCube to SAP HANA optimized, and the second method makes it so you can use mass conversion. Let's see how both of these methods work.

Converting a Single InfoCube

Begin by entering the Data Warehousing Workbench. From here, select the Info-
Cube you want to convert to an SAP HANA-optimized InfoCube. Using the context menu, select the DISPLAY option to open the DISPLAY INFOCUBE screen, as
shown in Figure 5.8. Select the CONVERSION TO SAP HANA-OPTIMIZED option
from the GOTO menu as shown in ❶ and ❷ of Figure 5.8. This converts the non-
SAP HANA InfoCube to an SAP HANA-optimized InfoCube.

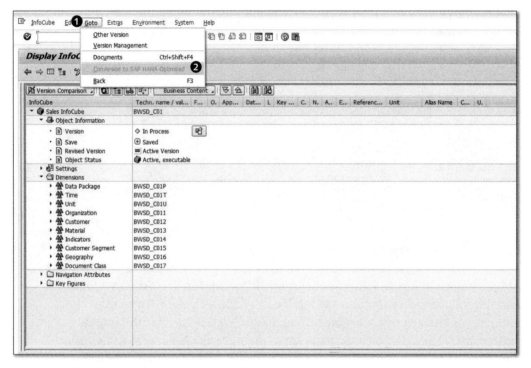

Figure 5.8 Converting a Single InfoCube to SAP HANA-Optimized

Mass Conversion

If you want to convert a number of InfoCubes/DSOs to an SAP HANA-optimized
structure, use Transaction RSMIGRHANADB. This starts the OPTIMIZED CONVER-
SION OF STANDARD OBJECTS TO SAP HANA-OPTIMIZED OBJECTS screen, as shown in
Figure 5.9.

Using this facility, you can convert standard InfoCubes/standard DSOs and
semantically partitioned objects to SAP HANA-optimized. Select the relevant

radio buttons as shown in ❶ of Figure 5.9. You'll also need to enter technical names of the objects here. If you're converting DSOs, there is an option to convert WITHOUT CHANGE LOG also, as shown in ❷ of Figure 5.9. There is another option to view the log of conversion activities ❸). After this is done, click on the EXECUTE icon ❹ to start the conversion. This will allow you to convert all your non-SAP HANA objects to an SAP HANA-optimized structure.

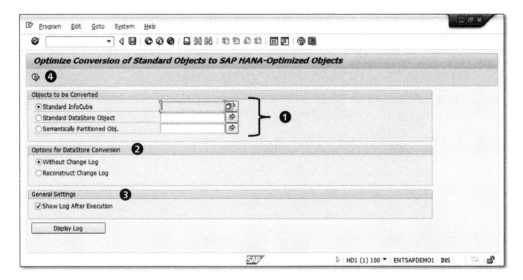

Figure 5.9 Mass Conversion to SAP HANA-Optimized Objects

5.2.3 Real-Time InfoCube

A *real-time InfoCube* has the ability to write data. Real-time InfoCubes are the basis for any planning application in SAP BW. The data stored in a real-time Info-Cube is also available for reporting.

While a standard InfoCube is optimized for reading data (i.e., reporting), a real-time InfoCube is optimized for writing data. Data generated or modified in a planning application is written to these types of cubes using an Application Programming Interface (API).

There are two ways in which you can load data into a real-time InfoCube: by using a planning application or through SAP BW staging. The real-time behavior of a real-time InfoCube can be changed to enable data loads to it. In other words, a real-time InfoCube can switch between the real-time mode and data load mode.

A real-time InfoCube is also classified as a data target. (More about this type of InfoCube is discussed in Chapter 12.)

5.2.4 VirtualProvider InfoCube

In a VirtualProvider InfoCube, data doesn't physically reside in the cube; instead, the InfoObjects in this InfoCube are linked to source fields. So when a query is executed on it, the data is read from the source system during runtime. This type of InfoCube isn't a data target because it doesn't store the data physically; however, it *is* an InfoProvider because queries can be built on it.

Because data is read directly from a source system when queries are executed, this type of InfoCube is useful for real-time reporting (i.e., reporting where the latest data from the source system should be visible in the reports). However, because it must request data from the source system, the performance of queries on Virtual-Provider InfoCubes can be poor (especially when large sets of data are requested). This type of InfoCube should be used sparingly, mostly for real-time reporting that requires only a small amount of data.

VirtualProviders in SAP BW Powered by SAP HANA

In a SAP BW system powered by SAP HANA, VirtualProviders are also used to consume SAP HANA models in SAP BW.

5.3 Creating an InfoCube

Requirements for ABCD Corp. point to a standard InfoCube, so this section explains the procedure for creating one. However, the procedure to create all types of InfoCubes is the same, so the following applies to creating the other types too.

5.3.1 Initial Setup

InfoCubes are created in the DATA WAREHOUSING WORKBENCH, which is started using Transaction RSA1. Select the INFOPROVIDER under MODELING from the navigator section, as shown in ❶ of Figure 5.10.

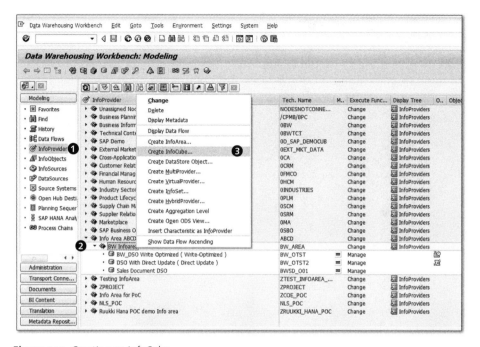

Figure 5.10 Creating an InfoCube

InfoCubes are created under an InfoArea. Select the InfoArea under which you want to create your InfoCube ❷. From the context menu, select CREATE INFOCUBE ❸. The CREATE INFOCUBE screen appears, as shown in Figure 5.11.

Enter the technical name (in our example, "BWSD_C01") and description (here, "Sales InfoCube") of the InfoCube (❶ of Figure 5.11). You can also use an existing InfoCube as a template to create a new InfoCube by entering the technical name of the existing InfoCube in the TEMPLATE field, as shown in ❸ of Figure 5.11.

As previously explained, there are three types of InfoCubes available in SAP BW. The type of InfoCube you want to create is defined in the INFOPROVIDER TYPE area of the screen. Select the appropriate checkbox to define the type of InfoCube.

When creating a standard InfoCube in SAP BW on a non-SAP HANA database, you'll also notice that there are two options related to SAP BW Accelerator (BWA) (see Figure 5.12). These options are only available if your SAP BW isn't on SAP HANA (because Figure 5.11 is captured from a SAP BW on SAP HANA system, it isn't showing these options).

Figure 5.11 Entering the Name and Description of the InfoCube

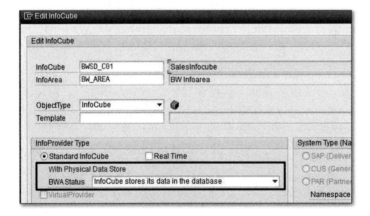

Figure 5.12 BWA Options for InfoCube

The following are the BWA STATUS options:

▶ INFOCUBE STORES ITS DATA IN THE DATABASE

▶ INFOCUBE ONLY STORES ITS DATA IN THE BWA

The first option is the default option, which we already discussed. The second option requires a connection to an SAP BWA system. Upon choosing the second option, definitions of the underlying tables are created in the SAP BW database; the data, however, is stored as a BWA index. Tables E and F and dimension tables are created on the SAP BW database, but data isn't stored in these tables. Data is loaded into this InfoCube using the standard data transfer process. This feature provides the flexibility to store data in SAP BWA and thus save space in the SAP BW database. As a result, options applicable for data storage and maintenance—such as compression, roll-up, and selective deletion—aren't available. Further InfoCube design can be much easier because you don't need to evaluate and explore relationships between characteristics for grouping them in a dimension. Dimensions are grouped with the requirements of the BEx Query Designer in mind. Queries designed on this type of InfoCube execute much faster because they read data directly from SAP BWA. There are two other main advantages associated with this kind of InfoCube:

▸ Reduction of space required in the database

▸ No need to create aggregates

VirtualProvider InfoCubes
Although we won't discuss this here, it's worth noting that a VirtualProvider InfoCube offers four different options based on how data is accessed: ▸ BASED ON DATA TRANSFER PROCESS FOR DIRECT ACCESS ▸ BASED ON BAPI ▸ BASED ON FUNCTION MODULE ▸ BASED ON AN SAP HANA MODEL (applicable for SAP BW powered by SAP HANA)

For our example scenario, select STANDARD INFOCUBE, and click on the CREATE icon, as shown in ❺ of Figure 5.11. As explained earlier, by default the SAP HANA-OPTIMIZED INFOCUBE checkbox is selected and grayed out. This means that all the newly created standard InfoCubes would be SAP HANA-optimized only. This takes you to the screen where you define the InfoCube (Figure 5.13).

The right side of the screen is the area where you can maintain the InfoCube definition. There are different sections visible on this screen, as follows:

▸ OBJECT INFORMATION
This section shows you general information about the InfoCube, such as VERSION and OBJECT STATUS.

▶ Settings

This section shows the type of InfoCube (❶ of Figure 5.13).

▶ Dimensions

You can maintain the dimensions of the InfoCube in this section ❷ of Figure 5.13. By default, it shows four dimensions; three of them (Data Package, Time, and Unit) are system-defined dimensions, and the fourth dimension (Dimension 1) is a placeholder for the user-defined dimension. As we've explained, it's mandatory to create at least one custom dimension; you can change the name of this dimension and attach characteristics to it.

▶ Navigation Attributes

This section lists all of the navigation attributes of the master data InfoObjects included in the InfoCube definition ❸ of Figure 5.13.

▶ Key Figures

The key figures of an InfoCube are included in the Key Figures section ❹ of Figure 5.13. (Remember, all InfoCubes must have at least one key figure.)

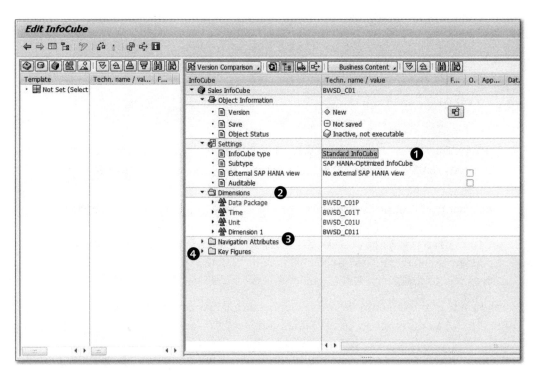

Figure 5.13 Edit InfoCube: Initial Screen

5.3.2 Using Templates for InfoObject Selection

As shown in Figure 5.14, the left side of the screen allows you to select InfoObjects (characteristics, key figures, and time characteristics) to be included in the InfoCube definition.

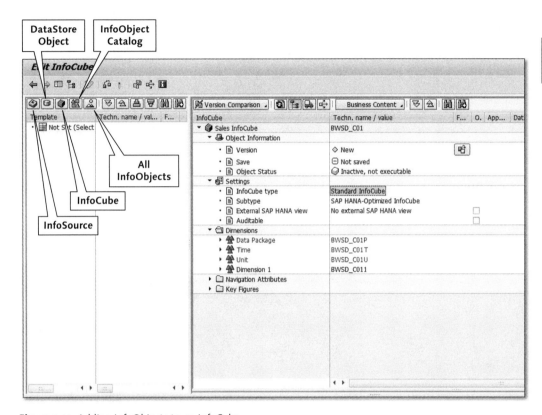

Figure 5.14 Adding InfoObjects to an InfoCube

There are several different templates available that you can use to select InfoObjects. These templates are shown in Figure 5.14 and explained here:

▶ ALL INFOOBJECTS
You can select InfoObjects for the InfoCube from the list of all available InfoObjects in the system.

▶ INFOOBJECT CATALOG
You can select InfoObjects for the InfoCube from a selected InfoObject catalog.

▶ INFOCUBE

You can use any of the existing InfoCubes as a template for selecting InfoObjects.

▶ DATASTORE OBJECT

You can use any of the existing DSOs as a template for selecting InfoObjects.

▶ INFOSOURCE

You can use any of the existing InfoSources as a template for selecting InfoObjects.

In the example shown in Figure 5.15, we explain the process of adding InfoObjects by using a DSO as a template. Select the DSO icon from the left side of the screen (❶ of Figure 5.15), and then select the DSO either by using the SEARCH option or by directly double-clicking from the list shown after clicking on the INFOAREA icon ❷. Select the BWSD_O01 DSO from the list ❸.

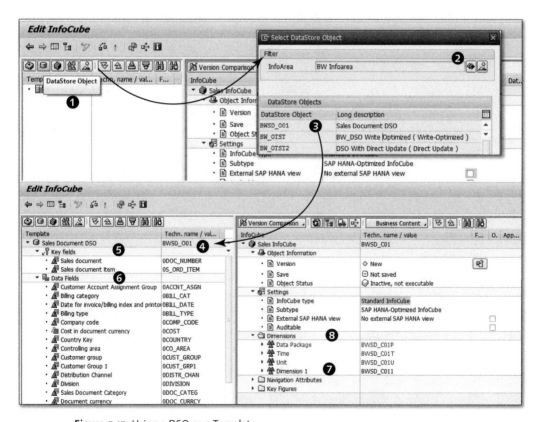

Figure 5.15 Using a DSO as a Template

Double-click on BWSD_O01. As shown in ❹ of Figure 5.15, SAP BW shows all of the InfoObjects reading the definition of BWSD_O01. It also classifies InfoObjects as Key fields ❺ and Data fields ❻.

The selection of a template doesn't add InfoObjects to dimensions. As shown in ❼ and ❽ of Figure 5.15, there are still four dimensions in the InfoCube, and no characteristics are yet assigned to them.

5.3.3 Editing Dimensions

Before we explain how to add new dimensions, let's explain the process of changing the description of Dimension 1, the placeholder name for the customer-defined dimension. (A dimension's description is visible in BEx Query Designer while designing a query based on an InfoCube and is a great help when working with queries.) As shown in ❷ of Figure 5.16, select the Properties option from the context menu of Dimension 1, under Dimensions (❶ of Figure 5.16).

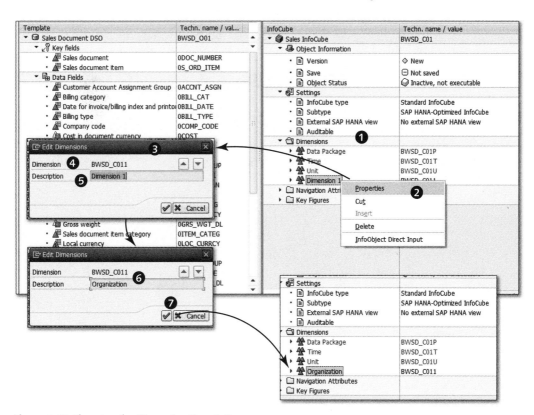

Figure 5.16 Changing the Dimension Description

The EDIT DIMENSIONS screen appears, as shown in ❸ of Figure 5.16. By default, the technical name BWSD_C011 is assigned to DIMENSION 1 ❹. The description of this dimension also appears as DIMENSION 1 ❺.

The technical names of dimensions follow a standard pattern, and you aren't allowed to edit them. Customer-defined and system-defined dimensions are treated in two different ways. For customer-defined dimensions, the technical name is *<Technical Name of InfoCube>x*, where *x* represents the dimension number. So, for the first dimension, the technical name is *<Technical Name of Info-Cube>1*; for the second dimension, it's *<Technical Name of InfoCube>2*; and so on.

The three system-defined dimensions are treated slightly differently:

▶ Data package: *<Technical Name of InfoCube>P*

▶ Time: *<Technical Name of InfoCube>T*

▶ Unit: *<Technical Name of InfoCube>U*

As an example, let's consider an InfoCube with the technical name BWSD_C01. The technical names of the customer-defined dimensions for this InfoCube are shown in Table 5.2.

Customer-Defined Dimension Number	Technical Name
First	BWSD_C011
Second	BWSD_C012
Third	BWSD_C013
Fourth	BWSD_C014
Fifth	BWSD_C015
Sixth	BWSD_C016
Seventh	BWSD_C017
Eighth	BWSD_C018
Ninth	BWSD_C019
Tenth	BWSD_C01A
Eleventh	BWSD_C01B
Twelfth	BWSD_C01C
Thirteenth	BWSD_C01D

Table 5.2 Technical Names for InfoCube Dimensions

Edit the description of the dimension as shown in ❻ of Figure 5.16. If you're using SAP BW without SAP HANA, then immediately beneath this, there are two checkboxes (Figure 5.17), which are explained next. These settings aren't applicable for SAP BW powered by SAP HANA.

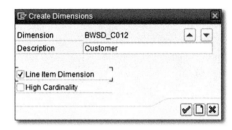

Figure 5.17 Dimension Properties

Line Item Dimension

In a business scenario, if you have a characteristic that can have a large number of distinct values, it's likely that the dimension table in which this characteristic is included contains an equally large number of records. In this case, the path from key figures in fact tables to DIM_IDs and then to SIDs can become critical for performance. The LINE ITEM DIMENSION setting simplifies this path.

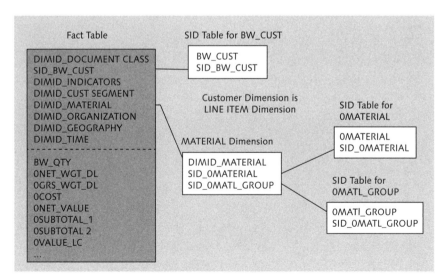

Figure 5.18 Line Item Dimension

When a dimension is set as a line item dimension, SAP BW doesn't create a dimension table for it. Instead, it directly connects the fact table with the SID table of that characteristic. For example, if the customer dimension is configured as a line item dimension, the fact table is directly connected to the SID table of InfoObject BW_CUST, as shown in Figure 5.18.

> **Note**
>
> For a line item dimension, the SIDs of the characteristic become the fact table key instead of the DIM_IDs in a non-line item dimension.

High Cardinality

When data volume stored in a table is huge, it's difficult to retrieve particular records or sets of records. Indexes are created on various columns of a table to improve the retrieval of the required record.

By default, SAP BW creates a bitmap index on each dimension column of a fact table, which is useful when the number of distinct values in a dimension isn't very high. However, in cases where distinct values *are* high, and the dimension table is at least 20% of the size of the fact table, SAP recommends choosing the HIGH CARDINALITY flag for the dimension. This setting changes the index type on the dimension to B-TREE.

This setting is more applicable if the SAP BW system uses the Oracle database. For non-Oracle systems, setting the HIGH CARDINALITY flag has no impact on the index type. The bitmap index is only used with Oracle, but there are some internal checks during the data load that determine different internal loading strategies.

When finished in the EDIT DIMENSION screen, click on the CONTINUE icon (refer to ❼ of Figure 5.16), or press ⎡Enter⎤ to return to the InfoCube definition screen.

5.3.4 Adding New Dimensions

In this section, we explain the process of adding new customer-defined dimensions to the InfoCube. To add a new dimension, call the context menu for the DIMENSIONS folder (❶ of Figure 5.19), and select the CREATE NEW DIMENSIONS option from the context menu ❷.

This action displays the CREATE DIMENSIONS screen, which lists a system-generated technical name for the new dimension ❸. By default, the description is listed as DIMENSION 2, as shown in ❹ of Figure 5.19.

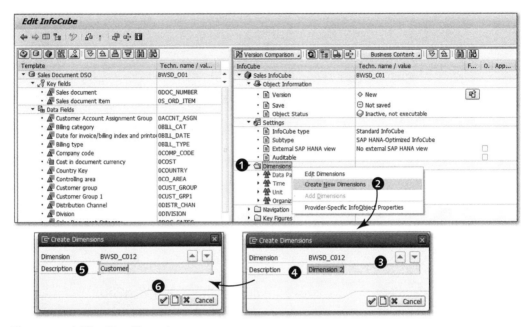

Figure 5.19 Adding New Dimensions

Enter the DESCRIPTION as "Customer" ❺. Now, because there are a large number of customers in ABCD Corp., this customer dimension should be a line item dimension. Select the LINE ITEM DIMENSION checkbox as shown earlier in Figure 5.17. (This step of selecting LINE ITEM DIMENSION is to be performed only if you're using a SAP BW system that is *not* on SAP HANA). Click on CONTINUE ❻ to return to the InfoCube definition screen.

The new customer dimension is now available as part of InfoCube BWSD_C01. Following this procedure, create the rest of the dimensions shown in Table 5.3, which were identified while developing the model based on the requirements of ABCD Corp.

> **Note**
>
> If you have SAP BW powered by SAP HANA, you can ignore the LINE ITEM DIMENSION and HIGH CARDINALITY flags because they aren't applicable.

Dimension Number	Description	Line Item	High Cardinality	Technical Name
DIMENSION 1	Organization	No	No	BWSD_C011
DIMENSION 2	Customer	Yes	No	BWSD_C012
DIMENSION 3	Material	No	No	BWSD_C013
DIMENSION 4	Indicators	No	No	BWSD_C014
DIMENSION 5	Customer Segment	No	No	BWSD_C015
DIMENSION 6	Geography	No	No	BWSD_C016
DIMENSION 7	Document Class	No	No	BWSD_C017

Table 5.3 Customer-Defined Dimensions for InfoCube BWSD_C01

After all of the dimensions are created, the InfoCube definition will look like the one shown in Figure 5.20.

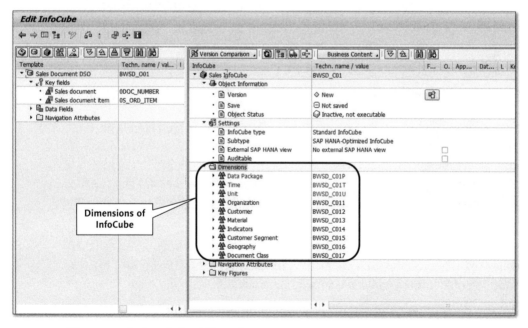

Figure 5.20 Custom-Defined Dimensions

5.3.5 Adding Characteristics to Dimensions

After the dimensions are created, you must assign characteristics to each dimension, per the extended star schema model created earlier. You can perform this task by using a template or by direct input.

As shown in Figure 5.21, using the DSO BWSD_O01 template gives you an already-populated list of InfoObjects.

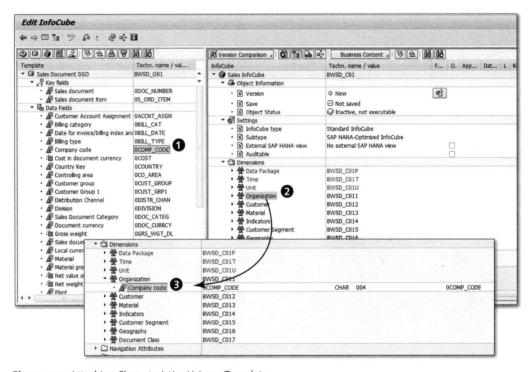

Figure 5.21 Attaching Characteristics Using a Template

Let's assign a few InfoObjects from this list as characteristics to the dimensions of the InfoCube. Select the InfoObject—0COMP_CODE (❶ of Figure 5.21)—and drag and drop it over the dimension, ORGANIZATION ❷. With this action, you assign the selected characteristic to the desired dimension ❸. To state this in SAP BW terminology, characteristic 0COMP_CODE is assigned to the organization dimension.

Another way to assign characteristics is by using the direct input method. Using this method, you can directly assign multiple characteristics to a dimension by entering their technical names. All of the dimensions of an InfoCube are visible under the DIMENSIONS folder (❶ of Figure 5.22). Select the dimension to which you want to assign characteristics ❷, and select the INFOOBJECT DIRECT INPUT option ❸.

This action displays the INSERT INFOOBJECTS screen ❹. Enter the technical names of the InfoObjects you want to assign as characteristics to the selected dimension ❺. Finally, click on the CONTINUE icon ❻ to return to the InfoCube definition screen. As you can see in Figure 5.23, all of the characteristics are now assigned to the ORGANIZATION dimension in the InfoCube definition.

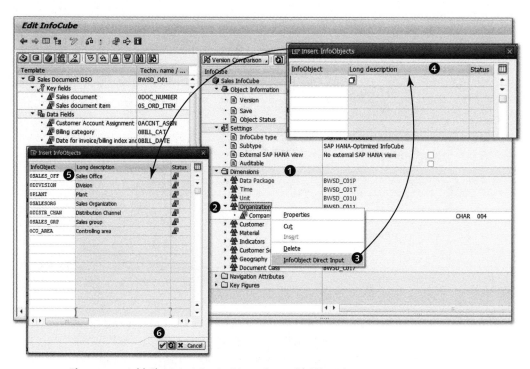

Figure 5.22 Add Characteristics to Dimensions with Direct Input

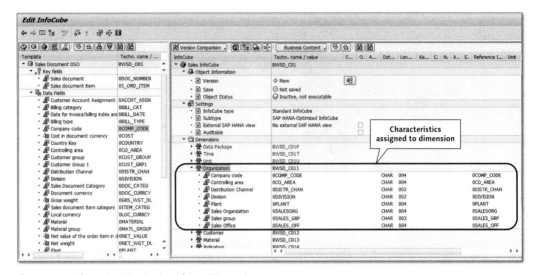

Figure 5.23 Characteristics Assigned to a Dimension

Using either the template procedure or the direct input procedure, assign characteristics to all of the dimensions of InfoCube BWSD_C01, as shown in Table 5.4.

Dimension	Characteristics
ORGANIZATION	0COMP_CODE 0DIVISION 0PLANT 0SALESORG 0DISTR_CHAN 0SALES_OFF 0SALES_GRP 0CO_AREA
CUSTOMER	BW_CUST
MATERIAL	0MATERIAL 0MATL_GROUP
INDICATORS	0ACCNT_ASGN
CUSTOMER SEGMENT	0CUST_GROUP 0CUST_GRP1
GEOGRAPHY	0REGION 0SALES_DIST

Table 5.4 Characteristics to Dimension Relationship for InfoCube BWSD_C01

Dimension	Characteristics
DOCUMENT CLASS	0BILL_TYPE 0ITEM_CATEG 0BILL_CAT 0DOC_CATEG
TIME	0CALMONTH 0CALQUARTER 0CALYEAR

Table 5.4 Characteristics to Dimension Relationship for InfoCube BWSD_C01 (Cont.)

5.3.6 Adding Key Figures to an InfoCube

Now we must add key figures to the InfoCube. Here again, we have two options to perform this task: the template method or the direct input method. Select the KEY FIGURES context menu shown in ❶ of Figure 5.24, and then select INFOOBJECT DIRECT INPUT ❷.

In the INSERT INFOOBJECTS screen ❸, enter the technical names of the key figures that should be added to the InfoCube ❹ (see Table 5.5). Select CONTINUE ❺ to return to the definition screen.

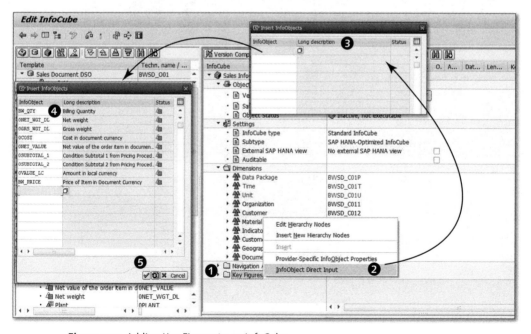

Figure 5.24 Adding Key Figures to an InfoCube

Key Figure	Description
BW_QTY	Billing quantity
0NET_WGT_DL	Net weight
0GRS_WGT_DL	Gross weight
0COST	Cost in document currency
0NET_VALUE	Net value of the order item in document currency
0SUBTOTAL_1	Subtotal 1 from pricing procedure for condition
0SUBTOTAL_2	Subtotal 2 from pricing procedure for condition
0VALUE_LC	Amount in local currency
BW_PRICE (see boxed note)	Price of item in document currency

Table 5.5 Key Figures

Note

Refer to Appendix B for information about creating the definition of InfoObject BW_PRICE.

After all of the key figures are assigned, you can see them under the KEY FIGURES section in the InfoCube definition (Figure 5.25).

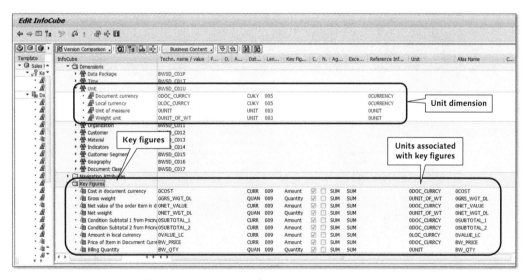

Figure 5.25 Key Figures and Units Assigned to the InfoCube

When you add a key figure to an InfoCube, the corresponding unit characteristic for that key figure automatically gets added to the UNIT dimension (Figure 5.25). You can see the units associated with each key figure on the right side of the key figure in the InfoCube definition. For example, the unit associated with key figure BW_QTY is 0UNIT and is added to the UNIT dimension.

5.3.7 Selecting Navigation Attributes

Some of the characteristics assigned to different dimensions of an InfoCube can be master data characteristics, which means they can have their own attributes. Some of these attributes may be configured as navigation attributes. All navigation attributes from all master data characteristics included in the InfoCube are available under the NAVIGATION ATTRIBUTES section of the InfoCube definition (❶ of Figure 5.26).

These navigation attributes aren't available for navigation by default. If you want to use any of the available navigation attributes in the InfoCube, you must explicitly select them using the ON/OFF column checkbox ❷. For the InfoCube BWSD_C01 example, we want to switch on navigation for the SALES OFFICE (0SALES_OFF) attribute of customer (BW_CUST) master data ❸.

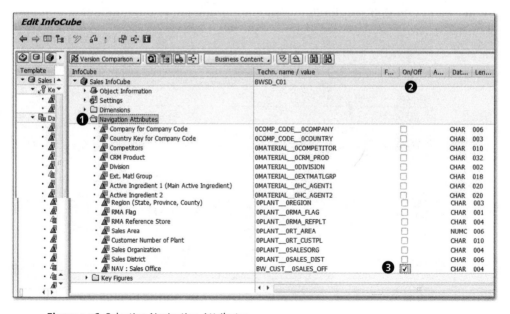

Figure 5.26 Selecting Navigation Attributes

5.3.8 Activating the InfoCube

The InfoCube design is now ready, and you can check its definition using the CHECK icon 🔓 on the dynamic menu bar. If no inconsistencies are found, the system gives a message that reads INFOCUBE BWSD_C01 IS CONSISTENT, which appears on the status bar. This means that you can activate the InfoCube definition using the ACTIVATE icon ▮ (❶ of Figure 5.27).

The activated InfoCube BWSD_C01 can be seen under InfoArea BW_AREA, as shown in ❸ of Figure 5.27.

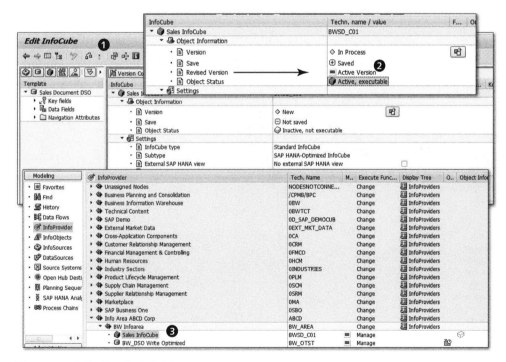

Figure 5.27 Activating the InfoCube

Having explained the design and creation of a standard InfoCube, let's now discuss some finer aspects of its design.

5.4 Provider-Specific Properties

The properties corresponding to different InfoObjects included in the InfoCube definition can be altered to suit specific requirements for an InfoCube. You can take advantage of this design aspect to meet some typical business requirements. For instance, assume that our example scenario requires that the 0MATERIAL characteristic be displayed with MEDIUM TEXT AND KEY when used in queries, and that the input help (F4 search) should use the VALUES IN MASTER DATA TABLE setting. These settings are available when creating/configuring InfoObject 0MATERIAL. The settings configured at the InfoObject level apply to all of the InfoCubes in which they're used. So, if InfoObject 0MATERIAL has other settings than the required ones, the InfoCube where it's used will apply them by default. However, it's possible to change these settings for an InfoCube. In this section, we discuss this process for both single InfoObjects and multiple InfoObjects.

5.4.1 Setting Provider-Specific Properties for a Single InfoObject

Because the InfoCube is already activated, go to the edit mode of the InfoCube. From the Data Warehousing Workbench, call the context menu for InfoCube BWSD_C01, and select CHANGE (Figure 5.28).

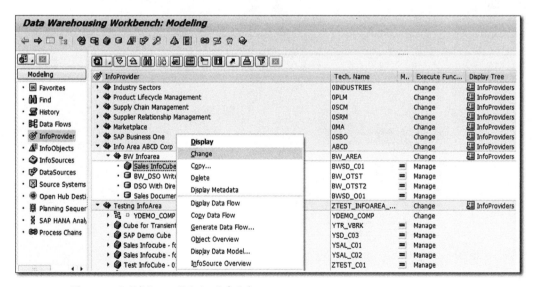

Figure 5.28 Editing an Existing InfoCube

This opens the InfoCube definition in edit mode. Call the context menu for InfoObject 0MATERIAL, and select PROVIDER-SPECIFIC PROPERTIES, as shown in Figure 5.29.

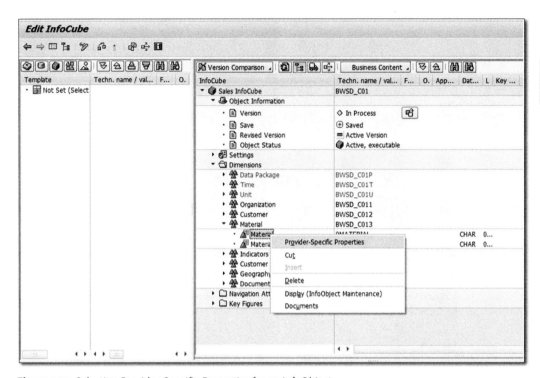

Figure 5.29 Selecting Provider-Specific Properties for an InfoObject

This action displays the PROVIDER-SPECIFIC PROPERTIES OF THE INFOOBJECT screen shown in ❶ of Figure 5.30. Different object-specific properties are visible ❷. To set the required properties of InfoObject 0MATERIAL, select the DISPLAY dropdown menu ❸, and select TEXT AND KEY AS MEDIUM TEXT ❹. This setting influences the display for 0MATERIAL only in this specific InfoCube ❺. Click on the CONTINUE icon ❻ to return to the definition screen.

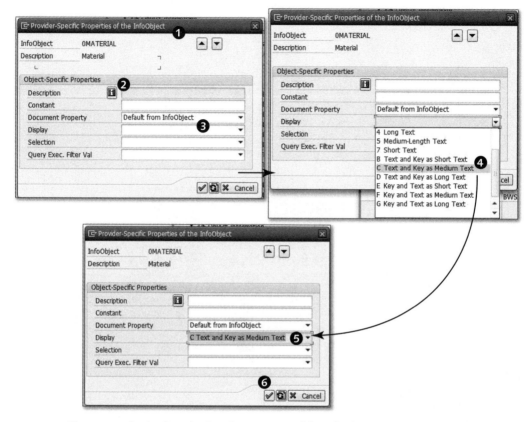

Figure 5.30 Setting Provider-Specific Properties of the InfoObject

5.4.2 Setting Provider-Specific Properties for Multiple InfoObjects

Open the context menu for the DIMENSIONS folder in the InfoCube definition (Figure 5.31), and select PROVIDER-SPECIFIC INFOOBJECT PROPERTIES.

The PROVIDER-SPECIFIC PROPERTIES OF THE INFOOBJECT screen is visible, as shown in Figure 5.32. Using this screen, you can maintain the provider-specific properties of multiple InfoObjects. After you've completed the process, check, save, and activate the InfoCube.

> **Note**
>
> To use the InfoCube, you must activate its definition every time you make changes to it.

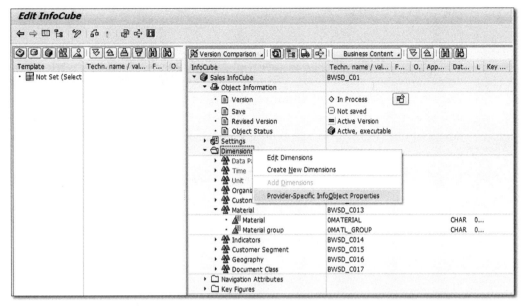

Figure 5.31 Provider-Specific Settings for Multiple InfoObjects

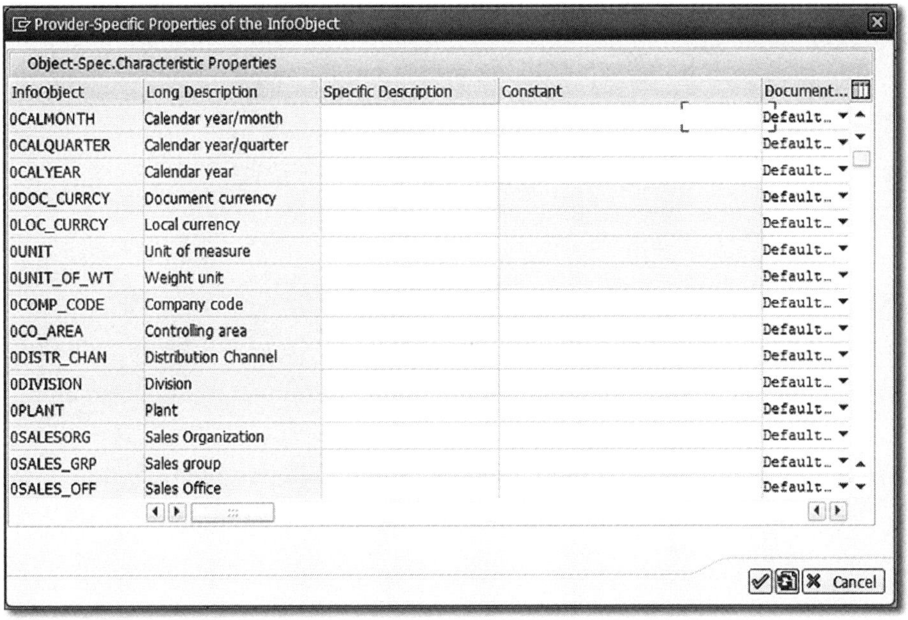

Figure 5.32 Maintain Provider-Specific Properties for Multiple InfoObjects

5.5   Summary

In this chapter, we explained the modeling of an InfoCube based on the unique architecture of the extended star schema, the types of InfoCubes, and the procedure for creating an InfoCube. We introduced some new information in SAP BW 7.4 regarding SAP HANA-optimized InfoCubes and the process of converting non-SAP HANA-optimized InfoCubes to SAP HANA-optimized objects. We then detailed some of the finer aspects of designing an InfoCube; specifically, provider-specific settings.

In subsequent chapters of this book, you'll learn more about the relevance and usage of the different settings explained in this chapter. In the following chapter, we explain the concept of InfoProviders.

Understanding InfoProviders and their design is essential for making use of the flexibility these objects provide in your overall BI solution architecture.

6   InfoProviders

Other than the basic InfoCubes and DataStore Objects (DSOs), several other Info-Providers are available in SAP BW:

- MultiProviders
- InfoSets
- VirtualProviders
- Semantically partitioned objects (SPOs)
- HybridProviders
- Transient providers
- Analytical indexes
- CompositeProviders
- Open Operational DataStore (ODS) views

Some of these are simply based on a logical definition and don't store any data physically. In some cases, these are based on a combination of two or more data targets such as InfoObjects (characteristics with master data), DSOs, and Info-Cubes. These InfoProviders answer many business queries and save on efforts to extract and store the data. They provide flexibility in managing a data warehouse and offer scalability and efficiency. Queries can be created on the InfoProviders using standard query tools supplied by SAP BW. In this chapter, we provide an overview of these InfoProviders and explain possible scenarios where you might use them.

6.1   MultiProviders

Normally, the design of a data target such as an InfoCube or DSO is based on one business process; for example, an InfoCube for sales billing process data and another InfoCube for sales order process data. In this way, SAP BW may have multiple InfoCubes, each supporting an individual business process. Business information requirements may invite a situation where data from two different InfoCubes needs to be joined.

SAP BW supports queries based on a single InfoProvider. To support reporting requirements across multiple data providers, you don't need to load data from individual data providers to the new data provider. The system provides a better way to handle this situation, by way of a MultiProvider.

6.1.1   Introduction to MultiProviders

Because a MultiProvider exists only as a logical definition, it doesn't physically store data. The data lies in the underlying data providers, which define the MultiProvider. You can create a MultiProvider based on the following objects, as shown in Figure 6.1 (note that all possible objects aren't shown in this figure):

▸ DSOs

▸ InfoCubes

▸ SPOs

▸ HybridProviders

▸ InfoObjects

▸ InfoSets

▸ Aggregation levels

▸ Transient providers

▸ VirtualProviders

MultiProviders can be created based on any combination of these objects, for example, InfoCube to InfoCube (not limited to two InfoCubes), InfoCube to InfoObject, or DSO to InfoCube. Again, the number of objects included in the definition of a MultiProvider isn't limited to two.

Figure 6.2 shows an example of including two InfoCubes in a MultiProvider: one on planning data and the other on actual sales. While the actuals InfoCube stores the data from actual sales, the plan InfoCube stores the data on sales planning. Another example of creating a MultiProvider based on InfoCubes and InfoObjects is having the sales InfoCube and the InfoObject 0MATERIAL. A query on such a MultiProvider might be used to identify slow-moving material.

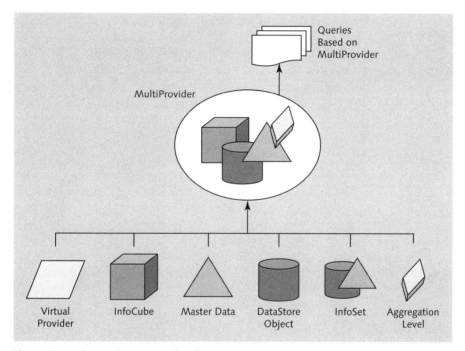

Figure 6.1 MultiProvider: A Logical Definition

You can also use a MultiProvider when the InfoCube you're creating becomes very large due to high data volume. In this case, you can split the InfoCube into identical smaller InfoCubes based on values of a logical characteristic such as fiscal year or company code. For reporting purposes, it's recommended that you create MultiProviders based on these InfoCubes and create queries on the Multi-Provider. With newer version of SAP BW, instead of breaking a large InfoCube into multiple physical small InfoCubes, you can use an SPO, which is explained in Section 6.4.

A MultiProvider provides the following benefits:

▶ **Flexibility**
Designing InfoCubes based on individual business processes is much simpler

than creating one complex InfoCube for multiple business processes, and it allows for the combination of various InfoCubes at a later stage. A MultiProvider allows you to keep your InfoCubes design simple and small.

▸ **Simple and easy**
Small InfoCubes are easy to maintain.

▸ **Faster results**
The system uses parallel processing when executing queries on a MultiProvider. As shown in Figure 6.2, when a query is executed on the planned sales versus actual sales MultiProvider, the system internally starts multiple subqueries in parallel. After the results of these queries are available, they are combined using the union operation and presented to the user.

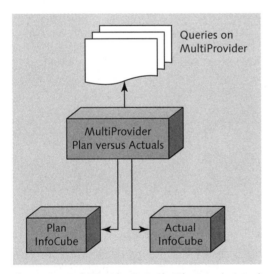

Figure 6.2 MultiProvider Example: Plan versus Actual

6.1.2   Designing MultiProviders

Having explained MultiProviders and their advantages, we'll now explain the step-by-step process of creating a MultiProvider in SAP BW.

Creating MultiProviders

Our example scenario requires that ABCD Corp.'s BI solution can report the status of actual sales compared to the planned sales forecast to ascertain whether company sales are on target or whether action is needed to address variance. We'll use a sales InfoCube, which stores actual sales data, and we'll use a planning InfoCube, which stores the plan data. Let's now proceed with the creation of a MultiProvider based on plan versus actual sales.

Note

To explain the concept of a MultiProvider, we've referred to InfoCube BW_PLAN. For our example scenario, this InfoCube stores the sales planning data. This real-time Info-Cube is discussed in detail when we explain the SAP BW Integrated Planning component in Chapter 12. If you want to practice creating a MultiProvider and the steps mentioned in the following section, first create InfoProvider BW_PLAN by referring to Chapter 12, Section 12.2.1. The definition of InfoCube BW_PLAN and the corresponding InfoObjects (BW_PROD, BW_VAL) is shown in Figure 12.7 in that section.

From the DATABASE WAREHOUSING WORKBENCH screen (Transaction RSA1), select INFOPROVIDER from the MODELING section, as shown in ❶ of Figure 6.3. A Multi-Provider is created under an InfoArea, so select BW_INFOAREA ❷. Open the context menu of BW_INFOAREA, and select CREATE MULTIPROVIDER ❸.

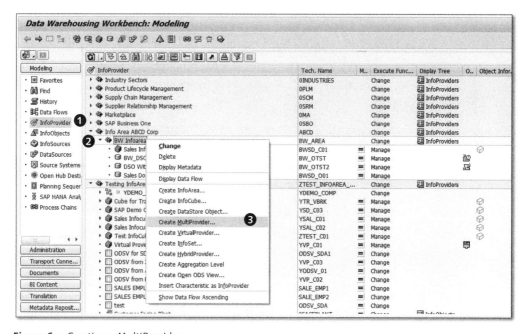

Figure 6.3 Creating a MultiProvider

The CREATE MULTIPROVIDER pop-up box appears, as shown in ❶ of Figure 6.4. You need to provide the unique technical name and description of the MultiProvider. Enter the technical name "BWSD_MUL1" ❷, and enter the description "Sales Actuals Vs Plan MultiProvider" ❸. Click on the CREATE icon ❹.

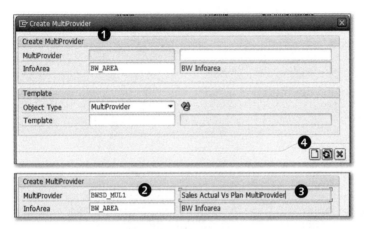

Figure 6.4 Creating a MultiProvider: Adding a Name and Description

The next screen is MULTIPROVIDER: RELEVANT INFOPROVIDERS , as shown in Figure 6.5. Because a MultiProvider is based on different data targets and/or InfoProviders (as shown earlier in Figure 6.1), this screen offers you selections based on the data targets and/or InfoProviders you want to include in the definition of the MultiProvider.

Different tabs are available based on various relevant InfoProviders (❶ of Figure 6.5). These tabs allow you to select various basic providers for the MultiProvider. For our example, select INFOCUBE BWSD_C01 (SALES INFOCUBE) and INFOCUBE BW_PLAN (SALES PLANNING CUBE) ❷.

Because there may be a large number of data targets and/or InfoProviders available in the system, three different display options are available to list them ❸. By default, the system uses the DISPLAY ALL INFOPROVIDERS (PLACE SELECTED FIRST) option. The search feature is also available to find specific InfoProviders ❹.

After the required InfoProviders are selected, click on the CONTINUE icon ❺ to move ahead.

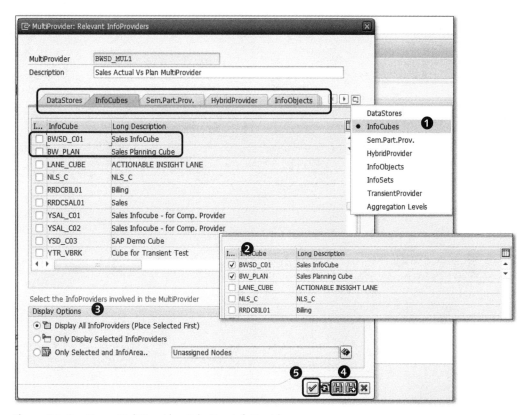

Figure 6.5 Creating a MultiProvider: Selecting InfoProviders

Defining MultiProviders

The system takes you to the EDIT MULTIPROVIDER screen, as shown in Figure 6.6. The initial definition of MultiProvider BWSD_MUL1 is shown with included InfoCubes (BWSD_C01 and BW_PLAN) ❶. Four default dimensions are shown ❷: DATA PACKAGE, TIME, UNIT, and DIMENSION 1. This screen also offers a section to include NAVIGATION ATTRIBUTES ❸ and KEY FIGURES ❹.

Because both InfoCubes support different business processes, their definitions ought to be different. However, a few characteristics and key figures are common between the two. Table 6.1 provides a list of characteristics and key figures from both of the InfoCubes.

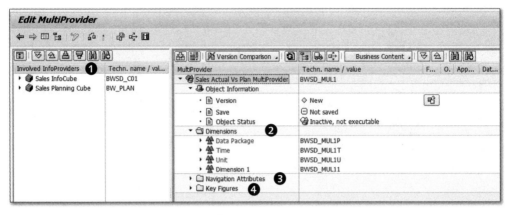

Figure 6.6 Edit MultiProvider Initial Screen

Type	Technical Name in BWSD_C01	Technical Name in BW_PLAN
Characteristics	0COMP_CODE	Not Available
	0DIVISION	0DIVISION
	0PLANT	Not Available
	0SALESORG	0SALESORG
	0DISTR_CHAN	Not Available
	0SALES_OFF	Not Available
	0SALES_GRP	Not Available
	0CO_AREA	Not Available
	BW_CUST	Not Available
	0MATERIAL	Not Available
	0MATL_GROUP	0MATL_GROUP
	0ACCNT_ASGN	Not Available
	0CUST_GROUP	Not Available
	0CUST_GRP1	Not Available
	0REGION	Not Available
	0SALES_DIST	Not Available
	0COUNTRY	Not Available
	0BILL_TYPE	Not Available
	0ITEM_CATEG	Not Available
	0BILL_CAT	Not Available

Table 6.1 Comparison of Definitions for Designing MultiProviders

Type	Technical Name in BWSD_C01	Technical Name in BW_PLAN
	0DOC_CATEG	Not Available
	Not Available	BW_PROD
Time Characteristics	0CALMONTH	Not Available
	0CALQUARTER	0CALQUARTER
	0CALYEAR	0CALYEAR
Key Figures	BW_QTY	Not Available
	0NET_WGT_DL	Not Available
	0GRS_WGT_DL	Not Available
	0COST	Not Available
	0NET_VALUE	Not Available
	0SUBTOTAL_1	Not Available
	0SUBTOTAL_2	Not Available
	0VALUE_LC	Not Available
	BW_PRICE	Not Available
	Not Available	BW_VAL

Table 6.1 Comparison of Definitions for Designing MultiProviders (Cont.)

We can see that only a few characteristics of InfoCube BWSD_C01 are available in the InfoCube BW_PLAN. One of the basic conditions in designing a MultiProvider is to have the identical technical name of the characteristics across Info-Cubes (or other included data targets).

All of the characteristic InfoObjects included in InfoCube BW_PLAN have the same InfoObject in InfoCube BWSD_C01, except BW_PROD. BW_PROD is used to refer to a product or material, similar to the use of InfoObject 0MATERIAL of InfoCube BWSD_C01. The two InfoObjects, BW_PROD and 0MATERIAL, can't be matched while designing a MultiProvider. Although including such non-matching InfoObjects is possible in a MultiProvider definition, queries using them don't produce the proper results when such disjointed characteristics are used.

When defining the MultiProvider, we'll include the following characteristics and key figures:

▶ 0SALESORG

▶ 0DIVISION

- 0MATL_GROUP

- BW_PROD

- 0CALQUARTER

- 0CALYEAR

- 0NET_VALUE (actual value)

- BW_VAL (planning value)

The dimensions of InfoCube BWSD_C01 and InfoCube BW_PLAN are shown in
❶, ❷, and ❸ of Figure 6.7. In this figure, characteristics within the ORGANIZATION
for SALES PLANNING CUBE dimension are shown in detail. Because a MultiProvider
exists as a logical definition and doesn't physically store data, the design of various dimensions isn't as vital as it is during the design of a standard InfoCube.
Dimension design while creating a standard InfoCube is a crucial step because
standard InfoCubes store data physically.

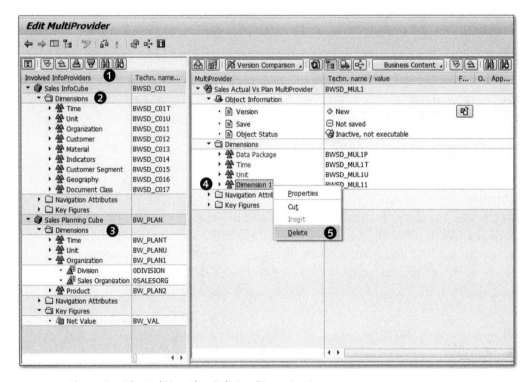

Figure 6.7 Edit MultiProvider: Deleting Dimension 1

A small error in dimension design can seriously and negatively affect the performance of queries. (Note that dimension design is crucial for SAP BW on non-SAP
HANA databases.) This doesn't apply to creating a MultiProvider, but attaching
characteristics in logical groupings in various dimensions helps BEx Query
Designer—so it's still recommended that you design dimensions.

First, let's delete dimension 1, which is created by default by SAP BW. Select
Dimension 1, as shown in ❹ of Figure 6.7, and open the context menu. Next,
select Delete ❺.

You can either create new dimensions or directly drag and drop dimensions from
any of the InfoCubes, as shown in Figure 6.8. Select the Organization dimension
❶, and then drag and drop it over Dimensions ❷. The outcome of this activity is
that the Organization dimension is available in MultiProvider BWSD_MUL1,
with both the characteristics (Sales Organization and DIVISION) ❸ of the base
InfoCube (BW_PLAN/Sales Planning Cube).

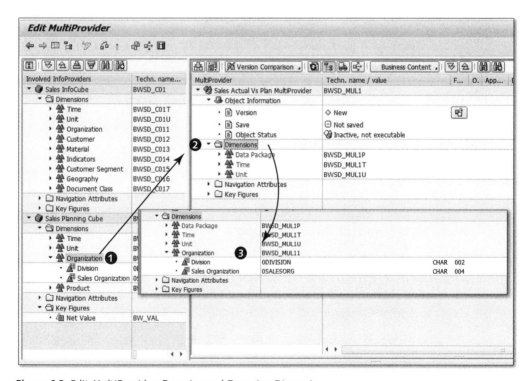

Figure 6.8 Edit MultiProvider: Dragging and Dropping Dimension

Now, drag and drop the PRODUCT dimension and the characteristics 0CALQUAR-TER and 0CALYEAR from the TIME dimension of InfoCube BW_PLAN to the TIME dimension of MultiProvider BWSD_MUL1. Also drag and drop key figures BW_VAL and 0NET_VALUE from the InfoCube to the MultiProvider.

The final design of MultiProvider BWSD_MUL1 is shown in Figure 6.9.

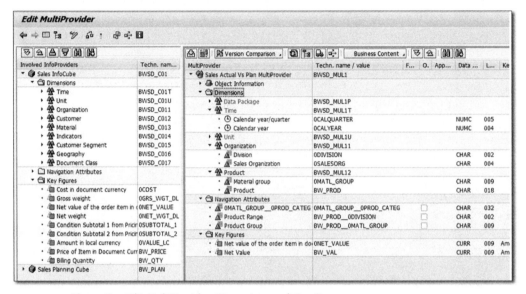

Figure 6.9 Edit MultiProvider: Dimensions and Key Figures

Identifying Characteristics

Now you need to identify each of the characteristics included in the MultiProvider and match them to the characteristics or navigation attributes of the base InfoCube. We'll explain this process next.

Click on the IDENTIFY CHARACTERISTICS icon, as shown in ❶ of Figure 6.10. The IDENTIFICATION OF PARTICIPATING CHARACTERISTICS/NAV. ATTR. box appears ❷. It shows each characteristic included in the MultiProvider and offers the matching characteristics or navigational attributes available from the included InfoCube.

This box shows the characteristic 0CALQUARTER ❸ from the MultiProvider and offers matching characteristic 0CALQUARTER from the SALES INFOCUBE (BWSD_C01) ❹. It also offers the characteristic 0CALQUARTER from the SALES PLANNING

CUBE (BW_PLAN) ❺. You need to confirm this matching by selecting the check-box ❻.

You can select the next characteristics from the MultiProvider using the NEXT icon ❼. This process needs to be completed for all of the characteristics included in the MultiProvider.

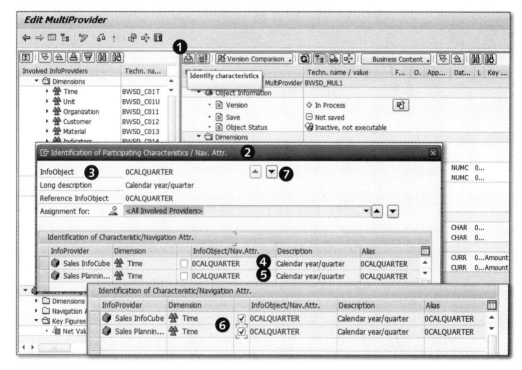

Figure 6.10 Edit MultiProvider: Identifying Characteristics

Now let's discuss the options for including characteristics in a MultiProvider, such as including characteristic 0DIVISION (see ❶ of Figure 6.11). 0DIVISION from the SALES INFOCUBE can be matched with 0DIVISION and BW_PROD_0DI-VISION (0DIVISION is the navigation attribute of BW_PROD) from the SALES PLANNING CUBE ❷. You need to decide whether you want to match the 0DIVI-SION characteristics of InfoCube BWSD_C01 with the 0DIVISION characteristics of InfoCube BW_PLAN or with the 0DIVISION navigation attribute of BW_PROD. Select 0DIVISION characteristics from both of the InfoCubes ❸.

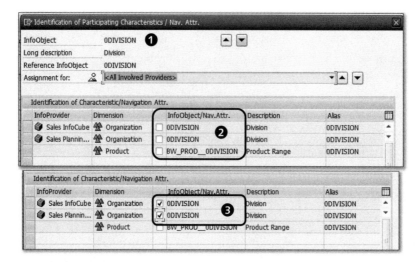

Figure 6.11 Edit MultiProvider: Identifying Characteristics from Multiple InfoCubes

You might also have a scenario where the characteristics can't be matched to characteristics or a navigation attribute in another InfoCube or data target included in the definition of a MultiProvider. For example, characteristic BW_PROD is included in the MultiProvider definition (❶ of Figure 6.12) and offered only from the SALES PLANNING CUBE InfoCube ❷ because there's no matching characteristic available in the Sales InfoCube. In this case, you select the characteristics as we've shown in ❸ of Figure 6.12.

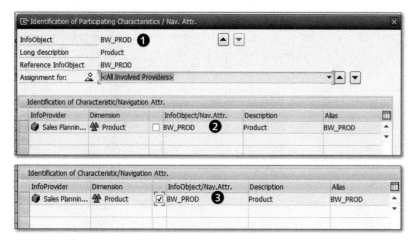

Figure 6.12 Edit MultiProvider: Identify Characteristics from Only One InfoCube

The final identification of characteristics is shown in Table 6.2.

MultiProvider Characteristics	Offer from InfoCube BWSD_C01	Offer from InfoCube BW_PLAN	Selected from InfoCube BWSD_C01	Selected from InfoCube BW_PLAN
0CALQUARTER	0CALQUARTER	0CALQUARTER	0CALQUARTER	0CALQUARTER
0CALYEAR	0CALYEAR	0CALYEAR	0CALYEAR	0CALYEAR
0SALESORG	0SALESORG	0SALESORG	0SALESORG	0SALESORG
0DIVISION	0DIVISION	0DIVISION BW_PROD__0DIVISION	0DIVISION	0DIVISION
BW_PROD	N/A	BW_PROD	N/A	BW_PROD
0MATL_GROUP	0MATL_GROUP	0MATL_GROUP BW_PROD__0MATL_GROUP	0MATL_GROUP	0MATL_GROUP

Table 6.2 Identification of Characteristics in a MultiProvider

Matching Key Figures

After all of the characteristics included in a MultiProvider are matched, you also need to match the key figures. Click on the SELECT KEY FIGURES icon, as shown in ❶ of Figure 6.13. The SELECTION OF KEY FIGURES INVOLVED box ❷ appears, and the system lists each key figure involved in the MultiProvider. The system offers the BW_VAL key figure ❸ from the SALES PLANNING CUBE ❹. Because there's no matching key figure available in the Sales InfoCube, the system doesn't show any second key figures. Select BW_VAL ❺. You can go to the next key figure by clicking on the NEXT OBJECT icon ❻.

The final identification of key figures is shown in Table 6.3.

MultiProvider Key Figure	Offer from InfoCube BWSD_C01	Offer from InfoCube BW_PLAN	Selected from InfoCube BWSD_C01	Selected from InfoCube BW_PLAN
BW_VAL	N/A	BW_VAL	N/A	BW_VAL
0NET_VALUE	0NET_VALUE	N/A	0NET_VALUE	N/A

Table 6.3 Identification of Key Figures

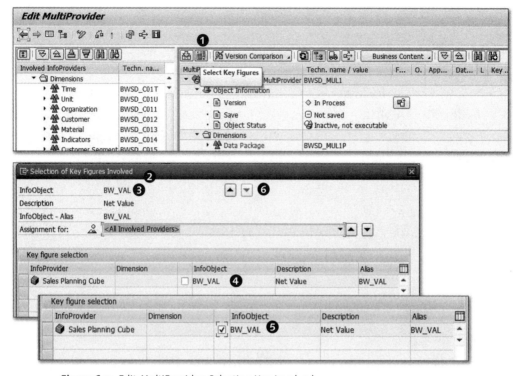

Figure 6.13 Edit MultiProvider: Selecting Key Involved

When identifying key figures, you can select key figures from both of the base InfoCubes (while including them in a MultiProvider). Selecting the same key figure (i.e., a key figure with the same technical name) from both of the InfoCubes would result in the summation of key figure values in the MultiProvider for the same values of characteristics.

Now click on the CHECK icon 🔍, as shown in ❶ of Figure 6.14, to check the definition of the MultiProvider. If everything is okay, the system reports a message ❷. At this moment, the MultiProvider is still not in ACTIVE status, so click on the ACTIVATE icon ❸. After it's successfully activated, the system changes the status of the MultiProvider to ACTIVE, EXECUTABLE ❹.

After successful activation of MultiProvider BWSD_MUL1, it's available under the BW INFOAREA, as shown in Figure 6.15.

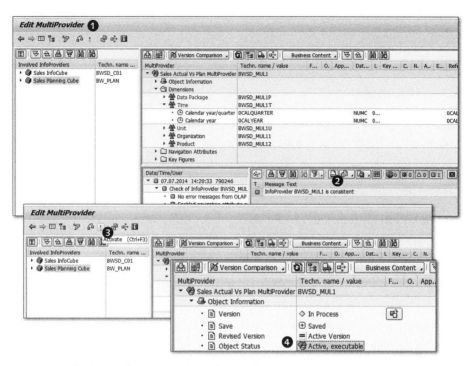

Figure 6.14 Checking and Activating the MultiProvider

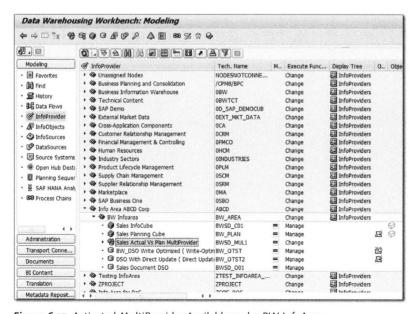

Figure 6.15 Activated MultiProvider Available under BW InfoArea

Now that we've covered the MultiProvider, let's move on to another InfoProvider: the InfoSet.

6.2   InfoSets

An InfoSet exists only as a logical definition, and thus doesn't physically store data. Queries can be created on an InfoSet using standard query tools supplied by SAP BW, and they get the data from underlying objects or sources. These sources can be InfoObjects (characteristics with master data), DSOs, or InfoCubes.

When it comes to InfoSets, you may be wondering how they differ from Multi-Providers. Are they a subset of MultiProviders? Why does SAP BW have another object of the same nature? Can't we accomplish the same task by using a Multi-Provider? The fundamental difference between the two is that MultiProviders use a union operation, while InfoSets use a join operation. Depending on your specific requirements, you may need either a MultiProvider or an InfoSet.

You can do most recent reporting using queries on an InfoSet. When you load master data into an InfoObject, the latest data loaded isn't immediately available for reporting because it's stored in the M (modified) version in the underlying tables associated with the InfoObjects. There is a process of activating master data, which turns an M version into an A (active) version. By default, only active version data is read to query, and only the InfoSet allows you to query on data that isn't active. The setting is shown in Section 6.2.5, where we explain the global properties of an InfoSet.

Usage Restriction
The following are restrictions in using an InfoSet: ▸ You can't define an InfoSet when the InfoCube is a right operand of a left outer join.   ▸ SAP doesn't support InfoSets containing more than two InfoCubes.   ▸ InfoCubes containing noncumulative key figures can't be part of an InfoSet.

In this section, we'll explain the types of joins, their implications and limitations, and the concept of transitive attribute reporting. We'll then describe the step-by-step procedure for creating InfoSets, including discussions of additional navigational capabilities and global properties.

6.2.1 Type of Joins

Using the join operation in InfoSets enables you to combine results from different underlying sources. In this section, we'll introduce you to the different types of joins found in InfoSets.

Inner and Left Outer Joins

By default, an InfoSet uses the inner join operation. An inner join checks the data in all underlying sources for the joining condition, and if it's available in all, it's passed to the result set.

InfoSets also offer outer joins, which can be used in some typical scenarios, such as for products that aren't being sold frequently (explained with an example later in this section). In this case, you can create an InfoSet based on InfoObject 0MATERIAL (which contains the material master data) and the DSO (in which material actual sales data is stored).

Although the basic idea of inner and left outer joins is simple, it's important to understand the difference between them. Let's look at an example.

Consider a scenario where an InfoObject for a customer (let's call it T1) has a sales office as an attribute. This sample data is shown in Table 6.4.

Customer Number	Sales Office
C1	SO1
C2	SO2
C3	SO3
C4	SO1
C6	SO2

Table 6.4 Customer InfoObject with Sales Office Attribute

The sales DSO (let's call it T2) contains the billing quantity information by customer and by month, as shown in Table 6.5.

Month	Customer Number	Billing Qty
10.2015	C1	100
10.2015	C2	120

Table 6.5 Data Sales DSO: Billing Quantity by Customer and by Month

Month	Customer Number	Billing Qty
10.2015	C3	150
10.2015	C5	140
10.2015	C6	110

Table 6.5 Data Sales DSO: Billing Quantity by Customer and by Month (Cont.)

When the InfoSet on T1 and T2 is created with an inner join on the customer number, the result looks similar to Table 6.6.

Customer Number	Sales Office	Month	Billing Qty
C1	SO1	10.2015	100
C2	SO2	10.2015	120
C3	SO3	10.2015	150
C6	SO2	10.2015	110

Table 6.6 Result of Making an InfoSet on T1 and T2 with an Inner Join

Note
The record for customers C4 and C5 isn't included in the result set because the data isn't available for these customers in both of the sources included in the InfoSet definition.

When the InfoSet on T1 and T2 is created with a left outer join on the customer number, while keeping the customer InfoObject on the left of the outer join, the result looks similar to Table 6.7.

Customer Number	Sales Office	Month	Billing Qty
C1	SO1	10.2015	100
C2	SO2	10.2015	120
C3	SO3	10.2015	150
C4	SO1	N/A	N/A
C6	SO2	10.2015	110

Table 6.7 Result of Making an InfoSet on T1 and T2 with a Left Outer Join

As you can see from these tables, there's a significant difference between the results produced depending on the type of join used, and it's essential to choose the right join for your reporting requirements.

As we've stated previously, the join selected between two InfoProviders included in an InfoSet definition is an inner join by default. However, you can change that to a left outer join if required. Select the InfoProvider T00002, and open the context menu, as shown in ❶ of Figure 6.16. Click on the LEFT OUTER JOIN option ❷.

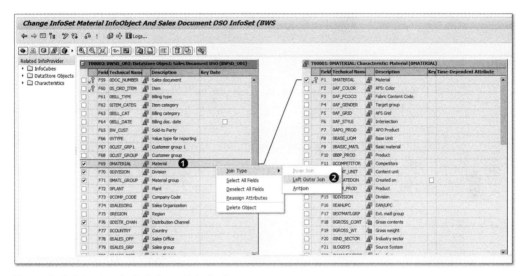

Figure 6.16 Selecting the Left Outer Join Option

The screen changes, as shown in Figure 6.17. Now the join shows the LEFT OUTER JOIN.

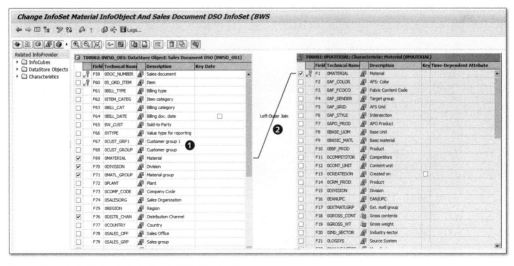

Figure 6.17 Left Outer Join in the InfoSet Definition

In this way, an inner join can be easily converted to a left outer join. Note, however, that where you select *from* is important. The selection process keeps the InfoProvider T00001 to the left side of the join. The query on this left outer join brings all of the rows from InfoProvider T00001, regardless of whether the matching value for the join condition (in our example, material) is available in InfoProvider T00002 or not.

Temporal Joins

InfoSets also offer a unique concept known as a *temporal join*, which is made available when an InfoSet is created with one of the InfoProviders that's included as an InfoObject with *time-dependent attributes*. In our example, InfoObject BW_CUST has 0SALESEMPLY as a time-dependent attribute. When we include Info-Object BW_CUST when creating the InfoSet, the temporal join can be used. We'll illustrate this with example data in Table 6.8 and Table 6.9.

Customer Number	Sales Office	Sales Employee	Valid From	Valid To
C1	SO1	EMP1	01-Jan-99	31-Dec-12
C1	SO1	EMP2	01-Jan-13	31-Mar-15
C1	SO1	EMP3	01-Apr-15	31-Dec-99
C2	SO2	EMP4	01-Apr-11	31-Mar-15
C2	SO2	EMP2	01-Apr-15	31-Dec-99
C3	SO1	EMP3	01-Jan-12	31-Dec-99

Table 6.8 Sample Master Data in InfoObject BW_CUST

Billing Document Number	Billing Date	Customer Number	Billing Qty
1234	25-Mar-15	C1	100
1235	25-Mar-15	C2	120
1236	25-Mar-15	C3	150
2115	03-Apr-15	C1	340
2116	03-Apr-15	C2	200
2117	03-Apr-15	C3	100

Table 6.9 Sample Data in DSO BWSD_O01

An InfoSet is created using InfoObjects BW_CUST and DSO BWSD_O01 with the customer number as the join between the two. The BILLING DATE field is used as a key date. (To understand how to set the key date, see the checkbox shown in ❹ of Figure 6.23, later in Section 6.2.3.)

The result of the query based on this InfoSet is shown in Table 6.10.

Billing Document Number	Billing Date	Customer Number	Sales Employee	Billing Qty
1234	25-Mar-15	C1	EMP2	100
1235	25-Mar-15	C2	EMP4	120
1236	25-Mar-15	C3	EMP3	150
2115	03-Apr-15	C1	EMP3	340
2116	03-Apr-15	C2	EMP2	200
2117	03-Apr-15	C3	EMP3	100

Table 6.10 Result of Query

As you can see, the value of the SALES EMPLOYEE field is derived using the value of the billing date for each billing document number, as well as the value of the sales employee between the valid from and valid to dates for the same customer in BW_CUST.

Anti Joins

From SAP BW 7.3, a new type of join is introduced for InfoSets: the *anti join s*. An anti join is a type of join that is used to identify which data from an InfoProvider isn't contained in another InfoProvider. As an example, let's look at a material InfoObject that contains the data shown in Table 6.11 (for simplicity, only the material key is shown). Another DSO contains sales order data, as shown in Table 6.12 (for simplicity, only the sales order number information and the material information are shown).

Material
21000
31000

Table 6.11 Material Master Data for the Anti Join Example

Material
41000
51000
61000

Table 6.11 Material Master Data for the Anti Join Example (Cont.)

Sales Order Number	Material
100	21000
101	41000
102	21000
103	51000

Table 6.12 Sales Order Data for the Anti Join Example

When creating an InfoSet using these two tables, the DSO is defined as an anti join on the material field. When you execute the queries on an InfoSet that uses this anti join, you're provided with a list of the master data entries in the material field that don't appear in the DSO; in our example, these are 31000 and 61000 (Table 6.13).

Result Data
31000
61000

Table 6.13 Result of the Anti Join

6.2.2 Transitive Attribute Reporting

One of the capabilities of an InfoSet is allowing *transitive attribute reporting*, which is the process of reporting on a second-level attribute. As shown in Figure 6.18, InfoObject BW_CUST has several attributes, one of which is 0SALESEMPLY. In addition, InfoObject 0SALESEMPLY has its own attributes, one of which is 0CITY. Because of this relationship, 0CITY is known as a *transitive attribute* of BW_CUST.

While designing an InfoCube, you can switch on 0SALESEMPLY as the navigation attribute of BW_CUST and use 0SALESEMPLY in the query design wherever BW_

CUST is part of the InfoCube. But you can't use the attributes of 0SALESEMPLY (for example, 0CITY) in the query design when BW_CUST is part of the InfoCube.

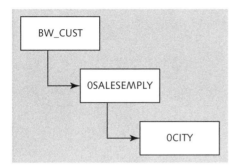

Figure 6.18 The Transitive Attribute of BW_CUST: 0CITY

In this scenario, you can use the InfoSet to get the information related to the transitive attribute.

6.2.3 Designing InfoSets

In the reference scenario, we have a requirement for analyzing which products of ABCD Corp. aren't getting sold in specific markets. This analysis requirement can be addressed using an InfoSet as explained next.

Creating InfoSets

To begin, open the DATABASE WAREHOUSING WORKBENCH screen using Transaction RSA1. Under MODELING in the navigation section, select INFOPROVIDER, as shown in ❶ of Figure 6.19. InfoSets are created under an InfoArea. From the tree section of the screen, select the InfoArea to which you want to attach your InfoSet ❷. In this example, BW INFOAREA is selected.

Using the context menu of BW INFOAREA, click on the CREATE INFOSET option ❸. The CREATE INFOSET box appears, as shown in Figure 6.20.

InfoSets require a unique technical name and description, as shown in ❶ of Figure 6.20. The technical name of the BW_AREA InfoArea in which the InfoSet would be grouped is displayed in the INFOAREA field ❷. The START WITH INFO-PROVIDER section ❸ offers three choices: DATASTORE OBJECT, INFOOBJECT, and INFOCUBE.

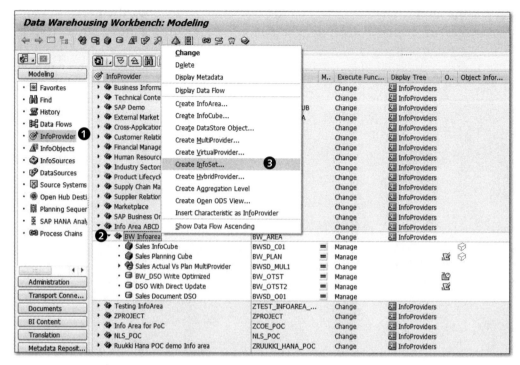

Figure 6.19 Creating the InfoSet

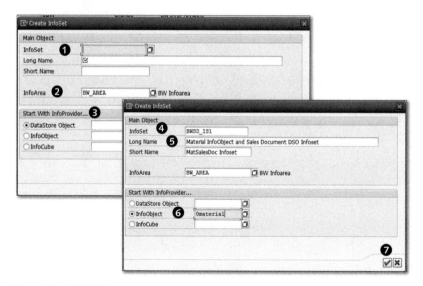

Figure 6.20 Initial Screen

In this example, we'll use the technical name "BWSD_IS1" ❹ and the description "Material InfoObject and Sales Document DSO Infoset" ❺. You can also choose to supply a short description, but only the long description is mandatory. We'll use "MatSalesDoc Infoset" in the SHORT NAME field.

The START WITH INFOPROVIDER area allows you to supply the technical name of the first source you want to include in the definition of InfoSet BWSD_IS1. In our example, we want to include an InfoSet based on InfoObject 0MATERIAL and DSO BWSD_O01. Select the INFOOBJECT radio button, and enter the name of the InfoObject "0material" ❻. Now click on the CONTINUE icon ☑ ❼. The resulting screen is shown in Figure 6.21.

InfoObject 0MATERIAL is included as part of InfoSet BWSD_IS1. SAP BW internally allocates the number T00001 to the first object that is included in this definition (see ❶ of Figure 6.21). For the subsequent objects you include, it gives the number T00002, and so on.

All attributes of InfoObject 0MATERIAL are shown in the vertical box format. The technical name of the attribute is shown in the TECHNICAL NAME column ❹.

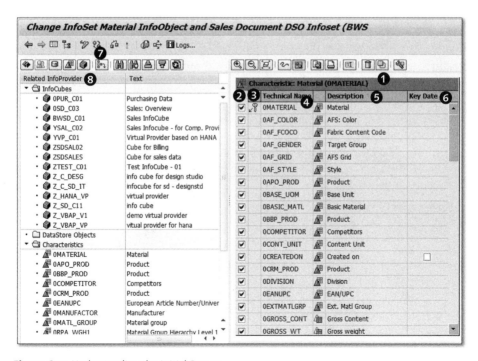

Figure 6.21 Understanding the Initial Screen

Not all columns have titles, so we've numbered them to explain their significance. Column ❷ of Figure 6.21 allows you to decide whether you want to include particular attributes of the 0MATERIAL InfoObject in the final definition of the InfoSet. By default, SAP BW includes all of the attributes. Column ❸ indicates whether the particular InfoObject is a key. For example, InfoObject 0MATERIAL is the key for InfoObject 0MATERIAL; for a DSO, all of the key fields are indicated as a key with a key icon 🔑. Columns ❹ and ❺ indicate the technical name and description of the attributes, respectively. Column ❻ indicates whether the field is included or excluded while defining the result for a temporal join. The checkbox is only shown when the field is a date field; for example, for field 0CREATEDON, the checkbox is shown, which is a date field.

The RELATED INFOPROVIDER section ❽ gives the list of InfoObjects, DSOs, and InfoCubes that can be used to join 0MATERIAL; that is, all of the objects of which 0MATERIAL is a part and that are available for making an InfoSet join with InfoObject 0MATERIAL.

Defining InfoSets

Now you're ready to include your next source in the definition of InfoSet BWSD_IS1. Select the INSERT INFOPROVIDER icon 📇, as shown in ❼ of Figure 6.21. The INSERT INFOOBJECT pop-up box appears, as shown in ❶ of Figure 6.22. Three choices (DATASTORE OBJECT, INFOOBJECT, and INFOCUBE) are available as InfoSet definitions and can include either of the objects. Our example InfoSet is based on InfoObject 0MATERIAL and DSO BWSD_O01.

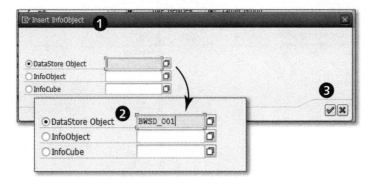

Figure 6.22 Inserting a Second Source

Next, select the DataStore Object radio button (if not selected already), and enter the technical name "BWSD_O01," as shown in ❷ of Figure 6.22. Now click on the Continue icon ☑ ❸.

The screen now changes, as shown in Figure 6.23. The DSO BWSD_O01 is displayed ❶. This time, the technical number attached to DSO BWSD_O01 is T00002, and column ❷ shows the Key icon for 0DOC_NUMBER and 0S_ORD_ITEM. These two InfoObjects are configured as key fields of DSO BWSD_O01. Column ❸ shows the technical name of the InfoObjects of DSO BWSD_O01. Column ❹ shows the key date.

Now both sources are available in the screen. We need to decide which fields to include in the InfoSet definition, and how to join the InfoSet. There are two ways you can select/deselect fields in the InfoSet definition. The first way is to select the individual checkbox to exclude or include it in the definition of the InfoSet. By default, SAP BW includes all of the fields in the definition of the InfoSet, so you need to uncheck the checkbox in the first column. This may be cumbersome when you want to include only a few required fields in the definition of an InfoSet.

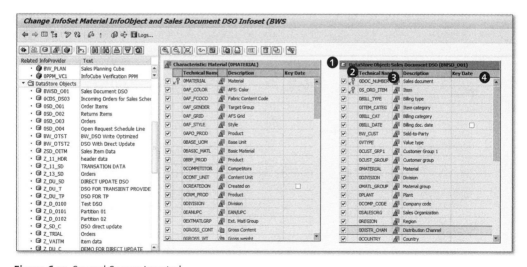

Figure 6.23 Second Source Inserted

The second way is to deselect all of the checkboxes using one single click and include only those that are required. First, open the context menu by right-clicking anywhere on the source object for which you want to deselect all of the fields. For example, we want to deselect all of the fields for the 0MATERIAL source object. Open the context menu by right-clicking somewhere near the spot shown in ❶ of Figure 6.24, and then select DESELECT ALL FIELDS ❷. You can perform similar steps on the BWSD_O01 source object and deselect all of the fields of DSO BWSD_O01.

All of the fields from both included source objects are now deselected. Now select only the required fields by selecting the checkbox available in the first column. As shown in ❸, we've selected only fields 0MATERIAL, 0MATL_CAT, and 0MATL_TYPE from source object T00001 (all fields aren't displayed in this screen).

In a similar way, the fields 0MATERIAL, 0DIVISION, 0MATL_GROUP, 0DISTR_CHAN, 0SALES_OFF, BW_QTY, and 0UNIT are selected from source object BWSD_O01 ❹.

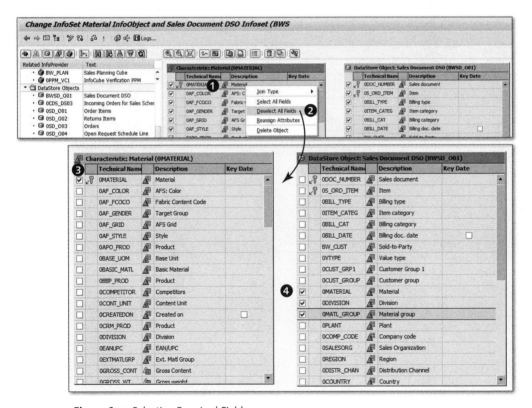

Figure 6.24 Selecting Required Fields

Joining Source Objects

The next step after selecting the fields is to join the two source objects. You can join a field from one source object to the same field or a field with a similar data type and length of another source field. This process is very simple. In our example, we want to join the 0MATERIAL field from the T00001 source object to the 0MATERIAL field of the T00002 source object. Select the 0MATERIAL field of T00001, keep the left mouse button pressed, and drag the mouse over to the 0MATERIAL target field of T00002. The dragged mouse icon pointer changes from the normal pointer icon ⌖ to a pencil icon ✎. Drop it on the target field.

SAP BW now creates a join between the 0MATERIAL field of the T00001 source object and the 0MATERIAL field of the T00002 source object. This is shown as a link from ❶ to ❷ in Figure 6.25. Internally, SAP BW makes this a join condition similar to *T00001.0MATERIAL = T00002.0MATERIAL*.

If required, you can create another join condition between the two fields of T00001 and T00002; however, our example scenario doesn't require another join condition. This completes the steps required to configure an InfoSet.

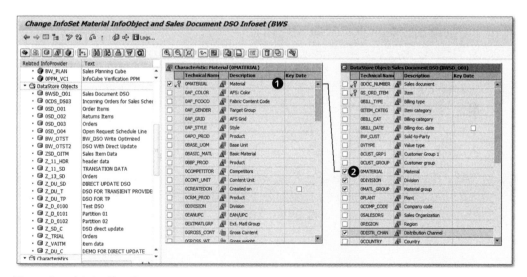

Figure 6.25 Joining Two Sources

Checking and Activating

Now check the definition using the CHECK icon ⌖, as shown in ❶ of Figure 6.26.

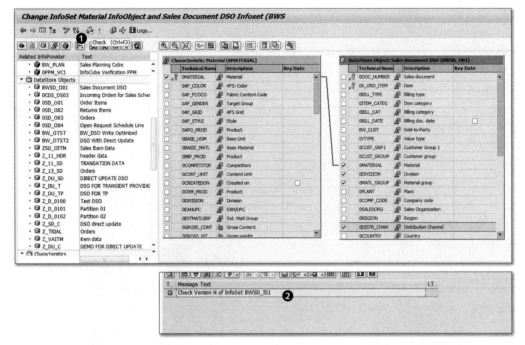

Figure 6.26 Checking the Definition of an InfoSet

Checked messages are available at the bottom of the screen, as shown in ❷ of Figure 6.26. Because the checking of InfoSet BWSD_IS1 hasn't resulted in any error messages, we can now activate the InfoSet definition in the SAP BW system.

To activate, click on the ACTIVATE icon, as shown in ❶ of Figure 6.27. Activation messages are shown in the lower section of the screen in a separate area ❷.

The final activation message is shown at the bottom of the screen ❸. Now the definition of the InfoSet is available for further use, for example, for creating a query based on this InfoSet or for creating a new MultiProvider that includes InfoSet BWSD_IS1.

As you can see in Figure 6.28, the newly created InfoSet BWSD_IS1 is available under BW INFOAREA BW_AREA.

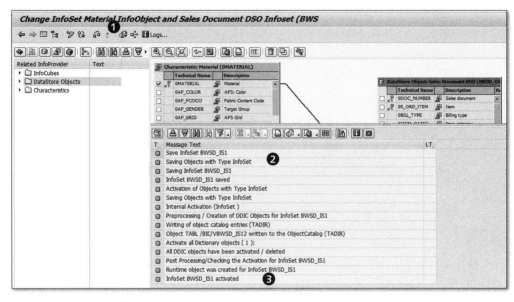

Figure 6.27 Activating the InfoSet

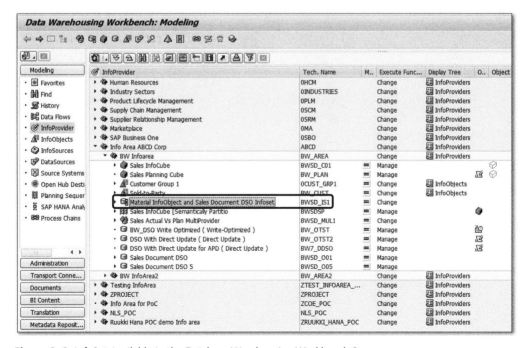

Figure 6.28 InfoSet Available in the Database Warehousing Workbench Screen

Changing the InfoSet Visual Setting

The InfoSet creation screen offers two types of display:

- Network display
- Tree display

So far we've seen the network display. You can change between the two settings by using the menu path SETTINGS • DISPLAY. The SETTING: INFOSET MAINTENANCE box appears, as shown in Figure 6.29. Select the HIERARCHY DISPLAY (TREE CONTROL) radio button ❶. Click on the CONTINUE icon ☑ ❷.

Setting: InfoSet Maintenance...
InfoSet maintenance can be performed in the network (data flow control) or in the tree (tree control).
While the network display is clearer, the tree display is readable for screen readers and more suitable for the visually impaired.
The change takes effect when InfoSet maintenance is started again.
Display Network (Data Flow Control)
Hierarchy Display (Tree Control)
1
2

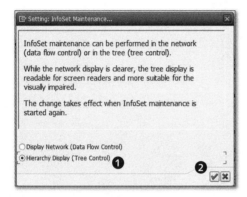

Figure 6.29 Changing the InfoSet Maintenance Screen Setting

The effect of this setting is visible the next time you open the InfoSet from the DATABASE WAREHOUSING WORKBENCH screen for editing. The screen should look like Figure 6.30.

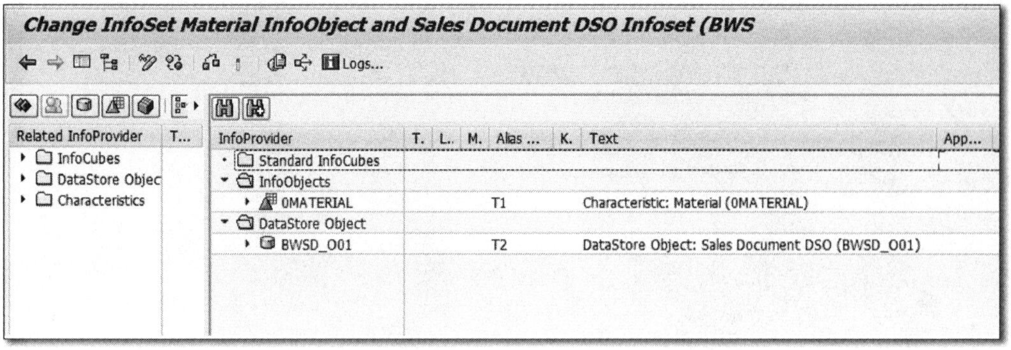

Change InfoSet Material InfoObject and Sales Document DSO Infoset (BWS
Logs...
Related InfoProvider
T...
InfoCubes
DataStore Objec
Characteristics
InfoProvider
T.
L..
M.
Alias ...
K.
Text
App...
Standard InfoCubes
InfoObjects
0MATERIAL
T1
Characteristic: Material (0MATERIAL)
DataStore Object
BWSD_O01
T2
DataStore Object: Sales Document DSO (BWSD_O01)

Figure 6.30 InfoSet Display in Tree Mode

The screen shown in Figure 6.30 is similar to what is explained in the LINK MAINTENANCE screen in the following section. The rest of the functionality remains the same.

6.2.4 Additional Navigation Capabilities

There are a few settings available for creating and editing an InfoSet. These settings are typical for the InfoSet only, so they are explained in detail in this section. Start the InfoSet definition in change mode. In the DATABASE WAREHOUSING WORKBENCH screen (Transaction RSA1), under MODELING in the navigation section, select INFOPROVIDER, as shown in ❶ of Figure 6.31. Select BW INFOAREA BW_ AREA ❷. Using the context menu of InfoSet BWSD_IS1 ❸, select the CHANGE option ❹. The CHANGE INFOSET screen appears (Figure 6.32).

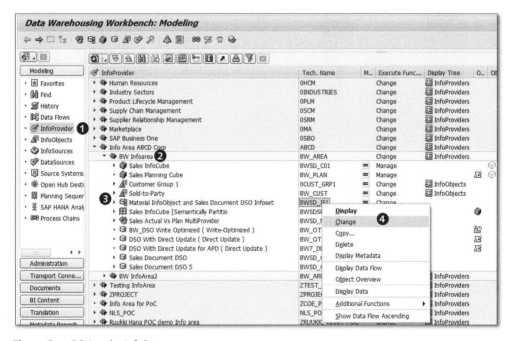

Figure 6.31 Editing the InfoSet

Auto Arrange

As you can see in ❶ of Figure 6.32, the join between two source objects isn't properly visible. Click on the AUTO ARRANGE icon 🖼 ❷. The resulting screen is shown in the lower part of Figure 6.32, where you can view the join properly ❸ and ❹. In the process, you may also observe that before executing AUTO ARRANGE, source object T00001 on the left side of the screen has moved to the right, and source object T00002 has moved to the left of the screen. This movement doesn't affect the functionality of the InfoSet.

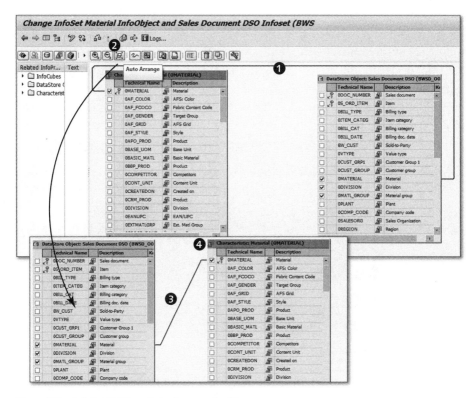

Figure 6.32 InfoSet Editing: Auto Arrange Facility

Navigator

When you're in the InfoSet change screen, sometimes all of the source objects won't fit on one screen. For example, as shown in Figure 6.33, the rightmost column (e.g., KEY DATE) isn't visible. There are three ways to adjust this view. The first method is to use the standard horizontal scroll bar available on any SAP BW screen, and scroll to the right side. The second method is to use the ZOOM OUT icon 🔍, which reduces the size of the font to accommodate more visible area on the same screen. There is also a ZOOM IN icon 🔍 that increases the size of the font to accommodate less visible areas on the same screen with more clarity.

The third method is to use the NAVIGATOR function. Click on the SHOW/HIDE NAV-IGATOR icon 🖼, as shown in ❶ of Figure 6.33. The result is that SAP BW adds a small box titled NAVIGATION ❷.

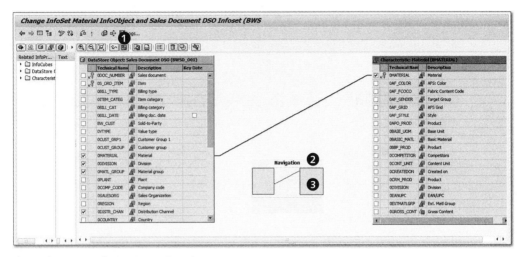

Figure 6.33 Using the Navigator Function

Here you can drag the navigation square box ❸ to the rightmost side of the NAV-IGATION box. The resulting screen is shown in ❶ of Figure 6.34. The content on the extreme right-hand side of the InfoSet definition screen is now visible ❷.

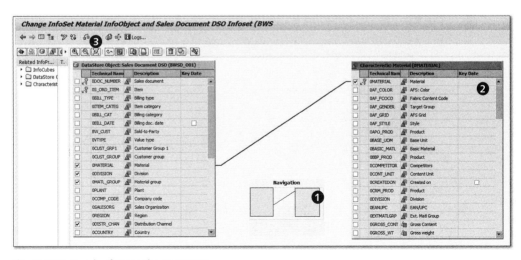

Figure 6.34 Result of Using the Navigator

Link Maintenance

When an InfoSet definition has two or more source objects and multiple joins, it may become difficult to move up and down or left and right to maintain the different joins involved in the definition of the InfoSet. An alternative way to maintain the join is by using link maintenance. Click on the LINK MAINTENANCE icon ⟲, as shown in ❸ of Figure 6.34. The LINK MAINTENANCE pop-up box appears (Figure 6.35).

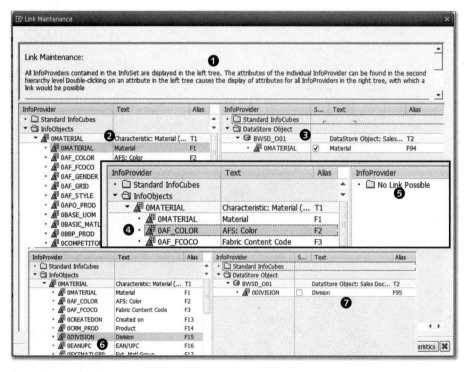

Figure 6.35 Link Maintenance

A brief description regarding the link maintenance functionality is shown in ❶ of Figure 6.35. A list of the included InfoProviders in the definition of the InfoSet is also given ❷. The right side panel is initially empty.

Expand the definition of InfoProvider 0MATERIAL, and double-click on the 0MATERIAL field ❷. The result of this action is shown on the right panel. The right panel now shows the 0MATERIAL field of DataStore object BWSD_O01 ❸.

This is the join we've created in our InfoSet, and the link maintenance functionality shows it in this simple way.

Double-click on the 0AF_COLOR field of InfoProvider 0MATERIAL ❹. This time, there's no matching field available in DataStore object BWSD_O01; on the right side, it's displaying No Link Possible ❺.

Double-click on the 0DIVISION field of InfoProvider 0MATERIAL ❻. On the right side panel, the 0DIVISION field of InfoProvider BWSD_O01 is displayed ❼. You can select the checkbox to create a join between the 0DIVISION field of InfoProvider 0MATERIAL and the 0DIVISION field of InfoProvider BWSD_O01.

Because our example InfoSet doesn't require this join, we'll leave it untouched.

6.2.5 Global Properties

A few properties are known as global properties for an InfoSet that can be accessed using the menu path GoTo • Global Properties. The InfoSet BWSD_IS1: Global Properties box appears, as shown in Figure 6.36. All four available settings are explained in this section.

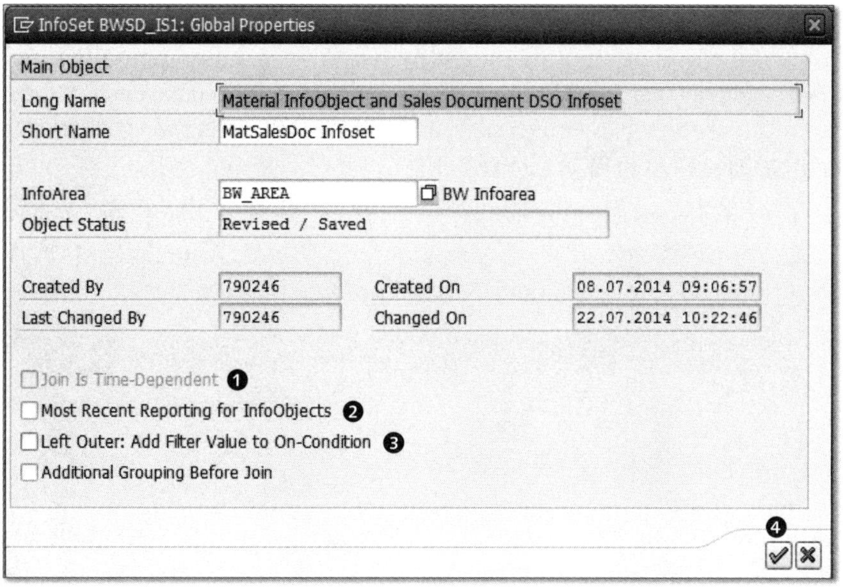

Figure 6.36 InfoSet Global Properties

Join Is Time-Dependent

This setting is display only (❶ of Figure 6.36). If any of the underlying InfoProviders included in the definition of the InfoSet is an InfoObject with a time-dependent attribute, this checkbox is checked, and the join created is known as a *time-dependent join*. In our example InfoSet, we've included InfoObject 0MATERIAL, but 0MATERIAL doesn't have any attributes that are time dependent, so this checkbox isn't available.

Most Recent Reporting for InfoObjects

An InfoSet can include an InfoObject as one of its underlying InfoProviders. In SAP BW, InfoObjects are used to store master data. The newly created master data (along with updated master data) is regularly loaded into this InfoObject. SAP BW doesn't make this newly loaded master data available to the queries right away. Newly loaded master data is first saved as an M version (modified version) in the underlying tables associated with the InfoObject. The data is only available for query after it's modified to become an A version (active version). To make newly loaded data active, you must process the attribute hierarchy change run, which is a normal part of the process when regular data loading takes place.

When you have a scenario where master data is loaded a number of times in SAP BW, there may be a delay in activating the newly loaded master data. However, using the settings available for InfoSets, you *can* report on this data, even if it isn't activated. To make this happen, check the MOST RECENT REPORTING FOR INFOOBJECTS setting, as shown in ❷ of Figure 6.36.

The first time the master data is loaded and activated, it's shown in Table 6.14. For the sake of simplicity, only a few columns are shown. Technically, SAP BW does have a few more columns to manage versions.

Customer Number	Version	City
C1	A	CITY-1
C2	A	CITY-2
C3	A	CITY-3

Table 6.14 Available Master Data

Now, the city of one customer has changed, and the newly loaded data (without the activation process) is shown in Table 6.15.

Customer Number	Version	City
C1	A	CITY-1
C2	A	CITY-2
C2	M	CITY-4
C3	A	CITY-3

Table 6.15 Data Loaded to Master: Activation Not Performed

If the InfoSet is queried with the configuration MOST RECENT REPORTING FOR INFOOBJECTS switched off, the result will be the data shown in Table 6.16.

Customer Number	City
C1	CITY-1
C2	CITY-2
C3	CITY-3

Table 6.16 Most Recent Reporting Not Configured

If the InfoSet is queried with the configuration MOST RECENT REPORTING FOR INFOOBJECTS switched on, the result will be the data shown in Table 6.17.

Customer Number	City
C1	CITY-1
C2	CITY-4
C3	CITY-3

Table 6.17 Most Recent Reporting Configured

Left Outer: Add Filter Value to On-Condition

This indicator (❸ of Figure 6.36) is useful if you've used a *left outer join* when defining the join in the InfoSet. It's used to control how a condition on a field of the left outer table is converted into a SQL statement while the query based on this InfoSet is executed. When the indicator is set, the condition is evaluated before the join. When the indicator isn't set, the condition is evaluated after the join.

The query result is different in both cases. You need to evaluate your reporting requirement and set the indicator accordingly.

Additional Grouping Before Join

By flagging the option for ADDITIONAL GROUPING BEFORE JOIN, the system is informed about the grouping of the key figures. When this flag isn't set, key figure grouping doesn't take place until the table contents are joined.

6.3 VirtualProviders

Businesses often want or need to analyze information in real time, which requires establishing a real-time connection with the data from a source system. This can be accomplished without storing data in data targets such as InfoCubes or DSOs because SAP BW has objects called *VirtualProviders*.

Like the MultiProvider and the InfoSet, VirtualProviders exist only as a logical definition. However, it's conceptually different from its counterparts because it doesn't source the data from existing data targets within the data warehouse but accesses the data in real time from the sources (see Figure 6.37).

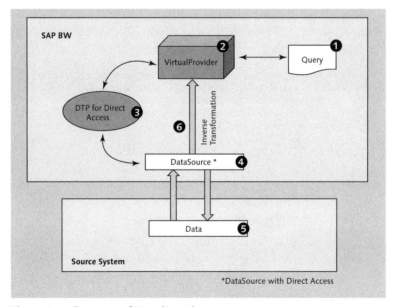

Figure 6.37 Illustration of VirtualProvider

We'll now explain the processes that enable reporting using a VirtualProvider. For instance, if we execute a query (see ❶ of Figure 6.37), the query is based on a

VirtualProvider ❷. The data for this query is then accessed in real time from the source system, using the direct access type data source ❹. The data is read from the source system ❺ and passed back to the query using the transformation ❻ and DTP for direct access ❸. Every navigation step in the query is a new process for reaching back to the source system for acquiring the relevant data set and relaying it to the query. The entire process of ETL happens in real time, and the data is converted to information and presented in the report. You can include the query variables to filter the data to be read from the source system. When a query is executed, the variable values are passed to the DataSource using inverse transformation.

The process of creating a VirtualProvider is very similar to creating a basic Info-Cube (see Chapter 5, Section 5.3). A radio button is available for defining a VirtualProvider with four available options:

▶ BASED ON THE DATA TRANSFER PROCESS FOR DIRECT ACCESS

▶ BASED ON BAPI

▶ BASED ON FUNCTION MODULE

▶ BASED ON A HANA MODEL (APPLICABLE FOR SAP BW ON HANA)

Note that conditions determine the applicability of a VirtualProvider. For instance, VirtualProviders should be used for scenarios that deal with a small data set, and the usage should be limited to a few users because the system has to execute the entire process from sourcing to presentation in real time.

VirtualProviders in SAP BW Powered by SAP HANA

In an SAP BW system powered by SAP HANA, VirtualProviders are also used to consume SAP HANA models in SAP BW.

6.4 Semantically Partitioned Objects (SPOs)

There may be scenarios where you're planning to store partitioned data based on certain characteristic values, such as data stored in identical InfoCubes, one for each sales organization, or data partitioned based on year. Prior to SAP BW 7.3, you could do this by creating these InfoCubes (one for each value of semantic partition) and then individually creating the transformations and DTPs for each of them, with one MultiProvider on top of it all. SAP provides a specific InfoProvider for this scenario: the *semantically partitioned object* (SPO). In this case, you simply define a reference data model, which can be a standard InfoCube or DSO, for the data target. Then you define the criteria for the semantic partition and the transformations. With this information, the SAP BW system automatically generates the partitioned data targets and corresponding transformations and DTPs. Thus, using an SPO eliminates the need for the creation of multiple smaller data targets with the same definition. Only the reference data model needs to be maintained, and the changes are reflected in the partitions automatically.

6.4.1 Creating SPOs

Semantic partitioning is a property of the InfoProvider, so you can define a standard InfoCube or a DSO as an SPO at the time of creating the data target. This step-by-step procedure is explained next.

An SPO is created in the DATABASE WAREHOUSING WORKBENCH screen, which is started using Transaction RSA1. Select INFOPROVIDER under MODELING from the navigator section, as shown in ❶ of Figure 6.38.

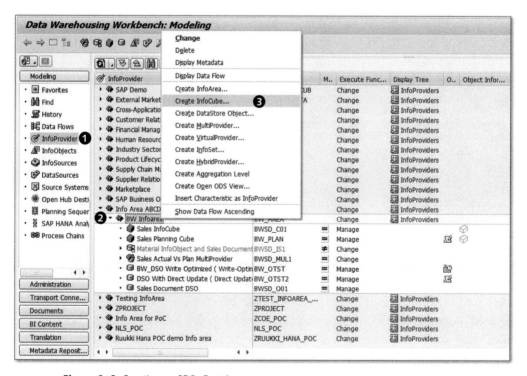

Figure 6.38 Creating an SPO: Part 1

Select the InfoArea under which you want to create your SPO ❷. From the context menu, select CREATE INFOCUBE ❸. The CREATE INFOCUBE screen appears, as shown in Figure 6.39.

Enter the technical name and description of the SPO (❶ of Figure 6.39). In our example, the SPO's technical name is "BWSDSP", and its description is "Sales InfoCube [Semantically Partitioned]". You can also use an existing InfoCube as a template to create a new SPO by entering the name of the existing InfoCube in the TEMPLATE field. In our example, InfoCube "BWSD_C01" is used as a template ❷.

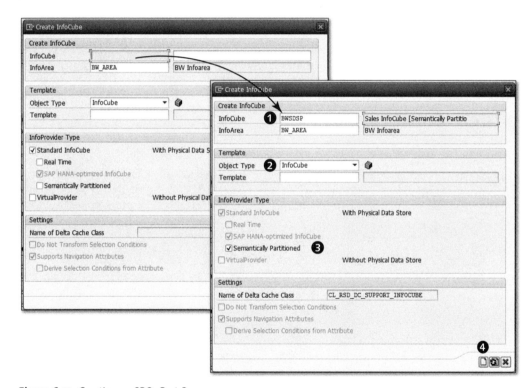

Figure 6.39 Creating an SPO: Part 2

Because this is a semantically partitioned InfoCube, select the SEMANTICALLY PARTITIONED property, as shown in ❸ of Figure 6.39. Click on the CREATE icon ❹. This takes you to the screen where you define the reference data model for the SPO (Figure 6.40).

6.4.2 Defining SPOs

In the left panel shown in ❶ of Figure 6.40, there are six steps to define and configure an SPO:

▶ MAINTAIN OBJECT

▶ MAINTAIN PARTITIONS

▶ START ACTIVATION

▶ CREATE TRANSFORMATION

▶ CREATE DATA TRANSFER PROCESSES

▶ CREATE PROCESS CHAINS

We consolidate our discussion of these steps into three major steps: managing partitions, creating transformations and DTPs for SPOs, and including SPOs in process chains.

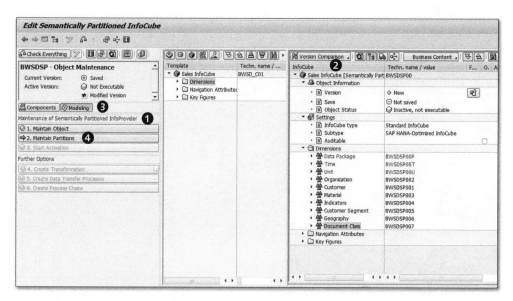

Figure 6.40 Editing an SPO

Managing Partitions

The right side of the screen, as shown in ❷ of Figure 6.40, displays the definition of InfoCube BWSD_C01, which is taken as the template. The system first creates the reference structure using InfoCube BWSD_C01 as the template. The system names this reference structure BWSDSP00 and refers to it when a new partition for an SPO is designed. All of the dimensions, navigational attributes, and key figures of BWSD_C01 are available here. As shown in ❸ of Figure 6.40, the MODELING section is selected by default. The COMPONENT section displays the included components of the SPO. Click on MAINTAIN PARTITIONS ❹ to open the SELECT PARTITIONING CRITERIA screen, as shown in Figure 6.41.

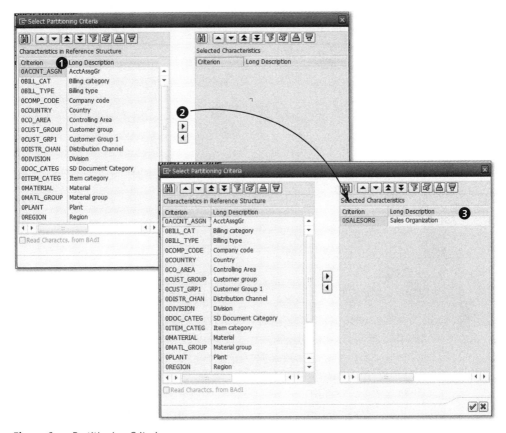

Figure 6.41 Partitioning Criteria

All of the characteristics of reference structure BWSDSP00 are displayed here (❶ of Figure 6.41). Select characteristics from the left-hand side that should be used to partition the data semantically; for our example, we use characteristic 0SALE-SORG (Sales Organization). Select 0SALESORG, and click on the TRANSFER icon ❷. Characteristic 0SALESORG is now available under SELECTED CHARACTERISTICS ❸. Click on the OK icon ❹ to continue with the definition of the SPO. This brings you to the MAINTENANCE OF CRITERIA FOR PARTITIONED OBJECT screen, as shown in Figure 6.42.

As shown in ❶ of Figure 6.42, the first partition is created by default and given the name PARTITION 01. Characteristic 0SALESORG is included as a partitioning characteristic ❷. By default, SINGLE VALUE is selected ❸, and a blank value is assigned to this partition ❹.

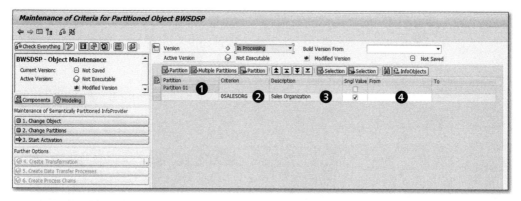

Figure 6.42 Creating Partitions

Our example needs three partitions based on sales organization 1000 (first partition), 2000 (second partition), and 3000 to 9999 (third partition). The procedure to configure this is shown in Figure 6.43.

Rename the first partition "SO 1000," as shown in ❶ of Figure 6.43. Also assign the value 1000 to sales organization in the FROM column ❷. To add a new partition, click on the PARTITION button ❸. This action adds one more blank partition, PARTITION 02 ❹. Rename this to "SO 2000" with the value 2000 assigned to it, as shown in ❺ and ❻. To add the third partition, repeat the process. Rename this new partition "Other SO" ❽, remove the SINGLE VALUE flag ❾, assign the value 3000 in the FROM column ❿, and the value 9999 in the To column. The final screen should look like the one shown in Figure 6.44.

While configuring partitions, the system offers a few facilities. In a scenario where you need to add multiple partitions at once, click on the MULTIPLE PARTITIONS button (❶ of Figure 6.44). Using the DELETE PARTITION button ❷, you can remove a partition. The ADD SELECTION button ❸ allows you to add selections to an existing partition; the DELETE SELECTION button ❹ allows you to remove selections from an existing partition.

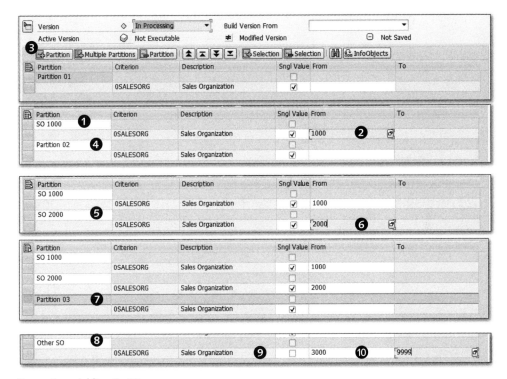

Figure 6.43 Adding Partitions

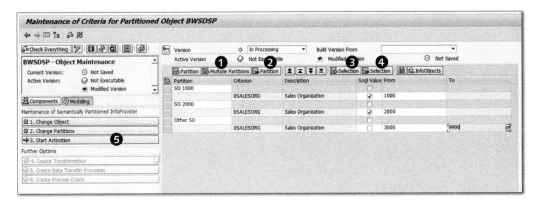

Figure 6.44 Partition Definition for an SPO

Our example scenario requires three partitions that are already configured and shown in Figure 6.44. Click on START ACTIVATION ❺ to activate the SPO and associated objects. This brings up the DISPLAY LOGS screen, as shown in Figure 6.45.

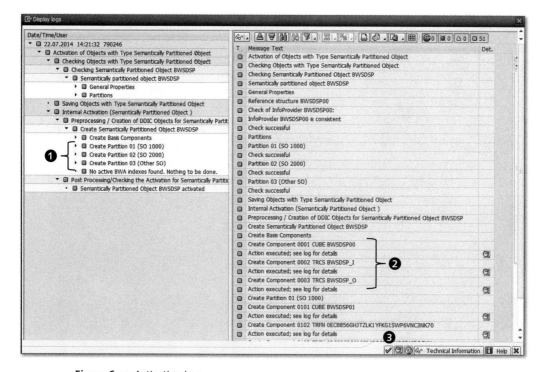

Figure 6.45 Activation Log

As shown in ❶ of Figure 6.45, three partitions are created. The system also assigns the names BWSDSP01, BWSDSP02, and BWSDSP03 to these partitions. All three partitions have the same structure as the reference structure BWSD-SP00. Along with these three partitions, the system also generates a few other components ❷.

Component BWSDSP_I is used in creating transformations, which is explained next. Click on CONTINUE ❸, and you're taken back to the MAINTENANCE OF CRITERIA FOR PARTITIONED OBJECT BWSDSP screen, as shown in Figure 6.46.

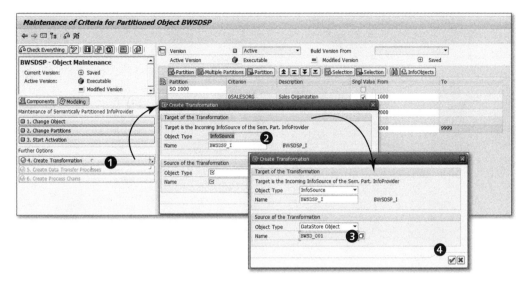

Figure 6.46 Creating a Transformation: Part 1

Creating Transformations and DTPs for SPOs

After maintaining partitions, the next activity is to create a transformation between the source and the defined SPO.

In our scenario, the source is the DSO BWSD_O01. Click on Create Transformation, as shown in ❶ of Figure 6.46 to open the Create Transformation screen. The system defaults the Target (InfoSource BWSDSP_I) ❷. This object is generated while activating the SPO (refer to ❷ of Figure 6.45), and internally connects to the SPO because there are multiple objects (depending on the partition created). Select DataStore Object as the source Object Type, and enter the name "BWSD_O01" ❸. Click on Continue ❹. This brings you to the Create Transformation screen, as shown in Figure 6.47.

As shown in Figure 6.47, the source of the transformation is DSO BWSD_O01 ❶, and the target is InfoSource BWSDSP_I ❷. After the required transformation is maintained, you need to activate it using the Activate icon ❸. You're back to the Edit Semantically Partitioned InfoCube screen, as shown in Figure 6.48.

> **Note**
>
> The transformation between a DSO and an InfoCube is explained in Chapter 7.

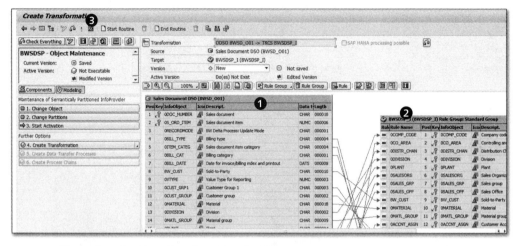

Figure 6.47 Creating a Transformation: Part 2

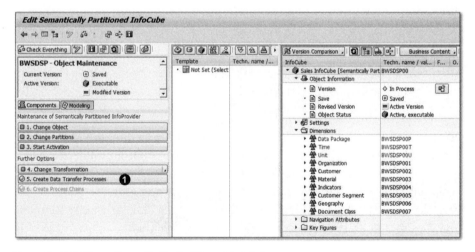

Figure 6.48 Editing a Semantically Partitioned InfoCube

After the transformation is created, you need to create the DTP between the source and the target. As shown in ❶ of Figure 6.48, click on the CREATE DATA TRANSFER PROCESSES option. This brings you to the GENERATE DATA TRANSFER PROCESSES screen, as shown in Figure 6.49.

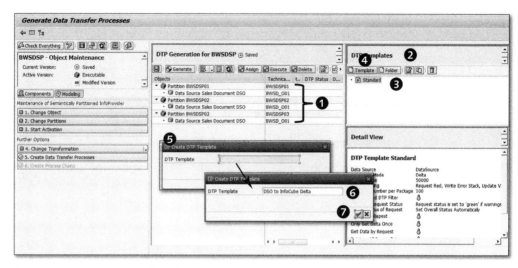

Figure 6.49 Generating Data Transfer Processes

As explained earlier, we've configured three partitions with the SPO BWSDSP. They are shown with their technical names: BWSDSP01, BWSDSP02, and BWSD-SP03 (❶ of Figure 6.49). Under each partition, DSO BWSD_O01 is listed as the source because we've created a transformation between DSO BWSD_O01 and InfoSource BWSDSP_I. This InfoSource was generated when the partitions were configured, and it connects all partitioned objects to a common source.

Now we need to create the DTP between the DSO and the SPO. The system offers DTP templates, as shown in ❷ of Figure 6.49; we'll create our own DTP template using the STANDARD template. Select the STANDARD template ❸, and click on the TEMPLATE button ❹. This action brings up the CREATE DTP TEMPLATE pop-up box ❺, where you should enter the name of the template ❻ and click on CONTINUE ❼. The system opens the EDIT PARAMETERS screen, as shown in Figure 6.50.

Depending on the template you choose, the DataSource of the template varies. Because we've selected the standard template, DATASOURCE is selected, as shown in ❶ of Figure 6.50. Ensure that you also select GENERATE AUTOMATICALLY as the DTP FILTER ❷, and change the DATA SOURCE field to DATASTORE OBJECT by using the dropdown list ❸. As soon as you make this change, the number of options will change based on the DataSource selected. For example, the EXTRACTION FROM option wasn't available when the DATA SOURCE field was the DATASOURCE object ❹. For our scenario, there's no need to change any other option. Click on the

Save button ❺, and you're returned to the Generate Data Transfer Processes screen with the newly created DTP template, as shown in ❶ of Figure 6.51.

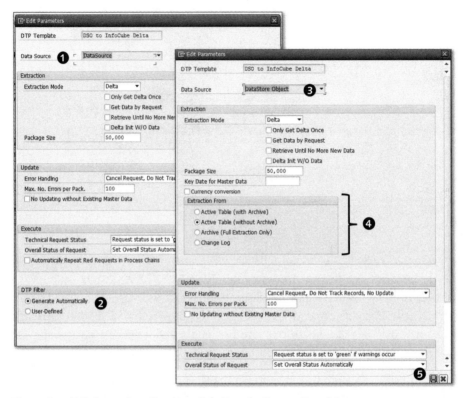

Figure 6.50 Edit Parameters: Copying a Data Transfer Process Template

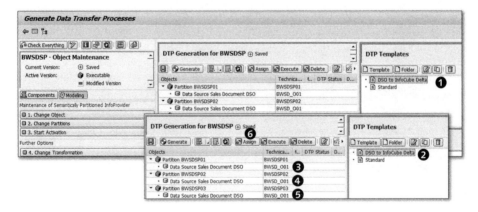

Figure 6.51 Assigning Data Transfer Processes

Now this DTP template needs to be assigned to the DataSource. Select the DTP template ❷, and also select DSO BWSD_D01 displayed under all three partition objects: BWSDSP01, BWSDSP02, and BWSDSP03 (❸, ❹, and ❺). Click on the Assign button ❻. This creates three different DTPs, as shown in ❶, ❷, and ❸ of Figure 6.52.

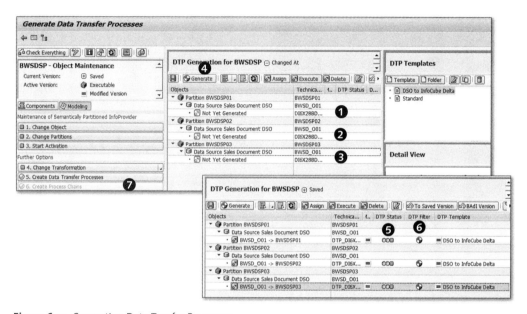

Figure 6.52 Generating Data Tranfer Processes

All of the DTPs generated are initially in inactive status; they need to be activated using the Generate button, as shown in ❹ of Figure 6.52. The system starts the generation of DTPs one by one. After all three DTPs are generated, they are shown as Active ❺. These DTPs have also taken into consideration the respective filter values for each of the partitions, which is displayed in the DTP Filter column ❻.

Including SPOs in Process Chains

Click on Create Process Chains, as shown in ❼ of Figure 6.52. This brings up the Generate Process Chains screen, as shown in Figure 6.53.

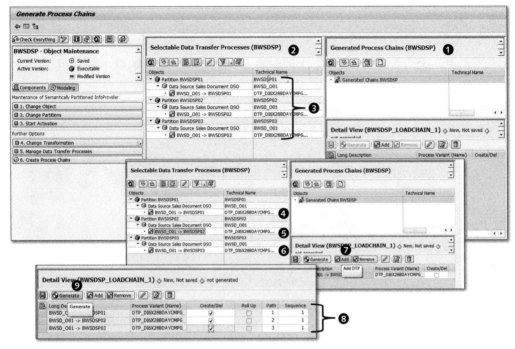

Figure 6.53 Generating Process Chains

On the right of the screen, the GENERATED PROCESS CHAINS (❶ of Figure 6.53) are displayed. In the middle of the screen, selectable DTPs are displayed ❷; these are the DTPs that were generated in the previous step. Select all three DTPs, as shown in ❹, ❺, and ❻. Click on the ADD button ❼, which adds all three selected DTPs to the DETAIL VIEW section ❽. Click on the GENERATE button ❾, which opens the MAINTAIN START PROCESS screen, as shown in Figure 6.54.

Click on the CHANGE SELECTIONS button, as shown in ❶ of Figure 6.54, which displays the START TIME pop-up box. Click on the IMMEDIATE button ❷, and then click on CHECK ❸ and SAVE ❹ to confirm the action. You're now back in the GENERATE PROCESS CHAINS screen, as shown in Figure 6.55.

Figure 6.54 Maintaining the Start Process and Execution Time

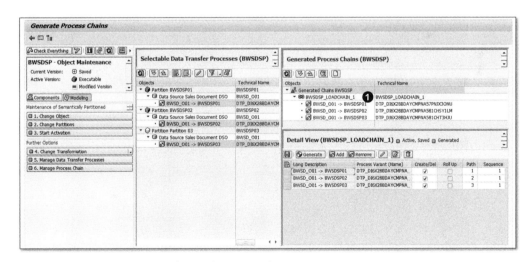

Figure 6.55 Generating Process Chains: Chain Created

You can now see that the system generated a process chain with the technical name BWSDSP_LOADCHAIN_1 and three DTPs under it (as shown in ❶ of Figure 6.55). You can view the process chain using Transaction RSPC, the details of which are shown in Figure 6.56. The execution of this generated process chain included deleting indexes for the InfoCube, executing the DTP (DSO to Info-Cube), and creating indexes for the InfoCube.

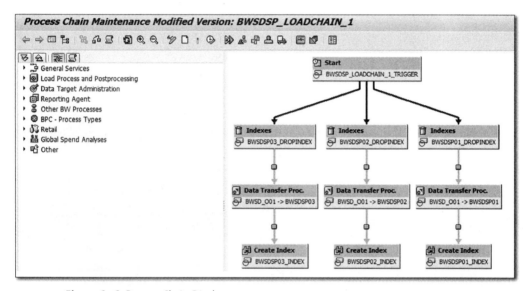

Figure 6.56 Process Chain Display

This step completes the configuration of the SPO. You can view the SPO in the DATABASE WAREHOUSING WORKBENCH screen by using Transaction RSA1, as shown in ❶ of Figure 6.57.

As shown in Figure 6.57, three InfoCubes (BWSDSP01, BWSDSP02, and BWSD-SP03) are shown under SPI BWSDSP (❷, ❸, and ❹). InfoSource BWSDSP_I and the transformation between the InfoSource and the three partitions are also shown. Just like other InfoProviders, SPOs can be used by BEx tools for querying and reporting.

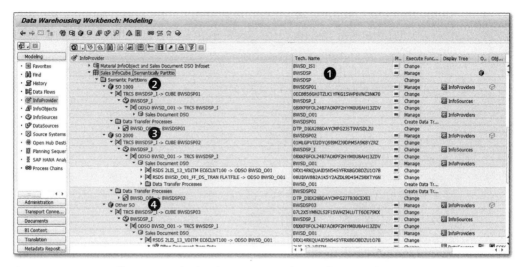

Figure 6.57 Semantically Partitioned InfoCube BWSDSP in the Database Warehousing Workbench Screen

6.5 HybridProvider

Sometimes, you'll need to combine real-time data with large volumes of historic data for reporting without compromising the performance of the reports. For larger data volumes, SAP Business Warehouse Accelerator (BWA) improves query performance. For real-time data, the solution could involve real-time data acquisition (explained in more detail in Section 6.5.1) or VirtualProviders (already explained in Section 6.3). The *HybridProvider* combines both of these components into one and presents it as a single InfoProvider for reporting. This combination allows data to be analyzed in real time along with the historical data and without much impact on performance. The HybridProvider was introduced with SAP BW 7.3.

A HybridProvider has two components: an InfoCube and an InfoProvider. The InfoCube stores the historical data and is loaded in BWA (although loading data into BWA isn't mandatory). The InfoProvider is used for real-time data. Based on the type of InfoProvider used to access real-time data, there are two types of HybridProviders:

▶ **HybridProvider based on DSOs**
   This HybridProvider is based on a combination of an InfoCube and a DSO. The

InfoCube stores the historical data, while new data is stored in the DSO using the real-time data acquisition (RDA) technique. This means that data is loaded in the DSO in real time through the real-time DTP, and then a DTP is used to load the data from this DSO to the InfoCube, as shown in Figure 6.58. RDA is only required if data is required in real time.

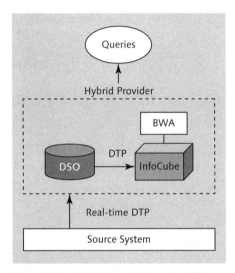

Figure 6.58 HybridProvider Based on DSO

When a query is executed on this HybridProvider, the system automatically determines what data is in the DSO and what part of the data can be accessed from the InfoCube.

▶ **HybridProvider based on direct access**
This type of HybridProvider is based on the combination of an InfoCube and a VirtualProvider. Historical data is stored in the InfoCube and is available through BWA, and new data is read from the source system through the VirtualProvider at the time of query execution. Again BWA isn't mandatory. The structure of both the InfoCube and the VirtualProvider is the same. Data is loaded into the InfoCube using the standard DTP, and a DTP for direct access is used between the DataSource and the VirtualProvider to access the real-time data. On execution of the query based on this type of HybridProvider, the system automatically determines whether the data requested resides in the InfoCube or has to be read from the source system using a VirtualProvider. A conceptual overview of this type of HybridProvider is shown in Figure 6.59.

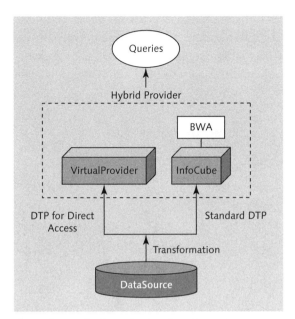

Figure 6.59 HybridProvider Based on Direct Access

Although the HybridProvider technically contains two separate InfoProviders within it, the system collectively treats it as one object. Also, after you define the HybridProvider, related objects, such as transformations and DTPs, are automatically generated. However, these generated DTPs and transformations can't be edited and should be used as generated by the system. The generated transformation between the DSO and the InfoCube (in the case of a HybridProvider based on a DSO) is always 1:1.

In this section, we explain the procedure of creating a HybridProvider. First, however, we start by explaining RDA, which is the concept leveraged in the functioning of a HybridProvider.

6.5.1 Real-Time Data Acquisition (RDA)

As shown in Figure 6.60, there are two ways to get data in real time: via the SAP source system and via external systems.

When data is accessed from the SAP source system, the SAP application (❶ of Figure 6.60) updates the data in the delta queue ❷ in real time. The daemon ❸ in SAP BW starts the InfoPackage for RDA ❹ at a defined interval, which can be configured while defining the daemon and could be as low as one minute. The InfoPackage for RDA then saves the data in the Persistent Staging Area (PSA) in SAP BW ❺. The daemon also controls the execution of the DTP for RDA ❻, which reads the data from the PSA and loads it into the DSO ❼. This DSO can become part of the HybridProvider.

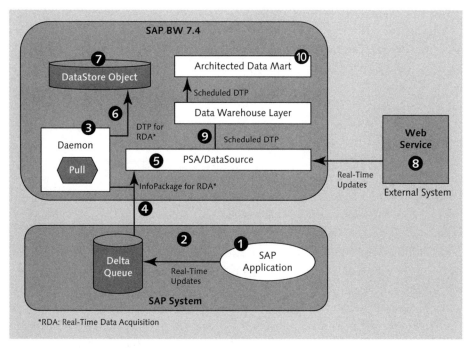

Figure 6.60 RDA Architecture

Daemons

Daemons are background activities that process InfoPackages and the DTPs assigned to them at regular intervals.

Persistent Staging Area (PSA)

A PSA is a transparent table whose structure is the same as that of the associated Data-Source. We discuss PSAs in more detail in Chapter 7.

When data is accessed from an external system, the external system Web Services ❽ push real-time data to the PSA of the DataSource ❺ on the SAP BW side. This

PSA data can be loaded using the DTP for RDA, the execution of which is controlled by the daemon. The data available in this PSA can also be loaded into the data warehouse layer using the scheduled DTP ❾. The data from the data warehouse layer can be further updated to an architected data mart using the scheduled DTP ❿.

6.5.2 Creating a HybridProvider

A HybridProvider is created in the DATABASE WAREHOUSING WORKBENCH screen, which is started using Transaction RSA1. Select INFOPROVIDER under MODELING from the navigator section, as shown in ❶ and ❷ of Figure 6.61.

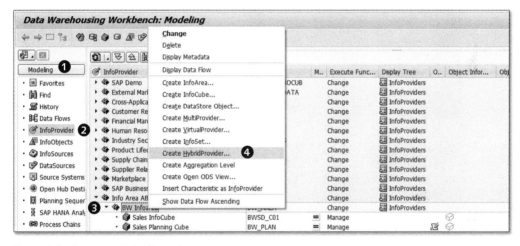

Figure 6.61 Creating a HybridProvider

Select the InfoArea BW_INFOAREA under which you want to create your Hybrid-Provider ❸. From the context menu, select CREATE HYBRIDPROVIDER ❹. The CREATE HYBRIDPROVIDER screen appears, as shown in ❶ of Figure 6.62.

Using a template (❷ of Figure 6.62) allows you to create a new HybridProvider based on an existing HybridProvider. The InfoCube is part of the definition of the HybridProvider, and the name of the InfoCube involved in the HybridProvider is shown under INVOLVED INFOCUBE ❸. The type of the HybridProvider is selected from HYBRIDPROVIDER TYPE ❹.

Enter the name of the HybridProvider as "BW_HP1" with the description "Sales Document Hybrid Provider" ❺. We're creating our HybridProvider based on the existing DSO BWSD_O04. You need to have created BWSD_O04 based on the definition per Table 6.18; the fields included in DSO BWSD_O04 are also shown in this table. Select BASED ON DATASTORE ❼.

Figure 6.62 Editing a HybridProvider: Part 1

Field Type	InfoObject	Description
Data Fields	0BILL_DATE	Date for invoice/billing index and printout
	BW_CUST	Sold-to party
	0MATERIAL	Material
	0DIVISION	Division
	0SALESORG	Sales organization
	0DISTR_CHAN	Distribution channel
	0SALES_OFF	Sales office
	BW_QTY	Billing quantity
	0UNIT	Unit of measure
	0DOC_CURRCY	Document currency
	0NET_VALUE	Net value of the order item in document currency

Table 6.18 Design of DSO BWSD_O04

Field Type	InfoObject	Description
Key Fields	0DOC_NUMBER	Sales document
	0S_ORD_ITEM	Sales document item

Table 6.18 Design of DSO BWSD_O04 (Cont.)

As soon as you select this, the system selects the name of the involved InfoCube (BW_HP1I), as shown in ➏ of Figure 6.62. To continue with the definition, click on the CREATE icon ➑. This brings you to the screen shown in Figure 6.63.

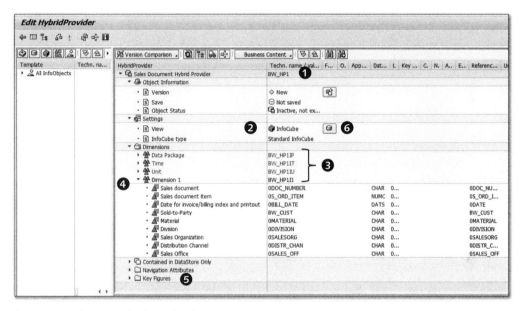

Figure 6.63 Editing a HybridProvider: Part 2

As shown in ➊ of Figure 6.63, the name of the HybridProvider is displayed. The system shows the INFOCUBE view ➋, which means that the system displays dimensions and key figures, as shown in ➌, ➍, and ➎. The system automatically creates the dimensions Data Package, Time, Unit, and Dimension 1, and all of the involved key figures are shown under the KEY FIGURE heading. You can jump to the DATASTORE OBJECT view by clicking on the DSO icon ➏. This switches the display to the DSO view of the HybridProvider, as shown in Figure 6.64.

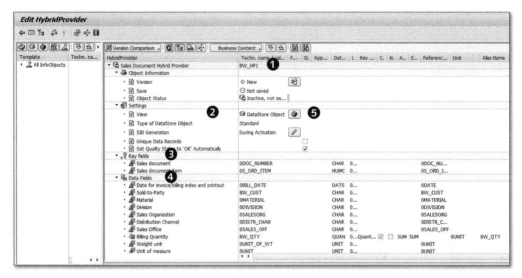

Figure 6.64 DataStore Object View of the Edit HybridProvider Screen

As shown in Figure 6.64, the definition of the DSO ❶ included in the HybridProvider is shown with Settings ❷, Key fields ❸, and Data Fields ❹. By clicking on the InfoCube icon ❺, you can switch back to the InfoCube view.

Click on the Activate icon to activate the HybridProvider. You can view the created HybridProvider using Transaction RSA1, as shown in Figure 6.65.

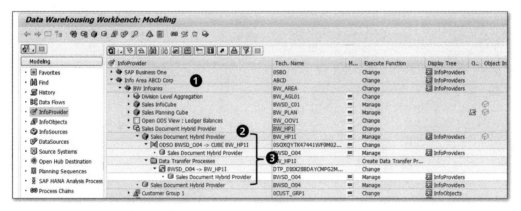

Figure 6.65 Created HybridProvider

The newly created HybridProvider BW_HP1 (❷ of Figure 6.65) is shown under the InfoArea BW_INFOAREA ❶. At the time of activating HybridProvider BW_HP1, the system also generated the associated transformation and DTP between DSO BWSD_O04 and InfoCube BW_HP1I ❸. The HybridProvider with direct access can be created following a similar procedure.

The HybridProvider provides the additional design flexibility of creating a data model with high-performance reporting on historical data combined with real-time data or data with reduced latency.

6.6   Transient Providers

Transient providers were introduced with the release of SAP BW 7.3. The objective behind transient providers is to provide the ability to perform ad hoc operational reporting directly on the SAP Online Transaction Processing (OLTP) system without the additional need to extract and stage the data in SAP BW; by using a transient provider, it's possible to report on real-time data (i.e., with zero latency). Using the transient provider, the standard BEx reporting tools can be used to create queries directly on the SAP OLTP tables and data. So, there's no need to have a separate SAP BW instance and to extract the data from the SAP OLTP system.

> **Note**
>
> In SAP BW powered by SAP HANA, the SAP HANA models published for consumption in SAP BW application are available as transient providers.

As a prerequisite to leverage the transient provider, the BI Client technical component must be installed on the same SAP OLTP system that has to be used for reporting; a transient provider by itself doesn't have any metadata, such as fields or InfoObjects. This InfoProvider is completely logical in nature and isn't visible in the DATABASE WAREHOUSING WORKBENCH screen. A conceptual overview of the transient provider is given in Figure 6.66.

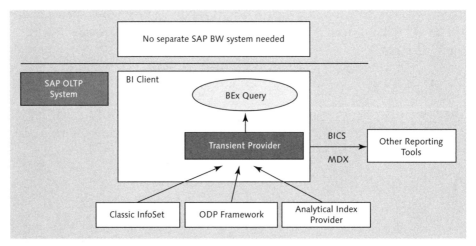

Figure 6.66 Transient Provider Concept

The source of data for a transient provider can be any of the following:

▶ A classic InfoSet in the OLTP system; these are client independent.

▶ DataSources from the SAP OLTP system; these are made available through the Operational Data Provisioning (ODP) framework.

▶ An analytical index created using the Analysis Process Designer (APD) (explained in Chapter 15).

Operational Data Provisioning (ODP)

ODP is a technical framework that's used to expose the standard SAP BW DataSources in the SAP OLTP system for third-party extraction tools (such as SAP Data Services) or to expose the SAP BW DataSources for operational reporting in the SAP OLTP system (as in the case of a transient provider).

As illustrated in Figure 6.66, the source from the preceding list is exposed as a transient provider to BEx Query Designer. From a BEx Query Designer perspective, this is just like any other regular SAP BW InfoProvider. All of the standard BEx Query Designer features are available when reporting on transient providers, too.

Apart from BEx reporting, transient providers can also be used to expose operational reporting to third-party reporting tools. For example, reporting tools from SAP BusinessObjects can connect with transient providers and thus get access to operational data in SAP OLTP systems. These third-party applications can leverage the standard BI Consumer Services (BICS) connectivity or the MDX connection.

Transient providers are thus an important method of achieving real-time reporting directly on an SAP OLTP system in a way that also allows you to utilize the complete set of features offered by BEx tools.

> **Note**
>
> You don't have to create any persistent metadata or data models when creating a transient provider. The characteristics and key figures used in the transient provider are automatically generated from the source field definitions.

6.7 Analytical Index

An analytical index is another type of InfoProvider that was introduced in SAP BW 7.3. This is an in-memory InfoProvider, which means that its data is stored directly in memory. Thus, an analytical index can be created directly in BWA or in an SAP BW system that uses SAP HANA as a database. An analytical index can be a source for a transient provider or for a CompositeProvider, and it can be used to address ad hoc reporting needs.

The creation of an analytical index takes place using an analysis process. We'll discuss more about analytical indexes and the procedure to create one when we explain analysis processes and the APD in Chapter 15, Section 15.2.

6.8 CompositeProvider

CompositeProviders are also new since SAP BW 7.3. The SAP BW CompositeProvider is used to bring the data together from in-memory data targets/InfoProviders. This InfoProvider can leverage both union and join operations to combine the data set. The base InfoProviders must reside in memory to be included in a CompositeProvider. It means that if you're using SAP BW on a non-SAP HANA database, then BWA is a prerequisite for a CompositeProvider. In such cases, only those SAP BW InfoProviders that reside in BWA can be part of a CompositeProvider. The BWA prerequisite for CompositeProviders is irrelevant if the SAP BW system uses the SAP HANA database.

There are three types of CompositeProviders, and each serves different requirements for different user groups and application areas: a central CompositeProvider, ad hoc CompositeProvider, and local CompositeProvider. We'll explain the
procedure to create a central CompositeProvider in the following section, and the
local CompositeProvider is explained in Chapter 10.

6.8.1 Creating a CompositeProvider

A CompositeProvider is created in the DATA WAREHOUSING WORKBENCH screen,
which is opened using Transaction RSA1. Select INFOPROVIDER under MODELING
from the navigator section, as shown in ❶ of Figure 6.67. Select the InfoArea
under which you want to create your CompositeProvider ❷. From the context
menu, select CREATE COMPOSITEPROVIDER ❸. The CREATE COMPOSITEPROVIDER
pop-up appears, as shown in Figure 6.68.

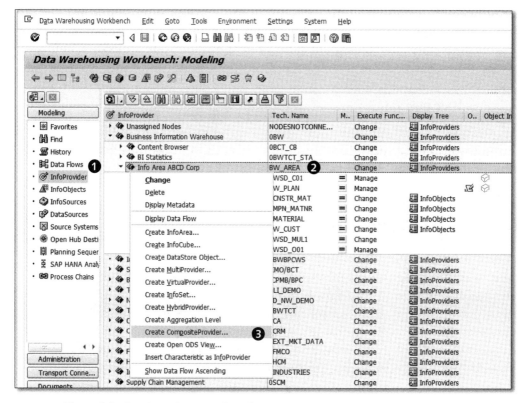

Figure 6.67 Creating a CompositeProvider

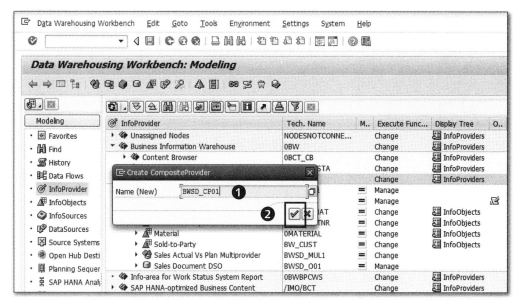

Figure 6.68 Entering the Technical Name for the CompositeProvider

Enter the technical name and description of the CompositeProvider (❶ of Figure 6.68). Click on the CREATE icon ❷. This takes you to the screen where you define the reference data model for the CompositeProvider (see Figure 6.69 in the next section).

To illustrate the creation of a CompositeProvider, let's assume a scenario where there is a business need to build a report that will show sales bonuses by sales office. This bonus calculation has to happen based on the sales commission percentage defined for each of the sales offices and the actual sales numbers. In SAP BW, the actual sales values are available in one of the InfoCubes (BWSD_C01), while sales commissions are stored in a separate master data InfoObject BW_SLCOM. To address this requirement, we would like to combine sales data and commission data in a CompositeProvider.

6.8.2 Defining CompositeProviders

The naming convention by SAP, that is, all CompositeProvider begin with "@3", is defaulted in the technical name for the InfoProvider in the right panel as shown in ❶ of Figure 6.69.

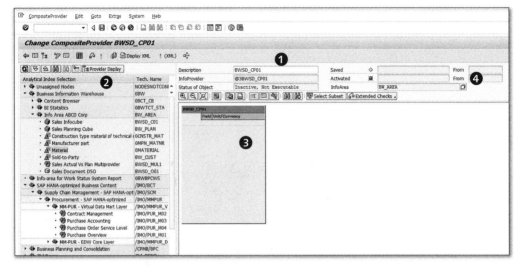

Figure 6.69 Reference Data Model for the CompositeProvider

The left panel provides all possible objects that could be used in creation of the CompositeProvider (❷ of Figure 6.69). The CompositeProvider is shown in the right panel ❸. We recommend identifying the CompositeProvider into a specific InfoArea by using the INFOAREA dropdown menu in the right panel ❹.

Inserting Objects

From the left side panel, select InfoCube BWSD_C01 (❷ in Figure 6.70), and drag and drop it into the right panel. In the pop-up that appears ❸, select a BINDING TYPE ❺. In this example, we chose UNION for the purpose referred to earlier. Click on the CONTINUE icon ❻, and the object is now available in the right panel (❶ of Figure 6.71).

Select the objects in BWSD_C01 that should be included in the CompositeProvider definition (❷ of Figure 6.71). From the context menu, select ADD SELECTED OBJECTS to add the selected objects to the CompositeProvider definition ❸.

All the characteristics of the inserted object are mapped 1:1 in the CompositeProvider (refer to ❸ of Figure 6.71).

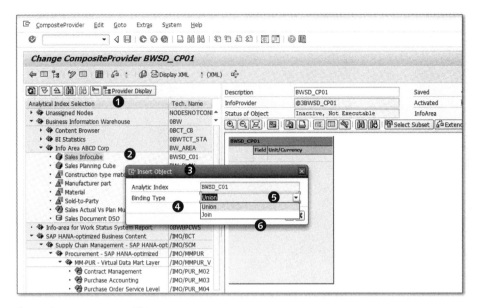

Figure 6.70 Inserting an Object

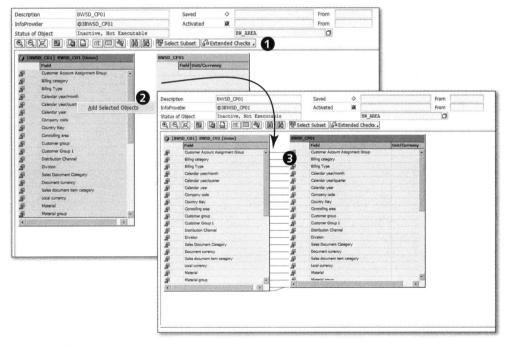

Figure 6.71 Defining a CompositeProvider: Part 1

Now identify other objects for the sales commission data from the panel on the left side by following the same process as for BWSD_C01. For this example, we selected BW_SLCOM (❶ of Figure 6.72) and chose JOIN in the BINDING TYPE field ❷.

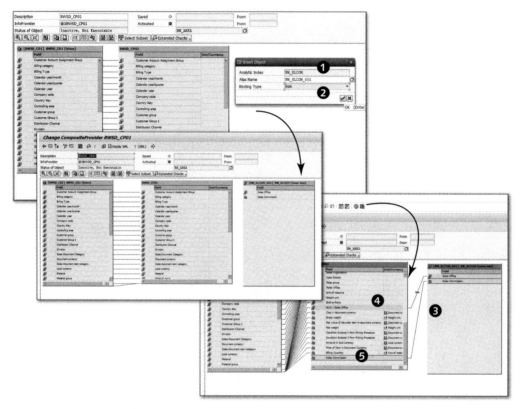

Figure 6.72 Defining a CompositeProvider: Part 2

The new object now is available in the right panel. The fields are mapped to the CompositeProvider via drag and drop (❸ of Figure 6.72). The join for SALES OFFICE ❹ is defined specifically while including the key figure for SALES COMMISSION ❺ in the CompositeProvider definition.

The EXTENDED CHECKS button (❶ of Figure 6.73) provides you options to analyze the defined joins and debug the definition of the CompositeProvider. Also, the context menu from the header of the inserted object gives you options to toggle between union and other join settings ❷.

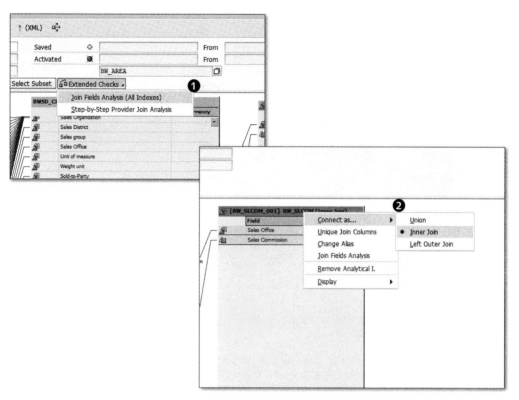

Figure 6.73 Defining a CompositeProvider: Part 3

Check the CompositeProvider using the CHECK icon (❶ of Figure 6.74), and take note of the system messages in the information panel that gets generated below ❷. When there are no errors reported, save the CompositeProvider by clicking on the SAVE icon in the menu bar ❸, and note the system messages in the information panel that gets generated below ❹. Finally, activate the CompositeProvider by using the ACTIVATE icon ❺, and note the system messages in the information panel that generated below ❻.

We recommend using the display data functionality to establish information output from the CompositeProvider. Click on the DISPLAY DATA icon (❶ of Figure 6.75) to see the options for filtering the data to be included or excluded in the output ❷. Choose the EXECUTE icon ❷, and check the output ❸.

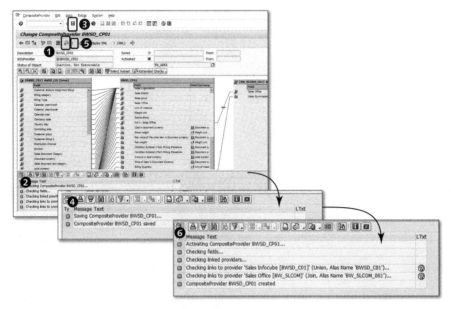

Figure 6.74 Saving and Activating a Composite Provider

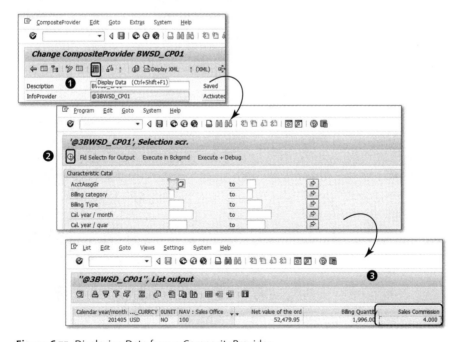

Figure 6.75 Displaying Data from a CompositeProvider

The newly created CompositeProvider is now available in the InfoArea BW_AREA within the DATA WAREHOUSING WORKBENCH screen (❶ Figure 6.76).

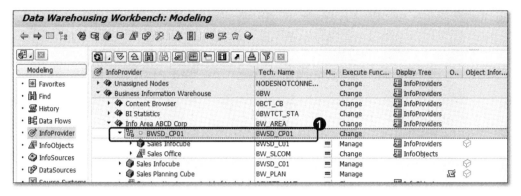

Figure 6.76 Newly Created CompositeProvider in the InfoArea

6.9   Open ODS View

The open ODS view (OOV), which was newly introduced in SAP BW 7.4, enables designers to build InfoProviders in a step-by-step manner. Until now, all the Info-Providers offered by SAP BW had to be designed using InfoObjects, which are the smallest building blocks of SAP BW and which are used in designing a number of other SAP BW objects. This makes it difficult to change the definition of an Info-Object after it's used in building other InfoProviders.

These InfoProviders give designers the flexibility to model InfoProviders based on source fields, and InfoObjects aren't mandatory. There is also a facility to attach an InfoObject to a field at the time of design to get benefits associated with the InfoObject (e.g., text of master data, navigational attributes, etc.). The main advantages of OOV are the following:

- ▶ Use of OOV as a VirtualProvider, with no data staging required
- ▶ Use of existing SAP BW objects to get additional information
- ▶ Flexibility of enhancing model
- ▶ Facility to load the data as the persistence layer

Prerequisite for the Open ODS View

Your SAP BW system must be on an SAP HANA database to use the open ODS view.

Let's now consider how to create OOV in an SAP BW system.

6.9.1 Creating an Open ODS View

As explained earlier, an OOV is a type of InfoProvider. An OOV is created in the DATABASE WAREHOUSING WORKBENCH screen, which is opened using Transaction RSA1. Select INFOPROVIDER ❶ under MODELING ❷ from the navigator section (see Figure 6.77).

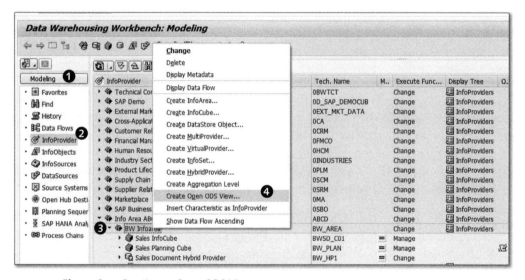

Figure 6.77 Creating an Open ODS View

An OOV is created under INFOAREA. Select InfoArea BW_INFOAREA ❸. From the context menu, select CREATE OPEN ODS VIEW ❹ to open the CREATE OPEN ODS VIEW screen as shown in ❶ of Figure 6.78.

You need to provide certain input while creating an OOV. Each OOV requires a unique name. Provide the name "BW_OOV1" and enter "Open ODS View – Ledger Balances" in the LONG DESCRIPTION field (❷ of Figure 6.79).

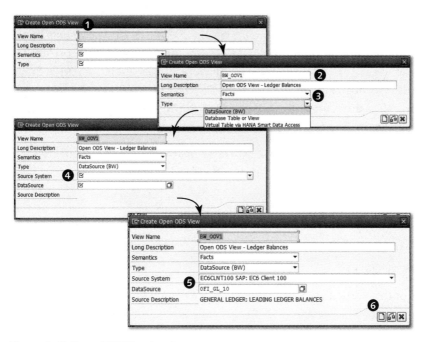

Figure 6.78 Open ODS View Input

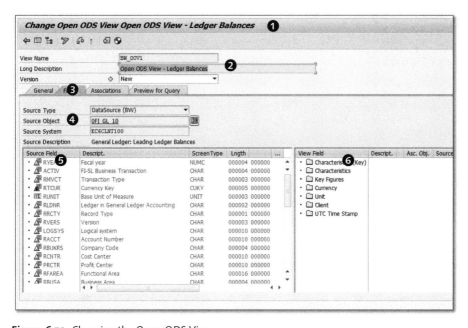

Figure 6.79 Changing the Open ODS View

An OOV is based on semantics, which are facts, master data, and texts, and we're creating an OOV based on facts, so click on the FACTS tab ❸. The details of the source are shown ❹. The OOV SOURCE TYPE field indicates what object stores the data: DataSource (BW), Database Table or View, or Virtual Table via HANA Smart Data Access. For our example OOV, select DataSource (BW) as the source type and 0FI_GL_10 as the source object. Once all of the details are added, click CREATE ❺, which opens the CHANGE OPEN ODS VIEW screen (Figure 6.78).

The VERSION field is initially shown as NEW. Below these fields, four tabs are available:

▶ GENERAL

▶ FACTS

▶ ASSOCIATIONS

▶ PREVIEW OF QUERY

The fields of this particular DataSource of source system EC6CLNT100 are shown under the SOURCE FIELD column ❺. Along with the field name, the description, screen type, and length of the field are also displayed. Under the VIEW FIELDS column ❻, the following seven folders are available:

▶ CHARACTERISTICS (KEY)

▶ CHARACTERISTICS

▶ KEY FIGURES

▶ CURRENCY

▶ UNIT

▶ CLIENT

▶ UTC TIME STAMP

You need to select source fields from the left side and move them to the right side under one out of seven sections. Let's see how it's done.

If you plan to move all the source fields from source to view, you can use the proposal feature. By clicking on the CREATE PROPOSAL icon (❶ of Figure 6.80), you can move all the source fields to the VIEW FIELD section. All the fields are moved from source to view based on their data types. You can remove the fields that aren't required from the VIEW FIELD section. If you require only a few fields to be taken from the VIEW FIELD section, you can take them one by one, as we'll describe next.

For example, let's move Account Number (RACCT field) to the CHARACTERISTICS (KEY) section. To do that, first select the RACCT field from the SOURCE FIELD section ❷, right-click to open the context menu, and select ADD TO CHARACTERISTICS (KEY) ❸. This action brings RACCT files under the VIEW FIELD section ❹. In the same way, get the RBUKRS field (COMPANY CODE) under the VIEW FIELD section.

You can use an OOV in two different ways:

▸ As a virtual query provider
▸ To store output of a virtual query into a DSO as persistence data

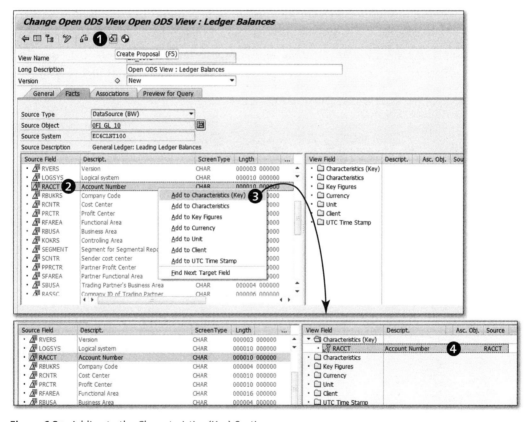

Figure 6.80 Adding to the Characteristics (Key) Section

If you plan to use an OOV to store data in a DSO as persistence, you need to move fields under the CHARACTERISTICS (KEY) section because these selected fields will define the key of the DSO. Our case requires storing data in a DSO, so we move the required fields under the CHARACTERISTICS (KEY) section. If you're going to use an OOV as only a virtual query provider, you need not move any fields under the CHARACTERISTICS (KEY) section.

Before we move the fields under the CHARACTERISTICS section, let's discuss how to open the PROPERTIES section for a field. There are number of ways to do it:

▸ From the menu bar, select UTILITIES • POSITION BY SINGLE CLICK (❶ of Figure 6.81). After selecting this option, whenever you click on a field under the VIEW FIELD column, the PROPERTIES section opens for the selected field.

▸ From the menu bar, select UTILITIES • POSITION BY DOUBLE CLICK. After selecting this option, whenever you double-click on a field under the VIEW FIELD column, the PROPERTIES section opens for the selected field.

▸ Select a field under the VIEW FIELD column for which you want to open the PROPERTIES section, and click on SHOW PROPERTIES icon (❸ of Figure 6.81).

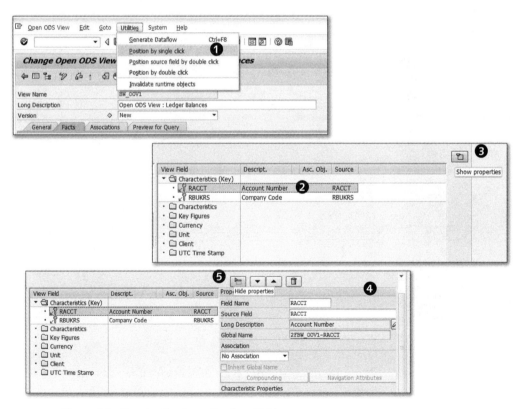

Figure 6.81 Opening the Properties for a Field

You can hide the PROPERTIES section by clicking the HIDE PROPERTIES icon ❺.

Now let's discuss how to add a field under the CHARACTERISTICS section of VIEW FIELD. Select the RBUSA (BUSINESS AREA) field ❶, and from the context menu, select ADD TO CHARACTERISTICS option ❷, as shown in Figure 6.82.

This action places the RBUSA field under the VIEW FIELD section as shown in ❸ of Figure 6.82. For each field under VIEW FIELD, you can set a number of properties. Open the PROPERTIES section ❹ using any of the methods explained earlier. You can set ASSOCIATION ❺, CHARACTERISTIC PROPERTIES ❻, and REPORTING PROPERTIES ❼ for each field. Each InfoObject created in SAP BW also has associated technical and semantic properties. You can take advantage of the associated properties of an InfoObject by associating fields of an OOV with the InfoObject. By associating the InfoObject with the fields, you can include InfoObject navigational fields and use the reporting properties in the design of the OOV.

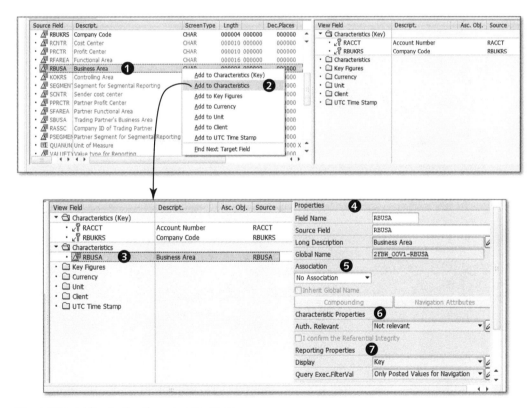

Figure 6.82 Adding to the Characteristics Section

You can also set the authorization relevance of the field, which helps in restricting certain data while viewing. Other properties are related to reporting, for example, displaying the data of fields as KEY, TEXT, or both.

As shown in Figure 6.83, you need to set the following fields when designing an OOV:

▶ CHARACTERISTICS (KEY)

　▶ RACCT

　▶ RBUKRS

▶ CHARACTERISTICS

　▶ RBUSA

　▶ RCNTR

　▶ KOKRS

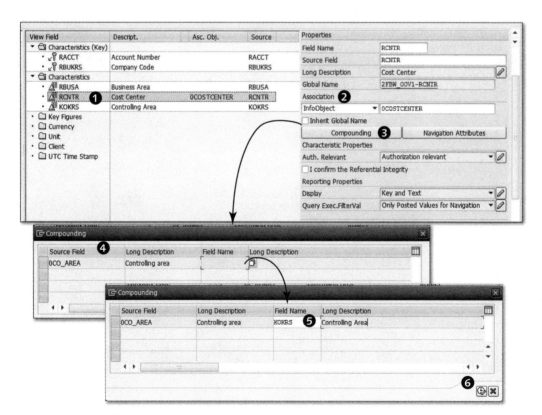

Figure 6.83 Setting Properties for a Field

Now let's see how to associate a field with an InfoObject and how to set a few properties. Select the RCNTR field from the VIEW FIELD section, and open the PROPERTIES section (❶ of Figure 6.83). In the ASSOCIATION dropdown, select INFO-OBJECT ❷, enter "0COSTCENTER", and press the ⌜Enter⌟ key. This associates Info-Object 0COSTCENTER to the RCNTR field, which activates the COMPOUNDING and NAVIGATION ATTRIBUTES buttons ❸.

Next, click on COMPOUNDING to open the COMPOUNDING box ❹. InfoObject 0COSTCENTER is compounded by CONTROLLING AREA (this is the standard SAP relationship) as already shown in this popup box. InfoObject 0CO_AREA is already available, so you only need to provide the appropriate field name for this InfoObject. Enter "KOKRS" in the FIELD NAME box ❺. Click on the CON-TINUE icon ❻.

You know from Chapter 3 that navigational attributes can be configured for Info-Object of type characteristics. Here, 0COSTCENTER has the type characteristics, and a few navigational attributes are defined for this InfoObject. While designing an OOV, SAP BW allows you to include navigational attributes so that it can be available while analyzing data on the OOV. To do this, click on the NAVIGATION ATTRIBUTES button as shown in ❶ of Figure 6.84.

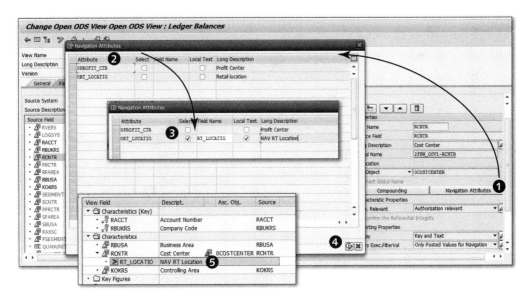

Figure 6.84 Adding Navigation Attributes

This action brings up the Navigation Attributes popup box ❷. Two navigation attributes are defined for InfoObject 0COSTCENTER as listed here. Select ORT_LOCATIO by selecting the checkbox in the Select column next to ORT_LOCATIO ❸. A field name is then proposed by the system. In this case, the field name is RT_LOCATIO. You can provide your own text for this field name as well. The same will appear in the query. To change the proposed text, select the Local Text checkbox, and type your own text. We've entered "NAV RT Location" as the long description text. Click on Continue ❹. The RT_LOCATIO field with the NAV RT Location text is now available under the RCNTR field ❺.

6.9.2 Adding Key Figures

Now let's discuss how to add key figures to an OOV. Select the BALANCE field as shown in ❶ of Figure 6.85. Using the context menu, select Add to Key Figures ❷. This action places the BALANCE field in the Key Figures section under the View Field column ❸. Each key figure is also associated with a number of properties ❹. A few of these properties are similar to characteristics, which are Association ❺ and Reporting Properties, but some properties, such as Aggregation ❻, are only available to key figures.

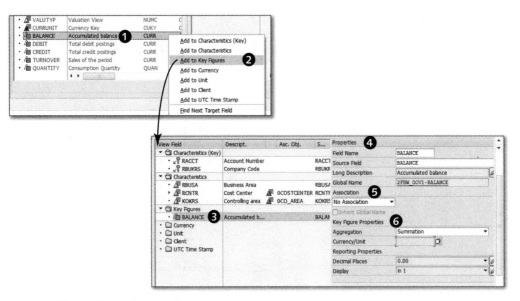

Figure 6.85 Adding Key Figure

Normally, a key figure is associated with a unit; for example, an expenditure during the year is 9 million US$. Here currency is the unit associated with the expenditure key figure, and the value is US$ for the currency unit. When designing an OOV, you can associate a unit for each key figure, as described next.

First, you need to add the field for unit under the VIEW FIELD section. For key figure BALANCE, the field associated for unit is RTCUR. Select the RTCUR field ❶, and from the context menu, select ADD TO UNIT ❷ as shown in Figure 6.86. This places the unit RTCUR field under the VIEW FIELD section under CURRENCY ❸. Now select the BALANCE field from the VIEW FIELD section ❹. Open the PROPERTIES section for the BALANCE field, and enter "RTCUR" in the CURRENCY/UNIT field ❺. This action associates the unit RTCUR field with key figure BALANCE.

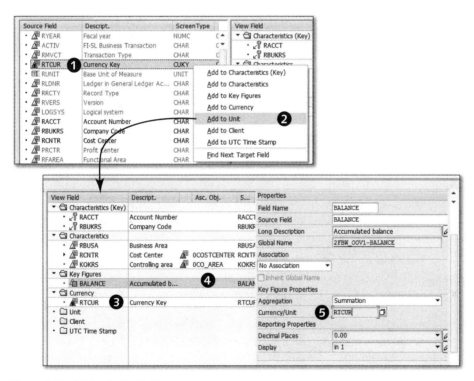

Figure 6.86 Adding to the Unit

6.9.3 Activating the Design

The example OOV design is now ready to be activated. Use the ACTIVATE icon as shown in ❶ of Figure 6.87 to make the OOV active ❷.

As indicated earlier, the OOV can also be used to store the data in a DSO. Let's see how the system helps you create a DSO and other related objects such as DTPs, transformations, and so on.

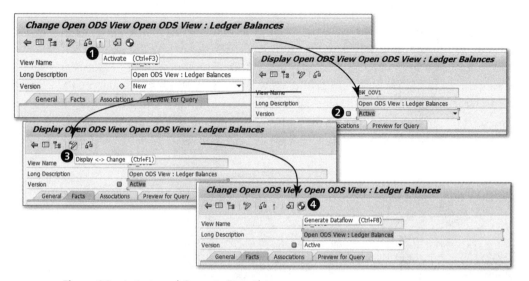

Figure 6.87 Activate and Generate Data Flow

You don't have to create the DSO from scratch; instead, you can create the DSO based on the OOV design. To do this, you need to go back to Change mode. Click on the DISPLAY < -- > CHANGE icon (refer to ❸ of Figure 6.87. Now you're in the CHANGE OPEN ODS VIEW screen. Click on the GENERATE DATAFLOW icon ❹. This action opens up a popup as shown in ❶ of Figure 6.88. The name of the DSO to be generated is proposed by the system, which, in our case, is 0FI_GL_1 ❷. Change this proposal to "BWOOV1" ❸. Also, in the DATA TYPES field, select BW DATA TYPES ❹, and keep the SOURCE OBJECT field set to AS IS ❺.

Click the CONTINUE icon ❻, which opens the CREATE DATA TRANSFER PROCESS screen to transfer data between DataSource 0FI_GL_10 and DSO BWOOV1 ❼. Keeping all the defaults as they are, click on the CONTINUE icon ❽. Another popup appears asking you to confirm the creation of a default transformation between DataSource 0FI_GL_10 and DSO BWOOV1.

Click on YES ❾ to create all the necessary objects, such as the DSO, DTP, and transformation. You can see your newly created OOV BW_OOV1 ❶ and DSO BWOOV1 ❷ under the INFOPROVIDER tree of your DATA WAREHOUSE WORKBENCH screen as shown in Figure 6.89. This OOV can be used in your query designer tool to create queries.

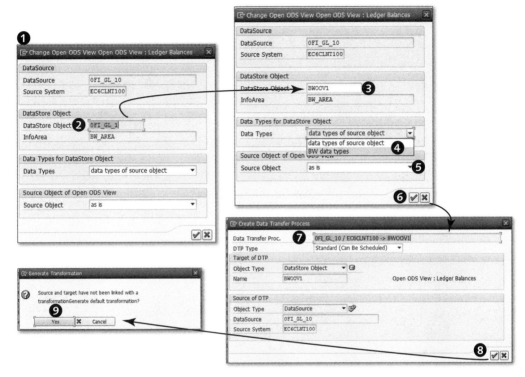

Figure 6.88 Automatic DSO/DTP/Transformation Generation for OOV

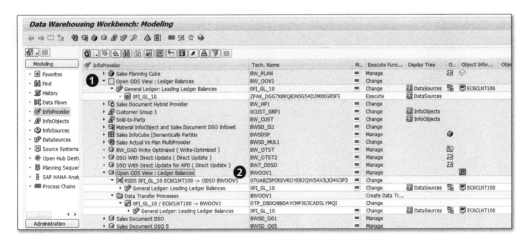

Figure 6.89 Newly Created OOV and DSO

6.9.4   Viewing Data with an Open ODS View

Now let's discuss how sample data can be viewed by default query using our newly developed OOV. In the DATABASE WAREHOUSING WORKBENCH screen, select the OOV BW_OOV1, and then select DISPLAY from the context menu. The DISPLAY OPEN ODS VIEW screen appears as shown in Figure 6.90.

On the menu bar, select GOTO • DEFAULT QUERY ❶ to open the QUERY MONITOR screen ❷. The query name is defaulted by the system ❸. In the QUERY DISPLAY field, there are a few display options, but for this example, choose HTML ❹. Now click on the EXECUTE button ❺. This action uses the definition of OOV, goes to the source system, executes the DataSource, retrieves data, and displays the data as output ❻. Because we've taken only one key figure (ACCUMULATED BALANCE) in the definition of this OOV, it's displayed ❼. Now you move the ACCOUNT NUMBER and NAV RT LOCATION from FREE CHARACTERISTICS to ROWS ❽. ACCUMULATED BALANCE ❾ is now shown for each ACCOUNT NUMBER and NAV RT LOCATION.

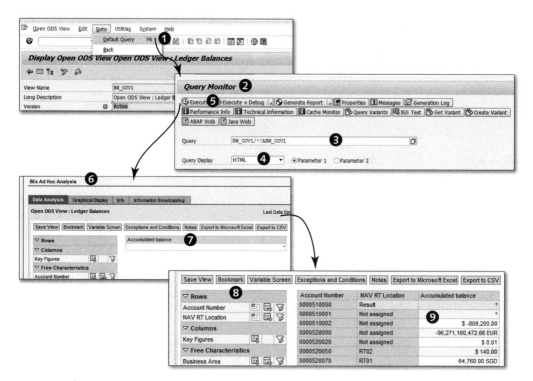

Figure 6.90 Querying on an OOV

6.10   Summary

In this chapter, we introduced you to several InfoProviders, including InfoProviders new to SAP BW 7.4. In certain cases, we discussed the procedures to create them and possible application scenarios for each of them; in other cases, we only briefly introduced them and then pointed you to the appropriate places in the book where we discuss them in more detail.

At this point, you should understand the concepts of modeling, data targets, and InfoProviders in SAP BW. With this foundation, we use the next chapter to explain the fundamental processes of extraction, transformation, and loading.

Extraction, transformation, and loading are essential to the management of data, and a thorough understanding of the ETL process is essential to getting the best out of your SAP BW system.

7 Extraction, Transformation, and Loading

In this chapter, we detail key ETL concepts, elements of the underlying ETL processes, and their realization within SAP BW. We explain the technical components and their functionalities that enable the efficient management of ETL processes using the following scenarios:

- Loading master data from a flat file to an InfoObject (to explain a basic ETL scenario)

- Loading transaction data from a flat file to a DSO (to cover a more specialized aspect of transformation)

- Loading data from a DSO to an InfoCube (to cover a complex transformation)

We also explain the details of temporary storage areas and error stacks. In the concluding section, we introduce the new graphical modeling tool, which helps the designer create data flow and data flow templates (DFTs). We have also included how a query can be used as the DataSource and how SAP HANA impacts the transformation and ABAP.

> **Note**
>
> The discussion of ETL is also continued in the next chapter, where we discuss the process of extracting data from SAP and non-SAP source systems.

7.1 Introduction to ETL

In this section, we begin by explaining the concept of the ETL process, including the basic elements that comprise ETL processes in SAP BW. We then move on to detail the interfaces in SAP BW that enable acquisition of data from heterogeneous sources. Next, we briefly introduce the transformation options in SAP BW that enable the transformation of data acquired from heterogeneous sources. Finally, we talk about the technical components of the loading process in SAP BW.

7.1.1   Elements in the ETL Process

Three essential subprocesses, as illustrated in Figure 7.1, comprise the ETL process: acquiring data from heterogeneous sources, transforming acquired data into the requisite format (e.g., consolidating data from different formats), and loading data to the data targets. This illustration only depicts the general process; some variants in this process are available to solve some typical scenarios.

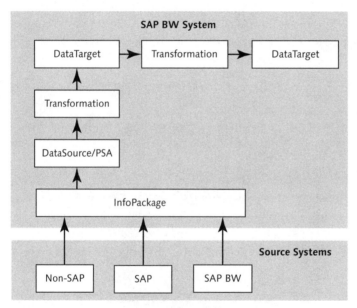

Figure 7.1 Overview of ETL Processes in SAP BW

The elements in the ETL processes are explained in the following list:

▶ **Source system**
   SAP BW is an OLAP system, so it doesn't generate any business transactions; business transactions are generated by OLTP systems. An OLTP source that supplies data to SAP BW is known as a *source system*. SAP BW is capable of data acquisition from a wide variety of source systems, such as data from flat files in ASCII and CSV formats, Database Management Systems (DBMSs), Relational

Database Management Systems (RDBMSs), multidimensional data, and data from legacy systems. SAP BW offers predefined, customizable extractors for application data from the entire SAP Business Suite; you can also design extractors for customized SAP applications. The source system can store various kinds of data (master data as well as transaction data).

▸ **InfoPackage**
An InfoPackage is the scheduler object defined for the combination of Data-Sources and source systems. You can supply various parameters while configuring InfoPackages, such as selection filters, parallel processing, the date of the extraction, and more. After the all the necessary objects are defined to load the data from the source system to the data target, you must execute the InfoPackage, which extracts data from the source system and saves the copy of the source system data into a persistent staging area (PSA). (A PSA is created when you activate your DataSource; it's a transparent table with the same structure as the associated DataSource. We discuss PSAs in more detail in Section 7.2.2.)

▸ **DataSource**
When data is extracted into SAP BW, it's related to specific master data or business transactions. You can't simply extract all data at once; because different types of data are stored in different objects with different structures (e.g., in relational databases, data is stored in tables), you must design an object known as a DataSource to extract specific data in a specific format. For example, to extract customer master data into SAP BW, you must design a DataSource expressly for this purpose. Because different kinds of source systems are supported by SAP BW, there are various ways to create DataSources; when a source system is from SAP (e.g., SAP ERP or SAP CRM), for example, there are special tools for just this task. Business Content offers ready-made DataSources, the majority of which offer delta capability that helps you in extracting only newly created data or changed records. This reduces the volume of data extraction and results in quicker loads.

▸ **Transformation**
Transformation converts the fields of the source into the format of the target. After the DataSource is created, you have data in the form of the source system, but you need to get it in a format appropriate for SAP BW. Transformation is this process.

▸ **Data transfer process (DTP)**
DTP controls the distribution of data after it's available in SAP BW. It reads the data from a PSA or another data target, transforms it, and supplies it to the

appropriate data target. After the InfoPackage has extracted and saved the data into a PSA, you must execute DTP. In this case, DTP reads the data available in PSA, passes the source system data through transformation, and loads the cleansed data to the appropriate data target. To extract data from the source system and load it into a data target on a regular basis, SAP BW offers a tool called the *process chain* that automates this activity. We discuss process chains in more detail in Chapter 14.

▶ **Data target**
A data target is an object in which data is stored using a data staging mechanism; examples include InfoObjects with master data, DSOs, and InfoCubes. In this chapter, we explain the process of how to load data into each of these data targets.

7.1.2 Data Acquisition Interfaces

As a leading BI solution, SAP BW is capable of acquiring data from a wide variety of sources; we detail the specific capabilities and technicalities of data acquisition interfaces in this section. SAP BW supports SAP as well as non-SAP systems, as shown in Figure 7.2. This figure also shows the data acquisition interfaces supported by the system.

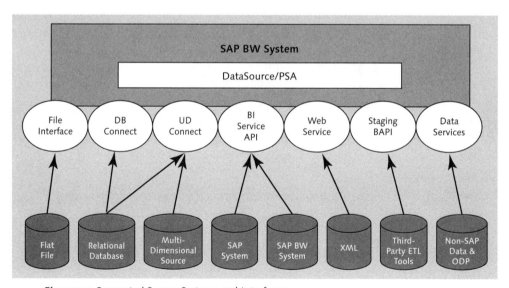

Figure 7.2 Supported Source Systems and Interfaces

► **File interface**

Both CSV (comma-separated values) and ASCII (American Standard Code for Information Interchange) file types are supported by the file interface. CSV files can be easily created using Microsoft Excel, but ASCII files are a little more difficult.

► **DB Connect**

With this interface, SAP BW supports extraction from a few popular RDBMSs, for example, Oracle, SQL Server, and IBM DB2. Check the SAP Service Marketplace to get the latest list of supported RDBMSs.

► **UD Connect**

Along with RDBMSs, this interface supports extractions from multidimensional DataSources such as Analysis Service, SAS, or Hyperion. UD Connect uses various Java Connectors available on the J2EE server, which is part of the SAP BW system. Installation of the J2EE server (Java stack) is essential to take advantage of UD Connect.

► **BI Service API**

Using this interface, you can extract master and transaction data from various SAP systems (SAP ERP, SAP CRM, etc.). In addition, this allows one SAP BW system to supply data to another SAP BW system.

► **Web Service(s)**

One of the most popular ways of exchanging data between different systems on the Internet is by defining data using XML; this can be used when you're required to extract data into SAP BW and the source application is Internet-based. SAP BW offers a tool to create web services that read the data from an XML format and store it in a PSA. After the data is available in a PSA, you can use the normal data staging mechanism to send it to the required data target.

► **Staging BAPI**

SAP BW uses staging Business Application Programming Interfaces (BAPIs) to extract data and metadata from legacy systems using SAP Data Services or other certified ETL tools.

► **SAP Data Services**

As of SAP BW 7.3 and SAP BusinessObjects BI 4.0, SAP Data Services is made available as a separate source system: Data Services. This source system type provides access to SAP Data Services *datastores* and *data flows*. With this functionality, the ETL capabilities of SAP Data Services can be seamlessly integrated with SAP BW to extract data from non-SAP sources. SAP Data Services uses operational data provisioning (ODP)/staging BAPIs to transfer data to other SAP systems such as SAP HANA and SAP BW.

► **SAP Landscape Transformation Replication Server (SLT)**
Real-time data from different sources can be extracted into SAP BW using this interface. It uses the trigger-based replication functionality of SAP LT Server to achieve this. It offers the ODP and web service interface, which we discuss in Chapter 8.

> **Note**
>
> SAP Data Services is also used for nonreal-time data provisioning to SAP HANA.

The preceding list should give you some perspective on the wide range of sources for data acquisition, which allows you to consolidate, cleanse, and integrate data from heterogeneous sources.

7.1.3 Transformation

SAP BW has multiple transformation options for the consolidation of data acquired from a wide variety of sources in different formats:

► **Direct assignment**
Also known as 1:1 transformations, this is used when source data is moved to a target without any changes.

► **Constant**
This is used when the source doesn't give a value for a specific field, and you want to supply a constant value for that field in all records in the target. For example, you may want to create a transformation where the company code for all records in the target is listed as 1000.

► **Formula**
This is used when the target value is derived using a formula, such as *value = price per unit × quantity.*

► **Initial**
This is used if you aren't interested in supplying values for a field; numerical fields will be populated with a zero, and character fields will be populated with a blank space.

▸ **Read master data**
This is best explained by example. Consider a target with two fields, MATERIAL and COLOR OF MATERIAL. Assume that the source data has a value only for the MATERIAL field, and that the master data for MATERIAL InfoObjects within SAP BW has values for COLOR (an attribute of a material). In this scenario, you use the read master data type of transformation, and the value for the COLOR field is read from the master data of the InfoObject.

▸ **Read from DSO**
This is similar to read master data, but characteristic data is read from the DSO.

▸ **Routine**
As the name suggests, this type of transformation is an ABAP code-based transformation. It provides flexibility for handling complex requirements that aren't met by the other types.

These options facilitate consolidation and harmonization of data from a very simple requirement to a highly complex one.

7.1.4   Loading

SAP BW has several components that help in managing the loading process with ease and efficiency:

▸ **InfoPackage**
An InfoPackage extracts and loads data into the entry layer (i.e., PSA). It specifies when and how to load data from a given source system and also helps you decide filter conditions for the data request from a source system.

▸ **DTP**
DTP determines how data transfers from one object to another within SAP BW in accordance with transformations, filters, the processing mode for optimizing and improving the performance of the transfer process, and separate delta processes for different targets. DTPs are used for standard data transfers, for real-time data acquisition, and for accessing data directly.

▸ **Error stack**
This transparent PSA table stores erroneous data records being transferred from source to target using DTP.

▶ **Temporary storage**
This table contains the data records processed with a request in a specific DTP processing step. The table contains correct records as well as erroneous records with a status display.

▶ **Monitor**
The monitor helps you track the entire ETL process in the various processing stages. DTPs and the InfoPackage loading processes are integrated into the monitor.

▶ **Process chain**
Process chains help you automate the ETL process. We explain this in detail in Chapter 14.

7.2 Loading Master Data from a Flat File to an InfoObject

In this section, we explain the entire process of loading master data from a flat file to an InfoObject. The section comprehensively covers the ETL process, from source system and DataSource creation, to data transformation, to loading, to the monitoring process. The process involves seven basic steps:

1. Create a flat file source system.

2. Create a DataSource.

3. Create and activate a transformation.

4. Create a DTP for loading master data.

5. Create an InfoPackage, and start data extraction.

6. Monitor data extraction to PSA.

7. Execute and monitor the DTP.

7.2.1 Creating a Flat File Source System

Creating a flat file source system is required to extract data from CSV and ASCII files. Source systems are created in the DATA WAREHOUSING WORKBENCH, which is started using Transaction RSA1. Select SOURCE SYSTEMS under MODELING, as shown in ❶ of Figure 7.3. A list of the different source system types supported by SAP BW is shown in ❷ of Figure 7.3.

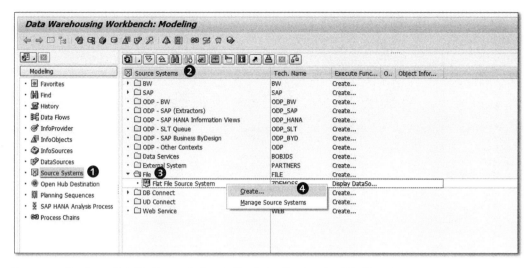

Figure 7.3 Creating a Flat File Source System in the Data Warehousing Workbench

For our example scenario, select FILE SOURCE SYSTEM ❸. From the context menu, select CREATE ❹. This action generates the CREATE SOURCE SYSTEM screen, as shown in ❶ of Figure 7.4.

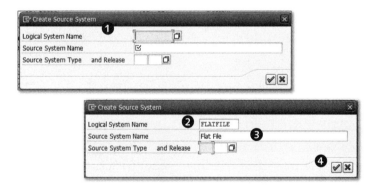

Figure 7.4 Create Source System

Enter the LOGICAL SYSTEM NAME ❷ and the SOURCE SYSTEM NAME ❸ of Figure 7.4. Because there is no real flat file system, enter a description in the SOURCE SYSTEM NAME field.

Click on the CONTINUE icon ❹ of Figure 7.4. The result of this action is shown in Figure 7.5, where FLAT FILE is available under the SOURCE SYSTEMS tree.

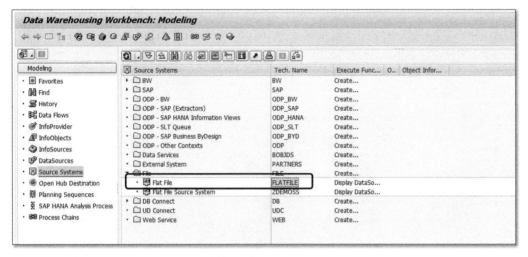

Figure 7.5 Source System Available in the Source System Tree

7.2.2 Creating a DataSource

Now that we've created a source system, we can create a flat file DataSource. A DataSource defines the source of data, its structure, and the technical details of the fields. We'll create a DataSource pertaining to customer master data. In our example, customer master data is available in a flat file (a CSV file). We want to load the data available in this file to InfoObject BW_CUST (which we created in Chapter 3).

To create a DataSource based on a flat file, select SOURCE SYSTEMS ❶ under MODELING, and then select FLAT FILE ❷. Open the context menu, and select DISPLAY DATASOURCE TREE ❸, as shown in Figure 7.6.

An application component hierarchy appears, as shown in ❶ of Figure 7.7. Just as InfoProviders are attached to InfoAreas, DataSources are attached to application components ❷. These application components are used for organizing the DataSource. As shown in Figure 7.7, you can create application components within other application components, depending on your requirements.

SAP Source Systems

For SAP source systems, the application component hierarchy is delivered as part of Business Content, and you simply need to replicate this hierarchy in the SAP BW system.

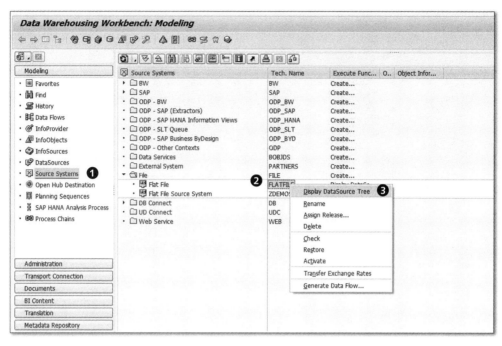

Figure 7.6 Displaying the DataSource Tree

In our example, you'll create a new application component simply to learn the process (normally, you would use the application component hierarchy replicated from the SAP source system). Select 0CRM (Customer Relationship Management), as shown in ❷ of Figure 7.7, and then select Create Application Component from the context menu ❸.

The Create Application Components screen appears as shown in ❶ of Figure 7.8. Enter the technical name (for this example, "BW_APP_COMP" ❷) and description ("BW Application Component" ❸) of the application component. Click on the Continue icon ❹. The result of this action is visible in ❺ of Figure 7.8. BW Application Component is now available under Customer Relationship Management, and the system has added the prefix "Z" to the technical name (❺), which indicates that it's a customer-defined application component.

You can now create a DataSource under the ZBW_APP_COMP application component. To do this, select the application component ❶, open the context menu, and select Create DataSource (❷ of Figure 7.9). The Create DataSource screen appears next as shown in ❸ of Figure 7.9.

Figure 7.7 Creating Application Components

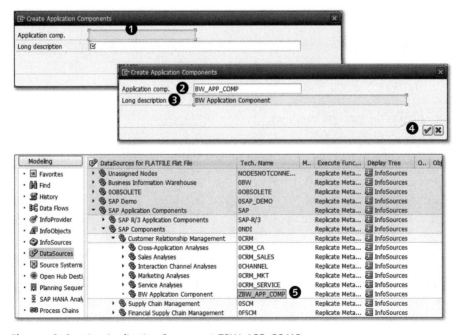

Figure 7.8 Creating Application Component ZBW_APP_COMP

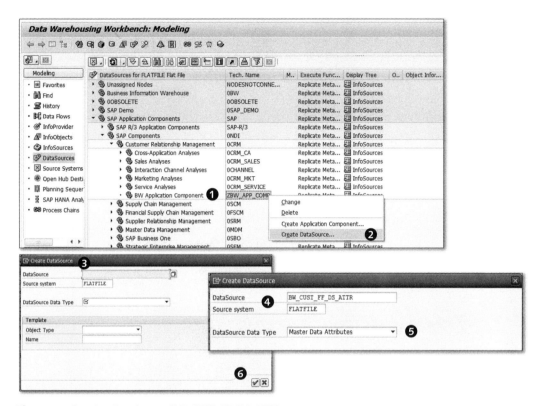

Figure 7.9 Creating DataSource BW_CUST_FF_DS_ATTR

Every DataSource requires a unique technical name. In this case, enter the technical name "BW_CUST_FF_DS_ATTR", as shown in ❹ of Figure 7.9. It's good practice to name the DataSource so that it easily indicates the DataSource and its contents. For example, in the current name, the first part (BW_CUST) indicates that this is for InfoObject BW_CUST; the next part (FF_DS) indicates that it's a flat file DataSource; and the last part (ATTR) indicates that the DataSource represents the attributes.

You need to choose the type of DataSource you're creating; there are three different types in the DATASOURCE DATA TYPE list box ❺ of Figure 7.9:

▶ TRANSACTION DATA
When data pertains to business transactions (such as sales order document data), you select this type of DataSource. The data target for this type of DataSource is either a DSO or an InfoCube.

▶ MASTER DATA ATTRIBUTES

When data pertains to master data attributes (such as customer attributes), you select this type of DataSource. The data target for this type of DataSource is either a characteristic InfoObject configured as master data or a DSO.

▶ MASTER DATA TEXTS

When data pertains to master data text (such as the name of a customer), you select this type of DataSource. The data target for this type of DataSource is a characteristic InfoObject configured with text.

In our example, we're loading customer attributes into InfoObject BW_CUST; thus, select MASTER DATA ATTRIBUTES for the DATASOURCE DATA TYPE ❺. Click on the CONTINUE icon ❻ of Figure 7.9.

The resulting screen has five different tabs (❶ through ❺ of Figure 7.10), which change depending on the source system. We'll discuss each of these tabs in more detail next.

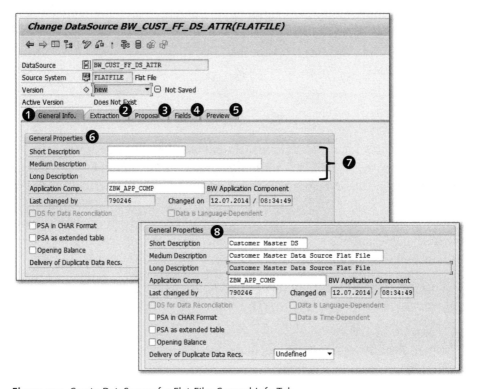

Figure 7.10 Create DataSource for Flat File: General Info Tab

General Info Tab

In this tab (❶ of Figure 7.10), you define general information and properties about the DataSource ❻, including short, medium, and long descriptions ❼. For our example, we provide the following:

▸ Short Description: "Customer Master DS"

▸ Medium Description: "Customer Master Data Source Flat File"

▸ Long Description: "Customer Master Data Source Flat File"

Other properties in this tab include the following:

▸ PSA in CHAR Format

▸ PSA as extended table

▸ Opening Balance

▸ Delivery of Duplicate Data Recs.

These fields aren't essential while creating a simple DataSource and aren't required for our scenario. The required details are entered as shown in ❽ of Figure 7.10.

Extraction Tab

The Extraction tab (❷ of Figure 7.10) allows you to configure the delta process, type of access, and real-time access you want to set for your DataSource (❶, ❷, and ❸ of Figure 7.11). Provide the actual name of the file, its location, and its type in the Adapter and File Name fields (❹ and ❺). We explain all major configuration settings in this tab next.

Delta Process

The Delta Process field describes all of the capabilities and restrictions of a DataSource. For flat files, SAP BW offers three different types of delta processes: Delta Only Via Full Upload (ODS or InfoPackage Selection), FIL0 (Delta Data with After Images), and FILE1 (Delta Data with Delta Images). Our example DataSource isn't supplying delta records, so choose Delta Only Via Full Upload (❶ of Figure 7.11).

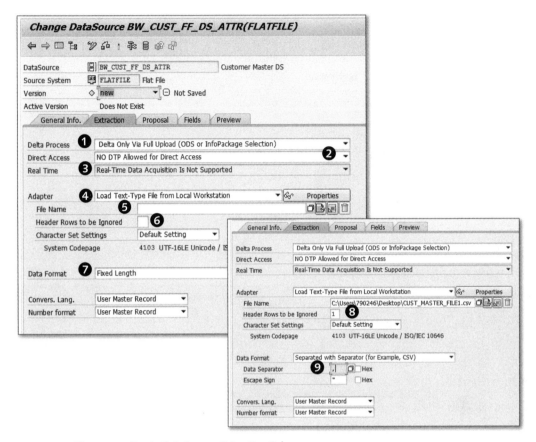

Figure 7.11 Create DataSource: Extraction Tab

The following is a brief description of the other two delta processes offered by SAP BW:

► **FIL0 (Delta Data with After Images)**
In this type, the DataSource only sends records that have new key figures or characteristics values. Data from this type of DataSource can't be loaded directly into an InfoCube; it must be loaded to a DSO first, and then the DSO will supply it to the InfoCube.

► **FILE1 (Delta Data with Delta Images)**
In this type, the DataSource only sends records with value changes for the key figures. Data from this type of DataSource can be directly loaded to a DSO and InfoCube.

Direct Access

There are two options for configuring DataSources with direct access: NO DTP Allowed for Direct Access (the default option) and Allowed, which is relevant when you plan to configure a VirtualProvider based on this DataSource (see Chapter 6 for more information about VirtualProviders). Most DataSources aren't capable of supporting direct access; also, the default setting for a DataSource for a flat file is NO DTP Allowed for Direct Access; choose this default option, as shown in ❷ of Figure 7.11.

Real Time

SAP BW allows you to access real-time data from the source system, a process handled by running a daemon. Because the DataSources based on flat files don't support real-time extraction, the field is uneditable (❸ of Figure 7.11).

Adapter

Adapters provide information about the type (text or binary) and location (local server or application server) of data. There are four options available when configuring flat files:

▶ Load Text-Type File from Local Workstation

▶ Load Text-Type File from Application Server

▶ Load Binary File from Local Workstation

▶ Load Binary File from Application Server

In our example, the file is available on a local workstation in CSV format, so we select LOAD TEXT-TYPE FILE FROM LOCAL WORKSTATION (❹ of Figure 7.11). When the file location is selected as a local workstation, you can't schedule the background job. To use background processing (and the process chain tool), the file must be located on the application server.

After you decide on the type of adapter, select the name and location of the physical file in which your data is available using the dropdown list (❺ of Figure 7.11). After you select a location, a full directory path is displayed ❻.

You may require that the file to be loaded be available with a new name (e.g., if you're loading customer master data every month, each new file created by the source system may have the month as part of its file name). In this scenario, you

299

can create the ABAP routine to generate the file name instead of hard-coding it. To do this, click on the CREATE ROUTINE FOR FILE NAME icon, which opens up the ABAP editor. Type "logic" in the ABAP editor to arrive at the file name dynamically. In our example, we hard-code the file name as shown in ❽ of Figure 7.11.

Figure 7.12 shows the sample data from the customer master file that we want to load into SAP BW. To eliminate confusion, it's always better to identify each column in the file using a column heading, as shown in Figure 7.12; however, these column headings don't become part of the customer master data, so you don't have to load the first row of this file. Indicate this by entering a number in the HEADER ROWS TO BE IGNORED text box shown previously in Figure 7.11.

	A	B	C	D	E	F	G	H	I
1	Customer	Customer GRP	Customer GRP1	Sales Group	Sales District	Sales Office	Sales Employee	Date From	Date To
2	100012	ST	WA	757	2717	3103	41	20100101	20121231
3	100012	ST	WA	757	2717	3103	42	20130101	99991231
4	100016	ST	UK	761	2402	3115	41	20090601	20101231
5	100016	ST	UK	761	2402	3115	43	20110101	99991231
6	100017	ST	UK	184	2218	1206	18	20120101	99991231
7	100018	RC	UK	821	1502	3407	44	20121201	99991231
8	100020	ST	WA	700	2140	3305	41	20100101	99991231
9	100022	RC	UK	762	2136	3114	41	20100101	99991231
10	100041	ST	UK	207	1908	1306	20	20000101	20011231

Figure 7.12 Sample Data Customer Master

As previously mentioned, text files can have two different formats, CSV and ASCII, and you must indicate the appropriate format in the DATA FORMAT field (refer to ❼ of Figure 7.11). By default, this field is filled with the FIXED LENGTH (or ASCII) option. However, because our example data is stored in CSV format, we change this using the dropdown list (refer to ❾ of Figure 7.11).

CSV format allows you to select your own separator (commas, semicolons, etc.) when creating the CSV file, and you must indicate what you've chosen in the DATA SEPARATOR field (refer to ❾ of Figure 7.11). In our example, we use the comma.

You can specify the language used to execute the conversion exit for the conversion language in the CONVERS. LANG. field. For our example, we use the default option (USER MASTER RECORD). Finally, you can specify the NUMBER FORMAT to be used, which indicates whether the separator indicates thousands or decimal points. We use the default setting, USER MASTER RECORD.

Proposal Tab

The PROPOSAL tab (Figure 7.13) reads records from the file you specified in the EXTRACTION tab and proposes the structure for the flat file and the technical specification of each field. The proposal given is solely based on the data available in the file and may not be 100% accurate.

The PROPOSAL ❶ and DATA ❷ areas of the screen are empty in the beginning. Click on LOAD EXAMPLE DATA ❸. By default, SAP BW sets the number of data records to be read as 10,000. Reduce the number to 10 or 12 because that's all you need from the flat file to report anomalies in structure.

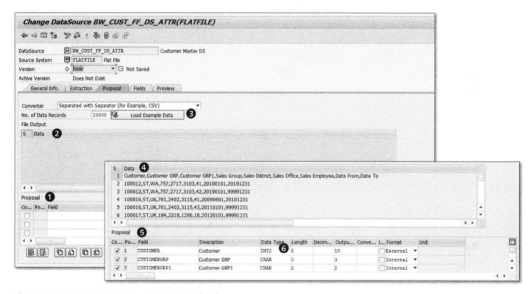

Figure 7.13 Create DataSource: Proposal Tab

When you click LOAD EXAMPLE DATA, the DATA and PROPOSAL areas are filled with information (❹ and ❺ of Figure 7.13). You can see from ❻ that the first field's data type is INT2, and the length is 5. As you may recall, our definition of Info-Object BW_CUST listed the data type as CHAR = 10 (refer to Chapter 3, Section 3.5.1), but the proposal given by the system is INT2 because the data available in the file is numerical. We'll describe how to change this incorrect information when we explain the FIELDS tab (next section). Even if some of the data is wrong, using the proposal function provides the list of fields in the correct sequence, so it's still useful.

For our example, we don't change anything on this tab, and move on to FIELDS. When moving to the FIELDS tab, a pop-up box displays a message asking if you want to copy your changes. Click on YES to continue.

Fields Tab

This is the tab where you finalize the structure of your DataSource. The data proposed by the system (in the PROPOSAL tab) also appears here (❶ of Figure 7.14), and you can overwrite, if necessary. It's important to make sure that the sequence of fields given in this screen is the same as in the actual data file. Because we've used the proposal function, we don't have to worry about this; however, we do need to correct the technical specifications of the fields proposed. The best way to do this is to enter the technical name of the InfoObject in the INFOOBJECT column. As we know from the data available in the actual data file, the first field pertains to the customer, which means InfoObject BW_CUST is used. Enter "BW_CUST" in the INFOOBJECT column ❷, and press Enter. The DEFAULTS FROM INFOOBJECTS pop-up box appears. Click on the COPY button, which reads the metadata definition of the InfoObject.

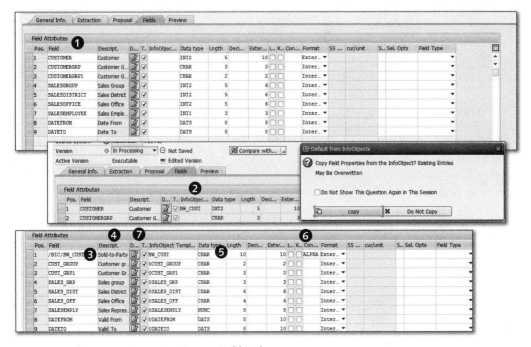

Figure 7.14 Create DataSource: Fields Tab

The result is shown in ❸, ❹, ❺, and ❻ of Figure 7.14. The system now reads the metadata from InfoObject BW_CUST, so the data type is changed from INT2 to CHAR. The conversion routine is also added as ALPHA, which was blank earlier.

Now enter the InfoObject for each row. Table 7.1 gives the technical name of each InfoObject to be entered in consecutive order. The DEFAULT FROM INFOOBJECTS pop-up box appears after entering each InfoObject name; click on COPY every time.

Position	Technical Name of InfoObject
1	BW_CUST
2	0CUST_GROUP
3	0CUST_GRP1
4	0SALES_GRP
5	0SALES_DIST
6	0SALES_OFF
7	0SALESEMPLY
8	0DATEFROM
9	0DATETO

Table 7.1 Technical Names of InfoObjects

Another important setting in this tab is shown in the T column (❼ of Figure 7.14), which stands for Transfer. A checkmark in this column indicates that you've chosen to include this field in the definition of the DataSource. Our example requires that all of the fields be included, so we leave all fields checked.

Finally, the SELECTION column is also an important element of the FIELDS tab. Configuring this setting for a particular field makes it possible to be used as a selection filter in the InfoPackage, which helps in filtering and extracting only the relevant data from the source system. As shown in ❶ of Figure 7.15, enter "X" in the SALES_OFF row because we do want to filter the extraction based on sales office.

You can now activate the DataSource using the ACTIVATE icon shown in ❶ of Figure 7.16. Activating the DataSource also creates the PSA associated with it (a PSA is technically a transparent table, and data is saved unchanged in it). There is no transformation between the source system and the PSA. In SAP BW, storing data in PSAs is mandatory in almost all of the ETL scenarios.

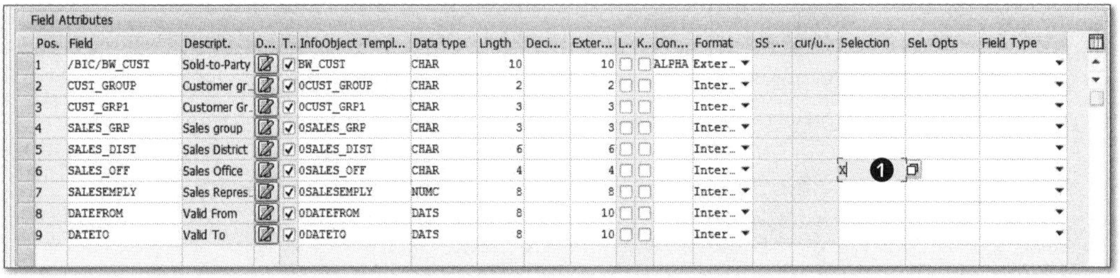

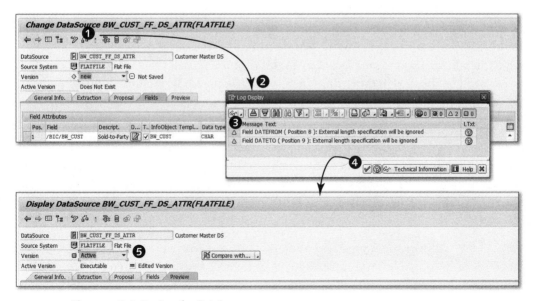

Figure 7.15 Field Tab: Selection Options

At the time of activation, the system may show you some log messages (❷ of Figure 7.16). These messages appear because of discrepancies in the specified field length; in positions ❽ and ❾ of Figure 7.15 shown earlier, the internal length (LENGTH column) is given as 8, and the external length (EXTERN column) is given as 10. The warning messages tell you that the system will use the internal length, ignoring the external length. As shown in ❸ of Figure 7.16, the symbol in front of both messages is yellow (which indicates a warning message); you can click on the CONTINUE icon ❹.

Figure 7.16 Activating the DataSource

After successfully activated, the version of the DataSource is changed from New to Active, as shown in ❺ of Figure 7.16.

Preview Tab

In the Preview tab, you can check whether your definition of the DataSource matches the actual data file definition; the tab allows you to see the data in the DataSource format before loading it to the SAP BW system (this can only be done, however, if the DataSource is active). Initially, no data is shown, and you can select the number of records you want to view (e.g., 1,000 records), and click on Read Preview Data ❸. The result of this action is shown in ❹ of Figure 7.17. SAP BW reads the actual data and displays the requested number of records, allowing you to make sure your DataSource is correct.

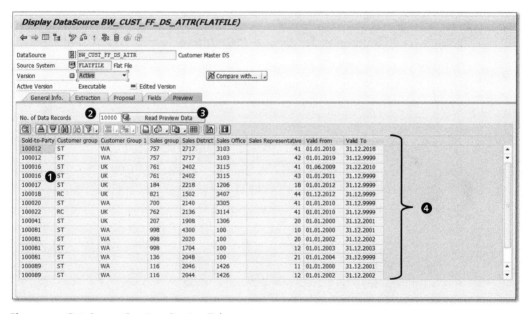

Figure 7.17 DataSource Creation: Preview Tab

The DataSource BW_CUST_FF_DS_ATTR is now ready to be used. Return to the Data Warehousing Workbench main screen by clicking on the Back icon. As you can see from Figure 7.18, the DataSource BW_CUST_FF_DS_ATTR is available under application component ZBW_APP_COMP.

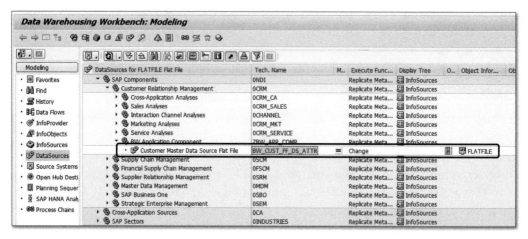

Figure 7.18 Newly Created DataSource Available in the Data Warehousing Workbench

7.2.3 Creating and Activating a Transformation

In this section, we describe the basic steps that a user must take to create a transformation, and we then go into the technical details of what the transformation process entails.

Basic Steps for Creating and Activating a Transformation

At this point in the process, your data target is InfoObject BW_CUST, and your DataSource is BW_CUST_FF_DS_ATTR. Now you must create the transformation between the data target and DataSource to convert the data format from source to the format required by the data target. This requires that the InfoObject be under an InfoProvider tree. First, select the INFOPROVIDER under MODELING, as shown in ❶ of Figure 7.19. Select INFOAREA BW_AREA ❷, open the context menu, and select INSERT CHARACTERISTICS AS INFOPROVIDER ❸. A pop-up box appears ❹ with an input box for entering the name of the InfoObject ❺.

Enter the technical name of the InfoObject, "BW_CUST" (❻ of Figure 7.19), and click on the CONTINUE icon ❼. The result of this action is shown in Figure 7.20; the InfoObject is available under the INFOPROVIDER tree in InfoArea BW_AREA (❶ of Figure 7.20). Expand the BW_CUST (text description: SOLD-TO PARTY) tree. This action shows three InfoProviders for BW_CUST: HIERARCHIES ❷, ATTRIBUTES ❸, and TEXTS ❹ of Figure 7.20. Recall that while configuring InfoObject BW_CUST (in Chapter 3), we configured it to have exactly these InfoProviders.

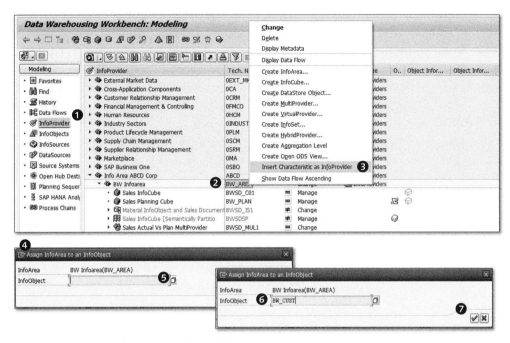

Figure 7.19 Inserting InfoObject as InfoProvider

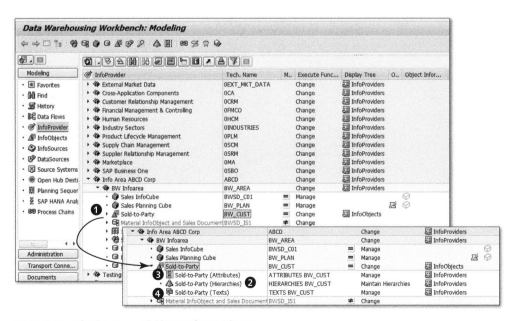

Figure 7.20 InfoObjects Available in InfoProvider Tree

Now that InfoObject BW_CUST is available in the INFOPROVIDER tree, a transformation can be created. In our example, we want to create a transformation between InfoObject BW_CUST and DataSource BW_CUST_FF_DS_ATTR. Select SOLD-TO PARTY (ATTRIBUTE), as shown in ❶ of Figure 7.21. Open the context menu, and select CREATE TRANSFORMATION ❷, which results in the ASSIGN INFOAREA pop-up box ❸. Provide the technical name of InfoArea BW_AREA ❹, and click on CONTINUE ❺. Because we've started the creation of the transformation from InfoObject BW_CUST (ATTRIBUTE), the target of the transformation is set to OBJECT TYPE = INFOOBJECT ❻, SUBTYPE OF OBJECT = ATTRIBUTE ❻, and NAME = BW_CUST ❻.

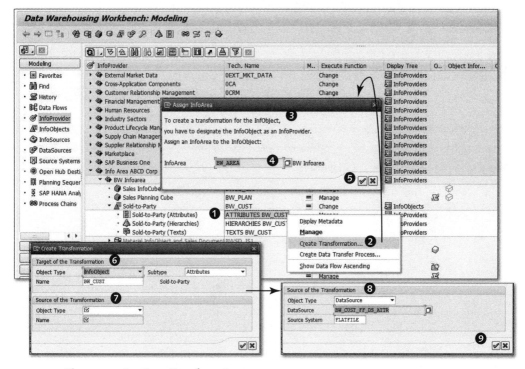

Figure 7.21 Creating a Transformation

Next, supply the necessary information in the SOURCE OF THE TRANSFORMATION area (❼, ❽ of Figure 7.21). The source can be any of the following:

▶ DATASOURCE

▶ INFOSOURCE

▶ DSO

- INFOCUBE
- INFOOBJECT
- INFOSET
- SAP HANA ANALYSIS PROCESS (HAP)
- MULTIPROVIDER
- SEMANTICALLY PARTITIONED INFOPROVIDER
- QUERYPROVIDER

InfoSources

The only object in this list we haven't previously discussed is *InfoSource*, which is a non-persistent structure consisting of InfoObjects that helps you to join two transformations. It doesn't store data, and you can't create queries based on it. In this way, it's neither an InfoProvider nor a data target.

Click on the CONTINUE icon ❾, which brings you to the CREATE TRANSFORMATION screen (Figure 7.22). On the left side of the screen is the source object of the transformation ❶; on the right is the target object of the transformation ❷. SAP BW is able to find the matching InfoObject for all of the fields from the Data-Source because all of the other InfoObjects are from Business Content. For Info-Object BW_CUST, the system may not be able to find the appropriate match; therefore, you may instruct the system that the /BIC/BW_CUST field should be connected to InfoObject BW_CUST.

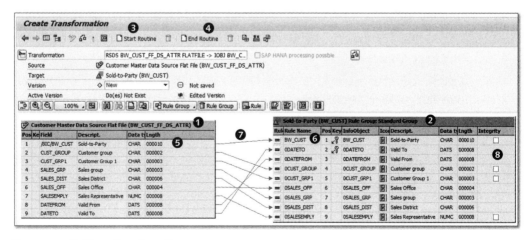

Figure 7.22 Making a Transformation

To accomplish this task, drag and drop /BIC/BW_CUST over InfoObject BW_CUST (❻ of Figure 7.22). This action completes the transformation and is known as a *direct assignment* transformation, which means that the data received by the DataSource field /BIC/BW_CUST is passed to InfoObject BW_CUST in as-is format (without any change). The other types of transformation are discussed in Section 7.3.2. The completed transformation is shown in ❼ of Figure 7.22.

The Technical Process of Creating and Activating a Transformation

Here we explain the technical process that occurs as a result of the user-performed steps discussed immediately before this (Section 7.2.3). At this stage, we simply introduce the basic concepts of transformation, keeping it simple. We'll introduce more complex transformation scenarios when we discuss the transformation between DSOs and InfoCubes in Section 7.4.

Start Routine

Before being transformed, each record passes through a *start routine*, as shown in ❸ of Figure 7.23. The start routine is a place where a developer can write ABAP code that transforms the data within a record according to requirements. The developer can work on a complete data package, defining variables, internal tables, and the values of both. The technique of filling internal tables in the start routine and then accessing them for individual transformation is a standard way to improve performance. The start routine is optional when defining transformation.

Semantic Groups

From a coding perspective, it's sometimes necessary to have a group of records in one data package (❶ in Figure 7.23). In this situation, you must define a *semantic group* ❷. Semantic groups also define the key of *error stacks*. (Error stacks are covered in Section 7.6.)

Transformation Types

After the start routine is completed, individual data records pass through a transformation ❹. The *transformation type* defines the treatment of the data. The direct assignment, constant, formula, initial, read master data, and routine types of transformations were defined in Section 7.1.3.

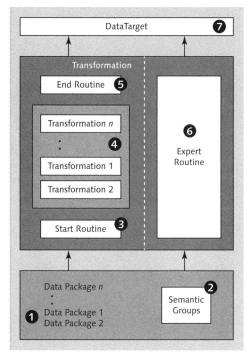

Figure 7.23 Overview of Transformation Process

End Routine

Data packages pass though start routines before passing through individual transformations, and through *end routines* (❺ of Figure 7.23) after all transformations are completed. The end routine is the place where all of the transformations are completed, and transformed values for all records are available. The end routine allows a developer to write ABAP code, if required; for example, you may require the deletion of a specific value in a record that is only available *after* the record has passed through transformation. You can use the end routine to perform a final quality check on a data record before it gets written to a data target ❼. Records that fail to meet quality checks can be deleted and aren't written to the data target. Like the start routine, the end routine is optional.

Expert Routine

In the expert routine (❻ in Figure 7.23), you don't use the rule types offered by SAP BW, and you code the transformation program yourself, including monitor messages. SAP recommends using the expert routine only if the standard functionality offered doesn't meet your requirements.

Activating a Transformation

Activate a transformation by clicking on ACTIVATE. Before activation, a version of the transformation is NEW. Successful activation changes the version to ACTIVE. Only active versions are used when loading data into a data target. Activating transformations actually generates an ABAP program that gets executed when a DTP is executed for loading data into a data target.

7.2.4   Creating a DTP for Loading Master Data

After activating a transformation, you must create the DTP. When you activate a transformation and return to the main screen ❶, an icon for DTP is available, as shown in ❷ of Figure 7.24.

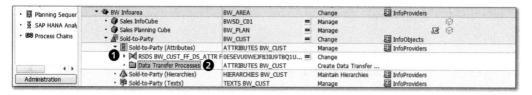

Figure 7.24 DTP Icon

Select DATA TRANSFER PROCESSES ❶, and then select CREATE DATA TRANSFER PROCESS (❷, from the context menu of Figure 7.25). The CREATE DATA TRANSFER PROCESS box appears ❸. Because you've started the creation of the DTP from the associated transformation, all of the required information is automatically supplied (❹ and ❺ of Figure 7.25). Click on the CONTINUE icon ❻.

The result of this action is the CHANGE DATA TRANSFER PROCESS screen shown in Figure 7.26. Three different tabs (❶, ❷, and ❸) are available, each of which we discuss next.

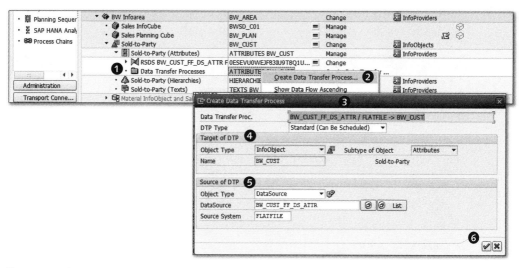

Figure 7.25 Creating DTP

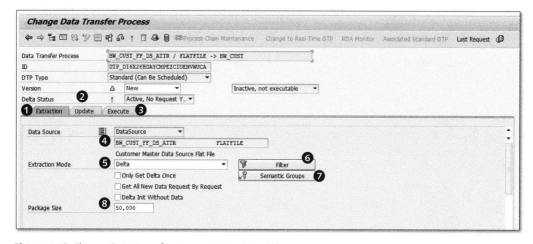

Figure 7.26 Change Data Transfer Process: Extraction Tab

Extraction Tab

The EXTRACTION tab provides details about the DataSource of the DTP, which is shown in ❹ of Figure 7.26. There are two different extraction modes ❺: FULL and DELTA. In the *full extraction mode*, all requests available in the associated PSA for the DataSource are loaded. In the *delta extraction mode*, the system loads only those requests from the associated PSA for the DataSource that are yet to be loaded to the data target. For our example, we use the DELTA mode.

There are several key elements of this screen:

▶ FILTER
The FILTER button ❻ allows you to select records based on selection conditions (e.g., you can decide to load data only for a specific month or sales office).

▶ SEMANTIC GROUPS
The SEMANTIC GROUPS button ❼ allows you to define keys for the extraction; data records with the same key are extracted in the same data package. Semantic keys also create a key for error stacks, which keeps track of erroneous records. These erroneous records can be corrected and loaded to a data target using an error DTP (we discuss this process in Section 7.6).

▶ PACKAGE SIZE
This field ❽ helps you change the parameters that control the bulk of extraction. Records from DataSources are extracted in a set, and the number of records in this set is called the *package size*. Determining the package size helps you control the extraction process and relate to the available processing capacity in the system; after a data set equal to the package size is extracted, the system starts loading it to a data target using another process. For our example, we don't change any default settings, and we keep the screen as shown in Figure 7.26.

Update Tab

Now click on the UPDATE tab (❷ of Figure 7.26), where the BW_CUST data target is shown in ❶ of Figure 7.27.

DTP offers various options for error handling, as shown in ❷ and described here:

▶ REQUEST RED, WRITE ERROR STACK, UPDATE VALID RECORDS
Using this option, you tell the system to isolate erroneous records in a data packet from the data load and to load only valid records into the data target. The entire set of data uploaded from the request remains unavailable for

reporting, and the request has a red status. An administrator can check the error records and then manually turn the uploaded request to green, making the data available for reporting. Erroneous records are written to an error stack that can be manually edited and loaded to a data target using an error DTP.

▶ Request Green, Write Error Stack, Update Valid Records
When you select this option, you instruct the system to make the valid data immediately available for reporting in the data target. Erroneous records are written to an error stack that can be manually edited and loaded to a data target using an error DTP.

▶ Cancel Request, Do Not Track Records, No Update (default)
If an error occurs, it's not assigned to any data record. This is the default option and quickest processing. No records are written to the error stack. The request has to be completely updated again.

▶ Cancel Request, Track First Incorrect Record, No Update
If an error occurs, the system highlights the incorrect record with a data record number. No records are written to the error stack. The request has to be completely updated again.

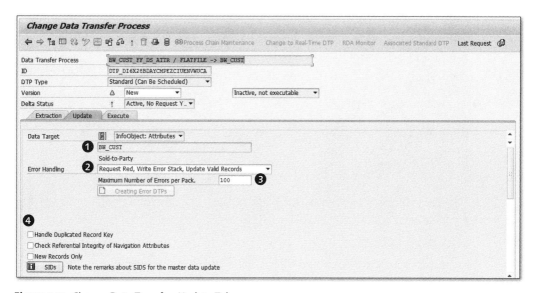

Figure 7.27 Change Data Transfer: Update Tab

We discuss the handling of errors more thoroughly in Section 7.6.

> ### Maximum Number of Errors per Pack
>
> The number of erroneous records that can be tolerated is entered in the MAXIMUM NUMBER OF ERRORS PER PACK. field, as shown in ❸ of Figure 7.27. The system terminates the DTP if the number of erroneous records exceeds the number entered here.

Another important setting on the UPDATE tab is the HANDLE DUPLICATED RECORD KEY checkbox (❹ of Figure 7.27). When set, this indicates that duplicate records should be handled in the order in which they occur in the data package. Finally, the last two settings are CHECK REFERENTIAL INTEGRITY OF NAVIGATIONAL ATTRIBUTES and NEW RECORDS ONLY. While the former allows you to check the referential integrity of navigational attributes, the latter can be used to improve data load performance in scenarios where the corresponding master data is loaded the first time, and there are no SIDs previously created in the system.

Our example doesn't require changing any settings on the UPDATE tab.

Execute Tab

Now click on the EXECUTE tab. This tab offers various processing modes, as shown in ❶ of Figure 7.28.

The *processing mode* describes in what order the processing of different steps occurs and also instructs the system whether the processing should be in synchronous or asynchronous mode; that is, it controls the degree of *parallel processing*.

> ### Synchronous Mode versus Asynchronous Mode
>
> In synchronous mode, the first process waits to invoke the second process until it receives a response from the second process. In asynchronous mode, the first process invokes the second process without waiting for a response from the second process.

Various processing modes are available in the system (although all of the processing modes may not be available at all times):

▸ SERIAL EXTRACTION, IMMEDIATE PARALLEL PROCESSING
In this case, data is processed asynchronously in a background process when a DTP is executed.

▸ SERIAL IN DIALOG PROCESS (FOR DEBUGGING)
This kind of processing is used by developers to debug transformations. As

shown in ❷ of Figure 7.28, different breakpoints are available. You can select them based on your requirements and select particular records for debugging.

► NO DATA TRANSFER; DELTA STATUS IN SOURCE: FETCHED
This is used when you want to transfer subsequent delta requests from the source to the data target without actually transferring the data to the data target.

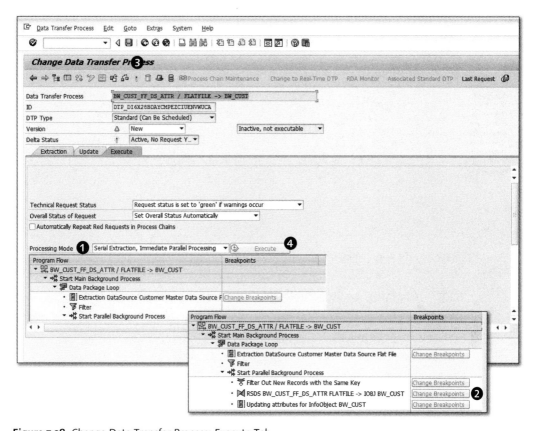

Figure 7.28 Change Data Transfer Process: Execute Tab

For our example, use the default settings shown in Figure 7.28. Activate your DTP using the ACTIVATE icon ❸.

The EXECUTE icon (❹ of Figure 7.28) is only available after activation of the DTP. At this point, however, we don't want to execute the DTP because we haven't yet extracted the data from the source system. (To do this, we must create an

InfoPackage for DataSource BW_CUST_FF_DS_ATTR, which is discussed next.) Using the BACK icon, return to the DATA WAREHOUSING WORKBENCH main screen. You can now see that the DTP created between DataSource BW_CUST_FF_DS_ ATTR and data target BW_CUST (attribute) is available (❶ of Figure 7.29).

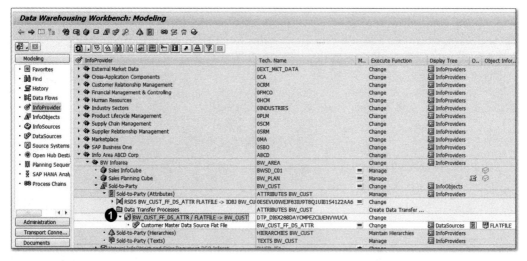

Figure 7.29 Newly Created DTP

7.2.5 Creating an InfoPackage and Starting Data Extraction

An InfoPackage is a scheduler object that, when executed, instructs SAP BW to extract data from a source system. It stores the extracted data in the first layer of SAP BW, which is the PSA. To create an InfoPackage, select the DataSource from the source system under which you want to create it. For our example, select DataSource BW_CUST_FF_DS_ATTR, which is attached to the FLATFILE, as shown in ❶ of Figure 7.30.

Open the context menu, and select CREATE INFOPACKAGE ❷. This action results in the CREATE INFOPACKAGE screen (❶ of Figure 7.31), which also displays the SOURCE SYSTEM ❷ and DATASOURCE ❸ under which the InfoPackage is created. Enter the INFOPACKAGE DESCRIPTION ❹, and click on the SAVE button ❺.

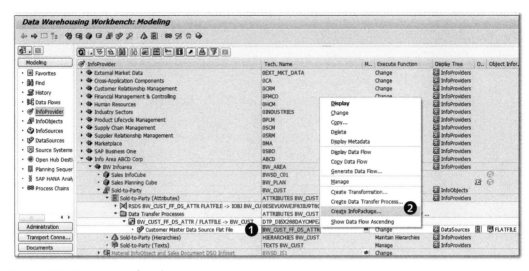

Figure 7.30 Creating an InfoPackage

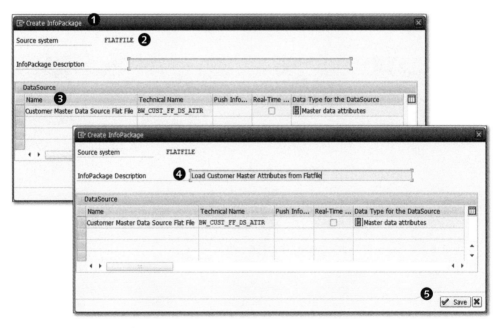

Figure 7.31 Entering an InfoPackage Description

This action opens up the InfoPackage maintenance screen shown in Figure 7.32. The five different tabs here are explained next.

Data Selection Tab

The DATA SELECTION tab (❶ of Figure 7.32) is displayed by default. This screen also shows details such as the DATASOURCE, DATA TYPE, and SOURCE SYSTEM for which the InfoPackage is created ❷. Each InfoPackage is given a unique technical name by the SAP BW system, which always starts with ZPAK_*.

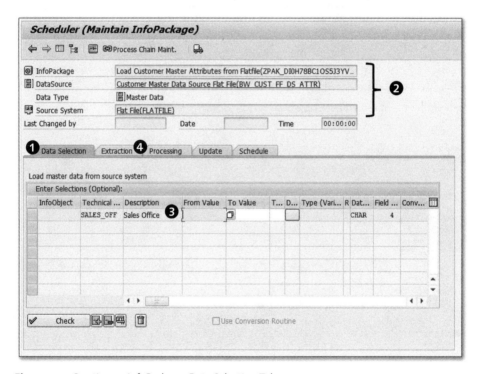

Figure 7.32 Creating an InfoPackage: Data Selection Tab

As shown in ❸ of Figure 7.32, this is the only field offered for filtering records based on the value for SALES_OFF. This was configured when creating Data-Source BW_CUST_FF_DS_ATTR, under the FIELD tab (refer to Figure 7.15). You can enter the value of a sales office as either a single value (e.g., 1768) or an interval (e.g., 1700 to 1799). The DataSource extracts data from the source system only for the entered values. Filling this field is optional; leaving it blank means that the system will extract all records from the source system. For our example, we keep the selection value blank.

Extraction Tab

Click on the EXTRACTION tab (❹ of Figure 7.32). The details of this tab are shown in Figure 7.33.

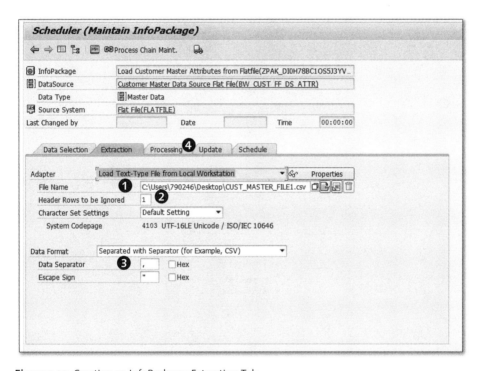

Figure 7.33 Creating an InfoPackage: Extraction Tab

This tab details information such as location, actual file name, type of file, and so on; the details are automatically provided based on the EXTRACTION tab of the DataSource definition (refer to Figure 7.11). You can change details such as file name, header rows to be ignored, data separator, and so on (❶, ❷, and ❸ of Figure 7.33). Most of the settings available on this tab page are editable, but nothing needs to be changed for our example.

Processing Tab

Now, click on the PROCESSING tab, which allows you to determine how the extraction is processed by the SAP BW system and where it's stored. As shown in ❶ of Figure 7.34, the data extracted is stored in a PSA. If required, data in a PSA can be manually modified before it's loaded into any data target.

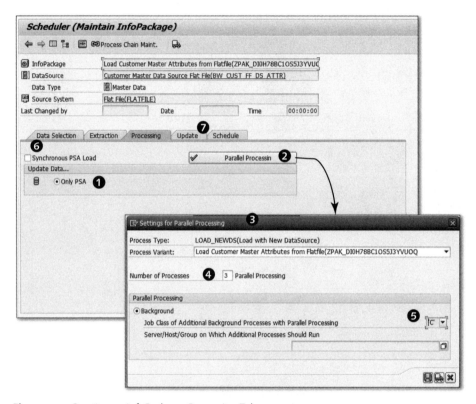

Figure 7.34 Creating an InfoPackage: Processing Tab

Parallel processing can be configured using this tab; click on PARALLEL PROCESSING ❷, which takes you to the SETTINGS FOR PARALLEL PROCESSING screen ❸. You can set the number of processes to be used for parallel processing ❹. By default, this number is set to 3. If you change this to 1, the extraction is processed serially. You can also process extractions serially by setting the SYNCHRONOUS PSA LOAD flag ❻.

During parallel processing, additional work processes are split off from the main work process. The parallel processes are usually executed in the background, and the job class for these background processes is set to C (low priority) by default ❺. B and A indicate a medium priority and a high priority, respectively.

Our example doesn't require any changes in the default settings.

Update Tab

Click on the UPDATE tab. This tab only has one setting, UPDATE MODE (❶ of Figure 7.35). The setting is determined by the delta capability of the DataSource associated with the InfoPackage. When the only update mode displayed is FULL UPDATE, you know that the associated DataSource isn't delta capable and will provide full data every time you extract. Now click on the SCHEDULE tab ❷.

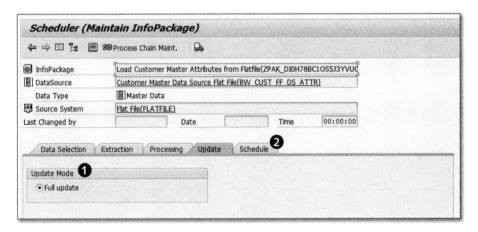

Figure 7.35 Creating an InfoPackage: Update Tab

Schedule Tab

The last tab is the SCHEDULE tab, which allows you to start the extraction by selecting the START DATA LOAD IMMEDIATELY radio button (❶ of Figure 7.36) and clicking on START ❻. Immediate extraction is done only once; if you want to extract data on a regular basis, select the START LATER IN BACKGROUND radio button ❷, and click on SCHEDULING OPTIONS ❸. This results in the START TIME box shown in Figure 7.36.

Various options are available here. You can start the job in the background by clicking on IMMEDIATE ❹; or, for extracting data on a regular basis, click on DATE/ TIME ❺. This action allows you to set the start date, time, and periodicity of extraction, which can be hourly, daily, weekly, monthly, and so on. After this is set, click on START ❻.

For our example, we want to extract the data immediately and only once, so we select START DATA LOAD IMMEDIATELY and click on START.

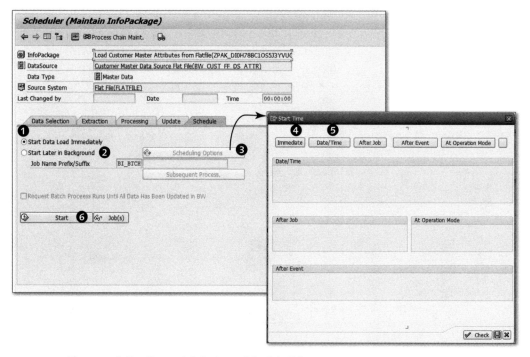

Figure 7.36 Creating an InfoPackage: Schedule Tab

7.2.6 Monitoring Data Extraction to the PSA

After the data extraction begins, you can click on the MONITOR icon shown in ❶ of Figure 7.37 to check the status of the data extraction.

The monitor shows a variety of information, such as the status of extraction, how many records have been extracted, the time taken by various steps involved in extraction, and so on. This detail is managed using three different tabs, each of which we discuss next. After explaining the tabs, we discuss the PSA MAINTE-NANCE icon, which is another important feature of the monitor.

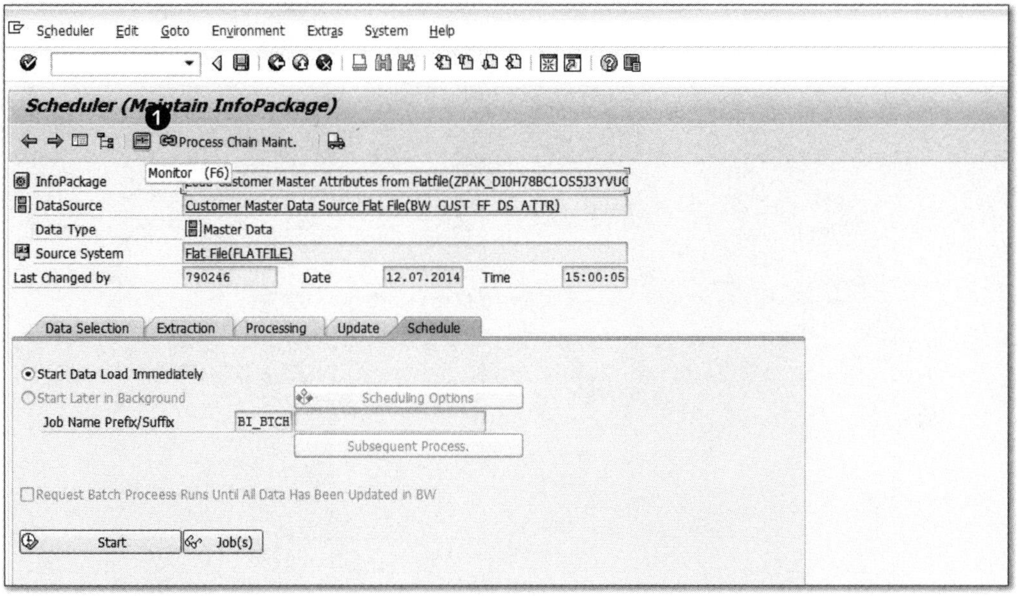

Figure 7.37 Monitor

Status Tab

The monitor automatically opens with the STATUS tab, which is shown in ❶ of Figure 7.38.

This screen shows both the TOTAL status and the TECHNICAL status ❷, and the progress of each is indicated by a traffic light:

► TECHNICAL status
A yellow light means processing isn't completed or is completed with a warning. A red light means that processing has encountered some error, or the maximum wait time has been exceeded. A green light means that processing has completed successfully.

► TOTAL status
The total status of a request is determined based on the technical status (of all technical parameters in the system) and the QM status (configurable and based

on quality processes). Using the QM status, the total status of the request can be changed.

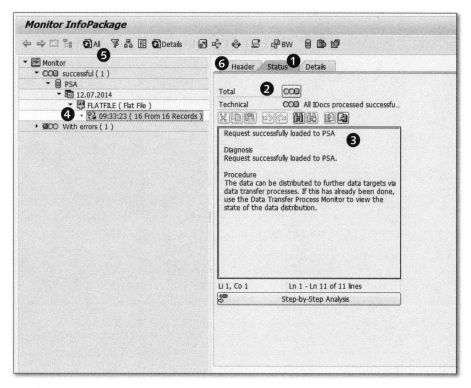

Figure 7.38 Monitor: Status Tab

The extracted data is stored in a PSA, and the number of records extracted is displayed in ❹ of Figure 7.38. By default, the monitor shows the details of the current extraction ❸, but this display can be configured using the FILTER icon ❺.

Header Tab

Click on the HEADER tab (❻ of Figure 7.38) to see the details of all of the objects involved in the extraction, as shown in Figure 7.39.

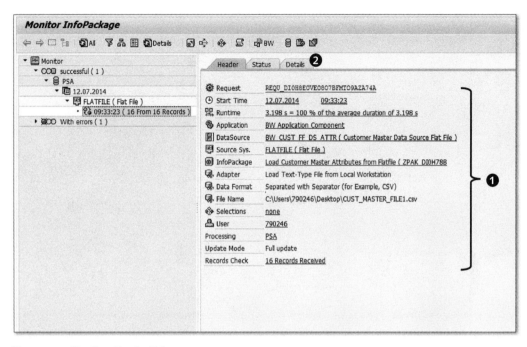

Figure 7.39 Monitor: Header Tab

The HEADER tab shows you information such as DataSource, source system, InfoPackage, update mode, selections, processing mode, user, date/time of the extraction, and runtime of the extraction ❶. Each extraction is assigned a unique request number, which you can use to identify each one. By default, this number starts with REQU_*.

Details Tab

The DETAILS tab (❷ of Figure 7.39) shows extraction details broken into various steps, as shown in Figure 7.40. When extraction is started by executing an InfoPackage, the request for extraction is sent to the source system. Messages during this phase (❶ of Figure 7.40), extraction messages ❷, the transfer of extracted records in the form of data packets ❸, and the processing of each data packet ❹ are all shown in Figure 7.40.

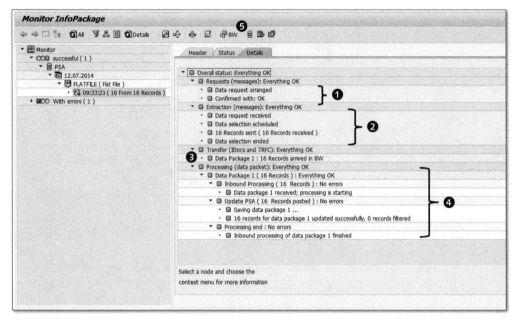

Figure 7.40 Monitor: Details Tab

PSA Maintenance

Another feature of the monitor is the ability to check the data stored in the PSA. To do this, click on the PSA MAINTENANCE icon shown in ❺ of Figure 7.40. This results in the PSA MAINTENANCE screen shown in Figure 7.41.

The PSA MAINTENANCE screen displays all data packets with the number of records in each one. Our example has only 1 data packet with 16 records (❶ of Figure 7.41), but, in practice, you'll probably have more than this. You can filter the records using the NO. OF RECORDS field ❷ and the WITH STATUS field ❸. You can also click on the FILTER icon ❹ to select specific record numbers. After you've filtered your records appropriately, select them, and click on the CONTINUE icon ❺ to view or edit them. The records are displayed as shown in ❶ of Figure 7.42. In our example, we want to edit data record 5 of data packet 1 (❷ of Figure 7.42) to change the value of the CUSTOMER GROUP1 field. Select this record number, and click on the CHANGE icon ❸. This displays the SINGLE RECORD CHANGE box ❹. Select the value of the CUSTOMER GROUP1 field, and change it from UK to "WA" (❺ and ❻). Click on the CONTINUE icon ❼. The changed value can be seen as shown in ❽. The system also indicates that the record has been changed with the icon shown in ❽ of Figure 7.42.

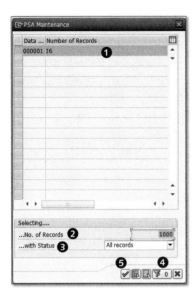

Figure 7.41 PSA Maintenance

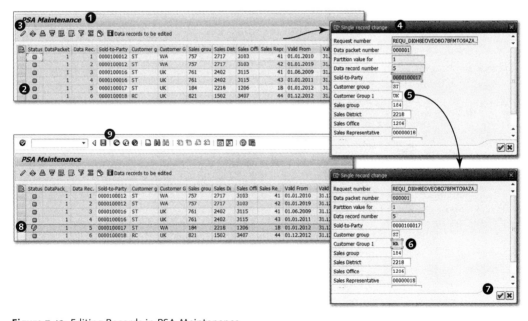

Figure 7.42 Editing Records in PSA Maintenance

Save your changes, and use the BACK icon to return to the monitor screen.

7.2.7   Monitoring the DTP

At this point, you've executed the InfoPackage and loaded the master data from the flat file to the PSA. Now you need to execute the DTP. The job of the DTP is to read the data from the PSA and pass it to the data target (InfoObject BW_CUST), transforming it in the process. You can directly jump to the associated DTP from the monitor screen by clicking on the DISPLAY DTP icon shown in ❶ of Figure 7.43.

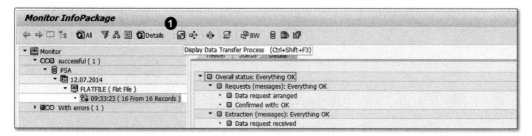

Figure 7.43 Starting the DTP

This displays the CHANGE DATA TRANSFER PROCESS screen shown in Figure 7.44. Click on the EXECUTE tab ❶ (recall our discussion of this tab from Section 7.2.4), and click on the EXECUTE button ❷. This results in the REQUEST STATUS box ❸.

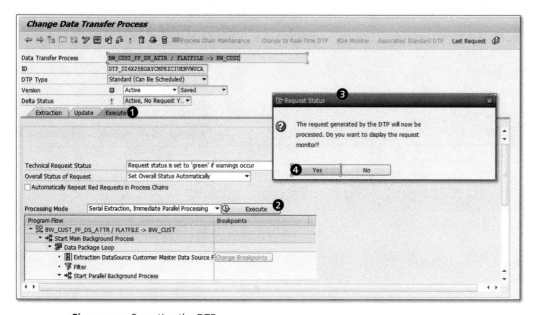

Figure 7.44 Executing the DTP

Click on Yes ❹, and the Monitor: Data Transfer Processscreen is displayed (Figure 7.45). The Monitor screen has two different tabs, Details and Header. We describe both of these next, and then discuss the InfoProvider Administration screen.

Details Tab

By default, you're shown the Details tab, which displays the unique request number of this DTP (❶ of Figure 7.45). More details about the DTP ❷ are organized by data packet. Different steps carried out during the DTP—extraction, filter, transformation, and updating—are shown here. The technical and overall status set for the request is shown in ❸ of Figure 7.45, and the duration of each step is shown in ❹ of Figure 7.45.

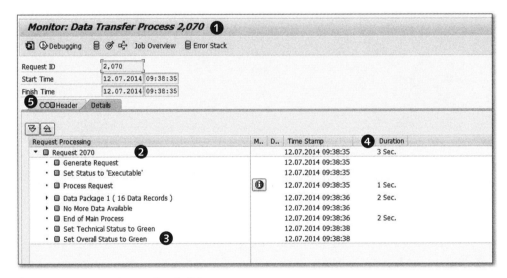

Figure 7.45 Monitor Screen: Details Tab

Header Tab

Click on the Header tab (❺ of Figure 7.45), and the screen shown in Figure 7.46 is displayed.

The Header tab shows all of the settings used for running this DTP (❶ of Figure 7.46). The master data from the flat file is now successfully loaded into tables associated with InfoObject BW_CUST.

InfoProvider Administration Screen

To view the loaded master data, click on the ADMINISTER DATA TARGET icon (❷ of Figure 7.46). The INFOPROVIDER ADMINISTRATION screen appears (❶ of Figure 7.47).

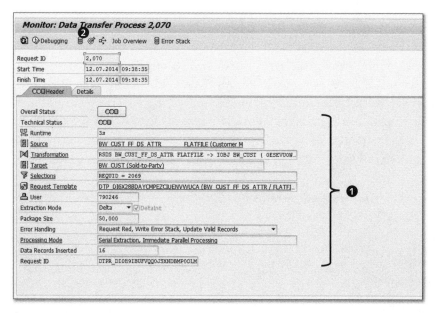

Figure 7.46 Monitor Screen: Header Tab

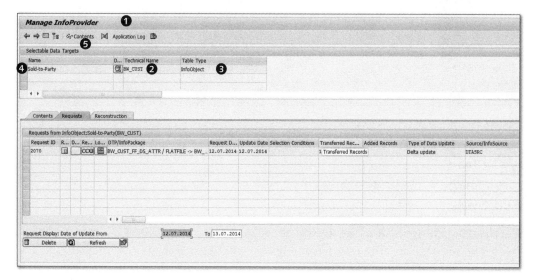

Figure 7.47 InfoProvider Administration Screen

As you can see, the InfoProvider is listed as INFOOBJECT BW_CUST (❷ and ❸ of Figure 7.47). You can select the InfoProvider by clicking on the start of the line ❹. A number of administrative tasks can be performed using the functionalities available in the lower part of Figure 7.47, but the details of this go beyond the scope of this chapter. Instead, these topics are addressed in Chapter 14.

7.2.8 Maintaining Master Data

From Figure 7.47, click on the CONTENTS button ❺ to open the next screen in a browser, as shown in ❶ of Figure 7.48, where you can maintain master data.

> **Note**
>
> In older versions of SAP BW, master data maintenance is carried out from the SAP GUI.

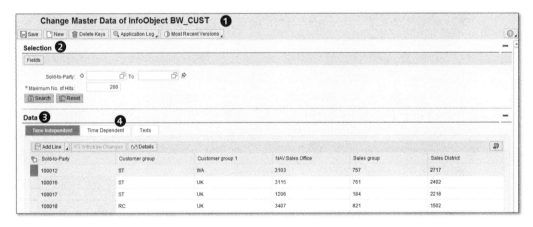

Figure 7.48 Change Master Data: Selection Screen

As shown in ❷ of Figure 7.48, the master data selection screen displays SOLD-TO-PARTY for making selections; this is where you select values for filtering master data records. By default, 200 records are displayed. As shown in ❸ of Figure 7.48, only values of TIME INDEPENDENT attributes of BW_CUST are displayed. Time-dependent attributes are shown under the TIME DEPENDENT tab ❹. Recall that when we defined the attributes of InfoObject BW_CUST (Chapter 3), we defined the sales employee attribute as time-dependent. The VALID TO and VALID FROM fields are available for selection as a result of this. The time-dependent data is shown in ❶ of Figure 7.49.

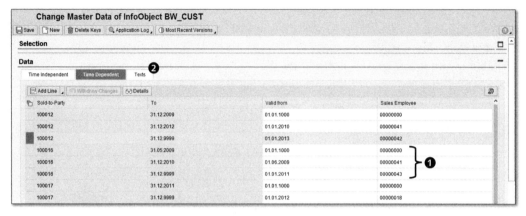

Figure 7.49 Master Data from InfoObject BW_CUST

As you can see from ❶ of Figure 7.49, there are multiple records for one sold-to party (100016). This is due to the time-dependent sales employee attribute; a separate record is created for each time period assigned to a sales employee. Thus, 100016 has one record from January 1, 1000 (a standard date used by the system to indicate the past), to May 31, 2009; another record from June 1, 2009, to December 31, 2010; and a third record from January 1, 2011, until the present (which is indicated using the date December 31, 9999). The three different time periods coincide with the assignment of different sales employees; no employee was assigned during the first period, employee 41 was assigned during the second period, and employee 43 is currently assigned.

The preceding data in InfoObject BW_CUST is due to the input records shown in Figure 7.50. As shown, there are two different sales employees assigned to the sold-to-party (100016) during two different time periods.

Customer	Customer GRP	Customer GRP1	Sales Group	Sales District	Sales Office	Sales Employee	Date From	Date To
100016 ST		UK	761	2402	3115	41	20090601	20101231
100016 ST		UK	761	2402	3115	43	20110101	99991231

Figure 7.50 Sample Master Data for Customer 100016

We've now completed the loading of master data attributes into InfoObject BW_CUST from the flat file, but we still need to load the master data text. To do this, simply replicate the activities we performed for the master data attributes:

1. Create a DataSource for loading text.

2. Create a transformation between this DataSource and InfoObject BW_CUST (text).

3. Create a new DTP between this DataSource and the InfoObject.

4. Create an InfoPackage for the newly created DataSource.

5. Execute the InfoPackage.

6. Execute the DTP.

Now you'll be able to perform a one-time load of master data from a flat file into an InfoObject. In reality, you'll need to load master data periodically, and the process for this uses process chains (see Chapter 14).

7.3 Loading Transaction Data from a Flat File to a DSO

In this section, we discuss the steps involved in loading transaction data from a flat file into a DSO. Because many of these steps are similar to the steps involved in loading master data, we won't go into much detail here; we'll mostly use this example to explain the different types of transformations in more detail. The transformation types dealt with in this section are related to requirements of ABCD Corp., including using a fixed company code as a single company, creating an indicator for a value type that isn't captured in the OLTP system, and using the value of customer groups stored in customer master records but not supplied in the flat file transaction DataSource.

DSOs generally store transaction data at the granular level. They can also store master data if required. Our example scenario requires transaction data in SAP BW, and we use DSO BWSD_O01 for storing it. Our transaction data is available in a flat file, so we load it to the DSO from the flat file.

Recall from Chapter 4 that we created DSO BWSD_O01. To load transaction data in DSO BWSD_O01, follow these steps:

1. Create a flat file source system. This process was explained in Section 7.2.1. We'll use this same source system in this example.

2. Create an application component and transaction DataSource. We created an application component and DataSource in Section 7.2.2. We'll reuse the application component, but the DataSource for the DSO needs to be created. This process is described in more detail later in this section.

3. Create and activate the transformation between the DataSource and the DSO. The basic process of creating a transformation remains the same, but this time, we use a more complex example. This is described in more detail later in this section.

4. Create and activate the DTP between the DataSource and the DSO. The process of creating a DTP remains the same.

5. Create and execute the InfoPackage. The process of creating an InfoPackage remains the same.

6. Execute the DTP to load the data into the DSO. The process of executing the DTP remains the same.

Again, steps 1, 4, and 5 in this process are similar to what we've already discussed, so we won't revisit them. Instead, we focus on steps 2 and 3.

7.3.1   Creating a Transaction DataSource

Referring to earlier in this chapter, ensure that FLATFILE is selected as your source system. Select application component ZBW_APP_COMP (refer to ❶ of Figure 7.9), and select CREATE DATASOURCE from the context menu. In the CREATE DATASOURCE box, enter the input parameters given in Table 7.2. Click on the CONTINUE icon.

Input Parameter	Input Given
DATASOURCE	BWSD_O01_FF_DS_TRAN
DATASOURCE DATA TYPE	Transaction Data

Table 7.2 Input Parameters for Creating a Transaction DataSource

General Info Tab

In the GENERAL INFO. tab (❶ of Figure 7.51) of the CHANGE DATASOURCE screen, enter the short description, medium description, and long description ❷.

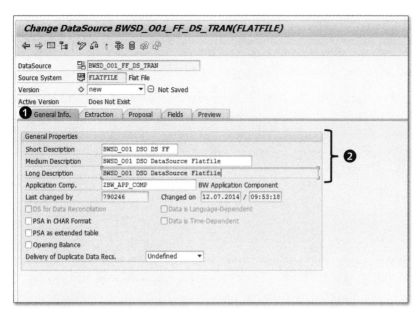

Figure 7.51 Transaction DataSource Creation: General Tab

Extraction Tab

In the EXTRACTION tab, enter the parameters shown in Table 7.3.

Input Parameter	Input Given
DELTA PROCESS	FIL0 DELTA DATA (AFTER IMAGES)
GENERIC DELTA	(Don't use)
DIRECT ACCESS	NO DTP ALLOWED FOR DIRECT ACCESS
REAL TIME	REAL-TIME DATA ACQUISITION IS NOT SUPPORTED
ADAPTER	LOAD TEXT-TYPE FILE FROM LOCAL WORKSTATION
FILE NAME	F:\ETL\BILLING TRANSACTION DATA FILE1.CSV (Make sure that file path matches the location where you save this file.)
HEADER ROWS TO BE IGNORED	3
DATA FORMAT	SEPARATED WITH SEPARATOR (FOR EXAMPLE, CSV)
DATA SEPARATOR	,

Table 7.3 Input Parameters for the Extraction Tab

There's usually a large volume of transaction data; as such, loading the full file may not be practical. With this in mind, we select FIL0 DELTA DATA (AFTER IMAGES). When a DataSource is created with this setting, you get the option of initialization, and subsequently delta, when extracting using an InfoPackage.

Our example scenario gets the data in a flat file for newly created and changed records. The fields of the changed record contain the latest information, so it's appropriate to select type FIL0. In addition, because the DSO update type is set to overwrite, the data sent from the DSO to the InfoCube is loaded with the correct values. By default, DSO is set to overwrite mode.

Proposal Tab

Now click on the PROPOSAL tab. Clicking on the LOAD EXAMPLE DATA button (refer to ❸ of Figure 7.13) provides information from the system; recall, however, that the system simply reads your file to get the data type and may not always be 100% accurate. As such, we rely on the InfoObject definition in the FIELDS tab.

Fields Tab

In the FIELDS tab, the system has proposed fields and listed them in sequence. As shown in ❶ of Figure 7.52, field SALESDOCU (or VBELN) is listed in position 1. The definition of this field comes from the InfoObject; we enter the associated InfoObject in ❷. Enter "0DOC_NUMBER" and press [Enter]. Select YES in the resulting pop-up box; the change is shown in ❸. The mapping of the field to the InfoObject (i.e., field VBELN to InfoObject 0DOC_NUMBER) is based on analysis of business content and the metadata repository.

You must follow this same process—that is, typing the InfoObject name, pressing [Enter], and selecting YES—for each position in Figure 7.52. Enter the names shown in Table 7.4.

Position	InfoObject
1	0DOC_NUMBER
2	0S_ORD_ITEM
3	0BILL_TYPE
4	0ITEM_CATEG

Table 7.4 InfoObjects to Be Entered in the Fields Tab

Position	InfoObject
5	0BILL_CAT
6	0BILL_DATE
7	BW_CUST
8	0CUST_GROUP
9	0MATERIAL
10	0DIVISION
11	0MATL_GROUP
12	0PLANT
13	0COMP_CODE
14	0SALESORG
15	0REGION
16	0DISTR_CHAN
17	0SALES_OFF
18	0SALES_GRP
19	0SALES_DIST
20	BW_QTY
21	0NET_WGT_DL
22	0GRS_WGT_DL
23	0UNIT_OF_WT
24	0UNIT
25	0DOC_CATEG
26	0COST
27	0LOC_CURRCY
28	0DOC_CURRCY
29	0ACCNT_ASGN
30	0CO_AREA
31	0NET_VALUE
32	0SUBTOTAL_1
33	0SUBTOTAL_2
34	0VALUE_LC
35	0COUNTRY

Table 7.4 InfoObjects to Be Entered in the Fields Tab (Cont.)

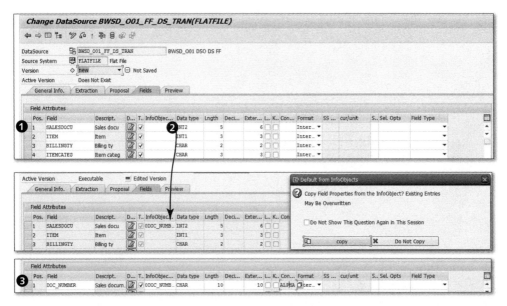

Figure 7.52 Create Transaction DataSource: Fields Tab

After this is completed, you can activate the DataSource by clicking on the ACTI-VATE icon (❶ of Figure 7.53). The activated DataSource ❷ (BWSD_O01_FF_DS_TRAN) is now available under the application component ZBW_APP_ COMP ❸.

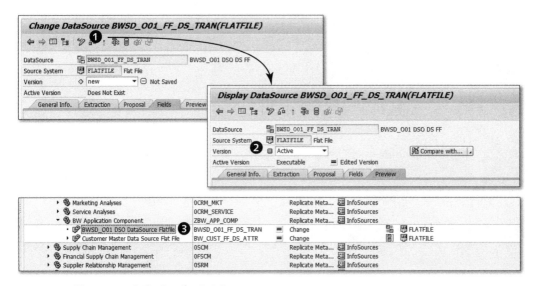

Figure 7.53 Activating the DataSource

Preview Tab

After the DataSource is activated, you can use the PREVIEW tab to see whether your configuration is correct. You should always confirm the configuration before using the DataSource in a transformation.

7.3.2 Creating a Transformation between a DataSource and a DSO

Here we again address the process of creating a transformation; however, in this section we focus on the creation of a transformation between a DataSource and a DSO. In addition, we expand our discussion from Section 7.2.3 to focus on four specific types of transformation: a direct assignment transformation from a Data-Source, a constant transformation, a read master data transformation, and a formula transformation. We conclude our discussion with a brief explanation of the difference between key figure transformations and characteristic transformations.

Creating a Direct Assignment Transformation from a DataSource

Now that you've configured your DataSource, you can create the transformation between DataSource BWSD_O01_FF_DS_TRAN and DSO BWSD_O01. You can begin creating a transformation from the context menu of the data target or the context menu of the DataSource; earlier in the chapter, we started from the context menu of the data target (in this case, an InfoObject), so this time we start from the DataSource.

From the DATA WAREHOUSING WORKBENCH screen, select DATASOURCES (❶ of Figure 7.54). Make sure that your DataSource tree is shown for the FLATFILE ❷; if it isn't, refer to Figure 7.6 to fix this. Select DataSource BWSD_O01_FF_DS_TRAN ❸, and select CREATE TRANSFORMATION ❹ from the context menu. This action results in the CREATE TRANSFORMATION screen ❺. The target of the transformation area is blank ❻ because we started the process from the DataSource. Input the TARGET OF THE TRANSFORMATION information as shown in ❽, and click on the CONTINUE icon ❾.

This results in the CREATE TRANSFORMATION screen shown in Figure 7.55, which allows you to create a transformation using drag and drop. As shown in ❶ of Figure 7.55, the source and target object are available as shown on the left and right, respectively ❷. SAP BW automatically matches the field of the DataSource to the InfoObject and proposes the transformation based on metadata available in the system. This is a direct assignment transformation, meaning that the data from the DataSource is passed to the target InfoObject without any modification of values. If required, you can change this proposed transformation.

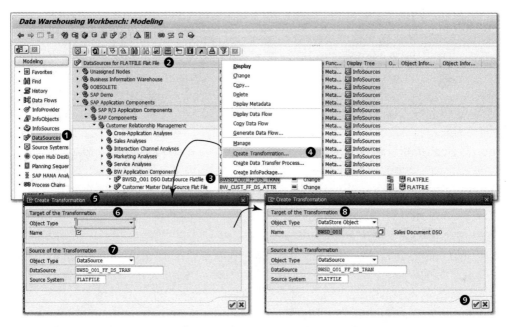

Figure 7.54 Creating a Transformation between a DataSource and a DSO

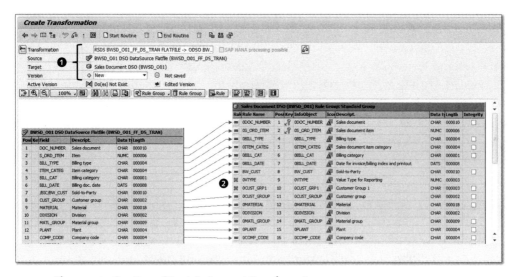

Figure 7.55 Creating a Direct Assignment Transformation

For our example, there are a few other direct assignment transformations from DataSource to DSO; the detail mapping from field to InfoObject is given in Table 7.5.

Field	InfoObject
DOC_NUMBER	0DOC_NUMBER
S_ORD_ITEM	0S_ORD_ITEM
BILL_TYPE	0BILL_TYPE
ITEM_CATEG	0ITEM_CATEG
BILL_CAT	0BILL_CAT
BILL_DATE	0BILL_DATE
/BIC/BW_CUST	BW_CUST
CUST_GROUP	0CUST_GROUP
MATERIAL	0MATERIAL
DIVISION	0DIVISION
MATL_GROUP	0MATL_GROUP
PLANT	0PLANT
SALESORG	0SALESORG
REGION	0REGION
DISTR_CHAN	0DIST_CHAN
COUNTRY	0COUNTRY
SALES_OFF	0SALES_OFF
SALES_GRP	0SALES_GRP
SALES_DIST	0SALES_DIST
/BIC/BW_QTY	BW_QTY
NET_WGT_DL	0NET_WGT_DL
GRS_WGT_DL	0GRS_WGT_DL
UNIT_OF_WT	0UNIT_OF_WT
UNIT	0UNIT
DOC_CATEG	0DOC_CATEG
COST	0COST
LOC_CURRCY	0LOC_CURRCY

Table 7.5 Transformation: Field to InfoObject Direct Assignment

343

Field	InfoObject
DOC_CURRCY	0DOC_CURRCY
ACCNT_ASGN	0ACCNT_ASGN
CO_AREA	0CO_AREA
NET_VALUE	0NET_VALUE
SUBTOTAL_1	0SUBTOTAL_1
SUBTOTAL_2	0SUBTOTAL_2
VALUE_LC	0VALUE_LC

Table 7.5 Transformation: Field to InfoObject Direct Assignment (Cont.)

Constant Transformation

There are two InfoObjects, 0VTYPE and 0CUST_GRP1, which have not had any transformation proposed by the system (❷ of Figure 7.55). The reason for this is that there are no fields in the DataSource that map to these two InfoObjects (as shown earlier in Table 7.4). As such, we must derive the value for these two Info-Objects using the formula and read master data transfer types (recall our discussion of the different types of transformations in Section 7.3).

As shown in ❶ of Figure 7.56, the COMP_CODE field is mapped to InfoObject 0COMP_CODE using a direct assignment transformation. We want to change the transformation type to *constant*, so our first step is to delete the proposed rule. Select InfoObject 0COMP_CODE as shown in ❶, open the context menu, and select DELETE RULE ❷. Click on YES in the resulting pop-up box ❸. The X in ❹ of indicates that no rule is assigned to InfoObject 0COMP_CODE.

To create a new transformation, select 0COMP_CODE, open the context menu, and select RULE DETAILS ❺.

This action results in the RULE DETAILS screen shown in Figure 7.57. As you can see, the target InfoObject ❶ is shown as 0COMP_CODE. Because we've deleted the transformation rule in the previous step, the RULE TYPE field lists NO TRANS-FORMATION ❷.

Target Fields

Normally, transformations have only one target field (as shown in ❸ of Figure 7.57). There may, however, be a situation where you can have more than one, such as when doing unit or currency translations for key figures.

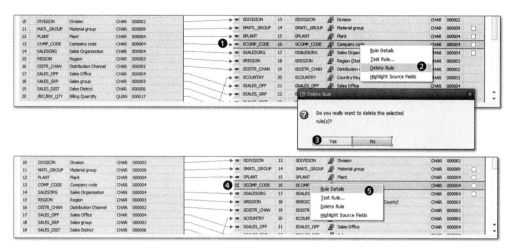

Figure 7.56 Deleting the Transformation Rule

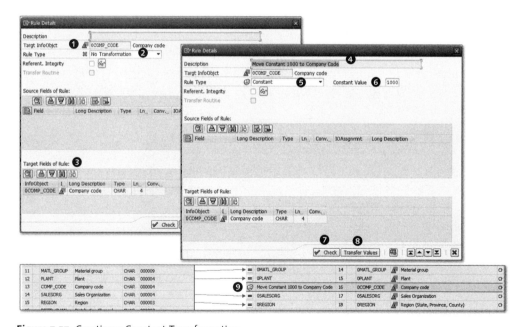

Figure 7.57 Creating a Constant Transformation

Give a proper description for the transformation type, as shown in ❹ of Figure 7.57. Use the dropdown list available for the RULE TYPE, and select CONSTANT ❺. You can now enter the value for the company code in the CONSTANT VALUE field ❻.

Check your transformation by clicking on the CHECK button ❼, and then click on TRANSFER VALUES ❽ to transfer the rule change to your transformation. As shown in ❾, a new rule is now available.

Read Master Data Transformation

Now we must configure the transformation for InfoObject 0CUST_GRP1 because the transaction data file doesn't contain the value of this field (again, refer to Table 7.4). Recall that Customer GRP1 is an attribute of InfoObject BW_CUST; that is, for each customer, the value of Customer GRP1 is available as part of the customer master data. As such, tables associated with InfoObject BW_CUST contain these values for each customer. In this kind of scenario, the *read master data* transformation type should be used. There is no need to write a single line of code to get this value. We'll explain this with an example first, and then show you the step-by-step configuration.

Figure 7.58 shows the document data from the input file that is relevant for our example. It's composed of four fields: VBELN (document number), POSNR (item number), KUNAG (customer number), and KDGRP (customer group 1). The data target has five InfoObjects, and four of them are associated with fields from the input data. The other InfoObject, 0CUST_GRP1, doesn't have a corresponding field in the input file.

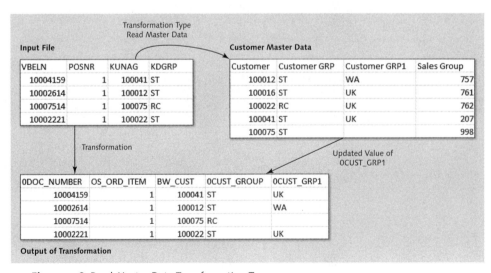

Figure 7.58 Read Master Data Transformation Type

Again, recall that the customer master data (InfoObject BW_CUST) has a value for InfoObject 0CUST_GRP1 for each customer. Using the read master data transformation type, the system searches the customer number of each input record, and if one is found, updates InfoObject 0CUST_GRP1 with the corresponding value.

To configure this, select InfoObject 0CUST_GRP1 (❶ of Figure 7.59), and select RULE DETAILS ❷ from the context menu. The RULE DETAILS pop-up box appears that shows the details of the target InfoObject ❸; provide a DESCRIPTION for the rule ❹. Now select READ MASTER DATA from the RULE TYPE dropdown list ❺, and instruct the transformation to read the attribute of InfoObject BW_CUST by clicking on the icon shown in ❻.

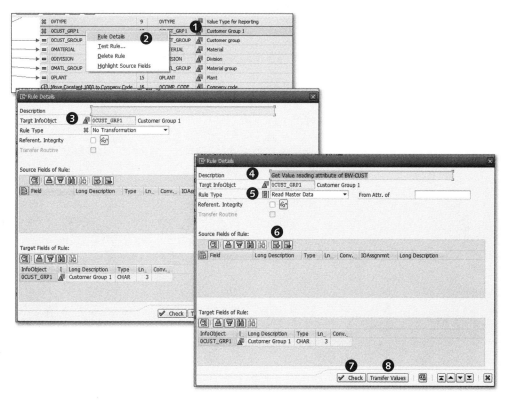

Figure 7.59 Read Master Data Transformation: Part 1

This results in the list are shown in ❶ of Figure 7.60, which lists all of the fields from the source object. Select /BIC/BW_CUST ❷, which is available under the SOURCE FIELDS OF RULE area ❸. Because we need to read the master data from the

InfoObject, you must type "BW_CUST" in IOAssgnmnt (InfoObject Assignment) ❹. Press Enter, and select From Attrib. Of ❺. Now press F4, which places the BW_CUST value into this field ❺.

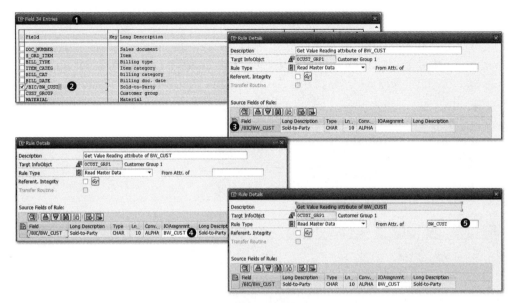

Figure 7.60 Read Master Data Transformation: Part 2

You can check your transformation by clicking on the Check button shown earlier in ❼ of Figure 7.59, and then clicking on Transfer Values (❽ of Figure 7.59) to transfer the rule changes for target InfoObject 0CUST_GRP1 to your transformation. As shown in ❶ of Figure 7.61, the new rule is now available for target InfoObject 0CUST_GRP1.

3	BILL_TYPE	Billing type	CHAR	000004			0BILL_DATE	7	0BILL_DATE	Date for invoice/billing index and printout
4	ITEM_CATEG	Item category	CHAR	000004			BW_CUST	8	BW_CUST	Sold-to-Party
5	BILL_CAT	Billing category	CHAR	000001			0VTYPE	9	0VTYPE	Value Type for Reporting
6	BILL_DATE	Billing doc. date	DATS	000008	❶		Get Value Reading attribute of BW_CUST	10	0CUST_GRP1	Customer Group 1
7	/BIC/BW_CUST	Sold-to-Party	CHAR	000010			0CUST_GROUP	11	0CUST_GROUP	Customer group
8	CUST_GROUP	Customer group	CHAR	000002			0MATERIAL	12	0MATERIAL	Material
9	MATERIAL	Material	CHAR	000018						

Figure 7.61 Read Master Data Transformation Configured

Formula Transformation

As we established in Chapter 1, ABCD Corp. requires that whenever the value of a record in the billing document goes above $10,000 USD, the transaction is identified as a high-value transaction, and the billing document is marked with an indicator to differentiate it from those with lower transaction values. We've used InfoObject 0VTYPE for identifying the record as high value or low value. When using transformations, we need to derive the value for InfoObject 0VTYPE because the data for this is also not available from the DataSource. We perform this derivation using the NET VALUE field and the *formula* transformation type. Assume the following:

▸ If the net value is equal to 0, value type = 000.

▸ If the absolute net value is greater than or equal to 10,000, value type = 001.

▸ In all other cases, value type = 002.

Select the target object 0VTYPE (❶ of Figure 7.61) in the transformation screen, and double-click on it to open the RULE DETAILS screen (alternatively, you can open the context menu). The rule details for 0VTYPE are shown in Figure 7.62.

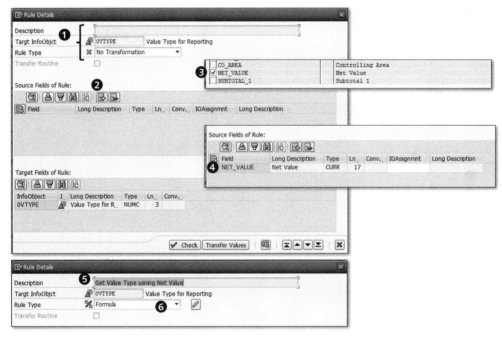

Figure 7.62 Selecting the Formula Transformation Type

To use the NET VALUE field to derive the value of 0VTYPE, you must add the field under SOURCE FIELDS OF RULE. To do this, click on the icon shown in ❷ of Figure 7.62. This results in the area shown in ❸. Select NET_VALUE, and click on the CONTINUE icon. NET_VALUE is now available under SOURCE FIELDS OF RULE ❹.

Enter a description for this transformation rule ❺, and then select FORMULA from the RULE TYPE dropdown list ❻. This action results in the formula builder screen shown in Figure 7.63.

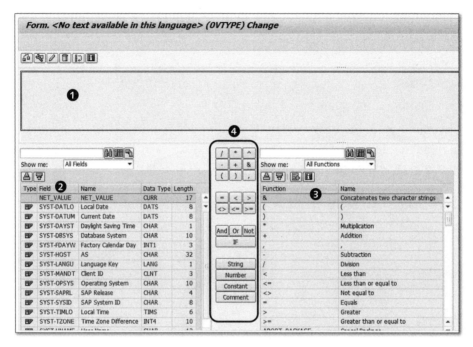

Figure 7.63 Formula Builder

The formula builder is a simple but powerful tool that allows nonprogrammers to create simple or complex formulas. It's divided into four different areas: an area to define your formula (❶ of Figure 7.63), an area where you can select the fields for the transformation ❷, standard functions ❸, and various operators used to define formulas ❹.

To derive values of 0VTYPE using NET_VALUE, click on OPERATORS ❹, FIELDS ❷, and FUNCTIONS ❸ to include it in the formula definition area. You may need to enter a value using the keyboard. Double-click to select the FIELD and FUNCTION (❷ and ❸).

The formula we want to create using the formula builder is the following:

IF(NET_VALUE >= 10,000 OR NET_VALUE <= 10,000-, '001', IF(NET_VALUE = 0, '000', '002'))

The building of the formula is shown step-by-step in Figure 7.64 and continued in Figure 7.65:

1. Click on the IF button ▭ IF ▭.
2. Double-click on the NET VALUE button ▭NET_VALUE▭.
3. Click on operator >=.
4. Click on the NUMBER icon, and enter "10000"; the definition area now changes to ▭ Number ▭.

The cursor position is very important when defining a formula. Moving the cursor one position to its right must be done explicitly, before any other click; this is also shown under the ENTER MANUAL VALUE column in Figure 7.64 and Figure 7.65.

The final formula is shown in the formula definition area of Figure 7.66. You can use the CHECK icon ❶ to check for any syntax errors. In addition, the formula builder offers an expert mode, which you can access by clicking on the icon shown in ❷. The expert mode allows you to create formulas using the keyboard.

Button to Click on Formula Builder	Enter Manual Value	How Formula Looks
IF		IF(| ,)
NET_VALUE		IF(NET_VALUE | ,)
Number	10000	IF(NET_VALUE >= 10,000 | ,)
>=		IF(NET_VALUE >= | ,)
Or		IF(NET_VALUE >= 10,000 OR | ,)
NET_VALUE		IF(NET_VALUE >= 10,000 OR NET_VALUE | ,)
<=		IF(NET_VALUE >= 10,000 OR NET_VALUE <= | ,)
Number	-10000	IF(NET_VALUE >= 10,000 OR NET_VALUE <= 10,000- | ,)
	Move the cursor one place right	IF(NET_VALUE >= 10,000 OR NET_VALUE <= 10,000- | ,)
String	001	IF(NET_VALUE >= 10,000 OR NET_VALUE <= 10,000-, '001' |)
	Move the cursor one place right	IF(NET_VALUE >= 10,000 OR NET_VALUE <= 10,000-, '001' |)

Figure 7.64 Building a Formula Using Formula Builder: Part 1

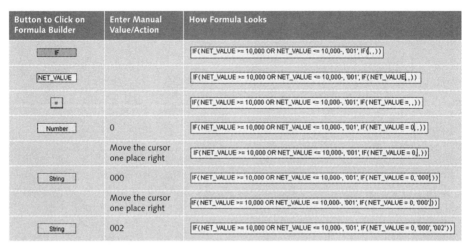

Button to Click on Formula Builder	Enter Manual Value/Action	How Formula Looks
IF		IF(NET_VALUE >= 10,000 OR NET_VALUE <= 10,000-, '001', IF(,,))
NET_VALUE		IF(NET_VALUE >= 10,000 OR NET_VALUE <= 10,000-, '001', IF(NET_VALUE,,))
=		IF(NET_VALUE >= 10,000 OR NET_VALUE <= 10,000-, '001', IF(NET_VALUE =,,))
Number	0	IF(NET_VALUE >= 10,000 OR NET_VALUE <= 10,000-, '001', IF(NET_VALUE = 0,,))
	Move the cursor one place right	IF(NET_VALUE >= 10,000 OR NET_VALUE <= 10,000-, '001', IF(NET_VALUE = 0,,))
String	000	IF(NET_VALUE >= 10,000 OR NET_VALUE <= 10,000-, '001', IF(NET_VALUE = 0, '000',))
	Move the cursor one place right	IF(NET_VALUE >= 10,000 OR NET_VALUE <= 10,000-, '001', IF(NET_VALUE = 0, '000',))
String	002	IF(NET_VALUE >= 10,000 OR NET_VALUE <= 10,000-, '001', IF(NET_VALUE = 0, '000', '002'))

Figure 7.65 Building a Formula Using Formula Builder: Part 2

Click on the BACK icon to exit the formula builder and revert to RULE DETAILS ❸, and click on TRANSFER VALUES ❹ to transfer the formula to the transformation between the DataSource and DSO. You're now back to the main transformation screen.

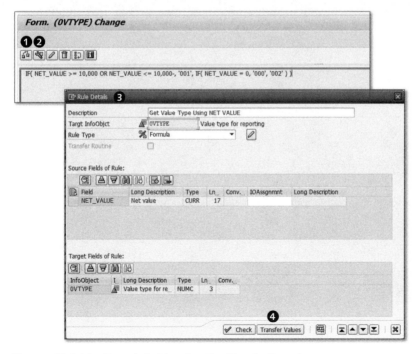

Figure 7.66 Exiting Formula Builder after Checking the Formula

The transformation type formula is indicated with the icon shown in ❶ of Figure 7.67. Now you can check whether the transformation created is correct by clicking on the CHECK icon ❷ of Figure 7.67.

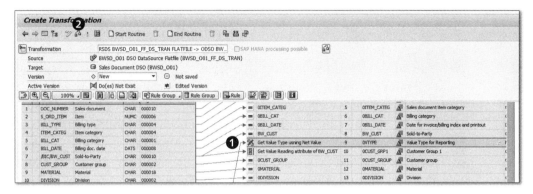

Figure 7.67 Formula Transformation Type Icon

Now you're ready to activate your transformation. Click on the ACTIVATE icon. On successful activation, the version of the transformation changes to ACTIVE ❶. Now return to the main DATA WAREHOUSING WORKBENCH screen. You can view the transformation between DataSource BWSD_O01_FF_DS_TRAN and DSO BWSD_O01, as shown in ❷ of Figure 7.68.

Figure 7.68 Activating the Transformation

You need to create InfoPackages for extracting data, and these InfoPackages will have INITIALIZATION set in the UPDATE tab, which needs to be changed to DELTA

MODE after the successful initialization. Then execute the DTP for transfer of data from PSA to DSO. Finally, activate the loaded request into the DSO and then load it into the InfoCube.

Characteristics versus Key Figure Transformations

Data targets can have characteristics as well as key figures, and the rule details we've discussed in this section have been specific to characteristics. Rule details for key figures are similar, but they offer the additional option of aggregation, as shown in ❸ of Figure 7.69. The AGGREGATION option specifies how key figures should be stored when the key fields (of DSOs) and characteristics (of InfoCubes) have the same value. There are two options available for key figure InfoObjects in the data field of a DSO: OVERWRITE and SUMMATION (we also discussed this in Chapter 4). By default, the AGGREGATION option for key figures of a DSO is set to OVERWRITE. Because our DataSource delta process is set to AFTER IMAGE, all key figures of the DSO must be set to OVERWRITE. The RULE DETAILS box for the key figure displays TARGET INFOOBJCT (❶ of Figure 7.69) and RULE TYPE ❷.

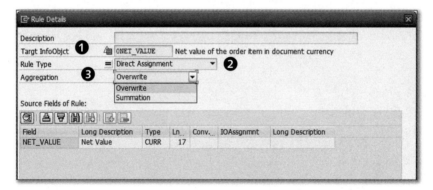

Figure 7.69 Aggregation for Key in Rule Details

7.4   Loading Data from a DSO to an InfoCube

In the previous section, we discussed the process of loading data to a DSO. Now we want to understand the process of loading a DSO (in our example, BWSD_001) to an InfoCube (in our example, BWSD_C01). The main difference between these two types of objects is that DSOs store data at the document level, and Info-Cubes store data at an aggregated level. As a result, some of the details (document number, item number, date) are removed from the InfoCube definition. In this section, we've used the routine transformation type for meeting another analysis requirement of ABCD Corp. to analyze the price of a material. This needed a transformation because it isn't being supplied by the source.

In this case, the DSO becomes the source of data, so we can say that the source system is SAP BW. There are two steps required to complete the task at hand:

1. Create and activate the transformation between the DSO and InfoCube. The process of creating a transformation remains the same as discussed previously; however, we cover additional functionality in this section.

2. Create and execute the DTP between the DSO and the InfoCube. The process of creating the DTP remains the same.

As you can see, this process doesn't have a step involving the creation of a source system because the source system is SAP BW (i.e., the *myself* system), and this connection is automatically created. There is also no step required to create a DataSource because the data is already available in the DSO, which acts as the DataSource. As such, the only step we need to address is the creation of a transformation between the DSO and the InfoCube.

In the DATA WAREHOUSING WORKBENCH screen, select the INFOPROVIDER section shown in ❶ of Figure 7.70; then select InfoCube BWSD_C01 from the INFOPRO-VIDER tree ❷. From the context menu, select CREATE TRANSFORMATION ❸, which results in the CREATE TRANSFORMATION box ❹.

The target object and name are displayed ❺, and the source object and name are blank ❻. Select DATASTORE OBJECT from the OBJECT TYPE dropdown list, and enter "BWSD_O01" ❼.

Click on the CONTINUE icon ❽, which displays the CREATE TRANSFORMATION screen in Figure 7.71. The source (sales document DSO BWSD_O01) and target (sales InfoCube BWSD_C01) objects are displayed ❶. Because the source is a DSO, the left side of the screen displays the names of InfoObjects instead of fields. The system offers direct assignment transformation whenever the name of the Info-Object in the source and target matches.

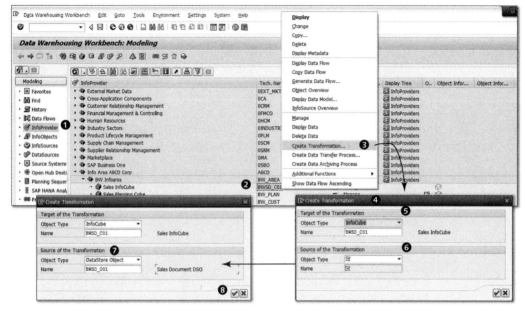

Figure 7.70 Creating the Transformation for the InfoCube

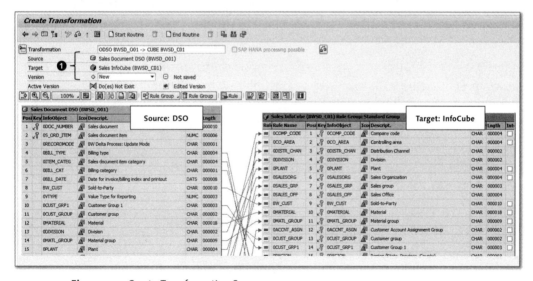

Figure 7.71 Create Transformation Screen

Per the requirement scenario for ABCD Corp., we apply two types of transformation while loading the data from the DSO to the InfoCube, one using the time conversion transformation and the other using the routine transformation.

7.4.1 Time Conversion Transformation

The DSO contains a billing date InfoObject (0BILL_DATE), whereas in the Info-Cube, we've decided not to store the data at the date level because it's granular and not required in most analyses; instead, we store it at the month, quarter, and year levels. So, we must match the source InfoObject 0BILL_DATE to target Info-Objects 0CALMONTH, 0CALQUARTER, and 0CALYEAR. This type of transformation is known as a *time conversion*.

As shown in ❶ of Figure 7.72, the system doesn't propose any transformations for the target InfoObjects because there are no matching source InfoObjects available. To fix this, you must associate 0BILL_DATE with the three target InfoObjects (0CALMONTH, 0CALQUARTER, and 0CALYEAR). Select 0BILL_DATE ❷, and drop it over 0CALMONTH. Repeat this process for 0CALQUARTER and 0CALYEAR. The result of these activities is shown in ❸ of Figure 7.72.

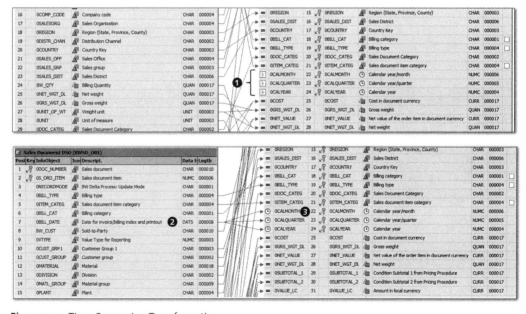

Figure 7.72 Time Conversion Transformation

7.4.2 Routine

Our example InfoCube has a BW_PRICE key figure (indicating the price of an item in the document currency), as shown in ❶ of Figure 7.73. The DSO that acts as a

DataSource doesn't have any key figures that match BW_PRICE, so we must derive the value of this key figure using values from 0NET_VALUE and BW_QTY by an ABAP code program. This type of transformation is known as a *routine transformation*. We could alternatively meet the same requirement using a formula transformation type.

Open the RULE DETAILS pop-up box by double-clicking on BW_PRICE, as shown in ❶ of Figure 7.73. The InfoObject and rule type are displayed ❷. (Unlike DSOs, InfoCubes don't allow overwriting; aggregation only offers summation.) Enter an appropriate description ❸. Because this key figure has a currency associated with it, we use the ROUTINE WITH UNIT transformation type ❹, which results in the display of currency information ❺. The target currency is 0DOC_CURRCY because this is associated with BW_PRICE ❻.

> **Routine versus Routine with Unit**
>
> The Routine transformation type allows you to return only one value. When you have a key figure associated with a unit or currency, you must use the Routine with Unit type for the system to return both values.

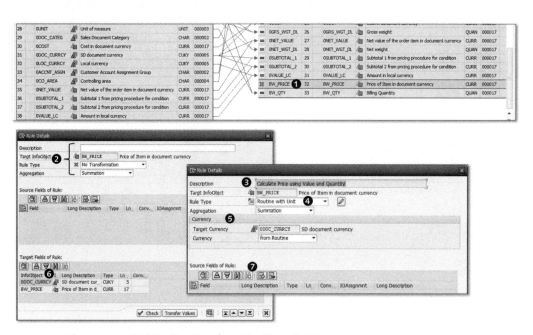

Figure 7.73 ABAP Routine Transformation Type: Part 1

Because we need to use the values of 0NET_VALUE, BW_QTY, and 0DOC_CUR-RCY in the ABAP routine, click on the icon shown in ❼ of Figure 7.73. This action results in the pop-up box shown in ❶ of Figure 7.74. Select InfoObjects BW_QTY, 0UNIT, 0DOC_CURRCY, and 0NET_VALUE, as shown in ❶. Click on the CONTINUE icon, and you can see that the selected fields are available under SOURCE FIELDS OF RULE ❷, making them available for use in an ABAP routine for any calculation.

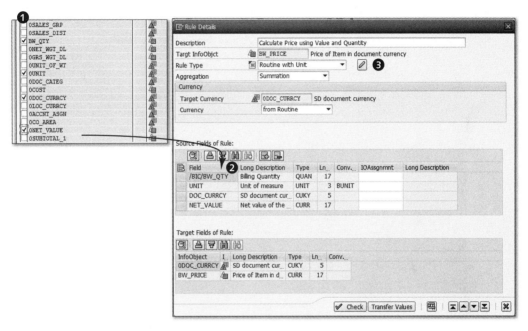

Figure 7.74 ABAP Routine Transformation Type: Part 2

Click on the CHANGE icon ❸ to invoke the ABAP editor (Figure 7.75). In the ABAP routine, we calculate the value of BW_QTY by using the following formula:

BW_PRICE = NET_VALUE / BW_QTY.

ABAP routines follow certain naming conventions. The input values are available in the ABAP routine with the prefix `source_fields_rule` or `source_fields` and the internal name of the InfoObject; for example, InfoObject 0NET_VALUE is referred to as `source_fields_rule-net_value`. There's normally one return value of an ABAP routine, which is available in the RESULT field. Whenever you use the ABAP routine with the unit transformation type, you get one more return value for the unit or currency value.

Replace the lines shown in ❶ with the lines shown in ❷ of Figure 7.75. Check your ABAP routine using the CHECK icon ❸, and save the ABAP routine.

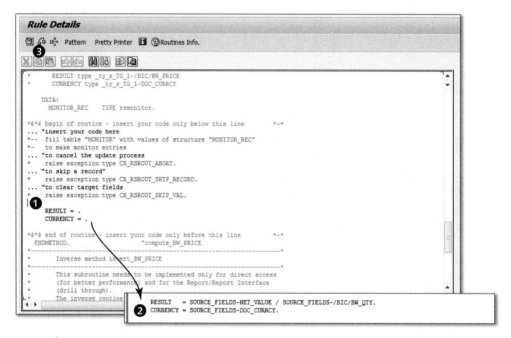

Figure 7.75 ABAP Routine

Return to the RULE DETAILS box using the BACK icon, and click on TRANSFER VALUES to return to the main transformation screen (Figure 7.76). The ABAP routine transformation type is attached to BW_PRICE ❶. Activate the transformation by clicking on the ACTIVATE icon ❷. Upon successful activation, the version is displayed as ACTIVE ❸.

Use the BACK icon to return to the Data Warehousing Workbench, and the newly created transformation is displayed. To extract data from the DSO, you must create a DTP between the DSO and InfoCube; we've already discussed this earlier in the chapter, so we won't cover it again here.

Execute the DTP. Upon successful completion of the DTP execution job, data is loaded into InfoCube BWSD_C01. We can now create SAP Business Explorer (BEx) queries and evaluate billing data. (The creation of queries is covered in subsequent chapters.) A number of administrative tasks can also be performed on this InfoCube, which are covered in Chapter 14.

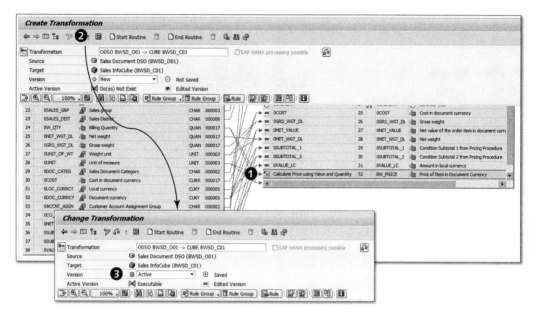

Figure 7.76 Activating the Transformation

7.5   Query as DataSource

In this chapter, we've discussed loading data into an InfoObject, DSO, and Info-Cube. The source of data used during the loading of data into an InfoObject and DSO was DataSource; for the InfoCube, we used a DSO as a source of data. However, SAP BW also gives another option here as well, which is to use a query as DataSource. Normally, a query is considered an output, but here we'll go through the steps needed to use a query as a DataSource to load the data into the DSO.

To begin, let's assume that you've created a query (query creation is explained in Chapter 9). Now, you'll also need a standard DSO that can store the data of query. In our scenario, we created a query called BWSD_C01_QUERY01, which is based in InfoCube BWSD_C01.

From here, use Transaction RSRT to start the QUERY MONITOR , as shown in ❶ of Figure 7.77. Enter the name of the QUERY that you want to use as the DataSource. In our scenario, we entered "BWSD_C01_QUERY01" ❷. Click on the PROPERTIES-button ❸. This opens the QUERY PROPERTIES dialog box ❹. The QUERY IS USED AS INFOPROVIDER setting ❺ isn't set by default, so you need to set it ❻ and then click on CONTINUE ❼. After this, you're back to the QUERY MONITORscreen. Now start the Data Warehousing Workbench by using Transaction RSA1.

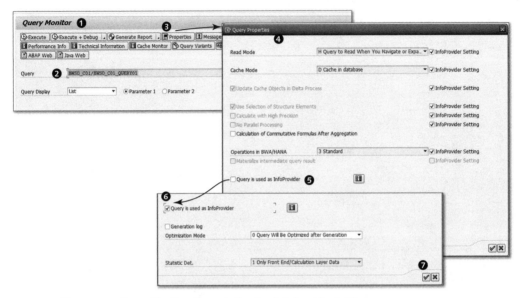

Figure 7.77 Query Monitor: Query Is Used as InfoProvider Setting

You're now in the DATA WAREHOUSING WORKBENCH screen. From the MODELING-area, select INFOPROVIDERas shown in ❶ of Figure 7.78. Select the DSO in which you want to load the data from the query. We'll select BWSD_O22 ❷. From the context menu, select CREATE DATA TRANSFER PROCESS. This brings up the CREATE DATA TRANSFER PROCESS screen, as shown in ❸. The TARGET OF DTP area shows DSO BWSD_O22 ❹ as we initiate the creation of DTP using the context menu of the DSO. Once here, we need to select a source of DTP ❺. From the OBJECT TYPE dropdown, select QUERY ELEMENT ❻. Now, click on the DATASOURCE dropdown. This brings up a list of queries in a separate pop-up box, as shown in ❼. Select query BWSD_C01_QUERY01 ❽, and then click on CONTINUE ❾.

With this action, your SOURCE OF DTP is now set to query BWSD_C01_QUERY01, as shown in ❶ of Figure 7.79. Click onCONTINUE ❷. This brings you to the GEN-ERATE TRANSFORMATION pop-up ❸. Click on YES ❹, and the system generates a default transformation between the query and DSO. You may change this setting as needed. Next, we come to the CHANGE DATA TRANSFER PROCESS screen, as shown in ❺ of Figure 7.79. The EXTRACTION tab showsQUERYPROVIDER selected in the pre-vious step as SOURCE OBJECT ❻. Activate DTP by clicking on the ACTIVATE icon ❼.

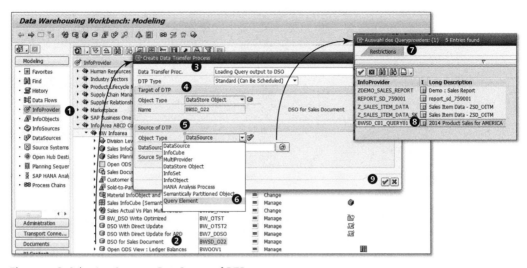

Figure 7.78 Selecting Query as DataSource of DTP

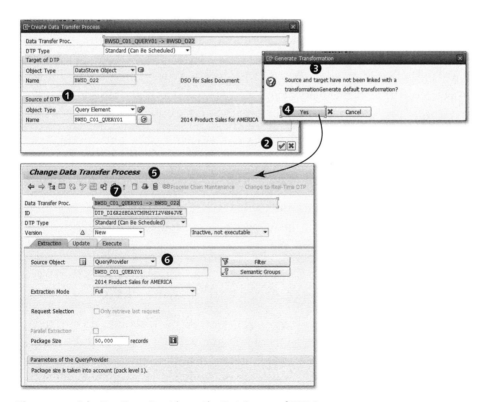

Figure 7.79 Selecting QueryProvider as the DataSource of DTP 2

This completes your configuration for using query as a DataSource. In the DATA WAREHOUSING WORKBENCH screen, you can now view the data flow from the query to the DSO, as shown in ❶ of Figure 7.80.

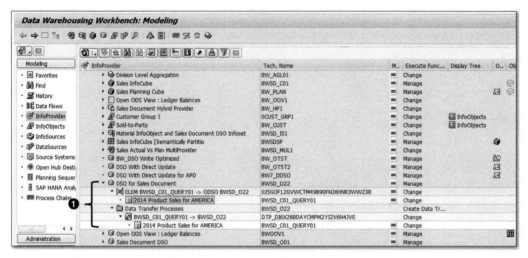

Figure 7.80 Query as DataSource in the Data Flow

This functionality proves very useful when you have a complex query and want to save the output of the query at a particular time (e.g., at month end) for future reference. There are limitations, however; you can't use query as a DataSource if it's using the following:

▶ Noncumulative key figures

▶ Input-ready variables

Now that you understand the basic ETL process using a flat file, we'll explain the two technical components of the loading process: temporary storage areas and error stacks.

7.6 Temporary Storage Areas and Error Stacks

When loading data into a data target, the system includes a number of standard checks to make sure everything is going smoothly; you can also customize checks based on your requirements. If any of these checks result in the identification of errors, SAP BW stores the erroneous records in a separate container called the *error stack*. After these records are corrected, they are again loaded into the data target using a special DTP called the *error DTP*. The overall position of the error stack during the loading process is shown in Figure 7.81.

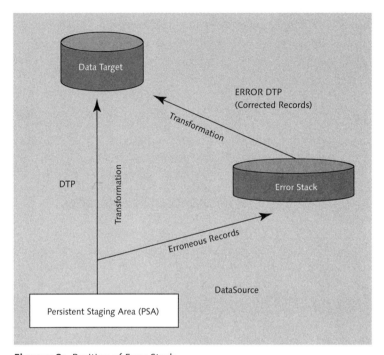

Figure 7.81 Position of Error Stack

In this section, we explain the temporary storage area (which is an important part of correcting erroneous records), the process of configuring standard integrity checks and viewing the errors that result from these checks, and the process of loading corrected records via the error DTP.

7.6.1 Temporary Storage

At this point, we should introduce another function offered by SAP BW: *temporary storage*. Once configured, this function stores data in various stages of transformation in a separate area known as the temporary storage area, which contains both correct and erroneous records and displays their current status. During complex transformations, this informs you of the exact processing step in which problems are encountered.

You can configure temporary storage from the DTP configuration screen, as shown in Figure 7.82. Use the menu path GOTO • SETTINGS FOR DTP TEMPORARY STORAGE ❶. This action results in the SETTINGS FOR DTP TEMPORARY STORAGE box ❷, which allows you to trace records to various levels of detail ❸. You can define the step in the sequence of processing substeps to fill the temporary storage ❹. Standard processing substeps are available here, and you can select multiple steps, if required. As shown in ❺, you can instruct the system when to delete data stored in the temporary storage area.

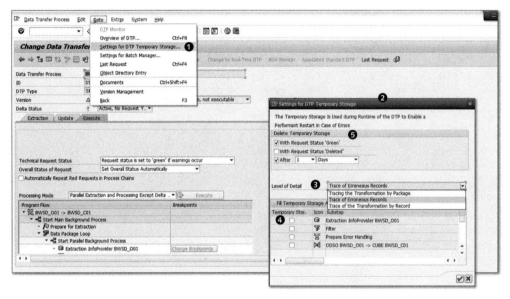

Figure 7.82 Configuring Temporary Storage

> **Note**
>
> Configuring the temporary storage functionality is optional.

7.6.2 Configuring Integrity Checks and Viewing Errors in Temporary Storage

InfoObject BW_CUST has one attribute: 0CUST_GRP1. When loading master data for InfoObject BW_CUST, the flat file has a value for the 0CUST_GRP1 attribute for each value contained in InfoObject BW_CUST. We want the system to check the value of 0CUST_GRP1 for each customer; this check is performed in the master data table of InfoObject 0CUST_GRP1. If the value isn't found in the table associated with InfoObject 0CUST_GRP1, the master data record of InfoObject BW_CUST should be stored in the error stack.

Let's explore this concept more thoroughly by using an example. Figure 7.83 shows a new data file to be loaded into InfoObject BW_CUST. There are three customers, each with a different value for Customer GRP1. Assume that at this moment, Customer GRP1 value WA is already loaded as master data (in tables associated with the Customer GRP1 InfoObject), but values BK and AP aren't loaded as Customer GRP1 master data.

	A	B	C	D	E	F	G	H	I
1	Sold-to Party	Customer GRP	Customer GRP1	Sales Group	Sales District	Sales Office	Sales Employee	Date From	Date To
2	100095 ST		WA	757	2717	3103	41	20000101	20081231
3	100096 ST		BK	757	2717	3103	42	20090101	99991231
4	100097 ST		AP	757	2717	3103	40	20090101	99991231

Figure 7.83 Sample Data for Error Stack

As we said, we must configure an integrity check so that the system checks the value of InfoObject 0CUST_GRP1 for each respective value of the customer. You therefore select the INTEGRITY checkbox shown in ❶ of Figure 7.84.

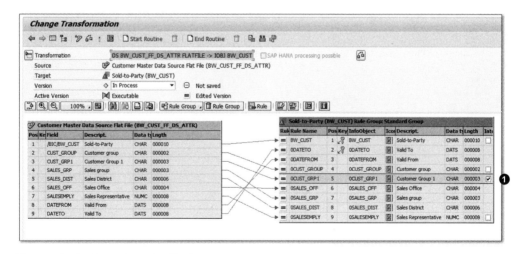

Figure 7.84 Setting an Integrity Check

Now that the checkbox is selected, you can load the data from the sample file to the PSA. The data in the PSA is shown in Figure 7.85. There is no error yet; transformations aren't executed while moving data to a PSA.

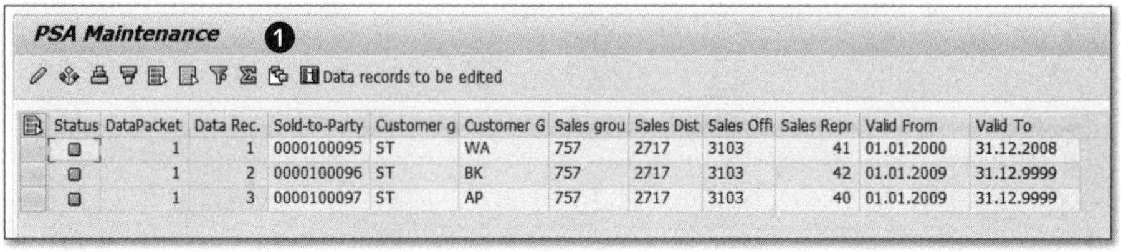

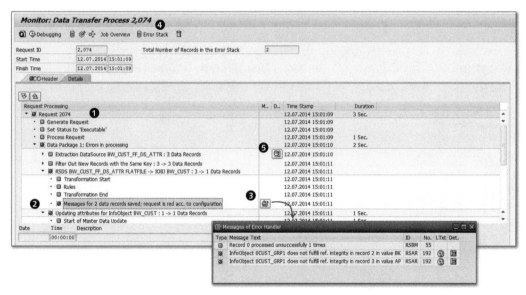

Figure 7.85 Data Loaded into PSA without Error

Now execute the DTP, and start the DTP monitor. This time, the DTP is unsuccessful, which is indicated by the red status in ❶ of Figure 7.86 (the load failed because the BK and AP values aren't loaded as part of the Customer GRP1 master data). As shown in ❷, the displayed message indicates that loading has encountered an error. (You can see the detailed message by clicking on the icon shown in ❸.)

Figure 7.86 Error during Loading

Viewing the records in the error stack is the same as viewing the data in the PSA; to do so, click on the ERROR STACK button ❹. This displays the ERROR STACK box shown in ❶ of Figure 7.87. Each data packet and its number of records are listed ❷. Select the data packet, and click on the CONTINUE icon ❸, which opens the box shown in ❹. All of the erroneous records from the selected data packet are listed in this screen. To view the error details for a particular record, select the record and double-click on the icon shown in ❺. The error detail for the selected record is shown in another pop-up box ❻. To correct value errors, select the record, and then click on the CHANGE icon.

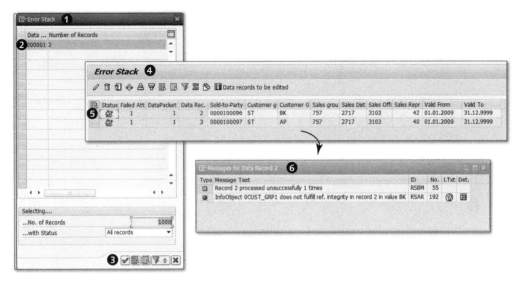

Figure 7.87 Data in the Error Stack

To view records in temporary storage, click on the icon shown in ❺ of Figure 7.86. The result of this action is the DISPLAY TEMPORARY STORAGE screen shown in Figure 7.88. Each record has a status in the form of an icon ❶:

▶ ▣: This icon indicates that the record has no errors.

▶ ▤: This icon indicates that the record is erroneous and stored in the error stack.

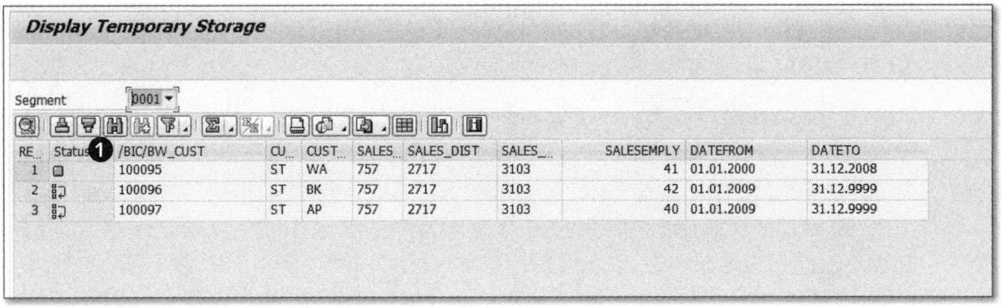

Figure 7.88 Records in Temporary Storage

7.6.3 Creating and Monitoring the Error DTP

To fix the errors in this example, you must load the BK and AP values as master data for InfoObject 0CUST_GRP1; assume that this has now been done. After the errors have been corrected, you can create the error DTP. In the DISPLAY DATA TRANSFER PROCESS screen, select the UPDATE tab (❶ of Figure 7.89). Click on the CREATING ERROR DTP button ❷, and the error DTP is created ❸. (You can switch to a standard DTP by clicking on the ASSOCIATED STANDARD DTP button ❹.)

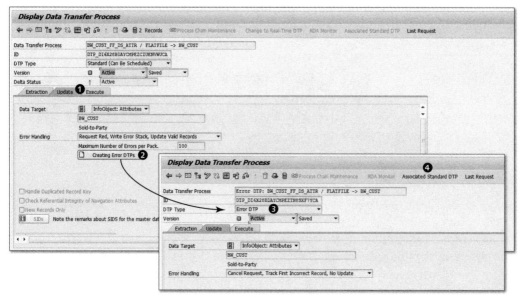

Figure 7.89 Creating an Error DTP

Refer to ❶ of Figure 7.90, which shows the DTP TYPE as ERROR DTP. Select the EXECUTE tab ❷, and start the execution of the error DTP by clicking on the EXECUTE button ❸.

This brings you to the MONITOR screen of the error DTP, as shown in Figure 7.91. This time, instead of extracting records from a DataSource, the system is extracting them from the error stack ❷. Because the error has been addressed, the request status is successful (green) ❶, and the system deletes the record from the error stack.

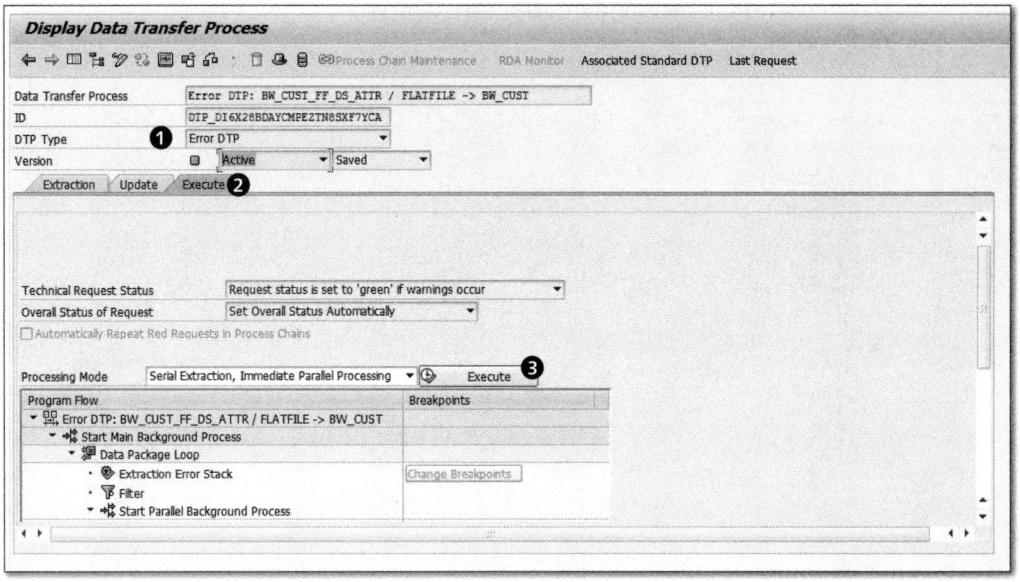

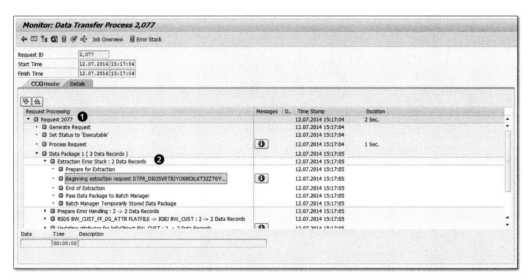

Figure 7.90 Executing Error DTP

Figure 7.91 Monitoring the Error DTP

The error DTP can be seen in the DATA WAREHOUSING WORKBENCHscreen under data target BW_CUST, as shown in ❶ of Figure 7.92. The same error DTP can be used every time the standard DTP encounters errors (after taking corrective action, of course).

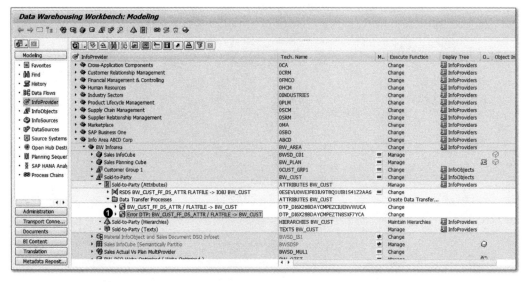

Figure 7.92 Error DTP in the Data Warehousing Workbench

7.7 Graphical Modeling

From version 7.3, SAP BW offers a functionality called *graphical modeling* that allows you to create data flows and data flow templates (DFTs) using a graphical user interface (GUI). All the required navigation to create objects and bind them with related objects is available in the same tool, so there is no need for an SAP BW designer to jump from one menu to another to create different objects.

A *data flow* displays a set of metadata objects and their relationships, and can contain persistent and nonpersistent objects. SAP defines a *persistent object* as any object that is already saved in the metadata tables in the database and that can also be displayed in the object tree of the Data Warehousing Workbench, for example, DSOs and InfoCubes in an InfoProvider tree. A *persistent object* can be part of many data flows, the way an InfoCube can be part of many MultiProvider definitions. SAP defines nonpersistent objects as objects that have been created with attributes, such as objects; a DSO is again an example (DSOs can be either persistent or nonpersistent). These objects haven't been stored in the database, and they can only be used and displayed in the data flow in which they were created. They can't be displayed in any other object tree of the Data Warehousing Workbench.

Data flows can be saved as a DFT if the data flow only contains nonpersistent objects. A DFT describes a data flow scenario with all required objects and can serve as scenario documentation.

In this section, we'll walk you through the process of creating a DFT. We'll then show you how that DFT can be used to design a data flow.

7.7.1 Creating a Data Flow Template

To start creating a DFT, open the DATA WAREHOUSING WORKBENCH screen using Transaction RSA1. From MODELING (❶ of Figure 7.93), select DATA FLOWS ❷ to open the DATA FLOWS panel on the right side of the screen. All the available data flows and DFTs are displayed here. DFTs are created under InfoAreas, so select the InfoArea BW_AREA ❸. From the context menu, select CREATE DATA FLOW ❹. This brings up the CREATE DATA FLOW pop-up box ❺. Enter the data flow technical name and description ❻, and then click on OK ❼.

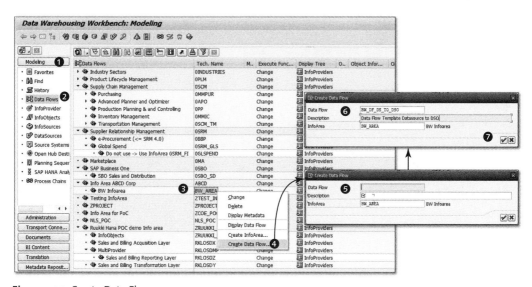

Figure 7.93 Create Data Flow

This brings up the EDIT DATA FLOW screen, as shown in Figure 7.94. The left panel ❶ displays all the objects that can be included when defining a data flow or DFT. This includes InfoCubes, DSOs, InfoObjects, DataSources, and so on. The right panel is where you can actually define the data flow or DFT.

In our example, we create a DFT where a DataSource is connected to the DSO. To do this, first click on the DATASOURCE icon (❷ of Figure 7.94). Drag and drop this icon onto the right panel ❸. The result of this action is shown in ❹.

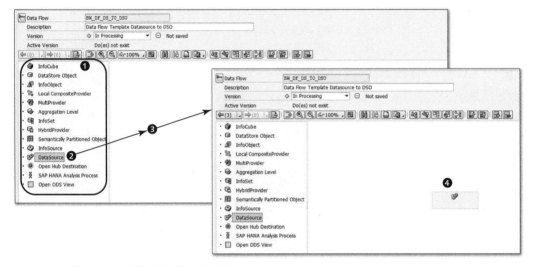

Figure 7.94 Edit Data Flow: Part 1

Now select DATASTORE OBJECT from the left panel, as shown in ❶ of Figure 7.95. Drag and drop this DSO into the free space available in the right panel ❷. This makes the DSO available on the right panel ❸.

Both source and target objects are available in the right side panel, and the next step is to connect them. Click on DATASOURCE (❶ of Figure 7.96), and drag it toward the target object—which, in our scenario, is a DSO ❷—and connect it to the DSO. The resulting data flow is shown in ❸, and the established connection is shown by the TRANSFORMATION icon. The data flow is now ready; all you need to do is save it as a template, so it can be used in creating future data flows.

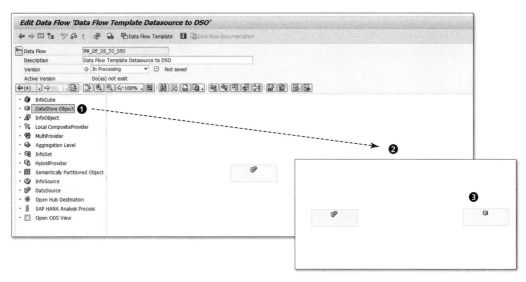

Figure 7.95 Edit Data Flow: Part 2

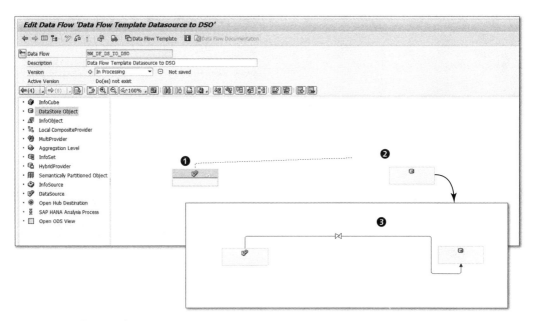

Figure 7.96 Edit Data Flow: Part 3

To do this, select DATA FLOW • SAVE AS TEMPLATE, as shown in ❶ of Figure 7.97. This brings up the SAVE AS DATA FLOW TEMPLATE box ❷; recall that the system has already supplied the entries. Click on OK ❸, which saves this data flow as a template ❹. The version is now changed to SAVED from NOT SAVED ❺.

To be used again, the template now needs to be activated. Click on the ACTIVATE icon (❻ of Figure 7.97). After successful activation of the template, the ACTIVE version is changed to EXECUTABLE ❼. This DFT BW_DF_DS_TO_DSO is now ready to use for designing another data flow.

Note

The template has objects that are nonpersistent.

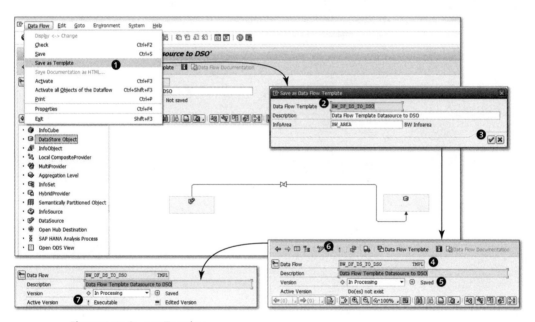

Figure 7.97 Save as Template

The new DFT BW_DF_DS_TO_DSO is available under InfoArea BW_AREA (❶ of Figure 7.98). The icon associated with this template ❷ differentiates the data flows from the DFTs in the list displayed under the InfoArea.

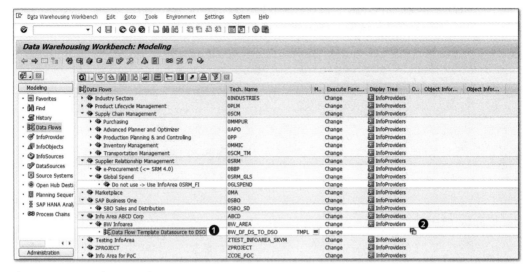

Figure 7.98 Data Flow Template

7.7.2 Creating a Data Flow

Now that we've created a DFT, we can use that template to create a data flow. Start the DATA WAREHOUSING WORKBENCH using Transaction RSA1. From MODELING (❶ of Figure 7.99), select DATA FLOWS ❷. On the right side panel, you can see the DATA FLOW and DATA FLOW TEMPLATE already available in the SAP BW system under their respective InfoAreas. Select InfoArea BW_AREA ❸, and select CREATE DATA FLOW ❹ from the context menu. This shows the CREATE DATA FLOW pop-up box. Enter a technical name and description ❺, and click OK ❻ to proceed. This action brings up the EDIT DATA FLOW screen, as shown in Figure 7.100.

As you can see, the edit panel (right side panel) is initially blank. Click on the DATA FLOW TEMPLATE button (❶ of Figure 7.100), which brings up the APPLY DATA FLOW TEMPLATES screen. This pop-up displays three different sections; the first two classify the template categories (SAP DATA FLOW TEMPLATES ❷ consists of SAP-provided templates, and DATA FLOW TEMPLATES ❸ consists of user-defined templates), and the third (DATA FLOWS, not shown on this screen) includes data flows.

For our scenario, click on the DATA FLOW TEMPLATE section, and select and expand InfoArea BW_AREA to reach the required DFT. You may use the SEARCH button (❹ of Figure 7.100) to find the DFT we created earlier. Select BW_DF_DS_

TO_DSO ❻, and click on Continue ❼. This action displays the selected DFT definition on the right-hand panel, as shown in ❷ of Figure 7.101.

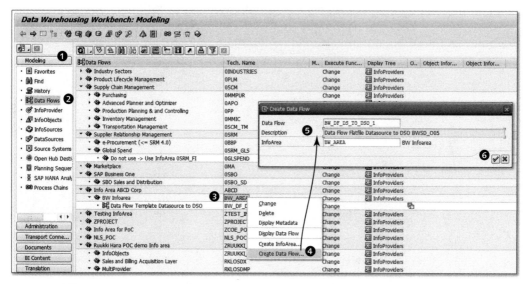

Figure 7.99 Create Data Flow

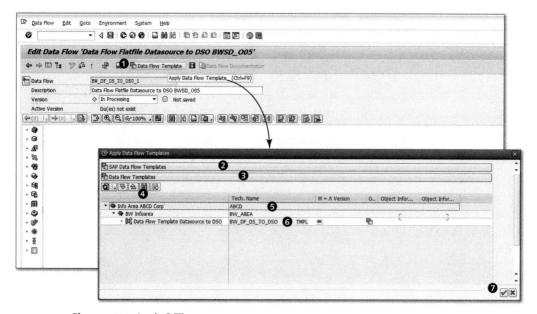

Figure 7.100 Apply DFT

The selected template shows the objects included and their relationship, but doesn't yet bind the objects to persistent objects. Click on CONTINUE (❸ of Figure 7.101) to proceed.

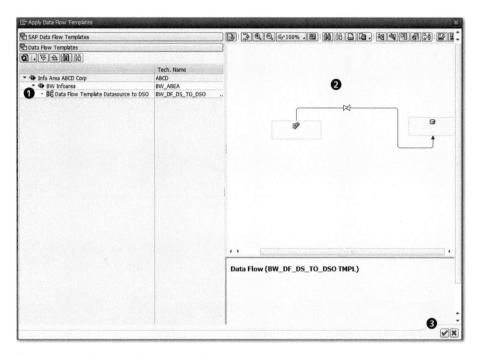

Figure 7.101 Objects and Their Relationship

While binding, you can choose between two different methods. First, you can choose the object that is already available in the system. Second, you can decide to create a new object and bind it to the data flow object. Next, we explain the step-by-step instructions for both methods.

Choosing an Object Available in the System

First, select the DataSource (❶ of Figure 7.102) from the context menu, and select the USE EXISTING OBJECT option ❷. In our example, we use the existing DataSource BWSD_O05_FF_DS_TRAN (which is a copy of DataSource BWSD_O01_FF_DS_TRAN). This action opens the EDIT DATA FLOW pop-up ❸, which displays all of the DataSources. Select DataSource BWSD_O05_FF_DS_TRAN ❹, and click on the TRANSFER SELECTION button ❺. This action binds persistent object BWSD_O05_FF_DS_TRAN to the DataSource object of the DFT, as shown in ❶ of Figure 7.103.

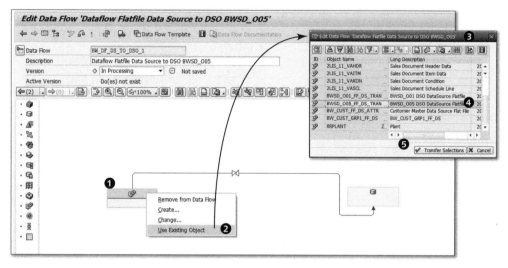

Figure 7.102 Choosing the DataSource

As shown in ❶, ❷, and ❸ of Figure 7.103, when binding DataSource BWSD_
005_FF_DS_TRAN, the system also adds attached objects to the DataSource. Here
the attached objects are INFOPACKAGE ❷ and SOURCE SYSTEM ❸. With this, we've
bound the existing object in the DFT.

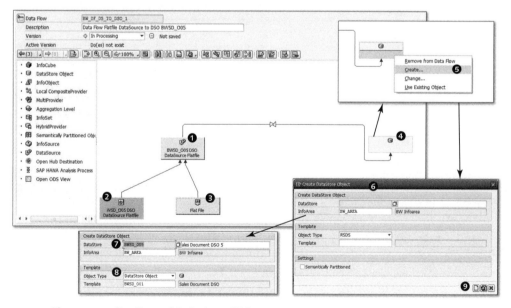

Figure 7.103 Creating and Assigning a DSO

Creating and Binding a New Object

Now let's use another method to bind a persistent object to the DSO. Select the DSO (❹ of Figure 7.103), and then select CREATE ❺ from the context menu. This action brings up the CREATE DATASTORE OBJECT screen ❻.

Enter "BWSD_O05" as the DSO technical name with the description "Sales Document DSO 5" (❼ of Figure 7.103). Also select DATASTORE OBJECT as the OBJECT TYPE and BWSD_O01 as the TEMPLATE ❽. Click on CREATE ❾ to proceed. This brings up the EDIT DATASTORE OBJECT screen, as shown in Figure 7.104.

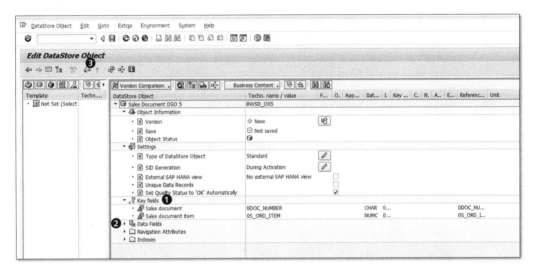

Figure 7.104 Editing the Assigned DSO

Because we've used BWSD_O01 as the template while creating DSO BWSD_O05, all of the settings of BWSD_O01 are displayed (❶ and ❷ of Figure 7.104). Without changing any settings, activate DSO BWSD_O05 by clicking on the ACTIVATE icon ❸. After the DSO is activated, use the BACK button to go back to the DATA FLOW EDIT screen, which is shown in Figure 7.105. The newly assigned DSO BWSD_O05 is now visible in the data flow (❶ of Figure 7.105).

The next step is to assign a transformation to the data flow. To do this, select TRANSFORMATION, and then select CREATE from the context menu (❷ of Figure 7.105). This action opens the CREATE TRANSFORMATION box ❸, which contains all of the required information, for example, target of the transformation and source of the transformation. (Remember that we've already assigned persistent objects to both the source and the target.) Click on CONTINUE ❹ to proceed. The resulting screen is shown in ❺, along with the transformation.

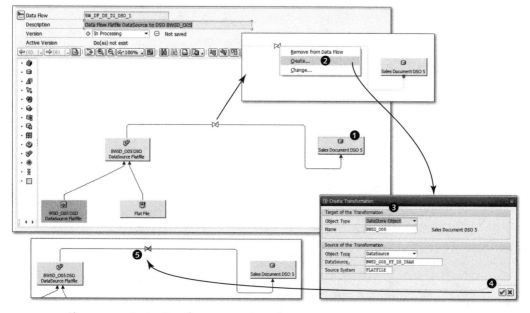

Figure 7.105 Assign Transformation to Data Flow

With this, we've completed the creation of a data flow using the DFT. Use the BACK button to go back to the main DATA WAREHOUSING WORKBENCH screen, which is shown in Figure 7.106.

To view the newly created data flow BW_DF_DS_TO_DSO_1 (❹ of Figure 7.106), select MODELING ❶, then DATA FLOWS ❷, and look under BW_INFOAREA ❸. All of the persistent objects that were assigned while designing the data flow can also be seen here ❺.

Graphical modeling is a very powerful tool that can be used to easily create from simple to very complex data flows.

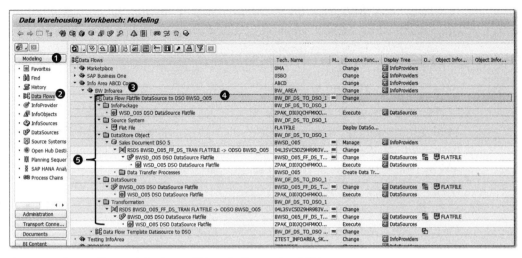

Figure 7.106 Data Flow and Persistent Objects in Transaction RSA1

7.8 Special Topics for SAP HANA

This section is applicable if your SAP BW system is powered by an SAP HANA database. In this section, we discuss specific topics related to transformations on SAP HANA. We'll explain how to design transformations and discuss how to take advantage of SAP HANA while designing a transformation, as well as what functionalities are offered by SAP BW on SAP HANA. Specifically, we'll be covering two special topics: SAP HANA-optimized transformation, and optimizing ABAP routines.

7.8.1 SAP HANA-Optimized Transformation

You can design a transformation based on your reporting needs and the way data is offered from a source. This transformation can vary from simple to complex. The execution of a transformation may be time-consuming; however, if you're using an SAP HANA database, this may improve the time required to execute the transformation.

By default, SAP BW performs transformations on an application server. At the time of activating a transformation, SAP BW checks to see if it can perform the task on an SAP HANA database. There are certain transformation that can't be performed on an SAP HANA database, so if they are included as part of your transformation, you can't instruct the system to perform them.

In this section, we'll explain how to check the system and what settings are needed to instruct the system to perform a transformation on an SAP HANA database. Figure 7.107 shows a transformation between a DataSource and a DSO. The SAP HANA PROCESSING POSSIBLE flag informs you that a transformation can be performed on an SAP HANA database, as shown in ❶ of Figure 7.107.

From here, click on the CHECK icon ❷ of Figure 7.107. The system will then perform certain checks, and if all the checks are passed, a message stating THE TRANSFORMATION CAN BE PROCESSED IN SAP HANA will appear ❸. The following objects aren't supported in SAP HANA, some of them are listed here:

- Rule groups
- ABAP routines (rule types Routine, Characteristic Routine, Start Routine, End Routine, and Expert Routine)
- Query as InfoProvider as source of transformation
- Conversion Routine PERI7
- UNIT Conversion with Quantity DSO

If one of the nonsupported transformation objects is used, the system won't allow you to set the SAP HANA PROCESSING POSSIBLE flag ❶ of Figure 7.107. If you are unable to perform this in the system, a log will be generated to indicate why.

In our scenario, because the message indicates that a transformation can be processed in SAP HANA, let's now activate this transformation. To begin, click on the ACTIVATE icon (❹ of Figure 7.107). The transformation is now ACTIVE ❺ and the SAP HANA PROCESSING POSSIBLE flag ❻ for SAP HANA processing is set.

Next you need to create a DTP. Go back to the MODELING section of the DATA WAREHOUSING WORKBENCH screen, and select INFOPROVIDER (❶ of Figure 7.108). Select the DSO icon ❷. From the context menu, select CREATE DATA TRANSFER PROCESS ❸. This action opens the CREATE DATA TRANSFER PROCESS dialog box. The details of a DTP are defaulted ❹. It doesn't require any change, so click on CONTINUE ❺.

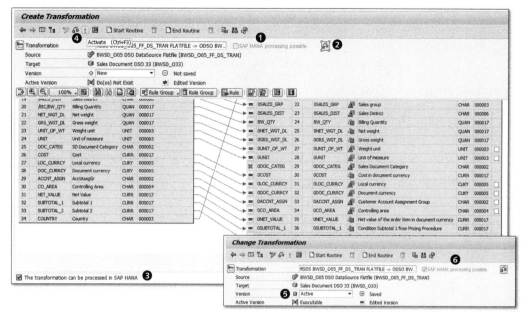

Figure 7.107 SAP HANA Optimized Transformation: Part 1

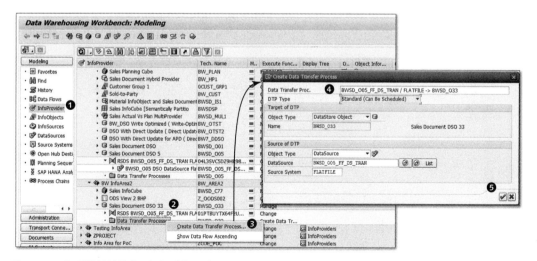

Figure 7.108 SAP HANA Optimized Transformation: Part 2

The next screen is CHANGE DATA TRANSFER PROCESS (❶ of Figure 7.109). Because this set of transformations will be processed in SAP HANA, you can see a new entry in the PROCESSING MODE dropdown: SAP HANA EXECUTION ❷. This particular option is only available if the transformation can be processed in an SAP HANA database. Click on the ACTIVATE icon ❸ to activate the DTP ❹. Click on the EXECUTE button ❺ to process the transformation in an SAP HANA database.

This way, you can use the SAP HANA database to process your transformation. The following targets are supported in this scenario:

- DSOs (standard and write-optimized)
- Semantically partitioned objects (SPOs) based on a DSO
- Open hub destinations with database tables

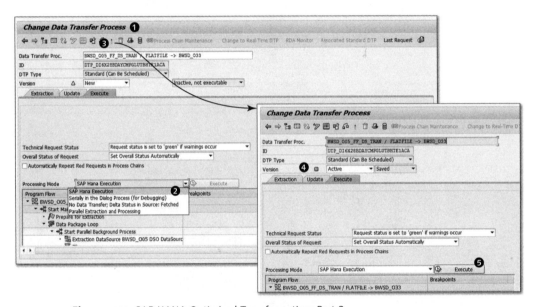

Figure 7.109 SAP HANA Optimized Transformation: Part 3

7.8.2 Optimizing Custom ABAP Routines on SAP HANA

This is applicable in a scenario in which either you're planning to implement or already use SAP BW powered by SAP HANA and want to optimize the custom ABAP routine.

You may have used your own ABAP routine in the transformation to satisfy your requirements, and you may have used some best practices of ABAP while developing that code. However, what is best practice for ABAP on a non-SAP HANA system may not be true when switching to an SAP HANA-based system. Here, SAP has provided a tool to alleviate these differences called the *ABAP Routine Analyzer*, which will analyze your code and recommend areas of improvement.

Prerequisite

To begin, download the latest version of the tool from SAP Note 1847431. SAP regularly updates this, so check for the latest version from the SAP Service Marketplace.

This note provides a code in ABAP that your ABAP developer will be able to implement. The tool provides a code for SAP BW 7.x (takes care of 7.x transformation, etc.) and SAP BW 3.x (takes care of 3.x update rules, transfer rules, etc.).

Once implemented, use Transaction SE38 as shown in ❶ of Figure 7.110. This will start the ABAP EDITOR: INITIAL SCREEN ❷. Initially, the PROGRAM field is empty ❸. Enter "ZBW_ABAP_ANALYZER" ❹. Then click on the EXECUTE icon ❺.

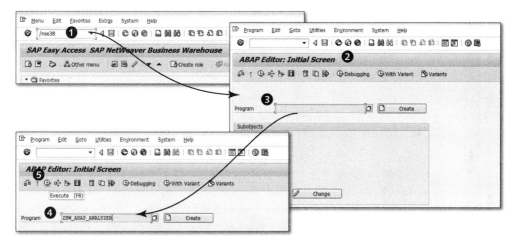

Figure 7.110 Starting the ABAP Editor

The screen that appears next is the SAP BW ABAP Routine Analyzer (❶ of Figure 7.111), which displays various options in nine tabs (only seven are visible initially, and the CHECKS tab ❷ is displayed by default). However, you can click on the rightmost icon ❹ to display all the available tabs. All of the available tab options appear in list form ❺. You can directly jump to any of the tabs from here.

Under the CHECKS tab, various checkboxes are available for you to select settings. By default, CHECK PROCESS CHAINS is set. At the same time, the settings on transformation, update rules, and transfer rules aren't available for you to select ❸. We explain next how to set them.

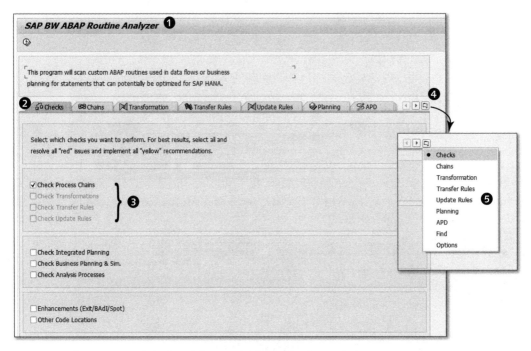

Figure 7.111 SAP BW ABAP Routine Analyzer: Part 1

Select the CHAINS tab as shown in ❶ of Figure 7.112. The various selection criteria for selecting the PROCESS CHAIN are displayed ❷. Click on the TRANSFORMATION tab ❸. You can see that the transformation isn't available for you to select ❹. To make it available for selection, click on the CHECKS tab ❺. Deselect the CHECK PROCESS CHAINS checkbox ❻. As soon as you deselect, the checkbox for transformation updates the rules, and the transfer rules are available for your selection ❼. Now, select CHECK TRANSFORMATIONS ❽, and click on the TRANSFORMATION tab again.

Back in the TRANSFORMATION tab shown in ❶ of Figure 7.113, the transformations are now available for you to select ❷. There are various settings, but the simplest is TRANSFORMATION ID. You can select a single transformation or multiple transformations. Here we'll select one and analyze it.

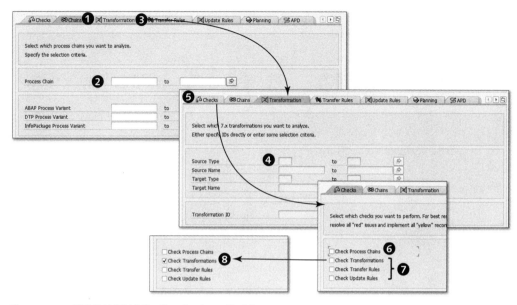

Figure 7.112 SAP BW ABAP Routine Analyzer: Part 2

Each transformation you activate in the system is given an ID. As shown in ❸ of Figure 7.113, the TRANSFORMATION ID is available on the right side of the transformation icon. Select the transformation ID you want to analyze, and enter the same in the TRANSFORMATION ID field under the TRANSFORMATION tab ❹.

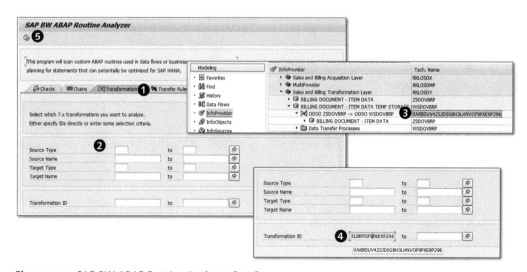

Figure 7.113 SAP BW ABAP Routine Analyzer: Part 3

Click on the EXECUTE icon ❺ to start analyzing the selected transformation. A log for analysis is displayed in ❶ of Figure 7.114.

The log is divided in two parts. An overview is shown on the left side, and a MESSAGE TEXT area is displayed on the right side (❸ of Figure 7.114). The MESSAGE TEXT area may display an icon for some messages ❹. Clicking on this icon takes you to the respective screen for the message (e.g., message CLICK ON DETAILS TO EDIT TRANSFORMATION… takes you to the EDIT TRANSFORMATION screen for that particular transformation).

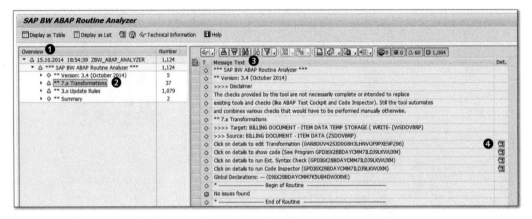

Figure 7.114 ABAP Routine Analyzer Log: Part 1

The log messages are displayed in four different colors:

▸ **Green icon**
Check is successful; no further action is necessary.

▸ **Yellow icon**
General findings; follow the recommended action.

▸ **Red icon**
Critical findings; highly recommends to follow the suggested action and adjust the ABAP code.

▸ **Gray icon**
This is an informational message.

For the red and yellow messages, the system proposes recommendations to address the issue.

As shown in Figure 7.115, the log shows general findings, information, and success. Incidentally, there is no red message given by our Analyzer for the selected transformation.

As shown in ❶ of Figure 7.115, messages are shown in yellow for general findings. You can get to this screen by expanding the 7X transformation on the left of the OVERVIEW section. You can double-click on any of the messages in the OVERVIEW section ❷. If there are further details available for selected message, the information is displayed on right-hand panel ❸.

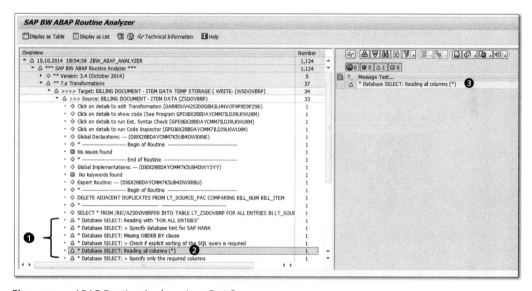

Figure 7.115 ABAP Routine Analyzer Log: Part 2

This tool helps you find the optimization required for SAP HANA, but it's not a replacement for other tools such as the ABAP Code Inspector.

7.9 Summary

In this chapter, we explained the process of ETL, focusing on three major processes:

▸ Loading master data from a flat file to an InfoObject

▸ Loading transaction data from a flat file to a DSO

▸ Loading data from a DSO to an InfoCube

We then explained error stacks and the graphical modeling tool. We then explained how a query can be used as a DataSource followed by explanation of error stacks and the graphical modeling tool. The chapter concluded with topics including SAP HANA-Optimized Transformation and optimizing ABAP code on SAP HANA.

8   Data Extraction from Source Systems

As you'll recall from earlier chapters, a DataSource is a structure where source system fields are logically grouped together and contain information related to extraction, transformation, and loading (ETL). Four types of DataSources exist: for transaction data, for master data attributes, for master data texts, and for master data hierarchies. If the source system is SAP ERP, replicating DataSources creates identical DataSource structures in the SAP BW system.

In this chapter, we continue our ETL discussion from the previous chapter by focusing on the specific details of extraction from source systems. The majority of the chapter discusses extraction from SAP source systems—because this is the most common SAP BW use case—and we focus on two main methods of accomplishing this extraction: using Business Content (with logistics DataSources as our example) and using a generic DataSource. In the last section, we briefly discuss the process of data extraction from non-SAP systems. We will also introduce extracting data using Operational Data Provisioning (ODP), and briefly go over the Operational Delta Queue (ODQ) and SAP LT Replication Server (SLT).

8.1   Configuring an SAP Source System for Extraction

Before you can extract data from an SAP source system, specific settings must be configured in the SAP ERP source system, including the activation of the DataSources in Business Content and the performance tuning of the extraction process.

To begin, select Transaction SBIW in the source system. The screen that appears is shown in Figure 8.1. This displays various settings and configuration options related to data extraction from SAP ERP to SAP BW. As shown in the figure, some of these settings can be called directly using a transaction code (e.g., Transaction RSA7 for CHECK DELTA QUEUE ❶), while other settings can only be invoked using the menu path (e.g., MAINTAIN CONTROL PARAMETERS FOR DATA TRANSFER ❺). Transaction RSA5 ❷ allows you to transfer a business content data source from delivered mode to active mode. Transaction RSO2 ❸ helps develop and maintain generic DataSources. You can maintain DataSource and application component hierarchy with Transaction RSA6 ❹.

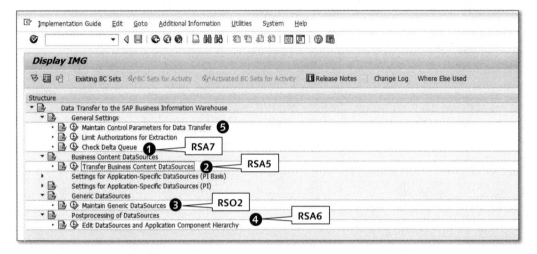

Figure 8.1 Settings in the SAP ERP Source System

For our case study, we need to use the DataSource that extracts the billing transaction data; the Business Content DataSource for billing transaction data (with item level information) is 2LIS_13_VDITM. To use this DataSource, you must first activate it.

To activate a DataSource, use Transaction RSA5 in the SAP ERP source system. All of the Business Content DataSources (transaction as well as master data) are listed in a hierarchical manner (❶ of Figure 8.2) and grouped together based on the functional area or business process. These groups are called *application components.*

The DataSource for billing item information ❷ falls under the SD (Sales and Distribution) application component. Place the cursor on the required DataSource ❸, and then click on ACTIVATE DATASOURCES ❹ to activate the selected DataSource. You can view all active DataSources by using Transaction RSA6 (Postprocess DataSources and Hierarchy) ❺.

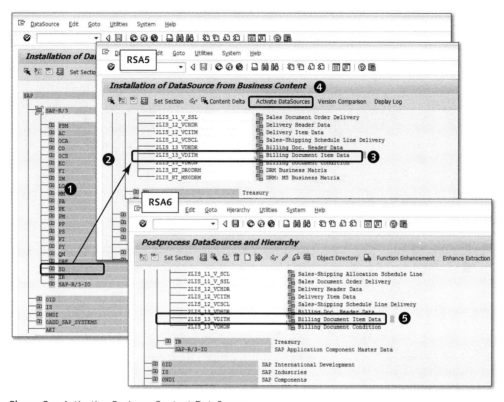

Figure 8.2 Activating Business Content DataSource

8.2 Using SAP Business Content for Extraction: Logistics DataSources

SAP ERP has a number of logistics applications, so, as part of Business Content, SAP provides a number of DataSources that are related to logistics.

SAP Business Content

SAP Business Content is a library of predelivered SAP BW solutions (DataSources, ETL logic, cubes, reports, queries, and more) that is included with SAP BW.

These DataSources require special attention because their extraction follows a well-defined process that uses a special framework: the *Logistics Cockpit*. Figure 8.3 gives an overview of the Logistics Cockpit.

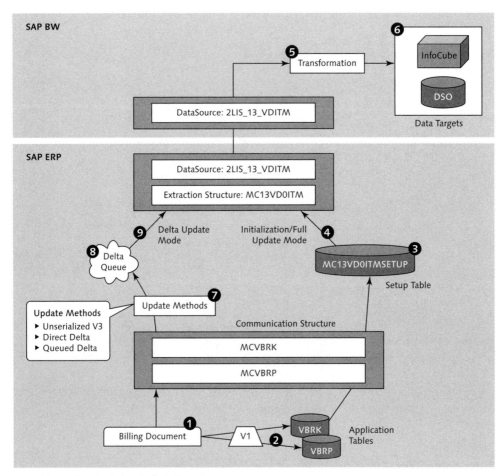

Figure 8.3 Logistics Cockpit Overview

Note

ABCD Corp. has an analysis requirement based on a billing application that is part of the Logistics Cockpit. The standard billing application allows you to create, change, or delete billing documents, as shown in ❶ of Figure 8.3. Each of these activities results in addition, modification, or reduction to the multiple billing documents stored in the billing application tables (tables VBRK and VBRP in ❷ of Figure 8.3).

Next, we discuss several topics relevant to data extraction using the Logistics Cockpit.

8.2.1 Initialization

In most cases, the SAP ERP system is in place before the SAP BW system, and therefore it has historical data for applications. SAP BW requires this historical data to carry out a trend analysis.

Almost all of the logistics-related applications offer delta-capable DataSources. To identify the new data (or changes to the existing data from history) from the historical data, the two sets of data are distinguished using a process called *initialization*, which sets a point of reference for the historical data and also gives the option to load this historical data to SAP BW. To use the delta capability of the DataSource, this process of initialization (❹ of Figure 8.3) must be carried out. Any new data generated after an initialization is identified as *delta data*. Next we discuss the steps involved in this process.

Filling Setup Tables

To move historical data from an SAP ERP system to an SAP BW system, you must fill up the setup tables (i.e., copy the historical data based on the selection condition from the application tables, and replicate it in the setup tables) in the SAP ERP system (❸ of Figure 8.3). The data in the setup tables is read either during the initialization process or during the full update mode. The setup tables are filled for the entire application component, not for individual DataSources; you use selection conditions to filter the relevant data from underlying application tables.

Executing an InfoPackage with the INITIALIZE WITH DATA TRANSFER option reads the data from the setup table and passes it to data targets ❻ in SAP BW after applying transformations ❺. The setup table is also used to extract the data in full update mode.

Deleting Data from Setup Tables

After initialization is completed successfully, you no longer need the data in the setup table, so it can be deleted using Transaction LBWG. Depending on the volume of data in the underlying tables and the selection criteria entered while filling up the setup table, the time it takes to complete this activity varies.

When the setup tables for an application are being filled, it's possible for transactions occurring in SAP ERP to change the transaction data, which could cause an inconsistency between the data in SAP ERP and the data in SAP BW. To avoid this situation, it's best to lock transactions that can interfere with the data being extracted in a setup table while the setup tables are being filled.

8.2.2 Delta Loads

After successful initialization, delta records get captured and passed to an area known as the delta queue, which stores records that are ready to be extracted by SAP BW after the InfoPackage is executed in delta mode (❽ of Figure 8.3). There are three different update methods for processing this data (❼, ❽, and ❾):

▶ **Unserialized V3**

This method stores posted document data in an update table using the *V3 collective run,* which happens before the data is written to the delta queue. Another V3 collective run then reads the data from the update table without considering the sequence and transfers the data to the delta queue ❽. Because this method doesn't retain the sequence in which records were generated, you shouldn't load data with this update type directly into a DataStore Object (DSO). This is used when serialization of data isn't required.

V3 Collective Run

The *V3 collective run* or the *V3 update* is the periodic job that transfers delta information to the delta queue.

▶ **Direct delta**

In this update method, every time a document in the SAP ERP system is created, changed, or deleted, the change is directly written to the delta queue. The direct delta method assigns a high priority to updates and is generally used only for the most critical ones. SAP recommends using this method when the maximum number of document changes (creation, modification, or deletion) is less than 10,000 per day for the application.

▶ **Queued delta**

This method uses the extraction queue to accumulate the posted document data. A collective run is required to read the data from the extraction queue and transfer it to the delta queue. Unlike the unserialized V3 method, this method guarantees the sequence of records because the order in which the changes are made in the SAP ERP system is preserved in the extraction queue. This method can be used when the number of documents posted is large, and serialization is also required.

8.2.3 Data Extraction

Start the Logistics Cockpit using Transaction LBWE. As shown in ❶ of Figure 8.4, all of the logistics applications available in the SAP ERP system are listed here. Each application is identified with a unique number; for example, 02 for Purchasing, 03 for Inventory Controlling, and so on.

SAP delivers an extraction structure for each DataSource. If SAP ERP has an active logistics information system (LIS), you can use additional fields from the LIS communication structure in the extraction structure of the DataSource by clicking on the MAINTENANCE link (❷ of Figure 8.4) of the DataSource.

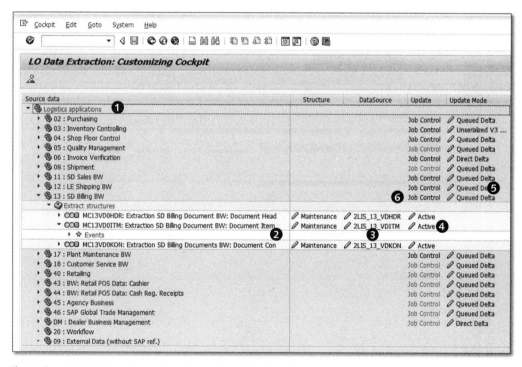

Figure 8.4 Logistics Data Extraction: Customizing the Cockpit

You can customize a DataSource by clicking on its technical name (❸ of Figure 8.4). Customization options include selecting fields, hiding fields, configuring for inversion, and allowing fields to be used in SAP exits (e.g., for calculation) (Figure 8.4). This is discussed in more detail in Section 8.3.2.

You activate a DataSource by clicking on the INACTIVE link shown in ❹ of Figure 8.4. (Incidentally, our system has all the DataSources in ACTIVE status, so it's shown in ACTIVE status instead of INACTIVE). By setting this to ACTIVE, the data is written into extraction structures online and also in setup or restructure tables. Only active state DataSources can be used for filling up a setup table or capturing deltas.

You set the update mode for the application by clicking on the UPDATE MODE (QUEUED DELTA, in our example) as shown in ❺ of Figure 8.4. Depending on the UPDATE MODE set, you may need to schedule the job for application by clicking on JOB CONTROL ❻. This moves the delta records from the update table/extraction queue to the delta queue. (The direct delta update method doesn't require this job.) When the InfoPackage with delta update mode is executed from SAP BW for this DataSource, the delta records available in the delta queue are passed to SAP BW.

These steps complete the configuration for this screen. When you activate Data-Source 2LIS_13_VDITM and successfully complete the initialization, the system starts writing all creations/modifications/deletions of billing documents into the extraction queue. When the collective run job is executed, all of the records from the extraction queue are moved to the delta queue. In general, the collective run job is scheduled to move data regularly. In our example, the job is scheduled with the IMMEDIATE option. After the maintenance of the DataSource with the required update mode in Transaction LBWE is completed, the data starts to flow into the delta queue via various paths corresponding to the mode selected.

8.3   Using Generic DataSources for Extraction

Having SAP ERP (and other SAP systems such as SAP CRM, SAP SCM, etc.) as a source system is the best way to gain the most from Business Content, which offers an extremely large number of DataSources that support a wide range of analysis requirements. For those requirements that aren't met by using Business Content, you can create a DataSource based on your own logic. These custom DataSources are called *generic DataSources*.

A generic DataSource must be created when Business Content doesn't deliver an extractor that can extract the required data to SAP BW (e.g., if a customer created his own tables and stored the data in them using his own application). The source system used here is SAP ERP, but the process of creating a generic DataSource is similar for all SAP source systems.

Start Transaction RSO2 in SAP ERP to open up the MAINTAIN GENERIC DATA-SOURCES screen shown in Figure 8.5.

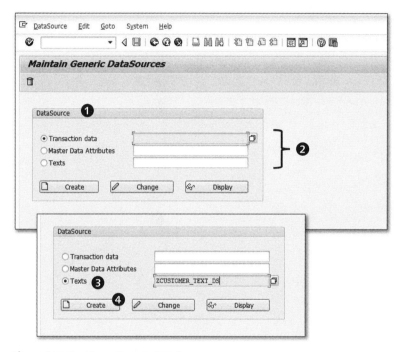

Figure 8.5 Creating a Generic DataSource

This transaction allows you to create the following three types of DataSources ❶ and ❷:

▶ TRANSACTION DATA
This type of DataSource is used for transaction data. The extracted data is loaded to a DSO or an InfoCube in SAP BW.

▶ MASTER DATA ATTRIBUTES
This type of DataSource is used for master data attributes. The extracted data is loaded to an InfoObject (configured with master data attributes in SAP BW).

▶ TEXTS

This type of DataSource is used for master data in a textual format (as opposed to master data attributes), such as a customer name or the description of a material code. Extracted data is loaded to InfoObjects (configured with master data text in SAP BW).

In Chapter 7, we created a master data and transaction DataSource. This time, we'll select a TEXT DataSource (❸ of Figure 8.5). Enter the technical name of the DataSource, and click on the CREATE button ❹. This action opens the screen shown in Figure 8.6.

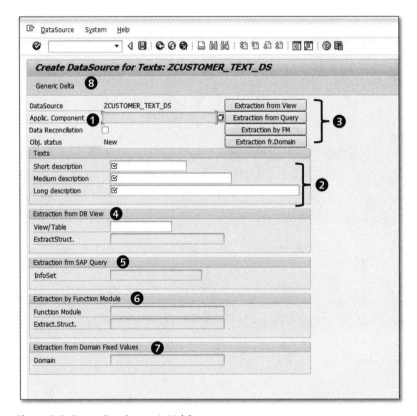

Figure 8.6 Create DataSource Initial Screen

Next, we explain the settings for a generic DataSource, the steps required to actually create the DataSource, how to make the DataSource delta-capable, and finally, how to test the DataSource.

8.3.1   Settings for Generic DataSources

We'll now explain the different parts of the screen shown in Figure 8.6.

Applic. Component Field

Just as in SAP BW, a DataSource is attached to an application component in SAP ERP. SAP delivers a standard structure of application components, which is known as the application component hierarchy. You can add more nodes to the delivered application component hierarchy or create your DataSource under a standard node. The application component hierarchy can be seen by clicking on the dropdown icon on the extreme right, as shown in ❶ of Figure 8.6.

Data Reconciliation Field

SAP offers a number of standard DataSources in Business Content that help reconcile the data in an SAP BW data target with the live data available in the SAP ERP system. DataSources configured with the DATA RECONCILIATION setting pass the data to a VirtualProvider in SAP BW, and a MultiProvider is created on the original data target and VirtualProvider. A query is created on the MultiProvider to compare key figures from the original data target and the virtual InfoCube. Generic DataSources can also be used for this kind of scenario.

Texts Area

A DataSource is described using text. You can attach a short, medium, and/or long description to a DataSource (❷ of Figure 8.6).

Extraction Options

As shown in ❸ of Figure 8.6, there are four different options available to create a DataSource, which you select based on how your data is stored:

▶ EXTRACTION FROM VIEW
  If data is stored in a single table or set of tables that are related via a common key, you can select this option. Then enter the details in the EXTRACTION FROM DB VIEW area ❹. (This option is selected by default.)

▶ EXTRACTION FROM QUERY
  SAP queries allow users to define and execute custom evaluations of data in the

SAP system; they are easy to use and don't require knowledge of ABAP coding. When the data required is available upon execution of an SAP query, you can create a DataSource based on this query. Selecting this option allows you to enter the details of the SAP query name in the EXTRACTION FROM SAP QUERY area ❺.

▶ EXTRACTION BY FM
Use this method when data to be extracted is available in multiple tables, and the relationship between them is complex. ABAP programming knowledge is required because this method requires the creation of a function module. Selecting this option allows you to enter the details of a function module in the EXTRACTION BY FUNCTION MODULE area ❻.

A function module has only a few input parameters (all optional) and returns output to the calling program or object. The sample function module delivered by SAP, `RSAX_BIW_GET_DATA_SIMPLE`, will give you an idea about what import and export parameters are required, as well as some hints about how logic should be written. A function module can be developed using Transaction SE37.

▶ EXTRACTION FR. DOMAIN
This option is only available when you're creating a text DataSource. Domains store a fixed set of values for text; for example, to record someone's marital status, you can use a domain that stores fixed values:

▶ M: Married

▶ U: Unmarried

▶ W: Widower

▶ D: Divorcee

You create a DataSource based on a domain to load master data text into an InfoObject in SAP BW. Selecting this option allows you to enter the details of the domain in the EXTRACTION FROM DOMAIN FIXED VALUES area ❼.

Generic Delta Button

By default, generic DataSources aren't delta-capable; they always provide a full data set based on selection criteria. To change this, click on the GENERIC DELTA button shown in ❽ of Figure 8.6. We describe more about this button in Section 8.3.3.

8.3.2   Creating Generic DataSources

Now that we've reviewed the screen details, let's create a generic text DataSource based on table ZCUST_TEXT in SAP ERP. Select the appropriate application component from the dropdown list; in our example, we select SAP-R/3-IO, as shown in ❶ of Figure 8.7.

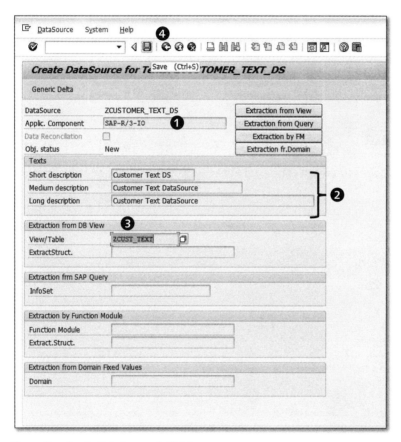

Figure 8.7 Create DataSource: Initial Screen

Enter the short, medium, and long text in the text boxes ❷. Enter "ZCUST_TEXT" in the VIEW/TABLE text box ❸. The extraction structure is created by the system by reading the definition of the table entered. Now click on SAVE ❹. The resulting screen is shown in Figure 8.8.

The DataSource can be customized based on the settings shown next.

ExtractStruct. Field

The extraction structure of the DataSource is created and given a unique name by the SAP ERP system, as shown in ❶ of Figure 8.8. The extraction structure contains fields included in the definition of the DataSource.

Direct Access Field

A DataSource with direct access can be used in configuring a VirtualProvider. By default, a generic DataSource is configured for direct access. Values 1 and 2 in the Direct Access field allow direct access; value D in this field doesn't allow direct access. For our example scenario, no change is required (❷ of Figure 8.8).

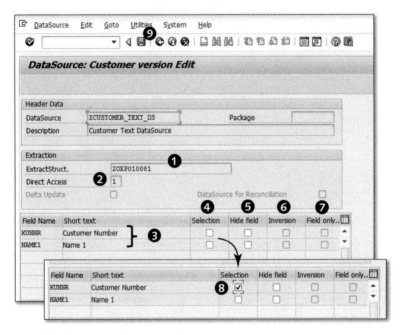

Figure 8.8 Configuring DataSource Fields

Customizing DataSource Fields

Fields included in the DataSource definition of table ZCUST_TEXT are shown in ❸ of KUNNR (Customer Number 1) and NAME1 (Name 1). Four different settings are available for each field:

▶ SELECTION ❹

Checking this checkbox allows you to enter selection values for this field in the InfoPackage created for this DataSource in SAP BW. For our example scenario, we flag this for the KUNNR field, as shown in ❽ of Figure 8.8.

▶ HIDE FIELD ❺

If you don't want to pass a specific field value to SAP BW, you can select this indicator.

▶ INVERSION ❻

The INVERSION setting is only valid for transaction DataSources and is applicable to fields that are numeric in nature and that allow reverse postings in the SAP ERP application.

▶ FIELD ONLY KNOWN IN CUSTOMER EXIT ❼

This setting is used specifically when you include additional fields in the already-available DataSource. Using this setting, you can define whether the value of that specific field should be passed on to SAP BW or should just be available in the customer exit.

After these settings are configured, click on SAVE ❾. Click on the BACK icon twice, which brings you back to the main screen for DataSource creation (refer to Figure 8.5).

The creation of a generic DataSource is now complete. The created DataSource is now available in the application component hierarchy node SAP-R/3-IO, as shown in Figure 8.9.

You can access the generic DataSource ZCUSTOMER_TEXT_DS with Transaction RSA6. To use this DataSource in SAP BW, you must replicate it. The process of replication can be started from SAP BW, as explained next.

1. Start Transaction RSA1.

2. From MODELING, select SOURCE SYSTEMS.

3. From the right panel, select the SAP ERP system in which the DataSource has been created.

4. Using the context menu, select DISPLAY DATASOURCE TREE. The application component hierarchy tree is displayed.

5. Select the application component under which you've created the DataSource in the SAP ERP system (e.g., SAP-R/3-IO).

6. Use the context menu to select REPLICATE DATASOURCE.

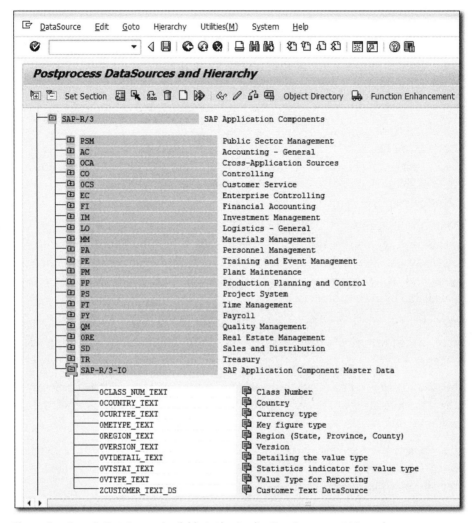

Figure 8.9 Generic DataSource Available in the Application Component Hierarchy

8.3.3 Making Generic DataSources Delta-Capable

As mentioned earlier, a generic DataSource doesn't offer delta capability. Every time you extract the data using a generic DataSource, it extracts the full set of data, which may not be practical when the data volume is large. Use Transaction RSO2 to create a generic DataSource. Provide the DataSource name and click on the CRE-ATE button. The resulting screen is shown in Figure 8.10. Generic DataSources can be converted into delta-capable DataSources using the GENERIC DELTA button (❷ of Figure 8.10).

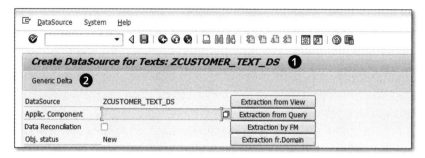

Figure 8.10 Create DataSource: Initial Screen

When you click on the GENERIC DELTA button, a pop-up box appears, as shown in Figure 8.11.

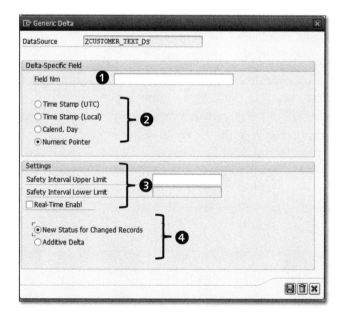

Figure 8.11 Settings Available for Creating Delta-Capable Generic DataSources

Next, we divide our discussion of the fields on the screen based on the screen's two main areas: DELTA-SPECIFIC FIELD and SETTINGS.

Delta-Specific Field Area

Making a delta-capable DataSource requires a delta-relevant field that supports delta identification and enables the delta capability. Enter the name of that field in FIELD NM shown in ❶ of Figure 8.11. The system uses four different types of fields to recognize delta records ❷: TIME STAMP (UTC), TIME STAMP (LOCAL), CALEND. DAY, and NUMERIC POINTER. The assumption regarding the generic delta Data-Source is that the value of the field declared here increases monotonically over time. When a delta-relevant field (e.g., a timestamp) exists in the extraction structure, the system determines the data volume transferred in the delta mode by comparing the maximum value transferred with the last load to the amount of data that has entered the system after the maximum value of the last load. Only those records that have a higher value are identified as delta records.

Settings Area

In ❸ of Figure 8.11, you can see the fields for setting a safety interval. The purpose of a safety interval is to make the system extract records (with the next extraction) that appear during the extraction process but aren't extracted (perhaps because they haven't been saved at the time of extraction).

SAFETY INTERVAL LOWER LIMIT defines the safety pointer value for the lower limit. For example, assume that the delta-relevant field is a numeric pointer whose last-read numeric pointer was 1000. Also assume that when the next delta extraction begins, the current numeric pointer is 1100. If the safety interval for the lower limit is set to 10, the selection interval is set by the system for delta, 990 to 1100 (subtracting the safety interval value of 10 from the lower limit of 1000 makes the lower value of the selection interval 990). The selection interval is used as a filter to extract the records using the DataSource. When the extraction is successfully completed, the pointer is set to 1100.

> **Note**
>
> Due to the overlapping selection interval, setting this safety interval results in duplicate records in the subsequent delta extraction. As such, you should not load data extracted from this DataSource directly into an InfoCube; you must load the data to a DSO and then to an InfoCube.

SAFETY INTERVAL UPPER LIMIT defines the safety pointer value for the upper limit. Let's now assume that the delta-relevant field is a numeric pointer whose last-read numeric pointer was 1000. Also assume that when the next delta extraction begins, the current numeric pointer is 1100. If the safety interval for the upper limit is set to 10, the selection interval set by the system for delta is 1000 to 1090 (subtracting the safety interval value of 10 from the upper limit of 1100 makes the upper value 1090). The selection interval is used as a filter to extract the records using the DataSource. When the extraction is successfully completed, the pointer is set to 1090.

> **Note**
>
> Setting this safety interval doesn't result in duplicate records in the subsequent delta because there's no overlapping in the selection interval. You can directly load the data extracted by this DataSource into an InfoCube.

There are two remaining fields in the SETTINGS area (❹ of Figure 8.11):

▶ NEW STATUS FOR CHANGED RECORDS
A DataSource with this setting indicates that a record to be loaded returns the latest value for all characteristics and key figures. The data from this type of DataSource can be loaded to a DSO and InfoObject with master data in SAP BW.

▶ ADDITIVE DELTA
The DataSource with this setting indicates that records to be loaded only return changes to key figures that can be aggregated. The data from this type of DataSource can be loaded to a DSO and InfoCube in SAP BW.

8.3.4 Testing DataSources Using the Extractor Checker

After a DataSource is created in the source system, you may want to check its accuracy. For this, SAP has provided a tool called the Extractor Checker. Start Transaction RSA3 in SAP ERP to bring up the EXTRACTOR CHECKER S-API screen shown in Figure 8.12.

Enter the name of the DataSource you want to test in the DATASOURCE field, as shown in ❶ of Figure 8.12. You have two options ❷ for the execution mode:

▶ DEBUG MODE
Helps in starting the debugger and takes you through step-by-step execution of the underlying DataSource program.

► Aᴜᴛʜ. Tʀᴀᴄᴇ

Used for tracing authorization while accessing various tables and objects used by the underlying DataSource program.

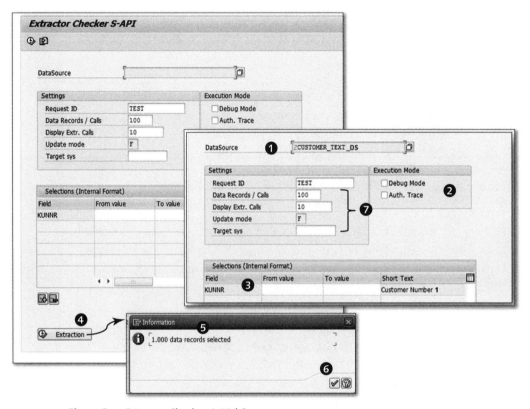

Figure 8.12 Extractor Checker: Initial Screen

The selection fields flagged when you created the DataSource are also available here. KUNNR is available for selection ❸.

You can restrict the number of records to be extracted by configuring the Dᴀᴛᴀ Rᴇᴄᴏʀᴅs / Cᴀʟʟs and Dɪsᴘʟᴀʏ Exᴛʀ. Cᴀʟʟs parameters. By default, 1000 records are extracted.

Click on the Exᴛʀᴀᴄᴛɪᴏɴ button ❹ to simulate the execution of the DataSource. The system extracts the records and displays them in the pop-up box that appears with details on the number of records extracted ❺. Now click on the Cᴏɴᴛɪɴᴜᴇ icon, which results in the screen shown in Figure 8.13.

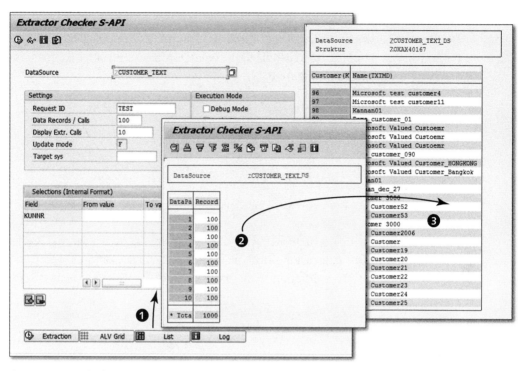

Figure 8.13 Result of Extractor Checker

The DataSource has extracted the records based on the selection criteria. If you want to see the records extracted, click on the LIST (OR ALV GRID) button ❶. The screen shown next ❷ provides the number of extracted records for each data package. Our example table, ZCUST_TEXT, on which the DataSource is defined, has extracted 1000 records in 10 data packages. Double-click on any of the data packages to view the details of the extracted records ❸.

8.4   Data Extraction from Non-SAP Systems

The open architecture of SAP BW gives it the flexibility to extract data from a large variety of sources, including relational database management systems (RDBMSs), which are a very popular way of storing business application data. To extract data from an RDBMS, SAP BW offers two different mechanisms: DB Connect and UD Connect.

8.4.1 DB Connect

DB Connect allows the extraction of data from a number of popular RDBMSs into the SAP BW system; the latest list of supported RDBMSs can be obtained from the SAP Service Marketplace (Figure 8.14).

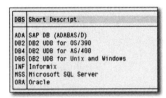

Figure 8.14 List of RDBMSs Supported by DB Connect

To extract data from an RDBMS using DB Connect, database-shared libraries (DBSL) of the source database must be installed on each application server in the SAP BW landscape. Two different scenarios of this are illustrated in Figure 8.15.

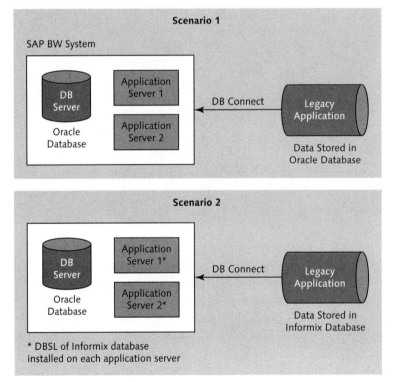

Figure 8.15 DB Connect Overview

In the first scenario, both source application data and SAP BW data are stored on an Oracle RDBMS; as such, there is no need to install a DBSL on the SAP BW system's application server. In the second scenario, the source application data is stored using an Informix RDBMS, but the SAP BW server stores data in an Oracle RDBMS. In this case, Informix's DBSLmust be installed on the SAP BW application server.

You also require a database-specific DB client with the database manufacturer in both scenarios. Execute the steps as follows:

1. Create a source system for the external database using DB Connect.
2. Create a DB Connect source system from the SOURCE SYSTEM section of MOD-ELING in the Data Warehousing Workbench. Different kinds of RDBMSs expect various parameters for source system connections; SAP Notes are available for connecting to each supported RDBMS (see *http://service.sap.com/notes*).
3. Create a DataSource by selecting a view or table from the source RDBMS.
4. Create a transformation between the DataSource and the data target.
5. Create a data transfer process (DTP) between the DataSource and the data target.
6. Create an InfoPackage for the DataSource (connected to the DB Connect source system).
7. Execute the InfoPackage.
8. Execute the DTP.

These steps load the data into the SAP BW data target, which can be a master data InfoObject, DSO, or InfoCube.

8.4.2   UD Connect

UD Connect allows the extraction of data stored in multidimensional structures (such as those created by Hyperion or Cognos). It also allows data extraction from RDBMSs. The prerequisite for using UD Connect is the installation of the J2EE engine in the SAP BW system. The steps for extracting data using UD Connect are the same as those of DB Connect.

8.5   Introduction to Operational Data Provisioning/ Operational Delta Queue

SAP BW 7.4 allows you to extract data from both SAP and non-SAP source systems. With SAP BW 7.4, you can connect SAP systems using the Operational Data Provisioning (ODP) framework mentioned previously. The ODP framework uses the Provider/Subscriber method. In SAP BW, you can create a source system with the type ODP. SAP delivers DataSources that are capable of using this method of extraction.

The unique features of this method are the following:

▶ Unified configuration and monitoring for providers and subscribers covering different types

▶ Highly compressed data in the Operational Delta Queue (ODQ)

▶ Optional loading into a Persistent Staging Area (PSA)

▶ Improved loading performance

▶ Scheduled or real-time data acquisition

▶ Capability to extract once and deploy to multiple targets

▶ Timestamp-based recovery mechanism

▶ Retention period for ODQ

To extract data using the ODP framework, you need to first configure the SAP source system in SAP BW by using one of the appropriate source system types: ODP-BW, ODP-SAP (extractor), ODP-SLT queue, and so on. You also need to have a DataSource from this source system, which you can accomplish in one of two ways:

▶ Replicate the DataSource from a connected source system to SAP BW.

▶ Create the DataSource manually.

In this section, we use the second method and show the step-by-step creation of a DataSource from the ODP source system. Here we assume that an ODP-SAP (extractor) source system is already created in SAP BW. We've created and named our source system ODPECC. Before following the steps described in the next section, make sure your Basis administrator has created this source system.

8.5.1 Creating a DataSource Using the ODP Source System

To create the DataSource, open the Data Warehousing Workbench using Transaction RSA1. Select DataSources under Modeling as shown in ❶ of Figure 8.16. On the right panel, you can view the list of DataSources under BW Application Component. Select the ODPECC type for the source system by clicking on ⊠. ❷. Select the BW Application Component ZBW_APP_COMP ❸. Use the context menu to select Create DataSource ❹. This opens the Create DataSource in ODP source system ODPECC pop-up box ❺.

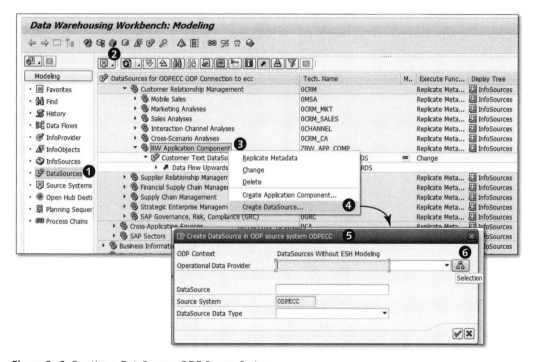

Figure 8.16 Creating a DataSource: ODP Source System

Click on 🔣 (❻ of Figure 8.16) to open another pop-up screen as shown in ❶ of Figure 8.17. This displays the application component hierarchy ❷ from the selected source system. Expand the SAP node and go to the Sales and Distribution (SD) node. Under this node, select the SAP standard DataSource Sales Document Item Data (2LIS_11_VAITM) ❸. For each DataSource, the Semantics column displays a one-character value. For example, in the Semantics column for

DataSource 2LIS_11_VAITM, F stands for TRANSACTION DATA/FACTS. The details of all the semantic values are given here:

- ▸ F: TRANSACTION DATA/FACTS
- ▸ P: MASTER DATA/ATTRIBUTES
- ▸ Q: TIME DEPENDENT MASTER DATA/ATTRIBUTES
- ▸ T: TEXT
- ▸ H: HIERARCHY

Click on the CONTINUE button ❹, which brings you back to the CREATE DATA-SOURCE IN ODP SOURCE SYSTEM ODPECC screen ❺. The required details are filled in by the system. Click on CONTINUE ❻.

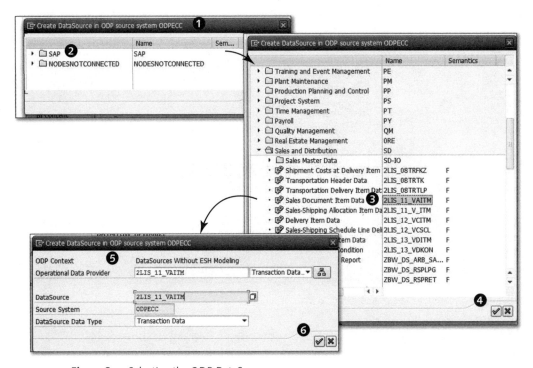

Figure 8.17 Selecting the ODP DataSource

The CHANGE DATASOURCE screen appears as shown in ❶ of Figure 8.18. This screen is similar to the CREATE DATASOURCE screen explained in Chapter 7, Section 7.2.2.

In this section, we explain what's new for an ODP source system and the minimum configuration required to create DataSources of this type.

First, provide the short, medium, and long descriptions ❹ for the DataSource in the GENERAL PROPERTIES tab. One noticeable difference from the earlier CREATE DATASOURCE screen is the ADAPTER field in the EXTRACTION tab ❻. Select EXTRACTION FROM SAP SYSTEM BY OPERATIONAL DATA PROVISIONING. There is no need to change other settings.

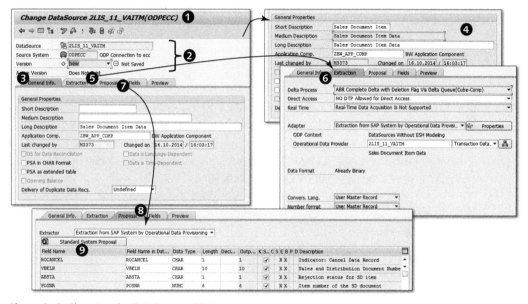

Figure 8.18 Changing the DataSource: ODP

Next, click on the FIELDS tab to open the next screen shown in Figure 8.19.

8.5.2 Activating the DataSource

The fields of DataSource 2LIS_11_VAITM are displayed ❶ and ❷. The various settings here have already been explained in Section 8.3.2. Click on the ACTIVATE icon (❸ of Figure 8.19) to activate this DataSource. This changes the DataSource VERSION from NEW to ACTIVE ❹. You can now use this DataSource to develop additional data flows.

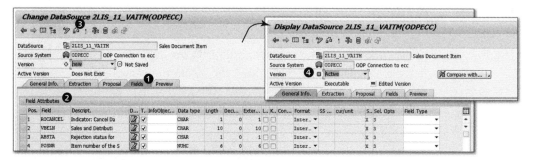

Figure 8.19 Activating the ODP DataSource

8.5.3 Source Data

One of the benefits of using an ODP DataSource is that you can skip loading the source data in a PSA because loading data into a PSA is optional. Here, you don't need to create an InfoPackage; you can directly create a DTP. As shown in ❶ and ❷ of Figure 8.20, DataSource 2LIS_11_VAITM is available under BW APPLICATION COMPONENT ZBW_APP_COMP. Using the context menu on DataSource 2LIS_11_VAITM, select CREATE DATA TRANSFER PROCESS.

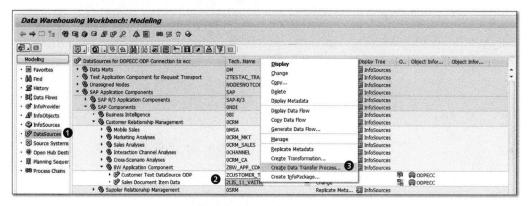

Figure 8.20 Creating a DTP on the ODP DataSource

You'll see the CREATE DATA TRANSFER PROCESS screen as shown in ❶ of Figure 8.21. The SOURCE OF DTP ❸ is already selected as DATASOURCE 2LIS_11_VAITM from the ODPECC source system because we started creating the DTP from there. The target selected here is DATASTORE OBJECT ZSD_ORD ❷. The design of this standard DSO is given in Appendix B. Click on CONTINUE ❹. This opens the GENERATE TRANSFORMATION pop-up box ❺. The message states that there is no transformation available between DataSource 2LIS_11_VAITM (from the ODPECC source system) and DSO ZSD_ORD. The system also asks whether to create a default transformation. Click on YES ❻ to generate a default transformation.

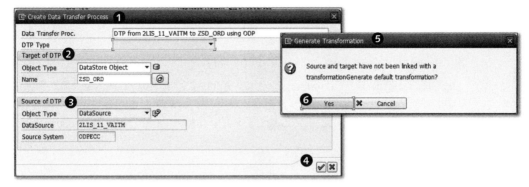

Figure 8.21 Creating a DTP/Transformation on an ODP DataSource

Next, the CHANGE DATA TRANSFER PROCESS screen appears as shown in ❶ of Figure 8.22. You need to initialize the delta for this DataSource, which helps to extract only delta records from the source system. Because this DataSource is delta enabled, it offers the DELTA selection in the EXTRACTION MODE field ❹.

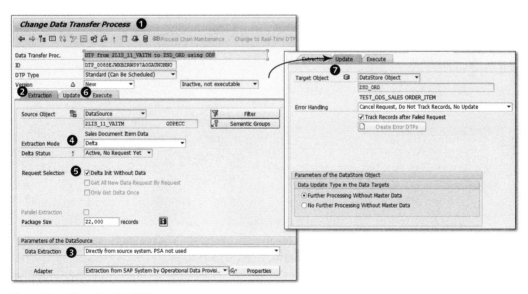

Figure 8.22 Changing the DTP

We aren't interested in extracting the historical records and want to start the delta from this point in time, so we set the DELTA INIT WITHOUT DATA flag ❺. Under the PARAMETERS OF THE DATASOURCE area ❸, the DIRECTLY FROM SOURCE SYSTEM, PSA NOT USED option is selected in the DATA EXTRACTION field. Click on the UPDATE tab ❻. The TARGET OBJECT of the DTP is shown as DATASTORE OBJECT ZSD_ORD ❼.

8.5.4 Activating and Executing the DTP

Now activate the DTP by clicking on the ACTIVATE icon as shown in ❸ of Figure 8.23. This changes the VERSION of the DTP to ACTIVE ❹. Now you can see the full data flow with the DataSource, target DSO, transformation, and DTP (❺ and ❻).

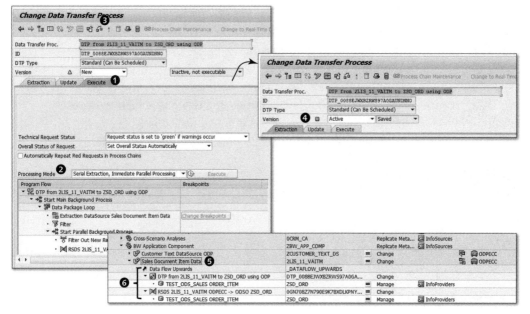

Figure 8.23 DTP Activated

After the DTP is activated, you need to execute it. This doesn't extract any data from the source system because you selected DELTA INIT WITHOUT DATA earlier in the process (❺ of Figure 8.22). However, this action does activate the delta queue on the source system side. Start Transaction ODQMON in the source system to open the MONITOR DELTA QUEUES screen, as shown in ❶ of Figure 8.24. You can monitor the delta queue using different filters such as PROVIDER, SUBSCRIBER, SUBSCRIBER

TYPE, QUEUE, REQUEST SELECT., ❷ and so on. This is the default view, and two different queues are displayed. One of them is 2LIS_11_VAITM ❸, which became active when you executed the DTP.

After the queue is activated, you can subsequently execute the DTP in delta mode, which only extracts newly created and modified records from the source system.

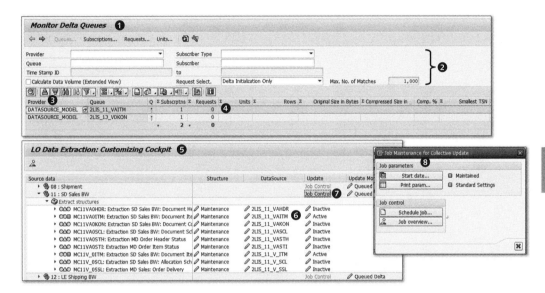

Figure 8.24 Operational Delta Queue and the LO Cockpit

> **Note**
>
> To use delta mode, follow these steps:
>
> 1. On the source system side, execute JOB CONTROL (see ❻, ❼, and ❽ of Figure 8.24).
> 2. On the SAP BW side, execute the DTP in delta mode.

8.5.5 Operational Delta Queue

ODQ is an offering with ODP that allows a common monitor for multiple subscribers to view extractions. The current delta queue mechanism (Transaction RAS7) is also available. ODQ offers the following benefits over the previous mechanism:

▶ ODQ displays more information such as number of units, records, size, compression factor, and so on.

▶ Data is stored in a compressed format.

▶ One queue is used for many SAP BW subscribers.

▶ A retention period can be maintained.

▶ There's no need to remove the old mechanism because ODQ is an additional mechanism.

▶ Both mechanisms can be used simultaneously.

As shown in ❶ of Figure 8.25, you can view data in the ODQ by queue, subscriber, request, and unit. Depending on the data, the compression ratio will vary; here, the compression ratio is 59.3% ❸. Finally, you can view the data available on the ODQ ❹.

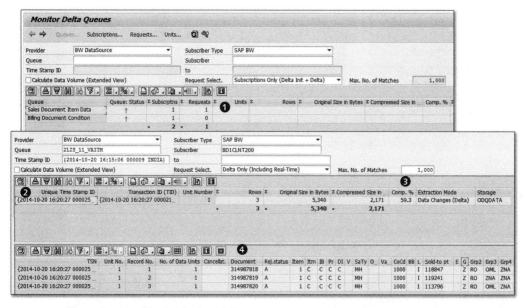

Figure 8.25 Looking Inside the ODQ

ODP/ODQ are new ways of extracting from SAP that offer a number of benefits, such as reducing the footprint (avoiding PSA), controlling the retention period, and so on.

8.6   SAP LT Replication Server for SAP BW

The introduction of SAP Landscape Transformation Replication Server (SLT) makes it possible to extract data from SAP and non-SAP sources in real time. The trigger-based replication functionality helps in achieving this. SLT offers two interfaces for transferring data:

▶ **Operational Data Provisioning (ODP)**
  Using this interface, you can transfer the data from SAP systems into SAP BW. DataSources based on simple tables/views containing minimal extractor logic are supported. The trigger-based mechanism moves the data to the ODQ, which resides on the SLT server. SAP BW can subscribe to this ODQ. Using DTPs or InfoPackages, you extract data from the ODQ. As explained in the previous section, a PSA is optional while using the ODP framework.

▶ **Web Service**
  Using this interface, you can transfer data from SAP as well as non-SAP systems into SAP BW. Again, DataSources based on simple tables/views containing minimal extractor logic are supported. The trigger-based mechanism moves the data to the ODQ, which resides on the SLT server. In this case, SLT replicates data in a Web Service DataSource that resides in SAP BW. From SAP BW, you use the DTP to move the data to the required data target.

An overview of SLT is depicted in Figure 8.26.

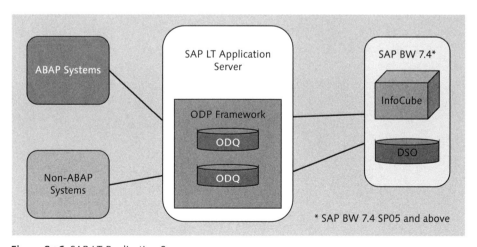

Figure 8.26 SAP LT Replication Server

8.7 Summary

In this chapter, we described the details of data extraction from SAP source systems, specifically focusing on the Logistics Cockpit and using generic DataSources. We also included a brief discussion of data extraction from non-SAP systems, introducing DB Connect and UD Connect. We concluded the chapter by exploring ODP/ODQ and SLT.

In the next chapter, we'll describe the BEx Query Designer and its functionalities.

Reporting and analysis is an integral part of a BI solution. In this chapter, we discuss the BEx Query Designer, which is used to create queries for reporting and analysis in SAP BW.

9 Creating Queries Using BEx Query Designer

Companies employ BI solutions to have visibility and control across their entities, functions, and business processes by providing decision makers with correct information in the right format. In the previous chapters of this book, you've learned about the data warehousing capabilities of SAP BW. We now explain the process of transforming data into information by presenting the data in reports that generate useful insights and help users make informed decision at the right time.

Making an informed decision often involves analysis of data from multiple perspectives and in an easily understandable format. SAP BW offers a flexible set of tools that can be used to create queries and reports and to present data to users along with extensive analysis options. These tools collectively form the Business Explorer (BEx) component of SAP BW. After the queries are created using *BEx Query Designer*, reporting and analysis can be performed using either Microsoft Excel (*BEx Analyzer*) or a web browser (*BEx Web Application Designer*). In this chapter, we will focus specifically on BEx Query Designer; for information about BEx Analyzer and BEx Web Application Designer, see Chapter 10 and Chapter 11, respectively.

Our example company, ABCD Corp., wants to support its sales process with reporting and analysis from SAP BW. To make the right decision, the company needs to find answers to the following questions (among others):

- What products are selling in different sales organizations?
- Which product lines or specific products are selling the most or the fewest?
- How do ABCD Corp.'s current year sales compare to the previous year?
- What are the top 10 best-selling products?

Also, the auditors of ABCD Corp. require the solution to provide traceability to the specific billing documents for a customer and, when necessary, to analyze instances of variances. This sales document-level investigation needs to be addressed in SAP BW rather than going into the transactional system for the detailed information, and it can be done using the BEx toolset.

In this chapter, we explain how to create queries in SAP BW using BEx Query Designer, as well as the different functions that can be built on a query for effective analysis. We take you through the procedure to define filters and variables in the query, and also explain the use of restricted and calculated key figures. Additional analysis features such as exceptions and conditions are illustrated with examples, followed by a detailed explanation of the report-to-report interface. Throughout the chapter, we'll explain these features by referring to the just mentioned requirements for ABCD Corp.

However, before we dive into a specific discussion of BEx Query Designer, let's spend a few minutes understanding the overall BEx toolset.

9.1 BEx Tools Landscape

As mentioned earlier, BEx is a set of tools that can be used to query, report, and analyze data available through different SAP BW InfoProviders. Figure 9.1 shows how the BEx component is structured.

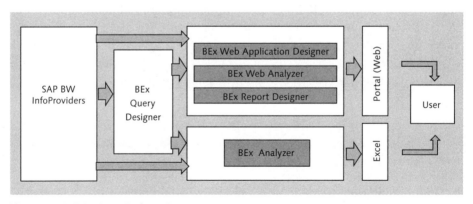

Figure 9.1 SAP Business Explorer Component

In SAP BW, data is made available for reporting through InfoProviders. An Info-Provider can store data physically (e.g., standard InfoCubes, real-time InfoCubes, master data InfoObjects, and DataStore Objects [DSOs] all store data physically) or can be a logical InfoProvider, which doesn't store any data physically (e.g., virtual InfoProviders, MultiProviders, CompositeProviders, InfoSets, and aggregation levels).

The BEx tool that is used to create queries on InfoProviders is *BEx Query Designer*. This is a user-friendly development tool that enables you to create queries using simple drag-and-drop functionality on characteristics and key figures from InfoProviders. BEx Query Designer also allows you to create different reusable query elements, which can be used across different queries.

Queries created in BEx Query Designer are used to present data to users for reporting and analysis through various tools (see Figure 9.1). The BEx tools that are used for reporting and analysis are described here:

▶ **BEx Analyzer**
Using BEx Analyzer, you can create an Excel-based reporting and analysis application based on one or multiple queries built in BEx Query Designer. Also, it supports ad hoc analysis directly on the InfoProvider. The application created using BEx Analyzer is saved as a workbook, which can be made available to multiple users.

▶ **BEx Web Analyzer**
BEx Web Analyzer is a powerful web-based application that can access data from a query built in BEx Query Designer or can even access data directly from InfoProviders for ad hoc analysis. Users can access BEx Web Analyzer through a portal or web browser.

▶ **BEx Web Application Designer**
BEx Web Application Designer is used to create web-based reporting and analysis applications. These applications are built using a variety of subcomponents called *web items*. This includes items to present data in different formats, such as tables and charts, or items to facilitate analysis of data such as filters, dropdowns, navigation blocks, and so on. Web applications created using BEx Web Application Designer are saved as web templates and are made available to users through a portal or web browser.

▶ **BEx Report Designer**
BEx Report Designer is a tool with features to generate formatted reports from SAP BW data. BEx Report Designer was removed from the SAP BW roadmap shortly after release 7.0, so we don't discuss it in this book.

The queries, reports, and web applications created using the BEx components from older versions of SAP BW (SAP BW 3.x and older) are executed on the ABAP stack of SAP BW. The BEx reports and applications created using SAP BW 7.x BEx components, however, use the Java stack of SAP BW when those reports and applications are run in the web environment.

> **Note**
>
> The BEx tools that were made available starting with release 7.0 contain additional features and are more advanced than the 3.x set of tools. In this book, we don't cover the 3.x versions, but focus on the 7.x versions.

9.2   Introduction to BEx Query Designer

Queries built on data provided by different InfoProviders enable structured analysis of data, and BEx Query Designer is the tool to create such queries in SAP BW. This tool has evolved into a user-friendly development tool, providing enriched features to support business analytical needs in different forms.

BEx Query Designer is a standalone application, so you don't need to log in to the SAP BW frontend applications. It can be launched directly from the START menu of your computer using the following path: START • PROGRAMS • BUSINESS EXPLORER • QUERY DESIGNER (❶ of Figure 9.2). Select the SAP BW system, and log in using the user ID and password ❷.

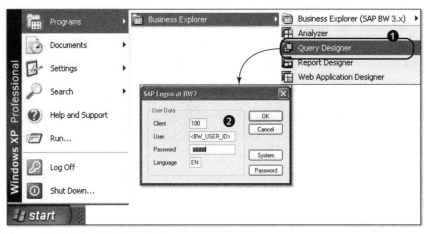

Figure 9.2 Starting BEx Query Designer

Now we'll explain the different components of BEx Query Designer and the menu functions.

9.2.1 BEx Query Designer Screen Layout

When you log in to BEx Query Designer, the default screen appears as shown in Figure 9.3.

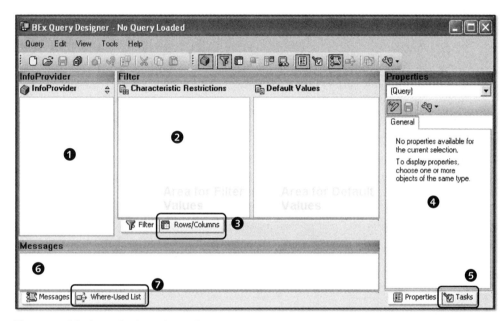

Figure 9.3 BEx Query Designer Screen Layout

The screen layout sections include INFOPROVIDER, MESSAGES, FILTER, and so on. These screen areas and their uses are explained next.

InfoProvider

A query has to be built on an InfoProvider. The InfoProvider definition upon which the query is built is displayed in the INFOPROVIDER area of BEx Query Designer (❶ of Figure 9.3). This becomes the base for the query because you can drag the necessary elements (characteristics, key figures, attributes, etc.) from the INFOPROVIDER area into the query definition.

Filter

If the query has to be restricted to certain characteristic values, then those filter restrictions are defined in the FILTER area of BEx Query Designer (❷ of Figure 9.3). The static filters are defined in the CHARACTERISTIC RESTRICTIONS sections. The default values for which the query should be first executed are defined in the DEFAULT VALUES area.

Rows/Columns

The layout of the query is defined on the ROWS/COLUMNS tab of BEx Query Designer (❸ of Figure 9.3). This screen area is displayed in Figure 9.4. The characteristics and key figures to be included as rows or columns in the report layout are specified in the ROWS and COLUMNS areas, respectively. If there are characteristics that you don't want to include in the default view of the query, but you want to make those fields available for drilldown if needed, such characteristics are added to the FREE CHARACTERISTICS area on the ROW/COLUMNS tab. The PREVIEW section provides a preview of the query structure and layout.

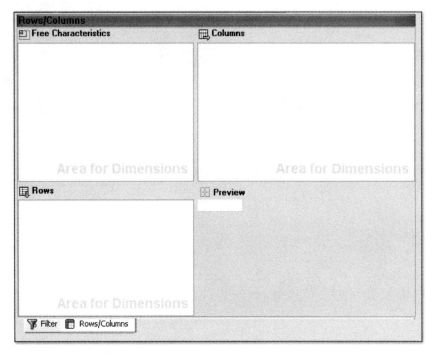

Figure 9.4 Rows/Columns Screen Areas

Properties

All components of the query (including the query itself) have their own sets of properties, descriptions, display settings, and so on, which determine the behavior of that element. The properties for the selected query element are visible in the PROPERTIES screen area of BEx Query Designer (refer to ❹ of Figure 9.3).

Tasks

For different components of a query, there are different tasks or actions that can be performed. These tasks vary based on the element that is selected. Different tasks related to the selected item are listed in the TASKS area, so you can find all relevant actions for an object listed under TASKS. In case of errors, the possible corrective actions and error help are also visible in the TASKS area (refer to ❺ of Figure 9.3).

Messages

Different messages, such as errors, warnings, or other information related to the query, are displayed in the MESSAGES area (refer to ❻ of Figure 9.3).

Where-Used List

A query or its reusable components can be used in multiple other objects such as workbooks, web templates, and so on. When you use the where-used list for the query or a reusable component, the list of all of the objects where the component or query is used is displayed in the WHERE-USED LIST area of BEx Query Designer (refer to ❼ of Figure 9.3).

9.2.2 BEx Query Designer Menu Bar

Having reviewed the basic screen sections, let's now look at the functions available under the BEx Query Designer menu bar (see Figure 9.5).

The following are the five menu options available in the menu bar:

❶ QUERY

The functions under this menu option allow you to create, save, open, check, execute, and delete a query.

❷ EDIT

Different editing functions are available using this menu option. Also, you can toggle between the display only and edit mode of the query.

❸ VIEW

The functions under this menu option allow you to display different screen areas as well as toolbars. You can also toggle between different options to display the technical name and description of query elements.

❹ TOOLS

The SAVE ALL function under this menu option saves the query definition as well all other reusable components that are created while working on the query.

❺ HELP

Functions under this menu option provide error help and also provide access to SAP online documentation.

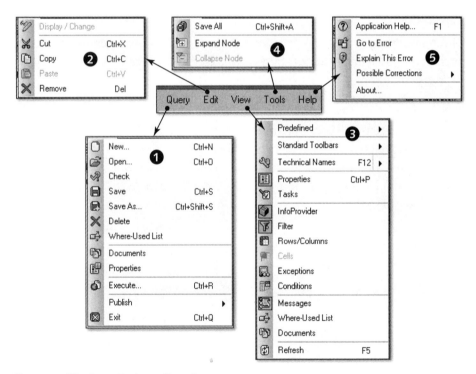

Figure 9.5 BEx Query Designer Menu Bar

9.3   Creating a Simple BEx Query

Let's begin creating a simple query based on the sales InfoCube (BWSD_C01) that we created earlier in Chapter 5. When you log in to BEx Query Designer, you see a default screen as shown earlier in Figure 9.3. To create a new query, you can either use the menu QUERY • NEW or click on the NEW toolbar icon shown in Figure 9.6.

Figure 9.6 Creating a New Query

As mentioned earlier, a query in SAP BW has to be based on an InfoProvider. When you create a query, a window pops up asking you to select an InfoProvider (see Figure 9.7). On this screen, you can navigate through the InfoAreas to select the InfoProvider on which you want to create the query ❶ and then click on the OPEN button ❷ to return to the BEx QUERY DESIGNER screen.

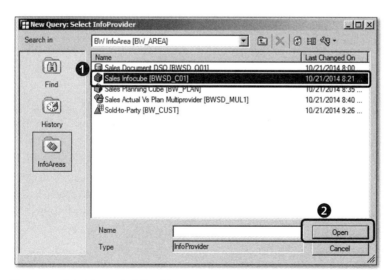

Figure 9.7 Selecting an InfoProvider

The definition of the selected InfoProvider becomes visible in the INFOPROVIDER area of BEx Query Designer (see Figure 9.8).

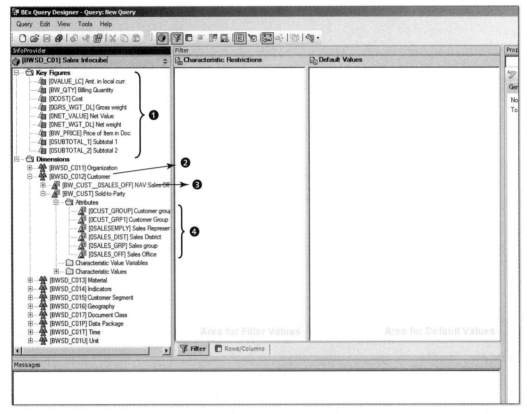

Figure 9.8 InfoProvider Definition in BEx Query Designer

You can see all of the key figures (❶ of Figure 9.8) and characteristics grouped within their respective dimensions ❷ in BEx Query Designer. The master data navigation attributes, which are selected in the InfoCube definition, appear in BEx Query Designer grouped with the master data characteristic in the same dimension ❸. You can also see additional information about the characteristics of the InfoCube, such as the attributes (if the characteristic is master data), variables, and values ❹.

Let's now create a query to answer the following analysis requirements for ABCD Corp. business analysts:

▶ What were the yearly net sales for all products sold in the year 2014 for Sales Organization 3000 (AMERICA)? (Show the data by division, material group, and product.)

▶ Can the values be seen by calendar quarter, if needed?

▶ Can the same data be viewed by division, customer group, and product, if needed?

9.3.1 Defining Filters

From these requirements, it's clear that the query needs to be *restricted* to year 2014 and sales organization 3000. These restrictions can be applied on the FILTER area under the CHARACTERISTIC RESTRICTIONS section. So if you want to restrict the query results for the calendar year, drag and drop the Calendar Year characteristic from the INFOPROVIDER area to the CHARACTERISTIC RESTRICTIONS area (❶ of Figure 9.9). Then, select RESTRICT ❷ from the context menu of the characteristic to define the restrictions.

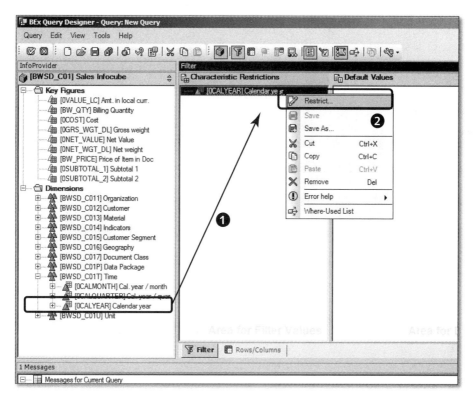

Figure 9.9 Adding a Characteristic for Query Restrictions

After you select RESTRICT, a selection window pops up where you can define the values with which you want to restrict the characteristic (see Figure 9.10).

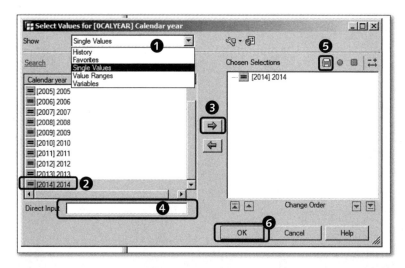

Figure 9.10 Selecting Filter Values for a Characteristic

You can restrict the characteristic with either a single value or a range, or you can choose to use a variable to restrict the characteristic. Select the appropriate option from the SHOW dropdown (❶ of Figure 9.10).

Highlight the desired value from the list ❷, and add it to the selections by clicking on the arrow button ❸. You can also make a selection by directly entering the value in the DIRECT INPUT box ❹ and then clicking on the arrow button.

Using the SAVE button ❺, you can save this selection as a variant in your favorites so that you can use it in the future. Finally, click on OK ❻ to confirm the selection and return to the query definition. You can see that the CALENDAR YEAR characteristic is now restricted for year 2014 (see Figure 9.11).

Figure 9.11 Calendar Year Restriction

Similarly, you can restrict the query for the SALES ORGANIZATION = 3000 (AMER-ICA) characteristic as shown in Figure 9.12.

Figure 9.12 Adding the Sales Organization Restriction

Having defined these filters, we've now restricted the result data set of the query to year 2014 and to sales organization 3000 as mentioned in the example requirements.

9.3.2 Defining Rows and Columns

The layout of queries is defined in the ROW/COLUMNS area of BEx Query Designer. The four sections under the ROW/COLUMNS area are explained next:

▶ ROWS
All those characteristics that need to appear as rows in the query display should be dragged and dropped into this area.

▶ COLUMNS
The characteristics or key figures that form the columns of the query display should be dragged and dropped into this area.

▶ FREE CHARACTERISTICS
Those characteristics that don't need to be displayed in the default query result when the query is executed—but can be brought into the result display as needed—should be dragged and dropped into the FREE CHARACTERISTICS area. Free characteristics can be added to the rows (drilldown) or to the columns (drill-across) after the query is initially executed.

▶ PREVIEW
A preview of the query layout, based on the rows and columns of the query definition, is displayed in this section.

Based on our example requirements, the report (the query output) should show the data by division, material group, and material, so these characteristics should be dragged into the Rows section (❶ of Figure 9.13). The sales value should be displayed as a column, so drag the key figure NET VALUE (0NET_VALUE) to the COLUMNS area ❷.

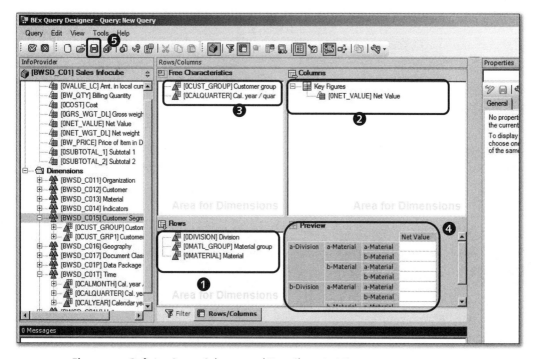

Figure 9.13 Defining Rows, Columns, and Free Characteristics

The requirements also mention that the analysts want to see the data by customer group or calendar year/quarter, if needed. This means you have to place these two characteristics as free characteristics ❸. The preview of the layout can be seen in the PREVIEW section ❹.

The query is now ready. To save this query definition, click on the SAVE button ❺. You can also use choose QUERY • SAVE from the menu bar to save the query. Specify the technical name and the description of the query in the pop-up box and click on the SAVE button to save the query (see Figure 9.14).

The MESSAGES area in BEx Query Designer displays a message indicating that the query was successfully saved (see Figure 9.15).

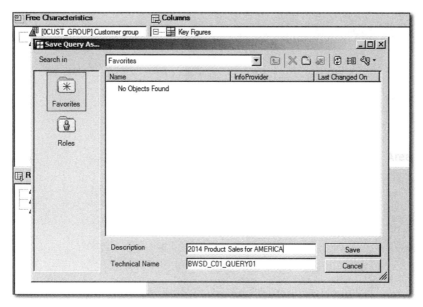

Figure 9.14 Saving the Query Definition

Figure 9.15 Success Message after the Query Save

In the next subsection, we'll see how to execute this query and perform analysis on the data.

9.3.3 Executing Queries and Analyzing Data

After the query is defined and saved, you can execute it by clicking on the Execute button shown in Figure 9.16 or by following the menu path Query • Execute.

When you execute a query, a new web browser window opens to displays the result of the query, as shown in Figure 9.17. It uses the ad hoc analysis template from BEx Web Analyzer to display the query result. (We discuss BEx Web Analyzer in detail in Chapter 10.)

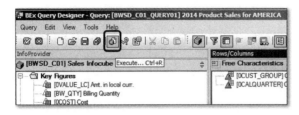

Figure 9.16 Executing a Query

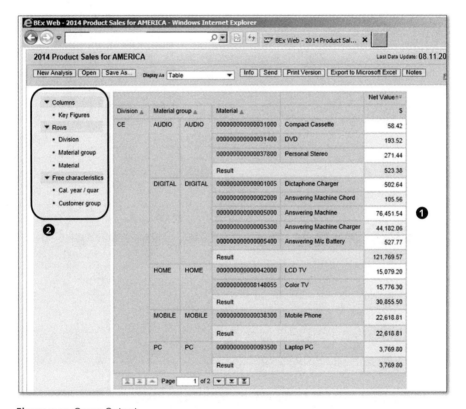

Figure 9.17 Query Output

Query Execution on SAP BW Powered by SAP HANA or SAP BW with SAP BW Accelerator

When a query is executed, the execution time at a broad level includes time taken to read and aggregate the data from the underlying data target, perform OLAP calculations, and prepare the data for output.

If you have SAP BW powered by SAP HANA or are using the SAP BW Accelerator, then the steps involve reading data from the data target, aggregating data, and performing OLAP calculations (with some exceptions) in-memory, resulting in significant query performance improvement.

Transaction RSRT is used to set the query properties that define how a query will be executed. This is an important transaction for debugging the query output and for performance tuning.

You can see that the query output is displayed per the example requirements. The query displays the net sales value (year 2014 and sales organization 3000) for all of the products by division and material group (❶ of Figure 9.17).

The query elements included in the rows, columns, and free characteristics of the query definition are visible on the left side of the screen ❷. These elements can be used to further analyze the data displayed in the query.

For example, if an analyst wants to see the net sales data by calendar quarter, he can simply drag CAL. YEAR/QUAR from FREE CHARACTERISTICS and drop it in COLUMNS, as shown in ❶ of Figure 9.18.

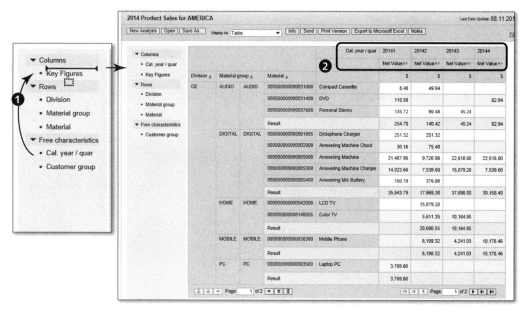

Figure 9.18 Drill-Across by Calendar Quarter

As a result, the query output is now modified to show the net sales by calendar quarter ❷. This action of adding a characteristic to the columns of the query is called *horizontal drilldown*. If you add a characteristic to the rows of the query, this action is called *vertical drilldown*.

For example, if an analyst now wants to see the data by customer group instead of material group, this navigation can be performed in two steps. First, remove MATERIAL GROUP from the layout; then, drill down by CUSTOMER GROUP. You can also directly swap the display of the MATERIAL GROUP characteristic with CUSTOMER GROUP, as shown in ❶ of Figure 9.19.

As a result of this navigation, the query output is refreshed to display CUSTOMER GROUP in the result area, and the MATERIAL GROUP characteristic is added to FREE CHARACTERISTICS ❷.

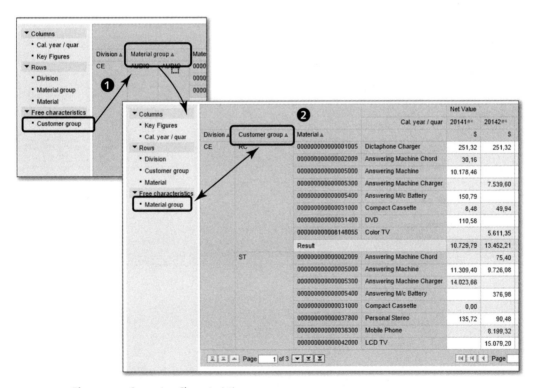

Figure 9.19 Swapping Characteristics

9.4   Introduction to OLAP Variables

The simple query that was discussed in the previous section determined material sales for the year 2014. As such, we designed the query to restrict the characteristics for all calendar years to value 2014. What if a user now modifies the requirement as follows?

▸ Show sales for all of the material that belongs to the material group selected by the user.

▸ Don't fix the query to year 2014; instead, the user should be able to select the year for which the query should be executed. However, the user entry should default to the previous year value; that is, if the current year is 2014, then the default value should be 2013, and when the year changes to 2015, the default value should be 2014.

These and other similar requirements are addressed using OLAP variables in SAP BW. Variables can be used for characteristics, texts, hierarchies, and so on, and using them in a query makes it more flexible. The most common use of variables in a query is to provide users with a prompt (or selection screen) where users can decide the parameters for which the query should be executed. Many other types of variables are also available in SAP BW.

OLAP variables are reusable objects, so variables created for a query can also be used in all of the InfoProviders in the system. In this section, we explain different types of OLAP variables and the different ways they can be processed in a BEx query.

9.4.1   Types of Variables

Variables in SAP BW are context dependent, which means the type of variable actually depends on the type of object for which it's defined. Following are different types of variables and the objects where they can be used.

Characteristic Value Variables

These types of variables are used to restrict characteristic values, which can be used in defining filters for a query. The characteristic variables created on a characteristic are available across all InfoProviders, wherever that characteristic is used. For example, a characteristic value variable can be used on a calendar year characteristic if the user wants to select the year while executing the query.

445

Text Variables

Text variables provide flexibility in displaying the text description of the query, as well as different query elements. This type of variable can be used where you define the text or description of a query or another query component.

For example, a text variable can be used to dynamically generate the key figure column name based on the year value; that is, if the query is executed for Year = 2015, then the key figure column name should be displayed as Net Sales 2015. When the same query is executed for year 2016, the key figure column name should be Net Sales 2016.

Hierarchy Variables

Hierarchies are used in a query either to restrict a characteristic or to display query results using a hierarchy. Hierarchy variables are used to select a hierarchy in the query.

Hierarchy Node Variables

Hierarchy node variables can be used wherever a characteristic is restricted using a specific node of a hierarchy. For example, if a customer characteristic has a hierarchy based on region, then by using a hierarchy variable, the user can select a specific region node, and the query is executed for all of the customers belonging to the selected region node.

Formula Variables

These variables can be used wherever there is a numeric input in the query definition, for example, in formulas, calculated key figures (CKFs), exceptions, and/or conditions. Let's take an example where you have a query that should display average sales per day for a month, selected by the user.

For this requirement, you have to define a formula where the total sales value for the selected month has to be divided by the number of days in that month. In this scenario, you can use a formula variable that represents the number of days in the selected month and divide the monthly total sales with the variable value.

The procedure to create different types of variables is discussed in Section 9.5.

9.4.2 Processing Types of Variables

We've seen different types of variables in the previous subsection. All of these variables are passed with a value (depending on the type of variable) when the query is executed. The values can be passed to these variables in different ways. The way in which a variable gets its value depends on the *processing type* of the variable. The processing type governs the process that fills the variable with a value when the query is executed.

SAP BW offers the following five different ways to process variables:

▶ Manual entry/default value
▶ Replacement path
▶ Authorizations
▶ Customer exit
▶ SAP exit

These processing types are explained next.

Manual Entry/Default Value

The variable created with the manual entry/default value processing type allows the variable value to be entered manually in the beginning of the query execution. You can also define the default values for the variable so that when the query is executed, the variable is prepopulated with the default value, or if the variable isn't enabled for user entry, the query is executed for the default values mentioned in the variable.

In Figure 9.20, the characteristic variables for the Year and Sales Organization characteristics are enabled for user input. Users can manually enter the values for these two variables and execute the query for these values by clicking on OK.

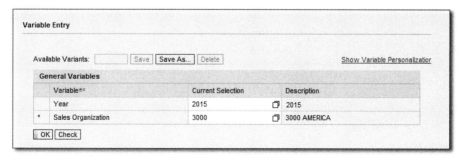

Figure 9.20 Manual Entry/Default Value Variables

This processing type is available for all variable types mentioned earlier.

Replacement Path

Variables defined using the replacement path processing type are replaced automatically with the value(s) defined in the variable when the query is executed. A variable with replacement path processing can be replaced using one of the following options:

▸ Replace with a characteristic/attribute value.

▸ Replace with the values returned by another query.

▸ Replace with the value of other variable.

Take an example of a formula variable that represents the number of days in the month (selected by the user) and then divide the monthly total sales key figure by the value of the formula variable. In this case, you can define a formula variable with the replacement path processing type. And in the definition, you specify that the value of the formula variable should be replaced with the value of the Number of Days attribute of the Calendar Month characteristic.

Another example of the replacement path variable is illustrated in Figure 9.21. Query 1 shows a list of all customers who bought the top ten selling materials; it needs to be executed with the material characteristic restricted to the top ten materials. There's another query (Query 2) that shows the top ten materials when executed.

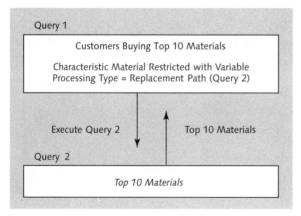

Figure 9.21 Example for Replacement Path Processing Type

To address the given requirement, you can restrict the material characteristic in Query 1 with a characteristic value variable using the replacement path processing type. The definition of this variable will include Query 2 as a source of material values. So whenever Query 1 is executed, Query 2 will also be executed in the background to determine top ten material values for this variable.

This processing type isn't available for hierarchy node variables.

Authorizations

Variables with the authorizations processing type are automatically populated from the authorizations of the user. This type of processing is useful if you want to provide restricted access to a query. When a user executes a query with the authorization variable in it, he can see only the data that he's authorized to see.

For example, consider a scenario where you want plant managers to see the data only for their plants. In the query definition, you can define a characteristic value variable on the plant characteristic with the processing type set as the authorizations processing type. When the U.S. plant manager executes the query, the plant characteristic is automatically restricted for Value = US.

This processing type is available only for characteristic value variables and hierarchy node variables.

Customer Exit

If the preceding SAP-delivered processing types don't satisfy your requirements, and you want to create your own logic to populate the variable values, then you can use the customer exit processing type. With this type, you can define the custom logic for the variable using ABAP coding. SAP has provided a function module exit EXIT_SAPLRRS0_001 to write the ABAP logic for customer exit variables.

This processing type is available for all variable types mentioned earlier.

SAP Exit

This processing type is used in variables that are readily delivered by SAP as a part of standard Business Content. This type of variable is for use only. You can't create variables with the SAP exit processing type.

Table 9.1 consolidates the different types of variables and the applicable processing types.

	User Entry/ Default Value	Replacement Path	Authorizations	Customer Exit
Characteristic Value	✓	✓	✓	✓
Text	✓	✓	X	✓
Hierarchy	✓	✓	X	✓
Hierarchy Node	✓	X	✓	✓
Formula	✓	✓	X	✓

Table 9.1 Variable Types and Applicable Processing Types

9.5 Creating OLAP Variables Using the Variable Editor

To create variables, SAP BW provides a context-dependent *Variable Editor*. Using the Variable Editor, you can create, change, and delete variables. *Context dependent* means that it provides you the option to create variables based on the object from which you called the editor. For example, when you call the editor from a characteristic restrictions screen, it automatically selects the variable type as a characteristic value. When you call the editor from the formula screen, it automatically selects the variable type as a formula variable and removes the option for the authorizations processing type (because this type isn't allowed for formula variables).

In this section, we explain the use of the Variable Editor to create some of the important and most commonly used variables.

9.5.1 Characteristic Variables: Manual Entry/Default Value

To create a characteristic variable, access the Variable Editor from the INFOPROVIDER area, as shown in Figure 9.22.

Expand the characteristic on which you want to create the variable, and select the NEW VARIABLE option from the context menu of the CHARACTERISTIC VALUE VARIABLES folder.

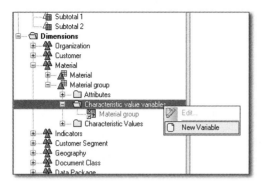

Figure 9.22 Accessing the Variable Editor from the InfoProvider Area

Alternatively, you can create a variable directly from the Characteristic Restrictions screen. Choose Variables from the dropdown option (see Figure 9.23) on the selection screen for the selected characteristic.

For our example scenario, let's create a variable based on the material group characteristic. After you select Variables from the Show dropdown, the list is refreshed to the variable values available for the selected characteristic (❶ of Figure 9.24).

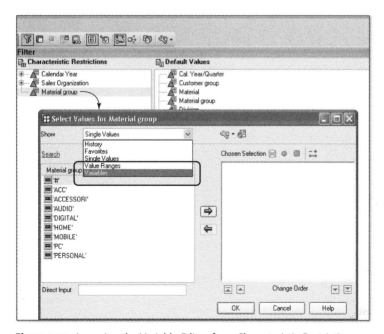

Figure 9.23 Accessing the Variable Editor from Characteristic Restrictions

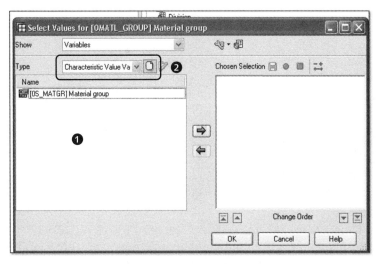

Figure 9.24 Creating a New Characteristic Variable

To create a new characteristic variable, select the characteristic value variable from the TYPE dropdown, and then click on the CREATE icon (❷ of Figure 9.24). This action takes you to the CHANGE VARIABLE screen (see Figure 9.25).

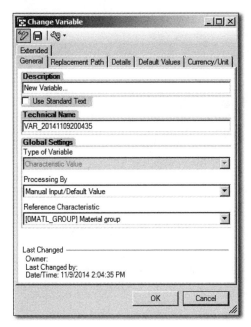

Figure 9.25 Variable Editor Screen

The different tabs visible in the CHANGE VARIABLE screen are described here:

► GENERAL
Provides basic information about the variable, such as name and description, processing type, and so on.

► REPLACEMENT PATH
On this tab, you define the replacement settings for a variable with a replacement path processing type. For all other processing types, this tab is grayed out.

► DETAILS
This tab is used to define additional settings for a variable. The DETAILS tab is applicable for all processing types, except the replacement path processing type.

► DEFAULT VALUES
This tab is used to define default values for a variable and is applicable only for those variables with the manual entry/default value processing type.

► CURRENCY/UNIT
This tab is applicable only for formula variables and is used to define the dimension for the variable value; that is, whether the numeric value is an amount, price, date, time, and so on.

► EXTENDED
This is a display tab only and displays the internal system ID of the variable.

Maintain the description ❶ and technical name ❷ of the variable as shown in Figure 9.26.

The TYPE OF VARIABLE (❸ of Figure 9.26) is already determined by the editor based on the element from which the Variable Editor is called. In this case, the editor is called from a characteristic, so the variable type is prepopulated as CHARACTERISTIC VALUE.

Select the processing type of the variable from the PROCESSING BY dropdown menu ❹. The characteristic visible in the REFERENCE CHARACTERISTIC field ❺ is the base for the variable. The remaining definition for this variable is defined on the DETAILS tab, as shown in Figure 9.27.

On the DETAILS tab, you decide what the variable represents from the available options (❶ of Figure 9.27). You can also define if the variable should be an optional variable (the user can run the query without entering a value for this variable), a mandatory variable (the user must enter a value for this variable), or a mandatory variable where the initial value isn't allowed (# isn't accepted as an input for the variable) ❷.

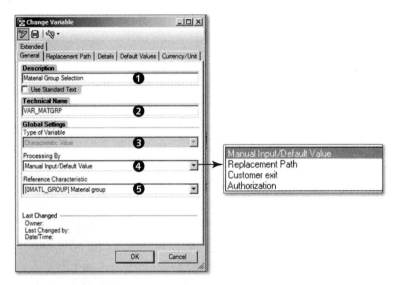

Figure 9.26 Maintaining the General Tab for VAR_MATGRP

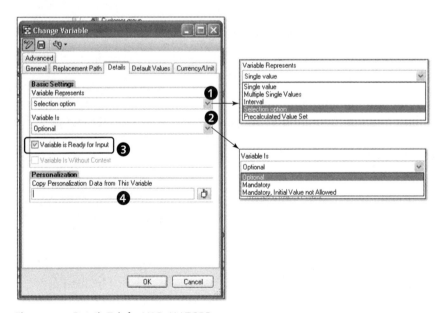

Figure 9.27 Details Tab for VAR_MATGRP

> **Note**
>
> If a query containing a characteristic value variable with optional entry is executed, and a user leaves the variable blank, then the query is executed for all values of that characteristic.

The VARIABLE IS READY FOR INPUT checkbox is an important setting for a variable (❸ of Figure 9.27). If this setting is checked, then the variable appears on the selection screen when the query is executed, and the user can input the values for the variable. If the box is unchecked, the user can't input the value for the variable, so the query is executed using the default values of the variable. For our example variable, we need the user to select MATERIAL GROUP, so VARIABLE IS READY FOR INPUT is checked.

If you want to copy the personalization setting of an existing variable to this new variable, you can do so by including the existing variable under the PERSONALIZATION section ❹ of the DETAILS tab.

Finally, if you want to maintain the default values for the variable, those can be maintained on the DEFAULT VALUES tab (see Figure 9.28).

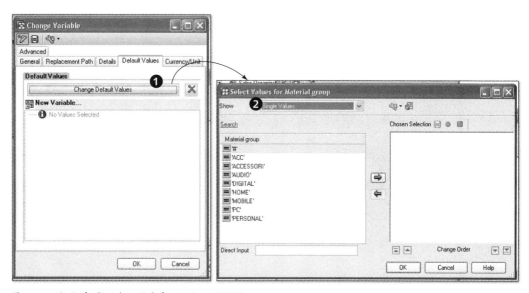

Figure 9.28 Default Values Tab for VAR_MATGRP

Click on the CHANGE DEFAULT VALUES button (❶ of Figure 9.28) so you can assign the default values to the variable using the selection screen ❷.

455

Finally, save the definition by clicking on the SAVE icon, as shown in ❶ of Figure 9.29.

Figure 9.29 Saving the VAR_MATGRP Variable

The newly created VAR_MATGRP variable is now displayed in the variables list of the material group characteristic (❷ of Figure 9.29) and can be used to restrict the characteristic in the query.

9.5.2 Characteristic Variables: Replacement Path

To define a replacement path variable, select REPLACEMENT PATH as the processing type from the PROCESSING BY dropdown (❶ of Figure 9.30) on the GENERAL tab of the CHANGE VARIABLE screen.

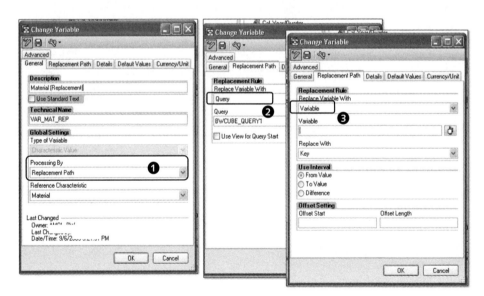

Figure 9.30 Creating the Characteristic Value Replacement Path Variable

For the selected processing type, the REPLACEMENT PATH tab is now enabled. On this tab, you can specify whether the variable should be replaced with the value from a query (❷ of Figure 9.30) or replaced with a value from another variable ❸. The corresponding settings for the selected option can be made on the same tab.

9.5.3 Characteristic Variables: Customer Exit

The customer exit processing type is commonly used for characteristic variables. We explain the procedure to create this type of variable with an example where the user wants to select the year for which the query should be executed. However, the user entry should be populated by default for the previous year value; that is, if the current year is 2015, then the default value should be 2014, and when the year changes to 2016, the default value should be 2015.

To address this requirement, you can create a variable based on the year characteristic with the customer exit processing type (❶ of Figure 9.31). A customer exit variable can be built in two steps. The first step is to define the variable using the Variable Editor, and the second step is to write the ABAP logic in a customer exit.

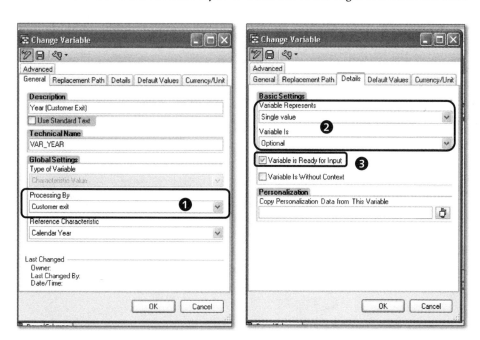

Figure 9.31 Defining a Variable with the Customer Exit Processing Type

Define the variable as shown in Figure 9.31. The query has to be run for one year only, so the variable should represent a single value ❷. Note that because a user wants to determine the year value for which the query should be executed, you have to select the VARIABLE IS READY FOR INPUT checkbox ❸. Finally, save the variable definition.

To write the ABAP logic for customer exit variables, SAP has provided the function module exit EXIT_SAPLRRS0_001 in SAP BW. This exit can be accessed only through a project for SAP enhancement. The project can be created using Transaction CMOD in SAP BW (❶ of Figure 9.32).

The project used for customer exit query variables should contain the enhancement RSR00001 ❷, which makes the exit EXIT_SAPLRRS0_001 available under components of the project ❸. Double-click on FUNCTION EXIT to enter the code. The FUNCTION BUILDER screen for the exit is displayed, as shown in Figure 9.33.

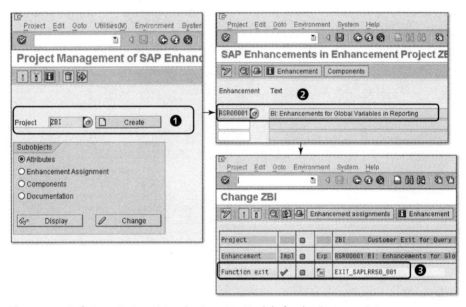

Figure 9.32 Defining a Project Using the Function Module for the Customer Exit

SAP has provided include ZXRSRU01 as a separate placeholder for all of the custom code. Double-click on this include to enter it in edit mode, and add the code from Listing 9.1 to the include.

```
when 'VAR_YEAR'.
DATA YEAR(4).    " Data Declaration
```

```
IF i_step = 1. " For default value
YEAR = sy-datum+0(4). " Get Year from system date
YEAR = YEAR - 1. " Get Previous Year
  l_s_range-low =  YEAR.
  l_s_range-sign = 'I'.
  l_s_range-opt  = 'EQ'.
  append l_s_range to e_t_range.
  exit.
endif.
```

Listing 9.1 Include Program

Figure 9.33 INCLUDE to Write Custom Logic

Save and activate the include program.

A customer exit variable can be defined in this manner. When the query using this variable is executed, this logic is executed first, and the previous year is derived based on the system data. Also, because the variable is marked as ready for input, a user can see the default value of this variable as the previous year and can change it to some different value if needed.

9.5.4 Formula Variables

To create a formula variable, you can access the Variable Editor from the CHANGE FORMULA screen while defining a query (see Figure 9.34). You can see a folder for formula variables under the AVAILABLE OPERANDS section of the formula editor. Select NEW VARIABLE from the context menu to create a new formula variable ❶. A new variable is created in the folder. To define this variable, select EDIT from the context menu of the new variable ❷.

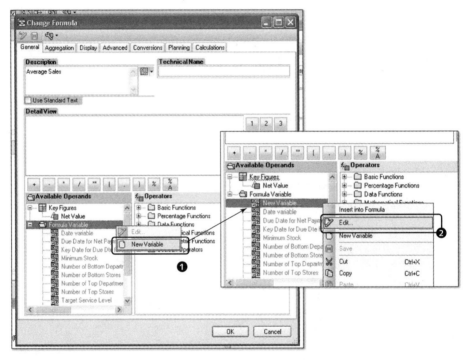

Figure 9.34 Accessing the Variable Editor from the Change Formula Screen

For example, you want to create a formula variable that should return the total number of days for the selected calendar month. To achieve this, you have to set the PROCESSING BY field of the formula variable as REPLACEMENT PATH (❶ of Figure 9.35) and the REFERENCE CHARACTERISTIC field as CALENDAR YEAR/MONTH ❷. The details for this variable are maintained on the REPLACEMENT PATH tab. Maintain the settings as shown in Figure 9.35.

Also, the CURRENCY/UNIT tab becomes applicable for the formula variable. On this tab, you can define the dimension for the numeric value stored in the variable (see Figure 9.36). Because the numeric value stored in the formula variable we've defined (number of days in a month) is purely a number, the dimension can be set as NUMBER.

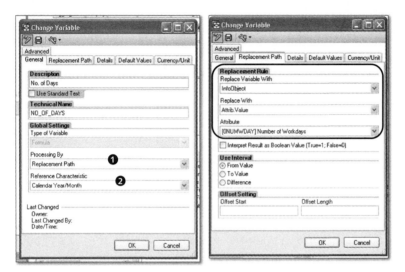

Figure 9.35 Defining the Formula Variable

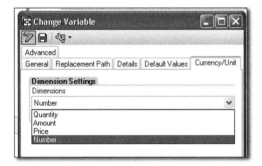

Figure 9.36 Currency/Unit Tab

Save the variable, and it's available to be used in the query definition.

9.5.5 Text Variables

Text variables can be used if you want to have flexible descriptions for different query elements. You can use a variable in the description wherever there is a

461

VARIABLE icon ☒ available. To call the Variable Editor, click on this icon (❶ of Figure 9.37), and then click on NEW VARIABLE ❷.

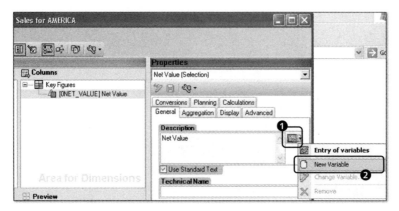

Figure 9.37 Calling the Variable Editor for a Text Variable

Let's take an example where you want the column description for the net value key figure to be dynamically populated with the year for which the query is executed. To achieve this, you have to set the processing type of the text variable as REPLACEMENT PATH and the REFERENCE CHARACTERISTIC as CALENDAR YEAR (see ❶ of Figure 9.38).

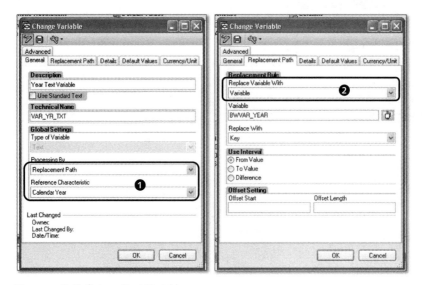

Figure 9.38 Defining a Text Variable

The details for this variable are maintained on the REPLACEMENT PATH tab. Maintain the settings as shown in Figure 9.38. Note that in this example, we're replacing the text variable with the value of calendar year entered in another characteristic variable ❷.

9.6   Creating Filters

Filters are used to restrict query execution to a specific data set. These restrictions can be applied on a set of characteristics together. You can also save the filter defined in one query as a reusable object that is available for all other queries built on that InfoProvider.

Let's look at an example where users want to see sales data with the following restrictions:

▶ **Year**
Users should be able to select the value for the year. However, the selection screen should show the previous year as the default value.

▶ **Division**
Users should be able to select the division for which they want to see the data.

▶ **Country**
Users should be able to run the query only for selected entries.

▶ **Sales document category**
The values displayed in the report should not include the sales from sales documents with document category N.

To create these restrictions in a query, first drag the relevant characteristic into the CHARACTERISTIC RESTRICTIONS area of the query, and then call the restrictions window from the context menu of the characteristic (❶ of Figure 9.39).

There are different options available on this screen to restrict a characteristic ❷:

▶ HISTORY
The restrictions you've recently used are saved here.

▶ FAVORITES
This view shows you all of the selections you've saved earlier as your favorites.

► SINGLE VALUES

Use this option if you want to restrict the characteristic with a single value or multiple single values.

► VALUES RANGES

Select this option for restrictions involving a value range or multiple value ranges.

► VARIABLES

Select this option to restrict the characteristic with different variables available for the selected characteristic.

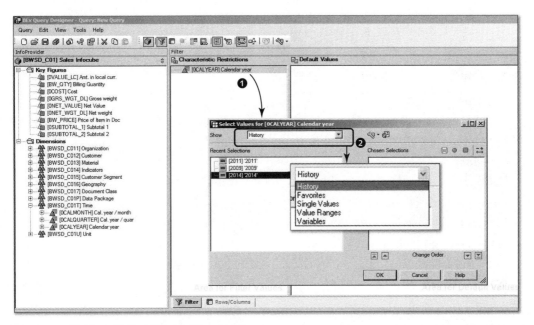

Figure 9.39 Restricting a Characteristic

Using the example mentioned earlier, select the CUSTOMER EXIT variable for YEAR, as shown in ❶ of Figure 9.40.

Use the arrow button ❷ to include the variable in the selection. Finally, click on the OK button ❸ to return to the query design.

Some additional functions are available on the selection screen with respect to the values selected for the characteristic. These functions are shown in Figure 9.41.

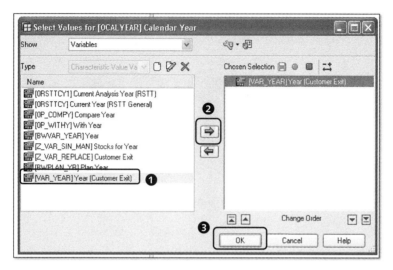

Figure 9.40 Restricting with a Variable

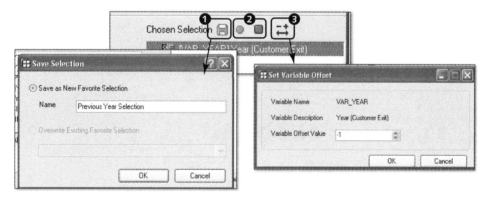

Figure 9.41 Additional Functions on the Selection Screen

If you want to use the selected values frequently, then you can save those values under your FAVORITES list by clicking on the SAVE button (❶ in Figure 9.41).

The red and green buttons ❷ are used to exclude or include the values from the selection.

If you want to define an offset on the selection value, you can use the offset option for the selection. Click on the OFFSET button ❸, and maintain the desired offset for the selected value.

Restrictions can be maintained for different characteristics together in a query. For the given example, you can drag the other characteristics, such as DIVISION, COUNTRY, or DOCUMENT CATEGORY, and restrict them per the logic (see Figure 9.42).

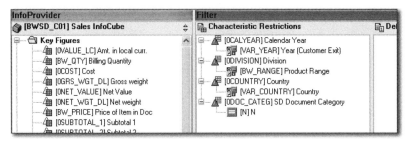

Figure 9.42 Filter Defined for Multiple Characteristics

Note that in Figure 9.42, the SD DOCUMENT CATEGORY characteristic is excluded for the value N. After this filter is defined for a query, it can be saved as a reusable component to be used in other queries built on the same InfoProvider (Figure 9.43).

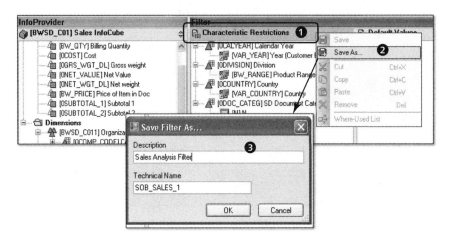

Figure 9.43 Saving the Filter as a Reusable Component

To save this filter, right-click the CHARACTERISTIC RESTRICTIONS bar to open the context menu (❶ of Figure 9.43), and select SAVE AS ❷. Maintain the description and technical name ❸ for the filter, and save it as a reusable component.

Note
The saved filters are available as selection objects in the SAP BW metadata.

Now, if you create a new query on the same InfoProvider, the saved filters are visible under the FILTER folder in the INFOPROVIDER area of the designer (❶ of Figure 9.44).

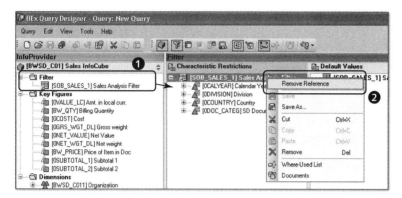

Figure 9.44 Reusing Saved Filters

To reuse the already existing filters, you have to select, drag, and drop the filter into the CHARACTERISTIC RESTRICTIONS area. If you make any changes to this filter in this query, those changes will be reflected in all of the queries that are using the same filter. So if you want to make any changes that are specific only for that query, you must remove the reference for the filter used in the query. To do this, open the context menu for the filter, and select REMOVE REFERENCE to detach the filter (❷ of Figure 9.44).

9.7 Creating Structures

Structures, which are identified with the STRUCTURES icon 📱, are basic structural components of a BEx query that are used to define the layout of the query for a row or column. There are two types of structures based on the type of components contained in a structure:

▸ Key figure structures

▸ Characteristic structures

We discuss each of these structures in the next sections and also explain how to reuse them.

9.7.1 Key Figure Structures

Key figure structures include the components that are based on a key figure such as basic, formula, restricted, and calculated key figures. A key figure structure is automatically created in a query when you drag and drop key figures from the InfoProvider screen to the query rows/columns. This structure is named KEY FIGURES by default (see Figure 9.45).

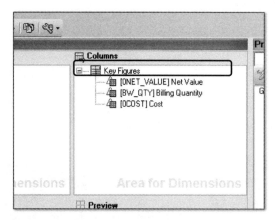

Figure 9.45 Key Structure

Each component included in a key figure structure should include a key figure. This means you can include key figures, formula key figures, selection with key figures, restricted key figures (RKFs), and calculated key figures (CKFs) in a key figure structure. But a characteristic or a selection without a key figure can't be included in the key figure structure.

> **Note**
>
> A maximum of two structures are allowed in a query definition, and only one of those can be a key figure structure.

9.7.2 Characteristic Structures

Characteristic structures are optional in query definition and are used if you want to display a specific number of characteristic values in a specific sequence. To create a new structure, select NEW STRUCTURE from the context menu of the ROWS area (see Figure 9.46).

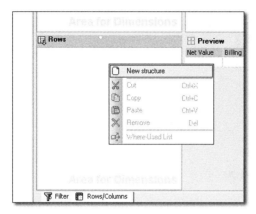

Figure 9.46 Creating a New Structure

You can add structural components to the structure by selecting an option from the context menu of the structure (see Figure 9.47).

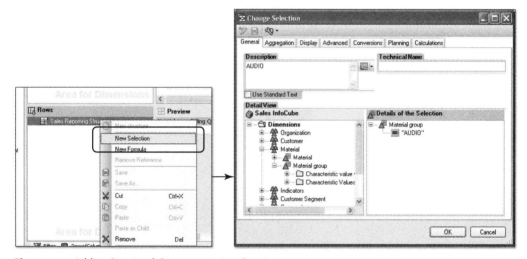

Figure 9.47 Adding Structural Components to a Structure

When you use two structures in a query, you can additionally define a separate logic (selections or formula) for each cell formed due to the intersection of the two structures. This logic will override the cell values generated implicitly from the intersection of structures. Click on the CELL DEFINITION icon (❶ of Figure 9.48), or use the menu path VIEW • CELLS. This option is activated only when there are two structures in the query.

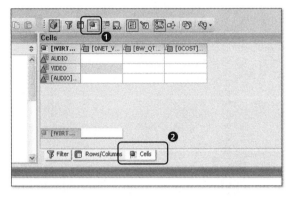

Figure 9.48 Cell Definition

When cell definition is enabled, an additional CELLS tab area is visible on the BEx Query Designer layout (❷ of Figure 9.48).

9.7.3 Reusing Structures

ABCD Corp. uses the value, quantity, and cost key figures most commonly in all of its queries. If you've used these key figures in a query, and they are part of the key figure structure, you can save this structure as a reusable component, which can be included in other queries on the same InfoProvider. To save the structure, select SAVE As from the context menu, and save it after providing the appropriate technical name and description (see Figure 9.49).

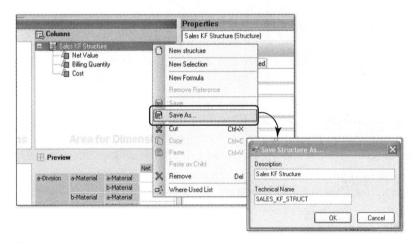

Figure 9.49 Save the Structure for Reuse

When you create a new query on the same InfoProvider, this saved structure is visible under the STRUCTURES folder in the INFOPROVIDER tab (❶ of Figure 9.50).

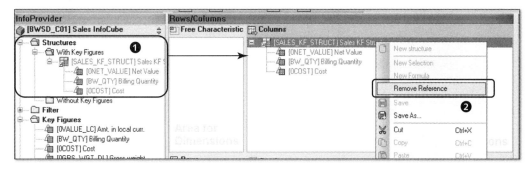

Figure 9.50 Reusing Structures

The structure can be directly pulled into the ROWS/COLUMNS area to use in the new query. However, if you make changes to this structure, they will be reflected in all queries that use it. If you want to make changes to the structure that are specific to only one query, you should detach the definition in the query by selecting REMOVE REFERENCE from the context menu ❷.

Reusable structures built for commonly used collections of key figures or characteristics (e.g., a plan/actual variance set of key figures or a year-on-year comparison scenario) can make query development easier and faster.

9.8   Creating Selections and Formulas

Characteristics and key figures from an InfoProvider can be directly dragged into the ROWS/COLUMNS area to define a query, but sometimes using the elements just as they are available in the InfoProvider isn't enough. Take the example of the report shown in Figure 9.51.

In this case, the net value key figure is used in both columns, but each column is restricted by a specific characteristic value (Year = 2014 and 2013, respectively). This kind of requirement can be addressed using selections in the query key figure structure.

Let's add one more field to the query shown in Figure 9.51. Per the requirements, the analysts now want to compare 2014 sales with respect to sales values from the year 2013 (see Figure 9.52). This additional column involves a calculation logic that needs to be defined in the query. This and similar requirements that involve calculations can be addressed using formulas in the query key figure structure.

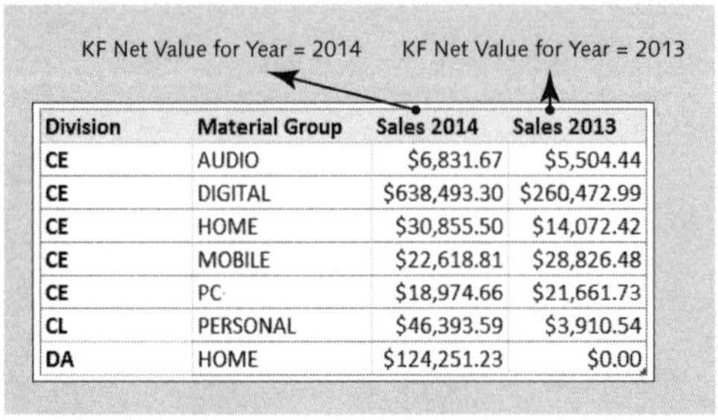

KF Net Value for Year = 2014   KF Net Value for Year = 2013

Division	Material Group	Sales 2014	Sales 2013
CE	AUDIO	$6,831.67	$5,504.44
CE	DIGITAL	$638,493.30	$260,472.99
CE	HOME	$30,855.50	$14,072.42
CE	MOBILE	$22,618.81	$28,826.48
CE	PC	$18,974.66	$21,661.73
CL	PERSONAL	$46,393.59	$3,910.54
DA	HOME	$124,251.23	$0.00

Figure 9.51 Columns Restricted with Year Values

{(Sales 2014 – Sales 2013)/Sales 2013}*100

Division	Material Group	Sales 2014	Sales 2013	YoY Comparison (%)
CE	AUDIO	$6,831.67	$5,504.44	24.11
CE	DIGITAL	$638,493.30	$260,472.99	145.13
CE	HOME	$30,855.50	$14,072.42	119.26
CE	MOBILE	$22,618.81	$28,826.48	-21.53
CE	PC	$18,974.66	$21,661.73	-12.40
CL	PERSONAL	$46,393.59	$3,910.54	1,086.37
DA	HOME	$124,251.23	$0.00	0.00

Figure 9.52 Column Based on a Formula

In this section, we explain the process of creating selections and formulas for the query using the example described previously.

9.8.1 Selections

To begin, get all of the characteristics needed to define the query in the Rows section (❶ of Figure 9.53), and also drag NET VALUE, which is needed to define the query. When you add the first key figure to the columns, the key figure structure is automatically created ❷.

You can restrict this key figure by applying selections to it. Double-click on the key figure, or select EDIT from the context menu for the key figure ❸. This action opens a selection screen for the key figure as shown in Figure 9.54.

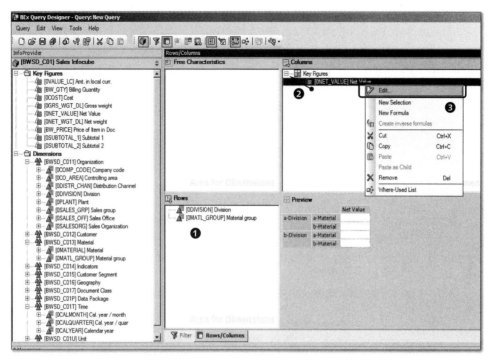

Figure 9.53 Editing the Key Figure

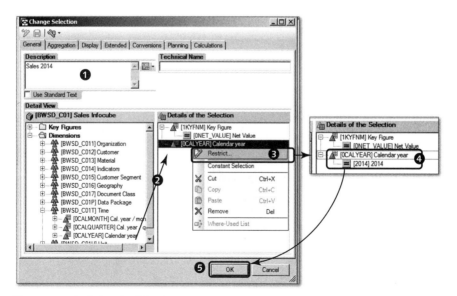

Figure 9.54 Defining the Selection

In this screen, you can maintain the description for the structure element (❶ of Figure 9.54). Then, select CALENDAR YEAR from the InfoProvider definition visible on the left side, and drag it to the DETAILS OF THE SELECTION area on the right side ❷. Here you can restrict the characteristic to the desired value using the RESTRICT option from the context menu ❸. Restrict CALENDAR YEAR to value 2014 ❹, and click on OK ❺ to return to the query definition.

> **Note**
>
> You can also use characteristic variables in the selection.

To create a new selection, use the NEW SELECTION option from the context menu (❶ of Figure 9.55). This will create a new SELECTION2 component in the key figures structure ❷. Double-click or select EDIT from the context menu to define this selection.

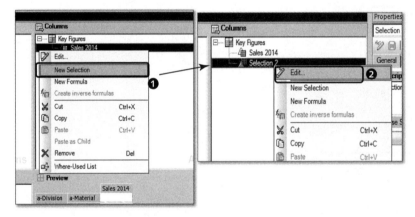

Figure 9.55 Creating a New Selection

As explained earlier, define this selection for Sales 2013 as shown in Figure 9.56.

When you create a new selection like this, you also have to specify the key figure in the selection.

> **Note**
>
> You can add only one key figure for a selection element, and because it's part of a key figure structure, you must have a key figure in all selections under this structure.

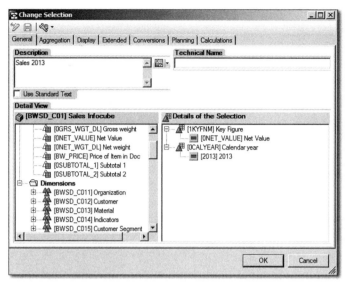

Figure 9.56 Defining a New Selection

Both of the columns are now ready per the requirement (see Figure 9.57).

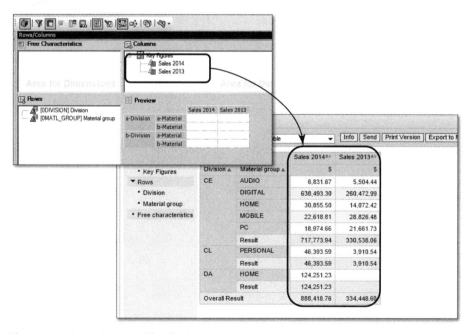

Figure 9.57 Query Output with Selections

475

You can address more complex requirements using selections involving multiple characteristics and variables and by using include/exclude and offset features.

9.8.2 Formula

Let's now move on to the next requirement, which is to add a column that compares the 2014 and 2013 values in the YoY COMPARISON (%) column (refer to Figure 9.52). This type of calculation is addressed using the formula component in the structure. To create a formula, select NEW FORMULA from the context menu, as shown in ❶ of Figure 9.58.

This action creates a new formula component in the key figure structure. To define the calculation for this formula, double-click or select EDIT from the context menu ❷. The CHANGE FORMULA screen appears in the pop-up where you can define the logic (see Figure 9.59).

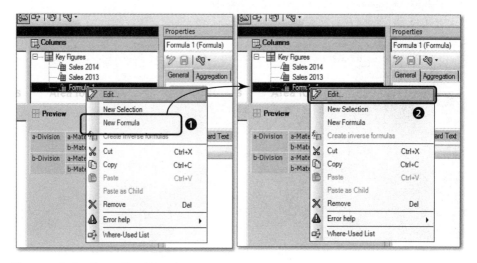

Figure 9.58 Creating a New Formula

Maintain the description of the component on this screen (❶ of Figure 9.59).

The DETAIL VIEW section shows the formula definition ❷, and on the bottom-left side of the screen is a list of all of the available operands ❸ that can be used in the formula. The operands can be any available key figures for the InfoProvider or any formula variables.

On the bottom-right side of the screen, there is a list of operators that could be used to define the formula ❹. These functions are grouped together into the following categories:

▸ BASIC FUNCTIONS

▸ PERCENTAGE FUNCTIONS

▸ DATA FUNCTIONS

▸ MATHEMATICAL FUNCTIONS

▸ TRIGONOMETRIC FUNCTIONS

▸ BOOLEAN OPERATORS

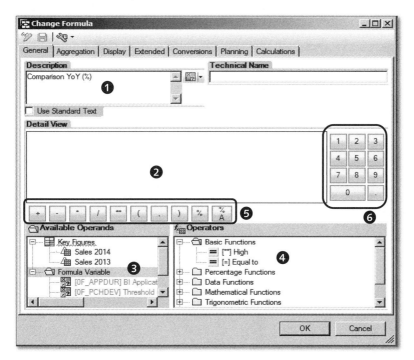

Figure 9.59 Formula Editor: Change Formula Screen

To add it to the formula, you select any operator and operand from the bottom part of the screen and double-click. You can also use the basic operators ❺ and the number pad ❻ to define a formula.

Let's create a formula for the comparison column mentioned in our example. The logic is shown here:

((2014 Value – 2013 Value) / (2013 Value))×100

This logic can be built for the formula as shown in Figure 9.60.

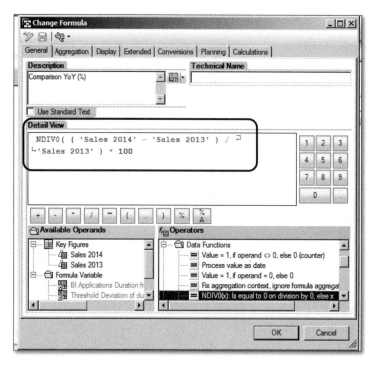

Figure 9.60 Define the Formula

Note that the NDIV0(x) function is used to handle the scenario when the denominator is zero. In this case, the formula will return the value 0 instead of x. The result of the query is shown in Figure 9.61.

Now you know the procedure to create selections and formulas in a BEx query. There are situations where the same selections or formula definitions are used in multiple queries. In these situations, you can obviously create the selections and formulas separately for each query. However, a better option is available in the form of RKFs and CKFs, where you can create selections and formulas that can be used in multiple queries. In the subsequent sections, we'll explain the procedure for creating RKFs and CKFs.

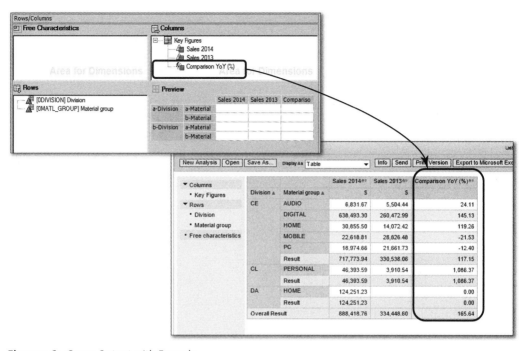

Figure 9.61 Query Output with Formula

9.9 Creating Key Figures

The selections and formulas discussed in the previous section are local elements of the query. Both selections and formulas can also be defined at the InfoProvider level and are then available to all the queries defined on that InfoProvider. The selections defined at the InfoProvider level are called restricted key figures (RKFs), and the formulas defined on the InfoProvider level are called calculated key figures (CKFs). We discuss both in this section.

9.9.1 Restricted Key Figures

RKFs are reusable query elements where the selection definition can be built on the InfoProvider itself, thus making the definition available for all of the queries on that InfoProvider.

To illustrate, let's take the example of a selection called "Mexico sales," which displays the key figure value for net sales where Country = Mexico. This particular definition is used in multiple queries on the Sales InfoCube. It makes sense to create a RKF for it so you don't have to create the same key figure again and again for each query.

RKFs are created directly on the InfoProvider definition visible in the INFOPROVIDER area (see Figure 9.62). Open the context menu for the KEY FIGURES folder in the INFOPROVIDER area, and select NEW RESTRICTED KEY FIGURE from the context menu.

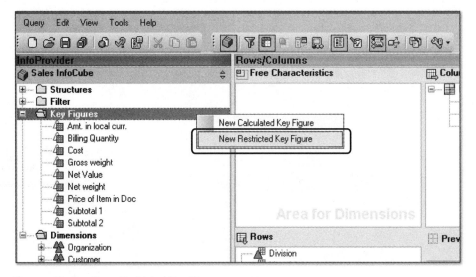

Figure 9.62 Creating a Restricted Key Figure

You have to provide the RKF a suitable description (❶ of Figure 9.63) and technical name ❷ in the definition screen.

Define the selections for the RKF per the example requirement stated earlier, where Key figure = Net Sales for Country = Mexico ❸. Save the RKF by using the SAVE button on the toolbar.

The saved RKF is now visible under the RESTRICTED KEY FIGURES folder in the INFOPROVIDER area (see Figure 9.64).

This RKF is defined at the InfoProvider level and is available for all of the queries that are defined on this InfoCube. To reuse the RKF in a query definition, you simple drag and drop the RKF to the desired location in the query definition (ROWS or COLUMNS area).

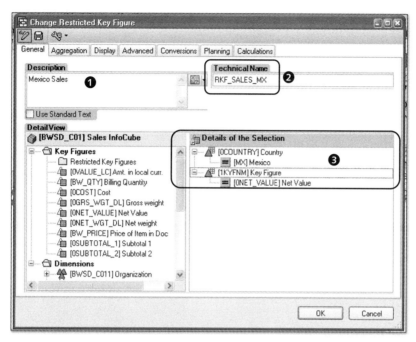

Figure 9.63 Defining the Restricted Key Figure

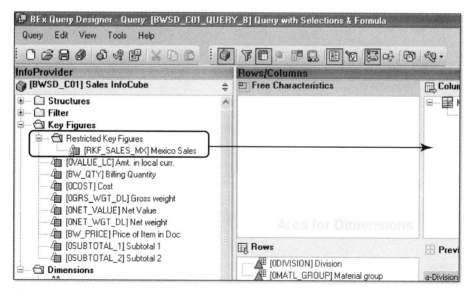

Figure 9.64 Reusing a Restricted Key Figure

9.9.2 Calculated Key Figures

Similar to RKFs, calculated key figures (CKFs) are defined at the InfoProvider level. CKFs facilitate the reuse of a formula definition across different queries on the InfoProvider. CKFs can be created using the NEW CALCULATED KEY FIGURE option from the context menu of the KEY FIGURES folder in the INFOPROVIDER area (refer to Figure 9.62).

Define the CKF in the pop-up box, as shown in Figure 9.65 by entering the description and the technical name for the CKF ❶. Further, define the formula logic in the DETAIL VIEW section for the CKF ❷. After the definition is complete, click on the SAVE button on the toolbar ❸.

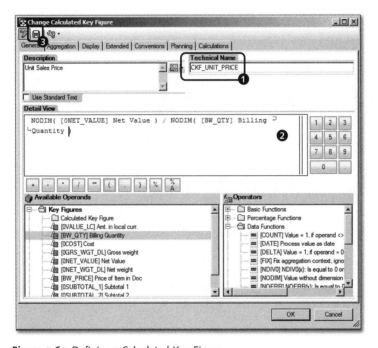

Figure 9.65 Defining a Calculated Key Figure

The newly defined CKF is available in the INFOPROVIDER area under the CALCU-LATED KEY FIGURES folder (see Figure 9.66).

The definition in the CKF is available for reuse in all of the queries that are built on that InfoProvider. To use the CKF during query designing, you simply drag and drop the selected CKF into the desired query area (ROWS or COLUMNS area).

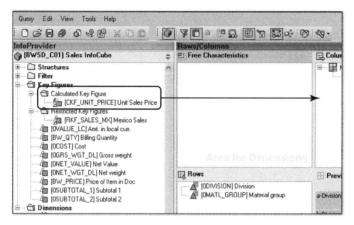

Figure 9.66 Reusing a Calculated Key Figure

9.10 Properties of Query Elements

All components of a query (including the query itself) have their own set of properties, which include settings for description, display, data access, calculation, and so on. These properties determine the behavior of that element. The properties for the selected query element are visible in the PROPERTIES area of BEx Query Designer. Also, you can select a query element for which you have to define the properties from the dropdown available in the PROPERTIES area (see Figure 9.67).

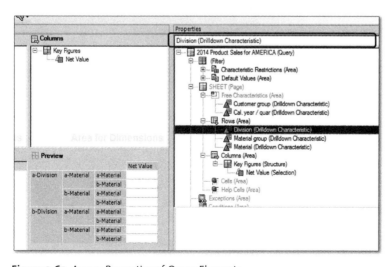

Figure 9.67 Access Properties of Query Elements

In this section, we explain the properties of a BEx query and the query elements (characteristics and key figures).

9.10.1 Setting Properties of Characteristic Query Elements

In this section, we explain the different properties that correspond to a characteristic query element. Select the characteristic for which you want to define the properties, as shown previously in Figure 9.67.

The properties for the selected characteristic element will appear in the Properties area, as shown in Figure 9.68. There are five different tabs available. Let's discuss each of these tabs one by one.

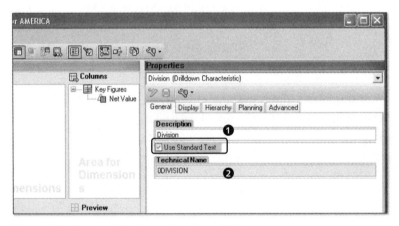

Figure 9.68 Characteristic Properties: General Tab

Characteristic Properties: General Tab

In the GENERAL tab (refer to Figure 9.68), you maintain the description ❶ of the characteristic of that query. The same description will be visible in the query output when the query is executed. If you select the USE STANDARD TEXT checkbox, the description as mentioned in the InfoObject definition is selected.

You also see the technical name ❷ of the characteristic on this PROPERTIES tab.

Characteristic Properties: Display Tab

In this tab, you control the display-related settings of the characteristic in the query (see Figure 9.69). There are three sections available on this screen.

In the VALUE DISPLAY section, you can select the way characteristic values should be displayed ❶. Also, in the TEXT VIEW field, you can specify which text (short, medium, or long) should be displayed.

In the SORTING section ❷, you define how the characteristic should be sorted (ascending or descending) in the query output.

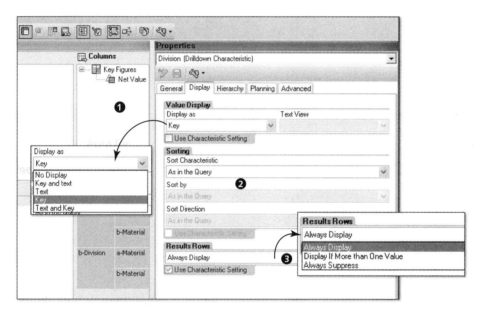

Figure 9.69 Characteristic Properties: Display Tab

The RESULT ROWS section ❸ allows you to set the display options of the totals (result rows) in the query output.

Characteristic Properties: Hierarchy Tab

If the characteristic for which properties are being maintained contains hierarchies built on it, then you can set different properties on the HIERARCHY tab. On this tab, you can select the hierarchy to be used in the query, and you can define the display and sorting settings for the selected hierarchy.

Characteristic Properties: Planning Tab

The options specific to planning on hierarchy nodes are available on the PLAN-
NING tab of characteristic properties. This setting is relevant for input-ready queries only. Input-ready queries in planning are explained in Chapter 12.

Characteristic Properties: Advanced Tab

The properties related to data access and data selection are maintained on the
ADVANCED tab of the characteristic properties (see Figure 9.70).

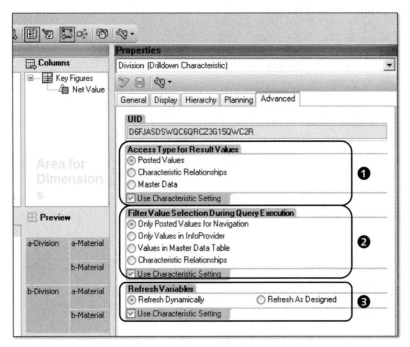

Figure 9.70 Characteristic Properties: Advanced Tab

Under the ACCESS TYPE FOR RESULT VALUES section (❶ of Figure 9.70), you can
define what values of the characteristic should be displayed in the query output.
These options are explained here:

▶ POSTED VALUES
   Use this option to display only posted values of the characteristics (per the
   query definition) in the query output.

▸ CHARACTERISTIC RELATIONSHIPS

Use this option to display the data per the characteristic relationships. Characteristic relationships are discussed in detail in Chapter 12.

▸ MASTER DATA

Use this option to display all of the characteristic values from the master data, whether transaction data exists for those values or not.

Similarly, in the FILTER VALUE SELECTION DURING QUERY EXECUTION section ❷, the setting determines the list of values you would get while selecting a filter value during query execution. You can also make variable refresh settings under the REFRESH VARIABLES section ❸.

9.10.2   Setting Properties of Key Figure Query Elements

In this section, we take a look at different properties for key figure query elements. The PROPERTIES screen for a query element involving a key figure shows seven different tabs (see Figure 9.71). These tabs and important properties are explained next.

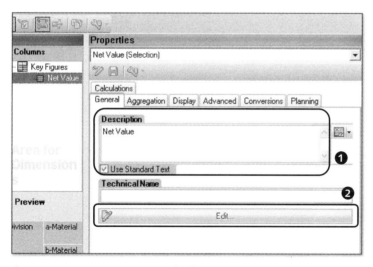

Figure 9.71 Key Properties: General Tab

Key Figure Properties: General Tab

You maintain the description and technical name for the query element on this tab (refer to ❶ of Figure 9.71). The description maintained here is visible in the query output. If you want to keep the default description from the key figure InfoObject description, select the USE STANDARD TEXT checkbox. Additionally, you can edit the definition of the element by clicking on the EDIT button ❷.

Key Figure Properties: Aggregation Tab

On this tab page, you can specify how the aggregation should take place for the key figure when the query is executed. This tab is enabled only for formula type query elements or CKFs (see Figure 9.72).

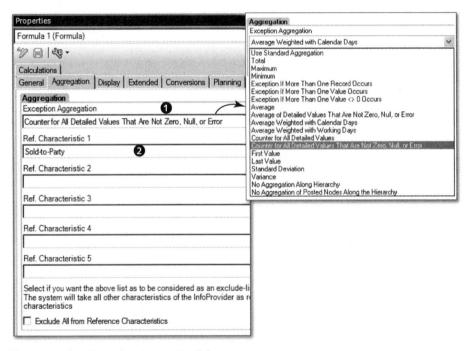

Figure 9.72 Key Properties: AggregationTab

By default, the key figures are aggregated using standard aggregation. In a standard aggregation, the data read from the InfoProvider is first aggregated by the characteristics included in the rows/columns of the query. Then the formula is applied to the data after this aggregation. The EXCEPTION AGGREGATION option ❶ allows you to define whether you want to aggregate the data in a specific manner and with respect to the reference characteristic. The different options of EXCEPTION AGGREGATION are available under the dropdown shown in Figure 9.72.

If you choose to use an exception aggregation, then you have to specify one of the characteristics from the InfoProvider as the reference characteristic against which the formula will be calculated ❷.

For example, if you want to calculate the number of customers who are buying a particular material, you create a formula with the net value key figure. Then, in the properties of the formula, you select Exception Aggregation as Count <> 0 and Customer as the Reference Characteristic.

If you have to perform exception aggregation with reference to multiple characteristics, you can define up to five reference characteristics on the AGGREGATION tab.

Key Figure Properties: Display Tab

On the DISPLAY tab of the properties, you have different options available to control the display of the key figure value in the query output (see Figure 9.73).

Use the settings under the HIDE section ❶ if you want to hide the key figure in the output. There is also an option available to highlight the key figure value under the HIGHLIGHT section ❷. Additional settings related to the number of decimal places, scaling factor, and so on, can also be set on this DISPLAY tab.

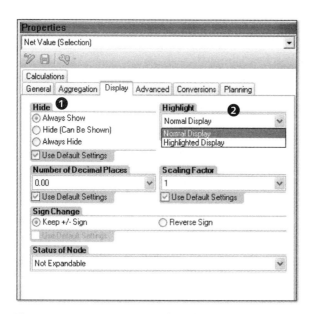

Figure 9.73 Key Properties: Display Tab

Key Figure Properties: Advanced Tab

The CONSTANT SELECTION setting on the ADVANCED tab of a key figure query element (❸ of Figure 9.74) is available only for elements of selections and RKFs. It's used if you want to keep the characteristic selections mentioned in the definition of the selection or RKF as constant. This means that during the query execution and navigation, the restrictions applied to the key figure don't change.

This setting is particularly important if you want to use a key figure value as a fixed reference for comparison with other key figures. Take an example where the business analysts at ABCD Corp. want to compare the sales for different material groups with respect to the sales for Material Group = DIGITAL. The report would look like the screen shown in Figure 9.74. As you can see, the DIGITAL SALES column has a constant value for all of the rows (❶ of Figure 9.74), and this value is nothing but the sales value where Material Group = DIGITAL ❷. As a result, the comparison can now easily be achieved using a simple formula.

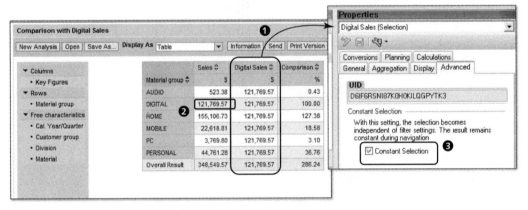

Figure 9.74 Constant Selection

In this case, the CONSTANT SELECTION setting ❸ was used on the DIGITAL SALES (SELECTION).

Key Figure Properties: Conversions Tab

The settings on the CONVERSIONS tab (see Figure 9.75) are useful if there is an amount or quantity key figure included in the query element definition, and you need to convert the amount or quantity in a uniform currency or unit.

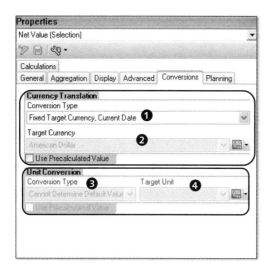

Figure 9.75 Key Properties: Conversions Tab

The Currency Translation section of this tab is available for amount key figures. Here, you can define the way the amount needs to be converted by specifying the Conversion Type (❶ of Figure 9.75) and the Target Currency ❷ to which the key figure value is translated.

If the key figure is a quantity key figure, the Unit Conversion section of this tab is enabled. Similar to the settings for currency translation, here you have to define the Conversion Type ❸ and the Target Unit ❹ as parameters for unit conversion.

Key Figure Properties: Planning Tab

The Planning tab allows you to set the properties for a key figure included in an input-ready query. The Planning tab and the significance of all the available settings are explained in Chapter 12.

Key Figure Properties: Calculations Tab

The Calculations tab allows you to define the way you want the results and the single values to be calculated for the report output (see Figure 9.76).

The option you choose in the Calculate Result As area (❶ of Figure 9.76) will actually recalculate the result per the selected option. Similarly, the option you select under CALCULATE SINGLE VALUES AS ❷ will influence the way single values are recalculated for the query output display.

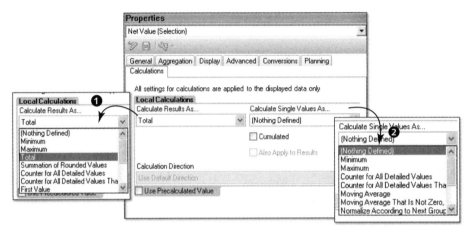

Figure 9.76 Key Properties: Calculations Tab

9.10.3 Query Properties

Different properties that are defined at the query level are discussed in this section. To display the query properties, select the query node from the dropdown available in the PROPERTIES area (❶ of Figure 9.77).

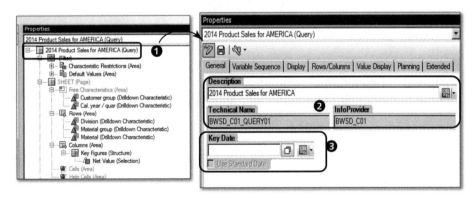

Figure 9.77 Query Properties: General Tab

There are seven different tabs where you can set the query properties. These tabs are explained next.

Query Properties: General Tab

The GENERAL tab of query properties displays the technical name and allows you to maintain the description of the query (refer to ❷ of Figure 9.77). This description is visible to the report user when the query is executed. You can also use text variables for flexible query description.

If the query involves any time-dependent master data, then the date specified in the KEY DATE field is used to derive the values from the time-dependent data ❸. You can maintain any specific date as a key date in the query, or you can use a characteristic variable on the date as a more flexible option. If nothing is included in the KEY DATE settings for a query, then the date of query execution is considered as the key date for that query.

Query Properties: Variable Sequence Tab

The VARIABLE SEQUENCE tab displays a list of all of the variables that are enabled for user entry. You can change the order in which the variables should appear on the selection screen when the query is executed.

Query Properties: Display Tab

The display-related settings for the query are maintained on the DISPLAY tab (see Figure 9.78).

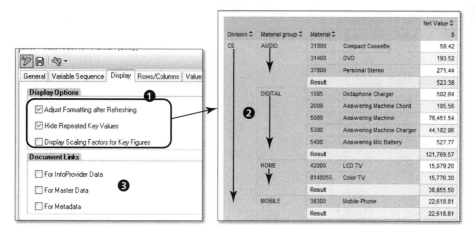

Figure 9.78 Query Properties: Display Tab

The formatting, display of key values, and display of scaling factors settings are done in the DISPLAY OPTIONS section (❶ of Figure 9.78). HIDE REPEATED KEY VALUES is typically the most frequently used display setting for a query. When you select this setting, the key values (characteristic values in the query) that are repeated in successive records are hidden, and only the first record displays the characteristic value, which is repeated. The values for DIVISION and MATERIAL GROUP ❷ are repeated for multiple records, so only the first record shows the value and hides the repeated values in the query display.

You can also choose if you want to provide document links in the query by selecting the options in the DOCUMENT LINKS section ❸.

Query Properties: Rows/Columns Tab

As the name suggests, this tab allows you to maintain settings related to rows and columns displayed in the query result (see Figure 9.79).

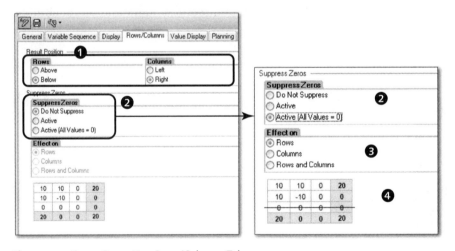

Figure 9.79 Query Properties: Rows/Columns Tab

The position of the result rows and result columns in a query is determined based on the settings maintained under the RESULT POSITION section (❶ of Figure 9.79). You can also decide to suppress the zero values from the query output in the SUPPRESS ZEROS section ❷. Further, you can decide whether to apply the suppression to rows or columns or both rows and columns in the EFFECT ON section ❸. This tab also displays a preview ❹ of the settings chosen on this tab.

Query Properties: Value Display Tab

The settings related to key figure display, such as display of +/– signs or display of zero values, are maintained on the VALUE DISPLAY tab.

Query Properties: Planning Tab

The PLANNING tab is relevant only to the input-ready queries where you can make the setting to open the query in change mode. This means users can enter and change the key figure values that are enabled for input. Chapter 12 covers input-ready queries and this setting in more depth.

Query Properties: Extended Tab

The ALLOW EXTERNAL ACCESS TO THIS QUERY setting on this tab (❶ of Figure 9.80) determines whether the query can be executed through the Object Linking and Embedding DB for OLAP (ODBO). As the name suggests, this setting has to be checked to allow external tools access to the query using ODBO.

The BY EASY QUERY checkbox ❷ allows external access for the query for static and unformatted consumption. A BEx query released as an easy query can be used in Simple Object Access Protocol (SOAP) services.

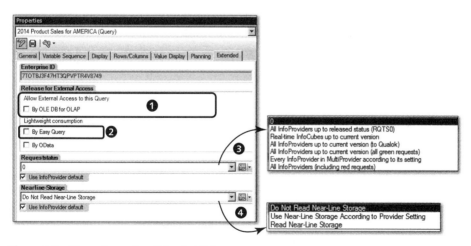

Figure 9.80 Query Properties: Extended Tab

This tab also allows you to configure how the data has to be read from the Info-Provider when the query is executed (❸ of Figure 9.80).

If the SAP BW solution involves near-line storage (NLS) then the setting for whether to read the data from NLS or not can be configured in the NEARLINE-STORAGE section ❹.

9.11   Creating Conditions

Conditions allow you to filter the data that is finally displayed in the query result, based on the parameters defined in the condition. This is an OLAP function provided by BEx to aid information analysis in SAP BW.

For example, the business analysts of ABCD Corp. want to see their top 10 best-selling products. In this section, we'll see how a condition built in the query helps address this requirement. We explain the procedure for creating a condition on a BEx query next.

Conditions are maintained in the CONDITIONS area of BEx Query Designer. To display this area, click on the CONDITIONS toolbar icon (❶ of Figure 9.81). The CONDITIONS area appears ❷.

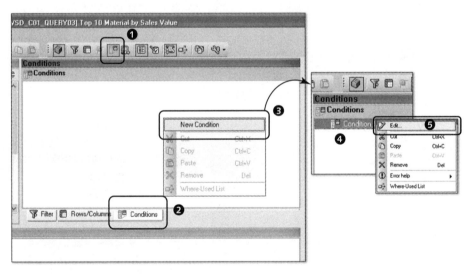

Figure 9.81 Creating a New Condition

To create a new condition, open the context menu from the CONDITIONS area, and select NEW CONDITION ❸. This creates a new condition with a system-generated description ❹. To edit and define this condition, double-click on it, or select EDIT from the context menu ❺.

The CHANGE CONDITION screen appears (see Figure 9.82). The condition defined is applied only if the CONDITION IS ACTIVE checkbox is selected. You can now maintain the description for the condition ❶. Click on the NEW button ❷ to create a new condition parameter, where you can define the logic for the condition.

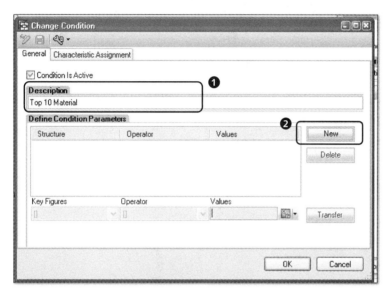

Figure 9.82 Changing a Condition

Define the condition parameter as shown in Figure 9.83. You have to specify three fields to define a condition parameter. First, select the KEY FIGURES on which this condition should be applied ❶. Then select an OPERATOR from the list of available operators for a condition ❷. For our example, we're selecting the operator TOP N. (Had the requirement been to show only those materials where total sales is more than $1,000 USD, you could have chosen the operator GREATER THAN.) Then select the value for the condition ❸. In this case, we have to display the top 10 materials, so we enter the value "10". However, you can make this condition more flexible by using a variable for the value ❹.

Click on the TRANSFER button ❺ after the parameter is defined. The defined condition is now visible, as shown in ❶ of Figure 9.84. Click on the CHARACTERISTIC ASSIGNMENT tab ❷ to configure more settings for the condition.

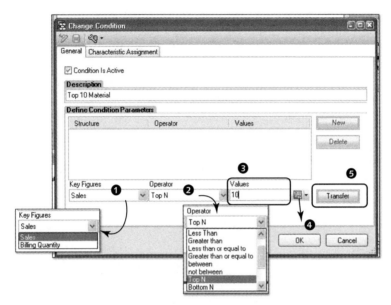

Figure 9.83 Define Condition Parameter

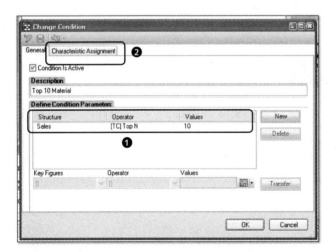

Figure 9.84 Going to the Characteristic Assignment Tab

On the CHARACTERISTIC ASSIGNMENT tab, you define how the condition should be applied to the query result (❶ of Figure 9.85). For the ALL CHARACTERISTICS IN THE DRILLDOWN INDEPENDENTLY setting, the condition will be applied to the characteristics that are used in the drilldown of the query. You can also choose to apply the condition to the MOST DETAILED CHARACTERISTIC ALONG THE ROWS or the MOST DETAILED CHARACTERISTIC ALONG THE COLUMNS. If you want that condition to be applied to some specific characteristics only, you select the INDIVIDUAL CHARS. AND CHAR. COMBINATIONS option. Here you can select the characteristics for which the condition should be evaluated ❷.

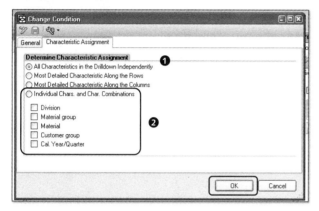

Figure 9.85 Maintaining Characteristic Assignments for a Condition

Click on OK to complete the condition definition (see Figure 9.85).

When you execute the query with this definition and material in the query drill-down, the condition evaluates the result and displays the records that satisfy the condition. See Figure 9.86, where the condition has evaluated the top 10 records by sales value and filtered the relevant query output.

Material		Sales $	Billing Quantity NO
81460	Air Conditioner	116,400.12	169.00
5000	Answering Machine	76,451.54	2,028.00
92000	Electric Shaving M/c	44,761.28	2,378.00
5300	Answering Machine Charger	44,182.06	1,758.00
38300	Mobile Phone	22,618.81	80.00
8148055	Color TV	15,776.30	39.00
42000	LCD TV	15,079.20	12.00
63000	Dish Washer	4,832.13	15.00
93500	Laptop PC	3,769.80	6.00
81480	Washing Machine	3,018.98	8.00
Overall Result		348,549.57	6,949.00

Figure 9.86 Query Output with Condition

9.12 Creating Exceptions

Like conditions, the exception is another OLAP feature with which you can highlight the cells in the query output if the value is beyond the threshold mentioned in the exception definition. For example, consider a scenario where you want to create a report that will highlight the cells in the query output in green if the sales value is *more than $1000 USD*, and in red if the sales value is *less than $200 USD*. This visualization can be achieved using exceptions in the query.

Display the EXCEPTIONS area in BEx Query Designer by clicking on the EXCEPTIONS icon, as shown in ❶ of Figure 9.87. In the EXCEPTIONS area ❷, create a new exception by selecting NEW EXCEPTION from the context menu.

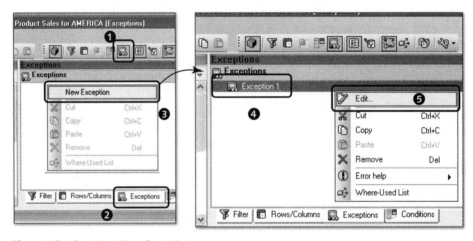

Figure 9.87 Creating a New Exception

An exception with a system-defined default description is created ❹. To edit and define this exception, select EDIT from the context menu ❺. Maintain the description for the exception (❶ of Figure 9.88).

Click on the NEW button ❷ to define the threshold values for the exception. Define the exception values by maintaining the fields as shown in Figure 9.89. Select the alert level ❶, for example, GOOD1 for green or BAD1 for red. Then select the OPERATOR from the dropdown ❷ to define the exception, and then specify the threshold value in the VALUE field ❸. You can also use a variable for the value to make the exception more flexible ❹. Finally, click on the TRANSFER button ❺ to transfer the defined exception. All of the defined exceptions are visible ❻.

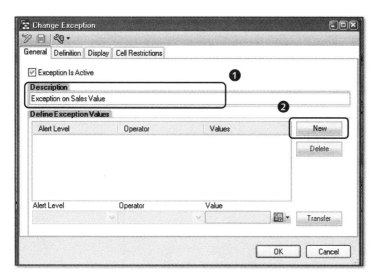

Figure 9.88 Changing the Exception

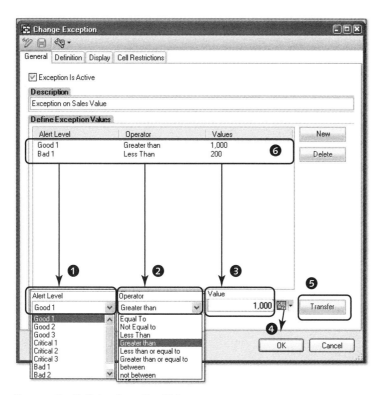

Figure 9.89 Defining Exception Values

After the exceptions are defined, you then select the query element on which this exception should be defined on the DEFINITION tab (see Figure 9.90). In our example, we want to highlight the exception on sales, so select SALES from the KEY FIGURE dropdown. If you want all of the key figures to be evaluated for this, select ALL STRUCTURE ELEMENTS. You can also use the BEFORE LIST CALCULATION setting if you want the exception to be determined before the local calculations are performed in the query.

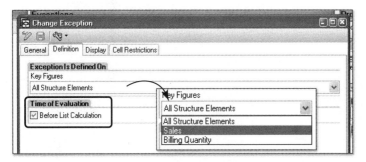

Figure 9.90 Change Exception: Definition

The DISPLAY tab contains the settings where you can define the query elements that should be highlighted for the exception (see Figure 9.91). If you select EXCEPTION AFFECTS DATA CELLS ❶, then you can select which data elements should be highlighted for this exception ❷. Similarly, if you select EXCEPTION AFFECTS CHARACTERISTIC CELLS ❸, you can specify whether the rows or columns or both rows and columns should be highlighted if an exception occurs.

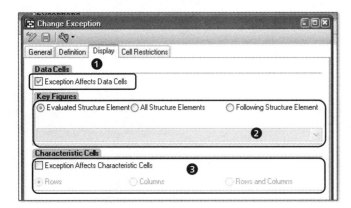

Figure 9.91 Exceptions: Display Tab

On the CELL RESTRICTIONS tab, you define the data set that should be evaluated for the exception. The EXCEPTION AFFECTS EVERYTHING option (❶ of Figure 9.92) will apply the exception to all of the records in the query output, whereas the EXCEPTION ONLY AFFECTS RESULTS option will evaluate and hence highlight only the result rows of the query output. You can also define specific cell restrictions if you want the exception to be evaluated for only a specific set of data. To create this restriction, click on the NEW button ❷, and then define and transfer the restriction using the fields and the TRANSFER button ❸.

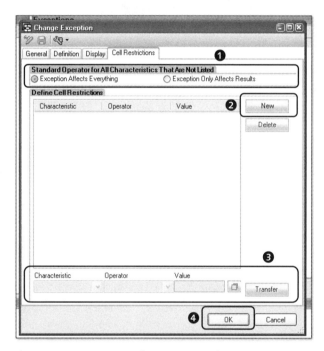

Figure 9.92 Exceptions: Cell Restrictions Tab

Finally, click on OK ❹ to complete the exception definition.

When you save and run this query, the exception evaluates the query output based on the settings and highlights the fields as mentioned in the exception definition (see Figure 9.93).

Exceptions can be effectively used for analyzing a huge set of data. Using exceptions, the business analyst can quickly focus on the values that are highlighted in the query output, accelerating the analysis process.

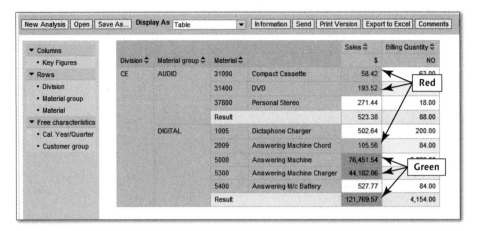

Figure 9.93 Query Output: Exceptions

9.13 Configuring Report-to-Report Interfaces

As we mentioned at the beginning of the chapter, the auditors of ABCD Corp. need a solution that can analyze instances of variances on specific sales documents. This billing document-level investigation needs to be addressed in SAP BW rather than by going into the transactional system for detailed information.

Consider a scenario where you have a report on an InfoCube that shows you the sales by customer, but the data is consolidated at the customer and material level, so there's no sales document-level information available in the InfoCube. At the same time, however, there is a DSO in which the detailed information is stored separately in SAP BW. To get a list of all sales documents for the selected customer when needed, SAP BW offers the report-to-report interface (RRI).

For the given example, say there's a customer sales query on the InfoCube that shows sales for different customers (❶ of Figure 9.94), and there's another query built on the DSO with detailed information that shows sales document details ❷. Using RRI, you can pass a specific value of customer from the customer sales query to the sales document query, which will show the documents for that specific customer. In this case, the query on the InfoCube sends the information to another query; hence, it's called the *sender* ❶. Meanwhile, the query on the DSO is executed based on the information received from the sender, so the DSO query is called the *receiver* ❷. The sender will send the value of the selected customer

(BW_CUST) to the receiver to display the sales documents for that customer ❸. This is also termed a *jump target*.

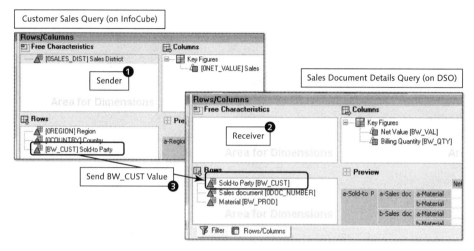

Figure 9.94 The Report-to-Report Interface Concept

Use Transaction RSBBS to open the MAINTAIN SENDER/RECEIVER ASSIGNMENT screen (see Figure 9.95).

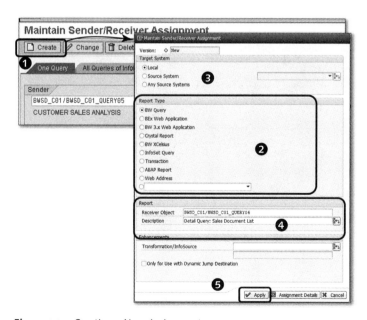

Figure 9.95 Creating a New Assignment

The RRI settings can be maintained for a specific query as well as for all of the queries on an InfoProvider. Select the ONE QUERY tab, and then select the sender query (refer to Figure 9.95).

After you select the sender query, click on the CREATE button ❶ to create a new sender/receiver assignment. A pop-up will appear where you can define the assignment. In the MAINTAIN SENDER/RECEIVER ASSIGNMENT pop-up box, define the receiver information. The receiver can be queries and web applications from BEx as well as from older versions of SAP BW (3.x and older). The receiver can also be a transaction, a report, or a web address. Different options are shown in ❷. For our example, select the BW QUERY option as the receiver.

Select whether the receiver is in the same system as that of the sender or in some different system ❸, and define the receiver query ❹. For our example, the DETAIL QUERY: SALES DOCUMENT LIST is maintained as the receiver. Click on the APPLY button ❺ to complete this configuration and return to the main screen. This newly created assignment is now visible in the RECEIVER section, as shown in Figure 9.96.

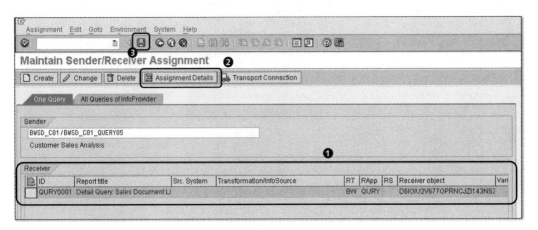

Figure 9.96 Going to Assignment Details

You now have to maintain the specific parameters of this assignment where you specify how the information will be exchanged between the sender and the receiver. Select the assignment (❶ of Figure 9.96), and click on the ASSIGNMENT DETAILS button ❷. This opens the FIELD ASSIGNMENTS pop-up box, as shown in Figure 9.97.

On the FIELD ASSIGNMENTS screen, you actually define how the information will be passed from the sender to the receiver. Select the type of assignment ❶, and specify the InfoObject name as the FIELD NAME ❷. Maintain the SELECTION TYPE ❸, and select the checkbox in the REQUIRED column ❹, so that the receiver query is called and executed only if it's called for a customer value.

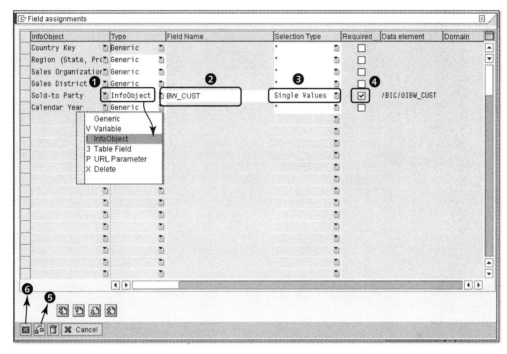

Figure 9.97 Maintaining Field Assignments

Check the details by using the 🔍 icon shown in ❺ of Figure 9.97, and finally complete the assignment and close this window using the CLOSE icon ❻. The RRI definition is complete, and you can now save this definition using the SAVE button shown earlier in ❸ of Figure 9.96.

Figure 9.98 shows the use of RRI, which has just been defined. RRI is available for the characteristic value for which it's defined (❶ of Figure 9.98). For this example, you can see in that the GOTO section in the context menu for customer value 100075 shows RRI for Detail Query: Sales Document List ❷. Select the RRI query, and it will call the receiver query and display the detailed list of all sales documents. As you can see from ❸, the value 100075 for the customer is passed as a parameter from the sender to the receiver. This is based on the field assignments defined for RRI.

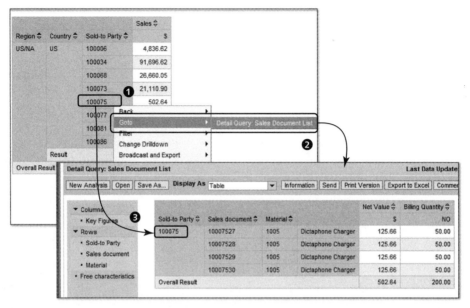

Figure 9.98 Using the Report-to-Report Interface (RRI)

Using RRI, you can provide additional features to perform detailed analysis on the data. Different types of jump targets can be assigned to a BEx query to make the analysis more flexible.

9.14   Summary

In this chapter, we discussed creating queries in BEx Query Designer: from simple queries, to the significance of OLAP variables in query design, as well as the different types and processing types of variables that can be used. Some common variable types were also discussed in detail.

As we explored additional features and query elements such as filters, selections, formulas, structures, RKFs, CKFs, and so on, we saw how different business requirements can be met using these elements. Because the properties of different query elements and the query itself have an influence on the query output, we also explained the significance of the different property settings in the context of real-life business scenarios.

Finally, we looked at features such as conditions, exceptions, and RRI, which can be built on a BEx query to make reporting and analysis on SAP BW data more flexible and effective.

In the next chapter, we'll discuss different modes of analyzing data using these BEx queries.

Reporting and analysis in SAP BW can be done in two main ways: via an Excel interface (using SAP BEx Analyzer) or a web interface (using SAP BEx Web Analyzer). We'll also look at the SAP BW Workspaces, which was introduced with SAP BW 7.3.

10 Reporting and Analysis Tools

In previous chapters, we explained the procedure of creating a query on InfoProviders, which can then be used to generate reports or perform data analysis. In SAP BW, you can perform analysis using a Microsoft Excel interface or a web interface. The SAP Business Explorer (BEx) application suite provides the following tools for this purpose:

- **BEx Analyzer**
  Using BEx Analyzer, you can run queries and perform ad hoc analysis in an Excel environment. BEx Analyzer is integrated with Excel by using an Excel add-in. You can also design your own analysis or planning application using the design option in BEx Analyzer.

- **BEx Web Analyzer**
  This is a reporting and analysis tool designed for a web environment. You can execute queries and perform ad hoc analysis using BEx Web Analyzer.

In addition to these two main reporting and analysis tools, SAP BW 7.3 and later versions offer new functionality targeted toward end users: *BW Workspaces*. BW Workspaces enable users to create their own ad hoc data models (composite providers) that can be based on SAP BW data as well as local user data. You can create queries on these data models and execute them from both BEx Analyzer and BEx Web Analyzer.

In this chapter, you'll learn about these tools. First, we explain how analysis can be performed in BEx Analyzer and the procedure used to build your own application. Then we discuss BEx Web Analyzer and the different analysis or ad hoc analysis options available on the web. We also have a brief discussion about information broadcasting, and, finally, we conclude with a discussion of BW Workspaces and composite providers.

10.1 Running Queries in BEx Analyzer

BEx Analyzer allows you to perform reporting and analysis in the Excel environment. BEx Analyzer is a standalone application that can be started by following Start Menu • All Programs • Business Explorer • BEx Analyzer, as shown in Figure 10.1.

Figure 10.1 Open BEx Analyzer

Starting BEx Analyzer opens an Excel session on your computer. BEx Analyzer functions are available in Excel through the Excel add-in. These functions can be seen by clicking on the Add-Ins tab on the Excel toolbar, as shown in ❶ of Figure 10.2.

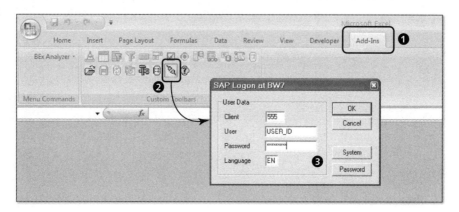

Figure 10.2 Connect to BEx Analyzer

Figure 10.2 displays the BEx Analyzer add-in in Microsoft Excel 2010. If you're using Microsoft Excel 2003, BEx Analyzer functions can be accessed as shown in Figure 10.3.

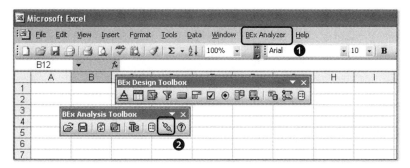

Figure 10.3 Connect to BEx Analyzer (Excel 2003)

The BEx ANALYSIS TOOLBOX and BEx DESIGN TOOLBOX are visible as two separate toolbars, and a new BEx ANALYZER menu is available in the Excel menu bar, as shown in ❶ of Figure 10.3.

To execute a query or to perform an analysis in BEx Analyzer, you must first establish a connection with the SAP BW system. To make a connection, click on the CONNECTION button (refer to ❷ of Figure 10.2 or ❷ of Figure 10.3). This opens the login screen for the SAP BW system; enter the login credentials to connect BEx Analyzer with SAP BW (refer to ❸ of Figure 10.2).

After the connection is established, all of the queries and InfoProviders from the connected SAP BW system are now available for reporting and analysis in BEx Analyzer.

With this accomplished, we'll now explain how to execute a query in BEx Analyzer, as well as the various functions of this application.

10.1.1 Executing a Query in BEx Analyzer

To execute an existing query from the connected SAP BW system, you have to first open the query (Figure 10.4).

Click on the BEx ANALYZER menu and select OPEN QUERY (❶ of Figure 10.4), which opens a pop-up screen. Navigate through the InfoAreas to locate the required query ❷, and click on OPEN ❸.

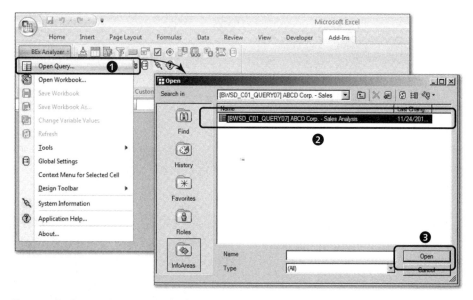

Figure 10.4 Open a Query in BEx Analyzer

This executes the selected query in BEx Analyzer. If the selected query has user entry variables included in it, the variable screen SELECT VALUES FOR VARIABLES appears, as shown in Figure 10.5.

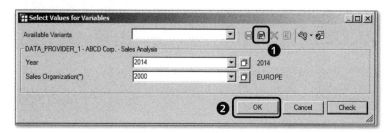

Figure 10.5 Select Values for Variables

Select the required values for the variables on this screen. If you want to save this selection for future use, you can save it as a variant using the button shown in ❶ of Figure 10.5. Finally, select OK ❷ to execute the query for the select variable values.

The query results are displayed in the Excel sheet, as shown in Figure 10.6.

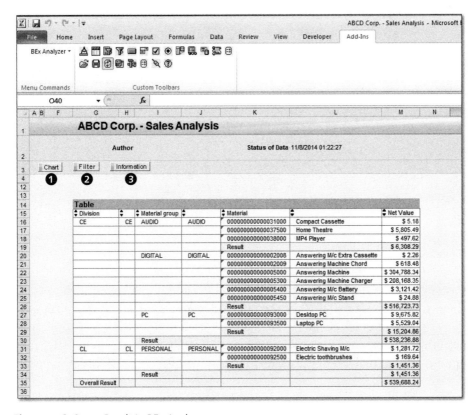

Figure 10.6 Query Result in BEx Analyzer

Along with the query result, you can also see the query description, the author of the query, and the status of the data in the InfoProvider. Figure 10.6 shows there are three buttons—Chart ❶, Filter ❷, and Information ❸—available in the display. Usage of these buttons is explained next.

Using the Chart button, you can convert the tabular display of data into a graphical display. As shown in Figure 10.7, the graph is displayed for the tabular data you saw earlier. You can now revert back to the tabular view by clicking on the Table button, as shown in Figure 10.7.

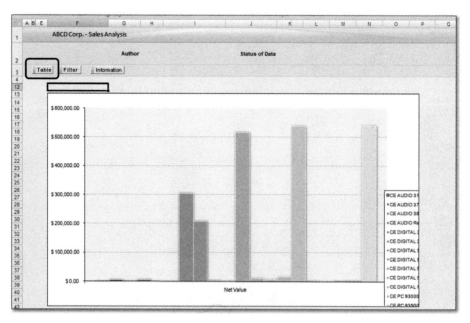

Figure 10.7 Graphical Display of Data

Clicking on the FILTER button displays a FILTER pane in the layout (Figure 10.8). Here, you can see a list of all of the query elements available in rows/columns/ free characteristics of the query. These can be used to filter the query result or to perform different navigations on the query result. (The different navigation options in BEx Analyzer are discussed in subsequent sections of this chapter.)

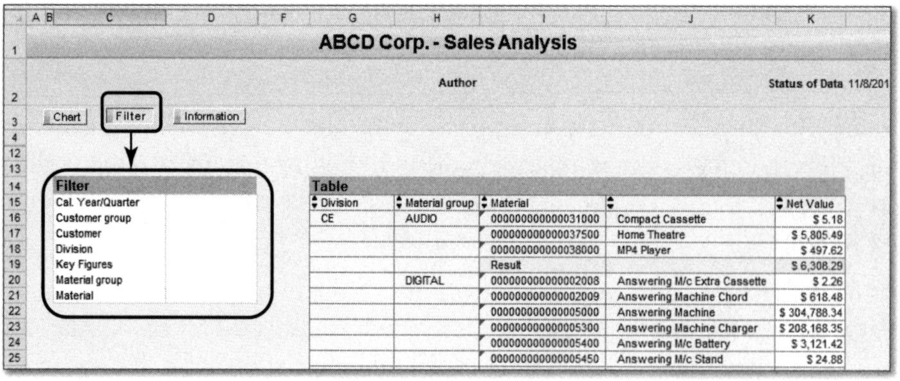

Figure 10.8 Filter Button in BEx Analyzer

The Information button displays the technical information about the query that is executed (Figure 10.9). This information includes details such as the technical name of the query and InfoProvider, different timestamps, and so on.

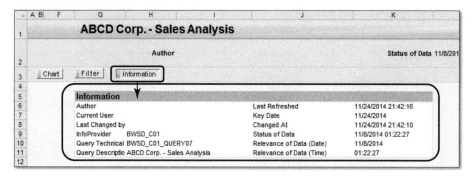

Figure 10.9 Information Button in BEx Analyzer

The Excel sheet with query results is called a *workbook*.

10.1.2 BEx Analyzer Analysis Functions

BEx Analyzer has two different sets of functions available in the form of two different toolbars: the Design toolbar and the Analysis toolbar. As shown in the boxed area of Figure 10.10, the top part of the BEx Analyzer functions are design functions and constitute the Design toolbar. The lower part of the BEx Analyzer functions constitutes the Analysis toolbar (shown enlarged in Figure 10.10). The significance of each of these buttons on the Analysis toolbar is discussed next.

❶ Open
This button is used to open an existing query or workbook in BEx Analyzer.

❷ Save
This button is used to save the workbook with the same name (Save Workbook) or as a different workbook (Save Workbook As). The Save View option stores the navigational state and the filter values for the selected query element.

❸ Refresh
This button refreshes the query results in the workbook. When the workbook is refreshed using this button, you can use the same button to pause the automatic refresh of the data in the workbook.

❹ CHANGE VARIABLE VALUES

This button is used if you want to call the variable selection screen for the selected query in the workbook.

❺ TOOLS

Use this button to open different BEx tools and applications.

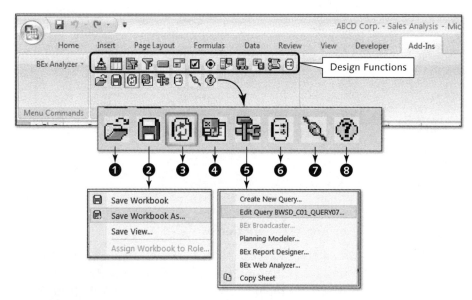

Figure 10.10 BEx Analyzer Analysis Toolbar

❻ GLOBAL SETTINGS

Use this button to maintain different settings for BEx Analyzer. There are four tabs available where you can maintain settings: BEHAVIOR, DEFAULT WORK-BOOK, TRACE, and STATISTICS (Figure 10.11).

❼ SYSTEM INFORMATION/CONNECT

Use this button (as you did earlier) to establish the connection between BEx Analyzer and the SAP BW system. If you click on this button after the system is connected, it gives you information about which system is connected and provides you with an option to disconnect the system.

❽ APPLICATION HELP

Use this button to display standard SAP help documentation.

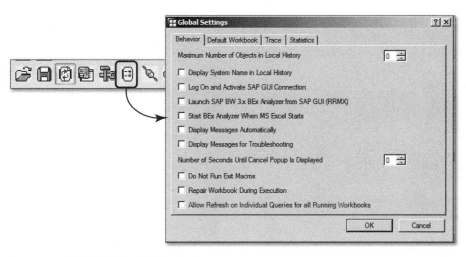

Figure 10.11 Global Settings for BEx Analyzer

10.2 Performing Information Analysis in BEx Analyzer

As we mentioned earlier, you can perform analysis and navigate through information to build your own view in BEx Analyzer. Two different options for analyzing data in BEx Analyzer are discussed in this section: filters and navigation options.

10.2.1 Applying Filters

As we mentioned earlier, the FILTER button is available in the workbook (❶ of Figure 10.12). Clicking on this button displays the FILTER pane with all of the characteristics and structures used in the query. You can use this pane to restrict the query result to the selected values of the characteristics or to the selected structure element. To apply the filter from the FILTER pane, select a characteristic or structure and choose SELECT FILTER VALUE from the context menu ❷.

You can also apply a filter by directly entering the value of the characteristic in the Excel cell ❸. Similarly, you can restrict the key figures to be displayed by selecting a specific key figure value from the key figures structure.

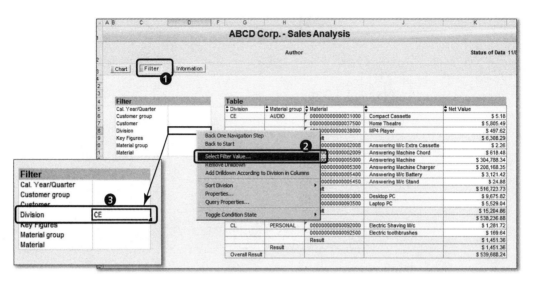

Figure 10.12 Applying Filters in a Workbook

10.2.2 Navigation Options

Apart from applying filters, many navigation options are available to perform intuitive analysis on the data displayed. These navigation options are discussed next.

Back One Navigation Step and Back to Start

Using the BACK ONE NAVIGATION STEP option (Figure 10.13), you can undo the latest navigation and revert back to the previous navigation state. For example, if you drill down by a characteristic and then choose this option, the drilldown will be removed, taking you to the previous state of navigation.

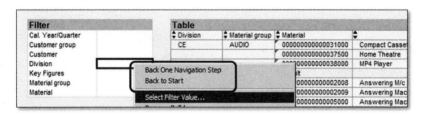

Figure 10.13 Navigating Backwards

Similarly, if you use the BACK TO START option (Figure 10.13), the system reverts all navigations performed and takes the navigation state to the initial one, as it was when the query was first executed.

Drilldown

Drilldown (either in rows or columns) is one of the most heavily used navigation options in data analysis. By using this feature, analysts can actually view data from different perspectives, as well as at different levels of detail.

For the example shown in Figure 10.14, if you want to see the sales values split by CAL. YEAR/QUARTER ❶, you can drill down by this characteristic in the columns. To perform this navigation, select ADD DRILLDOWN ACCORDING TO CAL. YEAR/QUARTER IN COLUMNS from the context menu of the CAL. YEAR/QUARTER characteristic ❷. As a result, the selected characteristic is added to the query, and the data is refreshed as the drilldown ❸.

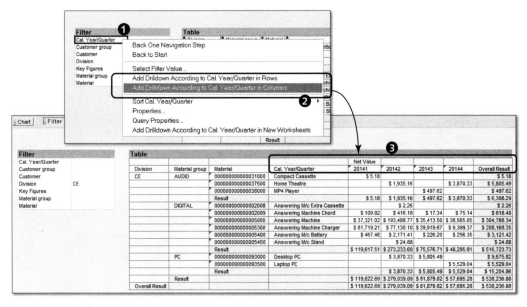

Figure 10.14 Drilldown Options

Similarly, ADD DRILLDOWN ACCORDING TO CAL. YEAR/QUARTER IN ROWS is also an option in the context menu ❷ and can be used if you want to add the drilldown in the rows.

If you want to remove a drilldown from the BEx Query Analyzer display, you can do so by selecting REMOVE DRILLDOWN, available in the context menu of the characteristic in the report layout (Figure 10.15).

Swap

The SWAP option is available to alter the position of a characteristic in the report by swapping it with another characteristic. For example, for the report shown in Figure 10.15, NET VALUE is displayed with respect to MATERIAL GROUP (❶ of Figure 10.15). If you want to display NET VALUE by CUSTOMER GROUP, you can swap MATERIAL GROUP with CUSTOMER GROUP.

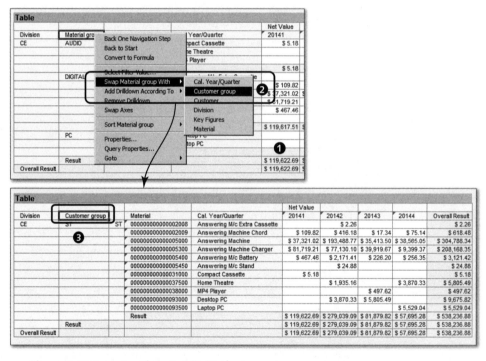

Figure 10.15 Swapping Characteristic Display

To do this, select SWAP MATERIAL GROUP WITH. The menu expands to show you a list of all of the characteristics used in the query, which can be selected for a swap. Select CUSTOMER GROUP from the list ❷, and the result is refreshed accordingly ❸.

Using Drag and Drop

BEx Analyzer also enables most of the navigations in the workbook using simple drag and drop actions. For example, if you want to add a characteristic to the drilldown, simply drag it from the FILTER pane, and drop it to the position in the report where you want it. The user is guided with a small arrow symbol pointing right (⟶) if it's a drilldown in columns, or pointing down (↓) if it's a drilldown in rows to know the exact impact of the drop.

To remove a drilldown, simply drag the column header out of the layout, and that characteristic will be removed from the display. To swap characteristics, drag the column header for that characteristic, and drop it over the characteristic with which you want to swap.

Applying filters is also very easy using drag-and-drop options. If you don't want to see the values for Division = CE, simply drag the value CE out of the layout in an empty cell. With this, the filter on the division characteristic automatically excludes this value. On the other hand, if you drag the CE value and drop it on the division characteristic in the FILTER pane, the division characteristic is restricted by that value.

This intuitive drag-and-drop feature expedites the navigation and analysis of data in SAP BW.

Some additional navigation functions are available in the context menu of selected cells in query results:

▶ CONVERT TO FORMULA
This function converts the result displayed in the report to a formula in Excel. Using this option, you can write your own formula functions in Excel to fetch the data directly from the SAP BW InfoProviders. The custom formatting done to the workbook in this case is retained because every time the query is refreshed, it retrieves only the values of the formula from the SAP BW server.

▶ KEEP FILTER VALUE
This function is available only for those cells with an actual characteristic value. Using this function, you can restrict the report result to that specific characteristic value for which the function is called. The report values are refreshed, and that characteristic is removed from the report display. For example, if you want to display only the values for Division = CE, select KEEP FILTER VALUE from the context menu of the cell containing CE. This restricts the report and removes DIVISION from the report display.

▶ SWAP AXES
Using this function, you can swap the query axes (rows and columns) with each

other. Thus, query elements defined in the rows are sent to columns, and query elements from columns are sent to rows.

▶ SORT
This function allows you to sort the selected characteristic values in ascending or descending order in the report display.

▶ GOTO
If there is any jump target defined on the query (RRI), the target is visible under the GOTO option in the context menu.

10.3 Local Properties and Formulas in BEx Analyzer

Apart from the filter and navigation options discussed in earlier sections, there are options available in the context menu to maintain the following:

▶ Local properties of a characteristic

▶ Local properties of a key figure

▶ Local query properties

▶ Local formulas

In this section, we discuss each of these concepts.

10.3.1 Local Properties of a Characteristic

To access the local properties of a characteristic, select PROPERTIES from the context menu of the characteristic (Figure 10.16). This opens up a properties dialog box where you can maintain the properties (Figure 10.17).

There are two tabs visible for Material Group: GENERAL and ATTRIBUTES. However, if the selected characteristic has hierarchies defined for it, an additional HIERARCHY tab is also displayed in the characteristic properties.

On the GENERAL tab page, you specify the properties related to display, sort order, result rows, or the access type for the values (❶ of Figure 10.17). The ATTRIBUTES tab is applicable only for those characteristics that have some attributes defined for them. On this tab ❷, you see a list of all of the attributes for the selected characteristic. If you want to display any of these attributes in the report, select them and bring them to the right side in the SELECTED ATTRIBUTES box, using the arrow keys ❷.

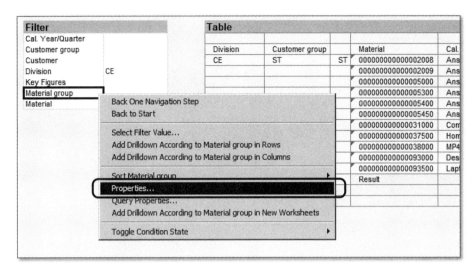

Figure 10.16 Local Properties for a Characteristic

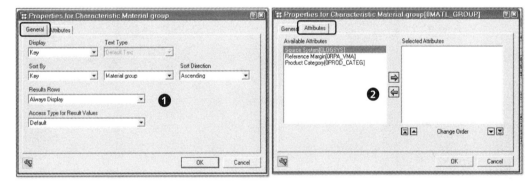

Figure 10.17 Maintaining Characteristic Properties

The properties maintained here are applicable to all values of the selected characteristic. However, the settings are local to this specific workbook only.

10.3.2 Local Properties of a Key Figure

Similar to the characteristics, the properties for a key figure query element can also be maintained locally in the workbook. The key figure properties can be called from the context menu of the *data cell* (a cell displaying key figure values) for the key figure (Figure 10.18).

Net Value					
	20141	20142	20143	20144	Overall Result
Cassette		$ 2.26			$ 2.26
hord	$ 109.82	$ 416.18	$ 17.34	$ 75.14	$ 618.48
	$ 37,321.02	$ 193,488.77	$ 35,413.50	$ 38,565.05	$ 304,788.34
harger	$ 81,719.21	$ 77,130.10	$ 39,919.67	$ 9,399.37	$ 208,168.35
y	$ 467.46	$ 2,171	Back One Navigation Step		$ 3,121.42
		$ 24	Back to Start		$ 24.88
	$ 5.18		Convert to Formula		$ 5.18
		$ 1,995			$ 5,805.49
			Properties...		$ 4,917.62
		$ 3,870	Query Properties...		$ 9,675.82
			Key Figure Definition		$ 5,529.04
	$ 119,622.69	$ 279,039			538,236.88
	$ 119,622.69	$ 279,039	Create Condition		538,236.88
	$ 119,622.69	$ 279,039	Goto ▶		538,236.88

Figure 10.18 Local Properties for Key Figures

The PROPERTIES dialog for a key figure consists of three different tabs: NUMBER FORMAT, CALCULATIONS, and SORTING (Figure 10.19).

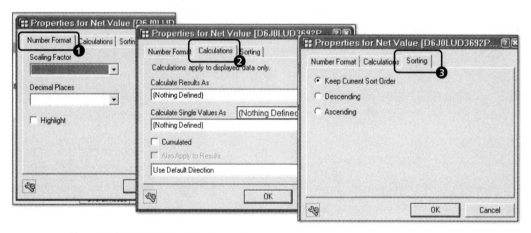

Figure 10.19 Maintaining Key Properties

The NUMBER FORMAT tab page contains the settings that correspond to the display behavior of the selected key figure (❶ of Figure 10.19). These settings include the scaling factor, decimal places, and highlighted display-related settings.

On the CALCULATIONS tab page, you can define the calculation behavior of the selected key figure. The key figure is locally recalculated based on the settings mentioned on this tab ❷. (Refer to Chapter 9 to review the significance of these key figure settings: CALCULATE RESULTS AS, CALCULATE SINGLE VALUES AS, etc.)

The sort order for the selected key figure is defined in the SORTING tab ❸ of the PROPERTIES dialog box.

10.3.3 Local Query Properties

Apart from the local properties that are defined for an individual characteristic or a key figure, you can maintain the properties for the query as well. To access the query properties, select QUERY PROPERTIES from the context menu of a filter/characteristic/key figure (Figure 10.20) used in the query.

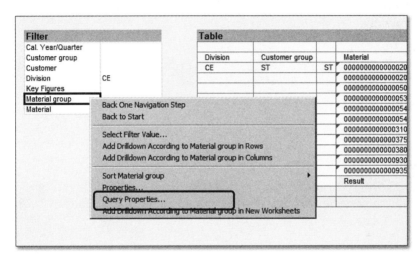

Figure 10.20 Local Query Properties

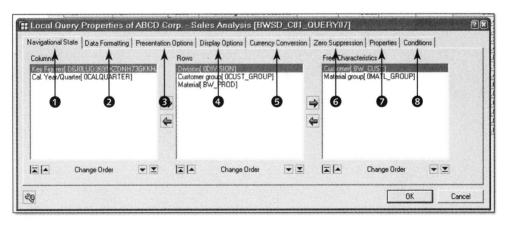

Figure 10.21 Maintaining Query Properties

The QUERY PROPERTIES window displays eight tabs where you can set properties to control the query behavior locally in the workbook (Figure 10.21):

❶ NAVIGATIONAL STATE
Controls the layout of the query. Here you can redefine the rows/columns/free characteristics in the query by moving the query elements using the arrow buttons.

❷ DATA FORMATTING
Allows you to define the way query results should be displayed in the workbook. You can specify if the query result should be displayed in a tabular format or in a multidimensional format on this tab page.

❸ PRESENTATION OPTIONS
Determines the presentation settings related to the position of results in the report, represented by +/– signs and zero values.

❹ DISPLAY OPTIONS
Allows you to maintain the scaling factors for key figure elements in the query. You can also maintain the setting to display the document links for objects such as data, metadata, and master data on this tab.

❺ CURRENCY CONVERSION
Allows you to perform currency translation locally in the workbook by maintaining the related settings.

❻ ZERO SUPPRESSION
Allows you to define settings to suppress rows/columns (or both) if all of the values in a particular row or column are zero.

❼ PROPERTIES
Provides general information about the query, such as the owner. The setting to toggle between change mode and display mode for an input-ready query is also available on this tab page.

❽ CONDITIONS
Displays the list of conditions that are built on the query and also the state of the condition (active/inactive). You can also build a local condition on the query in a workbook.

10.3.4 Local Formula

When analyzing data in a workbook, you sometimes need to perform some additional calculations on the existing key figure values. For example, consider a situation where you have a report displayed in a workbook that shows the net value for different materials for the entire year. However, during analysis, you need to know the average monthly net value for different materials. In BEx Analyzer, you can create a local formula to address such a requirement. In a local formula, you can define your own calculation, which remains local to the workbook.

The option to create a local formula in a workbook is available in the context menu for the key figure column header cell (Figure 10.22). Select Add Local Formula from the context menu of the key figure header ❶. This opens the Local Formula pop-up window where you define the formula logic.

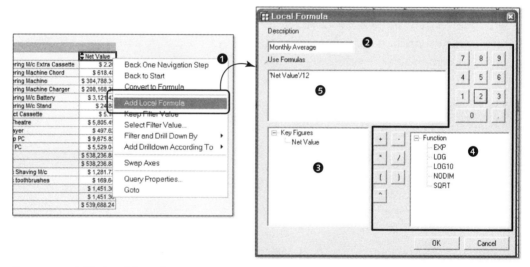

Figure 10.22 Add a Local Formula

Maintain the description for the new formula ❷. All of the key figure elements used in the query are listed under Key Figures ❸. You can define the formula using these key figures and the numbers and basic mathematical/scientific operators available on this screen ❹. The defined formula definition is visible ❺; for the example mentioned here, it is *(Net Value/12)*. Click on OK to complete the definition of the formula and to return to the workbook. As shown in Figure 10.23, an additional Monthly Average column is now visible in the report display.

Table						
⇕ Division	⇕ Customer group	⇕	⇕ Material	⇕	⇕ Net Value	⇕ Monthly Average
CE	ST	ST	000000000000002008	Answering M/c Extra Cassette	$ 2.26	$ 0.19
			000000000000002009	Answering Machine Chord	$ 618.48	$ 51.54
			000000000000005000	Answering Machine	$ 304,788.36	$ 25,399.03
			000000000000005300	Answering Machine Charger	$ 208,168.35	$ 17,347.36
			000000000000005400	Answering M/c Battery	$ 3,121.42	$ 260.12
			000000000000005450	Answering M/c Stand	$ 24.88	$ 2.07
			000000000000031000	Compact Cassette	$ 5.18	$ 0.43
			000000000000037500	Home Theatre	$ 5,805.49	$ 483.79
			000000000000038000	MP4 Player	$ 497.62	$ 41.47
			000000000000093000	Desktop PC	$ 9,675.82	$ 806.32
			000000000000093500	Laptop PC	$ 5,529.04	$ 460.75
			Result		$ 538,236.88	$ 44,853.07
	Result				$ 538,236.85	$ 44,853.07

Figure 10.23 Modified Layout with Local Formula

10.4 Saving and Reusing Workbooks in BEx Analyzer

After you've finished analysis in the workbook, you can save it on the SAP BW server so that you can later reuse the analysis or perform a new analysis. To save a workbook, click on the SAVE button, as shown in ❶ of Figure 10.24. Select SAVE WORKBOOK to save this workbook on the server.

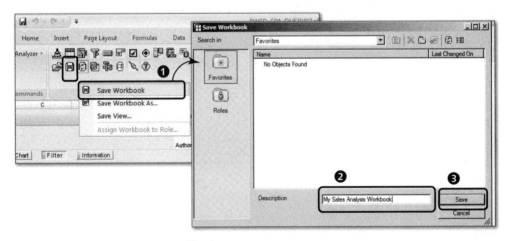

Figure 10.24 Save a New Workbook

Give a proper description to the workbook ❷, and click on SAVE ❸ to save the workbook in your favorites for future access. If you want to make this workbook available to other users, you can save it under a specific role (Figure 10.24). All of the users under that role can then access the same workbook for their analysis.

To open an already-saved workbook, click on the OPEN button, and select OPEN WORKBOOK from the menu (❶ of Figure 10.25). Select the workbook in the pop-up window ❷, and click on OPEN ❸ to open the workbook for analysis.

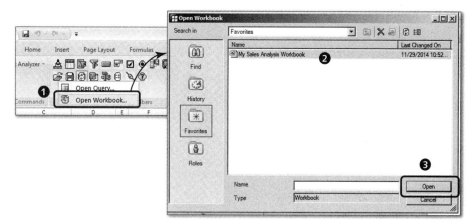

Figure 10.25 Open an Existing Workbook

To open an existing workbook, you must first connect to that SAP BW system. If you want to save the data locally so that you can refer to the data without connecting to the SAP BW system, you can do so by saving the Excel sheet using the normal Excel SAVE function (Figure 10.26).

Figure 10.26 Save the Workbook as a Local Copy

You can also connect your local workbook back to the SAP BW system by opening that Excel workbook in a BEx Analyzer session. The context menu on any of the query cells gives you the option to refresh the query (Figure 10.27). Selecting REFRESH shows the login screen where you can enter the login credentials and connect to the SAP BW system to perform online analysis of the data.

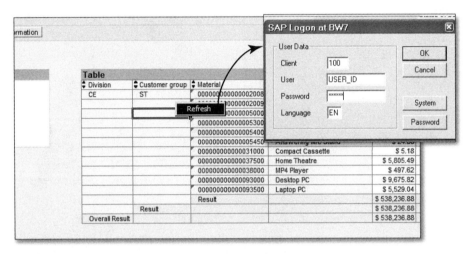

Figure 10.27 Reconnecting the Local Copy to the SAP BW System

10.5 Building an Analysis Application in BEx Analyzer

In addition to running existing queries, BEx Analyzer also allows you to build your own analysis applications with custom layouts and functions. In this section, we explain BEx Analyzer design functions and the procedure for building a simple analysis application. (BEx Analyzer can also be used to build a planning application in an Excel interface; this topic is covered in Chapter 12.)

10.5.1 BEx Analyzer Design Functions

When you start BEx Analyzer, you can see two different sets of functions available in the form of two different toolbars: the DESIGN toolbar and the ANALYSIS toolbar. As the name suggests, the ANALYSIS toolbar is used to perform analysis. (We discussed the use of this toolbar in Section 10.1.2.) The DESIGN toolbar, shown in Figure 10.28, is comprised of different design functions that can be used to design and build an application in BEx Analyzer.

The following are the different functions on the DESIGN toolbar (Figure 10.28):

❶ TOGGLE BETWEEN DESIGN MODE AND ANALYSIS MODE
Using this button, you can switch the workbook to the design mode and back to analysis mode from the design mode.

❷ INSERT ANALYSIS GRID
This button inserts the *analysis grid* design item in the workbook. The analysis grid is an important design item for workbooks; query results are displayed in the analysis grid, and it's where you perform different navigations on the data you're analyzing.

❸ INSERT NAVIGATION PANE
This button is used to insert the *navigation pane* in the workbook. The navigation pane design item displays all of the characteristics, key figures, and structure elements that can be used to perform navigation on the data. In the navigation pane, you can add/remove drilldown, filter values for characteristics, and so on.

❹ INSERT FILTERS
This design item allows you to display the list of all the filters applied to the query results. You can specifically select the query elements for which you want to display filters.

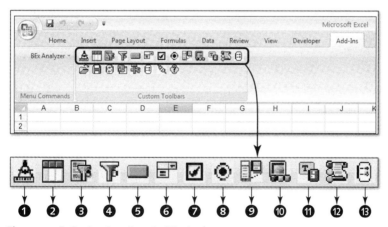

Figure 10.28 Design Functions in BEx Analyzer

❺ INSERT BUTTON
This design item adds a button to the application. You can configure a command that is assigned to this button so that it's executed when this button is clicked.

❻ INSERT DROPDOWN BOX
With this design item, you can provide users with a dropdown box to make a selection in the workbook.

❼ INSERT CHECKBOX GROUP
This design item inserts a checkbox group in the workbook. You can assign a query element to this checkbox group so that a list of values for that query element is displayed in the workbook. Users can then select multiple values for that element by using the checkbox option.

❽ INSERT RADIO BUTTON GROUP
With this design item, you can provide the user with an option to select a value for a specific query element using a radio button. The specific query element is assigned to the radio button group, and values of that element are visible to the user for selection.

❾ INSERT LIST OF CONDITIONS
If there are conditions defined on the query used in the workbook, you can display the list of all conditions using this design item. While performing analysis, the user can then toggle between the active and inactive states of each condition, if needed.

❿ INSERT LIST OF EXCEPTIONS
Similar to the list of conditions, if there are any exceptions defined on the query used in the workbook, this design item displays a list of them. These exceptions can be set as active or inactive during the analysis.

⓫ INSERT TEXT
This design item allows you to display different text elements for a query in the workbook. You can select from a list of different text elements that can be displayed in the workbook.

⓬ INSERT MESSAGES
In the course of navigation and analysis, there are different messages generated either by BEx Analyzer or by the SAP BW system. These messages can be error messages, warnings, or information. You can use this design item to display these messages in the workbook and make a selection about the type of messages to be displayed.

⓭ WORKBOOK SETTINGS
This function calls the WORKBOOK SETTINGS dialog, where you can maintain different settings on general workbook properties, display variables, and so on.

10.5.2 Building a Simple Analysis Application

Now that you're familiar with the basic design functions available in BEx Analyzer, we can build a simple analysis application for ABCD Corp. The analysts need a dropdown to select the material group characteristic and also an option to filter the results using a condition on high-value orders.

To create this custom analysis application, log in to BEx Analyzer and open a new Excel sheet from the Excel menu. This will enable all of the functions on the BEx DESIGN toolbar. Enter the heading "ABCD Corp. Sales Analysis" for the workbook, as shown in ❶ of Figure 10.29.

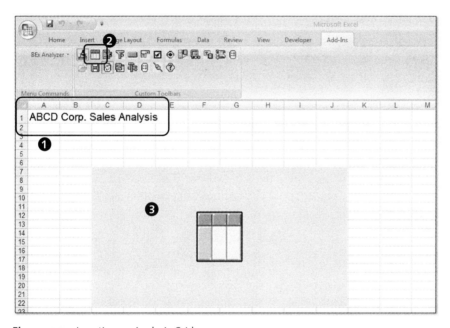

Figure 10.29 Inserting an Analysis Grid

To insert the analysis grid design item in the workbook, click on the icon shown in ❷ of Figure 10.29. This adds the analysis grid to the workbook ❸. Double-click on the design item to call the properties dialog as shown in Figure 10.30. You must assign a data provider to the analysis grid, which acts as a source of data to the design item. Create a new data provider by clicking on the CREATE button ❶, which opens another pop-up. Based on our example scenario, we assign the SALES ANALYSIS query to the data provider using the button ❷ of Figure 10.30. Finally, give a name to the data provider ❸, and click on OK ❹ to return to the PROPERTIES screen. After the assignment of the data provider is complete, you can also define some additional settings for the analysis grid by selecting appropriate check-boxes, as shown in Figure 10.30. Finally, click on the OK button ❺ to return to the workbook.

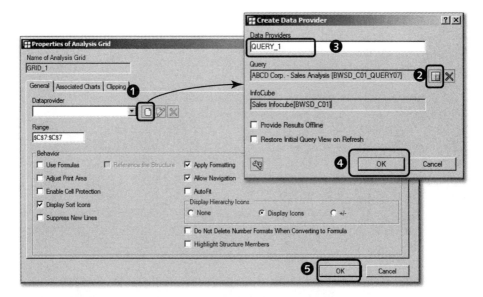

Figure 10.30 Setting Properties of an Analysis Grid

Multiple Queries in a Workbook

You can add multiple analysis grid design items in a workbook, each of which can be assigned to a different data provider. In other words, you can actually perform analysis on data from multiple queries together in a single workbook.

If the query assigned to the data provider in the analysis grid (❶ of Figure 10.31) contains some user entry variables, you must maintain these variables. To do this, click on the VARIABLES button ❷ on the ANALYSIS toolbar. This shows you the screen where the values for those variables can be maintained.

Select the cell where you want to add the dropdown box in the workbook, and then click on the dropdown button in the DESIGN toolbar (❶ of Figure 10.32). The dropdown box design item is added to the workbook ❷.

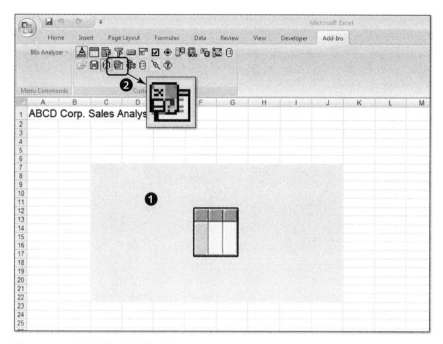

Figure 10.31 Maintain Variable Values

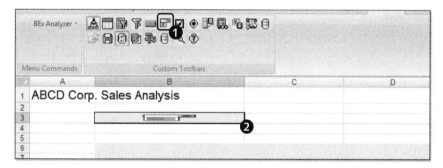

Figure 10.32 Insert Dropdown Box Design Item

Open the PROPERTIES OF DROPDOWN BOX dialog by double-clicking on the item. The PROPERTIES OF A DROPDOWN BOX dialog contains three tabs. On the GENERAL tab page (❶ of Figure 10.33), you assign the data provider to the dropdown and select the location of the dropdown in the workbook. On the SELECTION tab page ❷, you assign the specific query element (characteristic/structure) to the dropdown, and set the read mode of the characteristic. You can also maintain some display-related settings on this tab. For example, you can choose if you want to display the label of the characteristic and whether an ALL VALUES entry should be visible in the dropdown or not. On the AFFECTED DATA PROVIDER tab page ❸, select the data provider that will be impacted by the selection made using this dropdown box. Finally, click on OK to return to the workbook.

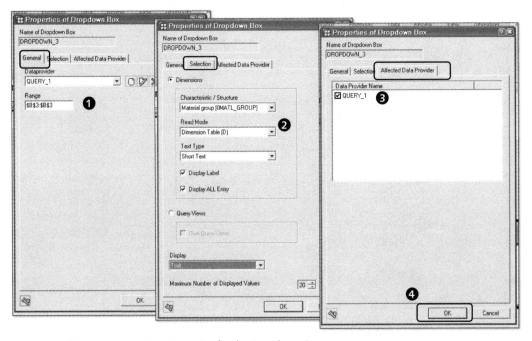

Figure 10.33 Setting Properties for the Dropdown Box

Dropdown Box for Query Views

If multiple query views are defined on a selected data provider, you can provide a dropdown box in the workbook that will give you a list of views created on that query. The user can then select a specific query view from this dropdown, and the affected data provider gets refreshed accordingly. To achieve this, you have to select the QUERY VIEWS option on the SELECTION tab of the PROPERTIES OF DROPDOWN BOX page (❷ of Figure 10.33).

Now, insert a button design item in the workbook using the function button from the DESIGN toolbar (❶ of Figure 10.34). Double-click on the newly inserted button ❷ in the workbook to call the properties screen for it.

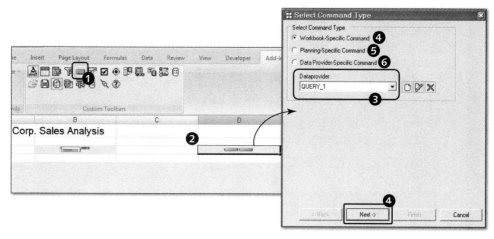

Figure 10.34 Inserting the Button Design Item

Assign the data provider to the design item ❸. For a button design item in a workbook, you can assign custom commands to be performed when this button is clicked. There are three types of commands that can be assigned to a button: WORKBOOK-SPECIFIC COMMAND, PLANNING-SPECIFIC COMMAND, and DATA PROVIDER-SPECIFIC COMMAND. The different commands available under each of these categories are listed here:

▶ WORKBOOK-SPECIFIC COMMANDS

  ▷ PROCESS VARIABLES (with an option to enable DISPLAY OF PERSONALIZED VARIABLES; this command calls the variable screen)

  ▷ TOGGLE DRAG AND DROP

  ▷ DISABLE DRAG AND DROP

  ▷ ALLOW DRAG AND DROP

▶ PLANNING-SPECIFIC COMMANDS

  ▷ SAVE

  ▷ TRANSFER VALUES

  ▷ EXECUTE PLANNING FUNCTION

  ▷ PLANNING: EXECUTE SEQUENCE

  ▷ RESET AREA

  ▷ REFRESH

> **Note**
>
> The planning-specific commands are explained in more detail in Chapter 12.

- ▶ DATA PROVIDER-SPECIFIC COMMANDS
  - ▶ EDIT (sets the input-ready data provider in edit mode)
  - ▶ DISPLAY (sets the input-ready data provider in display mode)
  - ▶ FILTER COMMAND
  - ▶ ASSIGN QUERY/QUERY VIEW

For our example scenario, select WORKBOOK-SPECIFIC COMMAND (❶ of Figure 10.35) for the inserted design item, and click on NEXT ❷. On the next screen, select PROCESS VARIABLES from the list of WORKBOOK-SPECIFIC COMMANDS ❸, and click on NEXT. The next screen displays the static parameters for the selected command. You can also maintain the text and range for the button in the workbook ❺. Finally, click on OK to return to the workbook.

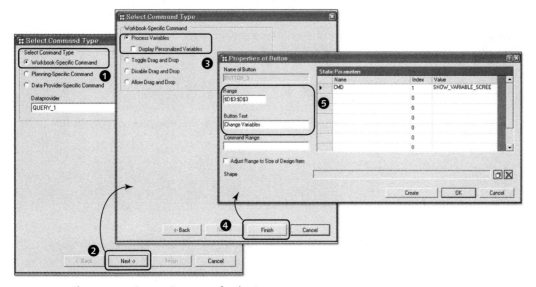

Figure 10.35 Setting Properties for the Button

Insert the *list of conditions* design item using the button shown in ❶ of Figure 10.36. Call the properties for the inserted design item by double-clicking on the inserted item ❷, and assign the data provider to the item ❸. Finally, click on OK to return to the workbook ❹.

The custom analysis application is now ready for use. To begin the analysis, click on the button shown in ❶ of Figure 10.37. This exits the design model and switches to the analysis mode. After you switch to the analysis mode, the workbook is refreshed with data, as shown in Figure 10.37.

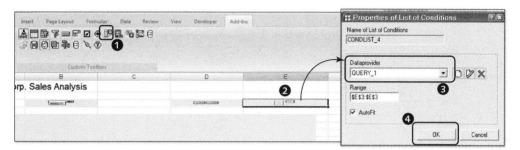

Figure 10.36 Inserting a List of Conditions

Figure 10.37 Working with Custom Analysis Application

You can see from ❷ that there is a dropdown box option available for the material group characteristic, as well as a CHANGE VARIABLES button ❸. When clicked, this button calls the variable entry screen ❹. The user can change the values of the variables and then refresh the data in the workbook by clicking on OK on the variable screen. You can also see the list of conditions built on the query displayed in the workbook ❺.

For analysis, you can toggle between the active and inactive states of the condition by clicking on the icon shown in ❶ of Figure 10.38. The query result is refreshed without the condition, as shown in Figure 10.38. You can revert the condition back to the active state by clicking once on the same icon (❷ of Figure 10.38).

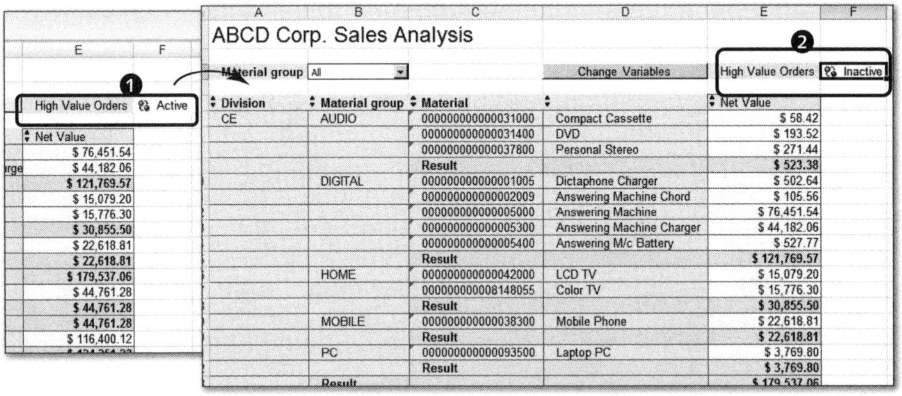

Figure 10.38 Toggle between Condition States

This custom analysis application can be saved on the SAP BW server for future use. Use the SAVE WORKBOOK command from the toolbar (Figure 10.39) to save this workbook.

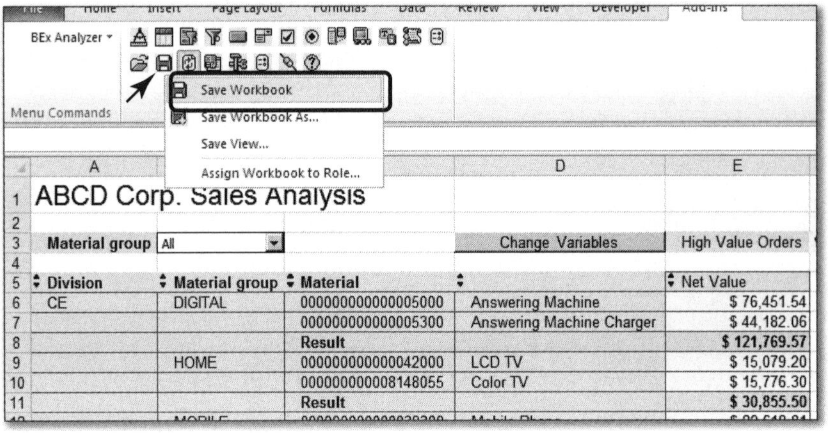

Figure 10.39 Save Workbook

As you've seen from this section, you can use available design items to build a custom application using BEx Analyzer, thereby providing an interactive and flexible analysis interface for business users.

10.6 Running Queries in BEx Web Analyzer

In an organization, diverse users accessing a set of data might want to see the same data in different ways or analyze that data in an ad hoc manner. BEx Web Analyzer is available to fulfill these ad hoc query and analysis requirements in a web environment. This is a powerful web-based application that can access data from a query built in BEx Query Designer or even from an InfoProvider for ad hoc analysis.

You can access BEx Web Analyzer either through a portal or directly through the web browser. The standard REPORTING ANALYSIS AND PLANNING (*com.sap.ip.bi.bi_showcase*) portal role (❶ of Figure 10.40) includes BEx Web Analyzer ❷. Click on the link to open it.

Figure 10.40 Accessing BEx Web Analyzer

Next we discuss how to create a new analysis with BEx Web Analyzer and then explain the different functions available.

10.6.1 Creating a New Analysis with BEx Web Analyzer

The default layout of BEx Web Analyzer is shown in Figure 10.41. Using the buttons available on the top toolbar, you can create a new analysis or open an existing one. To open a new analysis, click on the NEW ANALYSIS button ❶, and the OPEN window appears. Here you can select the data provider for your analysis from the available tab pages ❷. Ad hoc analysis can be performed on different types of data providers; you can open an existing query or InfoProvider for one of the views based on your specific need. Select the type of object from the dropdown ❸.

Analysis on Data from External Systems

Using BEx Web Analyzer, you can also perform analysis on data from external systems, which can be connected using XMLA or ODBO interfaces (❹ of Figure 10.41). For this, the external system must first be defined in the portal. Portal administrators usually perform this task for you.

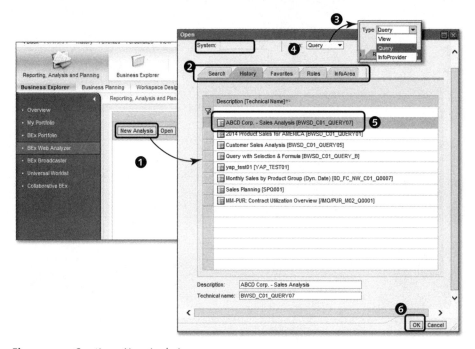

Figure 10.41 Creating a New Analysis

Navigate through the InfoProviders to locate the data provider ❺, and click on OK ❻ to run the analysis. If the data provider involves some user-entry variables, the variable entry screen is displayed where you can maintain the values of different variables (Figure 10.42). You can save this selection as a variant for future use by using the SAVE As button ❶. Click on OK ❷ to run the analysis with the selected variable values.

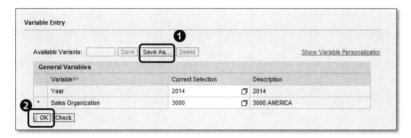

Figure 10.42 Entering Variable Values

Data from the InfoProvider is displayed in the tabular format on the right side of the screen (❶ of Figure 10.43). All query elements, such as characteristics in rows/columns and key figure structures, are visible in a navigation pane on the left side ❷.

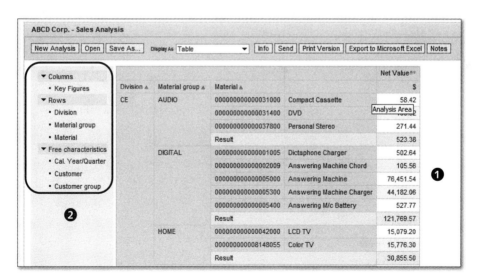

Figure 10.43 BEx Web Analyzer Layout

10.6.2 BEx Web Analyzer Functions

The buttons available on the top of the analysis provide some additional functions to assist with analysis:

▶ DISPLAY AS
Selecting an option from the DISPLAY AS dropdown, you can display the analysis result as a graphic, a table, or as both a table and graphic together (Figure 10.44).

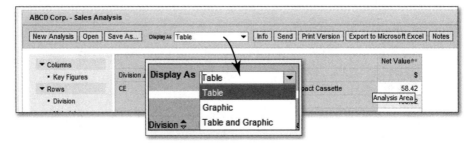

Figure 10.44 BEx Web Analyzer Function: Display Graphic

▶ INFORMATION
This button displays the information about the data provider used in the analysis. Apart from the metadata corresponding to the data provider (❶ of Figure 10.45), the information screen also displays the current state of filters on the data provider. This includes static filters, dynamic filters, and restrictions applied to the data provider using variables ❷.

▶ SEND
If the person performing analysis wants to share the results with another person, he can use the SEND button (❶ of Figure 10.46) to distribute this analysis. The SEND function actually calls the Broadcasting Wizard from BEx Broadcaster, which allows you to create these distribution settings. The data from the current analysis can be distributed in different output formats ❷. (Details about BEx Broadcaster and information broadcasting are discussed in Section 10.9.)

▶ PRINT VERSION
This function (❸ of Figure 10.46) allows you to prepare the analysis for printing. You can make print-specific settings, add headers/footers, and generate a PDF that can be printed ❹.

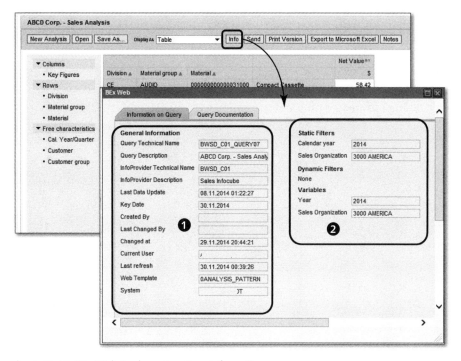

Figure 10.45 BEx Web Analyzer Function: Information

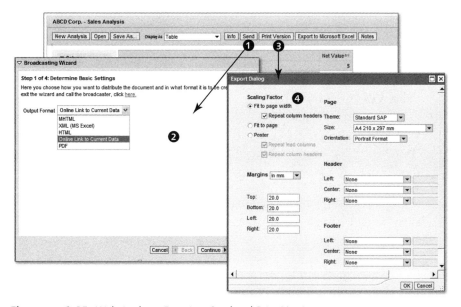

Figure 10.46 BEx Web Analyzer Function: Send and Print Version

▶ EXPORT TO EXCEL
Use this function (❶ of Figure 10.47) to download the analysis in Excel.

▶ COMMENTS/NOTES
You can create or maintain comments/documents for the data provider using the COMMENTS (or NOTES) function button (❸ of Figure 10.47). All of the existing documents created on the data provider are displayed for viewing and editing ❹.

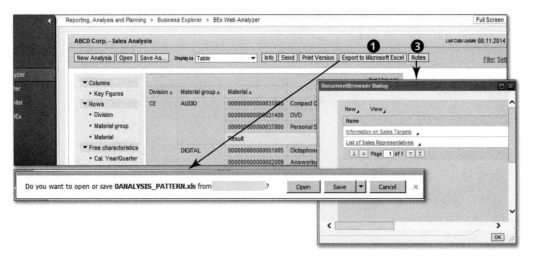

Figure 10.47 BEx Web Analyzer Function: Export to Excel and Comments

10.7 Performing Information Analysis in BEx Web Analyzer

Using BEx Web Analyzer, you can navigate through data (using drilldown, using filters, changing the layout, calculating key figures in a different way, etc.) to analyze it from various perspectives. These navigations can be performed via drag and drop or via context menu options. Similar to BEx Analyzer, context menu functions are available for query elements in the navigation pane (❶ of Figure 10.48), characteristic column headers ❶, specific characteristic values ❶, key figure headers ❷, and specific key figure values ❸. Drag and drop can also be used to navigate through data, which makes analysis very easy (minimizing the number of mouse clicks) and very interactive.

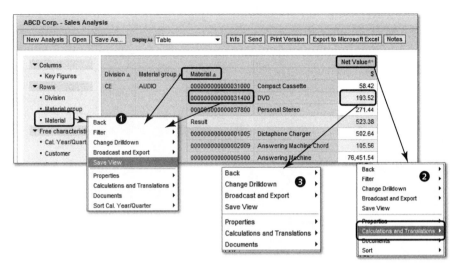

Figure 10.48 BEx Web Analyzer Context Menu Functions

Some of the commonly used navigations are described here:

▶ **Add drilldown**

To add a drilldown to the analysis (in rows or columns), you have to drag the relevant characteristic from the navigation pane and then drop it in the layout, as shown in ❶ of Figure 10.49. The same navigation can be achieved by placing the characteristic in the required section on the navigation pane ❷. In the example shown in Figure 10.49, the CAL YEAR/QUARTER characteristic is added to the columns (❸ and ❹).

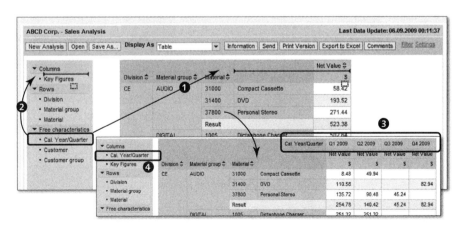

Figure 10.49 Navigation: Add Drilldown

▶ **Swap characteristics**

To swap characteristics, drag the characteristic and place it on the characteristic with which it is to be swapped. You can drag and drop in the analysis table (❶ of Figure 10.50) as well as in the navigation pane ❷. In the example shown in Figure 10.50, CUSTOMER GROUP is swapped with MATERIAL GROUP ❸.

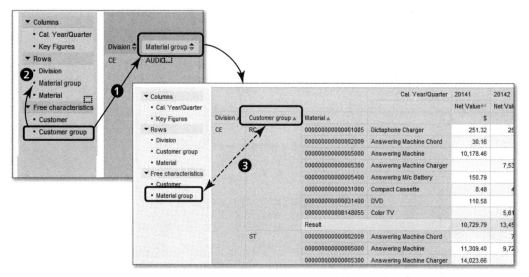

Figure 10.50 Navigation: Swap Characteristic

▶ **Exclude characteristic value**

In the example shown in Figure 10.51, if the analyst doesn't want the values for CAL. YEAR/QUARTER = Q1 2014 to be displayed in the analysis, he can remove this specific characteristic value by dragging the Q1 2014 characteristic value out of the layout (❶ of Figure 10.51). This puts an exclusion filter on the CAL. YEAR/QUARTER characteristic, and the query result is modified according to this exclusion ❷.

▶ **Remove result rows**

Using drag and drop, you can also remove the result values from the query result. By dragging the result row/column out of the result area (❶ of Figure 10.52), the specific result row will be removed from the query result display ❷.

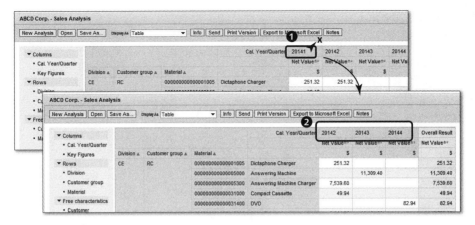

Figure 10.51 Navigation: Exclude Characteristic Value

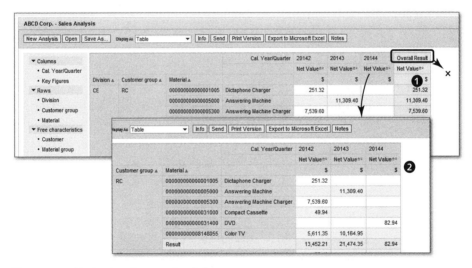

Figure 10.52 Navigation: Remove Result Rows

▶ **Filter by characteristic value**

Refer to the analysis shown in Figure 10.53. If you want to restrict the results for the CUSTOMER GROUP = RC characteristic value, simply drag the RC value and drop it over the CUSTOMER GROUP characteristic in the navigation pane ❶. This navigation is equivalent to the KEEP FILTER VALUE context menu function. The CUSTOMER GROUP characteristic is restricted for the RC value and is removed from the drilldown (❷ and ❸).

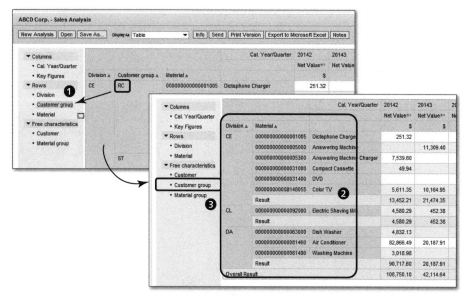

Figure 10.53 Navigation: Filter by a Characteristic Value

- ▶ **Remove drilldown**

  To remove a characteristic from the drilldown, you have to drag the characteristic header out of the layout area (❶ of Figure 10.54). The analysis is refreshed without that characteristic ❷, and the removed characteristic is added to the FREE CHARACTERISTICS area in the navigation pane ❸.

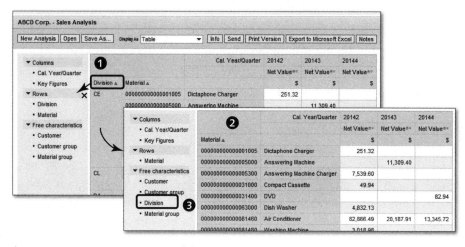

Figure 10.54 Navigation: Remove Drilldown

10.8 Analysis Filters and Settings in BEx Web Analyzer

Apart from all of the navigation options discussed previously, if you also want to work with the multiple filters applied to the data, a detailed filters view is available after you click on the FILTER link (❶ of Figure 10.55). This action displays all of the characteristics and structures used in the query, and you can specify the filter on the displayed data. The VARIABLE SCREEN button ❷ calls the variable selection screen and allows you to change the variable selection for the query.

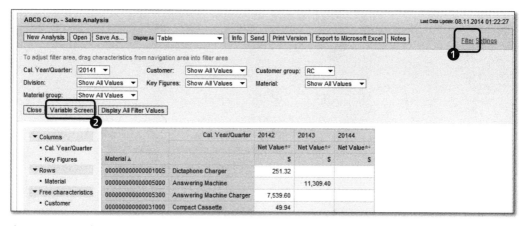

Figure 10.55 Analysis Filters

BEx Web Analyzer also allows you to maintain additional settings, which can be used to perform advanced analysis on data. Click on the SETTINGS link (Figure 10.55) to call the settings view.

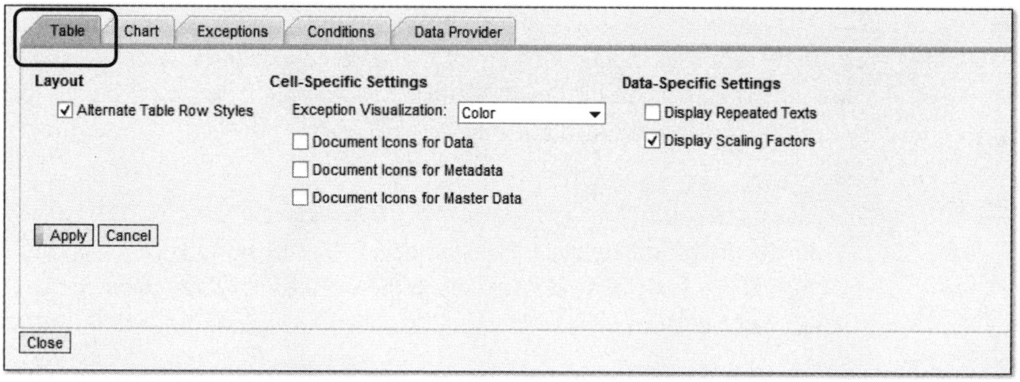

Figure 10.56 Analysis Settings Table

There are five tabs where you can maintain different types of settings for the data displayed in BEx Web Analyzer:

▶ TABLE
You can maintain the display settings for the tabular display of the data on this tab page (Figure 10.56).

▶ CHART
The settings related to the graphical display of the data in the analysis are maintained on this tab page (Figure 10.57). The details corresponding to the chart type, axis settings, legends, and so on are controlled here.

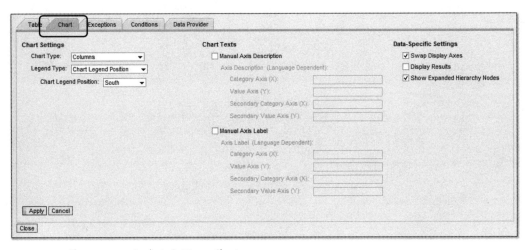

Figure 10.57 Analysis Settings: Chart

▶ EXCEPTIONS
This tab page shows the list of all exceptions defined on this data provider (Figure 10.58). You can toggle the state of the selected exception (active/inactive) using the TOGGLE STATE button ❶. You can also define new exceptions on the data provider using the ADD button ❷.

▶ CONDITIONS
This tab lists all conditions defined on the data provider (Figure 10.59). You can add, delete, or edit the details for a condition using the buttons provided here. The TOGGLE STATE button is used to switch the selected condition from active to inactive, or vice versa.

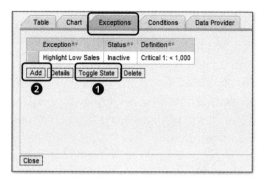

Figure 10.58 Analysis Settings: Exceptions

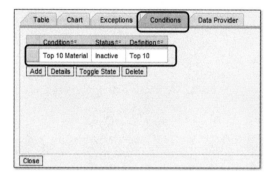

Figure 10.59 Analysis Settings: Conditions

▶ DATA PROVIDER

The settings related to the display of data elements from the data provider are maintained on this tab page (Figure 10.60). These include the settings for the position of the result rows, display settings for the result set, display settings for numbers, and settings related to the suppression of zero values in the analysis.

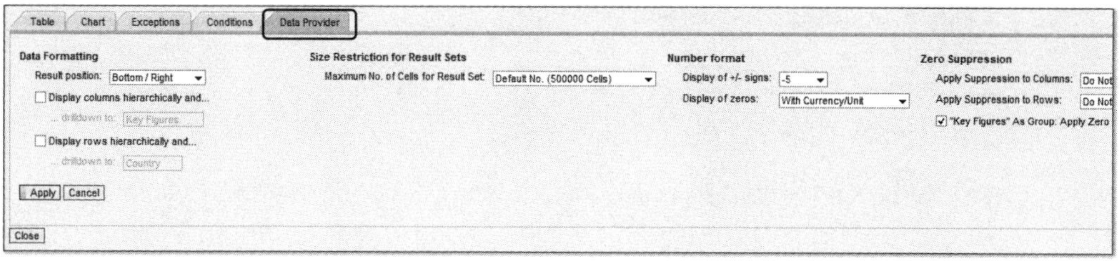

Figure 10.60 Analysis Settings: Data Provider

10.9 Information Broadcasting Using BEx Web Analyzer

The data, information, or analysis performed in BEx tools can be distributed (or *broadcasted*) to multiple users using information broadcasting. The BEx component that includes this function is called the *BEx Broadcaster*. In this section, we discuss the process of information broadcasting using BEx Web Analyzer, explain how to maintain broadcasting settings for different BEx objects, and then illustrate how to create a new setting in BEx Broadcaster.

10.9.1 Information Broadcasting in BEx Web Analyzer

The analysis done on BEx Web Analyzer can be broadcasted using the SEND button (❶ of Figure 10.61). Click on the button, and it opens a pop-up window from the BROADCASTING WIZARD.

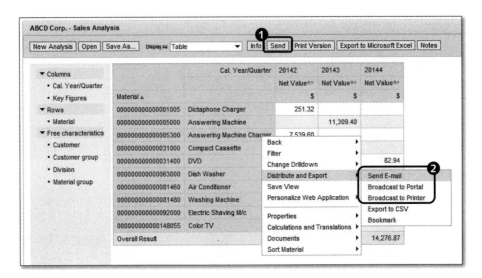

Figure 10.61 Calling BEx Broadcasting Wizard

The wizard can also be called from the DISTRIBUTE AND EXPORT context menu function, as shown in ❷ of Figure 10.61.

Select the OUTPUT FORMAT for broadcasting from the options available in the dropdown (❶ of Figure 10.62), and click on the CONTINUE button ❷ to proceed to the next screen.

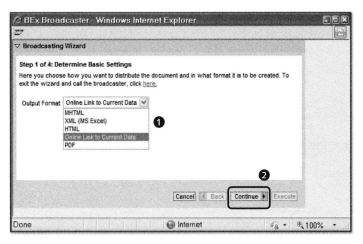

Figure 10.62 BEx Broadcaster: Determine Basic Settings

On the next screen, maintain the details of the broadcasting settings (Figure 10.63), which depend on the output format selected earlier. Include the EMAIL ADDRESSES ❶ of the intended recipients of this data, and create your own message, which will be sent to the users along with the information.

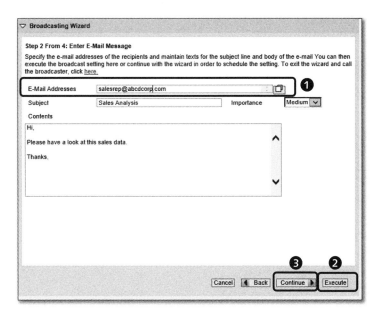

Figure 10.63 BEx Broadcaster: Maintain Message Settings

If this is a one-time broadcast, you can execute this setting directly from this screen using the EXECUTE button ❷. Click on the CONTINUE button ❸ if you want to save this setting for future use or want to schedule it to be executed automatically at some predefined time.

Save the broadcasting settings by providing a technical name and description (❶ of Figure 10.64), and click on CONTINUE ❷ to proceed to the next screen.

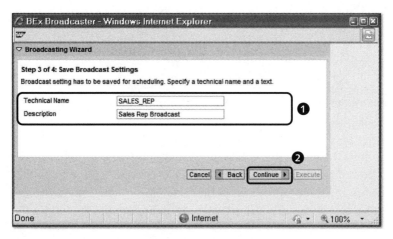

Figure 10.64 BEx Broadcaster: Save Broadcast Settings

On the next screen, you'll schedule the broadcasting setting by specifying the date and time for execution (❶ of Figure 10.65) Click on the SCHEDULE button ❷ to save the broadcasting and scheduling settings.

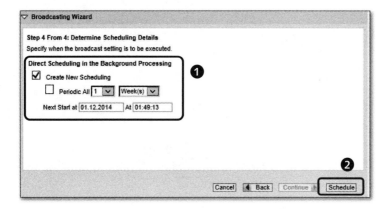

Figure 10.65 BEx Broadcaster: Determine Scheduling Details

10.9.2 Maintaining Broadcasting Settings on Different BEx Objects

The broadcasting settings on different objects in the BEx toolset can be maintained in BEx Broadcaster, which can be accessed from all BEx tools, as well from the BEx iView in the portal (Figure 10.66).

Figure 10.66 Accessing BEx Broadcaster from the Portal

To maintain the broadcasting settings on any BEx object, first select the object type from the dropdown (❶ of Figure 10.67), and then click on the OPEN button ❷ to select the specific object. This displays a list of the broadcasting settings that are defined and scheduled on the selected object ❸.

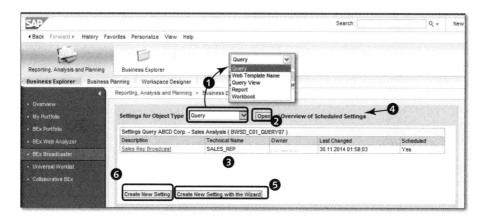

Figure 10.67 BEx Broadcaster Settings

To search and get an overview of all settings scheduled in the SAP BW system, click on the OVERVIEW OF SCHEDULED SETTINGS link ❹.

10.9.3 Creating a New Setting in BEx Broadcaster

To create a new setting, use the CREATE A NEW SETTING WITH THE WIZARD button (❺ of Figure 10.67), which takes you to the same BROADCASTING WIZARD that is accessed from the SEND button of BEx Web Analyzer. The CREATE NEW SETTING button ❻ allows you to create the setting in BEx Broadcaster.

Creating a setting in BEx Broadcaster instead of the Broadcasting Wizard provides you with some additional distribution types for broadcasting (Figure 10.68).

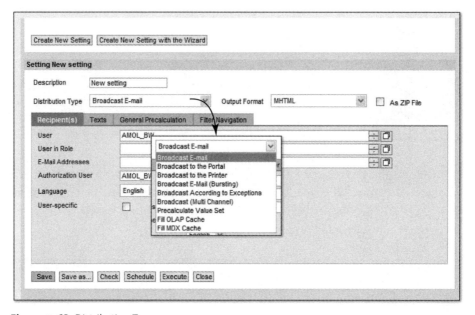

Figure 10.68 Distribution Types

These different distribution types are explained here:

▶ BROADCAST E-MAIL
Using this distribution type, you can broadcast information via email to multiple recipients.

▶ BROADCAST TO THE PORTAL
This distribution type allows you to save the precalculated analysis or post an online link to the analysis on the portal. Different users can then access the information using this saved information or the link.

▶ BROADCAST TO THE PRINTER
Using this distribution type, you can configure the print settings for the information contained in a select BEx object. BEx Broadcaster then sends the information to the output device maintained in the broadcasting settings at the scheduled time.

▶ BROADCAST E-MAIL (BURSTING)
If you want to distribute information to a specific set of users based on master data, you can use this distribution type. This type allows you to determine the recipients of the email based on the characteristic values (Figure 10.69).

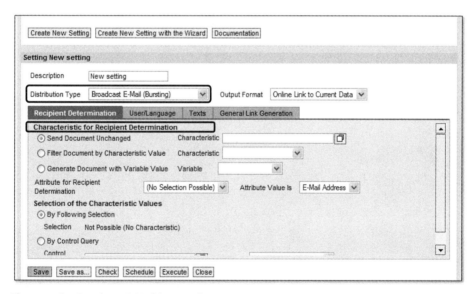

Figure 10.69 Broadcast E-Mail (Bursting)

▶ BROADCAST ACCORDING TO EXCEPTIONS
This distribution type broadcasts the data based on the exceptions defined on the selected BEx object and is especially useful if you want to send alerts to a set of recipients based on the threshold value defined in the exception (Figure 10.70).

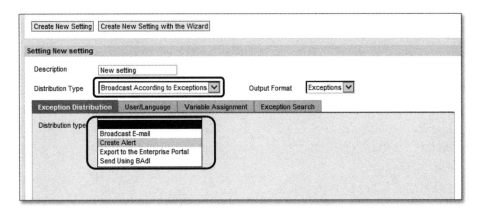

Figure 10.70 Broadcast According to Exceptions

▸ BROADCAST (MULTI CHANNEL)
This distribution type allows you to configure a broadcasting setting combining multiple channels of broadcasting (portal, email, print).

▸ PRECALCULATE VALUE SET
This distribution type is applicable for those OLAP characteristic variables that are filled using precalculated value sets. This broadcast setting determines the precalculated values that are then used to populate the variables with characteristic values.

▸ FILL OLAP CACHE
When the queries are executed in BEx, the data fetched by the query from the InfoProvider is retained in the OLAP cache. As a result, when the same set of data (or a subset of data in the OLAP cache) is requested again, the data is fetched from the OLAP cache instead of the InfoProvider. The query execution is actually faster in the latter case because the data is readily available in the OLAP cache. The distribution type FILL OLAP CACHE allows the specified query to run in the background to fill the OLAP cache, so the performance of that query can be improved.

▸ FILL MDX CACHE
Similar to the FILL OLAP CACHE type, this distribution type is used to provide better performance of external reports that are executed on a selected SAP BW query. Broadcast settings with this distribution type precalculate the query results and fill the MDX cache, which is used by external reports based on BEx queries (e.g., SAP Crystal Reports).

10.10 BW Workspaces

Empowering end users to perform their own analysis has always been a key factor that defines the success of business intelligence in an organization. The ability to link multiple sets of data and combine them with local data adds tremendous value for end users. For example, business users often want to add a new field or make a new set of data available for reporting, and it takes too long for the IT team to address the requirement—which furthers users' impressions that they can't control data. BW Workspaces (available from SAP BW 7.3 onward) address this challenge and present users with an opportunity to design their own foundation for reporting in a controlled environment (see Figure 10.71).

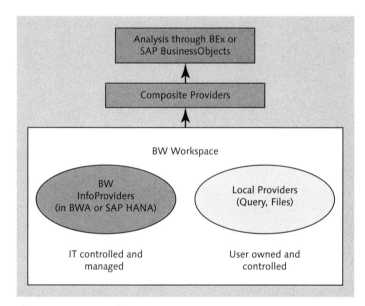

Figure 10.71 BW Workspaces

As illustrated, the foundation for ad hoc analysis can be data from SAP BW InfoProviders as well as from local providers. These InfoProviders must reside in memory, which means that if you're using SAP BW on a non-SAP HANA database, then SAP BW Accelerator (BWA) is a prerequisite to using BW Workspaces. In such cases, only those SAP BW InfoProviders that reside in BWA can be part of this foundation. Users can then create their own data models (called composite providers, explained later in the section) on this foundation.

> **Note**
>
> The BWA prerequisite for BW Workspaces is irrelevant if the SAP BW system uses the SAP HANA database.

To explain the use of BW Workspaces further, let's take a requirement from ABCD Corp.'s payroll department, which would like to calculate a one-time sales bonus for all of its sales offices. The bonus calculation must be based on the sales commission percentage defined for each of the sales offices and the actual sales numbers. In SAP BW, the actual sales values are available in one of the InfoCubes, while sales commission is stored in a separate data target. To address this requirement, we want to make the sales data and commission data available to users in a BW Workspace, where end users can create their own data model for analysis.

In the following sections, we explain how to define a BW Workspace and then create our own data model (a composite provider) based on the InfoProviders available in the BW Workspace.

10.10.1 Defining BW Workspaces

Individual BW Workspaces are defined and maintained through Transaction RSWSP in the SAP BW system (Figure 10.72). You can also use Transaction RSWSPW for mass maintenance of BW Workspaces.

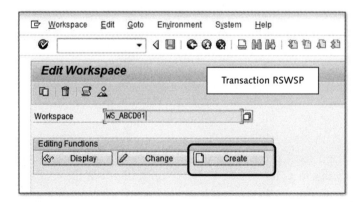

Figure 10.72 Workspace Maintenance (Transaction RSWSP)

Enter the technical name of the BW Workspace, and click on the CREATE button. The next screen shows where you can define the details for the BW Workspace

(Figure 10.73). There are five different tabs visible in a BW Workspace maintenance screen:

▶ SETTINGS

Define the basic settings for the BW Workspace on this tab, including the validity and contact details (❶ of Figure 10.73). Under the SETTINGS FOR MAIN PROVIDER section, you can specify whether the BW Workspace is based on a MultiProvider or a composite provider ❷. For the included main provider, all of the underlying base providers that are present in BWA are included in the BW Workspace. Also, only those characteristics and key figures from the base providers that are part of the main provider are available for the BW Workspace.

BW Workspaces also allow users to upload their own data files for analysis. The SETTINGS FOR LOCAL PROVIDERS section allows you to set the parameters for such local providers ❸.

Select the CREATION OF MASTER DATA ALLOWED checkbox if you want master data SIDs to be created for the data that is loaded locally ❹.

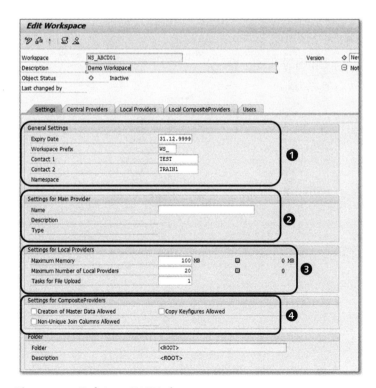

Figure 10.73 Defining a BW Workspace

▶ CENTRAL PROVIDERS

Within a BW Workspace, you can provide one or more InfoProviders for users to create ad hoc analysis scenarios. The InfoProviders made available in a BW Workspace are called *central providers*. For an InfoProvider to be defined as a central provider, it has to be present in memory. Thus, InfoProviders such as BWA-enabled InfoCubes, master data, and the analytical index can be added as central providers to the BW Workspace. These are defined in the CENTRAL PROVIDERS tab of the BW Workspace maintenance screen (see Figure 10.74). If you added a MultiProvider under the SETTINGS FOR CENTRAL PROVIDERS section on the first tab (❷ of Figure 10.73), then the basic providers (those present in BWA) from the included MultiProvider are already included as central providers.

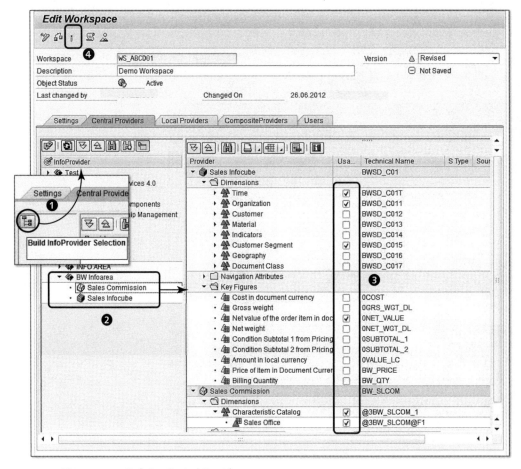

Figure 10.74 Defining Central Providers

Alternatively, you can also select individual InfoProviders from the INFOPROVIDER section. To display the INFOPROVIDER tree on the left side, click on the TREE icon shown in ❶ of Figure 10.74. Next, drag the selected InfoProviders to the right side of the screen to add those as CENTRAL PROVIDERS ❷. Here you can also decide to make only a selected few fields available to users and hide the others. For example, perhaps you don't want users to see the sales details at the CUSTOMER and MATERIAL level, and you also want to mask all key figures except NET VALUE. To do this, you can select the appropriate checkboxes ❸. The CENTRAL PROVIDERS defined on this tab are then visible to users for creating composite providers.

▶ LOCAL PROVIDERS
This tab shows a list of all user-defined local providers in the BW Workspace.

▶ COMPOSITE PROVIDERS
This tab shows a list of all the composite providers defined for the selected BW Workspace.

▶ USERS
This tab shows a list of all users who can access this BW Workspace.

After all of the details are defined, save and activate the BW Workspace (❹ of Figure 10.74). The active BW Workspaces are then visible to users for further use.

In the next section, we explain how business users can use a BW Workspace to define composite providers and then use these composite providers for analysis.

10.10.2 Creating a Composite Provider

Business users can work within the BW Workspace from the portal (SAP Enterprise Portal 7.0 or higher); the WORKSPACE DESIGNER is available as part of the standard REPORTING, ANALYSIS AND PLANNING tab (❶ of Figure 10.75).

Within the WORKSPACE DESIGNER, click on the MY WORKSPACE link ❷ to get an overview of all of the available central providers and local providers. You can also maintain the composite providers via this link.

The CREATE LOCAL PROVIDER link ❸ allows users to define an InfoProvider to load data locally either from flat files (CSV or Excel) or from a query or an SAP BW DataSource.

> **Note**
>
> The UI element *OfficeControl* needs to be installed on your SAP BW system to be able to upload the Microsoft Excel files as a local provider. Your Basis team should be able to configure this for you.

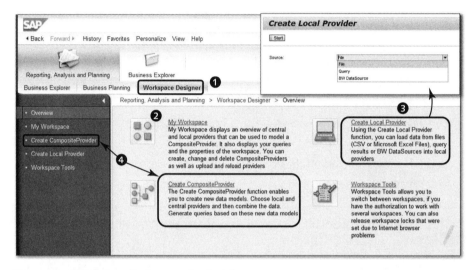

Figure 10.75 Workspace Designer on the Portal

To create a composite provider using available central providers and local providers, click on the CREATE COMPOSITEPROVIDER link, as shown in ❹ of Figure 10.75. The next screen will allow you to use one of the existing queries as a template for the composite provider. If you don't want to use a query as a template, click on the CONTINUE button (❶ of Figure 10.76) to proceed.

Maintain the name and description of the composite provider on the next screen (❷ of Figure 10.76). Select the providers you would like to use to create the data model ❸. Here you see a list of the central and local providers that you've created. For the given example, we select SALES COMMISSION and SALES INFOCUBE as the basis for defining the composite provider. Click on NEXT ❹.

The next step is to define the data model of the composite provider by defining connections between the previously selected central and local providers (Figure 10.77). Select the CONNECTION TYPE from the dropdown ❶ for each of the selected providers.

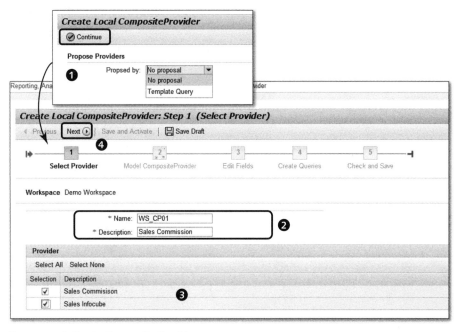

Figure 10.76 Create Composite Provider

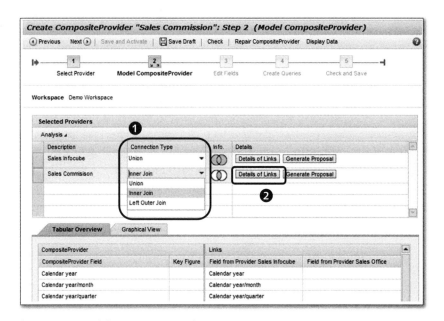

Figure 10.77 Model Composite Provider

You can either ask the system to generate a proposal for links by clicking on the GENERATE PROPOSAL button, or define the links yourself by clicking on the DETAILS FOR LINKS button ❷. This action will navigate you to the screen where link details are maintained (Figure 10.78).

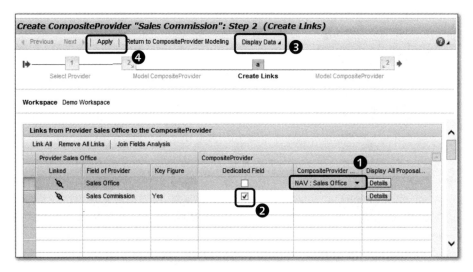

Figure 10.78 Defining Links for Composite Provider

Again, for our example requirement from ABCD Corp., we need to get the sales commission percentage value for each sales office from the sales commission provider. Therefore, the SALES OFFICE field from the SALES COMMISSION PROVIDER is mapped to the SALES OFFICE field from the COMPOSITEPROVIDER (❶ of Figure 10.78). The other field, SALES COMMISSION, is coming solely from the SALES COMMISSION PROVIDER; hence the DEDICATED FIELD checkbox is checked for this key figure ❷. To validate the links you've defined, you can preview the data by clicking on the DISPLAY DATA button. Click on the APPLY button to confirm the link definition ❹. This will take you back to the MODEL COMPOSITE PROVIDER screen. Now, you can select the GRAPHICAL VIEW tab to see the pictorial definition of the COMPOSITE PROVIDER (Figure 10.79).

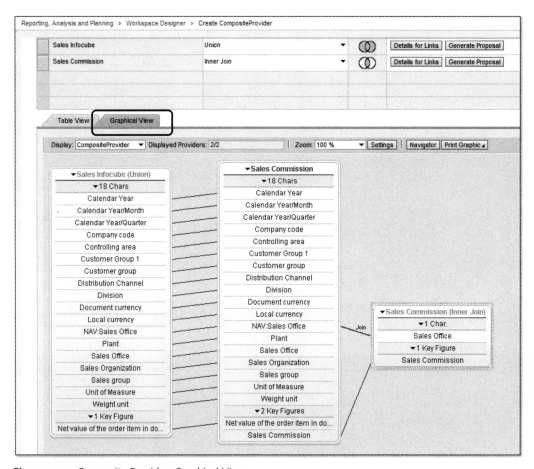

Figure 10.79 Composite Provider: Graphical View

You can edit the field descriptions on the next screen (Figure 10.80); the descriptions maintained will be visible in the query definition. You can also specify whether the key figure loaded from the local data will have a unit or currency assigned to it.

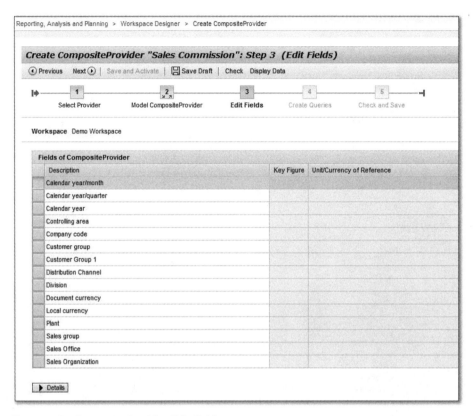

Figure 10.80 Composite Provider: Edit Field

After all of the fields are edited, you can choose to create queries on the composite provider (❶ of Figure 10.81). Here, you can define a standard query that will contain all of the characteristics and key figures from the composite provider. You can also select one of the existing queries from the assigned main provider as a reference query. (This step is optional because you can always create queries on the composite provider separately using BEx Query Designer.)

Finally, validate and save the definition of the composite provider (❷ of Figure 10.81). You'll see a confirmation that the definition is saved and activated successfully on the final screen ❸. As mentioned earlier, this composite provider is now accessible as one of the InfoProviders on which you can define your queries from BEx Query Designer (Figure 10.82).

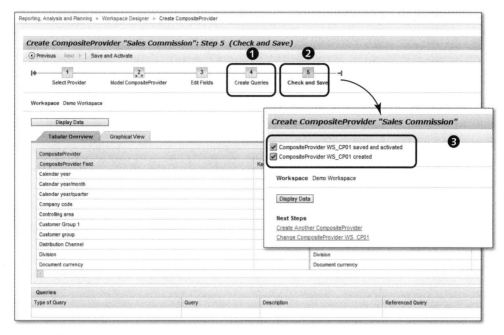

Figure 10.81 Saving the Composite Provider

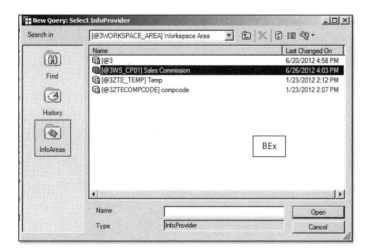

Figure 10.82 Composite Provider in BEx

The composite providers are available under @3WORKSPACE_AREA (WORKSPACE AREA), as shown in Figure 10.82. A query can now be created on this composite provider to address ABCD Corp.'s requirement to determine sales commission amounts for sales offices (Figure 10.83).

Note

You can also create composite providers from the SAP BW backend directly from Transaction RSA1 as discussed in Chapter 6.

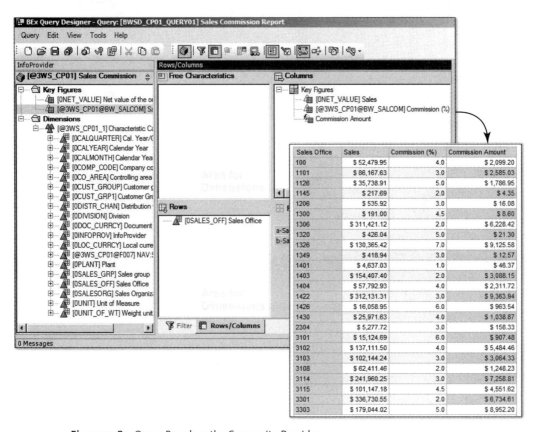

Figure 10.83 Query Based on the Composite Provider

In the process of addressing this requirement, we've explained how to use BW Workspaces, which allows you to create a data model and query on the fly without any backend development and change transports. Moreover, all of this can be done by business users themselves, alleviating dependency on the IT team and allowing them to manage their own ad hoc analysis requirements.

10.11 Summary

BEx Analyzer and BEx Web Analyzer provide reporting and analysis capabilities to business analysts in Excel and web environments, respectively, and this chapter has discussed the different analysis functions available in both tools. We also discussed the concept of information broadcasting and explained how a collaborative analysis can be performed using BEx Broadcaster functions. We concluded the chapter with a discussion of BW Workspaces, and saw with an example how this tool can be used for BI user empowerment.

The quality and ease of information access and data analysis are major evaluation criteria for any BI tool. The components discussed in this chapter highlight the capabilities of SAP BW in this respect.

In the next chapter, we discuss building web applications using BEx Web Application Designer.

Reporting and analysis features are important criteria to consider when evaluating a BI tool, and SAP BW offers a wide range of features. This chapter discusses BEx Web Application Designer, which is used to create custom web applications in SAP BW.

11   Creating Applications Using BEx Web Application Designer

In the previous chapters of this book, we explained the use of BEx Query Designer to create queries on different SAP BW InfoProviders. We also explained the different analysis options available in BEx, including BEx Analyzer and BEx Web Analyzer. Most importantly, the procedure to create a custom analysis application in Excel using BEx Analyzer was also discussed. In this chapter, we take you through BEx Web Application Designer, which is used to create custom analysis applications for a web environment. By the end, you'll be familiar with BEx Web Application Designer and the different options it gives you to create web applications.

11.1   BEx Web Application Designer Overview

BEx Web Application Designer is a standalone tool that can be accessed through the desktop without logging on to a SAP GUI. The web applications built using BEx Web Application Designer are based on HTML pages and can be based on data providers such as BEx queries, views, filters, or InfoProviders. The web applications created in this tool are saved as Extensible Hypertext Markup Language *(XHTML) documents*. These XHTML documents form the basis for the web application and are called *web templates*. Placeholders for all of the objects included in the web application, their properties, settings, and so on are translated into the XHTML format in the web template.

> **XHTML**
>
> XHTML is an extension of HTML and is based on XML rules.

11.1.1 Starting BEx Web Application Designer

Similar to other BEx tools, such as BEx Query Designer or BEx Analyzer, BEx Web Application Designer is a standalone tool that can be accessed through a desktop without actually logging into the SAP GUI. Follow the path START • PROGRAMS • BUSINESS EXPLORER • WEB APPLICATION DESIGNER to open the tool (see Figure 11.1).

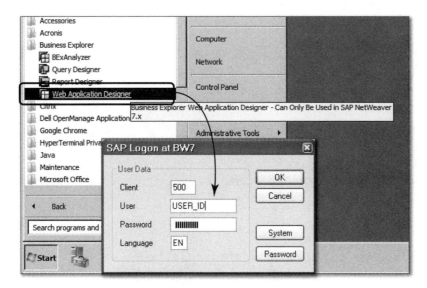

Figure 11.1 Open BEx Web Application Designer

The system prompts you for the login credentials for the SAP BW system. Enter the user ID and password, and log on to BEx Web Application Designer (see Figure 11.1).

On the entry screen, you see options to CREATE NEW WEB TEMPLATE or to OPEN EXISTING WEB TEMPLATE. A list of recently accessed web templates is also displayed for quick access (see ❶ of Figure 11.2). To open a new web template, click on CREATE NEW BLANK WEB TEMPLATE, or use the menu path WEB TEMPLATE • NEW ❷.

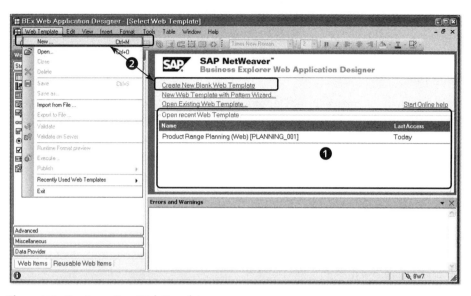

Figure 11.2 Creating a New Web Template

11.1.2 Different Screen Areas of BEx Web Application Designer

The web template screen in BEx Web Application Designer consists of different screen areas, as shown in Figure 11.3.

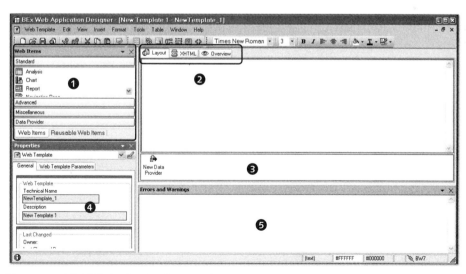

Figure 11.3 BEx Web Application Designer Screen Layout

The significance of each area in a web template design is explained in the following subsections.

Web Items

To facilitate easy and faster development of web applications, BEx Web Application Designer provides a bunch of prebuilt components called *web items*, which can be used directly in the web application. The web items are available in the WEB ITEMS area, as shown in ❶ of Figure 11.3. Each web item performs some design function or is linked to a data provider to perform some data function, such as displaying the data in tabular format, displaying the data in graphical format, and so on. Available web items are classified into three web item groups:

▶ STANDARD
This web item group contains the most commonly used web items for a web application, such as an analysis grid, chart, different filter and navigation components, and so on.

▶ ADVANCED
These components can be used to create more complex web applications. Web items such as containers, groups, tabs, and so on help you configure the web application in a sophisticated manner. You can also embed other web templates, documents, information items, and so on in the web template.

▶ MISCELLANEOUS
Different web items are used to add additional features to the web application. Web items such as list of conditions or list of exceptions provide additional analysis options. Similarly, web items such as menu bars, text, tickers, and so on add additional features to the web application.

All of these web items are explained later in Section 11.3.

Layout/XHTML/Overview Tabs

The layout of the web template is displayed under the LAYOUT tab of this area (see ❷ of Figure 11.3). You can add a web item to the web template layout using simple drag and drop from the WEB ITEMS area. The XHTML tab page displays the XHTML document, which is generated based on the web items added to the web template. You can add your own XHTML code on this tab for additional features or logic. The OVERVIEW tab page provides an overview of all of the components used in the web template. You can edit the components from the OVERVIEW tab page directly.

Data Provider

The section shown in ❸ of Figure 11.3 is used to manage the data providers in a web template. *Data providers* are those elements that act as a source of data for different web items. Queries defined in BEx Query Designer, query views, query filters, and SAP BW InfoProviders can be used as data providers in a web template. You can define a new data provider or change an existing data provider in this area. This also corresponds to the DATA PROVIDER section that is visible in WEB ITEMS area.

Properties

All of the web items and the web template itself have properties that control their behavior in the web application. These properties are maintained in the PROPERTIES pane shown in ❹ of Figure 11.3. For the web items based on a data provider, the data provider assignment is also maintained in the GENERAL tab of the PROPERTIES pane.

Other parameters for a web item/web template—DISPLAY, BEHAVIOR, and so on— are maintained on the WEB ITEM PARAMETERS tab of the PROPERTIES pane. Important properties of web items and web templates are discussed later in Section 11.5.

Errors and Warnings

This section on the screen displays error messages or warnings if there are any discrepancies in the definition of the web template (❺ of Figure 11.3).

11.2   Creating a Simple Web Application

To begin with, we take a scenario from our example company, ABCD Corp., and then address it by creating a web application using BEx Web Application Designer.

The analysts at ABCD Corp. want a *sales overview dashboard* where they can see quarterly material sales for a selected sales organization and year. The representation of the data has to be in both *tabular* and *graphical* format. They also need an easy-to-use *dropdown* feature where they can select a material group, and the table and graph should be refreshed for the selected value. There also needs to be the flexibility to change the selected sales organization or year if needed.

Next, we discuss the steps involved in creating a simple web application.

11.2.1 Creating a Data Provider

The basis for the web items displaying data in a web template is a data provider. As a first step, create the data provider that should be used by different web items in a web template. To create a data provider in a web template, click on the New Data Provider icon, shown in ❶ of Figure 11.4. The Maintain Data Provider box appears.

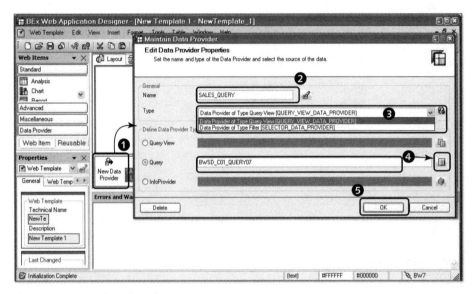

Figure 11.4 Create Data Provider

Give a name to the data provider (❷ of Figure 11.4). This data provider is referred to by different web items in the query using this name.

There can be different types of data providers. The queries defined in BEx Query Designer, query views, query filters, and SAP BW InfoProviders can be used as data providers in a web template. The Type dropdown ❸ allows you to select the data provider type. The Data Provider of Type Filter option is normally used while creating planning applications. (The use of this type of data provider is discussed in Chapter 12.)

If you select Data Provider of Type Query View, you can further select an option from among Query View, Query, or InfoProvider. For this example scenario, select the Query option, and select the query that should be used as a data provider using the Input Help button ❹.

Click on OK ❺ to complete the definition of the data provider and to return to the web template layout screen.

11.2.2   Using an Analysis Web Item

Before you begin adding different web items to the web template, first create a heading for the web application. You can enter the text directly into the template layout screen (❶ of Figure 11.5) and can control its display using the formatting toolbar ❷.

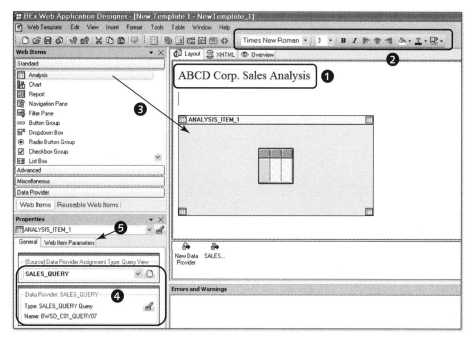

Figure 11.5 Adding the Heading and Inserting an Analysis Web Item

You can now start including required web items in the layout. The ANALYSIS web item is used when you have to display data in a tabular format in the web application. To add this web item to the template, drag it from the WEB ITEMS area, and place it in the layout (❸ of Figure 11.5).

Because the ANALYSIS web item displays data, it needs to be assigned to a data provider. The data provider assignment can be done on the GENERAL tab in the PROPERTIES area ❹. Click on the WEB ITEM PARAMETERS tab ❺ to maintain settings for the selected analysis web item. The WEB ITEM PARAMETERS tab for an analysis web item is shown in Figure 11.6.

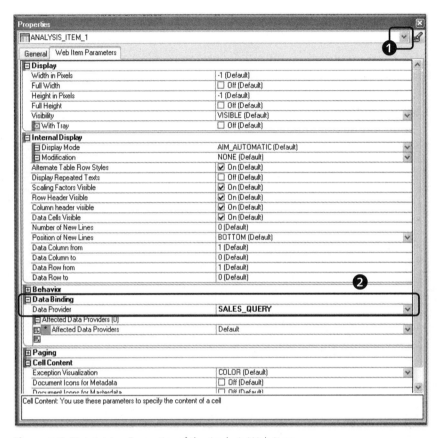

Figure 11.6 Maintaining Properties of the Analysis Web Item

You can change the name of the web item by clicking on the EDIT icon shown in ❶ of Figure 11.6. You can control the display and behavior of the web item in the application by setting different parameters on this screen.

Data Binding

If the web item is based on a data provider or changes to this web item can impact other data providers (affected data providers), then these settings for the web item are maintained under the DATA BINDING section of PROPERTIES (❷ of Figure 11.6).

11.2.3 Using a Dropdown Box

The analysts at ABCD Corp. want an easy-to-use dropdown feature so that they can filter the data displayed by selecting a value from the dropdown. To add a dropdown to the web template, drag the DROPDOWN BOX web item from the WEB ITEMS area, and drop it in the desired location in the web template (❶ of Figure 11.7).

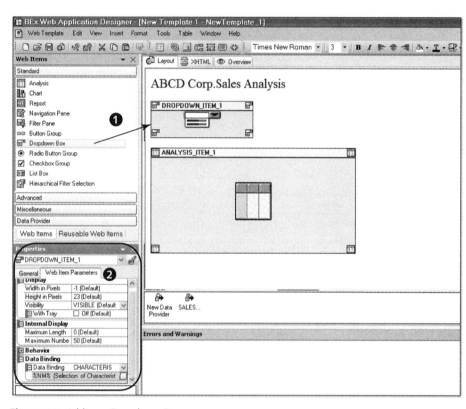

Figure 11.7 Adding a Dropdown Box

The parameters for this dropdown box can be maintained in the PROPERTIES area (❷ of Figure 11.7). The properties for this web item are maintained as shown in Figure 11.8. A dropdown box actually reads the contents from the object to which it's tied. The assignment is maintained under the DATA BINDING section, where the property DATA BINDING TYPE provides you with multiple options that can be used as a source of data for the dropdown box (❶ of Figure 11.8). Per the requirements, the dropdown box must display the values of the material group characteristic, so select the CHAR/STRUCTURE MEMBER option as the data binding type.

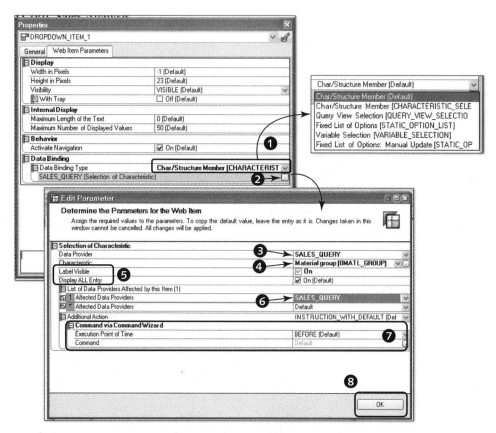

Figure 11.8 Maintaining Dropdown Box Properties

To define the selection of characteristic for the dropdown, click on the button shown in ❷ of Figure 11.8. The EDIT PARAMETERS box appears. Maintain the characteristic selection and set the following for SELECTED CHARACTERISTIC:

▶ DATA PROVIDER ❸
The data provider from where the dropdown box should read the characteristic value.

▶ CHARACTERISTIC ❹
Select the specific characteristic that will be assigned to the dropdown. Input help is available for this parameter.

▶ DISPLAY PARAMETERS SETTINGS ❺
The display-related settings, such as whether the label of the characteristic

should be visible or not, and whether to display the ALL entry, are maintained on this screen.

▶ AFFECTED DATA PROVIDERS ❻

This is one of the most important settings for the dropdown box because it determines which data providers within the web template should change per the specific value selected in the dropdown. If there are multiple data providers in the query, and you want more than one data provider to change due to the dropdown, you can maintain a list of different data providers under the AFFECTED DATA PROVIDERS section.

▶ COMMAND VIA COMMAND WIZARD ❼

The Command Wizard is one of the most powerful features available in BEx Web Application Designer. It enlists many useful commands that can be used to assign a specific action to a web item; for example, you can set exceptions to an inactive state whenever a value is selected in the dropdown box. Details about the Command Wizard and the different available commands are discussed in Section 11.4.

Finally, click on OK ❽ to complete the selection of characteristics and return to the web template layout.

11.2.4 Creating Charts

The CHART web item displays data from the data provider in graphical format. To add a chart to the web template, drag the CHART web item from the WEB ITEMS area into the layout (see ❶ of Figure 11.9). Assign the data provider to this web item in the PROPERTIES box ❷. The detailed setting for the graphical display is done in the WEB ITEM PARAMETERS tab of the PROPERTIES box ❸.

Different parameters that control the display, behavior, and other chart settings are maintained as a part of chart properties (see Figure 11.10).

The EDIT CHART option (see ❶ of Figure 11.10) opens up an EDIT CHART window, which is much like a chart wizard (similar to that of Excel). On this screen, you can select the type of chart from the numerous available chart types ❷ and configure the chart at a detailed level.

Maintain the DATA BINDING and chart-specific settings, as shown in ❸.

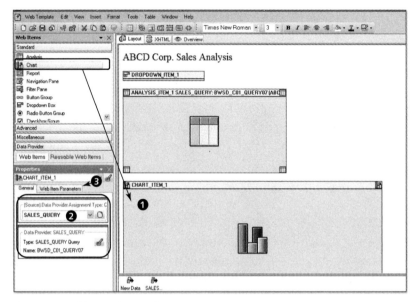

Figure 11.9 Adding a Chart Web Item

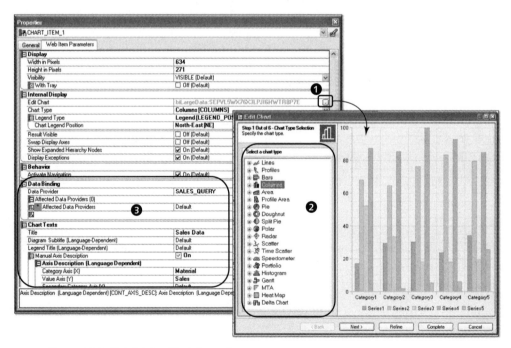

Figure 11.10 Maintaining Chart Properties

11.2.5 Adding a Command Button

Let's now address the requirement for analysts to be able to change the selected sales organization or year, if needed. This requirement means there must be a provision to call the variable screen. In this case, *calling the variable screen* is a command, and we'll use a button in the web application that will execute this command.

To add a button in the web template, drag the Button Group web item from the Web Items area into the layout, as shown in ❶ of Figure 11.11. Then go to the Web Item Parameters tab for the button group to configure the button group ❷.

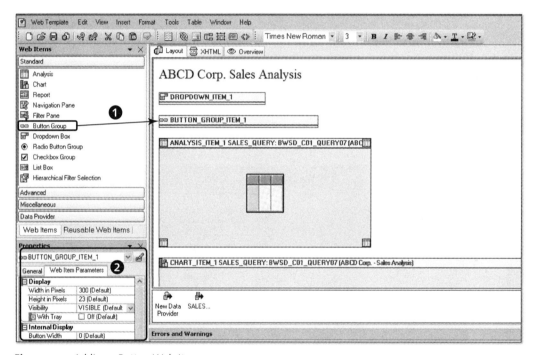

Figure 11.11 Adding a Button Web Item

Apart from maintaining the display settings for the button group (❶ of Figure 11.12), you must define a button (or multiple buttons) on this screen ❷.

To add a button, click on the button shown in ❸ of Figure 11.12. The Edit Parameter box appears, in which you define the button settings ❹. You also have to select one of the available button designs ❺.

Now that you've configured the button, the next step is to assign an action to it. You can either assign a command from the already available set of commands, or you can assign a custom JavaScript function to the button. We have to assign an action that will call the variable screen. This command is available in the Command Wizard, so select COMMAND VIA COMMAND WIZARD as the ACTION ❻. Click on the button shown in ❼ to call the Command Wizard.

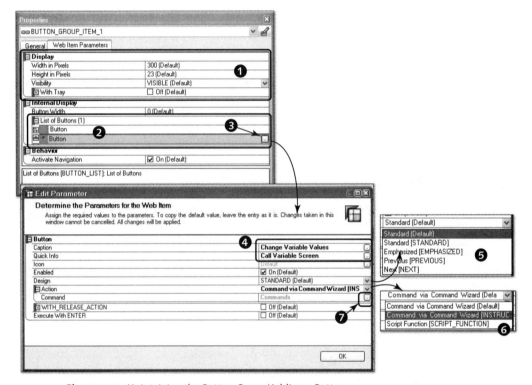

Figure 11.12 Maintaining the Button Group/Adding a Button

The Command Wizard includes a variety of commands that can be used in the web template to create effective applications for analysis or planning (see Figure 11.13). Based on the usage and applicability, these commands are grouped in four different sections, as shown in ❶ of Figure 11.13. (Again, these commands are discussed in more detail earlier in Section 11.4.)

For the example scenario, we need a command to call up the variable screen. This command is available under the COMMANDS FOR WEB TEMPLATES section (❶ of Figure 11.13). Select the OPEN VARIABLE DIALOG (OPEN_VARIABLE_ DIALOG)

command ❷, and click on the NEXT button to set the parameters for this command ❸. You can also maintain a list of frequently used commands as your favorites by selecting the checkbox in front of a command ❹. All commands where the checkbox is selected will appear on the FAVORITE COMMANDS tab page ❹.

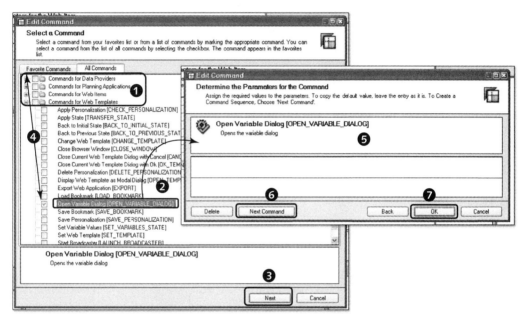

Figure 11.13 Assigning a Command

When you click on the NEXT button, the next screen appears based on the command selected. Each command has a different set of parameters that should be maintained for that command in the next screen ❺. For example, for the SET WEB TEMPLATE command, you have to define the web template name as a parameter. On the other hand, the OPEN VARIABLE DIALOG command doesn't need any parameters, so the next screen doesn't show any configuration.

You can also add more than one command to the same button so that a sequence of commands is executed when the button is clicked. Click on the NEXT COMMAND button ❻ to add new commands to the button. When finished, click on OK ❼, and return to the button definition screen (see Figure 11.14).

The selected command is now linked to a button (❶ of Figure 11.14). If you want a specific command to be executed when the user presses the Enter key, then check the EXECUTE WITH ENTER setting in the button configuration ❷.

Finally, click on OK ❸ to return to the web template design screen.

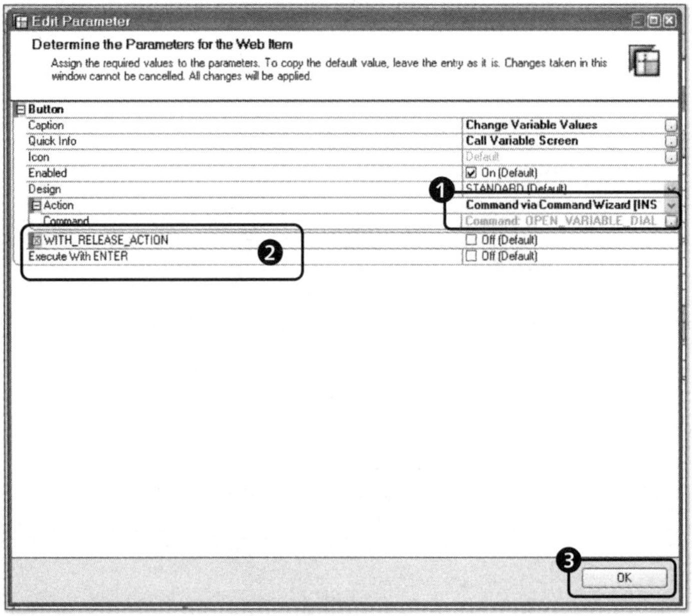

Figure 11.14 Complete Button Settings

11.2.6 Arranging Web Items

All of the web items needed in the web application are now included and are configured. You can now arrange the web items in the web template for a structured display. For example, you might want to display the dropdown and button next to each other, rather than displaying them in two separate rows.

For this and other similar purposes, BEx Web Application Designer allows you to use some standard XHTML elements in the web template.

To insert a table in the web template, first position the cursor where you want to insert it, and then click on the INSERT TABLE button on the toolbar, as shown in ❶ of Figure 11.15.

The EDIT HTML ELEMENT box appears, in which you can customize the element per the requirement (❷ in Figure 11.15). Finally, click on OK to return to the web template design screen. The table is inserted in the web template layout per the settings (❶ of Figure 11.16). To arrange the web items, simply drag them into the different cells of the table ❷.

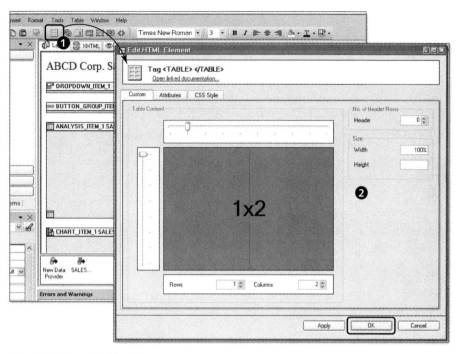

Figure 11.15 Insert Table Button

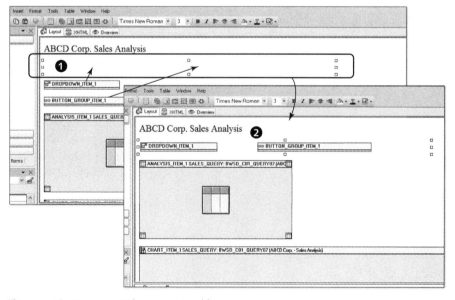

Figure 11.16 Arranging Web Items in a Table

11.2.7 Validating and Saving the Web Template

After the web template is designed, you can validate the definition of the web template using the options shown in ❶ of Figure 11.17. Use the VALIDATE option to validate the definition of the web template for consistency in the definition. The other option, VALIDATE ON SERVER, validates the web template definition as well as checks the consistency with respect to the data providers and other elements based on their definition on the server.

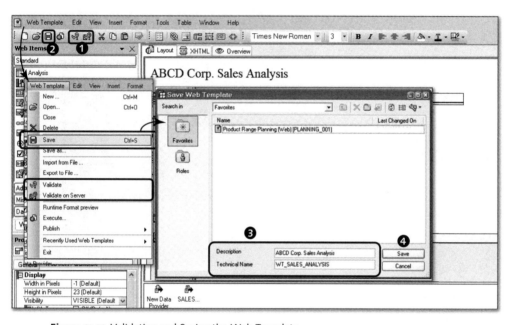

Figure 11.17 Validating and Saving the Web Template

After the definition of the web template is validated, save the web template using the SAVE icon (❷ of Figure 11.17). You can also use the menu option WEB TEMPLATE • SAVE to save the template. The SAVE WEB TEMPLATE box appears, in which you enter the description and technical name of the web template ❸. Click on the SAVE button ❹ to save the web template with the given name and description.

As you create the web template using different web items in the layout, the XHTML code is updated for all of the settings and configurations made to the web items. The XHTML code can be seen on the XHTML tab page (❶ of Figure 11.18). You can jump to the code relevant for a specific web item by selecting that web item from the dropdown.

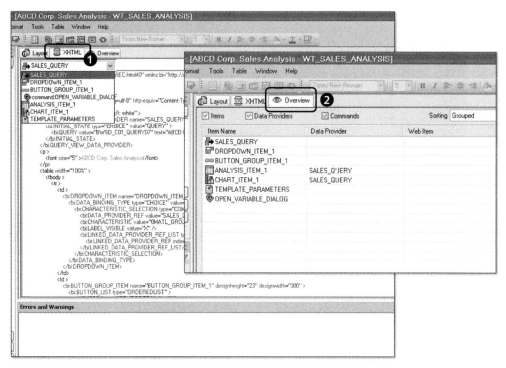

Figure 11.18 XHTML Tab and Overview Tab

The OVERVIEW tab page ❷ is more like a blueprint of the web template. This tab page lists all of the elements used in the web template. Any of these elements can be edited from this screen.

11.2.8 Executing the Web Template

Follow the WEB TEMPLATE • EXECUTE menu path to execute the web template, or use the EXECUTE button shown in ❶ of Figure 11.19. The web template is executed in a separate web browser window.

If any of the data providers in the web template include user entry variables, then the variable screen is displayed in the beginning, prompting users to make variable entries. Enter the variable selection ❷, and then click on the OK ❸ button to execute the web template.

The resulting web application is displayed in the web browser, as shown in Figure 11.20.

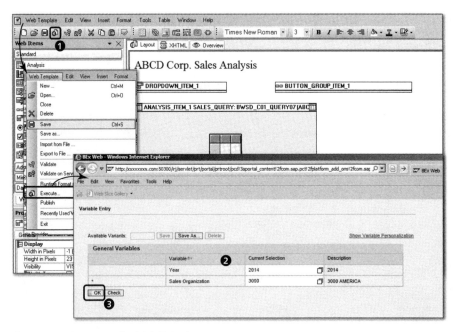

Figure 11.19 Executing the Web Template

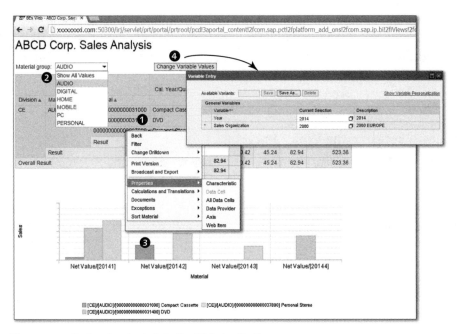

Figure 11.20 Performing Analysis in the Web Application

This web application, ABCD Corp. Sales Analysis, displays quarterly sales by material in a tabular format, and the different BEx navigation options are visible in the context menu for this web item (❶ of Figure 11.20). A MATERIAL GROUP dropdown ❷ is available to filter the results of the web application.

The data is displayed in graphical format ❸ based on the selections made in the drilldown. Finally, if you click on the CHANGE VARIABLE VALUES button ❹, the VARIABLE ENTRY box appears in which you change the values for sales organization and year.

11.3 Web Items

As we said earlier, web items are objects that can be readily used in web templates, and thus they eliminate the need to write XHTML code to create web applications. As you'll recall, a web item carries out a design function or is linked to a data provider. Again, the available web items are classified into three web item groups:

- Standard
- Advanced
- Miscellaneous

In this section, we'll discuss the web items available in BEx Web Application Designer and their use in creating a web application.

11.3.1 Standard Web Items

Standard web items are the most common and are discussed next.

Analysis

As we've seen while creating the web application in the previous section, the ANALYSIS web item is used to display the data from the data provider in a tabular format. All of the navigation functions we explained in BEx Web Analyzer (i.e., drag and drop, filters, drilldown, etc.) are supported by this web item. However, you can control whether these options are available to users by controlling the properties and context menu options for the web template.

This web item is based on a data provider, and the data provider is assigned to the web item on the GENERAL tab of the PROPERTIES pane (❶ of Figure 11.21). You can change the web item name by clicking on the ✐ button shown in ❷ of Figure 11.21.

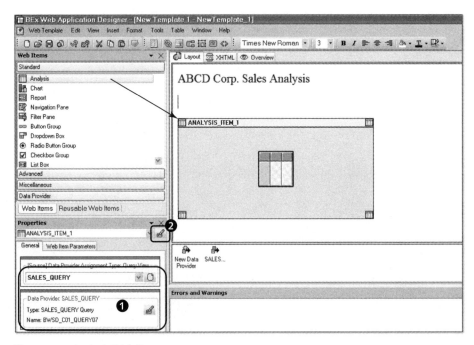

Figure 11.21 Analysis Web Item

Different parameters corresponding to the ANALYSIS web item are maintained on the WEB ITEM PARAMETERS tab. The parameters are grouped by category, as shown in Figure 11.22. You can maintain the display-related settings, such as length, width, and appearance of the web item by using the parameters under the DISPLAY section (❶ of Figure 11.22). The parameters that control the display of data within the analysis web item are available under INTERNAL DISPLAY ❷.

Using the parameters under the BEHAVIOR section ❸, you can decide if the navigation and analysis can be allowed for the analysis web item. Set the ACTIVE NAVIGATION parameter to OFF for fixed format and static reporting. Using the ROW SELECTION/COLUMN SELECTION parameters, you can select the rows or columns from the tabular display and then perform specific actions on the selected data.

Under the DATA BINDING section ❹, you maintain the reference data provider for the web item and a list of those data providers that are affected due to changes in this web item.

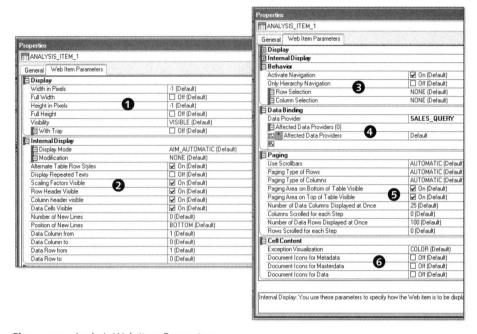

Figure 11.22 Analysis Web Item Parameters

The PAGING settings ❺ for an analysis web item define how the data should be displayed in the table format, and the CELL CONTENT section ❻ contains the parameters for the cells displayed in the analysis web item. Here, you can set the way exceptions should be displayed and control the display of document icons in the analysis display.

Chart

We discussed this web item while creating the web application in Section 11.2. The CHART web item is used to display the data in a graphical format and is based on a data provider. The different parameters shown earlier control the display, behavior, and so on for the chart. A wide variety of chart options is available in the BEx Web Application Designer. These charts/graphs can be customized using the chart wizard, which can be called from the chart properties (refer to Figure 11.10).

Report

Preformatted reports created in the BEx Report Designer can be inserted in a web application using the REPORT web item.

Navigation Pane

The NAVIGATION PANE web item can be used in the web application to provide users with an option to perform slice and dice, filters, and other operations on the data. The navigation state of the data provider (e.g., characteristics in rows/columns/free characteristic area, and position of key figures) is displayed in the navigation pane. In the properties of this web item, you can control the query elements to be displayed in the navigation pane (see Figure 11.23).

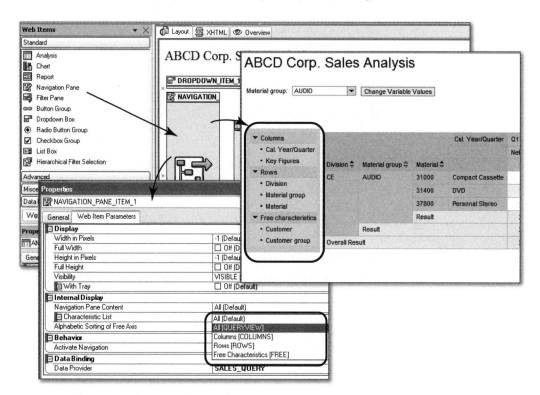

Figure 11.23 Navigation Pane Web Item

Filter Pane

The FILTER PANE web item is used if you want to let users select the values for selected characteristics or specific key figures from the key figure structure by applying a filter. The same web item can also be used to display the filter values for selected characteristics in the web application (see Figure 11.24).

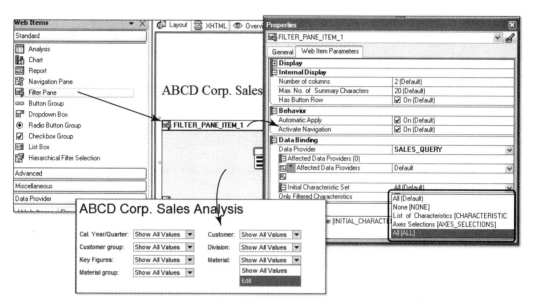

Figure 11.24 Filter Pane Web Item

Button Group

Earlier, we discussed the use of buttons while creating the web application for ABCD Corp. The main purpose of the BUTTON GROUP web item is to provide actions to the web application. Different commands that are available in the Command Wizard can be attached to a button. Multiple buttons can be included in a single button group, and each button in the button group can have a separate command/sequence of commands linked to it (see Figure 11.25). (Again, the Command Wizard and its different commands are discussed in Section 11.4.)

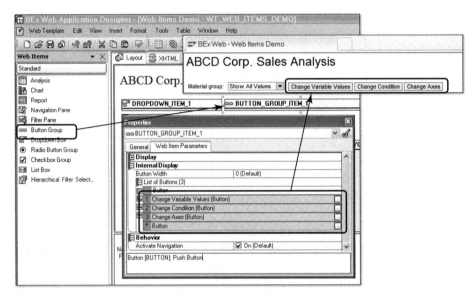

Figure 11.25 Button Group Web Item

Dropdown Box

The DROPDOWN BOX web item is used to provide an easy option for user selections. The use of the dropdown box was discussed when we explained the creation of a web application (refer to Figure 11.8). The dropdown box that was created was based on a characteristic. However, a dropdown box can be populated from multiple sources:

▶ CHARACTERISTIC VALUES
In this case, the dropdown list is populated from the selected characteristic of a data provider. The data provider display is controlled based on the value selected in the dropdown box.

▶ QUERY VIEW SELECTION
In this case, if there are views built on the data provider, then the dropdown displays the list of all those views from a selected data provider. Using this option, users can select different views of the data provider in the dropdown.

▶ FIXED LIST OF OPTIONS
Using this option, you can define your own values, which should appear in the

dropdown list, and then you can assign an action (a command) to each of the values added to the dropdown.

▶ FIXED LIST OF OPTIONS: MANUAL UPDATE
This option is similar to the FIXED LIST OF OPTIONS setting. The difference is that this web item also allows users to trigger manual updates.

▶ VARIABLE SELECTION
This option populates the dropdown list with the values for the selected BEx variable.

Radio Button Group

The RADIO BUTTON GROUP web item allows you to filter selected characteristic values using a radio button. Characteristic values for the selected characteristic are displayed in a group in the web application. In the WEB ITEM PARAMETER settings, you can control the number of values to be displayed and whether to display an ALL entry. This option is typically used if characteristics need to be restricted with a single value (see Figure 11.26).

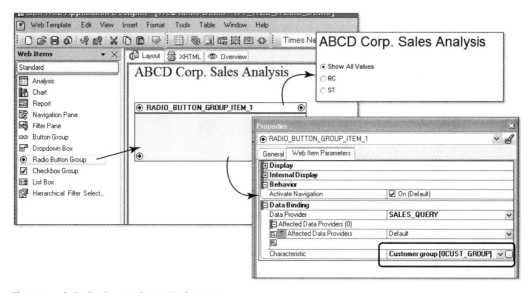

Figure 11.26 Radio Button Group Web Item

Checkbox Group

Using a CHECKBOX GROUP web item, you can display values for a selected characteristic that can be selected using checkboxes. This option is useful for selecting one or more values of a characteristic for which the data providers are filtered (see Figure 11.27).

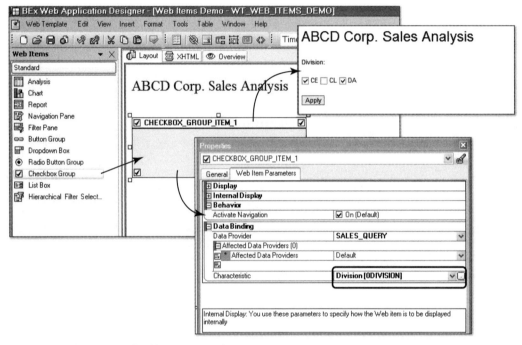

Figure 11.27 Checkbox Group Web Item

List Box

The LIST BOX web item is used if you want to select filters for a characteristic using a list box. You can select one or multiple values at a time as a filter (see Figure 11.28).

Hierarchical Filter Selection

The HIERARCHICAL FILTER SELECTION web item allows users to select filter values based on the hierarchy built on the selected characteristic. The user can expand or collapse the hierarchy and can select a specific node (or leaf) that is used to filter the attached data provider (see Figure 11.29).

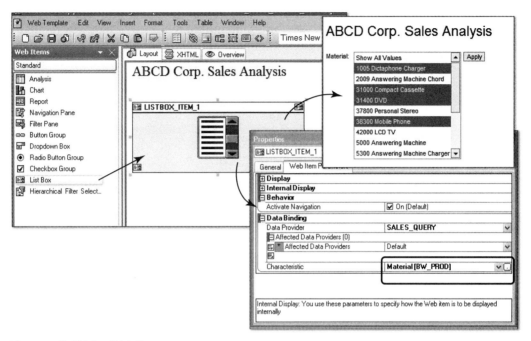

Figure 11.28 List Box Web Item

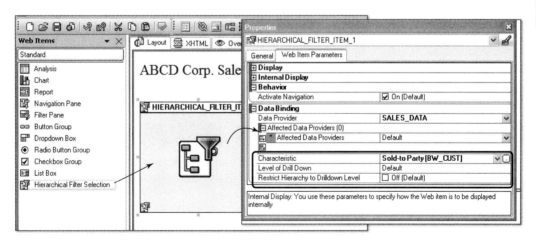

Figure 11.29 Hierarchical Filter Selection Web Item

11.3.2 Advanced Web Items

Advanced web items are used for more complex applications, such as a group or tab. The details are discussed next.

Web Template

The WEB TEMPLATE web item can be used to insert another web template into the web template definition (see Figure 11.30).

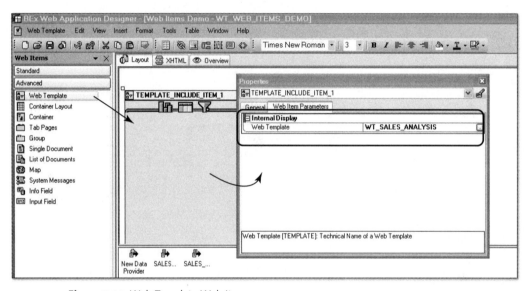

Figure 11.30 Web Template Web Item

Container Layout

You use the CONTAINER LAYOUT web item to place and space the different web items included in the web template. A CONTAINER LAYOUT is used to create an organized display for the web application. This web item offers you a grid to arrange the web items. Note that one cell in the grid accommodates only one web item.

Container

The CONTAINER web item is used to group contents from different web items together in the web template. For example, grouping items on different tab pages of the web application can be achieved using a container on each of the tabs.

Tab Pages

Use the TAB PAGES web item to organize the web items included in the web template across different tab pages (see Figure 11.31).

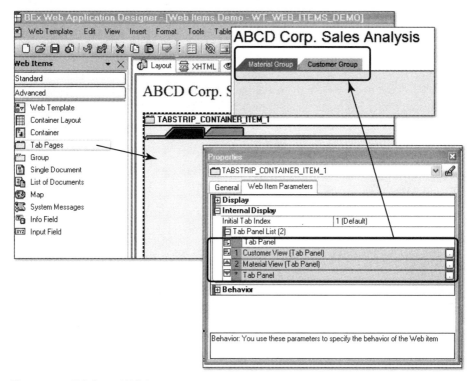

Figure 11.31 Tab Pages Web Item

Group

A GROUP web item is used to display the contents of the web application together as a group.

Single Document

Using the SINGLE DOCUMENT web item, you can embed a document in the web application that is maintained for the selected data provider. You can also specify the *document class* (i.e., InfoProvider, metadata, or master data) of the document, which should be displayed in the web application.

List of Documents

Use the LIST OF DOCUMENTS web item to display the list of documents corresponding to a data provider. This web item is context sensitive, so only those documents that are applicable to the current state of navigation for the data provider are shown in the list.

Map

You can use the MAP web item to display the data provider information on a map with respect to the geographical characteristic, such as country, region, state, and so on. Using this feature and web item is dependent on the geo-characteristics that form the basis for maps in SAP BW.

System Messages

Different system messages, errors, warnings, and information messages can be displayed in the web application by inserting the SYSTEM MESSAGES web item.

Display/Suppress Messages
The setting to display or suppress messages/errors/warning/information is configured at the web template level.

Info Field

The information regarding the user, data provider, filters, status of data, and so on can be displayed using the INFO FIELD web item. You can select the list of information parameters to be displayed in the web application in the web item properties.

Input Field

The INPUT FIELD web item provides you with a general user input field in the web application. Users can enter characteristic filter values, numeric values, and so on in this field, and this information can be read by other web items for processing in the web application.

11.3.3   Miscellaneous Web Items

Miscellaneous web items are used to add other features to web applications, as discussed next.

Data Provider Information

The DATA PROVIDER web item is used to generate XML for the query results or the navigation state of the data provider. This XML generation isn't visible to the user because the code is generated at the source of the web application. To view the generated XML, view the source for the web application.

Text

The TEXT web item is used to display general text, characteristic descriptions, or other text elements, such as queries, data providers, and user information, in the web application.

Link

Using the LINK web item, you can include a link in the web application and assign a command to the link that is executed when the link is accessed.

List of Exceptions

The LIST OF EXCEPTIONS web item displays the list of all exceptions defined on the data provider used in the web template. These exceptions can be set as active or inactive during the analysis.

List of Conditions

The LIST OF CONDITIONS web item displays a list of conditions defined on the data provider used in the web template. While performing analysis, the user can then toggle between the active and inactive states of each condition, if needed.

Menu Bar

The MENU BAR web item is used in a web template to build a menu bar for the web application. Using this web item, you can create your own menu options and provide action to each of these menu options by assigning commands.

Ticker

Using the TICKER web item, you can display data in the form of a ticker in the web application.

Properties Pane

Use the PROPERTIES PANE web item if you want to allow users to edit the properties of web items included in the web application during runtime.

Context Menu

While working in a web application, you can use different context menu options to perform analysis on the data displayed using the ANALYSIS web item or the NAVIGATION BLOCK web item. Using the CONTEXT MENU web item, you can control different menu options that should be made available to the user using the web application. You have an option to hide/display each function of the context menu in the properties of this web item.

Script

Using the SCRIPT web item, you can integrate a JavaScript into the web template.

Custom Extension

The CUSTOM EXTENSION web item is used to address some of the complex requirements that can't be addressed using any of the readily available web items. You can integrate custom ABAP code or HTML code with the web template, for example.

Reusable Web Items

Web items that are included and configured in a web template can be saved as REUSABLE web items in BEx Web Application Designer. These saved web items are available under the REUSABLE WEB ITEMS tab in the WEB ITEMS panel (❶ of Figure 11.32).

To save a web item for reuse, select SAVE AS REUSABLE WEB ITEM from the context menu of the web item ❷, and then save it after providing a technical name and description in the pop-up box ❸.

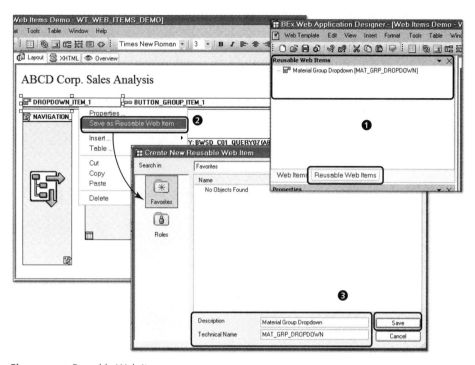

Figure 11.32 Reusable Web Items

11.4 Working with Commands

Assigning commands to different components and user actions is very important when creating a web application. You can assign commands to different web items included in the web template using custom JavaScript. However, to eliminate coding and reduce the complexity of development, BEx Web Application Designer provides a variety of ready-to-use commands. You can set your own parameters per the requirements for these commands, and you can assign these commands to web items using the Command Wizard.

You can call the Command Wizard from the ACTION section of the WEB ITEM PARAMETERS tab of the PROPERTIES box. Using these available commands makes the web application design an easy and intuitive process.

There are two tab pages in the Command Wizard (see Figure 11.33):

▶ ALL COMMANDS
All of the available commands in the Command Wizard are displayed on the ALL COMMANDS tab page.

▶ FAVORITE COMMANDS
You can select and add frequently used commands for easy access in the FAVORITE COMMANDS tab page. Simply select the checkbox next to a command to add it to the FAVORITES tab (see Figure 11.33).

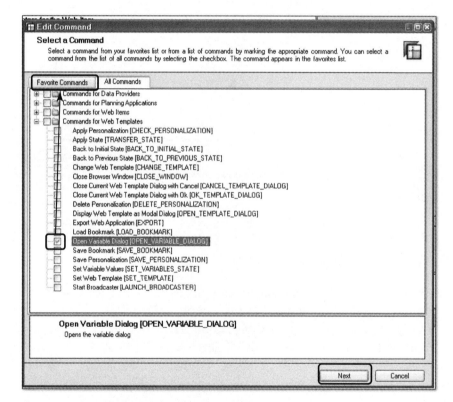

Figure 11.33 Command Wizard

Based on usage and applicability, these commands are grouped into four different sections:

▶ COMMANDS FOR DATA PROVIDERS

▶ COMMANDS FOR PLANNING APPLICATIONS

▶ COMMANDS FOR WEB ITEMS

▶ COMMANDS FOR WEB TEMPLATES

Each of the available commands has its own specific parameters to be defined. When you select a command and click on the NEXT button (see Figure 11.33), the next screen displays all of the parameters that can be set for the selected command. The description of the command and the parameters for that command are displayed in the Command Wizard to assist in development.

11.4.1 Commands for Data Providers

The commands that correspond to a data provider are grouped as COMMANDS FOR DATA PROVIDERS. Based on the application of the commands, they are further divided into subgroups. The list of all of the commands for data providers is given next.

Basic Data Provider Commands

The commands under BASIC DATA PROVIDER are listed in Table 11.1.

Command	Technical Name
REPORT-REPORT INTERFACE	RRI
SET DATA PROVIDER PARAMETERS	SET_DATA_PROVIDER_PARAMETERS
SET ZERO VALUE DISPLAY	SET_ZERO_PRESENTATION
SET SIGN DISPLAY	SET_SIGN_PRESENTATION
BACK TO INITIAL STATE	BACK_TO_INITIAL_DP_STATE
BACK TO PREVIOUS STATE	BACK_TO_PREVIOUS_DP_STATE
TRANSLATE CURRENCY	SET_CURRENCY_TRANSLATION
EXPORT DATA PROVIDER AS XML	EXPORT_XML

Table 11.1 Basic Data Provider Commands

Data Provider Commands for Axes

The commands related to the data provider axes, drilldowns, navigations, and so on are grouped as DATA PROVIDER COMMANDS FOR AXES. The commands under this group are listed in Table 11.2.

Command	Technical Name
SET HIERARCHICAL DISPLAY OF AXIS	SET_AXIS_HIERARCHY
SET POSITION OF RESULTS ROW	SET_RESULT_ALIGNMENT
SWAP AXES	SWAP_AXES
REMOVE DRILLDOWN	REMOVE_DRILL_DOWN
DRILL DOWN A CHARACTERISTIC	DRILL_DOWN
EXCHANGE CHARACTERISTICS/STRUCTURES	EXCHANGE

Table 11.2 Data Provider Commands for Axes

Data Provider Commands for Characteristics

The commands that correspond to the display and presentation of characteristic values in the data provider are grouped as DATA PROVIDER COMMANDS FOR CHARACTERISTICS. Table 11.3 lists the different commands that belong to this group.

Command	Technical Name
SET DISPLAY ATTRIBUTES	SET_ATTRIBUTES
SET PRESENTATION	SET_PRESENTATION
SET DISPLAY OF RESULTS ROW	SET_RESULT_VISIBILITY
SET SORTING	SET_SORTING

Table 11.3 Data Provider Commands for Characteristics

Data Provider Commands for Conditions/Exceptions

Commands related to exceptions and conditions, such as calling up the CONDITIONS/EXCEPTIONS dialog box or toggling between statuses, are grouped as DATA PROVIDER COMMANDS FOR CONDITIONS/EXCEPTIONS. Commands under this group are listed in Table 11.4.

Command	Technical Name
SET CONDITION	SET_CONDITION
SET STATUS OF A CONDITION	SET_CONDITION_STATE
SET EXCEPTION	SET_EXCEPTION

Table 11.4 Data Provider Commands for Conditions/Exceptions

Command	Technical Name
Set Status of an Exception	SET_EXCEPTION_STATE
Call Conditions Dialog	OPEN_CONDITIONS_DIALOG
Call Exceptions Dialog	OPEN_EXCEPTIONS_DIALOG

Table 11.4 Data Provider Commands for Conditions/Exceptions (Cont.)

Data Provider Commands for Data Cells

The commands grouped as COMMANDS FOR DATA CELLS (see Table 11.5) allow you to call the data cell properties or set local calculations for the data provider.

Command	Technical Name
Set Data Cell Properties	SET_DATA_CELL_PROPERTIES
Set Local Calculations	SET_LIST_CALCULATION

Table 11.5 Data Provider Commands for Data Cells

Data Provider Commands for Filter Values

Different commands that can be used to apply filters on the data providers or on a characteristic in the data provider are grouped together as DATA PROVIDER COMMANDS FOR FILTER VALUES. These commands are listed in Table 11.6.

Command	Technical Name
Remove All Filter Values	CLEAR_ALL_SELECTION_STATES
Call Input Help Dialog	OPEN_SELECTOR_DIALOG
Set Filter Value for a Characteristic	SET_SELECTION_STATE_SIMPLE
Set Filter Values	SET_SELECTION_STATE
Remove Filter Values for a Characteristic	CLEAR_SELECTION_STATE
Remove Filter Values for a List of Characteristics	CLEAR_SELECTION_STATES
Set Filter Values Using Different Sources	SET_SELECTION_STATE_BY_BINDING
Set Filter Values Using Filter	SET_SELECTION_STATE_BY_FILTER

Table 11.6 Data Provider Commands for Filter Values

Data Provider Commands for Hierarchies

Hierarchy-related commands are grouped as DATA PROVIDER COMMANDS FOR HIERARCHIES (see Table 11.7).

Command	Technical Name
EXPAND/COLLAPSE HIERARCHY NODES	SET_DRILL_STATE
SET HIERARCHY	SET_HIERARCHY
SET NODE ALIGNMENT	SET_NODE_ALIGNMENT

Table 11.7 Data Provider Commands for Hierarchies

Data Provider Commands for Open/Save Functions

The commands grouped under OPEN/SAVE FUNCTIONS are listed in Table 11.8.

Command	Technical Name
CALL OPEN DIALOG	LOAD
CALL SAVE DIALOG	SAVE_AS
SAVE QUERY VIEW	SAVE_VIEW

Table 11.8 Data Provider Commands for Open/Save Functions

Data Provider Commands for Documents

The commands for documents are grouped as DATA PROVIDER COMMANDS FOR DOCUMENTS and are listed in Table 11.9.

Command	Technical Name
OPEN DOCUMENT BROWSER	OPEN_DIALOG_DLG_DOC_BROWSER
OPEN DIALOG FOR NEW DOCUMENT	OPEN_DIALOG_DLG_NEW_DOCUMENT

Table 11.9 Data Provider Commands for Documents

11.4.2 Commands for Planning Applications

The commands that are grouped under COMMANDS FOR PLANNING APPLICATIONS are used when creating a web-based planning application. This includes commands to save and refresh data, commands to execute different planning functions, and so on. A list of all planning-related commands is given in Table 11.10.

Command	Technical Name
REFRESH DATA	REFRESH_DATA
SAVE CHANGED DATA	SAVE_DATA
RESET CHANGED DATA	RESET_DATA
SET DATA ENTRY MODE	SET_DATA_ENTRY_MODE
EXECUTE A PLANNING FUNCTION (SIMPLE)	EXEC_PLANNING_FUNCTION_SIMPLE
EXECUTE A PLANNING FUNCTION	EXEC_PLANNING_FUNCTION
EXECUTE A PLANNING SEQUENCE	EXEC_PLANNING_SEQUENCE_SIMPLE

Table 11.10 Commands for Planning Applications

Using these commands for planning applications is explained in detail in Chapter 12.

11.4.3 Commands for Web Items

Different web items used in the web template can also be modified from the web application. The commands listed in Table 11.11 belong to the COMMANDS FOR WEB ITEMS group.

Command	Technical Name
CALL CHART PROPERTIES DIALOG	OPEN_CHART_DIALOG
CALL PROPERTIES DIALOG	OPEN_DIALOG_PROPERTIES_PANE
SET WEB ITEM PARAMETERS	SET_ITEM_PARAMETERS
RESTORE INITIAL STATE	BACK_TO_INITIAL_ITEM_STATE
BACK TO PREVIOUS STATE	BACK_TO_PREVIOUS_ITEM_STATE
SET STATUS OF MODULE	SET_MODULE_STATE

Table 11.11 Commands for Web Items

11.4.4 Commands for Web Templates

The COMMANDS FOR WEB TEMPLATES group includes all commands that are applicable for a web template. Table 11.12 lists the different commands under this group.

Command	Technical Name
SAVE BOOKMARK	SAVE_BOOKMARK
LOAD BOOKMARK	LOAD_BOOKMARK
START BROADCASTER	LAUNCH_BROADCASTER
CLOSE BROWSER WINDOW	CLOSE_WINDOW
TRANSFER STATE	TRANSFER_STATE
SET VARIABLE VALUES	SET_VARIABLES_STATE
OPEN VARIABLE DIALOG	OPEN_VARIABLE_DIALOG
EXPORT WEB APPLICATION	EXPORT
CHANGE WEB TEMPLATE	CHANGE_TEMPLATE
DISPLAY WEB TEMPLATE AS MODAL DIALOG	OPEN_TEMPLATE_DIALOG
CLOSE CURRENT WEB TEMPLATE DIALOG WITH CANCEL	CANCEL_TEMPLATE_DIALOG
CLOSE CURRENT WEB TEMPLATE DIALOG WITH OK	OK_TEMPLATE_DIALOG
SET WEB TEMPLATE	SET_TEMPLATE
RESTORE INITIAL STATE	BACK_TO_INITIAL_STATE
RESTORE PREVIOUS STATE	BACK_TO_PREVIOUS_STATE
DELETE PERSONALIZATION	DELETE_PERSONALIZATION
SAVE PERSONALIZATION	SAVE_PERSONALIZATION

Table 11.12 Commands for Web Templates

11.5   Web Template Properties

Before we conclude this chapter, let's consider the different properties that can be set for a web template. Similar to all web items included in the web template, the web template itself has a set of parameters that can be set based on individual requirements. The different parameters available for a web template are shown in Figure 11.34.

You can control the display of various system messages, information, warnings, and error messages in the web application. The INTERNAL DISPLAY parameters (❶ of Figure 11.34) are set based on your requirements. The parameters that impact how the web template acts with respect to the variables included in its data providers are available under the BEHAVIOR section ❷.

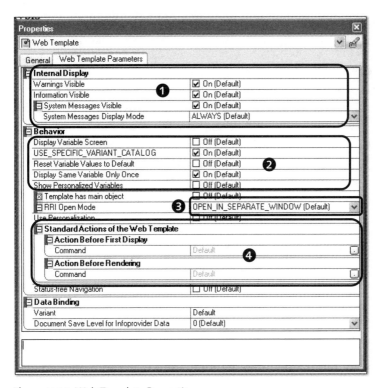

Figure 11.34 Web Template Properties

The RRI OPEN MODE parameter ❸ decides how the jump targets or RRI on the data provider should open when called in the web application. You can also assign commands to the web template that are executed before the first display or before the rendering of the web application ❹. As you can see, you can define the properties of the web application by specifying the parameter values for the web template.

SAP BusinessObjects Design Studio

For organizations using SAP BusinessObjects BI 4.0 or higher for reporting with SAP BW as a backend, SAP BusinessObjects Analysis is offered as a premium alternative to BEx tools. To create custom OLAP and planning web applications, SAP BusinessObjects Design Studio is a premium option to BEx Web Application Designer. An overview of SAP BusinessObjects reporting tools, including SAP BusinessObjects Design Studio, is provided in Chapter 13.

11.6 Summary

In this chapter, we explored how a web application can be created using BEx Web Application Designer, including the functions and use of the different web items that are available for web templates. Another important feature available in BEx Web Application Designer is the Command Wizard, which enlists numerous commands to be readily used in the web application. These commands can be linked to different web items to provide actions in the web application. The variety of web items and rich collection of ready-to-use commands in the Command Wizard makes the development of a web application an easy and intuitive task in BEx Web Application Designer.

In this chapter, we discuss the process of building a planning application with the help of a typical sales planning scenario.

12 Creating Planning Applications

Today's competitive global market makes most companies attempt to focus on their core business areas and synergize with trading partners in all possible forms of collaboration, information, and business process sharing. When doing this, it's important to create a business plan that is truly integrated; without integration, pitfalls often arise.

Planning can be done at different levels within an organization. If planning is done at a very high level, and the objective is to define business strategy and to define an organization's future direction, it's called *strategic planning*. A strategic plan often aims at a long-range time frame (e.g., 5 to 10 years). The planning for shorter time duration, say 1 or 2 years, is called *operational planning*. An operational plan can be by weeks, months, or quarters and is derived from the strategic plan. Planning at the operational level is specific to functional areas such as sales planning, financial planning, and so on. A plan addressing further details and focusing on the immediate future can be derived from the operational plan. This planning addresses execution-level details and is often the lowest level of planning in an organization.

Different organizations follow different approaches for planning. In some organizations, plan values for entire organizations are determined at the top-most level, and these high-level targets are then used to create targets for the lower levels of the organization. This approach is called *top-down planning*. A budget planning process typically follows the top-down approach. In another approach, the planning cycle begins at the lowest level of an organization, and then these goals at lower levels are aggregated as a basis of planning for the higher levels. This is called *bottom-up planning*. Finally, some organizations proceed with a hybrid approach for planning, which combines both top-down and bottom-up planning.

In this chapter, we discuss the process of building planning applications in SAP BW. By the end of the chapter, you'll be able to start the design and development on your own. However, note that there's no specific rule or a ready planning data model available for this process; instead, the system provides you with the building blocks needed for a planning application that can be flexibly used to build applications addressing a variety of scenarios.

To begin, we first give you an overview of the SAP BW Integrated Planning component and planning in general, including an example sales planning scenario for ABCD Corp. We'll then introduce you to the elements of a planning application and explain how to use these elements to actually build planning applications. Finally, we conclude with a discussion of some special planning functionality in SAP BW: planning locks and the behavior of real-time InfoCubes.

12.1 Introduction to the Integrated Planning Component and Planning Applications

One of the keys to building planning applications in SAP BW is the Integrated Planning component, which was introduced with the release of the SAP NetWeaver 2004s version of SAP BW. With Integrated Planning (BW-IP), you can build flexible planning applications that are integrated with typical SAP BW interfaces, ensuring homogeneity between reporting/analysis and planning. The key advantages of Integrated Planning are listed here:

▶ The Integrated Planning component is integrated with SAP BW's analytical features. This means you can use analysis features such as filters, slice-and-dice reporting, exception reporting, and so on while working on planning data.

▶ To build a planning application using Integrated Planning, you use the same design and development tools that are used to build analytical applications, such as BEX Query Designer, BEx Web Application Designer, and BEx Analyzer.

▶ OLAP variables are shared with SAP BW and thus are available in Integrated Planning. This once again ensures consistency of information between planning and reporting within SAP BW.

Figure 12.1 illustrates how the Integrated Planning component relates to the other areas of SAP BW. Both the reporting and planning applications use the same

OLAP engine for data processing, and they share InfoProviders, data models, transaction data, master data, OLAP variables, OLAP documents, and OLAP metadata. Also, Integrated Planning uses BEx Query Designer, BEx Web Application Designer, and BEx Analyzer for designing the planning user interface.

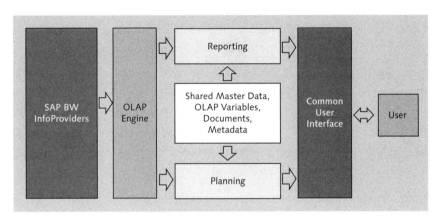

Figure 12.1 Integrated Planning as a Part of SAP BW

For a planning process to be more effective, it has to be integrated with business functions as a closed-loop process. This means that the plan has to be taken to the execution level, and then the outcome of the actions has to be measured against the plan values to evaluate the effectiveness of the plan. This enables a continuous improvement in the plan, leading to better execution. Figure 12.2 shows how SAP BW fits into this overall closed-loop planning scenario.

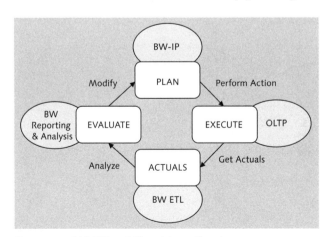

Figure 12.2 SAP BW and Closed-Loop Planning

When put into action, the planning done in Integrated Planning (BW-IP) forms the base for the execution that generates actual values. The execution happens in the transaction system (OLTP), and data is then extracted to SAP BW using its ETL process. The plan values and actual values, now both available in SAP BW, provide a platform for analyzing plan and actual data together, and SAP BW's reporting and analysis tools can then measure the plan performance. Such an analysis further leads to optimizing the plan, making it a closed-loop process.

To illustrate the different planning features of SAP BW, we've used a simple sales planning scenario within ABCD Corp. In this company, sales planning occurs on an annual cycle for all the three sales organizations: 1000 (APAC), 2000 (Europe), and 3000 (North America). Each sales organization plans for the sales figures of three different divisions or product ranges: consumer electronics (CE), daily appliances (DA), and consumer lifestyle appliances (CL).

This is a high-level plan for the organization, and the high-level values for each of the product ranges are transferred to different products belonging to them; each sales organization has a product range manager who is responsible for planning the sales of each product under his assigned product range. The plan for a year (January to December) is done by quarter, so there are four planning periods: quarter 1 (Q1), quarter 2 (Q2), quarter 3 (Q3), and quarter 4 (Q4). Figure 12.3 is a graphical representation of this scenario.

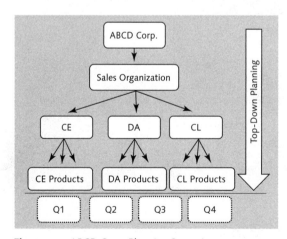

Figure 12.3 ABCD Corp. Planning Scenario

12.2 Elements of a Planning Application

A number of different components serve as the building blocks of any planning application. The relationship among these components is depicted in Figure 12.4.

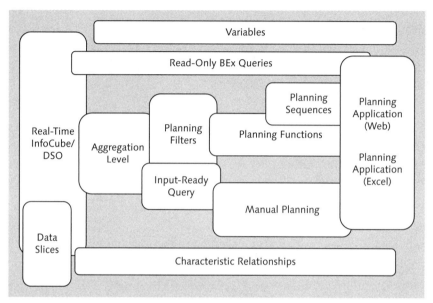

Figure 12.4 Planning Components and Their Dependencies

In the following list, we provide you with an overview of the different planning components and their relationships with each other:

▶ **Real-time InfoCube**
A *real-time InfoCube* has the ability to write data. As shown in Figure 12.4, a real-time InfoCube is the basis for any planning application in SAP BW. The data entered by different planners is saved into a real-time InfoCube, and data stored there is also available for reporting. To begin creating a real-time Info-Cube, see Section 12.2.1.

▶ **Planning-Enabled DSO**
As of SAP BW 7.30 SPS8, DataStore Objects (DSOs) of the direct update type can also be used for planning. These DSOs only have the active table, and, as illustrated in Chapter 4, Section 4.6, the Planning Mode has to be turned on to enable the direct-update DSO for planning. This option of using DSOs for

planning is particularly useful when certain planning functions are to be performed on the data at the record level instead of the aggregated data.

▶ **Characteristic relationships**
Characteristic relationships provide a means of maintaining data consistency in a planning application. Using characteristic relationships, you can build the logic to check, propose, or derive valid combinations of various characteristics values used in planning scenarios. As shown in Figure 12.4, characteristic relationships are defined at the InfoCube level. We will begin defining these characteristic relationships in Section 12.2.2.

▶ **Data slices**
Data slices are used to lock a specific set of plan data based on the characteristic selections defined at the InfoCube level, and they can be used to protect a set of data stored in a real-time InfoCube from changes. The data selected under data slices can't be changed during planning. Data slices are defined on the real-time InfoCube. Section 12.2.3 discusses data slices at greater length.

▶ **Aggregation levels**
Aggregation levels are InfoProviders specific to planning and are built on real-time InfoCubes (also on MultiProviders involving real-time InfoCubes). An aggregation level consists of a set of characteristics and key figures selected from the underlying InfoProvider, which are to be used for planning. As shown in Figure 12.4, the aggregation level forms the basis for all subsequent planning development. One real-time InfoCube can have multiple aggregation levels. To begin defining aggregation levels, see Section 12.2.4.

▶ **Planning filters**
Planning filters are defined on an aggregation level (see Figure 12.4). Using a planning filter, you can restrict the data contained in an aggregation level by maintaining selections for different characteristic values from the aggregation level. An aggregation level can have multiple planning filters, whereas a planning filter can relate to one and only one aggregation level. The creation of planning filters is discussed in Section 12.2.5.

▶ **Planning functions**
Planning functions are used to automatically create, change, and delete plan data based on the logic defined in the function. Some predefined (standard) functions are available in Integrated Planning, but you can define your own custom planning function if needed. A planning function is built on an aggregation

level but is always executed on a planning filter, so a planning function can be used by multiple planning filters based on the same aggregation level. The creation of planning functions is discussed in Section 12.2.6.

▶ **Planning variables**
Integrated Planning uses the same OLAP variables in building a planning application as are used in creating the queries. The variables are available for use in almost all of the planning components. Because the variables are dependent on the InfoObjects, after they are defined, they are available throughout for all planning components (Figure 12.4). OLAP variables are discussed in detail in Chapter 9.

▶ **Planning sequences**
Planning sequences are used to define an execution sequence for multiple planning functions. As shown in Figure 12.4, planning sequences are based on planning functions.

▶ **Manual planning**
Manual planning is a process where you manually create, change, and delete the plan data in a planning application. The process to build applications with manual planning using BEx Web Application Designer or BEx Analyzer are discussed in later sections of this chapter. As shown in Figure 12.4, manual planning applications are based on input-ready queries (defined next).

▶ **Input-ready query**
Input-ready queries form the basis for manual planning. These are queries where you can manually enter data, which then gets written to the real-time InfoCube or a planning-enabled DSO. Input-ready queries are built using BEx Query Designer. Input-ready queries are discussed further in Section 12.2.8.

All of these components come together to form *planning applications*, built by putting different planning components together so that users can perform manual planning as well as execute different planning functions. This can involve input-ready queries as well as read-only BEx queries (refer to Figure 12.4). Different planning functions and planning sequences can also be included in a planning application. An Excel-based planning application is built using BEx Analyzer, and a web-based planning application is built using BEx Web Application Designer.

You can create and maintain planning elements through Transaction RSPLAN, or you can create them directly from the DATA WAREHOUSING WORKBENCH screen (Transaction RSA1) (see Figure 12.5).

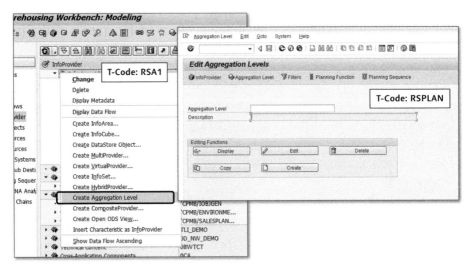

Figure 12.5 Maintaining Planning Components Using Transactions RSA1 and RSPLAN

In the following sections, we explain how these planning elements are created and discuss their use in detail.

12.2.1 Creating a Real-Time InfoCube

A real-time InfoCube forms the basis for planning applications in SAP BW. The procedure to create a real-time InfoCube is the same as that of a standard Info-Cube, as discussed in Chapter 5. The only difference is that while specifying the cube setting, you have to select the REAL TIME checkbox (Figure 12.6).

You can decide on the characteristics and key figures to be included in the real-time InfoCube based on the planning requirements. The primary factors that influence this decision are listed here:

▸ The entities that are needed to plan the data

▸ The entities that are needed for further analysis of the plan data

In the example scenario explained in the chapter introduction, these are the entities that ABCD Corp. uses to plan data:

▸ Sales organization

▸ Product range

▸ Product

▶ Calendar quarter

▶ Net value

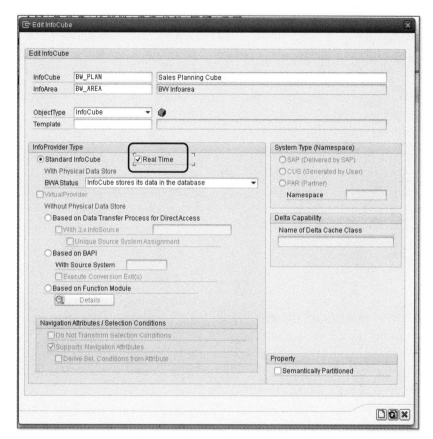

Figure 12.6 Creating a Real-Time InfoCube

Further, let's assume that ABCD Corp. needs the plan data to be analyzed by calendar year and also by the current and historical values of product group and product range. To address this requirement, the real-time InfoCube should include the following:

▶ Calendar year

▶ Product group as a characteristic for historical values

▶ Product group as a navigation attribute of product for current values

▶ Product range as a navigation attribute of product for current values

Having decided on the objects to be included in the InfoCube, you can now create the real-time InfoCube BW_PLAN, as shown in Figure 12.7.

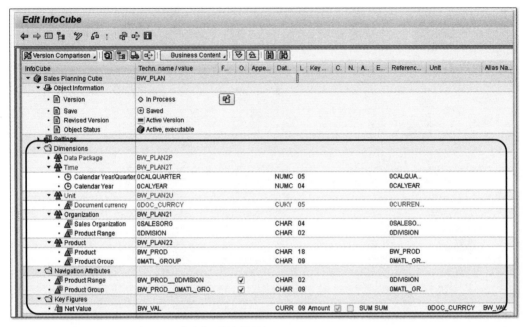

Figure 12.7 Real-Time InfoCube BW_PLAN

A standard InfoCube is optimized for reading data in a way that considers reporting performance. A real-time InfoCube, on the other hand, is optimized for writing data into it. The data generated or modified in a planning application is written to the cube using an API. In a practical planning scenario, more than one user can work simultaneously in the same planning application, meaning that multiple users can attempt to write data in the same real-time InfoCube. The API for real-time InfoCubes allows parallel writes to support multiple users simultaneously.

A real-time InfoCube can't be used for data loads using standard SAP BW data flow; however, the real-time behavior of a real-time InfoCube can be changed to enable data loads to it. In other words, a real-time InfoCube can switch between the real-time mode and data load mode.

In the DATA WAREHOUSING WORKBENCH screen (Transaction RSA1), select PLANNING-SPECIFIC PROPERTIES • CHANGE REAL-TIME LOAD BEHAVIOR in the context menu of the real-time Sales Planning Cube InfoCube (❶ of Figure 12.8) to open a box in which you can set the real-time load behavior of the InfoCube ❷.

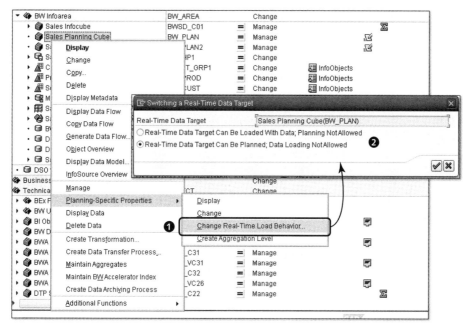

Figure 12.8 Changing Real-Time Load Behavior

If you select the REAL-TIME DATA TARGET CAN BE LOADED WITH DATA; PLANNING NOT ALLOWED radio button, the real-time InfoCube is switched to the read-only mode, and you can load the data to this InfoCube using regular SAP BW data load options. If you select the REAL-TIME DATA TARGET CAN BE PLANNED; DATA LOADING NOT ALLOWED radio button, the InfoCube is switched back to the write mode where planning can be performed. Data can't be loaded to the InfoCube in this mode using the data flow.

InfoProviders Used in Planning

Planning can be performed only on a real-time InfoCube or a planning-enabled DSO, but standard InfoCubes and data targets can be used in a planning application for reading data.

After you have the real-time InfoCube ready, you can start building the planning components on this InfoCube.

> **Note**
>
> After we give you a little more background about the different components of a planning application as well as the specifics of building planning applications, we'll briefly come back to the real-time InfoCube in Section 12.5.

12.2.2 Defining Characteristic Relationships

Characteristic relationships are used to build logic that checks, proposes, and derives valid combinations of characteristic values in a planning application. This is one of the most important features to consider when building a planning model. Before we show you how to create characteristic relationships, let's first explain their usage in a practical scenario.

Consider a planning scenario where you first select a region and then enter the plan values for the countries under that region. As shown in Figure 12.9, when you select a region, you can technically create a record for any country under that region. For example, as a planner for region NA, you could create a record for Germany—even though this is an invalid combination. On the other hand, the combination of region NA and country Canada *is* valid. If the characteristic relationship for this scenario is defined, every time you enter a value for a country, the system validates and accepts it, or displays an error based on the validation result (Figure 12.9).

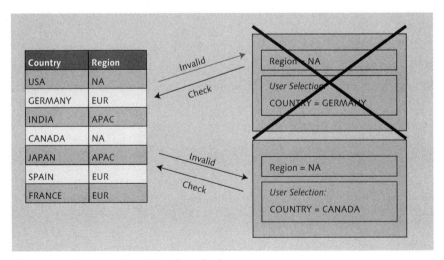

Figure 12.9 Characteristic Relationship: Check

The other use of characteristic relationships is to generate valid proposals based on business logic for planning applications. To explain this, let's take a look at the example shown in Figure 12.10, where the product range master data and the product master data both have three different values. You decide to provide the planning users with all possible combinations of product ranges and products to enter the plan values.

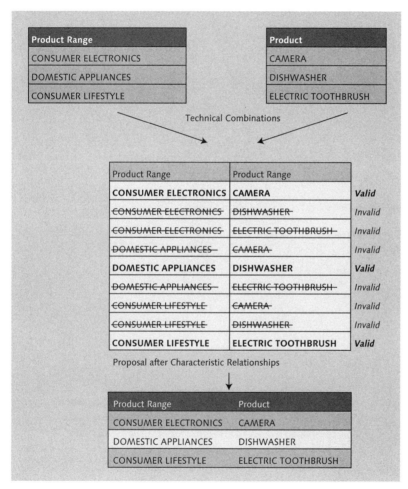

Figure 12.10 Characteristic Relationship: Propose

If you look at the technical combinations, nine different possible values can be generated for the given data, but not all make functional sense. For example, the combination of Product = Camera and Product Range = Domestic Appliances is an invalid combination from a functional point of view. In this case, the logic defined in the characteristic relationship for product master data allows the system to propose only the valid combinations for data entry.

Finally, you can also use the characteristic relationships to derive values of a characteristic based on values of another characteristic. For example, if the requirement is to maintain the plan values for products and their corresponding product group, you can avoid entering both the products and the product groups during planning (Figure 12.11).

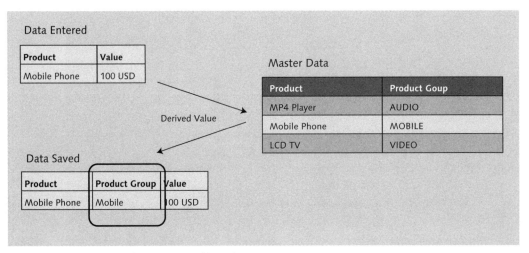

Figure 12.11 Characteristic Relationship: Derive

Using characteristic relationships, you can derive the value of a product group from product master data—if you know the product—so the data saved in the cube contains the derived value as well.

You can create characteristic relationships in the INFOPROVIDER section in Transaction RSPLAN (❶ of Figure 12.12).

Enter the InfoProvider on which the characteristic relationship has to be defined. In this case, we entered "Sales Planning Cube" in the DESCRIPTION field and "BW_PLAN" in the INFOPROVIDER field, which is the InfoProvider we created earlier (❷ of Figure 12.12). Then click on EDIT ❸ to move to the next screen, which shows the definition of the selected InfoProvider on the INFOPROVIDER tab (❶ of Figure 12.13).

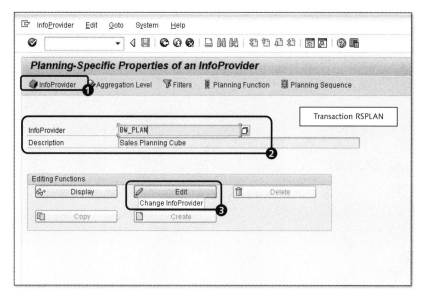

Figure 12.12 Selecting InfoProvider to Define the Characteristic Relationship

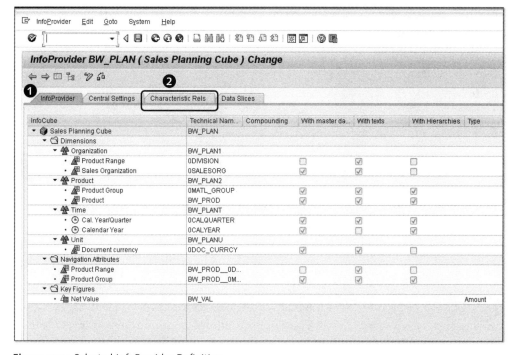

Figure 12.13 Selected InfoProvider Definition

The other three tabs that are displayed are CENTRAL SETTINGS, CHARACTERISTIC RELS, and DATA SLICES. To create a characteristic relationship, first click on the CHARACTERISTIC RELS tab (❷ of Figure 12.13). Then, click on the CREATE icon (❶ of Figure 12.14). This creates a new row for the characteristic relationship in the upper section of the screen ❷.

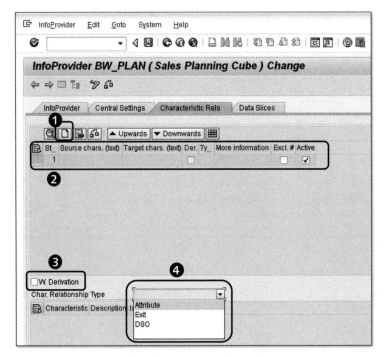

Figure 12.14 Creating a New Characteristic Relationship

The W DERIVATION checkbox ❸ allows you to define whether the characteristic relationship is used to derive values. This checkbox is left unchecked if the characteristic relationship is used only for check and proposal needs. In this case, we create a characteristic relationship to check the valid combinations of product (defined using the material InfoObject BW_PROD) and product range (defined using the division InfoObject 0DIVISION). Leave the W DERIVATION checkbox unchecked.

The next step is to select the base for the characteristic relationship ❹. The dropdown list provides four different options on which you can build the characteristic relationship:

▶ ATTRIBUTE
The validity of the data is based on the data existing in the selected master data. The characteristic and attribute values that are present in the master data are treated as valid for characteristic relationships.

▶ DSO
In this case, the base for the characteristic relationship is the data loaded in a DSO. All of the records that exist in the DSO are treated as valid for characteristic relationships.

▶ HIERARCHY
The validity of the characteristic values is based on the definition of the hierarchy structure. Only those characteristic hierarchies that contain external characteristics other than the main characteristic can be used as the base for the characteristic relationship.

▶ EXIT
If none of the preceding types can be used to meet the requirements, you can use characteristic relationships based on your own custom logic built using ABAP code. To build this, you have to implement the IF_RSPLS_CR_EXIT interface, or you can use the sample CL_RSPLS_CR_EXIT_BASE class as the template to create one.

In this example, we select ATTRIBUTE as the base for the characteristic relationship (❶ of Figure 12.15).

Select the master data characteristic to be the basis for the characteristic relationship ❷. The bottom side of the screen displays all of the attributes of the selected master data. Select the characteristic attributes that need to be validated under this characteristic relationship ❸. Note that the base master data characteristic BW_PROD is selected by default.

In this example, we want to check and propose the valid combinations of product (defined using the material InfoObject BW_PROD) and product range (defined using the division InfoObject 0DIVISION). Select the DIVISION checkbox under the IS USED column, as shown in ❸ of Figure 12.15. Save this definition of the characteristic relationship by clicking on the SAVE icon ❹.

This characteristic relationship allows and proposes only those combinations that exist in the master data BW_PROD. You can further set this characteristic relationship as inactive by deselecting the ACTIVE checkbox ❺. Also, you can decide if the characteristic relationship has to exclude the blank values (i.e., records with value = "#") by checking the Excl. # checkbox ❻.

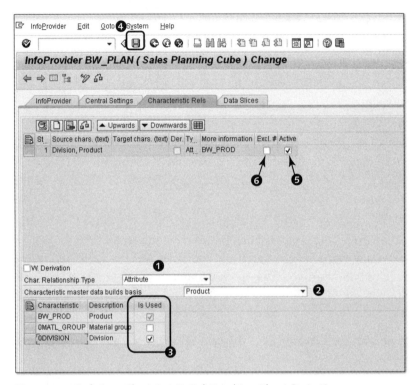

Figure 12.15 Defining a Characteristic Relationship without Derivation

The *derive* type of characteristic relationships can also be defined in a similar way. For our example scenario, the requirement is to allow users to enter the plan values for products (represented with the material InfoObject), and then derive the corresponding values of product groups (represented with the material group InfoObject) while saving the data into the real-time InfoCube. The procedure to create this specific characteristic relationship is explained next and illustrated in Figure 12.16.

Create a new characteristic relationship by clicking on the CREATE icon (❶ of Figure 12.16). We want to derive the product group from product values, so select the W DERIVATION checkbox ❷ for this characteristic relationship. Select ATTRIBUTE ❸ as the type of characteristic relationship. Select the characteristic that is used to derive the values for other characteristics ❹. This characteristic is marked as a source characteristic. Select the characteristics that are to be derived from the source characteristic. These characteristics are called *derived characteristics*. For our example, select MATERIAL GROUP ❺ as the derived characteristic.

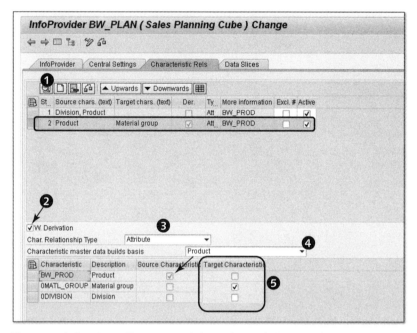

Figure 12.16 Creating a Characteristic Relationship with Derivation

Characteristic Relationships for Time Characteristics

The characteristic relationships for time characteristics are already built in Integrated Planning, so they don't need to be explicitly defined.

12.2.3 Defining Data Slices

Data slices are used to protect a specific set of data from changes in the real-time InfoCube. In a data slice, you can define restrictions on characteristics of the real-time InfoCube, and the data contained in those restrictions is then locked from any changes that could happen, either due to planning functions or due to manual planning.

To explain the use of data slices, let's take an example planning scenario in which you have both actual and plan data stored in the same cube, and you don't want users to change the actual data. This can be achieved by creating a data slice where the planning version characteristic is restricted to actuals to protect actual data from changes (❶ of Figure 12.17).

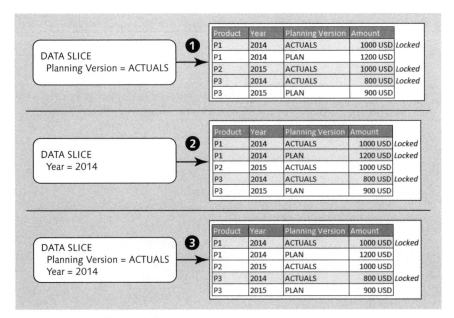

Figure 12.17 Data Slices

This also illustrates how restrictions defined in a data slice change the data locked for planning (❷ and ❸ of Figure 12.17). The condition formed for the locks is based on the AND logical condition between the values defined. For example, in ❸, all those records are locked where Planning Version = ACTUALS and Year = 2014.

Data slices are defined under the INFOPROVIDER section of Transaction RSPLAN. Click on the DATA SLICES tab page of the selected InfoProvider, as shown in ❶ of Figure 12.18.

Click on the CREATE icon to create a new data slice ❷. Maintain the description of the data slice ❸ as well.

In the TYPE dropdown list, select SELECTION ❹. This option allows you to maintain selections for different characteristic values that can be locked. If you want to define a custom and complicated logic for locking the plan data, you can define the data slice based on ABAP exits.

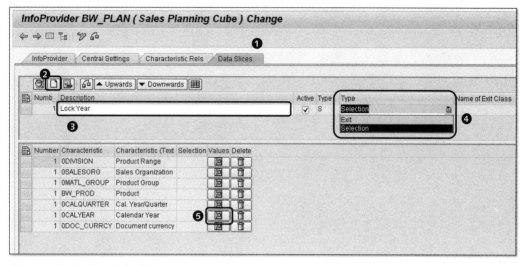

Figure 12.18 Creating Data Slices

In the lower part of the screen, you can see a list of all characteristics included in the cube. Here is where you specify the selections that need to be locked. For example, if you want to protect the data for Calendar Year = 2014, lock this selection. To do this, click on the INPUT HELP icon for the CALENDAR YEAR characteristic ❺. This opens the INPUT HELP pop-up window as shown in Figure 12.19.

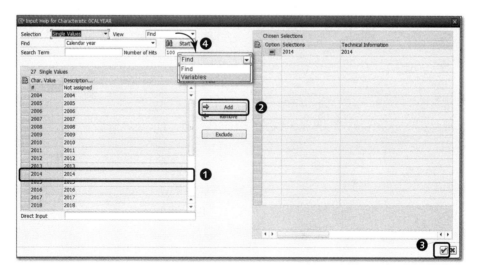

Figure 12.19 Defining Selections for a Data Slice

From the INPUT HELP screen, select the value 2014 (❶ of Figure 12.19), and click on ADD ❷ to include it in the chosen selections. Click on OK ❸.

After you've defined all of the necessary selections for the data slice, click on SAVE on the INFOPROVIDER tab (❶ of Figure 12.20).

If you're using the ACTIVE checkbox shown in ❷ of Figure 12.20, you can create multiple data slices on an InfoProvider and then toggle between the active and inactive modes.

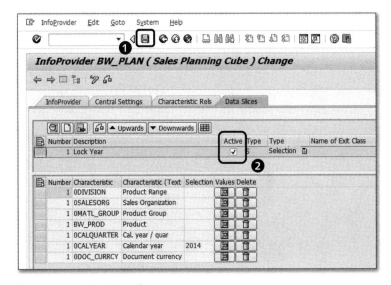

Figure 12.20 Saving Data Slices

12.2.4   Defining Aggregation Levels

Aggregation levels, indicated by the AGGREGATION LEVELS icon 🗇, are InfoProviders specific to planning and are built as a subset of an underlying InfoProvider. In a simple scenario, an aggregation level can be built directly on a real-time Info-Cube. In more complex situations, it's also possible to build an aggregation level on a MultiProvider. The prerequisite of the complex aggregation level is that the MultiProvider is based on at least one real-time InfoCube (see Figure 12.21).

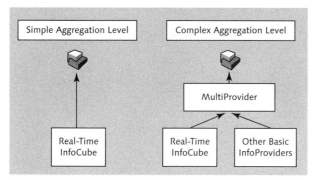

Figure 12.21 Types of Aggregation Levels

An aggregation level can be defined directly on top of the InfoProvider in Transaction RSA1 or can be defined from Transaction RSPLAN (refer to Figure 12.5) by selecting specific characteristics and key figures from the underlying InfoProvider that are to be used for planning. The selected key figure values are aggregated for characteristics selected in an aggregation level, thus ignoring the characteristics that aren't part of the aggregation level.

If some data is changed or edited for an aggregation level, the record is stored in the InfoCube as # (i.e., not assigned) for all characteristics that aren't included in the aggregation level. We explain this concept with the help of Figure 12.22.

The InfoCube stores the data for the following characteristics: PRODUCT RANGE, PRODUCT, and QUARTER (❶ of Figure 12.22). The aggregation level is defined at the product range and quarter level, so the data is aggregated for the characteristics that are included in the aggregation level ❷. Now, if the data is changed at this level, the changes to the data are saved in the cube ❸. The values for the product characteristic are not assigned (#).

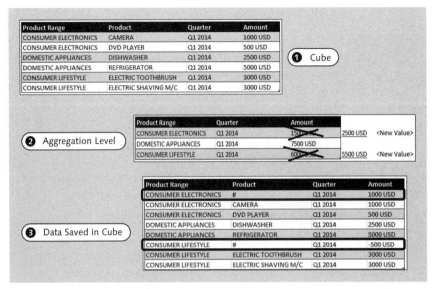

Figure 12.22 Not Assigned (#) Values

Let's explain how to create an aggregation level on a real-time InfoCube. For the example scenario explained earlier in this chapter, the planning is done at two different levels—the product range level and the product level—so we must create these two aggregation levels. Go to the AGGREGATION LEVEL section in Transaction RSPLAN (❶ of Figure 12.23), and click on CREATE ❷ to create a new aggregation level. The CREATE AGGREGATION LEVEL pop-up screen appears.

Enter the technical name in the AGGREGATION LEVEL field, enter the description of the aggregation level, and select the InfoProvider over which you want to build the aggregation level ❸. Click on OK ❹.

A list of all of the characteristics and key figures from the selected InfoProvider is displayed on the left side of the screen (❶ of Figure 12.24). You can define the aggregation level by dragging the specific characteristics and key figures from the left side to the right side of the screen ❷.

Note that the Product InfoObject isn't selected in the aggregation level because the planning is done at the product range level.

After you've defined the aggregation level, save it. You also have to activate the level to be able to use it for further planning development. Use the SAVE and ACTIVATE icons ❸ to save and activate the aggregation level.

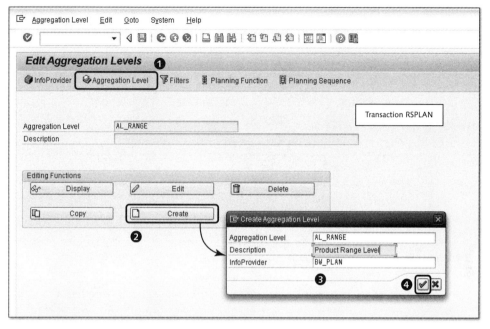

Figure 12.23 Create a New Aggregation Level

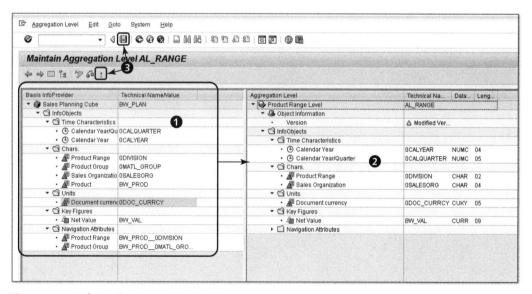

Figure 12.24 Defining the Aggregation Level

This aggregation level is now also visible in the DATA WAREHOUSING WORKBENCH screen (Transaction RSA1), linked to the InfoProvider on which it's created (see Figure 12.25).

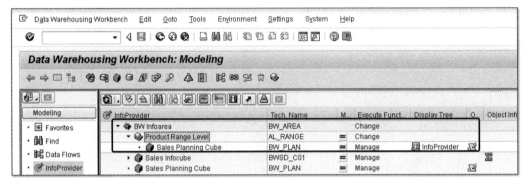

Figure 12.25 Aggregation Levels in Transaction RSA1

A similar procedure can be followed to build different aggregation levels. For example, you can create a new aggregation level with the technical name "AL_PROD" and the description "Product Level" on InfoCube BW_PLAN, as shown in Figure 12.26.

Figure 12.26 Creating an Aggregation Level for Product Level Planning

This level can be used to build the planning functions and layout, which will enable planning at the product level.

12.2.5 Creating Planning Filters

Planning filters are the subset of data contained in an aggregation level and are defined by putting specific selections on characteristics from the aggregation level. These filters can be used in input-ready queries either to restrict data or to execute a planning function. An aggregation level can have multiple planning filters, whereas a planning filter can relate to one and only one aggregation level.

When you execute a planning function on a planning filter, it's executed for only the data that is selected in the planning filter. For example, if you enter Year = 2014 in the filter and execute the delete planning function, only those records with the year listed as 2014 are deleted.

To create planning filters, go to the FILTER section in Transaction RSPLAN (❶ of Figure 12.27), and click on CREATE ❷. This gives you a pop-up screen where you define the filter.

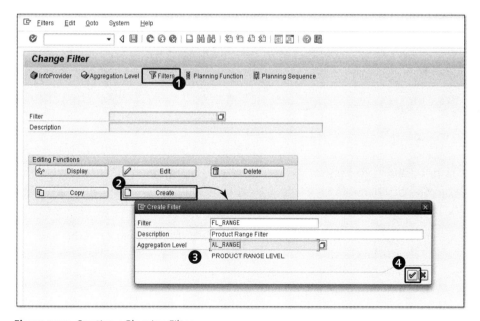

Figure 12.27 Creating a Planning Filter

Enter the technical name in the FILTER field, enter the description of the filter, and select the aggregation level over which you want to build the filter ❸. Click on OK ❹.

The next screen for filter definition is displayed as shown in Figure 12.28. You can maintain the filter here. If you want to apply a selection that includes time-dependent master data, then you can also define a key date that will be used to derive time-dependent values for the filter. The key date can be specified as a fixed date or can be derived using a variable ❶.

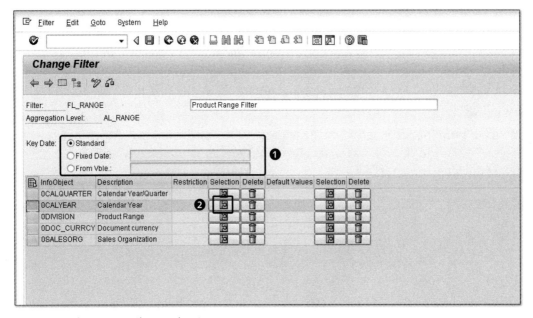

Figure 12.28 Change Filter Screen

The next step is to restrict the characteristics in the filter. Call INPUT HELP to define the characteristic restrictions by clicking on the button shown in ❷ of Figure 12.28. This opens the INPUT HELP pop-up window (Figure 12.29).

You can restrict the characteristic either with some fixed values or with characteristic variables. The OLAP characteristic variables built on the selected characteristic are available for restriction. In this example, we restrict the calendar year characteristic (0CALYEAR) with a variable.

Select VARIABLES from the VIEW dropdown list (❶ of Figure 12.29), and the list of variables built on the characteristic is displayed. Select the variable with which you want to restrict the characteristic ❷. Click on ADD ❸ to add the selected variable to the selections. You can also choose to exclude the selected values from the filter using the EXCLUDE button ❹. Finally, click on OK ❺ to get back to the main filter definition screen.

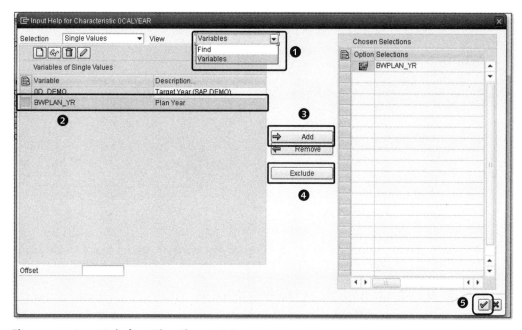

Figure 12.29 Input Help for a Filter Characteristic

In this case (Figure 12.29), the characteristic 0CALYEAR is restricted with a user entry variable, BWPLAN_YR, which has a single mandatory entry. The use of variables in filters increases the flexibility of the planning application because the filters—and the data for the planning—are determined at runtime.

Restrict the remaining characteristics of the FL_RANGE filter, as shown in Figure 12.30.

Note that the value for 0CALQUARTER is set to EXCL # (which means the value # is excluded from the filter) (❶ of Figure 12.30). The sales organization characteristic (0SALESORG) is also restricted with a user entry variable, BW_SORG, which has a single mandatory entry ❷.

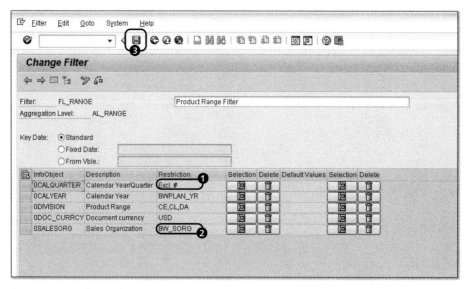

Figure 12.30 Defining Filter Restrictions

After you've maintained all of the necessary restrictions to the filter, save it using the SAVE icon ❸.

You can now build another planning filter, FL_PROD (Product Filter), on the product level aggregation level. The restriction is shown in Figure 12.31.

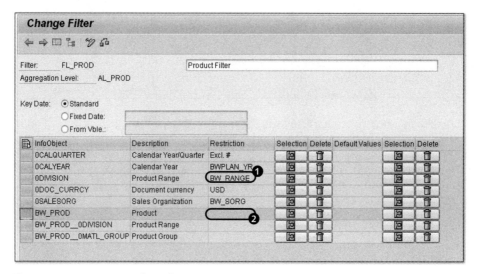

Figure 12.31 Creating a Product Filter

Here the product range (0DIVISION) characteristic is restricted with the BW_
RANGE user entry variable (❶ of Figure 12.31), which has a single mandatory
entry. Also, note that there is no restriction defined for the product (BW_PROD)
characteristic ❷. This means that all of the values of the product characteristic are
available for planning. During planning, we'll be using characteristic relationships for the validation and proposal of product values.

Creating Planning Filters from BEx Query Designer

Planning filters are the same as the filters built on queries using BEx Query Designer,
and they can also be created using this tool. If you're using BEx Query Designer to create planning filters, the aggregation level must be selected as the InfoProvider.

12.2.6 Creating Planning Functions

To facilitate automatic create/change/delete functions on plan data, Integrated
Planning delivers some standard functions for use in the planning model. It also
provides you the option to create or define your own custom planning function
using ABAP, if needed. A planning function is built on an aggregation level but is
always executed with a filter, so a planning function can be used by multiple planning filters based on the same aggregation level (see Figure 12.32).

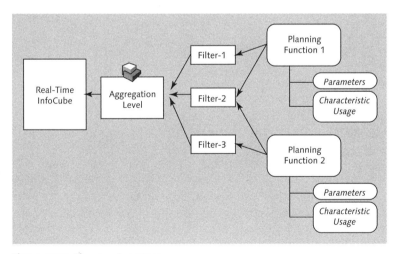

Figure 12.32 Planning Functions

A planning function can edit only data that belongs to a real-time InfoCube and
that is included in the filter over which the function is executed, often known as

data to be changed. However, a planning function can also read data from other types of InfoProviders or data that is out of the filter selection, just for reference. This is often known as *reference data.*

Before we explain each of the available standard functions, let's learn how to create a planning function based on an available standard function type. To create a planning function, go to the PLANNING FUNCTION section in Transaction RSPLAN (❶ of Figure 12.33), and then click on CREATE ❷. The CREATE PLANNING FUNCTION pop-up screen appears.

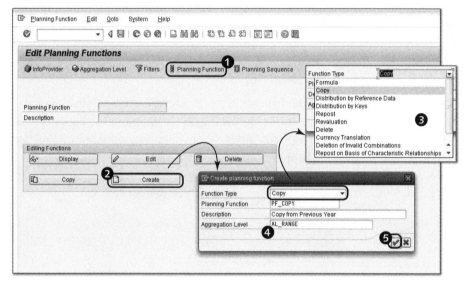

Figure 12.33 Creating a Planning Function

In the pop-up screen, select one of the available planning function types from the dropdown list (❸ of Figure 12.33). (We'll discuss each of these standard planning function types in subsequent sections.)

Enter the technical name in the PLANNING FUNCTION field, enter the description for the planning function, and select an aggregation level ❹ over which the planning function has to be created. After you define all of these settings, click on OK ❺ to create the planning function.

A planning function is created in two steps:

▸ Define characteristic usage.
▸ Define parameter values.

In the first step for defining characteristic usage, you can select different characteristics from the aggregation level that will be used in the planning function. A characteristic can be classified as a field to be changed or as a field to be used in conditions. The characteristics that aren't selected to be changed remain constant and aren't used and affected by the execution of the planning function.

To determine the fields to be changed, you have to first determine the characteristics for which the values are to be created/updated/deleted in a planning function. Let's look at the example shown in Figure 12.34.

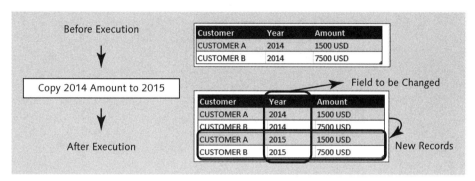

Figure 12.34 Field to Be Changed

Assume you want to copy the amount key figure from the year 2014 to 2015 for all customers. In this case, if you compare the records before and after the execution of the planning function, the value of the Year characteristic changes from 2014 to 2015. So, for the COPY function in this example, the year is selected as a field to be changed.

Using characteristics as fields for conditions, you can define distinct processing for different characteristic values of the field selected. For the example shown in Figure 12.35, you want to copy the year 2014 key figure values to the year 2015 values with a *revaluation*. However, you also want to define different processing logic for Customer A and Customer B. So, in this case (Figure 12.35), the CUSTOMER characteristic is the field for condition, and the YEAR characteristic is the field to be changed.

After the characteristics to be used in a planning function are identified, you can define the specific conditions and rules under parameters. You can define multiple parameters for different values of characteristics selected as fields for conditions. However, if no characteristic is selected for conditions, only one parameter is sufficient. In this case, the entire data in the selection is processed with the same parameters.

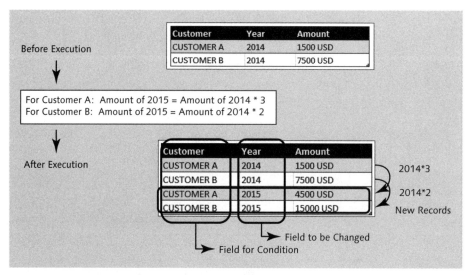

Figure 12.35 Field for Conditions

In the following sections, we explain the different types of standard planning functions available and their use in a planning model.

Copy

The COPY function is used to copy key figure values from one characteristic combination to other combination. In this function, you can define FROM values as the source for copying and TO values as the target.

FROM values are treated as reference data and are accessed only for reads by the COPY function, so it isn't necessary to include the FROM values in the filter over which the planning function is executed. On the other hand, upon execution of the copy planning function, the data in the TO values changes, so it's necessary to include the TO values of the data in the filter over which the function has to be executed.

Let's build a Copy function for our example scenario, assuming you want to copy the values from the previous year to the current year (Figure 12.36). The current year is entered by the user, and the previous year is derived from the current year.

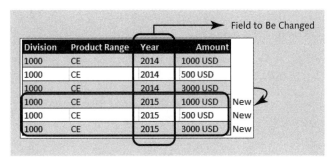

Figure 12.36 Copy Function Example

As shown in Figure 12.36, the field to be changed is YEAR. By specifying fields in conditions, you can also define parameters for different values of characteristics chosen for a condition.

Create a copy planning function by following the procedure explained in the beginning of Section 12.2.6. Enter the technical name "PF_COPY" and description "Copy from Previous Year" on the AGGREGATION LEVEL for product range planning (AL_RANGE). After you click on OK, you can define the characteristic usage for this planning function on the next screen (see Figure 12.37).

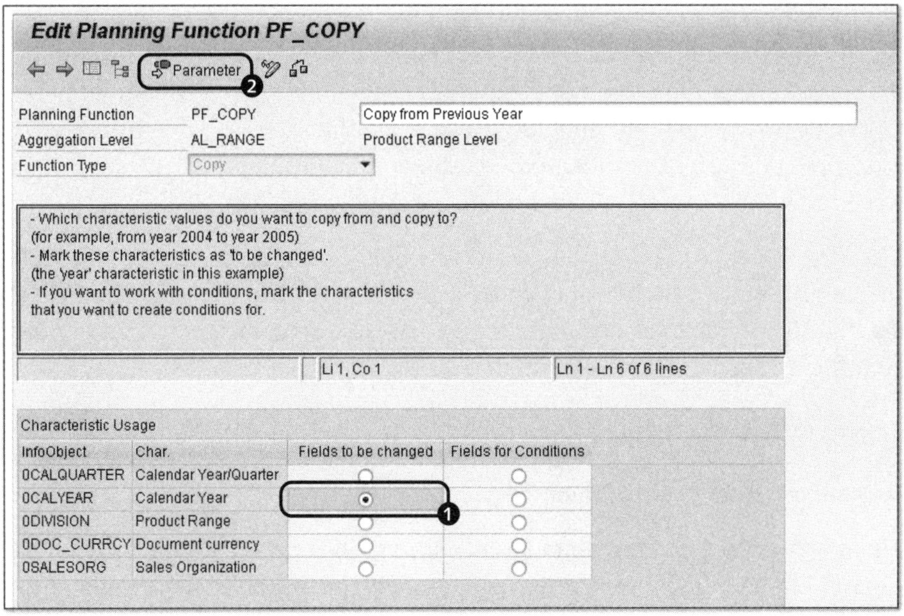

Figure 12.37 Characteristic Usage for the Copy Function

Select CALENDAR YEAR as the field to be changed, as shown in ❶ of Figure 12.37. Then click on PARAMETER ❷.

On the parameter screen, first select the key figures that need to be copied. For our example, select NET VALUE (BW_VAL), as shown in ❶ of Figure 12.38.

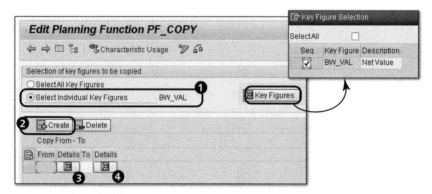

Figure 12.38 Defining Parameters for the Copy Function

To define the copy logic, you must specify the FROM and TO values for the COPY function. Click on CREATE ❷ to create the first row where you can specify FROM and TO values. Click on DETAILS ❸ to specify the FROM values for copying.

As mentioned earlier in this section, you must copy the values from the previous year based on the variable value entered by the user. The variable used here is BWPLAN_YR (refer to Section 12.2.5). We use the same variable to derive the FROM values for the COPY function. As shown in ❶ of Figure 12.39, select VARIABLES from the VIEW dropdown list, and select PLAN YEAR ❷.

The logic to derive the previous year can be built by setting an offset on the value of the user entry variable. Specify an offset of –1 in the OFFSET entry field ❸. Finally, click on ADD ❹ to choose the FROM value, and click on CONTINUE ❺ to return to the main planning function definition screen.

Similarly, to define the TO values, you can click on the button ▣ as shown in ❹ of Figure 12.38, earlier in this section. Select the same variable BWPLAN_YR without offset for the TO values.

Finally, save the planning function by clicking on the SAVE button as shown in Figure 12.40. If the prompt for maintaining the variable value (user entry) appears, then maintain an input value for the variable and save.

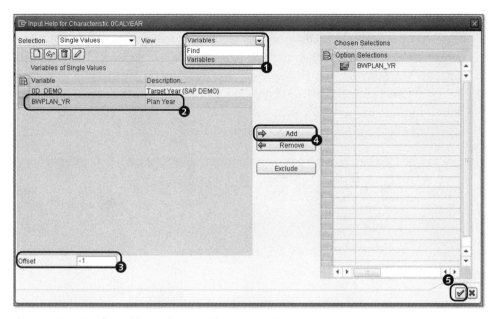

Figure 12.39 Use of Variables in the Copy Planning Function

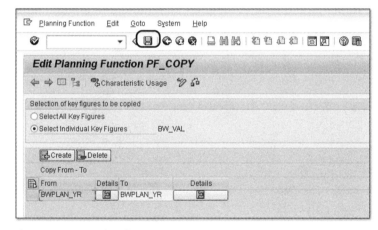

Figure 12.40 Save the Planning Function

Repost

The REPOST function is used to change the characteristic values of existing plan data included in the selection of planning functions. For example, assume client representative CR1 has some sales target for a customer in his sales area, but now the target has to be shifted to client representative CR2 because the customer served by CR1 has moved to the sales area where CR2 is responsible (Figure 12.41). The REPOST function is useful in such a scenario.

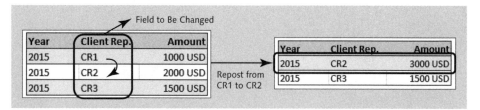

Figure 12.41 Example of Repost Function

In this case (Figure 12.41), the characteristic that is changed is CLIENT REPRESEN-TATIVE. You define the parameters for the selected fields to be changed by specifying the FROM and TO values. This means that FROM values will be replaced by TO values.

Upon execution, the reposted values are added to the existing values. As shown in Figure 12.41, when CR1 is reposted as CR2, the value $1000 USD from CR1 is added to CR2, making the total of CR2 $3000.

The REPOST function is defined and works in a way similar to that of the COPY function (see Figure 12.42). In this case, the FROM values are copied to the To values for the existing records in the given selection, and then the records with FROM values are deleted.

The REPOST function replaces Calendar Year with 2015 for all those records in the selection where Calendar Year is 2014.

> **Note**
>
> For a REPOST function, the FROM and TO values are always single values.

We've seen that the REPOST function actually affects the data that is included in both FROM and TO values. This means that for the REPOST function to work, both

FROM and TO values must be included in the filter on which the function is executed.

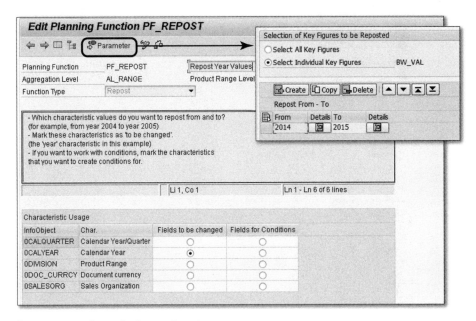

Figure 12.42 Defining the Repost Function

Repost by Characteristic Relationships

This standard planning function reposts values from characteristics based on the characteristic relationships. This function is particularly useful when you want to correct already-entered data and make it consistent with the characteristic relationship.

For example, consider a situation where you've defined a characteristic relationship that derives the value of product group from product. Data is entered at the product level, and product group is derived based on this characteristic relationship (Figure 12.43). So, if you enter a record for Product = LCD TV, the Product Group = Video value is derived.

Now assume that, due to some organizational restructuring in 2015, a new product group called Entertainment is introduced, and now Product = LCD TV belongs to Product Group = Entertainment. A new planning record that gets posted in 2015 for Product = LCD TV will get saved with Product Group = Entertainment in the cube, as shown in Figure 12.43. This new relationship makes the record 1 from year 2014 invalid. To correct the previously entered records, you must define the REPOST BY CHARACTERISTIC RELATIONSHIPS planning function.

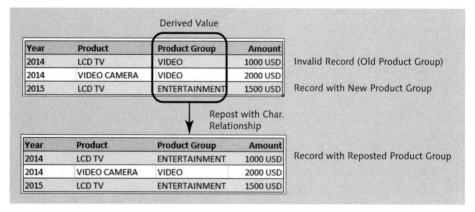

Figure 12.43 Repost with Characteristic Relationship

To define this function on an aggregation level, the aggregation level should *include all* of the InfoObjects from the real-time InfoCube. Also, you can create this function only on an aggregation level that is built directly on a real-time InfoCube.

You can define the characteristic used for this planning function by selecting the fields that need to be reposted as fields to be changed (Figure 12.44).

You have to define only the characteristic usage for creating this planning function. Because the values are reposted based on the logic derived in characteristic relationships, this planning function doesn't have any parameters.

Delete

This standard planning function is used to delete the key figure values of the data included in the selection. In the definition of the DELETE function, you have to specify the key figures that need to be deleted for selected records (Figure 12.45).

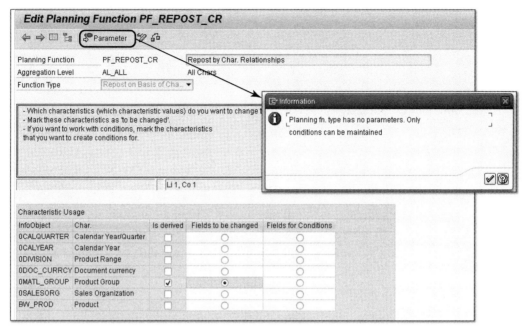

Figure 12.44 Define Function: Reposting with Characteristic Relationship

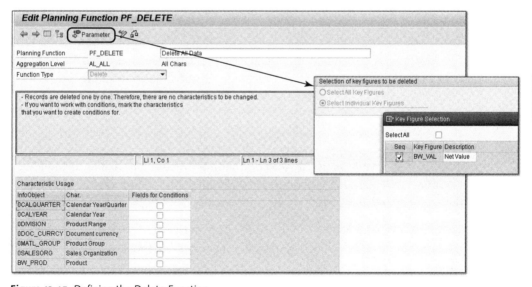

Figure 12.45 Defining the Delete Function

> **Note**
>
> When you delete a particular record using this planning function, it actually sets the key figures values to zero for that characteristic combination.

Generate Combinations

The GENERATE COMBINATIONS function type is used to generate blank records for an aggregation level. This function is dependent on characteristic relationships defined on the real-time InfoCube. The blank records are created for those combinations that are valid per the master data and characteristic relationship.

You don't have to define any parameters for this planning function. All valid combinations of characteristic values are generated based on characteristic restrictions defined and the filter over which this planning function is executed.

Delete Invalid Combinations

If you want to delete the key figure values for all of those records whose characteristic combinations aren't valid (as per characteristic relationships), you can use the DELETE INVALID COMBINATIONS standard planning function type. This function is based on the characteristic relationships defined on the real-time InfoCube.

This function is dependent on characteristic relationships and can be executed only on an aggregation level that includes all InfoObjects of the real-time InfoCube.

Forecasting

FORECASTING is one of the advanced planning functions available in Integrated Planning. This planning function uses different statistical forecasting methods to derive the plan values based on already-existing data (Figure 12.46).

To define a FORECASTING planning function, you first have to specify the key figure and the period for which you want to generate the forecast data (❶ of Figure 12.46). The next step is to define the set of historical data that should be used to derive the forecast values ❷. For this, you have to set the data range and selection for the historical data, as well as the key figure to refer to.

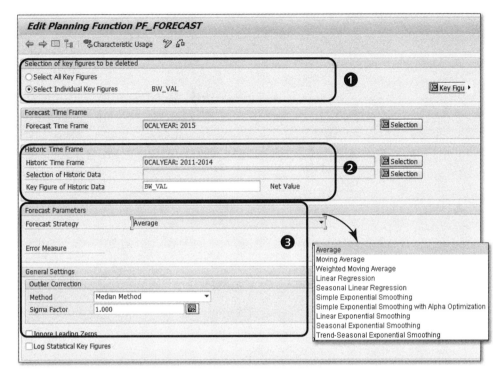

Figure 12.46 Forecasting Planning Function

Finally, you have to define the forecasting settings for the planning function ❸. Here you can select the STRATEGY from the available set of standard forecasting methods.

Revaluation

As the name suggests, the REVALUATION planning function type is used to recalculate key figure values for the records included in the selection. The key figure values can be increased or decreased by a percentage factor defined in the planning function. However, the characteristic values of data remain unchanged if this function is executed.

You can define a REVALUATION planning function for all of the key figures in the selected set of data (❶ of Figure 12.47). Also, you can define each key figure to be revaluated separately with a different revaluation factor.

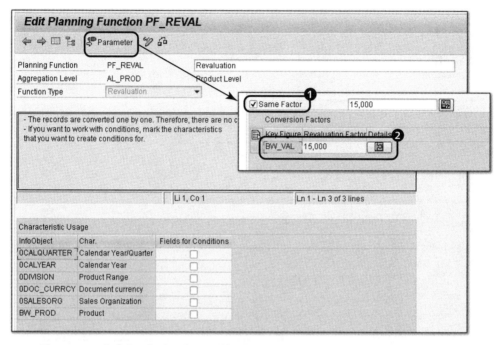

Figure 12.47 Defining the Revaluation Planning Function

Define the revaluation factor as shown in ❷ of Figure 12.47. The revaluation logic with which the new value is calculated can be represented as follows:

New Value = {1 + (Revaluation Percentage/100)} × Existing Value

To add more flexibility to the planning application, you can use user entry variables for the revaluation factor. The key figure values will be revaluated dynamically based on the user input.

Distribution by Key

In a typical top-down planning scenario, the values planned at a higher level are transferred to a lower level for planning. The DISTRIBUTION BY KEY function is used to distribute the values from one level of planning to another level of planning. This distribution can happen either based on some already existing reference data or by using a distribution key where the distribution weighting factors are defined.

We discussed the significance of NOT ASSIGNED (#) values in SAP BW in Section 12.2.4. The DISTRIBUTION BY KEY function can be used to bring consistency to the data between aggregation levels by eliminating not assigned (#) values.

In the case of the DISTRIBUTION BY KEY function, the characteristics that are used to distribute data are selected as fields to be changed. You have to then define the distribution weight with respect to the characteristics values by which distribution should take place.

To define the parameters for the DISTRIBUTION BY KEY function, you have to first select the key figures that need to be distributed (❶ of Figure 12.48).

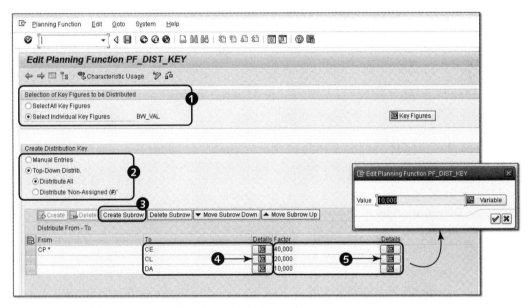

Figure 12.48 Defining the Planning Function Distribution with Key

Then you have to specify the source for the distribution function ❷:

▶ MANUAL ENTRIES
This option can be used if you want to distribute data from a specific characteristic value to one or more specific characteristic values. In this case, you maintain the FROM and TO values manually.

▶ TOP-DOWN DISTRIB.
This option follows the typical top-down distribution logic. The values for the

records in the selection are redistributed per the distribution key defined. There are two options for top-down distribution:

▶ DISTRIBUTE ALL: The total of the values in the selection is redistributed per the distribution key defined.

▶ DISTRIBUTE 'NOT-ASSIGNED (#)': Only the records where the characteristic value isn't assigned (#) are distributed to other records in the selection where the characteristic value exists. This option can be used to eliminate the # records by distributing their value to other records.

The next step is to maintain the distribution key. To create each new entry in the distribution key, click on CREATE SUBROW ❸. The specific To values of the characteristic can be selected by clicking on the DETAILS button ❹. The distribution factors are maintained in the FACTOR column ❺. However, you can also use variables to determine the distribution factors.

Note that the distribution weight is calculated based on the relative weight of the factors, so it isn't necessary for the sum of the factors to be 100%. For the example shown in Figure 12.48, the product range CE will get a value that is double the value product range CL will get. Similarly, product range DA will get a value that is half the value CL will get.

Distribution by Reference Data

The DISTRIBUTION BY REFERENCE DATA function is defined the same way as you define the DISTRIBUTION BY KEY planning function. Additionally, you have to select the characteristics that are used to define the reference data. The values included in the planning filter selection are distributed with respect to the mentioned reference data. The EDIT PLANNING FUNCTION parameter screen for distribution by reference data is shown in Figure 12.49.

Similar to the DISTRIBUTION WITH KEY function, you must select the key figure that needs to be distributed ❶. The next step is to define the reference data that should be used for distribution ❷. In the example shown in Figure 12.49, the net value key figure for the data in the selection is distributed per the data for calendar year 2014. Further, select the method of distribution ❸ from the available options. You can also define the error handling for this function if there is no relevant reference data ❹.

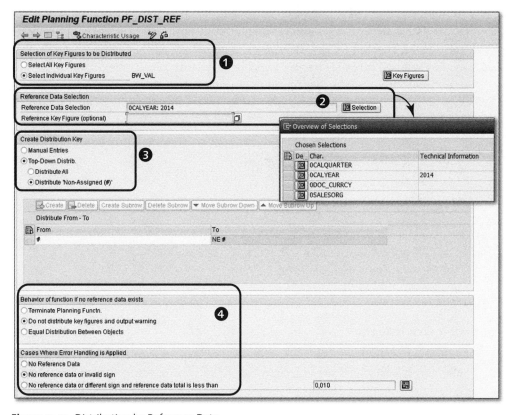

Figure 12.49 Distribution by Reference Data

Set Key Figure Values

The SET KEY FIGURE VALUES planning function is used to set key figure values for those records where the aggregated key figure values are empty. Similar to the DISTRIBUTION BY REFERENCE DATA function, this function also distributes the values per the reference data, but it applies the function to only those records where the key figure value is blank at the aggregation level.

Currency Translation

The CURRENCY TRANSLATION planning function type is useful in a scenario where planning is performed in multiple currencies. The values entered in different currencies can be translated to a uniform currency using this function.

To define the CURRENCY TRANSLATION function, specify the key figure that needs to be translated in the SOURCE KEY FIGURE column (❷ of Figure 12.50). Also include the TARGET KEY FIGURE where the translated values will be stored ❶. Both the source and target currency could be the same key figure; in this case, the translated values of the key figure overwrite the original values. You must also specify the CURRENCY TRANSLATION TYPE ❸, which decides how the values should be translated.

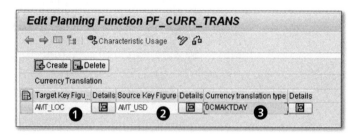

Figure 12.50 Currency Translation Function

Unit Conversion

This function is similar to the CURRENCY TRANSLATION function. It's used when planning is performed for a quantity involving multiple units of measure. Similar to the CURRENCY TRANSLATION function, to define the parameters of a UNIT CONVERSION planning function, you have to specify the source unit, target unit, and the unit conversion type.

Formula

This planning function is often referred to as the FOX (FORMULA EXTENSION) function. The FOX function provides you with an enhanced formula editor that you can use to define your own processing logic. Following are the different options for building a function in the formula editor:

▸ Data access read, write, or reference

▸ Ability to read the values from BEx variables and master data attributes

▸ Use of internal programming components such as internal variables and constants

▸ Standard formula functions (logical, Boolean, data, string, etc.)

▶ Loop functions

▶ Calls to ABAP function modules

The EDIT PLANNING FUNCTION parameter screen for the FORMULA planning function is shown in Figure 12.51.

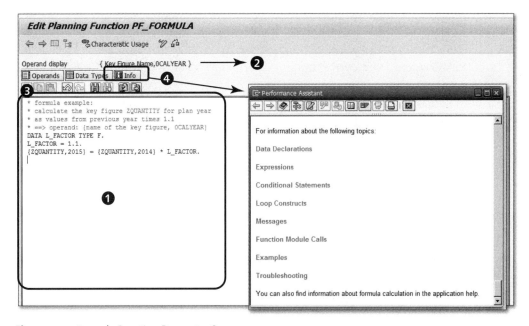

Figure 12.51 Formula Function Parameter Screen

You can write your planning function in the formula editor on the parameter screen (❶ of Figure 12.51). The operands for writing the formula are based on the key figure and characteristic usage settings for the function. We've used 0CALYEAR as the field to be changed, so the operand is {KEY FIGURE NAME, 0CALYEAR} ❷. You can also use the help available on operands when creating a formula ❸.

If you want to use additional programming elements to create the formula function, you can choose from a variety of elements available for FOX programming. The details about these program elements, input help for the selected program element, its syntax, and a brief description is available when you click on the INFO button ❹.

An example of the formula with operand {key figure name, 0CALYEAR} is {BW_VAL, 2015} = {BW_VAL, 2014}*1.25.

This formula calculates the values for key figure BW_VAL for the year 2015 by multiplying the corresponding 2014 values by a factor of 1.25.

For more complex formulas, you can use the available program elements. Click on the INFO button for more details.

12.2.7 Defining Planning Sequences

Planning sequences are used to compose execution plans for multiple planning functions, and the corresponding filter values over which those are to be executed. You can define planning sequences in Transaction RSPLAN under the PLANNING SEQUENCES section. In this section, we explain how to create planning sequences. We'll also explain how to test and debug one or more planning functions built in the planning model.

Creating Planning Sequences

To create a planning sequence, go to the PLANNING SEQUENCES section (❶ of Figure 12.52), and click on CREATE ❷. Enter the technical name and the description of the planning sequence ❸, and click on CONTINUE ❹.

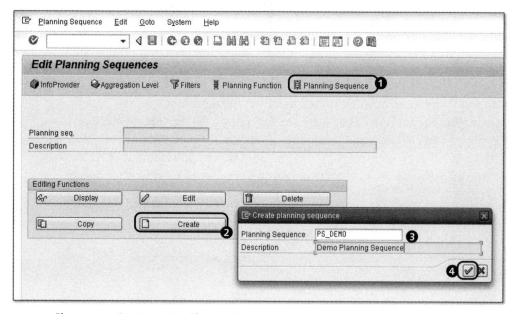

Figure 12.52 Creating a New Planning Sequence

In the next screen, define the planning sequence by adding planning functions and defining the sequence of execution (Figure 12.53). By clicking on the CREATE button ❶, you can add a new step in the planning sequence.

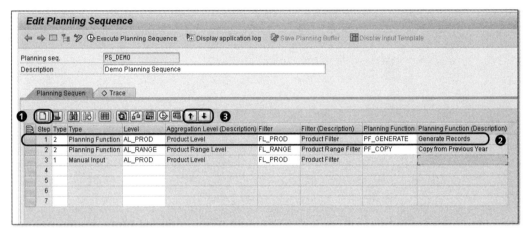

Figure 12.53 Defining the Planning Sequence

Select the AGGREGATION LEVEL, PLANNING FILTER, and PLANNING FUNCTION to define the steps in the planning sequence ❷. This way, you can add multiple steps to the planning sequence. You can also readjust the sequence of the planning functions with the help of the UP and DOWN buttons ❸.

Finally, save the planning sequence by clicking on the SAVE button on the tab page.

Testing Planning Functions and Planning Sequences

After the planning sequence is saved, you now have the option to execute it directly or to execute it without trace. You can test and validate the complete planning sequence or a selected planning function using this option. Before you execute any function or sequence, you have to first maintain the variable values involved in the planning function (❶ of Figure 12.54).

After the variable values are maintained, select a function to execute, and click on the EXECUTE button (❷ of Figure 12.54). If no step is selected, the complete planning sequence is executed.

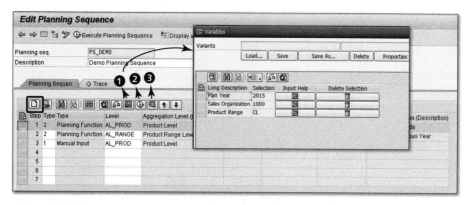

Figure 12.54 Executing the Planning Function or Sequence

When you click on the EXECUTION WITH TRACE icon ❸, the planning function is executed, and all of the actions performed by the planning function on the data can be traced.

After you execute the planning function, you can see the system messages displayed at the bottom part of the screen (❶ of Figure 12.55). This lets you know whether the planning function has been executed successfully.

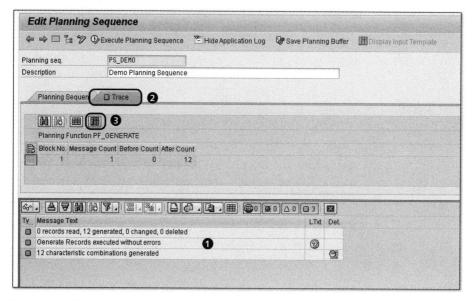

Figure 12.55 System Messages

If you execute the planning function with trace, then the trace information is available under the TRACE tab (❷ of Figure 12.55).

Select the block row, and click on the DETAILS icon ❸ to see detailed trace information and data. The system displays the state of a data record before and after change. Also, the new records that are created can be identified using the TYPE of the record (Figure 12.56).

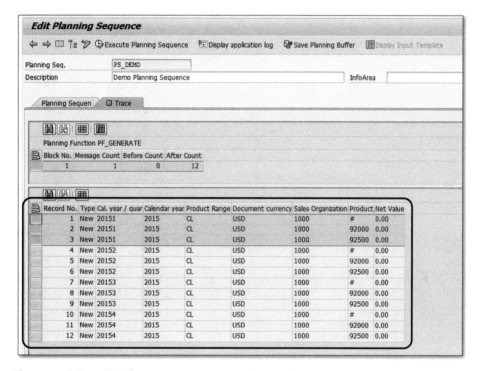

Figure 12.56 Trace Details

Execution with trace is a very important option available to debug and trace the planning functions and planning sequences.

12.2.8 Input-Ready Query

As we've seen in earlier sections, planning functions and planning sequences enable the automatic processing of data. Apart from this automatic processing, planning users also need an interface to manually edit data. This process is called *manual planning.* A planning application that includes manual planning can be built using either BEx Web Application Designer or BEx Analyzer, but the basis for all manual planning is an input-ready query.

An input-ready query is built in BEx Query Designer and is created the same way as a regular BEx query used for reporting. However, unlike a regular reporting query, an input-ready query can be built only on an aggregation level or a Multi-Provider that includes a simple aggregation level.

Open BEx Query Designer, and create a new query. When you navigate through the InfoAreas, you'll notice that the aggregation levels that are created in Transaction RSPLAN are also available as InfoProviders in BEx Query Designer. Select the [AL_RANGE] PRODUCT RANGE LEVEL level to create the query (Figure 12.57).

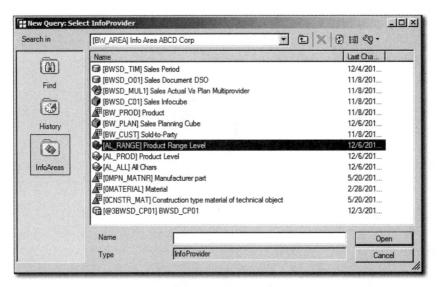

Figure 12.57 Creating a Query on the Aggregation Level

In the query definition screen, you can see that the planning filters defined in the PLANNING MODELER are available under the FILTER folder (Figure 12.58). Drag and drop the filter in the query definition.

Drag and drop all of the necessary characteristics and key figures from the aggregation level in the query definition (Figure 12.59).

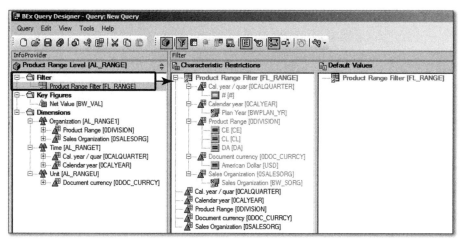

Figure 12.58 Filter for the Input-Ready Query

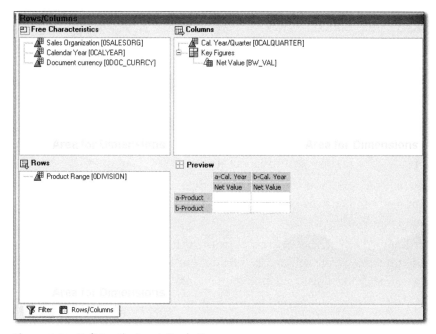

Figure 12.59 Defining the Input-Ready Query

For the user to be able to edit the key figure values, the key figure needs to be enabled for planning. Go to the key figure properties, and click on the PLANNING tab (Figure 12.60).

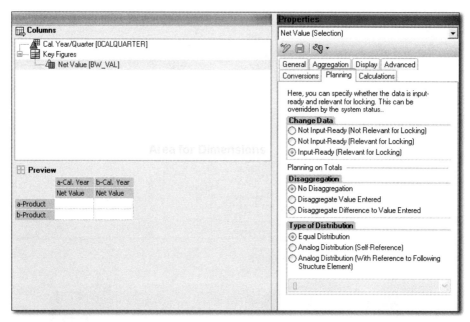

Figure 12.60 Key: Planning Properties

Different planning-related settings for the selected key figure are available on this tab:

▶ Change Data

Under this section, you can specify whether the selected key figure should be input ready or not. Three options are available:

▶ Not Input-Ready (Not Relevant for Locking): This option disables the input-ready property of the selected key figure; the data for that key figure won't be locked.

▶ Not Input-Ready (Relevant for Locking): This option disables the input-ready property of the selected key figure, but the data will be locked. This data can be changed using planning functions.

▶ Input-Ready (Relevant for Locking): With this option, the selected key figure is made input-ready, and the corresponding plan data is locked for other users.

▶ Disaggregation

In an input-ready planning layout, data is entered only at the lowest level of drilldown. However, if data is entered at result rows (i.e., at the aggregated level), the new result value has to be distributed to the lower-level records. This top-down distribution setting can be selected under this section.

▶ No Disaggregation: If this radio button is selected, the change of values at an aggregated level is disabled.

▶ Disaggregate Value Entered: For this setting, the new value entered at the aggregated level is disaggregated to lower records based on the type of distribution selected in the next section.

▶ Disaggregate Difference to Value Entered: For this setting, only the change between the new and the old value is distributed.

▶ Type of Distribution

In this section, you can specify the type of top-down distribution by using the following settings:

▶ Equal Distribution: The aggregated value is equally distributed across all of the records at the lower level.

▶ Analog Distribution (Self-Reference): The value is distributed in the same proportion as that of the existing data for the same key figure.

▶ Analog Distribution (With Reference to Following Structure Element): With this option, you can distribute the value with reference to the data for a specific structure element.

Also, you need to set the Startup View query property (visible under the Planning tab in Query Properties) to start the query in change mode. By selecting the checkbox shown in Figure 12.61, you set the query to be opened in input-ready mode when executed.

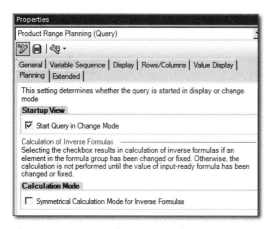

Figure 12.61 Starting the Query in Change Mode

Inverse Formulas

The *inverse formulas* are used when a formula in the input-ready query is enabled for input. For example, if you have a formula for the average monthly sales in a query, where the data in the real-time InfoCube is stored in key figure BW_VAL at calendar quarter level, then:

Avg. Monthly Sales = BW_VAL / 3

If this formula is made input-ready, then the user can input the value for monthly average sales. For this data to be saved in the InfoCube, the system needs to know how the entered value of Avg. Monthly Sales has to be translated into the base key figure BW_VAL.

In this particular case, an inverse formula has to be defined as:

BW_VAL = Avg. Monthly Sales × 3

Thus, when a user enters a value of $1000 in the input-ready formula, the inverse formula calculated the value for BW_VAL = $3000 to be saved in the real-time InfoCube.

Refer to SAP Note 1236347 for details on inverse formulas.

Also, you can define some additional settings for the characteristics involved in the query definition. For example, if you want to list all of the possible values of product range in the default view of the query, you set the ACCESS TYPE FOR RESULT VALUES property for the PRODUCT RANGE characteristic as MASTER DATA (Figure 12.62).

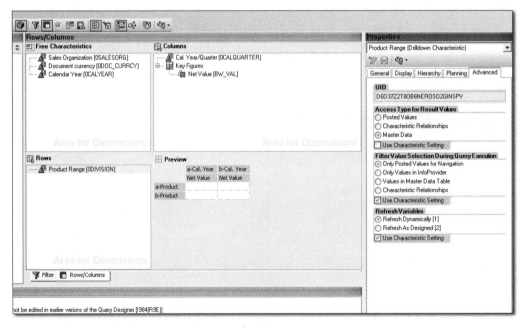

Figure 12.62 Characteristic Properties for Planning

Finally, save the query with the technical name "BW_PLAN_Q001" and enter the description "Product Range Planning".

12.3 Building Planning Applications

A *planning application* is built by putting different planning components together so that you can perform manual planning as well as execute different planning functions. This can involve input-ready queries as well as read-only BEx queries. Different planning functions and planning sequences can also be included in planning applications. An Excel-based planning application is built using BEx Analyzer, and a web-based planning application is built using BEx Web Application Designer. We discuss both of these in more detail in the following sections.

12.3.1 Excel-Based Planning Applications

In the sections covered so far in this chapter, we've seen how to create different elements involved in building a planning application. A planning application can include different planning objects, such as input-ready queries, planning functions, and planning sequences. In addition, a planning application can also include regular reporting queries based on InfoProviders other than real-time InfoCubes.

However, the most important part of building a planning application is to assemble these planning components together to form a user interface for the planning application. In this section, we explain how to create a simple Excel-based planning application with the help of our example product range planning scenario.

To start, open BEx Analyzer by choosing START MENU • PROGRAMS • BUSINESS EXPLORER • ANALYZER. Open a new Excel workbook, and switch to design mode by clicking on the icon shown in ❶ of Figure 12.63.

Maintain the heading for this application by editing the Excel cells ❷. For the input-ready query, insert an analysis grid ❸ from the BEx design toolbar. Assign the input-ready query to the analysis grid in the properties (accessed from the ANALYSIS GRID context menu) of the design item. For this, first create a new data provider by clicking on the CREATE button (❶ of Figure 12.64). Assign the input-ready query to the data provider using the QUERY icon ❷. Assign this data provider to the analysis grid item by clicking on OK ❸.

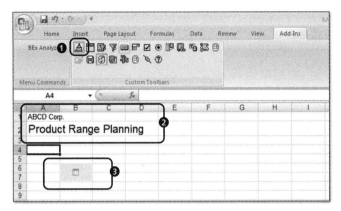

Figure 12.63 Creating a New Planning Application in BEx Analyzer

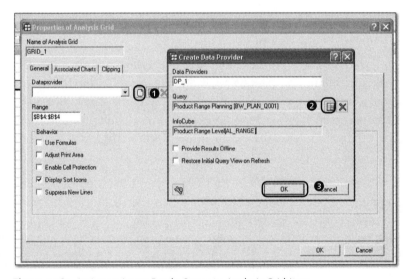

Figure 12.64 Assign an Input-Ready Query to Analysis Grid Item

With the previous step, the manual entry layout is made available in the application. Now, let's build some command buttons in this planning application. The first command button used in almost all planning applications is the SAVE command. Insert a button design item from the BEx design toolbar into the layout (❶ of Figure 12.65). We can assign the command to this button in the item properties. Go to the design item properties from the context menu of the newly inserted button, and select the PLANNING-SPECIFIC COMMAND radio button ❷. Then click on NEXT ❸ to define further settings.

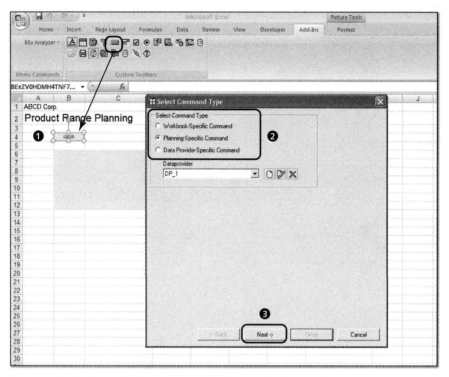

Figure 12.65 Assigning the Planning-Specific Command to Button Design Item

The next screen shows the different planning commands that can be assigned to the button (Figure 12.66). Select the SAVE radio button, and click on FINISH. This assigns the SAVE function to the button added.

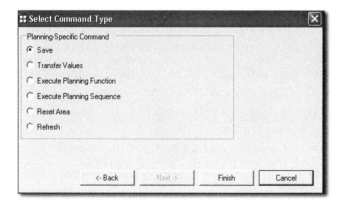

Figure 12.66 Select Command Type

You can further maintain the properties for this SAVE function assignment, as shown in Figure 12.67. You can define the cell range ❶ in the workbook to which the planning function button will be positioned. The display text for the button can be maintained in the BUTTON TEXT field ❷. The static parameters for the function are visible on the right side ❸. For the SAVE command, no additional parameters need to be defined. Maintain the properties for the button, and click on OK to complete the command assignment.

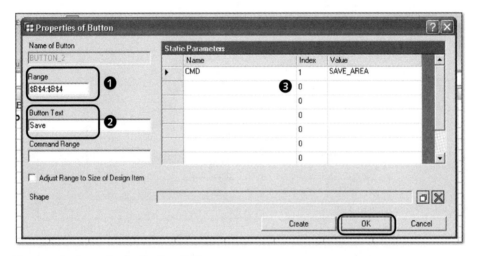

Figure 12.67 Properties for the Save Button

Let's now add another command button that will execute a planning function to copy the plan values from the previous year. The procedure is the same as shown previously in Figure 12.66. First insert the button design item in the workbook, and then select the EXECUTE PLANNING FUNCTION command type from the DESIGN ITEM PROPERTIES screen. Click on NEXT to further customize the properties.

On the next screen, first select the planning function and the data provider on which the planning function has to be executed. Select the planning function that needs to be assigned to the button, as shown in ❶ of Figure 12.68. Also select the data provider from the dropdown list on which the selected planning function should be executed; alternatively, you can create a new one if needed ❷. If the planning function includes variables, the list of those variables is displayed after you select the planning function ❸.

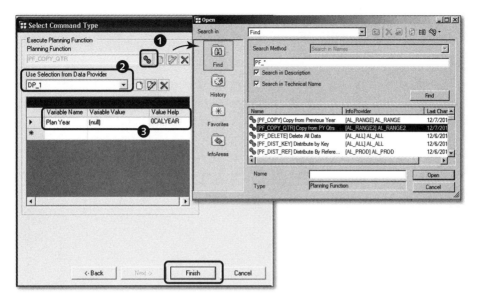

Figure 12.68 Selecting the Planning Function

Note

The PF_COPY_QTR planning function is used in Figure 12.68 as an example. It copies the quarterly sales values from the previous year to the quarterly sales values of the plan year entered. Because the data is read and copied at the calendar quarter level (example copy from Q1 2014 to Q1 2015), the CALENDAR YEAR/QTR characteristic is used as the fields to be changed in this function (refer to Figure 12.34 for an illustration of fields to be changed).

After you've defined the planning function and the data provider, click on the FINISH button to move to the next screen. This is where you can set the button properties and other parameters related to the planning function (Figure 12.69). Maintain the BUTTON TEXT ❶.

The STATIC PARAMETERS section on the right side of the screen lists all of the parameters associated with the planning function that you've selected earlier; you can maintain the values for those parameters that will remain static throughout. Also note that there are parameter entries for the variables used in the function. The VAR_NAME_1 parameter corresponds to the name of the variable, and the

VAR_VALUE_1 parameter corresponds to the value that this variable will store. The PF_COPY_QTR planning function, which we've selected here, uses the BWPLAN_YR variable. This is a user entry variable, so it isn't needed to define the static parameter for the variable value. Delete the VAR_VALUE_1 entry from the static parameters ❷, and click on OK to complete the planning function assignment to the button. You can assign the planning sequence and other planning-specific commands to the button in the same way.

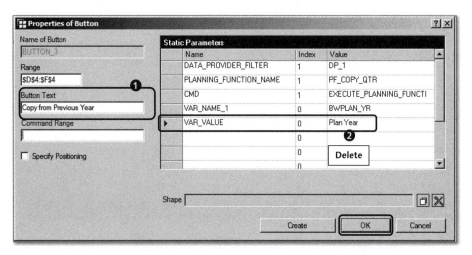

Figure 12.69 Maintaining Properties of the Button

Your simple application for product range planning at the divisional level is ready. Save the workbook, as shown in Figure 12.70. Maintain the mandatory variable values if the variable input screen prompts you to while saving the workbook. You can change these values anytime during later analysis and planning.

When this workbook is opened for planning, the application will appear as shown in Figure 12.71. You can enter or edit the plan values for the product ranges by calendar quarter ❶ for the plan year and by sales organization entered in the variable screen of the query. Also, you can execute the planning function by clicking on the COPY FROM PREVIOUS YEAR button ❷. Clicking on the SAVE button ❸ saves the changed data to the underlying real-time data target.

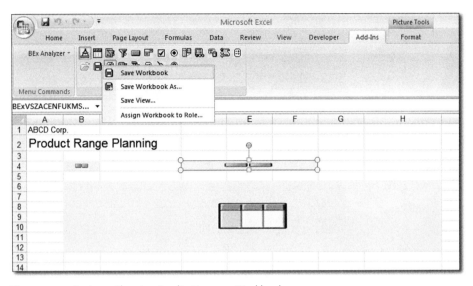

Figure 12.70 Saving a Planning Application as a Workbook

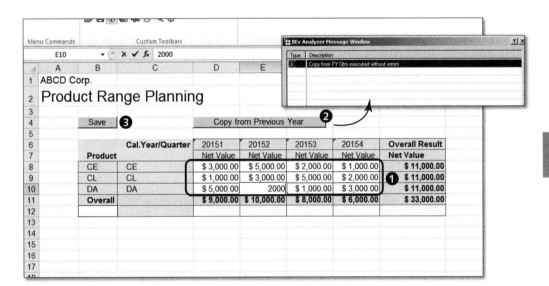

Figure 12.71 Working with Excel-Based Planning Applications

You can see the messages on the actions performed by a function on the information bar visible at the bottom of the workbook (see Figure 12.72).

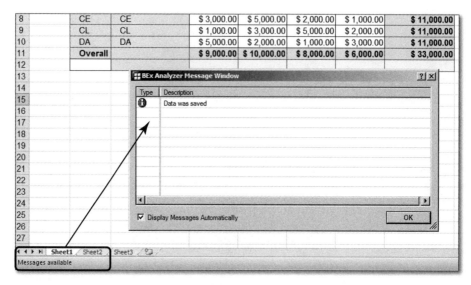

Figure 12.72 Displaying Messages

In this manner, you can create Excel-based planning applications in SAP BW. You can, of course, add more input-ready queries and functions. You can also build more complex planning applications by combining the planning components with the regular BEx analysis components—such as charts, exceptions, filters, navigation blocks, and so on—available in BEx Analyzer.

12.3.2 Web-Based Planning Applications

The web-based planning interface is built using BEx Web Application Designer, and users can access this planning interface from the portal or by using a direct URL. In this section, we explain various aspects of this development with the help of our example scenario, where the product range level planning happens through a web interface.

Open BEx Analyzer by choosing START MENU • PROGRAMS • BUSINESS EXPLORER • WEB APPLICATION DESIGNER, and then open a new web template. Create the heading for the planning application using the font options available in the web template (❶ of Figure 12.73).

Define a new data provider based on the input-ready query. Click on the NEW DATA PROVIDER icon shown in ❷ of Figure 12.73. In the pop-up screen, give a description for the data provider (❶ of Figure 12.74). Select the type of data provider as QUERY VIEW ❷, and assign the query to the data provider using the selection help ❸. Click on OK to complete the data provider creation. Generally, this type of data provider is based on the input-ready queries that are used to provide manual planning layouts in the planning application.

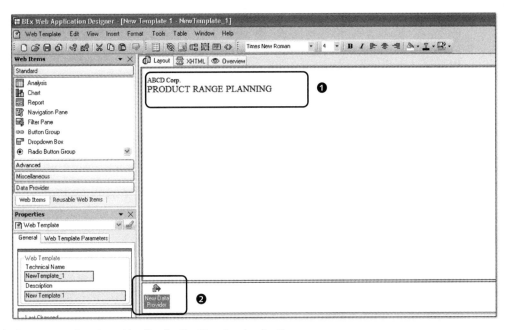

Figure 12.73 Creating a Heading for the Planning Application

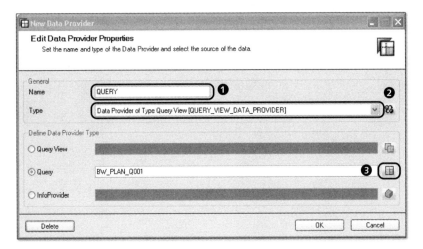

Figure 12.74 Defining a Data Provider for the Input-Ready Query

Another type of data provider needed in building a planning application is the filter type. This type of data provider is used in the execution of planning functions because planning functions are always executed on some filter. Create a new data provider, as shown in Figure 12.75. Give a name to the data provider ❶. Select the type of data provider as FILTER ❷, and assign the required filter to the data provider using the selection help ❸. Click on OK to complete the data provider creation.

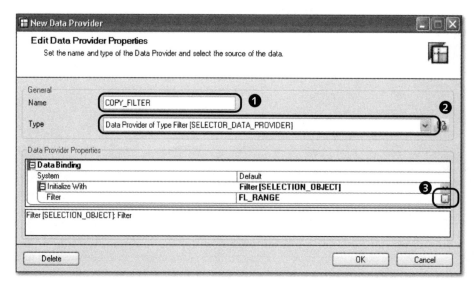

Figure 12.75 Defining the Filter Data Provider

Drag and drop the ANALYSIS web item into the web template (❶ of Figure 12.76). We'll use this web item to create the manual planning layout based on the input-ready query in the application. Assign the QUERY data provider, which you created in previous steps, to the ANALYSIS item ❷.

Drag and drop the BUTTON GROUP web item into the web template to add command buttons to the planning application (Figure 12.77).

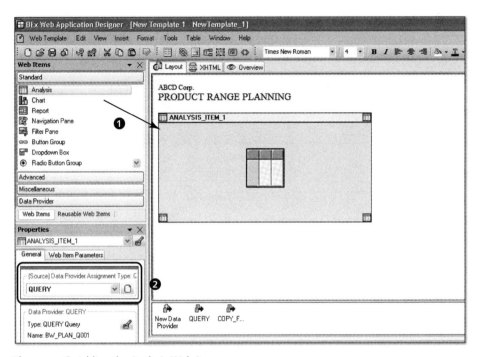

Figure 12.76 Adding the Analysis Web Item

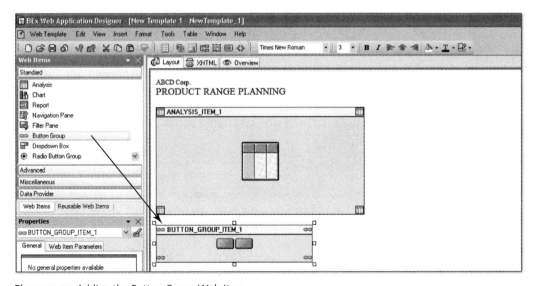

Figure 12.77 Adding the Button Group Web Item

The buttons for this button group are defined in the properties of the button group. Click on the icon shown in Figure 12.78 to add a new button to the button group.

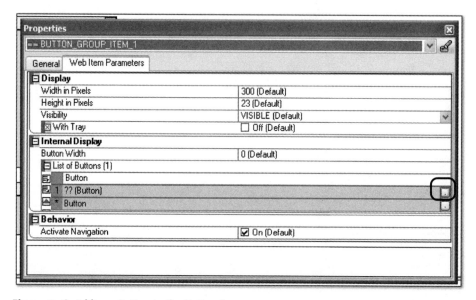

Figure 12.78 Adding a Button to the Button Group

Define the new button by maintaining the display caption and other button parameters, as shown in Figure 12.79. The most important part of button configuration is to assign an action to the button. This can be done using the commands from the Command Wizard available in BEx Web Application Designer. Select COMMAND VIA COMMAND WIZARD ❶ as the action for the button, and then click on the icon shown in ❷ to define the command settings.

You'll see a list of all of the available commands in the Command Wizard under the ALL COMMANDS tab (Figure 12.80).

All of the planning-related commands are grouped under the COMMANDS FOR PLANNING APPLICATIONS folder (❶ of Figure 12.80). These commands are explained here:

▶ EXECUTE A PLANNING FUNCTION (SIMPLE) (EXEC_PLANNING_FUNCTION_SIMPLE)
You can use this command to execute a planning function that can be based on the filter from a single data provider.

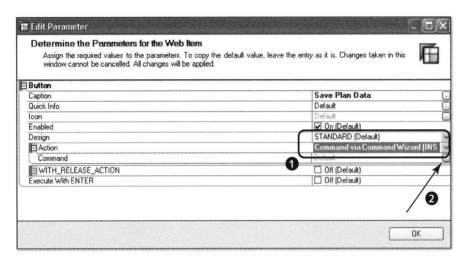

Figure 12.79 Defining Button Parameters

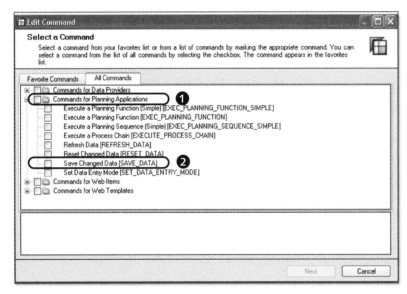

Figure 12.80 Planning Commands

▶ EXECUTE A PLANNING FUNCTION (EXEC_PLANNING_FUNCTION)
You can use this command if you want to execute a planning function and derive the filter for the planning function from multiple sources and data providers. You can independently define the source for each characteristic in the filter.

▶ EXECUTE A PLANNING SEQUENCE (SIMPLE) (EXEC_PLANNING_SEQUENCE_SIMPLE)
You can use this command to execute a planning sequence in the planning application.

▶ EXECUTE A PROCESS CHAIN (EXECUTE_PROCESS CHAIN)
You can use this command to execute a process chain with planning-related process steps.

▶ REFRESH DATA (REFRESH_DATA)
You can use this command to transfer the changed values to the buffer after checking the entries.

▶ RESET CHANGED DATA (RESET_DATA)
You can use this command to undo changes to data.

▶ SAVE CHANGED DATA (SAVE_DATA)
You can use this command to save data changes to the InfoCube after validation of the entries.

▶ SET DATA ENTRY MODE (SET_DATA_ENTRY_MODE)
You can use this command to switch between DISPLAY and CHANGE mode for a data provider based on an input-ready query.

For our example scenario, select the SAVE CHANGED DATA (SAVE_DATA) command (❷ of Figure 12.80), and then click on the NEXT button.

The parameters for the selected command can be defined on the subsequent screen (Figure 12.81). Because there are no parameters to define for the SAVE command, click on OK.

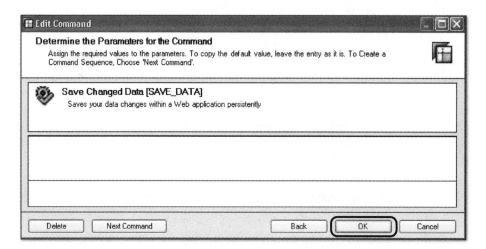

Figure 12.81 Parameter Screen for the Save Command

This takes you back to the button definition screen, where you can see the command assigned to the button under the ACTION settings (Figure 12.82). Click on OK to return to the button group web item properties screen.

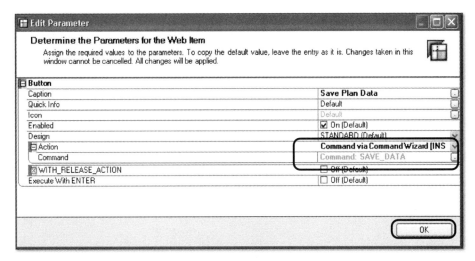

Figure 12.82 Save Button Definition

On the web item PROPERTIES screen, the first button to save the data is defined. Let's now add another button to execute a planning function to copy values from a previous year. Click on the button shown in Figure 12.83 to create another button.

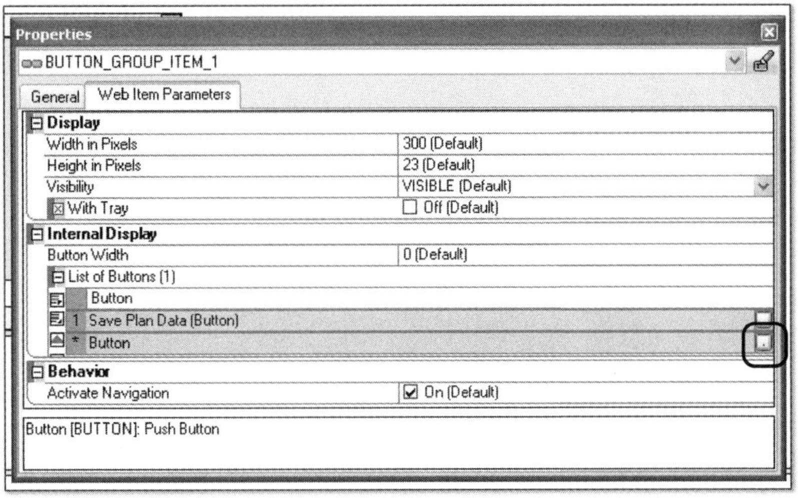

Figure 12.83 Adding a New Button

Define the parameters for the button, and click on the button shown in Figure 12.84 to go to the Command Wizard.

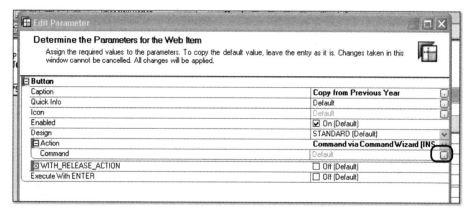

Figure 12.84 Defining Parameters for the Copy Button

Select the EXECUTE A PLANNING FUNCTION (SIMPLE) (EXEC_PLANNING_FUNCTION_SIMPLE) command (❶ of Figure 12.85), and then click on the NEXT button ❷.

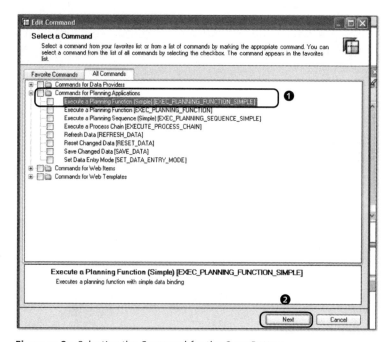

Figure 12.85 Selecting the Command for the Copy Button

Define the parameters for the planning function command on the next screen (Figure 12.86). The most important setting is to define the filter for the planning function. Select the COPY_FILTER data provider, which is based on a filter ❶. You can also maintain any default values for the variables used in the planning function under the VARIANT area of the screen ❷. Finally, assign the required planning function to the command using the selection help ❸. Click on OK to complete the command setting, and then click on OK on the button definition screen to confirm the definition.

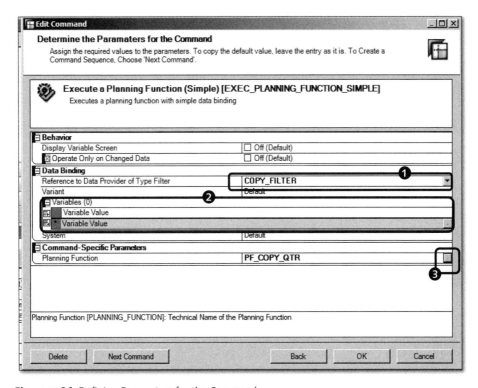

Figure 12.86 Defining Parameters for the Command

You can see both of the defined commands visible in the button group PROPERTIES screen (see Figure 12.87).

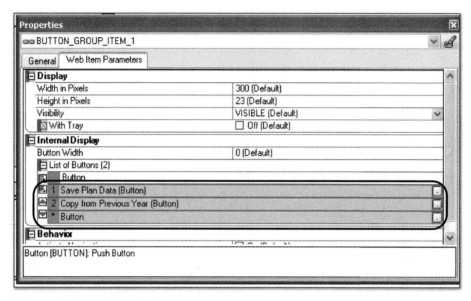

Figure 12.87 Button Group Properties

Your web-based application for product range planning at the divisional level is ready. Save the application by saving the web template (Figure 12.88).

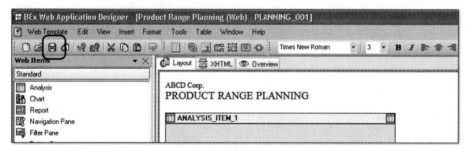

Figure 12.88 Save Planning Application

When you execute this web-based planning application, the VARIABLE ENTRY screen is invoked if variables are used in the application. Enter the variable selection, and click on OK to run the planning application (Figure 12.89).

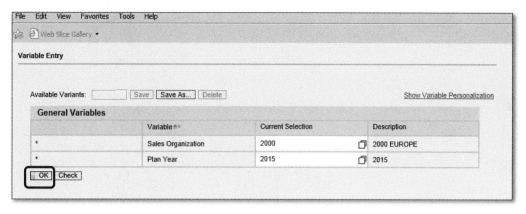

Figure 12.89 Entering Variables to Execute Planning Application

The planning application is executed for the given selection, as shown in Figure 12.90. You can enter or edit the plan values for the product ranges by calendar quarter (❶ of Figure 12.90) for the plan year and by sales organization, entered earlier in the variable screen. Also, you can save the changed data or execute the planning function by clicking on the available buttons ❷.

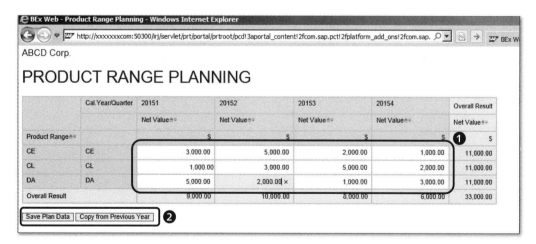

Figure 12.90 Working with a Web-Based Planning Application

A message is displayed based on the action performed in the planning application (Figure 12.91).

Figure 12.91 System Messages for the Action Performed

When you execute a planning function, the system messages are displayed showing the execution results for the planning function (Figure 12.92).

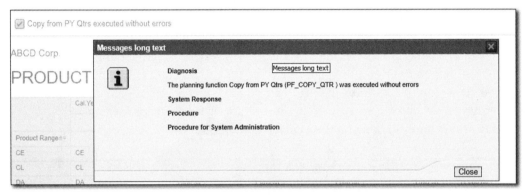

Figure 12.92 Execution Result for the Planning Function

In this manner, you can create and work with a web-based planning application created in SAP BW. Of course, you can add more manual planning layouts to the web template and add more functions and commands as necessary. Also, you can build more complex planning applications by combining the planning components with the regular BEx analysis components available in BEx Web Application Designer, such as charts, exceptions, filters, navigation blocks, and so on.

12.4 Planning Locks

SAP BW Integrated Planning allows you to build an application that can support planning operations in an organization. With this planning application, users can create and edit plan data. In a real-life scenario, multiple planners often are working on the same set of data at the same time, resulting in a conflict that can lead to data integrity issues. To address this situation, Integrated Planning uses the concept of planning locks. Using planning locks, the data selected by a user for editing is locked and made unavailable to all others who try to access the data with overlapping selections.

The data in a planning application is edited either by planning functions or by manual planning. In the case of planning functions, the entire data selection over which the planning function is executed is locked. In the case of manual planning, all of the data contained in the filter of the input-ready query used in the application is locked.

For two planners to work without locking each other, the data sets they are editing should be completely distinct; there will be a locking conflict even in the case of a slight overlap between the two data sets (as illustrated in Figure 12.93).

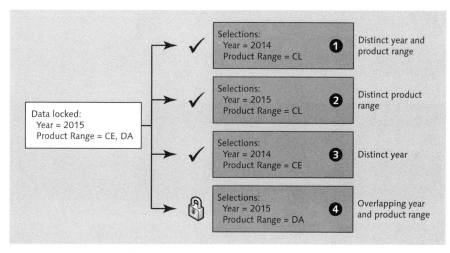

Figure 12.93 Examples of Planning Locks

> **Note**
>
> Data selections are locked regardless of whether there is already a data record in the cube for the given selection. This is done so that another planner can't create a new record and change the data for the given selection.

In most planning scenarios, planning data is accessed from different aggregation levels. These aggregation levels can use different characteristics, so the data on one aggregation level can be aggregated differently from the other aggregation level. In such a scenario, if a characteristic isn't included in one aggregation level, all of the values for that characteristic are locked. We'll explain this situation with an example in which we have two different aggregation levels product range and product. In the product range level, you don't have the product characteristic, so the data is aggregated without it.

Now let's assume that a user, Planner A, starts planning the data for division 1000 for all three product ranges (CE, DA, and CL) using the product range level. Because the product characteristic isn't included in the level, all values for PROD-UCT are locked (Figure 12.94). At the same time, Planner B is trying to access the data from the product level for division 1000, the CE product range, and Product = Camera. In this situation, Planner B gets a lock because there isn't a single characteristic without any overlap.

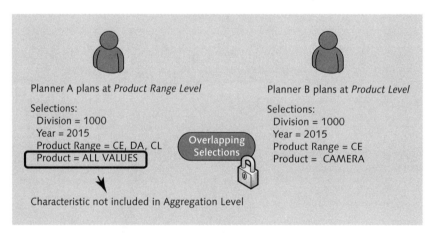

Figure 12.94 Locks on Different Aggregation Levels

Planning locks can be administered from Transaction RSLPLSE.

12.5   Changes to Data in Real-Time InfoCubes

In the previous sections, we explained the different ways in which you can automatically and manually change data using both planning functions and manual planning. This data that is changed, created, or deleted is stored in a real-time data cube; in fact, no record in an InfoCube is really changed or deleted. Instead, the changes to the plan data are managed by creating *additive delta* for the changes.

This is explained with an example in Figure 12.95. If a record is deleted from plan data, the deletion is actually stored by creating an additional record with the selected key figure value reversed ❶. If the key figure value for a record is increased (e.g., from $1000 to $1500), the change is stored in the cube by creating an additional record for the increased value, that is, $500 ❷. Similarly, if the key figure value for a record is decreased (e.g., from $1000 to $800), the change is stored in the cube by creating an additional record for the decreased value, that is, –$200 ❸.

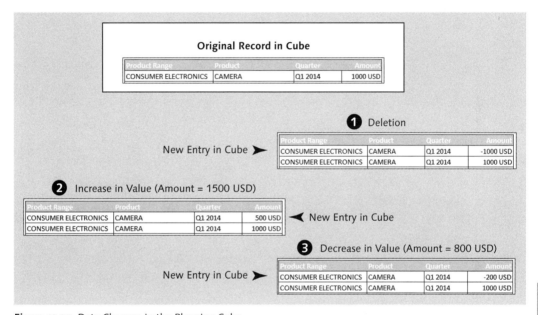

Figure 12.95 Data Changes in the Planning Cube

12.6 Summary

In the beginning of this chapter, we provided an overview of the planning process in an organization and discussed the significance of SAP BW and SAP BW Integrated Planning to address the closed-loop planning requirements. We then explained the different planning components involved in building a planning application and how these components are related to each other, including a discussion about the significance of each planning component and the procedure for creating them in an SAP BW system. These planning components can be put together to build a planning application that can be accessed by the end user, and we explained the two different ways to create these planning applications (Excel-based and web-based). Finally, we discussed the concept of locks in planning and how edited plan data is handled in a real-time InfoCube.

In the next chapter, we discuss the reporting options available in the SAP Business-Objects BI toolset.

The integration of SAP BW and SAP BusinessObjects BI provides more ways for users to present information. In this chapter, we discuss the SAP BusinessObjects BI reporting tools that can be used on top of SAP BW.

13 Reporting with the SAP BusinessObjects BI Suite

By now, you should clearly understand the role played by data warehousing in the early stages of business intelligence (BI). As time progresses, though, newer tools and technology options are changing the way information is consumed; thus, BI as we know it today is no longer confined to the boundaries of data warehousing. As Figure 13.1 depicts, BI has transitioned itself from primitive database queries written directly on Online Transaction Proccesing systems to the latest age of data exploration: mobile BI and real-time analytics. In the process, the maturity of information consumption has grown in parallel with the usage of business intelligence in day-to-day business decisions.

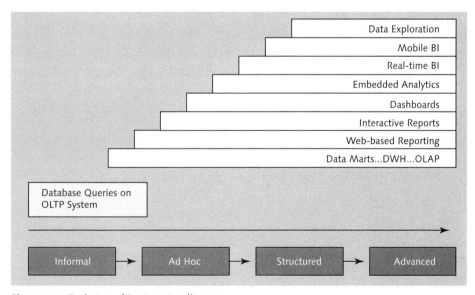

Figure 13.1 Evolution of Business Intelligence

Today, we see that the format in which data is presented isn't limited just to Excel-based reports. The following list shows various options that are available today:

► Excel-based reports

► Formatted reports

► Dashboards

► Operational reports

► Ad hoc analysis

► Advanced analysis

► Data exploration

► Reports on mobile devices

► Broadcasted reports

This list isn't all-inclusive but gives you a fair idea of the varied information consumption pattern in today's business scenarios. It also makes clear the need for tools that offer a similar variety of options to present data. The SAP BusinessObjects BI suite offers a range of reporting solutions that can be used to address this challenge. In this chapter, we familiarize you with the reporting solutions and tools that SAP BusinessObjects BI has to offer.

> **Note**
>
> Because this book focuses on SAP BW, we don't go into great detail about the SAP BusinessObjects BI suite. For more detailed coverage of this topic, including books about integrating SAP BusinessObjects BI with SAP BW and books on each of the different SAP BusinessObjects BI products, we recommend that you visit the Business Intelligence page at *www.sap-press.com/business-intelligence/*.

13.1 Overview of SAP BusinessObjects BI Products

SAP BusinessObjects BI aims to support a wide range of reporting, querying, and analysis needs. Some of the salient features of this toolset are listed here:

► **A common end-user experience**
Users get the same look and feel of the user interface (UI) across all of the reporting tools.

▶ **Enhanced options to report and present data**
Provides a comprehensive toolset to cover all reporting and data presentation needs.

▶ **Enhanced data access methods**
Brings data together from diverse data sources and makes it available as one common platform for reporting.

▶ **Availability of tools to support self-service reporting**
Facilitates ad hoc reporting and empowers users to create their own analysis.

Figure 13.2 provides an overview of the SAP BusinessObjects BI reporting tools.

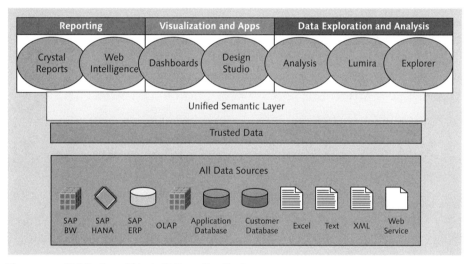

Figure 13.2 SAP BusinessObjects BI Reporting Tools

As the figure suggests, the SAP BusinessObjects BI tools can be used to report on data from virtually any data source, be it SAP or non-SAP data. This data is brought together and merged in the *unified semantic layer*. This layer is built using the *Information Design Tool (IDT)*, where data from underlying data sources is combined and offered to the following reporting tools for further consumption:

▶ SAP Crystal Reports (see Section 13.3)

▶ SAP BusinessObjects Web Intelligence (see Section 13.4)

▶ SAP BusinessObjects Dashboards (see Section 13.5)

▶ SAP BusinessObjects Analysis (see Section 13.6)

- ▸ SAP BusinessObjects Design Studio (see Section 13.7)
- ▸ SAP BusinessObjects Explorer (see Section 13.8)
- ▸ SAP Lumira (see Section 13.9)

SAP BusinessObjects BI also offers direct connectivity to SAP BW InfoProviders and SAP Business Explorer (BEx) queries, so the reporting tools just listed can be integrated with SAP BW. One final BI solution for business needs can be an amalgam of SAP BW and SAP BusinessObjects BI, where SAP BW is the backend and SAP BusinessObjects is used to present the data.

In the subsequent sections of this chapter, we take you through each of the critical components and reporting tools for SAP BusinessObjects BI. We also discuss some of the important features of each of the tools and their positioning in relation to information consumption needs.

13.2 The Unified Semantic Layer and the Information Design Tool

The Information Design Tool (IDT), new with release 4.0 of the SAP BusinessObjects BI suite, allows for the creation of a semantic layer that unifies data from diverse sources and presents it together for reporting. This semantic layer keeps report users away from the technical development at the backend DataSource and allows them to work with the represented entities in business language. Moreover, by using the IDT, you can include additional components such as calculated key figures (CKFs) and regulated key figures (RKFs) for reporting without actually making any changes to the underlying source of the data.

The semantic layer is comprised of SAP BusinessObjects universes, and the IDT is used to create and manage these universes. Reporting users connect to a universe when accessing a report. In addition to representing the reporting elements in a common business language, a universe also masks the complexity of underlying sources, data mappings, logic, and so on from the reporting users. In this section, we discuss the steps for configuring the semantic layer and publishing a universe:

1. Define a connection.
2. Define a data foundation.
3. Configure the business layer.
4. Publish the universe.

The first logical step in the creation of the semantic layer is to connect the IDT with desired data sources (see Figure 13.3). This connection can be either a relational connection ❶ or a connection to OLAP data sources ❷.

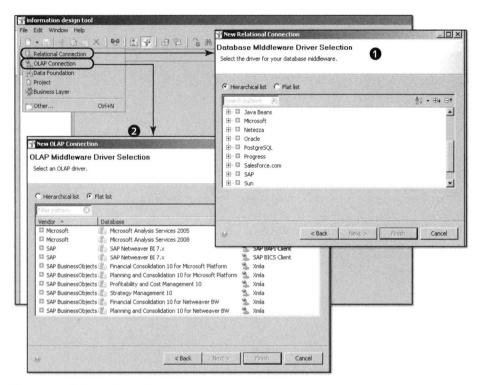

Figure 13.3 Define a Connection

After a connection is defined, you select the tables or schemas from the data source and model the data foundation for analysis. This is called a *data foundation*, which can be based either on tables from a single data source or on data from multiple sources (see Figure 13.4).

A single-source data foundation can be based on either a relational connection or an OLAP connection. To build a multi-source data foundation, you need a relational connection.

Within the data foundation, you can select the fields from one or multiple tables that are desired in the semantic layer for reporting (❶ of Figure 13.5). You also create the joins that define the relationships between these selected tables ❷.

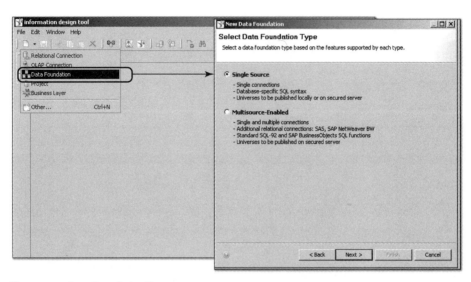

Figure 13.4 Data Foundation Types

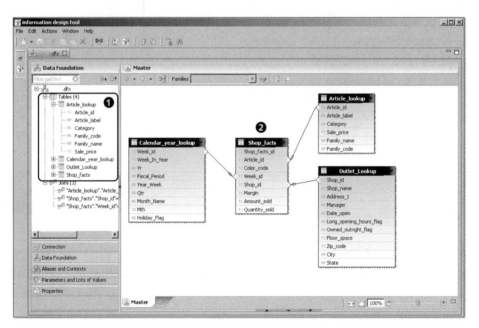

Figure 13.5 Defining Data Foundation

The short-listed fields from one or multiple sources and the joins connecting these tables result in a common foundation for creating the business layer.

The next step is to create the business layer on top of the data foundation; this layer will be visible to users. Because the data is already merged in the data foundation, the creation of the business layer isn't directly linked to the data sources or original source tables. All of the fields included in the data foundation are available in the business layer (❶ of Figure 13.6).

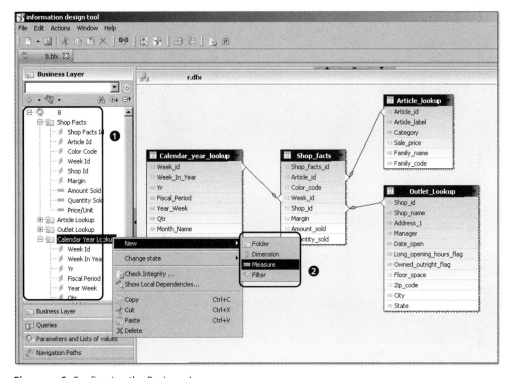

Figure 13.6 Configuring the Business Layer

While defining the business layer, you can choose fields and set them as dimensions (*characteristics* in SAP BW terminology) or measures (*key figures* in SAP BW terminology). In addition to the available fields from the data foundation, you can also choose to create additional folders, measures, dimensions, or filters (❷ of Figure 13.6).

After the business layer is configured, you can publish the universe (see Figure 13.7). A published universe is based on details from the defined connection, data foundation, and business layer; the technical complexity included in the IDT is invisible to users.

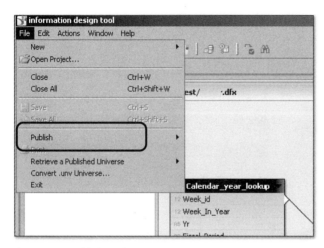

Figure 13.7 Publishing the Universe

A universe based on a single-source data foundation can be published locally (available only to you) as well as on the server (available for sharing with other users). A universe based on a multi-source data foundation must be published on the server.

This published universe can now be accessed through all of the SAP BusinessObjects BI reporting tools, which, as mentioned earlier, can also provide direct connectivity to SAP BW InfoProviders and BEx queries. Let's take a look at each of these reporting tools in the following sections of this chapter.

13.3 SAP Crystal Reports

SAP Crystal Reports is positioned to design and deliver highly formatted and pixel-perfect reports (see Figure 13.8). As of SAP BusinessObjects BI 4.0, SAP Crystal Reports is available in two versions. The first version is SAP Crystal Reports 2013, which is an individual version of the tool suitable for local analysis, usually undertaken by small organizations. However, the other version, SAP Crystal Reports for Enterprise, addresses the enterprise-level reporting needs that are suitable for large organizations.

Because of the better connectivity options it offers to SAP systems, the latter version is also more suitable for organizations that have SAP implementations (see Figure 13.9).

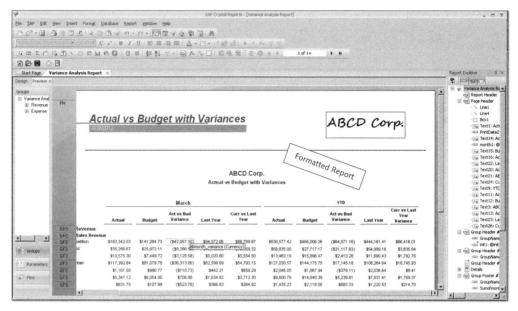

Figure 13.8 Example of Reporting with SAP Crystal Reports

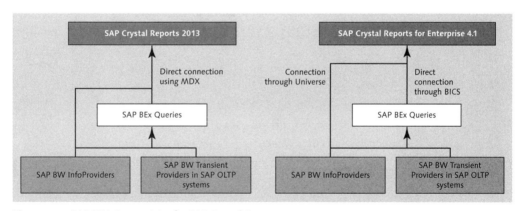

Figure 13.9 SAP BW Connectivity for SAP Crystal Reports

As shown in Figure 13.9, SAP Crystal Reports 2013 can connect to SAP BW Info-Providers and queries using an MDX connection. SAP Crystal Reports for Enterprise has a direct BI Consumer Services (BICS) connectivity to BEx queries. This direct connection ensures better performance by avoiding the additional MDX layer. The Enterprise version can also connect to SAP BW InfoProviders via the universe. This option leverages all of the benefits that come with the IDT discussed earlier.

SAP Crystal Reports emphasizes the formatting and display of data in the reports it offers. However, with this type of reporting, users have very limited ad hoc analysis capabilities.

13.4 SAP BusinessObjects Web Intelligence

SAP BusinessObjects Web Intelligence is one of the most widely used SAP BusinessObjects reporting tools. Users are empowered to build their own analysis (❶ of Figure 13.10), and all of the objects from the underlying universe and other sources are available for creating reports ❷.

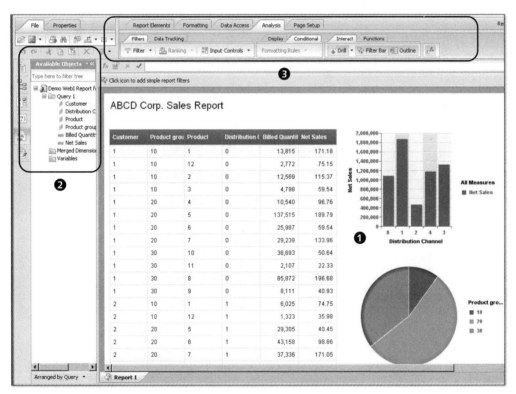

Figure 13.10 Example of Reporting with SAP BusinessObjects Web Intelligence

Apart from ad hoc analysis, this tool has several options to further customize reports. These include display, formatting, charts, filters, and so on (❸ of Figure 13.10) that offer additional choices to the user to create an effective report.

Several options are available to export reports and analysis created in SAP BusinessObjects Web Intelligence (❶ of Figure 13.11). Reports can also be shared with other users to reap the benefits of collaborative analysis ❷.

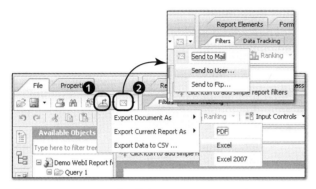

Figure 13.11 Export and Collaboration Options with SAP BusinessObjects Web Intelligence

Also one of the important features available in SAP BusinessObjects Web Intelligence is the DATA TRACKING option, which allows you to highlight any changes to the data (see Figure 13.12).

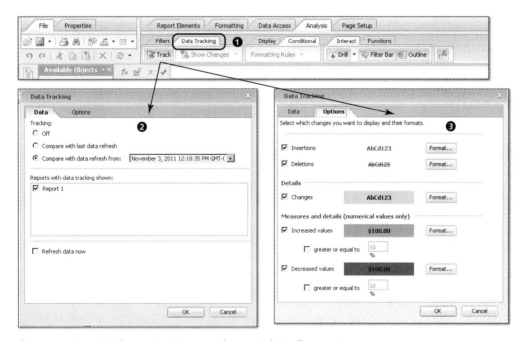

Figure 13.12 Data Tracking in SAP BusinessObjects Web Intelligence Reports

Under the DATA TRACKING tab (❶ of Figure 13.12), you can define the reference point against which data changes should be tracked ❷. You can also select the specific changes that you want to display in the report and define its format on the OPTIONS tab ❸.

Connecting SAP BusinessObjects Web Intelligence to SAP BW can be done in two ways, as shown in Figure 13.13.

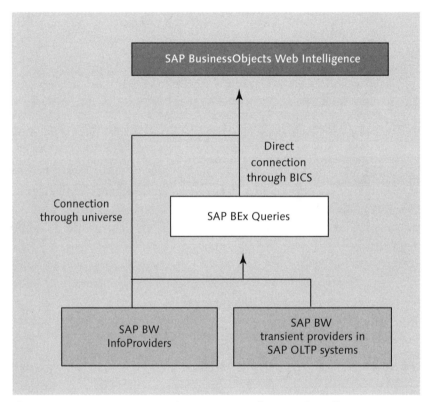

Figure 13.13 SAP BW Connectivity for SAP BusinessObjects Web Intelligence

For SAP BEx queries, SAP BusinessObjects Web Intelligence can connect using the native SAP BW BICS connectivity. Thanks to this direct connectivity, there's no need to connect through the universe layer. However, for SAP BW InfoProviders, SAP BusinessObjects Web Intelligence can access the data though the universe layer defined on top of the InfoProviders.

13.5 SAP BusinessObjects Dashboards

For those reporting needs where data visualization in the form of dashboards is a priority, SAP BusinessObjects Dashboards (formerly known as Xcelsius) is the tool of choice. It provides an intuitive and easy-to-use interface to create dashboards (see Figure 13.14).

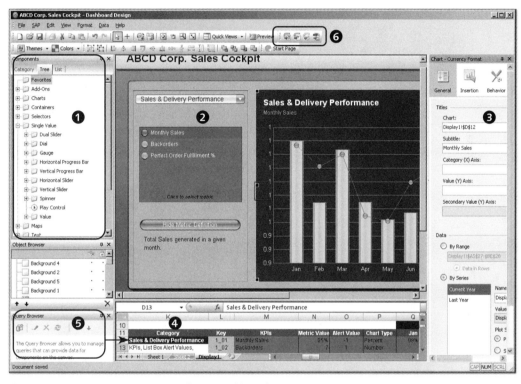

Figure 13.14 Designing SAP BusinessObjects Dashboards

To design dashboards, you can use a variety of components available under the COMPONENTS section in the designer (❶ of Figure 13.14). These components can be arranged on the right side of the screen ❷ in the manner that they are to be actually displayed on the dashboard. Each of these selected components in the dashboard has a set of configurable properties such as color, display, behavior, and so on ❸.

The data that feeds the dashboard is made available in the bottom part of the designer, which is based on Excel ❹. You have the option to populate this section with manual entries, local data sheets, or queries. The QUERY BROWSER ❺ is used to connect the dashboard to queries that provide data for the dashboard.

Dashboards can be published as Microsoft Word documents, PowerPoint presentations, and PDF files; they can also be emailed using Microsoft Outlook with the dashboard embedded in it ❻.

Figure 13.15 shows the options for connecting SAP BusinessObjects Dashboards to SAP BW. BEx queries can be accessed directly using the native BICS connection from SAP BW, and a universe layer can be leveraged to connect to SAP BW Info-Providers.

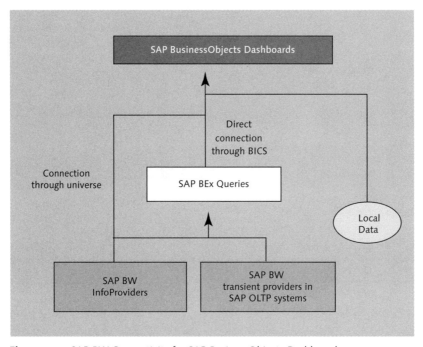

Figure 13.15 SAP BW Connectivity for SAP BusinessObjects Dashboards

13.6 SAP BusinessObjects Analysis

For users with advanced analytical needs where reporting is coupled with advanced multidimensional analysis of data, SAP BusinessObjects Analysis is the preferred option. For organizations that want to use SAP BusinessObjects BI as the frontend reporting tool and SAP BW as the backend, SAP BusinessObjects Analysis is positioned to be a premium alternative to BEx.

The products discussed in this section can be suitable SAP BusinessObjects alternatives for existing BEx tools as follows:

▸ SAP BusinessObjects Analysis, Edition for Microsoft Office (for SAP BEx Analyzer)

▸ SAP BusinessObjects Analysis, Edition for OLAP (for SAP BEx Web Analyzer)

This doesn't mean that the existing BEx tools will be discontinued. BEx tools are still part of the SAP BW roadmap and are used where SAP BusinessObjects BI isn't available. The implementation of SAP BusinessObjects reporting tools along with SAP BW is optional and simply offers a premium reporting alternative to BEx tools.

13.6.1 SAP BusinessObjects Analysis, Edition for Microsoft Office

This tool allows users to perform reporting and multi-dimensional analysis on one or more data providers in an Excel interface, allowing them to create Excel-based analytical and integrated planning applications. The client software has to be installed for each user to use this tool. A separate ANALYSIS toolbar is available in Excel as an add-in (❶ of Figure 13.16).

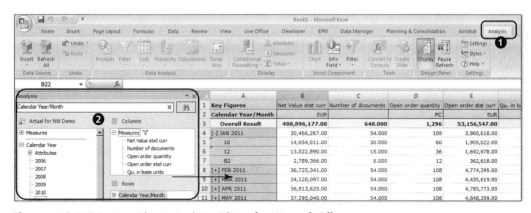

Figure 13.16 SAP BusinessObjects Analysis, Edition for Microsoft Office

The Excel edition is particularly popular because it works within a format that is quite familiar to analysts. It can connect to one or more data sources from more than one source system. With fields from the data sources (❷ of Figure 13.16), users can build their own analysis application that can include multiple cross-tabs, fields, conditions, local calculations, and so on. This analysis workbook, similar to a BEx Analyzer workbook, can be saved, shared, and reused. You can also publish this analysis in PowerPoint, meaning that presentations can have analysis embedded into them with a live connection to data sources.

SAP BusinessObjects Analysis can connect directly to SAP BW InfoProviders and BEx queries leveraging the native BICS connectivity. For the Microsoft Office edition, the connection with SAP BW can be directly managed through SAP GUI. Otherwise, if the SAP BusinessObjects BI platform is installed, it can also be used to connect to SAP BW InfoProviders and BEx queries (see Figure 13.17).

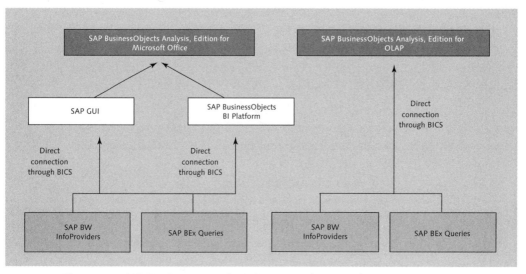

Figure 13.17 SAP BW Connectivity for SAP BusinessObjects Analysis

13.6.2 SAP BusinessObjects Analysis, Edition for OLAP

SAP BusinessObjects Analysis, Edition for OLAP, is the web-based version for performing interactive multi-dimensional analysis. Unlike the Microsoft Office version, this tool doesn't require that any client software be installed. An ideal option for web-based analysis, it enables end users to perform hierarchical reporting, cross-tab reporting, graphical analysis, conditional reporting, filters, and so on (see Figure 13.18).

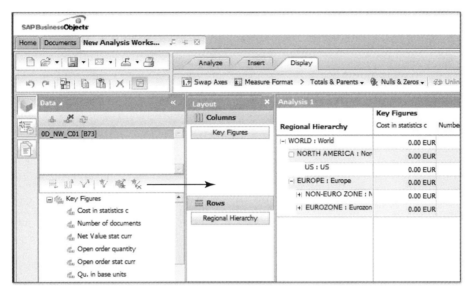

Figure 13.18 SAP BusinessObjects Analysis, Edition for OLAP

The UI for this product is intuitive, and most of the navigations can be performed using drag and drop. You can also include data from multiple sources and systems in one single analysis and view the results together.

The OLAP edition can connect directly to SAP BW InfoProviders and BEx queries using the direct BICS connectivity. In Chapter 9, we mentioned that to use BEx Web Analyzer, you need BI Java (a component of SAP Enterprise Portal) to be installed. In the case of SAP BusinessObjects Analysis, Edition for OLAP, there is no dependency on the BI Java usage type; thus, this tool can be an option for web-based SAP BW reporting when BI Java isn't available.

13.7 SAP BusinessObjects Design Studio

SAP BusinessObjects Design Studio is positioned in the SAP BusinessObjects product suite to create web-based analysis and planning applications. This tool comes with a repository of prebuilt design components (e.g., buttons, tabs, radio buttons) that can be used to create a web application.

It can be compared with BEx Web Application Designer in terms of positioning, but SAP BusinessObjects Design Studio offers far more flexibility and ease in terms of design, development, and deployment of web applications.

The UI for this tool is based on HTML5 technology, and the design environment offers a what you see is what you get (WYSIWYG) interface. It makes tasks like setting the visual layout of a web application and formatting the components a lot easier. Apart from the available design components, it's also possible to build a custom functionality using the script functions, if needed.

The applications created using SAP BusinessObjects Design Studio can be deployed on web browsers and mobile devices.

Similar to SAP BusinessObjects Analysis, Edition for OLAP, this product can also connect directly with SAP BW queries and InfoProviders leveraging BICS connectivity (refer to Figure 13.17).

13.8   SAP BusinessObjects Explorer

So far we've seen a few tools from the SAP BusinessObjects BI reporting portfolio that address varied reporting needs. In some cases, users are aware of what they're looking for and begin using the report that provides answers to their specific question. But quite often, users don't have any specific question in mind or have a completely ad hoc question. SAP BusinessObjects Explorer is probably the most suitable tool for such a situation. It allows users to explore large volumes of data with complete flexibility. It also allows users to pursue any ad hoc reporting need that they can address themselves using SAP BusinessObjects Explorer.

The SAP BW InfoProviders that are available in SAP BW Accelerator (BWA) can be accessed through SAP BusinessObjects Explorer. Specific dimensions and measures that need be exposed to end users are included in a logical component called *Information Spaces* (see Figure 13.19).

Data is made available to users via these Information Spaces. To facilitate ad hoc analysis, this tool also comes with an intelligent search feature that allows users to find any specific measure, characteristic, or other parameter from the available Information Spaces in SAP BusinessObjects Explorer.

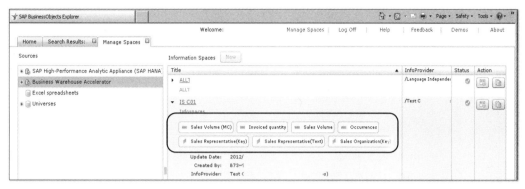

Figure 13.19 SAP BusinessObjects Explorer Information Spaces

SAP BusinessObjects Explorer connects directly with SAP BW InfoProviders that are in-memory in BWA (ACCELERATED DATA in Figure 13.20). For SAP BW powered by SAP HANA, all InfoProviders are in-memory and thus are available in SAP BusinessObjects Explorer. This enables users to explore huge volumes of data quickly.

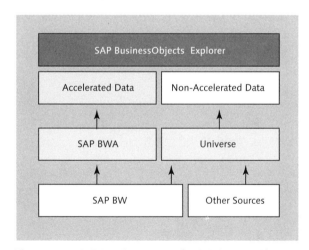

Figure 13.20 SAP BW Connectivity for SAP BusinessObjects Explorer

InfoProviders that aren't in BWA can also be made available to SAP BusinessObjects Explorer through the universe layer. Users can achieve this by creating a universe using the IDT on a SAP BW InfoProvider and then creating an Information Space on that universe.

Minimal training is required to use this tool because of its intuitive interface. In addition to ad hoc analysis and data exploration capabilities, the availability of this tool on mobile devices (smart phones, tablets) makes it a popular choice among end users.

13.9   SAP Lumira

SAP Lumira is a reporting tool that enables users to build data visualizations through an intuitive interface. End users can report on the data from diverse sources such as SAP BW, SAP HANA models, SAP BusinessObjects universes, and so on. SAP Lumira can also be used to connect directly with local DataSources such as flat files. This tool empowers end users to combine the enterprise data with local data and then perform local transformations on that data (e.g., adding new calculations, cleansing the data, etc.). This data is then used with ease to generate powerful infographics.

Visualizations created using SAP Lumira can be shared for collaboration via email or can also be published on the SAP BusinessObjects BI platform.

13.10   SAP BusinessObjects BI Launch Pad

In the previous sections, we introduced the SAP BusinessObjects BI reporting tools. The BI LAUNCH PAD screen acts as a self-service portal that provides a single point of access to all of these reporting tools (❶ of Figure 13.21).

Through the BI LAUNCH PAD screen, it's possible to create content using these reporting tools and manage it from one single place; users can work on different tools simultaneously using the tabbed browsing (❷ of Figure 13.21). Because content created from all of these tools is accessible from the BI LAUNCH PAD screen, users can search the repository to locate desired content ❸. Users can also create their own content by grouping components created from different tools into one single page. For example, a dashboard and an SAP BusinessObjects Web Intelligence report can be displayed together as user-defined custom content. This is called a *BI Workspace* (not to be confused with BW Workspaces, which we discussed in Chapter 10).

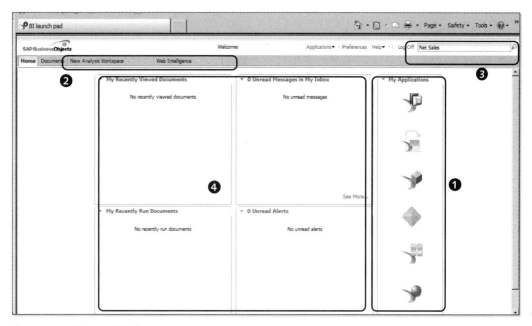

Figure 13.21 BI Launch Pad

The BI LAUNCH PAD screen provides a snapshot of recent user activity, such as recently accessed reports or documents. It also allows users to centrally manage the alerts and messages related to all the tools ❹. Use of the BI LAUNCH PAD screen provides ease of access to reporting tools and also promotes end-user empowerment toward content creation and management.

13.11 Summary

In this chapter, we gave you an overview of the spectrum of reporting tools available under the SAP BusinessObjects BI portfolio. We saw that each of these tools comes with a unique value proposition and use case. Various factors, such as information delivery mechanism, data presentation, and target audience, influence the decision to choose a particular tool—and a detailed discussion of these factors is necessary before making a selection. All of these tools can also be connected to SAP BW; as such, an enterprise-level BI solution can also be a combination of SAP BW and SAP BusinessObjects BI. In this case, SAP BW acts as a data warehouse, and SAP BusinessObjects reporting tools serve as frontend tools for information consumption. SAP BusinessObjects also comes with the BI Launch Pad, which acts as a single point of access to all of these reporting tools and allows users to manage content seamlessly.

Having covered the reporting aspects of SAP BW in this and the past few chapters, we now move on to discuss SAP BW administration and monitoring tasks.

In this chapter, we introduce some of the basic administration and maintenance aspects of SAP BW. Understanding these concepts will help you maximize efficiency when using the SAP BW solution.

14 Administration and Monitoring

A BI solution is only successful when it lives up to its purpose of delivering the right information at the right time by consuming the right amount of resources—consistently. Administration and maintenance activities ensure that a solution lives up to its purpose with minimal total cost of ownership (TCO) and high reliability in data quality and information security.

In this chapter, we cover the following topics related to administration and maintenance of SAP BW:

▶ DataStore Object (DSO) administration and maintenance

▶ InfoCube administration and maintenance

▶ Aggregates

▶ Compression

▶ Process chains

▶ Analysis authorizations

We conclude the chapter with a section that offers a quick summary of a few other administration and maintenance tasks.

> **Note**
>
> In addition to reading this chapter, we recommend that you consult the related reference material listed in Chapter 2 of this book.

14.1 DataStore Object Administration and Maintenance

Administration and maintenance tasks for data targets (both DSOs and Info-Cubes) are well organized in the DATA WAREHOUSE WORKBENCH screen by the use of buttons, icons, and tabs. This section provides an overview of the main tasks involved in DSO maintenance and performance improvement.

14.1.1 Manage InfoProvider Screen Tasks

Use Transaction RSA1 to reach the DATA WAREHOUSE WORKBENCH screen, and choose INFOPROVIDER within the MODELING tab on the left panel (❶ of Figure 14.1). Then choose SALES DOCUMENT DSO on the right panel ❷.

Figure 14.1 Managing a DSO

Click on the MANAGE option in the context menu ❸, and the MANAGE INFOPROVIDER screen appears (Figure 14.2). The upper part has the details of the InfoProvider, and the lower part has three tabs: CONTENTS, REQUESTS, and RECONSTRUCTION (❶ of Figure 14.2). The lowest part of the screen in each tab has relevant options for executing administration and maintenance tasks ❸.

We explain each of these three tabs next.

Figure 14.2 Administration Tasks for a DSO

Contents Tab

Viewing the contents of a DSO is one of the most regular tasks in its administration. As you know, a standard DSO has three different tables: the activation queue (new data) table, the active data table, and the change log table. The contents in these vary, and viewing it helps in the reconciliation of any reporting errors.

The lower part of the CONTENTS tab (❶ of Figure 14.3) provides buttons that allow you to view different types of content ❷. Click on the button for the chosen table (the NEW DATA button refers to the activation queue), and the system takes you to the DATA BROWSER: TABLE <TECHNICAL NAME> screen ❸. The selection screen contains fields for each of the InfoObjects in the DSO, along with the technical field value options relevant to the type of table. Click on the NUMBER OF ENTRIES button, and the system provides information about the number of entries. To make a complex selection, use the COMPLEX SELECTION icon . Make a selection for different InfoObjects on this screen, and click on the EXECUTE icon to view the contents of the activation queue (new data) table ❹.

The contents of the change log table can be viewed by following the same process (❶ to ❹ in Figure 14.4).

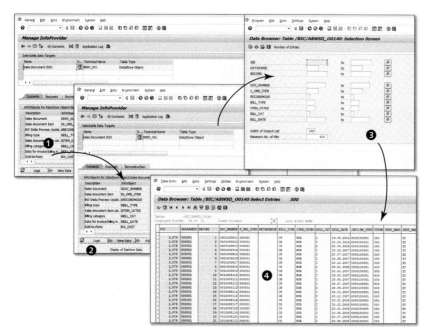

Figure 14.3 Viewing DSO Content: Active Data Table

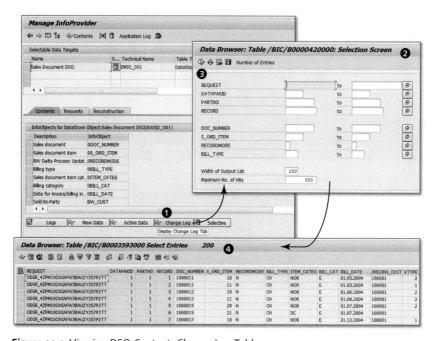

Figure 14.4 Viewing DSO Content: Change Log Table

Requests Tab

In Chapter 4, Section 4.2.2, we explained the process of activating requests in the system at the conceptual level. In this section, we explain the actual execution of the activation of a request in a DSO. This is a regular maintenance task that you perform using the REQUESTS tab (❶ of Figure 14.5).

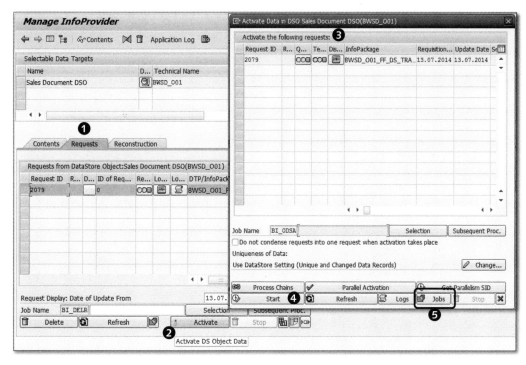

Figure 14.5 Activating a New Request in a DSO

The lower part of the REQUESTS tab has options relevant to executing the activation of requests ❷. Clicking on the ACTIVATE button opens the ACTIVATE DATA IN DSO <TEXT NAME OF DSO> screen, with a list and details of the requests to be activated ❸. In our example, the screen shows request 2079, including its QM and technical status. Select the request, and click on the START button ❹.

The JOBS button ❺ takes you to the SIMPLE JOB SELECTION screen (❶ of Figure 14.6), and the system prepopulates the entry box for the job name with a typical naming convention: BI_ODS <LONG TECHNICAL NAME>.

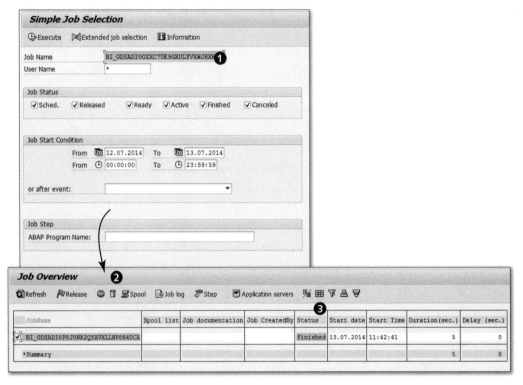

Figure 14.6 Activation Job Overview

To see the status of the activation job, click on the EXECUTE button, which takes you to the JOB OVERVIEW screen ❷. The status of the job can be monitored under the STATUS column ❸ of the table. The REFRESH button on the extreme left of the dynamic menu bar is used to refresh the status of the job. Jobs that are finished are labeled as such and highlighted in green ❸. A FINISHED status indicates that the request has been successfully activated.

Upon successful activation, the status of the request in the REQUESTS tab is reported with changes; see ❶ and ❷ of Figure 14.7 to view the status of request 2079 before and after activation, respectively. The data from the request is now available for reporting.

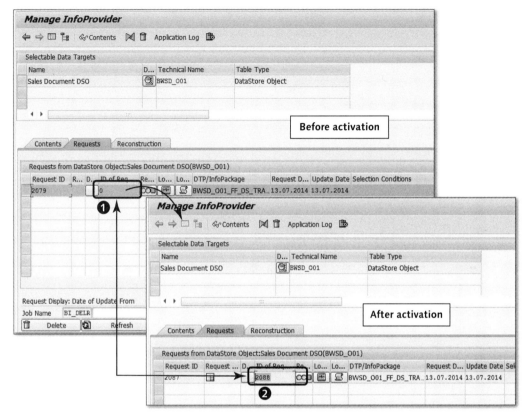

Figure 14.7 Activated Request in a DSO

You also have the option to activate multiple requests in one job. To do this, make sure the DO NOT CONDENSE REQUESTS INTO ONE REQUEST WHEN ACTIVATION TAKES PLACE checkbox is deselected. This causes the system to compress multiple requests into one.

When multiple requests are combined into one change log request, the individual request identifier (a separate request ID) is removed, and they appear as one request in the change log table. This necessitates that you delete all of the requests from the DSO that were condensed and activated as one to delete a single request from the DSO. Check the flag (❶ of Figure 14.8) if you require deletion of a single request from the DSO.

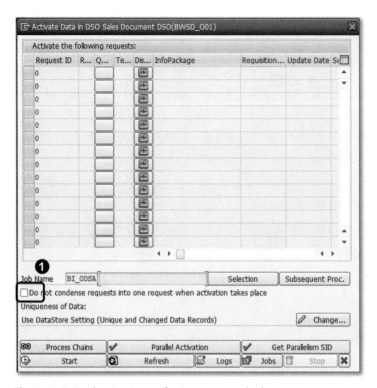

Figure 14.8 Condensing Option for Activating Multiple Requests

Reconstruction Tab

Some requests involve data that requires manual modification or cleansing. To maintain data integrity and consistency, the system doesn't allow any such changes for a single record; instead, the entire request must be deleted from the DSO. After this is done, you can perform data maintenance in the Persistent Staging Area (PSA). Reloading the corrected request from the PSA to the data target is known as *reconstruction* and is managed using the RECONSTRUCTION tab (❶ of Figure 14.9).

Note

The RECONSTRUCTION tab is only relevant for data targets that use the extraction, transformation, and loading (ETL) processes of SAP BW 3.x. It isn't relevant for those using the data transfer process (DTP) for data load.

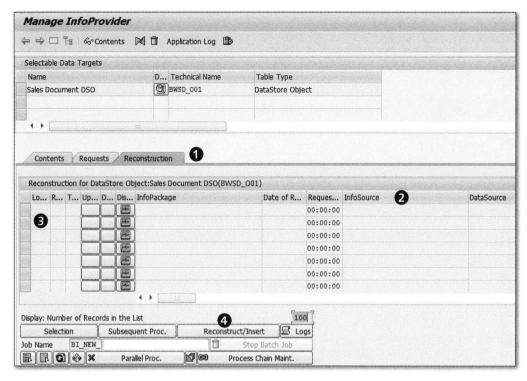

Figure 14.9 Reconstruction of a Request for a DSO

A request is only visible as a row item ❷ in the RECONSTRUCTION tab if it's deleted from the DSO. After deleting the request and making changes in the PSA, select the request ❸, and click on the RECONSTRUCT/INSERT button ❹.

14.1.2 Performance Improvement Tasks

Next we discuss some tasks that will help you improve the performance of the DSOs in your SAP BW system.

Deleting Change Log Data

As time goes by, data in the change log table builds up, negatively impacting activation processes in the system. To delete change log data, follow this menu path: ENVIRONMENT • DELETE CHANGE LOG DATA (❶ and ❷ of Figure 14.10).

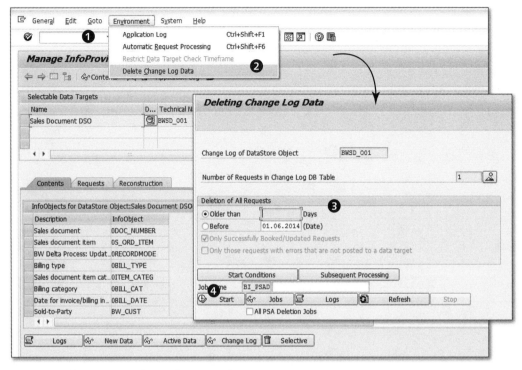

Figure 14.10 Deleting Change Log Data

The DELETING CHANGE LOG DATA screen opens, and you can select what data should be deleted based on how old it is or when it was loaded ❸. After making the selection and starting the conditions for the job, click on the START button ❹.

Automatic Processing of Requests in a DSO

To configure the system to process requests automatically, use the following menu path in the ADMINISTRATION screen of the DSO: ENVIRONMENT • AUTOMATIC REQUEST PROCESSING (❶ and ❷ of Figure 14.11).

The resulting screen ❸ provides options for automatic request processing in the form of flags about data quality, request activation, and loading data to the data target above the DSO ❹. After making your choices, save your changes ❺.

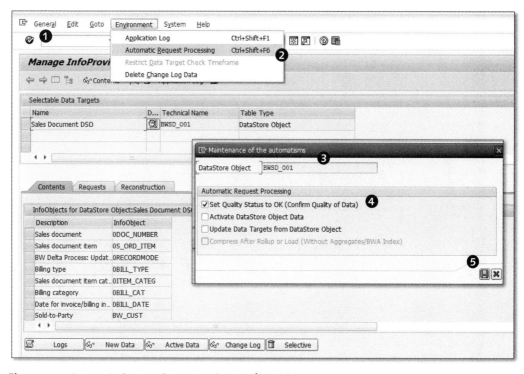

Figure 14.11 Automatic Request Processing Options for a DSO

Note

The administration of a DSO can vary based on its type. We explained the different types of DSOs in Chapter 4, Section 4.1.2.

14.2 InfoCube Administration and Maintenance

Some of the administration tasks performed for an InfoCube are similar to those performed for a DSO, but there are also tasks that are unique to an InfoCube. In this section, we discuss some basic administration and maintenance tasks contained in the MANAGE INFOPROVIDER screen, and then we cover some performance improvement tasks.

14.2.1 Manage InfoProvider Screen Tasks

To open the MANAGE INFOPROVIDER screen, click on the MANAGE option from the context menu of the InfoCube in the DATA WAREHOUSE WORKBENCH screen (Transaction RSA1) (❶, ❷, and ❸ of Figure 14.12).

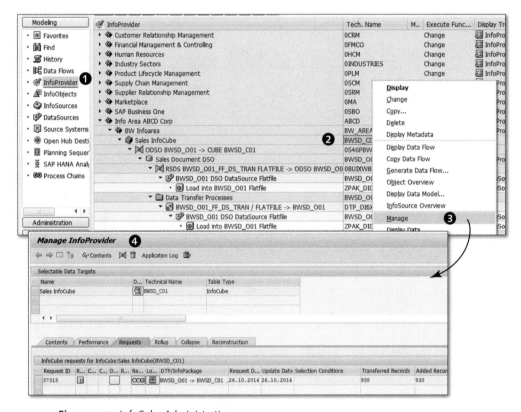

Figure 14.12 InfoCube Administration

The MANAGE INFOPROVIDER screen for the InfoCube has two parts ❹; the upper part contains the details of the InfoCube, and the lower part has six tabs: CONTENTS, PERFORMANCE, REQUESTS, ROLLUP, COLLAPSE, and RECONSTRUCTION. We explain each of these tabs next.

Manage an InfoCube on SAP HANA

If you're on an SAP HANA database, the MANAGE option offers four tabs for an SAP BW on SAP HANA system (i.e., CONTENTS, REQUESTS, COLLAPSE, RECONSTRUCTION).

Contents Tab

The CONTENTS tab (❶ of Figure 14.13) on the MANAGE INFOPROVIDER screen allows you to view the contents of the InfoProvider. This can be helpful in investigation and reconciliation of inaccurate data in reports. You can choose to see contents of the entire InfoCube or only the fact table of the InfoCube by clicking on the appropriate button ❷.

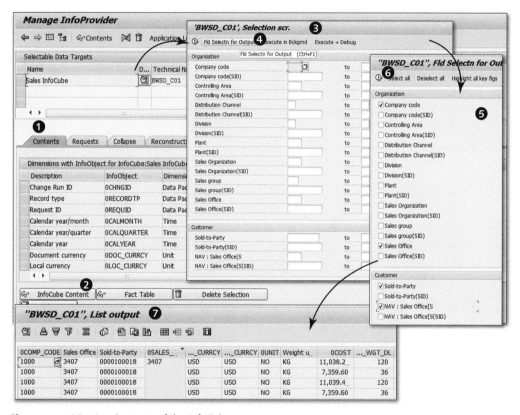

Figure 14.13 Viewing Contents of the InfoCube

When you click on the button for contents, the system takes you to a selection screen ❸ that has entry options for values of InfoObjects for each of the characteristics in the InfoCube. You have the option to choose the details in the output by flagging the appropriate characteristics and key figures ❺. After the selection is made, click on the EXECUTE icon ❻, and the contents of the InfoCube/fact table are displayed ❼.

Performance Tab

The performance-related settings and actions for an InfoCube are maintained on the PERFORMANCE tab (❶ of Figure 14.14). The upper part of the PERFORMANCE tab ❷ provides tools to maintain database indexes and aggregates indexes ❸; the lower part ❹ provides tools for managing database statistics. Optimal performance of an InfoCube is achieved by regular maintenance and updating of the indexes and statistics in a database. We discuss both of these topics next.

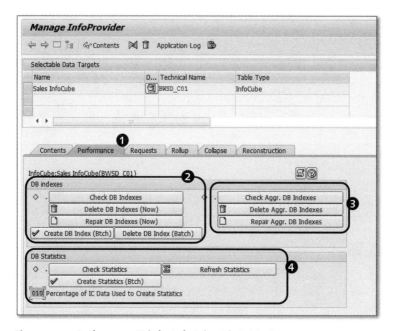

Figure 14.14 Performance Tab for InfoCube Administration

DB Indexes

Building database indexes on an InfoCube helps improve the performance of the queries built on that InfoCube. Within this tab, there are various options (❷ and ❸) that allow you to check and control the status of indexes for the fact tables of both the InfoCube and its aggregates (we explain the concept of aggregates in more detail in Section 14.3):

▶ CHECK DB INDEXES
This checks the status of the indexes on the database and compares it with the index definitions in the dictionary.

- ▷ Green light: This indicates that indexes exist and are correctly defined.

- ▷ Yellow light: This indicates that indexes exist but are the wrong type.

- ▷ Red light: This indicates that either (a) there are no indexes, or (b) there are indexes but they are incorrectly defined.

- ▶ DELETE DB INDEXES (NOW)
  This allows you to delete the available indexes.

- ▶ REPAIR DB INDEXES (NOW)
  This allows you to create missing indexes and repair faulty indexes.

- ▶ CREATE DB INDEX (BTCH)
  This allows you to schedule a background job that creates indexes on the fact table of the InfoCube. You can specify that indexes are deleted/rebuilt with each data load; however, the recommended approach is to manage this through process chains.

- ▶ DELETE DB INDEX (BATCH)
  This allows you to schedule a background job that deletes the indexes.

- ▶ CHECK/DELETE/REPAIR AGGR. DB INDEXES
  These buttons offer the same functionality as the preceding items in this list but are specific to aggregate fact tables.

> **Note**
>
> It's an SAP Best Practice to delete the indexes before loading the data to an InfoCube and then re-create those after the data load is complete. This helps improve the data load performance to that InfoCube.

When query or loading performance is subpar, a simple check of the indexes can help solve the problem.

DB Statistics

A database system can read data for a query from the underlying database table in a number of ways. Some of these are very costly (e.g., reading a large database table sequentially and getting only a few records as output), and others are less so (e.g., using indexes to read the required data very quickly). Because there may be a number of indexes available on the same table, database statistics can help the database optimizer get the optimal execution path for a query. On the other hand, if the statistics aren't up to date, the database optimizer may decide on the wrong path, costing time and resources. As such, one of the important tasks of an SAP BW administrator is to keep the database statistics up to date.

Using the CHECK STATISTICS button (❹ of Figure 14.14), you can check whether the database system has statistics for the InfoCube and whether they are up to date:

▸ Green light: Indicates that database statistics are available and up to date.

▸ Yellow light: Indicates that database statistics are available but not up to date.

▸ Red light: Indicates that database statistics are missing.

You can also control what percentage of InfoCube data should be used to create statistics; normally, it's sufficient to specify only 10% (❹ of Figure 14.14) because the job for creation of statistics consumes a lot of time and resources.

Requests Tab

In the REQUESTS tab (❶ of Figure 14.15), the lower part of the screen shows administration and maintenance task buttons for requests ❷, and the lowest part of the screen provides buttons for execution of these tasks ❸.

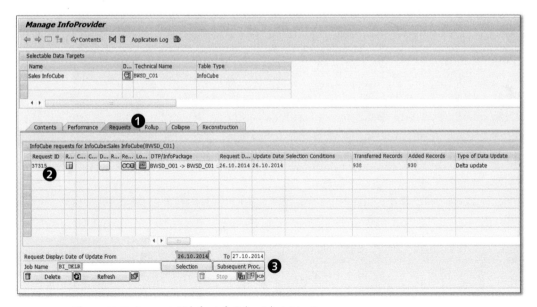

Figure 14.15 Requests Tab for InfoCube Administration

The FROM and TO fields help in limiting the display of requests to a specific period ❸. As you can see, this screen shows request 37315; the green light indicates that it's loaded and available for reporting. In the middle of the screen, columns report the details of the DTP and the date of loading into the InfoCube. The columns on the right report the number of records transferred and added to the InfoCube (938 and 930, respectively).

Rollup Tab

The ROLLUP tab (❶ of Figure 14.16) has buttons that replicate part of the InfoCube data into a summarized subset called an aggregate. We explain the concept of aggregates in more detail in Section 14.3.

The lower part of the ROLLUP tab ❷ now shows options related to rolling up requests into aggregates and other relevant tasks.

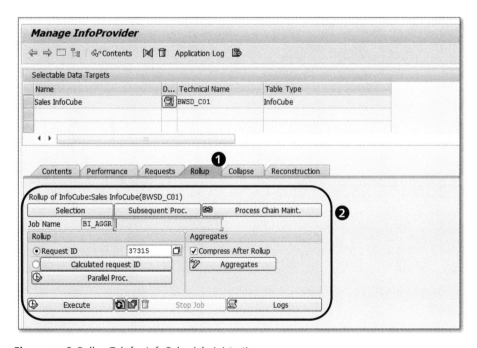

Figure 14.16 Rollup Tab for InfoCube Administration

The lowest part of the screen provides buttons to execute the rollup tasks and monitor the job or to analyze the job log for the rollup activity.

Collapse Tab

The COLLAPSE tab (❶ of Figure 14.17) has buttons that perform compression activities, which move InfoCube data into a summarized table (i.e., moving data from an F table to an E table) and aid in improving loading and reporting performance. We explain the concept of compression in more detail in Section 14.4.

The lower part of the COLLAPSE tab ❷ shows options for carrying out the collapse task, from calculating the request ID to selecting a job and its maintenance in the process chain (see Section 14.5).

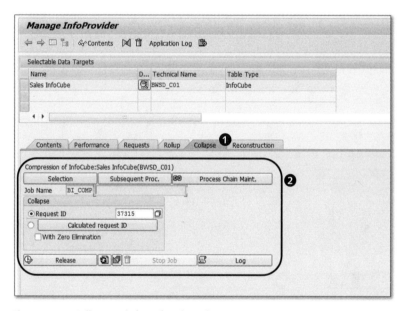

Figure 14.17 Collapse Tab for InfoCube Administration

The lowest part of the screen provides buttons to release and schedule the job for releasing the collapse activity, to monitor the collapse job, and to analyze the job log for compression activity.

Reconstruction Tab

The RECONSTRUCTION tab (❶ of Figure 14.18) in the MANAGE INFOPROVIDER screen of an InfoCube offers exactly the same options and functions as in a DSO. As a reminder, this tab is relevant for those data targets that use ETL processes of SAP BW 3.x.

A request is only visible as a row item ❷ in the RECONSTRUCTION tab if it's deleted from the InfoCube. After deleting the request and making changes in the PSA, select the request ❷, and click on the RECONSTRUCT/INSERT button ❸.

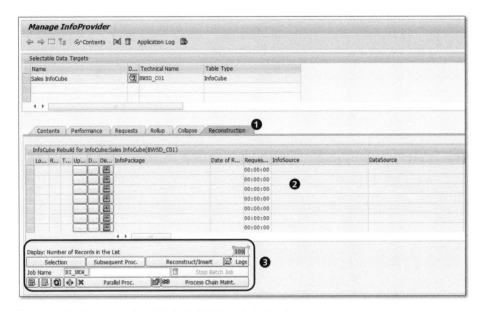

Figure 14.18 Reconstruction Tab for InfoCube Administration

14.2.2 Performance Improvement Tasks

One of the main ways to improve performance in InfoCubes is to automate request processing. Choose the following menu path within the administration screen of the InfoCube: ENVIRONMENT • AUTOMATIC REQUEST PROCESSING (❶ and ❷ of Figure 14.19). The resulting pop-up box ❸ allows you to set flags related to data quality, rollup, and compression of requests ❹.

Table 14.1 summarizes the main administration and maintenance tasks and their applicability to the specific data targets.

	Contents	Performance	Requests	Rollup	Collapse	Reconstruction
DSO	✓		✓			✓
InfoCube	✓	✓	✓	✓	✓	✓

Table 14.1 Summary of Administration and Maintenance Tasks for DSOs and InfoCubes

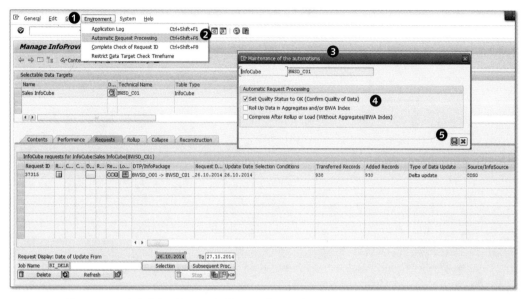

Figure 14.19 InfoCube: Automatic Request Processing

Now that we've covered administration and maintenance tasks for DSOs and InfoCubes, let's move on to the concept of aggregates, their relevance to performance improvement, and their management.

14.3 Aggregates

An *aggregate* is an object that stores a summarized subset of data in an InfoCube, grouped by a specific set of selected characteristics. When an appropriate aggregate for an InfoCube exists, summarized data can be read directly from the database during query execution, instead of having to perform this summarization during runtime. Aggregates generate the following direct benefits:

- Reduction in the volume of data to be read from the database
- Improvement of query execution time
- Reduction of overall load on the database during query execution

When you load data into an InfoCube, you must also load the data into aggregates; this is known as the *rollup* process. Without rollup, the data loaded in the InfoCube isn't available for reporting. The OLAP processor ignores requests that aren't rolled up into an aggregate to maintain reporting integrity.

On one hand, aggregates are the best option for boosting query performance because they reduce most of the processing time needed for aggregating the data read from the database. However, if they aren't created correctly, they can actually inhibit performance, due to the rollup process and realignment run (see Section 14.7.1 for more details on realignment runs).

> **Note**
>
> Aggregates aren't relevant or available when you have an SAP BW powered by SAP HANA system, because the data is available in-memory. Therefore, the option to create an aggregate isn't available.

There are multiple options for identifying and creating aggregates, such as manual creation or the use of the AGGREGATE button (which is found in the ROLLUP tab in the MANAGE INFOPROVIDER screen of an InfoCube; refer to Figure 14.16). In this section, we focus on manual creation of aggregates. To begin, choose MAINTAIN AGGREGATES from the context menu of the InfoCube (❶ and ❷ of Figure 14.20). If there are no aggregates defined for this InfoCube, the PROPOSALS FOR AGGREGATES pop-up box appears ❸. You can select GENERATE PROPOSALS for the system to propose aggregates, or you can click on the CREATE BY YOURSELF option to manually create the aggregate ❹.

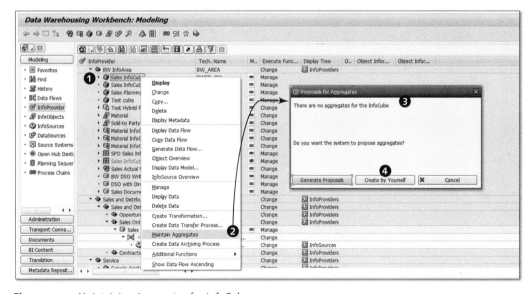

Figure 14.20 Maintaining Aggregates for InfoCubes

The system takes you to the maintenance screen for aggregates, which has two panels; the left panel shows the dimensions, characteristics, and navigation attributes of the selected InfoCube (❶ of Figure 14.21). From the dynamic menu bar, click on the CREATE NEW AGGREGATE icon 🗖. In the ENTER DESCRIPTION FOR AGGREGATE pop-up box ❷, enter the short and long description ❸ for the aggregate. Click on the CONTINUE icon ❹ to return to the MAINTAIN AGGREGATES screen ❺.

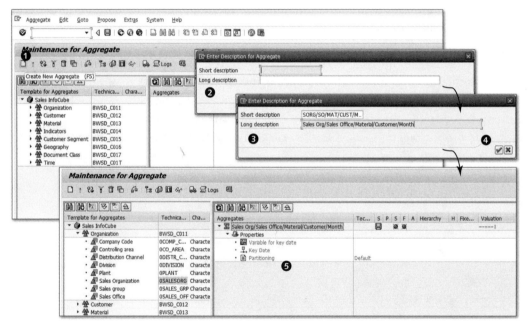

Figure 14.21 Creating an Aggregate

By clicking on the EXPAND icon ▶ to the left of the aggregate name (on the right panel), the properties for the aggregate are visible (❶ in Figure 14.22). On the left panel, all characteristics are available within their respective dimensions. For the purpose of explanation, we select the ORGANIZATION dimension; click on the EXPAND icon to open the SALES ORGANIZATION dimension, and all of the characteristics that are part of this dimension for InfoCube BWSD_C011 ❷ are listed.

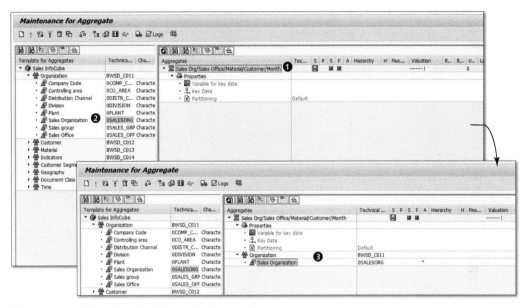

Figure 14.22 Adding Characteristics to the Aggregate

Drag and drop the 0SALESORG characteristic (in the left panel) into the SUMMA-TION icon ∑ at the top of the right panel. 0SALESORG and the organization dimension are added to the aggregate definition ❸. Repeat the drag-and-drop process for the remaining characteristics 0SALES_OFF, 0MATERIAL, BW_CUST, and 0CALMONTH. These characteristics and their respective dimensions are added to the aggregate definition.

Business requirements might call for analysis to determine whether an aggregate is needed for specific values of characteristics. For example, assume a specific group of users always runs the query for Sales Organization = Europe. In this case, the sales organization characteristic should be restricted to a fixed value of Europe in the aggregate. To do this, choose the option FIXED VALUE from the context menu of the characteristic in the aggregate definition (❶ of Figure 14.23), and select EUROPE from the list in the pop-up box. However, our scenario doesn't need to have a fixed value, so we don't use the option.

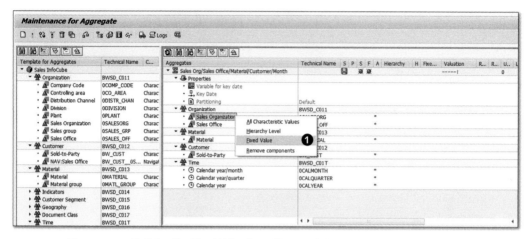

Figure 14.23 Defining the Fixed Value for a Characteristic in an Aggregate

Having defined the aggregate, you now need to check the definition of the aggregate for accuracy. Click on the CHECK icon (❶ of Figure 14.24).

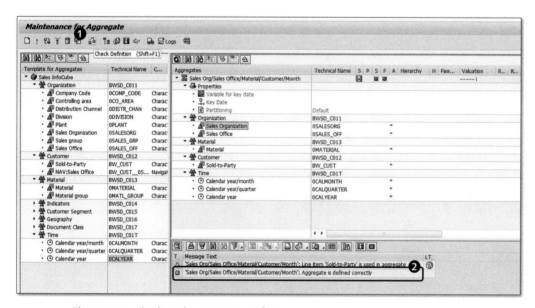

Figure 14.24 Checking the Aggregate Definition

The lower-right panel reports any messages that result from the process; a green light indicates that the aggregate has been defined correctly ❷. A correctly defined aggregate is like an empty box and isn't used by queries; it's just the definition for summarizing the subset of an InfoCube, and there's no data inside it.

Activation of the aggregate fills the aggregate with data from the InfoCube. To do this, click on the aggregate on the right panel, and then click on the ACTIVATE AND FILL icon on the dynamic menu bar (❶ of Figure 14.25). A pop-up box appears ❷; place the cursor on the row with the text definition of the aggregate ❸, and click on the START icon ❹.

Another pop-up box appears that gives you the options for when to time the execution of filling the aggregate ❺. The aggregation job can be started immediately by clicking on the IMMEDIATE button, or it can be started later by clicking on the LATER button ❻. In our example, we choose IMMEDIATE. After the job is complete, the status bar and log section indicate this with a message. An aggregate (with a technical name allocated by the system) is created for InfoCube BWSD_C01; as you can see, the resulting screen shows green boxes (❶ of Figure 14.26) as well as details about the valuation of the aggregate.

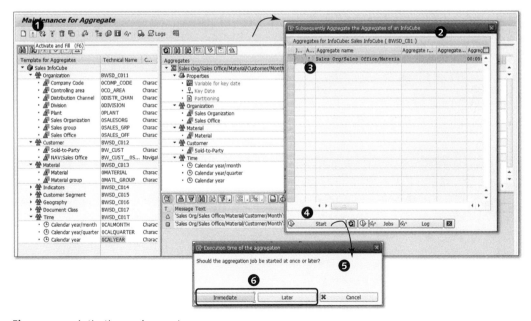

Figure 14.25 Activating an Aggregate

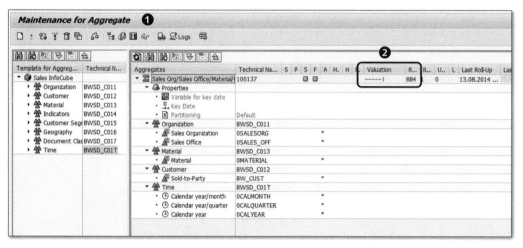

Figure 14.26 Valuation of Aggregates

The system evaluates aggregates using plus and minus signs (❷ in Figure 14.26); five plus signs (+++++) indicate the highest valuation, whereas five minus signs (-----) indicate the lowest valuation. Valuation is a good indicator for whether an aggregate is likely to serve its purpose in performance improvement, but it should not be the only factor to conclude whether you keep or delete an aggregate. (For more information on this, we recommend *Performance Optimization for SAP BW* (Shiralkar and Sawant [Espresso Tutorials, 2015].) One of the parameters for this valuation is the level of summarization, which can be checked in the RECORD SUMMARIZES column. The value here indicates how many records of the InfoCube (on average) correspond to the number of records in that aggregate. For a good aggregate, this value should be 10 or more.

After the aggregate is created and activated, the information for the InfoCube gets added to it. Compare the details in the OBJECT INFORMATION for InfoCube BWSD_C01—both before the aggregate is created (Figure 14.20) and then again after the aggregate is created. Note that the SUM icon is now visible for InfoCube BWSD_C01 (❶ of Figure 14.27).

Now compare the REQUESTS tab for InfoCube BWSD_C01 (Figure 14.15) with the same tab in Figure 14.27, and you'll notice that there are additional details reported ❷. To maintain integrity in reporting, the new InfoCube data isn't available for reporting until the request is successfully rolled up into all of the aggregates for the cube. After a successful rollup, the request record in the REQUESTS tab for the InfoCube will be marked with the OK status ☑.

Figure 14.27 InfoCube with Aggregate

14.4 Compression

The process of consolidating data loaded in the InfoCube after removing the request ID dimension is called *compression*. As the technical identifier is removed, multiple records are consolidated (or compressed) together. However, because request ID is the technical identifier for the data loaded, its removal in the compression process results in the loss of the ability to identify individual requests in an InfoCube. In other words, compression makes it impossible to delete individual requests from the compressed data in the InfoCube.

Request ID

The SAP BW system creates a new request ID whenever new data is loaded into an Info-Cube. If all data in a previously loaded request must be deleted, you can identify the data from an InfoCube with the help of the request ID. Although the request ID is helpful in identifying data, it also hampers the performance of a query.

The request ID is part of the data packet dimension, which is automatically created by the system when you create an InfoCube. The key of the fact table is a combination of all the dimension keys; so, in this way, the request ID is also a part of the fact table key. Request IDs are automatically generated by the system during extraction.

When new data is loaded into an InfoCube, it is first loaded into the F fact table of the InfoCube. Compressing the requests moves the data from the F fact table to the E fact table; in doing so, the system also sets the request ID to 0 and creates a single record from multiple records with the same combination of the remaining characteristics (Figure 14.28). When the request is successfully compressed, data for the compressed requests is deleted from the F fact table.

F - Table

Request ID	Customer	Material	CALMONTH	Quantity
19623	100050	20000	200601	200
19623	100050	30000	200601	300
19623	100050	50000	200601	500
19623	100200	20000	200601	220
19623	100200	30000	20(	Before Compression
19623	100200	60000	20(	
19640	100050	20000	200601	400
19640	100050	30000	200601	600
19640	100050	50000	200601	1000
19640	100200	20000	200601	440
19640	100200	30000	200601	660
19640	100200	60000	200601	1320

E - Table

Customer	Material	CALMONTH	Quantity
100050	20000	200601	600
100050	30000	20(	After Compression
100050	50000	20(	
100200	20000	200601	660
100200	30000	200601	990
100200	60000	200601	1980

* 12 records of F-Table compressed to 6 records in E-Table

Figure 14.28 Compression of Requests in an InfoCube

The advantage to compression is that a query has to read significantly fewer records; additionally, in relational database management systems (RDBMSs) that support physical partitioning, you can partition the E fact table according to time criteria. (For more information about partitioning, we recommend *Performance Optimization for SAP BW* (Shiralkar and Sawant [Espresso Tutorials, 2015].) The disadvantage is that request identifiers are lost, and you no longer identify or delete data pertaining to a specific request.

The data in an InfoCube can be compressed from the COLLAPSE tab on the MANAGE INFOPROVIDER screen (refer to Figure 14.17). Enter the request number in the REQUEST ID field; all requests previous to this one (and including this one) will be compressed. Click on the RELEASE button to start compression.

It isn't mandatory to compress all requests in an InfoCube, but we suggest doing so to improve performance and manage data storage space. You can also partially compress, depending on the frequency with which you're required to process the deletion of data from the InfoCube. After a request is successfully loaded into an InfoCube, and you know that it won't need to be deleted, you can compress it.

Compression improves loading performance and makes for faster aggregate rebuilding, although the reduction ratio between the number of records in the F table and E table depends on the granularity of data and the frequency of loading to the InfoCube. For example, if you've included characteristics such as document number, customer, material, and calendar day, the frequency of loading is once a day, so there won't be much reduction in records.

> **Compression: SAP BW Powered by SAP HANA**
>
> When you have an SAP BW powered by SAP HANA system, an InfoCube does not create two different fact tables (E and F). An InfoCube in an SAP BW powered by SAP HANA system has only one fact table, and a compression activity is available. In this case, the fact table is internally partitioned by the system. One partition keeps an uncompressed request while the other stores all the compressed requests. As explained earlier, during the compression process, the system moves data from one partition to another and also makes the Request ID = 0. There are two other partitions, but they are only relevant for noncumulative InfoCubes. These partitions are used by other processes to help improve system performance.

14.5 Process Chains

Recall that one of ABCD Corp.'s requirements was to implement automated process control, including the establishment of email alerts for occurrences of successes or failures in systemic processes. In this section, we discuss how that can be done using *process chains*.

Process chains are used extensively to automate most administration and monitoring tasks, such as transactional and master data loads, or index and statistic rebuilds. A process chain is a group of processes or system jobs that are linked together. Each process has a defined beginning point and end point, and the linkages between processes have a predetermined sequence that is governed by interdependent conditions assigned to a system-generated event. During execution, each process waits for the predecessor to complete based on the dependency assigned. Process chains can send email alerts based on events in the system, which makes management more efficient and eliminates mundane and manual efforts.

A typical process chain consists of a start process, individual application processes, and collectors. The *start process* defines the start of a process chain; other chain processes are scheduled to wait for a systemic event. *Application processes* refer to actual processes; they represent SAP BW activities that are typically performed as part of SAP BW operations. For example:

▶ Data load

▶ Attribute/hierarchy change run

▶ Aggregate rollup

▶ Reporting agent settings

Application processes also include custom ABAP programs that you can implement in your system; additionally, you can include process chains as processes in another process chain.

Finally, *collectors* are used to manage multiple processes that feed into one subsequent process. The collectors available for SAP BW are listed here:

▶ **AND**
All of the processes that are direct predecessors must send an event for subsequent processes to be executed.

▶ **OR**
At least one predecessor process must send an event. The first predecessor process that sends an event triggers the subsequent process.

▶ **EXOR (Exclusive Or)**
Similar to regular OR, but there is only *one* execution of the successor processes, even if several predecessor processes raise an event.

In this section, we explain the creation of a simple process chain and then the creation of email alerts related to that process chain.

14.5.1 Creating a Process Chain

Here we explain the creation of a simple process chain for automating transactional data, from the extraction of billing data from an SAP source system, to the loading process culminating in InfoCube BWSD_C01. To begin, you must first create the sequence of tasks you want the system to automatically process:

1. Start the process at 7:00am.

2. Execute the InfoPackage for extracting the delta load for the billing data from the source system.

3. Execute the DTP for loading the data from the PSA into BWSD_O01.

4. Activate the newly loaded request in BWSD_O01.

5. Delete indexes for BWSD_C01.

6. Execute the DTP for loading the data from the DSO (BWSD_O01) to the Info-Cube (DSO BWSD_C01). Send an email alert if the data load fails.

7. Create indexes for BWSD_C01.

8. Roll up the request into the aggregate.

SAP has developed more than 50 predefined standard process variants that you can use to develop process chains. Table RSPROCESSTYPES provides a view of all process types and specific attributes important to understanding how process types work.

Process chains are created using the process chain configuration utility, which you can find via Transaction RSPC or by clicking on the chain-link icon that appears on the menu bar in the DATA WAREHOUSE WORKBENCH screen. The process chain utility offers a planning view, a checking view, and a monitoring view, which allow you to build, check/test, and monitor process chains in real-time, respectively.

Choose the PROCESS CHAIN MAINTENANCE icon from the DATA WAREHOUSE WORK-BENCH screen toolbar, or use Transaction RSPC. The system takes you to the PROCESS CHAIN DISPLAY PLANNING VIEW screen (❶ of Figure 14.29). All of the existing process chains are listed here and organized under DISPLAY COMPONENT ❷. To create a new display component, select CREATE DISPLAY COMPONENT from the context menu ❷. The new display component requires a unique name and description; enter "BW_DC001" as the name in the APPLICATION COMP. field ❸ and "BW Display Component 001" as the LONG DESCRIPTION ❹. The newly created display component is now available ❺.

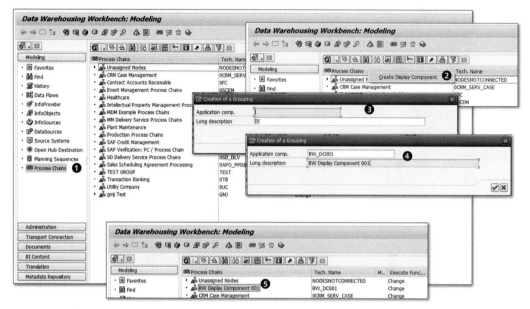

Figure 14.29 Creating a New Process Chain

You're back to the main screen of the process chain. Select display component BW_DC001, and then select CREATE PROCESS CHAIN from the context menu (❷ of 14.30). The NEW PROCESS CHAIN pop-up box is displayed ❸. Each process chain requires a unique name and description; enter the following ❹:

▶ PROCESS CHAIN: "BW_LOAD_BWSD_C01"

▶ LONG DESCRIPTION: "Load Data Into BWSD_C01"

Click on CONTINUE to confirm the inputs, and the system automatically opens a pop-up box for inserting a start process ❺. Click on the CREATE icon, and enter the following ❻:

▶ PROCESS VARIANTS: "START_BW_LOAD001"

▶ LONG DESCRIPTION: "Start Loading to BWSD_C01"

Click on the CONTINUE icon to confirm the entries. The system takes you to the MAINTAIN START PROCESS screen (❶ of Figure 14.31). The MAINTAIN START PROCESS screen has two radio buttons: DIRECT SCHEDULING and START USING META CHAIN OR API ❷.

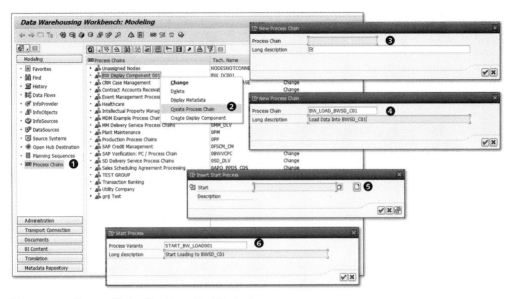

Figure 14.30 Process Chain: Creating a Start Variant

Figure 14.31 Process Chain: Maintaining the Start Process

There are also buttons that help you set the start time ❸; like any system job, there are multiple options for this ❹. When you finish choosing the appropriate settings, save your changes, and use the BACK icon to return to the PROCESS CHAIN MAINTENANCE screen. The panel on the right should now display the start process (Figure 14.32).

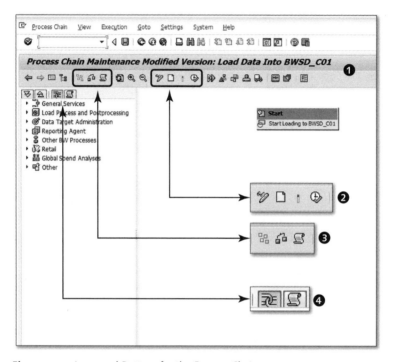

Figure 14.32 Icons and Buttons for the Process Chain

The dynamic menu bar on the screen (❶ of Figure 14.32) has icons for editing, creating, activating, and scheduling a process chain ❷, as well as icons for choosing the view of a process chain ❸. Click on the PROCESS TYPES icon 🎓 ❹. The left panel displays the list of all process types. The first process we want to execute is for data extraction from a source system; from the left panel, choose the EXECUTE INFOPACKAGE process type (❶ of Figure 14.33).

Drag and drop this process into the right panel; the INSERT EXECUTE INFOPACKAGE pop-up box appears ❷, as does another pop-up box with a list of all InfoPackages ❸. Select the BILLING DOCUMENT DATA/DELTA DataSource ❹, and click on the CONTINUE icon ❺ to confirm the selection. INSERT EXECUTE INFOPACKAGE has an

entry with the technical ID for the DataSource; confirm by clicking on the CON-
TINUE icon ❻. The right panel now has the START process item and the LOAD DATA
item (Figure 14.34).

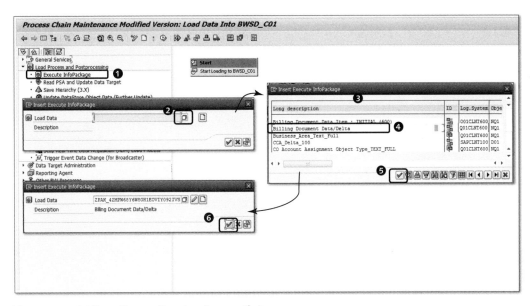

Figure 14.33 Adding a Process Type in a Process Chain

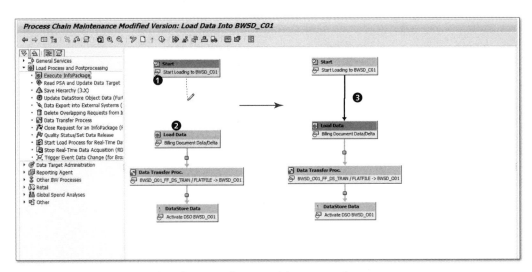

Figure 14.34 Establishing a Linkage between Elements of the Process Chain

To link the two processes for establishing the sequence, click on Start Process Chain (❶ of Figure 14.34), and drag the cursor down. A pencil with a dotted line appears on the screen ❷; drag the cursor to the Load Data box, and the system establishes a sequence ❸.

Repeat this process for all of the steps we listed at the beginning of this section.

14.5.2 Setting Email Alerts

We must also set up emails that alert solution administrators to the failure of a data load between the DSO and InfoCube. To do this, select the DTP item in the process chain that is responsible for loading the data from DSO BWSD_O01 to InfoCube BWSD_C01 (❶ of Figure 14.35). Open the context menu, and select Create Message ❷.

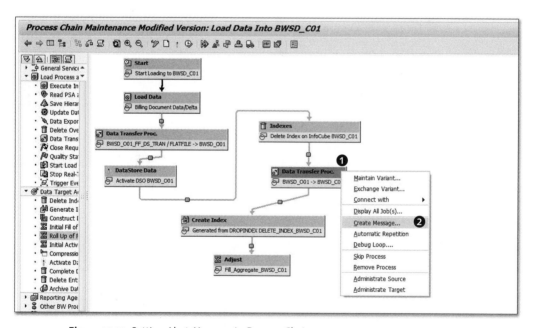

Figure 14.35 Setting Alert Message in Process Chains

In the Action For pop-up box, select the Errors radio button (❷ of Figure 14.36), and click on the Continue icon. In the Insert Send Message box ❸, you can choose an existing message from the dropdown list, or create a new one by clicking on the CREATE icon ❸. Now a SEND MESSAGE box appears, which has two fields. Enter the following ❹:

► PROCESS VARIANTS: "ERROR_MSG_BWSD_O01_C01"

► LONG DESCRIPTION: "Error Message Loading from DSO BWSD_O01 to InfoCube BWSD_C01"

Confirm the entries by clicking on the CONTINUE icon. The system opens the PROCESS MAINTENANCE: SEND MESSAGE screen ❺.

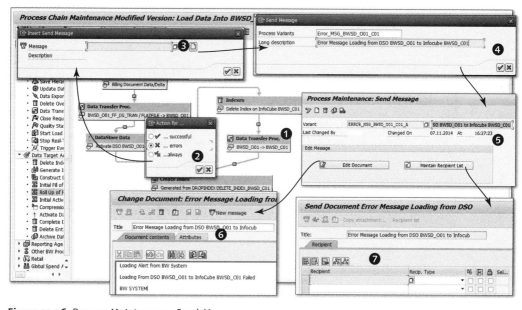

Figure 14.36 Process Maintenance: Send Message

The screen has two buttons: EDIT DOCUMENT and MAINTAIN RECIPIENT LIST. Click on EDIT DOCUMENT; the next screen has two tabs: DOCUMENT CONTENTS and ATTRIBUTES. In the DOCUMENT CONTENTS tab, type the text of the message ❻.

Save your changes, and use the BACK icon to return to PROCESS MAINTENANCE: SEND MESSAGE ❺. Click on MAINTAIN RECIPIENTS LIST, and the system opens a box where you can enter recipient email addresses and recipient types ❼. Click on the SAVE icon and the BACK icon; your email alert is now configured.

Check your process chain using the CHECK icon 🔍, and make any necessary corrections (i.e., any changes suggested by the system in the log). If there are no errors, save the process chain, and click on the ACTIVATE icon. A new process chain (technical name: BW_LOAD_BWSD_C01; text description: Load data into BWSD_C01) is ready to be scheduled. As you can see, the active process chain matches the steps stated in the beginning of the section (Figure 14.37).

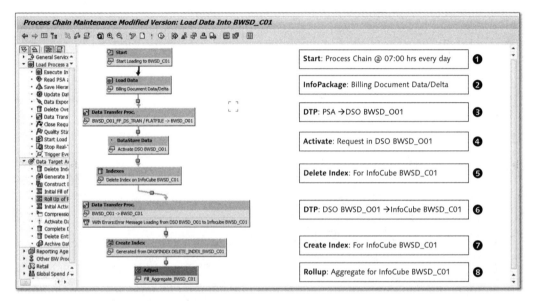

Figure 14.37 Overview of the Process Chain

Now schedule the process chain using the SCHEDULE icon ⊕, which will automate the process of data extraction from the SAP ERP system every day at 7:00am (❶ through ❽ of Figure 14.37).

14.6 Analysis Authorizations

The ABCD Corp.'s IT team requires that users have access to information relevant to their roles and that other users can't access privileged information without specific approval. Information security and authorization in SAP BW is a vast subject, and a full discussion is beyond the scope of this book. In this section, we specifically focus on creating an analysis authorization to meet the specific IT business requirement.

The latest version of SAP BW offers extremely refined information security governance. In general, authorizations relate to a set of authorization objects that ensure information security. There are primarily two classes of authorization in SAP BW: reporting and administration. *Reporting authorization objects* are used for field-level security, and *administration authorization objects* are used to secure administration functions, such as the creation of InfoObjects, the creation of queries, and so on.

For this basic introduction to reporting and analysis authorization, we explain how to do the following:

- Restrict access at a specific InfoCube level, so users won't be able to access any reports based on other objects (e.g., the DSO).

- Restrict access to the characteristics within an InfoCube. This feature ensures that users will be able to analyze data in a report that is based on a specific characteristic, for example, sales manager with user-ID TRAIN1 for 0SALES_OFF value 1422 (Figure 14.38).

Sales Manager	Sales Office	Sales 2009	Sales 2008	YoY Comparison (%)
TRAIN0	1000	Not Authorized	5,504,44	24.11
TRAIN0	1002	Not Authorized	0,472.99	145.13
TRAIN1	**1422**	$30,855.50	$14,072.42	119.26
TRAIN1	**1422**	$22,618.81	$28,826.48	-21.53
TRAIN1	**1422**	$18,974.66	$21,661.73	-12.40
TRAIN3	1421	Not Authorized	3,910.54	1,086.37
TRAIN3	1421	Not Authorized	$0.00	0.00

Figure 14.38 Analysis Authorization Restriction by Characteristics

- Restrict access to a specific node of a hierarchy of a characteristic within an InfoCube, so that users won't be able to view the data for any other node or set of nodes (Figure 14.39).

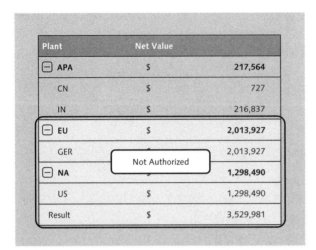

Plant	Net Value	
⊟ APA	$	217,564
CN	$	727
IN	$	216,837
⊟ EU	$	2,013,927
GER		2,013,927
⊟ NA	Not Authorized	1,298,490
US	$	1,298,490
Result	$	3,529,981

Figure 14.39 Analysis Authorization Restriction by Hierarchy and Hierarchy Node Figure

▸ Restrict access to specific key figures within an InfoCube, so that users won't be able to view the data on a row (or column) that has this specific key figure (Figure 14.40).

Plant	Quantity	Net Value
CN	48	726.92
GER	50236	Not Authorized
IN	663	21,6837.36
US	167807	1,298,707.78
Result	218754	3,530,198.84

Figure 14.40 Analysis Authorization Restriction by Key Figure

The following steps provide a quick overview of the process of creating an analysis authorization.

14.6.1 Step 1: Define the InfoObject

The first step is to define the InfoObject as relevant for authorization. Use Transaction RSD1, and go to the InfoObject maintenance screen in the BUSINESS

EXPLORER tab. Define the authorization-relevant characteristics. This will enable authorizations on characteristic values; for example, 0SALES_OFF (❶ of Figure 14.41).

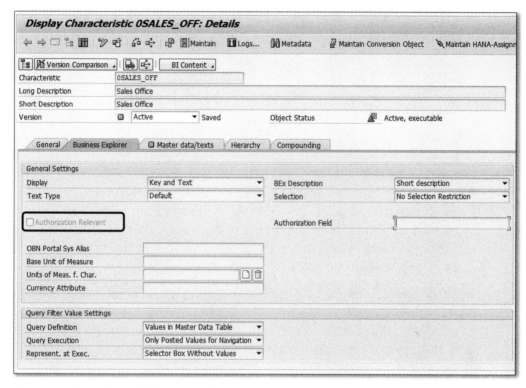

Figure 14.41 Authorization-Relevant InfoObject

14.6.2 Step 2: Create an Authorization Object

The second step is to create an authorization object. Use Transaction RSECAD-MIN. The system takes you to the MANAGEMENT OF ANALYSIS AUTHORIZATIONS screen (Figure 14.42).

This screen has three tabs for carrying out the management of analysis authorizations: AUTHORIZATIONS ❶, USER ❷, and ANALYSIS ❸. In the following steps, we deal with the AUTHORIZATIONS and USER tabs (the ANALYSIS tab is beyond the scope of this book).

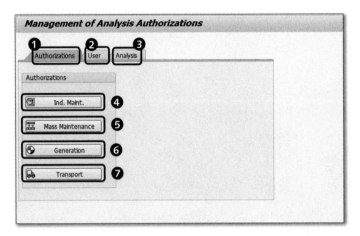

Figure 14.42 Management of Analysis Authorization

The AUTHORIZATION tab has four buttons for carrying out authorization-related tasks: IND. MAINT ❹, MASS MAINTENANCE ❺, GENERATION ❻, and TRANSPORT ❼. Click on the IND. MAINT. button, and the MAINTAIN AUTHORIZATIONS: INITIAL SCREEN appears (Figure 14.43).

In the AUTHORIZATION field, enter "BW_SD_A01" (❶ of Figure 14.43), and click on the CREATE button ❷. The next screen is MAINTAIN AUTHORIZATION: BW_SD_A01 CREATE. The screen has three fields for the authorization object's short, medium, and long descriptions ❸. Enter the following:

- SHORT TEXT: "Sales Office 1422"
- MEDIUM TEXT: "Sales Office 1422"
- LONG TEXT: "Sales Office 1422"

Click on the CREATE ROW icon ❹. The screen below now has a row open for entry; on the extreme right of the field, there is a dropdown list ❺ that lists all InfoObjects defined as relevant for the authorization ❺. Select the 0SALES_OFF row, and then click on the COPY icon ❻. The row in the screen now has an entry for InfoObject 0SALES_OFF ❼.

Double-click on the 0SALES_OFF row. The system takes you to a screen where you can enter the characteristics value or hierarchy value (Figure 14.44).

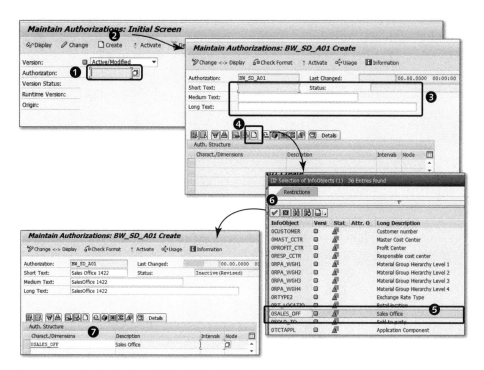

Figure 14.43 Create Analysis Authorization Object

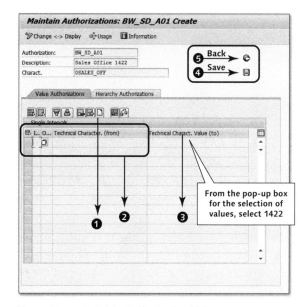

Figure 14.44 Maintain Authorization Values

Now choose the VALUE AUTHORIZATIONS tab, and click on the CREATE ROW icon (❶ of Figure 14.44), which opens a row editable in the table ❷. From the drop-down list ❸, choose a value to which to restrict the information in sales office reports (in our example, we use 1422). Click on the SAVE and BACK icons, respectively. Authorization object BW_SD_A01 is created, which allows analysis only for sales office 1422.

Table 14.2 gives authorization value options and the resulting behavior, with examples.

Authorization Value	Authorization Behavior
* (asterisk)	▶ Denotes a set of arbitrary characters ▶ Used alone to grant access to all values ▶ Used at the end of a value to specify a simple pattern (example: SAP*)
: (colon)	Allows access only to aggregated data (e.g., allows information on all sales areas only on an aggregated level—not on particular sales areas)
+ (plus)	▶ Denotes exactly one character ▶ Used at the end of a value to specify a simple pattern
# (hash)	Stands for an initial or unassigned value

Table 14.2 Authorization Value Options and Their Influence on Access Behavior

14.6.3   Step 3: Assign a User ID

The third step is to assign the authorization object to a user ID. Use Transaction RSECADMIN, and the system opens the MANAGEMENT OF ANALYSIS AUTHORIZA-TIONS screen. Click on the USER tab (Figure 14.45). You're now assigning the authorization object to a user ID for providing access to analysis on reports for sales office 1422.

The screen has two separate boxes: ANALYSIS AUTHORIZATIONS and NETWEAVER TRANSACTIONS (❷ of Figure 14.45). Click on the INDVL. ASSIGNMENT button ❷, and the system takes you to the BW REPORTING: INIT. SCREEN ASSIGNMENT OF USER AUTHORIZATIONS screen. Use the User "TRAIN1" (Figure 14.45) for the sales manager (for sales office 1422), and click on the CHANGE button (Figure 14.45). The system brings you to ASSIGNMENT OF USER AUTHORIZATIONS: EDIT ❸.

The following screen has two tabs: MANUAL OR GENERATED and ROLE-BASED ❹. By default, the system takes you to the MANUAL OR GENERATED tab; note that there is no row for authorization assignments in the ASSIGNED AUTHORIZATION table. In the NAME (TECHN.) field ❺, enter the name of the authorization object that you created ("BW_SD_A01", in our example), and click on INSERT. The authorization object is assigned to the user referred to in ❻. Click on the SAVE icon, and the system displays a message indicating successful assignment at the bottom of the screen. Use the BACK icon to return to MANAGEMENT OF ANALYSIS AUTHORIZATIONS.

Click on the ANALYSIS tab to check the authorization restriction for the user ID based on the authorization object. Authorization object BW_SD_A01 should be assigned to the user ID TRAIN1 for the sales manager responsible for sales office 1422.

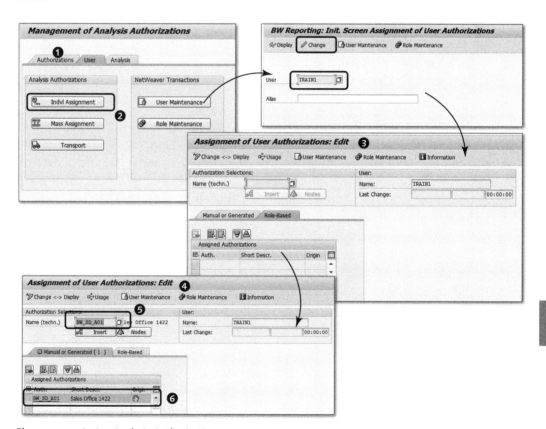

Figure 14.45 Assign Analysis Authorization

14.7   Other Administration and Maintenance Tasks

In this section, we briefly introduce some other administration and maintenance tasks without going into too much detail.

14.7.1   Executing an Attribute Hierarchy Change Run

Changes to master data can also result in changes to navigational attributes or hierarchies. Recall from Section 14.3 that aggregates can be built using navigational attributes and hierarchies, so it's absolutely essential that you adjust data in the aggregates after you load master data. So that reporting delivers consistent results, master data and hierarchies are kept in two versions: the active version (which you can see in the query) and the modified version (which at some point becomes the active version).

The *attribute hierarchy change run* (also called the *realignment run*) adjusts the data in aggregates and turns the modified version of the navigational attributes and hierarchies into the active version. If there are any changes to master data, they aren't available for reporting until the change run is executed and finished.

Let's understand this important concept with the help of an example. Assume that InfoObject BW_CUST represents customers and has a navigational attribute 0SALESEMPLY, which represents the sale employee responsible for those customers (recall that we've used BW_CUST in InfoCube BWSD_C01). Sales employee 67679999 is responsible for customer 100086 for a certain period of time, but eventually the sales employee is changed to 6768000. Meanwhile, you've designed an aggregate based on 0SALESEMPLY, the purpose of which is to boost the query performance of queries with this characteristic. Although employee 6768000 is responsible for customer 100086 currently, the aggregate built using 0SALESEMPLY will have sales figures for the previous sales employee associated with that customer, 67679999. So if the system activates new master data without adjusting the aggregate, there will be data inconsistency.

To avoid this, the system doesn't activate newly loaded master data before the attribute hierarchy change run has adjusted the aggregate. After the attribute hierarchy change run is finished, all of the new relationships are also adjusted in the aggregates. So, in our example, all of the sales figures pertaining to customer 100086 now correctly fall under employee 6768000.

The attribute hierarchy change run is a very important process. By executing it, not only do you activate newly loaded master data in the system, but you also adjust the aggregates.

14.7.2   Deleting Extra Aggregates

The AGGREGATES MAINTENANCE function should be called regularly to delete unused aggregates. This improves load performance because the rollup process and realignment runs consume system resources. We explained earlier how the realignment run is essential to maintaining information integrity.

An aggregate might be unnecessary for several reasons:

▸ There are similar aggregates that could be combined into one new aggregate.

▸ There are aggregates that are never used and are not base aggregates.

▸ There are aggregates with an insufficient reduction factor compared to the Info-Cube.

Aggregates are created especially for performance reasons, but unnecessary aggregates waste disk space and have to be regularly maintained via rollup and change runs, so it's important to regularly check your usage of your aggregates.

14.7.3   Deleting PSA Data

You need to determine a defined data retention period for data in PSA tables; the exact period depends on the type of data involved and your data uploading strategy. As part of this policy, establish a safe method to periodically delete data. If the PSA data isn't deleted on a regular basis, the PSA tables grow unrestricted. Very large tables increase the cost of data storage, the downtime for maintenance tasks, and the time required for uploading data. PSA deletion can be easily integrated in process chains.

14.7.4   Deleting DTP Temporary Storage

The deletion of DTP temporary storage is another action that can improve the performance of your system. This can be accomplished via DTP • DISPLAY • GOTO • SETTINGS FOR DTP TEMPORARY STORAGE. Based on the retention time frame for the temporary storage, choose the appropriate option within DELETE TEMPORARY STORAGE.

14.7.5 Using Report SAP_INFOCUBE_DESIGNS

Use Transaction SA37 to execute the SAP_INFOCUBE_DESIGNS report. The result shows the database tables of an InfoCube, the number of records in these tables, and the ratio of the dimension table size to the fact table size. If dimension tables are too large, they can cause badly performing table joins on the database level. As data volume grows and data allocation changes over time, this check should be executed regularly. Based on the results from this report, you can use the settings such as LINE ITEM dimension or HIGH CARDINALITY dimension to improve the performance of the InfoCube. These settings are explained in Chapter 5.

14.7.6 Checking Data Consistency

Use Transaction RSRV to analyze the important objects in the SAP BW system; this transaction also provides repair functionality for some tests. These tests only check the intrinsic technical consistency of objects, such as foreign key relations of the underlying tables, missing indexes, and so on; they don't analyze any business logic or semantic accuracy of data. Missing table indexes or inconsistencies in master data or transactional data can have a negative impact on your system performance or lead to missing information in your SAP BW reporting.

Again, as a reminder, we recommend reading the reference material mentioned in Chapter 2, which will teach you the techniques for optimizing your use of SAP BW.

14.7.7 Early Unload Concept for SAP BW Powered by SAP HANA

The early unload concept (introduced previously in Chapter 4, Section 4.5) is applicable to an SAP HANA database only. SAP BW systems normally store large amounts of data with SAP HANA. However, out of this, some large chunks of valuable data may not be accessed regularly. Because SAP HANA's memory isn't infinite, there may be a situation where SAP HANA's memory becomes bottlenecked.

The SAP BW system tries to handle this situation by off-loading some data from memory when this kind of bottleneck arises. It determines the data that hasn't been used recently and off-loads that first. It moves the data from memory to the SAP HANA file system. Thus, most inactive data is off-loaded first from memory in case of a memory bottleneck.

Most inactive data is stored in SAP BW in objects such as PSAs and write-optimized DSOs. They store data in a particular mode. Whenever new data is loaded in both of these objects, SAP BW creates a new partition and stores the data in this newly created partition. The system then selectively identifies inactive data (old partitions) and off-loads it from memory. However, data from the newest partition isn't off-loaded because it's needed for processes such as loading the data, and so on. Such processes use partition IDs to ensure that only the required data can be accessed, and the system optimizes the requirement of SAP HANA memory in this way.

> **Caution with Write-Optimized DSOs**
>
> Write-optimized DSOs with 3X dataflow does not use a partition ID while loading data, and hence full data is loaded into memory. The write-optimized DSO with a semantic key, configured with the DUPLICATE DATA RECORDS NOT ALLOWED setting is also not partitioned by the request ID, and therefore the entire data is loaded into memory.

In addition, SAP BW also provides a nonactive data monitor in the SAP HANA database that allows you to monitor the handling of inactive data. Here, you can set objects flagged as EARLY UNLOAD. Objects flagged with EARLY UNLOAD are displaced first from memory.

Flagging as Early Unload

Let's now see how we can set an object to be flagged as EARLY UNLOAD.

Begin by starting Transaction RSHDBMON, and you'll be brought to the screen shown in Figure 14.46. The system details such as system ID, version, platform, memory, CPU, and so on ❶ are shown. Below it, things like host name, services, and so on are shown ❷.

Click on the DETAIL VIEW icon ❸. This brings up the DETAIL SELECTION screen ❹. Here, you can filter the objects by object type and name ❺. In OBJECT TYPE, you can select the following from the dropdown list:

- INFOAREA
- INFOPROVIDER
- DATASOURCE
- ALL OBJECTS
- ALL OBJECTS WITH UNLOADS

You also have the option to perform EXACT SEARCH or SEARCH PATTERN ❻. These searches can be performed for tables set w/ EARLY UNLOAD or w/o EARLY UNLOAD ❼. As shown in ❶ and ❷ of Figure 14.47, our search options are provided.

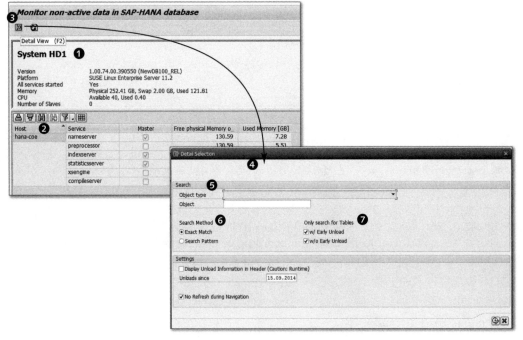

Figure 14.46 Non-Active Data Monitor in SAP HANA Database

As shown in Figure 14.47, the object type selected is InfoProvider and the object entered is "BWSD" with the SEARCH METHOD option shown as SEARCH PATTERN. Keeping all remaining settings as default, click on the EXECUTE icon ❸. The resulting screen is shown below ❹ of Figure 14.47.

Here, objects starting with the name BWSD are displayed, due to our search criteria. InfoProviders are listed in ❺ and their status is indicated in the EARLY UNLOAD flag 6. We can see also see that InfoProvider BWSD_C01 is flagged for early unload as well.

Now, let's flag DSO BWSD_O01 for early unload by clicking on it ❼. The resulting screen is shown in Figure 14.48.

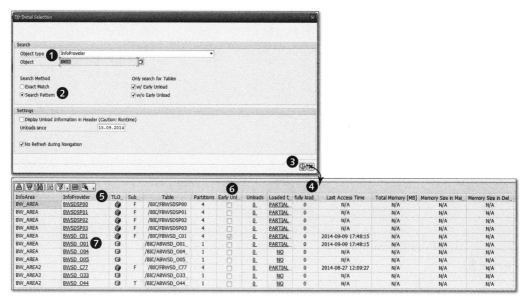

Figure 14.47 Non-Active Data Monitor: Search and Result

As shown in ❶ of Figure 14.48, two tables are shown to be associated with the selected DSO BWSD_O01. Select both of these tables ❷. Now, click on the LOAD/UNLOAD icon ❸. From the dropdown menu, select the ACTIVATE EARLY UNLOAD option ❹.

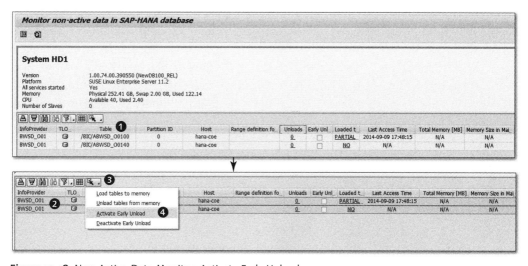

Figure 14.48 Non-Active Data Monitor: Activate Early Unload

This action finally sets the EARLY UNLOAD flag for DSO BWSD_O01, which is shown in ❶ and ❷ of Figure 14.49.

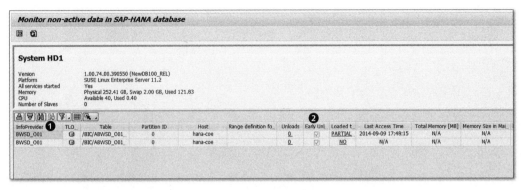

Figure 14.49 Nonactive Data Monitor: DSO Flagged for Early Unload

You now know how to set early unload for objects you wish to unclutter in SAP HANA's memory, based on your priorities. Using this concept of early unload, you can optimize SAP HANA system's memory usage.

14.8 Summary

In this chapter, we introduced the fundamental idea behind administration and maintenance tasks: ensuring your system lives up to its purpose of delivering the right information at the right time by consuming the right amount of resources—consistently. We began the chapter with a discussion of managing data targets (DSOs and InfoCubes), briefly explained the idea of aggregates and compression, and then moved on to a discussion of process chains and analysis authorizations. We concluded the chapter with a summary of other important administration and maintenance tasks.

In the next chapter, we explain some of the advanced features and functionality offered by SAP BW.

This chapter is meant to get you started with some of the advanced concepts of SAP BW as a data warehousing, reporting, and analysis tool.

15   Advanced Features

The previous chapters were designed to give you a basic understanding of SAP BW. In this chapter, we introduce you to some of the more advanced features offered by SAP BW, which are used to address complex and high-end analysis requirements and to maintain scalability of the solution. The topics covered in this chapter include the following:

- Open Hub
- The Analysis Process Designer (APD) and the analytical index
- Remodeling
- SAP HANA analysis process (HAP)

15.1   Open Hub

As a data warehouse, SAP BW can acquire data from a variety of sources and then store this data in data targets. SAP BW can also act as a source for the data that is acquired from other systems (SAP or non-SAP; Figure 15.1). In such a scenario, SAP BW acts as a *hub* that is *open* for the distribution of data to different destination systems.

Using the Open Hub service, you can transfer data from SAP BW InfoProviders to different destinations in either *full mode* or *delta mode*. The destination from where data is extracted is known as the *Open Hub Destination (OHD)*. An OHD is created and maintained in the Data Warehousing Workbench, under the MODELING section (❶ of Figure 15.2). The InfoArea tree is displayed on the right panel of the screen.

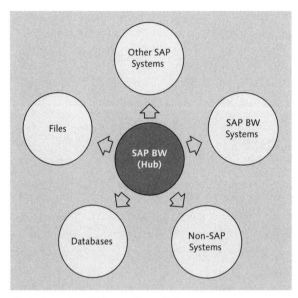

Figure 15.1 SAP BW as an Open Hub

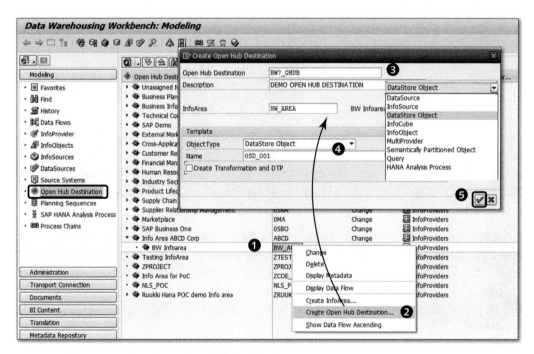

Figure 15.2 Creating an Open Hub Destination

To create an OHD, select CREATE OPEN HUB DESTINATION from the context menu of the InfoArea where you want to create it (❷ of Figure 15.2). A pop-up box appears for entering the technical name and description of the OHD ❸. To reduce development time, you can also use the object ❹ from which you're going to load data as a template to create the OHD definition. Click on the CONTINUE icon ❺ to continue with the OHD creation. The detailed OHD definition is maintained on the screen shown in Figure 15.3.

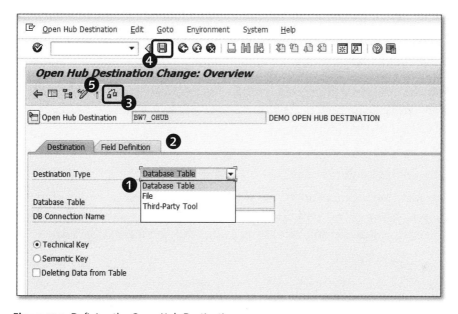

Figure 15.3 Defining the Open Hub Destination

The two tabs on the OHD definition screen are explained here:

▶ DESTINATION
The Open Hub service allows you to transmit data to various destinations. On the DESTINATION tab (❶ of Figure 15.3), you can define the destination where the data needs to be sent.

▶ FIELD DEFINITION
The fields and format in which the data has to be sent to the destination are defined in the FIELD DEFINITION tab ❷.

After the OHD is defined, check the definition ❸, save the definition ❹, and activate the definition ❺.

After the OHD is active, you can create a *transformation* and data transfer process (DTP) from the source to this OHD to transfer the data. The DTP for an Open Hub is the same as the regular DTP and can be scheduled the same way.

15.2 Analysis Process Designer

The Analysis Process Designer (APD) provides advanced analysis options in SAP BW. Data from a variety of InfoProviders (DataStore Objects [DSOs], InfoCubes, InfoObjects, as well as data providers such as BEx queries, etc.) can be linked together with logic and transformations to create additional information needed for business analysts. APD also supports data mining operations based on the data stored in SAP BW. In this section, we discuss the Analysis Workbench used in APD and also explain how to create an analysis process. Finally, we explain how to create an analytical index using APD.

15.2.1 Analysis Workbench

The creation and maintenance of analysis processes is done in the *Analysis Workbench,* which you access with Transaction RSANWB. You can also access this from the Data Warehousing Workbench by clicking on the APD icon shown in Figure 15.4.

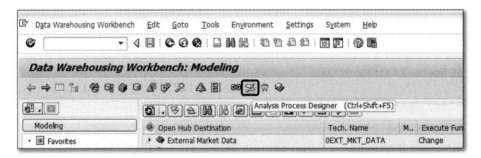

Figure 15.4 Accessing the Analysis Workbench

The Analysis Workbench has a default layout, as shown in Figure 15.5. To create a new analysis process, click on the CREATE icon (Figure 15.5), and select GENERAL from the APPLICATION/FOLDER list box.

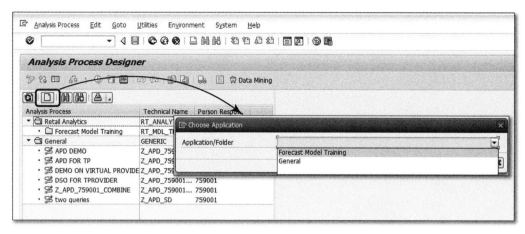

Figure 15.5 Creating an Analysis Process

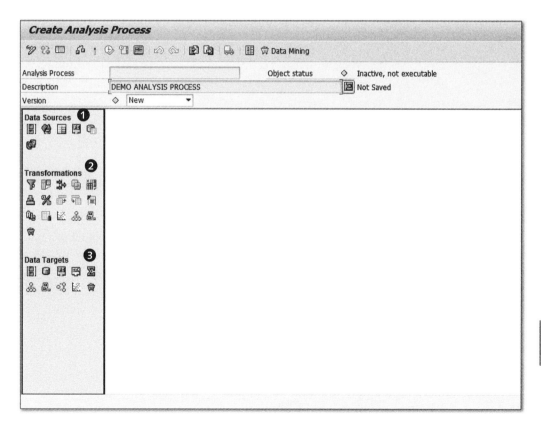

Figure 15.6 Components of an Analysis Process

This displays the CREATE ANALYSIS PROCESS screen (Figure 15.6). The left panel of the screen displays all of the components that can be used to build an analysis process, and the right panel displays the design area where the analysis process is built.

There are three types of components used in an analysis process:

❶ **Data sources**
The components from which data is read for further processing in an analysis process are categorized as DATA SOURCES. An analysis process can use master data, BEx queries, InfoProviders, flat files, or database tables as a DataSource.

❷ **Transformations**
Different analysis functions used on the data are grouped under TRANSFORMATIONS. These different transformations range from simple filter functions to more complex data mining functions.

❸ **Data targets**
The data processed and generated in an analysis process can be saved into different DATA TARGETS, such as direct update DSOs, master data attributes, flat files, analytical indexes, and so on. The data generated in an analysis process can also be fed to data mining models.

15.2.2   Creating Analysis Processes

Let's take a simple example where you want to perform some advanced analysis based on a query and master data. Assume that you want the output of the analysis to be stored in a direct update DSO.

Drag the QUERY icon from the DATA SOURCES area to the design area (❶ of Figure 15.7), and assign a query to this DataSource using the CHOOSE QUERY button in the pop-up box ❷. Press ⌨Enter, or click on the CONTINUE icon ❸ to return to the design screen.

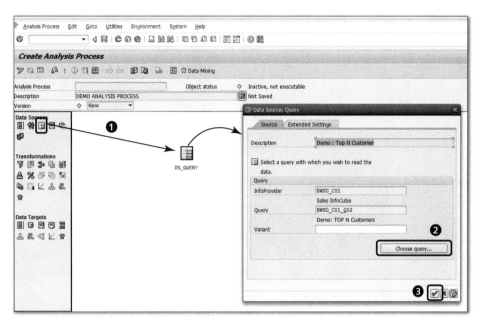

Figure 15.7 Adding a Data Source: Query

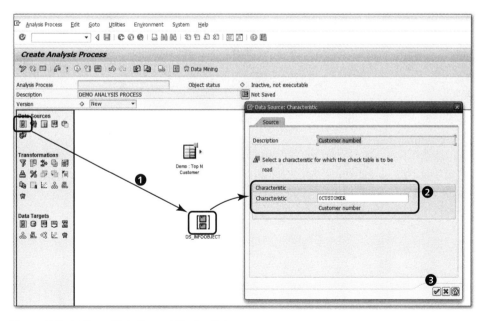

Figure 15.8 Adding a Data Source: Master Data

Drag another DataSource, MASTER DATA, to the design area (❶ of Figure 15.8), and assign the master data characteristic needed to perform the analysis ❷. Press Enter, or click on the CONTINUE icon ❸ to return to the design screen.

Drag the DSO WITH DIRECT UPDATE FOR APD icon from the DATA TARGETS area to the design area (❶ of Figure 15.9), and select the direct update DSO to where the data from the analysis process should be saved ❷. Press Enter, or click the CONTINUE icon ❸ to return to the design screen.

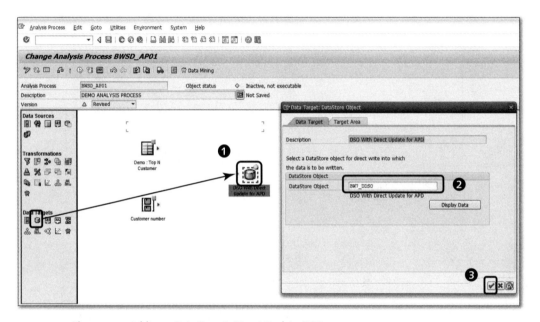

Figure 15.9 Adding a Data Target: Direct Update DSO

Drag the JOIN icon from the TRANSFORMATIONS area to the design area (Figure 15.10). The data from both DataSources will pass though this transformation before getting saved to the data target.

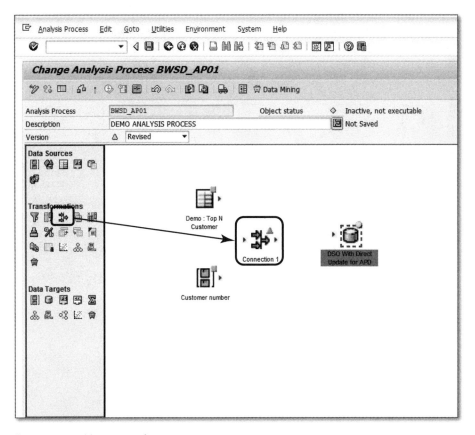

Figure 15.10 Adding a Transformation: Join

Create links between the components by dragging the mouse from one component to the other (❶ of Figure 15.11). You can now maintain the join conditions for both DataSources ❷, as well as the rules for mapping the transformed data to the fields in the data target ❸.

Check, save, and activate the analysis process. You can now execute the active analysis process.

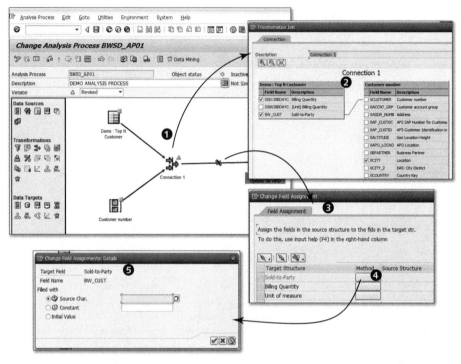

Figure 15.11 Defining Transformations

15.2.3 Creating Analytical Indexes

An analytical index is a data container that stores its data in a simple star schema. It operates in SAP BW on either SAP BW Accelerator (BWA) or on SAP HANA (in a column table), and it's used in creating a transient provider. Containing facts and characteristics (called dimensions) with attributes, an analytical index is suitable for ad hoc analysis.

> **Facts**
>
> Facts are key figures that are stored in the fact table of the star schema.

To create an analytical index, start the Analysis Workbench using Transaction RSANWB. The CREATE ANALYSIS PROCESS screen is displayed, as shown in Figure 15.12. We use the query BWSD_C01_QUERY01, which we designed in Chapter 9 as a DataSource for the APD. Select the QUERY icon (❶ of Figure 15.12), and drag and drop it on the right panel ❷. This action brings up the DATA SOURCE QUERY pop-up box, as shown in ❶ of Figure 15.13.

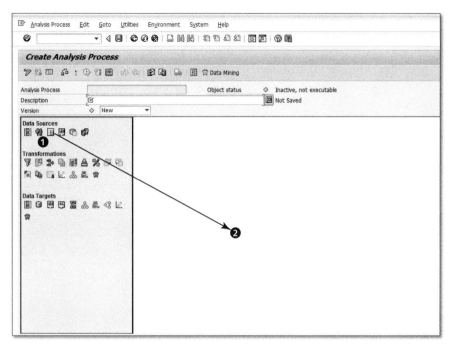

Figure 15.12 Creating an Analysis Process

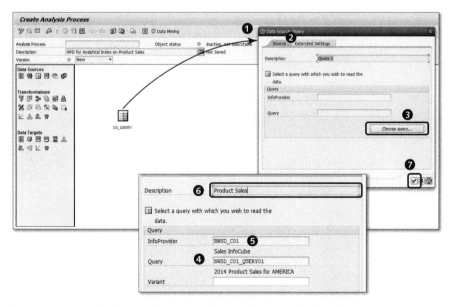

Figure 15.13 Analysis Process Designer: Assigning a Query as the DataSource

On the SOURCE tab ❷, select the query by clicking on the CHOOSE QUERY button ❸. Select query BWSD_C01_QUERY01 ❹, and the system shows the InfoProvider name ❺. Add the "Product Sales" description ❻, and then click on the CONTINUE ❼ icon to return to the main screen. The query is now assigned with the given details (❶ of Figure 15.14).

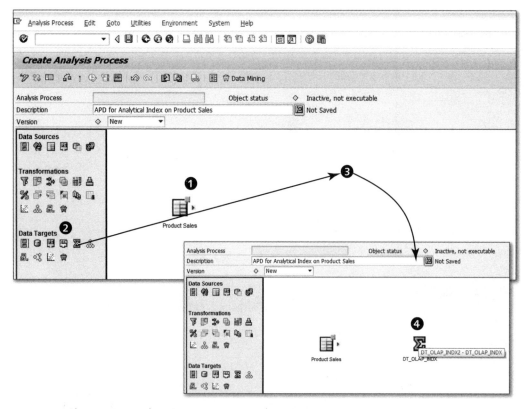

Figure 15.14 Analysis Process Designer: Selecting a Data Target

Now drag and drop the analytical index ❷ on the right panel ❸ to select it as the data target. This action brings up the ANALYTICAL INDEX DATA TARGET pop-up box, as shown in ❶ of Figure 15.15.

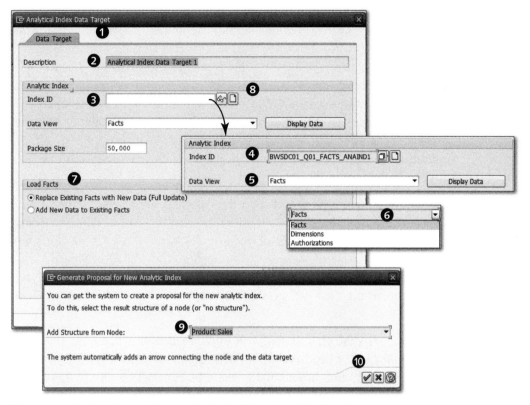

Figure 15.15 Analysis Process Designer: Assigning Values to a Data Target

The system proposes the description ANALYTICAL INDEX DATA TARGET 1 ❷. The INDEX ID field is blank initially ❸; enter "BWSDC01_Q01_FACTS_ANAIND1" ❹. Three data views ❻ are offered for creating the analytical index:

- FACTS
  The analytical index will expect data to be in the form of dimensions and facts. When loading data, you can select whether you want to replace the existing facts with new data or add new data to existing facts ❼.

- DIMENSIONS
  Specify the dimension whose attribute you want to load in the analytical index. You can specify which dimensions and the specific attributes of the dimensions that you want to include.

789

▶ AUTHORIZATIONS

Analytical indexes can also contain authorization data. The fields and the order of the fields when loading authorization data is very specific: attribute name (ATTR_NAME), user (USERNM), the technical name of the authorization (AUTH), InfoObject (IOBJNM), sign (SIGN), selection operator (OPTION), the lower limit selection value (LOW), and the upper limit selection value (HIGH). You can either extract the authorization data from an InfoProvider or extract an assignment of users and values from an Excel file. To extract analysis authorizations from an InfoProvider, you can use the Analysis Authorizations DataSource.

Select the FACTS data view ❺. Click on the CREATE icon ❽, which brings up the GENERATE PROPOSAL FOR NEW ANALYTICAL INDEX pop-up box. The DataSource available in the current APD is displayed in the ADD STRUCTURE FROM NODE box. Select PRODUCT SALES (which is the default action) (refer to ❻ of Figure 15.13), and click on CONTINUE ❿. This action connects product sales to the analytical index and opens the CREATE ANALYTICAL INDEX screen, as shown in ❶ of Figure 15.16.

On the PROPERTIES tab ❷, you assign an InfoArea ❸ to the analytical index. The analytical index won't be visible under the assigned InfoArea in the Data Warehouse Workbench, but it will help when making selections in BEx Query Designer. Enter the description "Analytical Index 1 [FACTS View] on BWSD_C01_QUERY01" ❹, and assign InfoArea BW_AREA ❺.

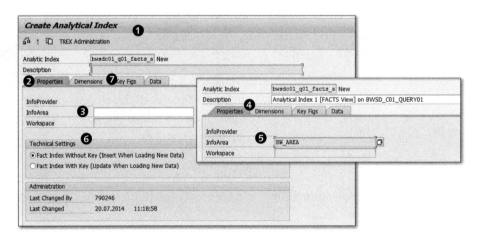

Figure 15.16 Analytical Index: Properties Tab

Under the Technical Settings area ❻, there are two options:

▸ Fact Index Without Key (Insert When Loading New Data)
If this option is selected, new data records are always added.

▸ Fact Index With Key (Update When Loading New Data)
If this option is selected, data records with the new key combination are added when the existing key combination is updated.

Select the default option, Fact Index Without Key (Insert When Loading New Data). Click on the Dimensions tab ❼, and the screen shown in Figure 15.17 is displayed.

As shown in ❶ of Figure 15.17, the system reads the definition of the query (which is taken as the DataSource) and displays the name accordingly. You can select the data type ❷ for each element of the query. If you've selected Fact Index With Key (refer to ❻ of Figure 15.16), you can flag the dimension as part of the key (❸ of Figure 15.17). This is grayed out because we've selected the Fact Index Without Key setting. You can define the attributes of each dimension ❹, and descriptive text ❺ can be entered for each element. There is also an option to assign an InfoObject ❻ to each element; if this is done, it means that fields are automatically assigned in the APD when connecting the source structure to the target structure. The Reference InfoObject flag ❼ is used by the transient Info-Object during OLAP reporting. Set the Authorization ❽ flag, and the system runs a check when executing and navigating queries on the transient provider to ensure that the user is authorized for all dimension data flowing into the result set. Click on the Key Figs tab ❾, and the screen shown in Figure 15.18 is displayed.

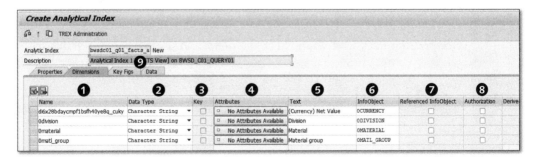

Figure 15.17 Analytical Index: Dimensions Tab

The structure of the key figure from the DataSource (query BWSD_C01_ QUERY01) is shown in Figure 15.18. The additional setting is for unit dimension ❻, which is applicable only for key figures.

The bottom part of this figure displays the DATA tab ❼; click on it to view details associated with the analytical index, such as number of records, memory size, and so on. The data in this tab isn't available in our example because we're still in the design phase of the analytical index; this will change after activation and execution of the analysis process.

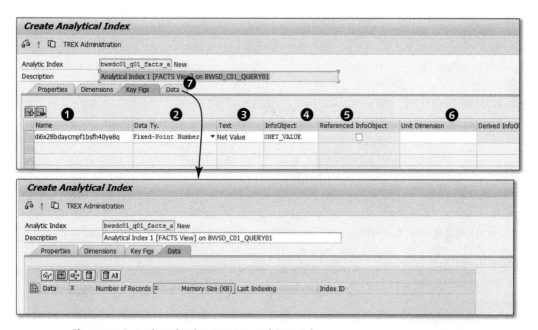

Figure 15.18 Analytical Index: Key Figs and Data Tabs

Click on the CHECK icon 🔧 to check the definition of the analytical index. After receiving confirmation that the definition is correct, click on the ACTIVATE icon 🔼.

As shown in ❶ of Figure 15.19, the status of the analytical index is changed from NEW to SAVED. The system has assigned a name to the InfoProvider: @3BWS-DC01_Q01_FACTS_ANAIND1 ❷. Use the BACK button to return to the ANALYTICAL INDEX DATA TARGET screen, as shown in Figure 15.20.

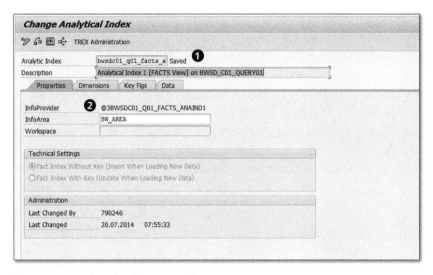

Figure 15.19 Analytical Index Activated

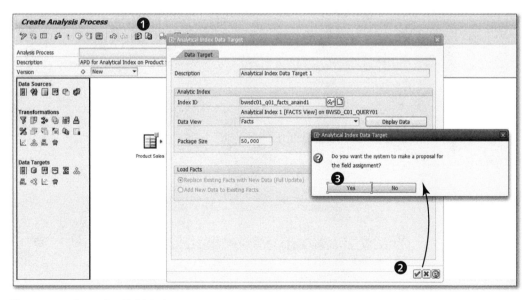

Figure 15.20 Proposing Field Assignments

Click on CONTINUE (❷ of Figure 15.20) to display the pop-up message box. Select YES ❸ to instruct the system to provide proposals for assigning the source structure to the target structure. Here the source is Query, and the target is Analytical

Index. Click on YES to join the query to the analytical index with transformations, as shown in Figure 15.21.

The transformation between source and target is shown in ❶ of Figure 15.21. Double-click on the icon, and the CHANGE FIELD ASSIGNMENT pop-up box appears ❷. On the right side, elements of the source structure are shown ❸, and on the left side, elements of the target structure are shown ❹. The transformation between individual elements is shown using the arrow button that points from right to left ❺. Double-click on the arrow button to view the individual transformation and edit it. The default transformation has a 1:1 assignment; click on CONTINUE ❻.

Now you need to activate the analysis process by clicking on the ACTIVATE icon ❼. This brings up a pop-up box where you can enter the technical name "BWSD_C01_Q01_APD1" (❽ and ❾); click on CONTINUE ❿.

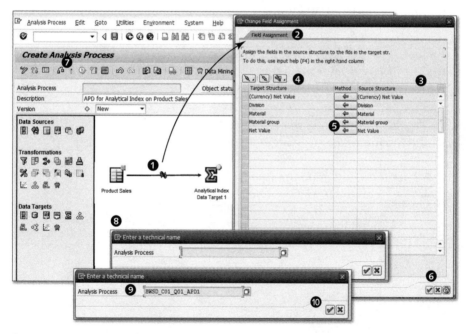

Figure 15.21 Activating Analysis Process

Creation of the analytical index is complete. The analysis process is shown in its active version (❶ of Figure 15.22). You can load data into the analytical index either by executing this analysis process or by including it as part of a process chain for loading data periodically into the analytical index.

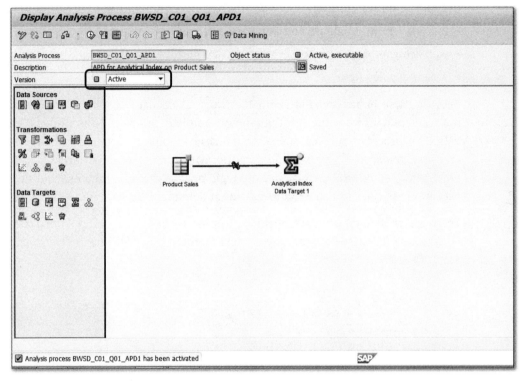

Figure 15.22 Analytical Index Activated

An analytical index is used in the creation of a transient provider and is a very useful tool for ad hoc analysis. Queries can be created on the basis of a transient provider.

Next we'll describe another feature of SAP BW 7.4.

15.3 Remodeling

When an InfoCube is in use for a long period (and therefore has a large quantity of data), it needs to be enhanced to meet new analysis requirements. Such enhancements might include the following:

- Adding a new characteristic and populating it with new values
- Replacing an existing characteristic with a new one
- Deleting a characteristic
- Adding a new key figure and populating it with new values
- Replacing an existing key figure with a new one
- Deleting a key figure

Because these enhancements result in structural changes to an InfoCube, you must delete data from the InfoCube before implementing, and then reload the data. This process can be cumbersome if a large amount of data must be deleted and then reloaded. The *remodeling* feature available in SAP BW allows you to build remodeling rules that define the logic behind the enhancement and then execute these rules to make changes without deleting the data.

To create or maintain the remodeling rules for an InfoCube, select ADDITIONAL FUNCTIONS • REMODELING from the context menu of the InfoCube in Transaction RSA1 (❶ of Figure 15.23).

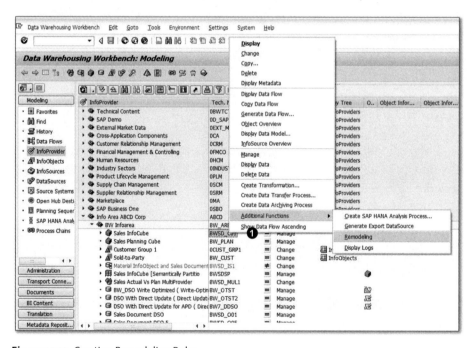

Figure 15.23 Creating Remodeling Rules

This takes you to the REMODELING TOOLBOX screen (❶ of Figure 15.24) where you can specify the type of object for which you want to write a remodeling rule. The following three options are available ❷:

▶ INFOCUBE

▶ DATASTORE OBJECT

▶ INFOOBJECT

Select the INFOCUBE radio button (if not already selected). Provide the name of the InfoProvider and remodeling rule. Here, we entered "BWSD_C01" as the InfoProvider and "REMODRULE" as the remodeling rule ❸. To create a new rule, click on the CREATE button ❹. A pop-up box appears in which you can enter the description of the rule ❺.

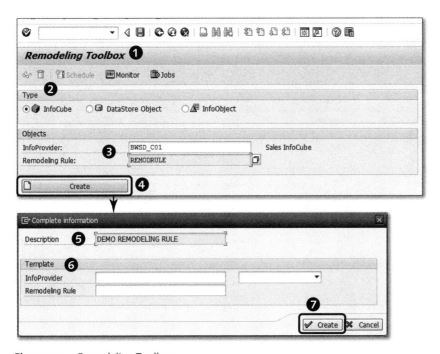

Figure 15.24 Remodeling Toolbox

Note

Although we are creating our own rule in this example, note that the system does provide an option to reuse an existing template ❻.

After the necessary information is entered, click on the CREATE button ❼. On the next screen, you can define the rule for the selected InfoCube (Figure 15.25). Click on the NEW icon ❶ to add an *operation* to the rule. The ADD A NEW OPERATION pop-up box appears in which you can select the type of operation you want to perform ❷. Maintain the INPUT ❸ and FILLING METHOD ❹ sections in the bottom part of the pop-up box.

Finally, click on the CREATE button ❺ to add the defined operation to the remodeling rule. If you want to perform multiple operations on the InfoProvider, you can add these operations in the same remodeling rule.

After it's completely defined, save the remodeling rule, and return to the previous screen. You can execute this rule by using the SCHEDULE button as shown in Figure 15.25.

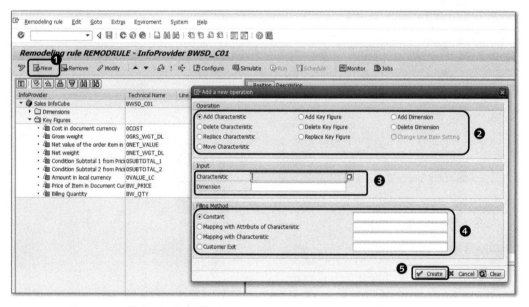

Figure 15.25 Defining Operations

InfoObject Remodeling

Only Characteristics InfoObjects can be remodeled. To carry out the remodeling of an InfoObject, select the INFOOBJECT radio button under the TYPE section (refer to ❷ of Figure 15.24). The following operations are offered:

- ▶ Activate/deactivate high cardinality
- ▶ Changing the time dependency of an attribute
- ▶ Changing the attribute type (display/navigation)
- ▶ Deleting compounding attribute

15.4 SAP HANA Analysis Process (HAP)

SAP BW allows you to extract data from a variety of system sources. This data is then stored in various ways in SAP BW (e.g., InfoCubes, DSOs, and InfoObjects). With the introduction of SAP BW powered by SAP HANA, you now have the power to analyze this data from different perspective and calculate ABC classes or scoring classes. Different libraries, such as the Predictive Analysis Library (PAL) and Application Function Library (AFL), can be used by SAP HANA to analyze large volumes of data quickly by using complex algorithms. To achieve this easily, SAP BW has introduced a feature called SAP HANA analysis process (HAP).

Prerequisites for SAP HANA Analysis Process

Make sure the following prerequisites are met before using HAP:
- ▶ You are on an SAP HANA database.
- ▶ You are using SAP BW 7.4 with SP5 or higher.
- ▶ The script server is started.
- ▶ The AFL is installed.

15.4.1 SAP HANA Analysis Process Inputs

To create a HAP, you must determine the inputs. A HAP is created in the DATA WAREHOUSING WORKBENCH screen, which can be started using Transaction RSA1. Select the SAP HANA ANALYSIS PROCESS ❷ under MODELING ❶ from the navigator section as shown in Figure 15.26.

From here, select the BW InfoArea ❸ under which you want to create your HAP. From the context menu, select CREATE SAP HANA ANALYSIS PROCESS ❹. The CREATE HANA ANALYSIS PROCESS screen appears, as shown in ❶ of Figure 15.27.

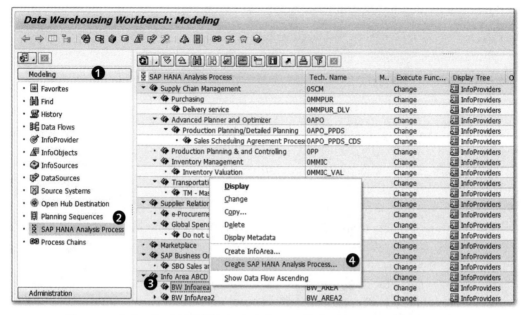

Figure 15.26 Creating SAP HANA Analysis Process Navigation

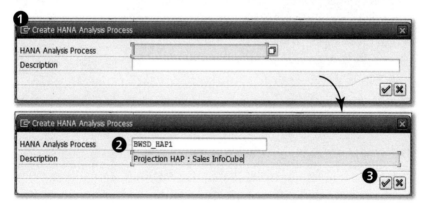

Figure 15.27 Providing the HAP Name and Description

Enter the technical name and description of the HAP ❷. In our example, the HAP's technical name is BWSD_HAP1, and its description is Projection HAP: Sales InfoCube. Click on CONTINUE ❸ to proceed. This takes you to the CREATE SAP HANA ANALYSIS PROCESS BWSD_HAP1 screen, as shown in ❶ of Figure 15.28. This screen has four different tabs:

- OVERVIEW

- DATA SOURCE

- DATA ANALYSIS

- DATA TARGET

By default, the OVERVIEW tab is shown ❸. The description and InfoArea name are defaulted from previous selections/input. The OVERVIEW tab requires three different kinds of input: DATA SOURCE ❹, DATA ANALYSIS ❺, and DATA TARGET ❻.

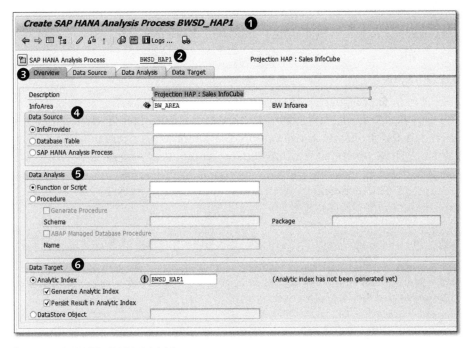

Figure 15.28 BWSD_HAP1: Initial Screen

Data Source

In the DATA SOURCE section (refer to ❹ of Figure 15.28), you need to provide the source of the data for HAP. The system offers you three different kinds of sources from for the data source:

- INFOPROVIDER

  - ANALYTIC INDEX

  - COMPOSITEPROVIDER

- ▸ DataStore Object
- ▸ InfoCube
- ▸ InfoObject
- ▸ MultiProvider
- ▸ Query Snapshots
- ▸ Semantically Partitioned Object
- ▸ Database Table
- ▸ SAP HANA Analysis Process

For our scenario, we used the input shown in ❶ of Figure 15.29.

Data Analysis

As shown in ❺ of Figure 15.28, you define what is used for data analysis as well. You can select FUNCTION OR SCRIPT. There are a number of prefabricated functions offered by SAP from which you can run the complex algorithm in an SAP HANA database. These functions are designed by SAP, so there's no need to write code. They are executed in an SAP HANA database, offering fast execution. SAP BW can execute SAP HANA functions from different libraries (e.g., AFL) and analyze the data stored in InfoProviders.

> **Procedure Choices**
>
> If the prefabricated functions provided by SAP aren't sufficient for your analysis, you can write your own algorithm either using your own SAP HANA database procedure or an ABAP-managed database procedure.

For our scenario, we used the inputs shown in ❷, ❸, and ❹ of Figure 15.29.

Data Target

The analyzed data is stored in the data target (refer to ❻ of Figure 15.28). In the DATA TARGET section, the following targets are available:

- ▸ Analytic Index
- ▸ DataStore Object
- ▸ Database table
- ▸ Embedded in Data Transfer Process

For our scenario, we used the input shown in ❺ of Figure 15.29.

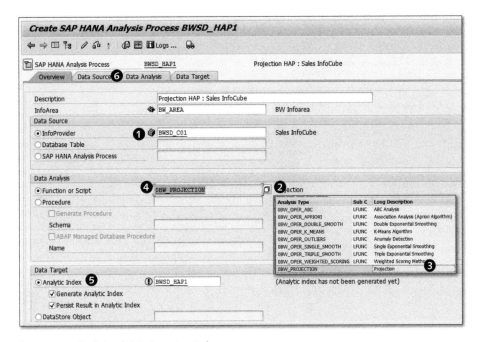

Figure 15.29 Defining HAP: Overview Tab

15.4.2 Creating SAP HANA Analysis Process

After you confirm the described inputs from the previous section, click on the DATA SOURCE tab, as shown in ❻ of Figure 15.29. The next screen available to you is shown in Figure 15.30.

In Figure 15.30, all of the InfoObjects included in the definition of InfoProvider BWSD_C01 are listed ❶. We now need to map the fields of the DataSource to data analysis to create the HAP:

1. Select the checkbox in front of the field required for DATA ANALYSIS, which in our example is 0MATL_GROUP ❷.

2. Select (or filter) the field value by clicking on the MULTIPLE SELECTION icon ❸. This brings up the MAINTAIN FILTER FOR INFOOBJECT 0MATL GROUP screen ❹.

3. For each key figure associated with a unit or currency, perform a unit/currency conversion.

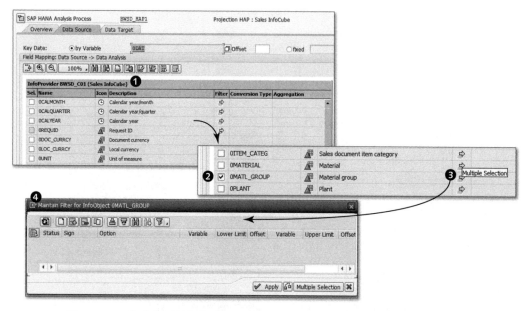

Figure 15.30 Defining HAP: Data Source

Now, we need to filter values for the InfoObject. Basically, for this example, we want to instruct the system to filter the data containing the material group value PC. To do so, follow these steps:

1. Click on the INSERT ROW icon as shown in ❶ of Figure 15.31. This opens up a new row ❷. Various options are now available for you to choose (e.g., SIGN, OPTION, VARIABLE, LOWER LIMIT, UPPER LIMIT, etc.).

2. Under the SIGN option, you can select INCLUSIVE or EXCLUSIVE. Select INCLUSIVE ❸ for our scenario.

3. Under OPTION, you can select one of the following:

   ▸ EQ: SINGLE VALUE

   ▸ GE: GREATER THAN OR EQUAL TO

   ▸ LE: LESS THAN OR EQUAL TO

   ▸ GT: GREATER THAN

   ▸ LT: LESS THAN

   ▸ NE: NOT EQUAL

▸ BT: BETWEEN

▸ NB: OUTSIDE THE INTERVAL

For our scenario, select EQ SINGLE VALUE ❹.

4. You can select a variable for LOWER LIMIT and UPPER LIMIT. For our example, select PC for LOWER LIMIT.

5. When applicable, you can set the OFFSET option.

6. Click on the APPLY button ❺.

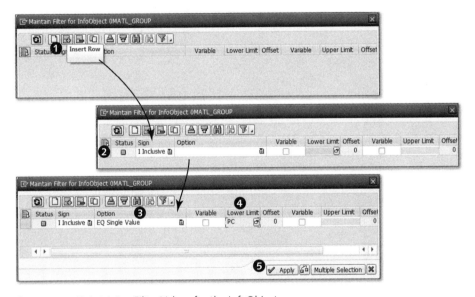

Figure 15.31 Maintaining Filter Values for the InfoObject

7. In ❶ of Figure 15.32, you can see that for InfoObject 0MATL_GROUP, the SEL. column is checked, and the FILTER icon has also changed color. Previously, the yellow arrow was shown with a green square below the yellow. The green color indicates that the filter value is selected for this InfoObject.

8. For our scenario, select the following InfoObjects:

▸ 0CALMONTH

▸ 0MATL_GROUP (along with the FILTER value just described)

▸ 0SALES_GRP

▸ 0NET_VALUE

▸ BQ_QTY

9. Click the DATA TARGET tab ❷ to reveal its two subtabs:

   ▸ DATA ANALYSIS

   ▸ ANALYTIC INDEX

   By default, the DATA ANALYSIS subtab is displayed ❸. All the fields selected from the DATA SOURCE tab are also shown under this tab as OUTPUT FIELDS.

10. Click on the ANALYTIC INDEX tab ❹.

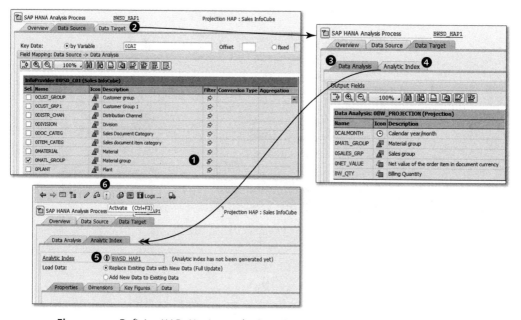

Figure 15.32 Defining HAP: Moving to the Data Target

11. For this example, we selected the analytic index as a data target in the OVERVIEW tab. The name that the system proposes for the analytic index is the same as that selected for HAP, which is BWSD_HAP1 ❺. The analytic index is still not generated. Only on activation will it be generated. You can either choose to delete the content of analytic index and replace it with new data or add new data to the existing data. For our example, select the default mode of REPLACE EXISTING DATA WITH NEW DATA (FULL UPDATE).

12. Activate the analytic index by clicking on the ACTIVATE icon ❻. This activates the analytic index BWSD_HAP1, as shown in ❶ of Figure 15.33.

By default, the DIMENSIONS tab ❷ contains details of the analytic index. You can see that `0calmonth`, `0matl_group`, and `0sales_grp` are shown under the DIMENSIONS tab. We selected five InfoObjects (see Figure 15.32) while designing our HAP. The system detects the InfoObject's characteristics data type and puts it under the DIMENSIONS tab while activating the analytic index.

13. From here, click on the KEY FIGURES tab ❸. In a similar fashion, the system detected the key figure InfoObjects and put them under the KEY FIGURES tab of the analytic index. In our selection, we have two key figure InfoObjects (i.e., `0net_value` and `bw_qty`), which are both displayed under the KEY FIGURES tab.

14. Click on the PROPERTIES tab ❺. The properties of the analytic index are shown here ❻. The system then assigns a name to the InfoProvider of the analytic index. The naming convention is prefixed by "@3". In our case, our analytic index name is BWSD_HAP1, and hence the name of the InfoProvider is @3BWSD_HAP1.

15. Click on the DATA tab ❼.

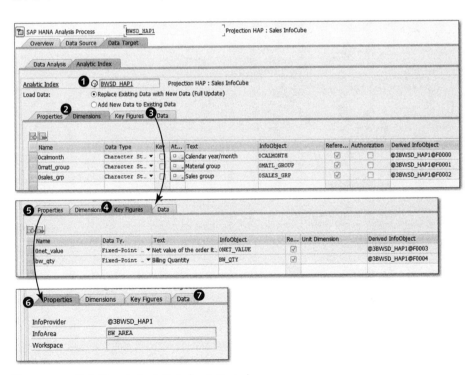

Figure 15.33 Data Target: Analytic Index Activated

16. As shown in ❶ of Figure 15.34, you're now on the DATA tab of the analytic index under DATA TARGET tab of HAP. The NUMBER OF RECORDS ❷ column is 0 because the HAP still isn't executed. Only after execution does the HAP read the data from the DataSource, pass through data analysis (function/script or procedure), and store in the data target. Now, let's execute it by clicking on the EXECUTE SYNCHRONOUSLY icon ❸. This action opens the INFORMATION MESSAGE dialog box, as shown in Figure 15.34. It informs you about the start of the HAP's execution, the number of rows updated or inserted, and successful execution of the HAP.

17. Click on CONTINUE ❹.

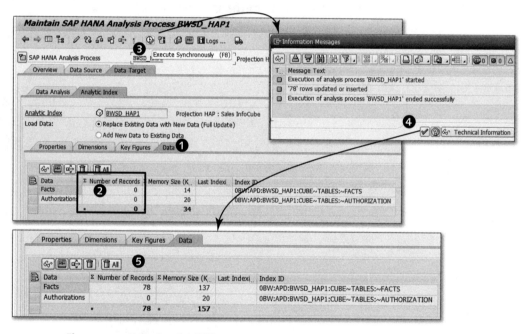

Figure 15.34 Executing the HAP

In the DATA tab ❺, the NUMBER OF RECORDS column for FACTS shows 78 (see Figure 15.34). We've successfully completed the configuration and execution of the HAP.

> **Note**
>
> You may also include the execution of the HAP in the process chain.

As shown in ❶ of Figure 15.35, you can see that newly created HAP BWSD_HAP1 is available in the DATA WAREHOUSING WORKBENCH screen.

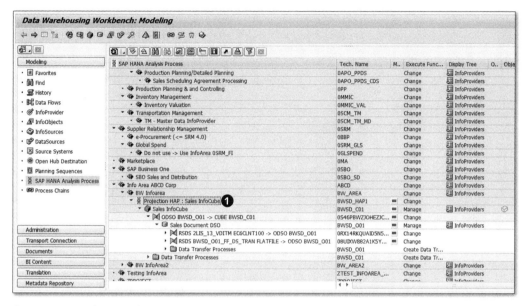

Figure 15.35 Newly Created HAP

15.5 Summary

This chapter briefly explained a few advanced features of SAP BW: Open Hub, the Analysis Process Designer and analytical indexes, remodeling, and the SAP HANA analysis process.

This concludes the book's main content, but turn to the appendices for additional information about metadata related to ABCD Corp.

Appendices

A   ABCD Corp. Case Study Data

Marketing Region	Country	Market Code
AMERICA	USA	NA
AMERICA	Canada	NA
EUROPE	UK	EU
EUROPE	Germany	EU
EUROPE	France	EU
ASIA-PACIFIC	China	APAC
ASIA-PACIFIC	India	APAC
ASIA-PACIFIC	Singapore	APAC
ASIA-PACIFIC	Australia	APAC
ASIA-PACIFIC	Japan	APAC
ASIA-PACIFIC	Saudi Arabia	APAC
ASIA-PACIFIC	South Africa	APAC
AMERICA	Mexico	NA

Table A.1 Countries in the Marketing Regions

Plant Location	Plant Code
USA	US
Germany	GR
China	CN
India	IN

Table A.2 Plants

Customer Code	Customer Name	Customer Group	City	Contact Name	Country
100017	Consumer Electronic Store	Store	Adeleaide	Georg Pipps	Australia
100071	Sound Systems	Store	Perth	Roland Mendel	Australia
100042	James	Store	Charleroi	Pascale Cartrain	Belgium
100051	Mike	Store	Bruxelles	Catherine Dewey	Belgium
100015	Comércio Mineiro	Store	São Paulo	Pedro Afonso	Brazil
100023	Familia Arquibaldo	Store	São Paulo	Aria Cruz	Brazil
100033	Gourmet Lanchonetes	Store	Campinas	André Fonseca	Brazil
100037	Hanari Carnes	Store	Rio de Janeiro	Mario Pontes	Brazil
100059	Que Delícia	Store	Rio de Janeiro	Bernardo Batista	Brazil
100060	Queen Cozinha	Store	São Paulo	Lúcia Carvalho	Brazil
100064	Ricardo Adocicados	Store	Rio de Janeiro	Janete Limeira	Brazil
100080	Tradição Hipermercados	Store	São Paulo	Anabela Domingues	Brazil
100088	Wellington Importadora	Store	Resende	Paula Parente	Brazil
100035	Great Eastern	Store	Tsawassen	Elizabeth Lincoln	Canada
100050	Mère Paillarde	Store	Montréal	Jean Fresnière	Canada
100082	Trans Canada	Store	Vancouver	Yoshi Tannamuri	Canada
100070	Simons	Store	København	Jytte Petersen	Denmark

Table A.3 Customers

Customer Code	Customer Name	Customer Group	City	Contact Name	Country
100083	Vaffeljernet	Store	Århus	Palle Ibsen	Denmark
100087	Wartian Herkku	Store	Oulu	Pirkko Koskitalo	Finland
100090	Wilman Kala	Store	Helsinki	Matti Karttunen	Finland
100009	Blondel père et fils	Store	Strasbourg	Frédérique Citeaux	France
100011	Bon app'	Store	Marseille	Laurence Lebihan	France
100021	Du monde entier	Store	Nantes	Janine Labrune	France
100025	Folies gourmandes	Store	Lille	Martine Rancé	France
100027	France restauration	Store	Nantes	Carine Schmitt	France
100044	La corne d'abondance	Store	Versailles	Daniel Tonini	France
100045	La maison d'Asie	Store	Toulouse	Annette Roulet	France
100056	Paris spécialités	Store	Paris	Marie Bertrand	France
100072	Spécialités du monde	Store	Paris	Dominique Perrier	France
100084	Victuailles en stock	Store	Lyon	Mary Saveley	France
100085	Vins et alcools Chevalier	Store	Reims	Paul Henriot	France
100001	Alfreds Futterkiste	Store	Berlin	Maria Anders	Germany
100008	Blauer See Delikatessen	Store	Mannheim	Hanna Moos	Germany
100019	Die Wandernde Kuh	Store	Stuttgart	Rita Müller	Germany

Table A.3 Customers (Cont.)

Customer Code	Customer Name	Customer Group	City	Contact Name	Country
100020	Drachenblut Delikatessen	Store	Aachen	Sven Ottlieb	Germany
100029	Frankenversand	Store	München	Peter Franken	Germany
100043	Königlich Essen	Store	Brandenburg	Philip Cramer	Germany
100046	Lehmanns Marktstand	Store	Frankfurt a.M.	Renate Messner	Germany
100052	Morgenstern Gesundkost	Store	Leipzig	Alexander Feuer	Germany
100054	Ottilies Käse-laden	Store	Köln	Henriette Pfalzheim	Germany
100061	QUICK-Stop	Store	Cunewalde	Horst Kloss	Germany
100078	Toms Spezialitäten	Store	Münster	Karin Josephs	Germany
100007	Bharat Elec-tronics Ltd.	Retail Chain	Mumbai	Bharat Patel	India
100055	Palekar & Sons	Store	Delhi	Amol Palekar	India
100074	SWS Associates	Store	Bangalore	S. W. Shiralkar	India
100040	Hungry Owl All-Night Grocers	Store	Cork	Patricia McKenna	Ireland
100028	Franchi S.p.A.	Store	Torino	Paolo Accorti	Italy
100049	Magazzini Alimentari Riuniti	Store	Bergamo	Giovanni Rovelli	Italy
100063	Reggiani Caseifici	Store	Reggio Emilia	Maurizio Moroni	Italy
100002	Ana Trujillo Emparedados y helados	Store	México D.F.	Ana Trujillo	Mexico
100003	Antonio Moreno Taquería	Store	México D.F.	Antonio Moreno	Mexico

Table A.3 Customers (Cont.)

Customer Code	Customer Name	Customer Group	City	Contact Name	Country
100013	Centro comercial Moctezuma	Store	México D.F.	Francisco Chang	Mexico
100036	GROSELLA-Restaurante	Store	México D.F.	Manuel Pereira	Mexico
100038	HILARIÓN-Abastos	Store	México D.F.	Carlos Hernández	Mexico
100047	LILA-Super-mercado	Store	México D.F.	Carlos González	Mexico
100048	LINO-Delicateses	Store	México D.F.	Felipe Izquierdo	Mexico
100057	Pericles Comidas clásicas	Store	México D.F.	Guillermo Fernández	Mexico
100079	Tortuga Restaurante	Store	México D.F.	Miguel Angel Paolino	Mexico
100067	Santé Gourmet	Store	Stavern	Jonas Bergulfsen	Norway
100091	Wolski Zajazd	Store	Warszawa	Zbyszek Piestrze-niewicz	Poland
100030	Furia Bacalhau e Frutos do Mar	Store	Lisboa	Lino Rodriguez	Portugal
100058	Princesa Isabel Vinhos	Store	Lisboa	Isabel de Castro	Portugal
100010	Bólido Comidas preparadas	Store	Madrid	Martín Sommer	Spain
100024	FISSA Fabrica Inter. Salchi-chas S.A.	Store	Madrid	Diego Roel	Spain
100031	Galería del gastrónomo	Store	Barcelona	Eduardo Saavedra	Spain
100032	Godos Cocina Típica	Store	Sevilla	José Pedro Freyre	Spain

Table A.3 Customers (Cont.)

817

Customer Code	Customer Name	Customer Group	City	Contact Name	Country
100066	Romero y tomillo	Store	Madrid	Alejandra Camino	Spain
100005	Berglunds snabbköp	Store	Luleå	Christina Berglund	Sweden
100026	Folk och fä HB	Store	Bräcke	Maria Larsson	Sweden
100014	Chop-suey Chinese	Store	Bern	Yang Wang	Switzerland
100065	Richter Supermarket	Store	Genève	Michael Holz	Switzerland
100004	Around the Horn	Store	London	Thomas Hardy	UK
100012	B's Beverages	Store	London	Victoria Ashworth	UK
100016	Consolidated Holdings	Store	London	Elizabeth Brown	UK
100022	Eastern Connection	Store	London	Ann Devon	UK
100041	Island Trading	Store	Cowes	Helen Ben-nett	UK
100053	North/South	Store	London	Simon Crowther	UK
100069	Seven Seas Imports	Store	London	Hari Kumar	UK
100006	Best Buy	Retail Chain	Portland	Fran Wilson	USA
100018	Costco	Retail Chain	Anchorage	Rene Phillips	USA
100034	Great Audio Systems	Store	Eugene	Howard Snyder	USA
100039	Hungry Coyote Import Store	Store	Elgin	Yoshi Latimer	USA
100062	Rattlesnake Canyon Grocery	Store	Albuquerque	Paula Wilson	USA

Table A.3 Customers (Cont.)

Customer Code	Customer Name	Customer Group	City	Contact Name	Country
100068	Save-a-lot Markets	Store	Boise	Jose Pavarotti	USA
100073	Home Depot	Retail Chain	Washington	Abraham Lincoln	USA
100075	Target	Retail Chain	Walla Walla	John Steel	USA
100076	The Big Cheese	Store	Portland	Liz Nixon	USA
100077	The Cracker Box	Store	Butte	Liu Wong	USA
100081	Trail's Head Gourmet Provisioners	Store	Kirkland	Helvetius Nagy	USA
100086	Walmart	Retail Chain	San Francisco	Jaime Yorres	USA
100089	White Clover Markets	Store	Seattle	Karl Jablonski	USA

Table A.3 Customers (Cont.)

Customer Group Code	Customer Group Name
ST	Store
RC	Retail Chain

Table A.4 Customer Groups

Product Code	Product Name	Product Range Name (Code)	Product Group Code
31000	Compact Cassette	Consumer Electronics	AUDIO
31500	DVD Player	Consumer Electronics	AUDIO
5200	Cassette – Answering Mc	Consumer Electronics	AUDIO
38000	MP4 Player	Consumer Electronics	AUDIO
37500	Home Theatre	Consumer Electronics	AUDIO
37800	Personal Stereo	Consumer Electronics	AUDIO
31300	Compact Disc	Consumer Electronics	AUDIO

Table A.5 Products

Product Code	Product Name	Product Range Name (Code)	Product Group Code
31400	DVD	Consumer Electronics	AUDIO
5000	Answering Machine	Consumer Electronics	DIGITAL
5400	Answering Machine Battery	Consumer Electronics	DIGITAL
5300	Answering Machine Charger	Consumer Electronics	DIGITAL
5450	Answering Machine Stand	Consumer Electronics	DIGITAL
2008	Answering Machine Extra Cassette	Consumer Electronics	DIGITAL
5500	Answering Machine Extra Cord	Consumer Electronics	DIGITAL
5510	Answering Machine Extra Handset	Consumer Electronics	DIGITAL
1009	Dictaphone Battery	Consumer Electronics	DIGITAL
1000	Dictaphone Pouch	Consumer Electronics	DIGITAL
1005	Dictaphone Charger	Consumer Electronics	DIGITAL
93000	Desktop PC	Consumer Electronics	PC
93500	Laptop PC	Consumer Electronics	PC
38300	Mobile Phone	Consumer Electronics	MOBILE
8148055	Color TV	Domestic Appliances	HOME
42000	LCD TV	Domestic Appliances	HOME
81460	Air Conditioner	Domestic Appliances	HOME
61000	Refrigerator	Domestic Appliances	HOME
21000	Video Camera	Domestic Appliances	HOME
63000	Dish Washer	Domestic Appliances	HOME
92000	Electric Shaving Machine	Consumer Lifestyle	PERSONAL
92500	Electric Toothbrushes	Consumer Lifestyle	PERSONAL
2009	Answering Machine Cord	Consumer Electronics	ACC
5000	Battery	Consumer Electronics	ACC

Table A.5 Products (Cont.)

Product Group Code	Product Group Name
AUDIO	Audio Systems and Equipments
DIGITAL	Digital Audio/Video Systems
HOME	Home Appliances
PERSONAL	Personal Systems
ACC	Accessories

Table A.6 Product Groups

Product Range Group Code	Product Range Group Name
CE	Consumer Electronics
DA	Domestic Appliances
CL	Consumer Lifestyle

Table A.7 Product Range Groups

Selling Channel Code	Selling Channel Name
DR	Direct
IT	Internet

Table A.8 Selling Channels

Billing Document Code	Type of Transaction
CR	On Credit
CH	On Cash

Table A.9 Types of Transactions

Billing Document Category Code	Type of Billing Transaction
DOM	Customer within USA
EX	Customer outside USA

Table A.10 Billing Types

Billing Value Limit	Billing Value Indicator Codes
Item without any cost	000
Item value $ 10000 USD	001
Item value , 10000 USD	002

Table A.11 Billing Value Indicators

B   Definitions of Additional InfoObjects for ABCD Corp.

For the example company discussed in this book, ABCD Corp., we have defined specific business requirements for sales analysis. If you want to develop the solutions to these requirements in your own system, you will need to create all essential objects. In Chapter 3, we give step-by-step instructions on how to create a number of these InfoObjects; in this appendix, we provide screenshots that show how to create the rest of them.

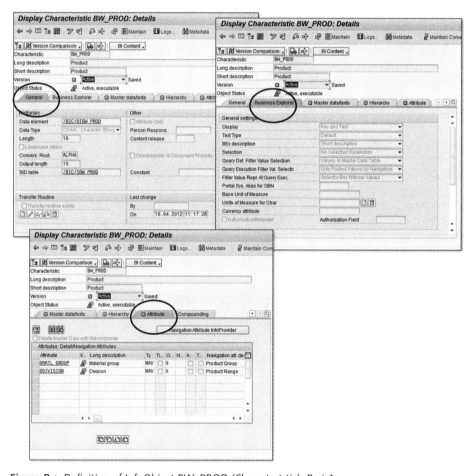

Figure B.1 Definition of InfoObject BW_PROD (Characteristic): Part 1

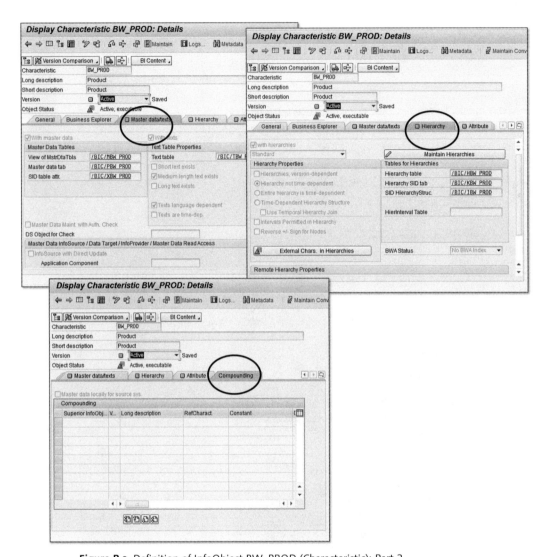

Figure B.2 Definition of InfoObject BW_PROD (Characteristic): Part 2

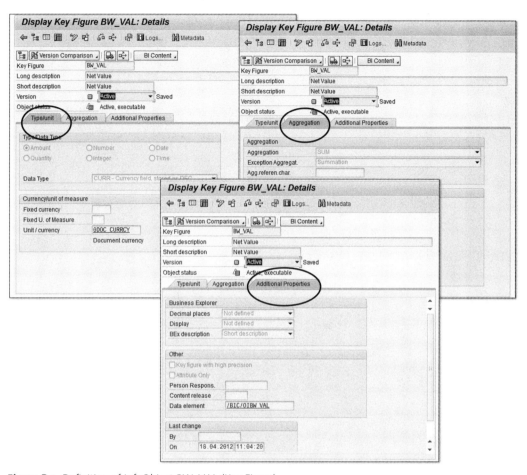

Figure B.3 Definition of InfoObject BW_VAL (Key Figure)

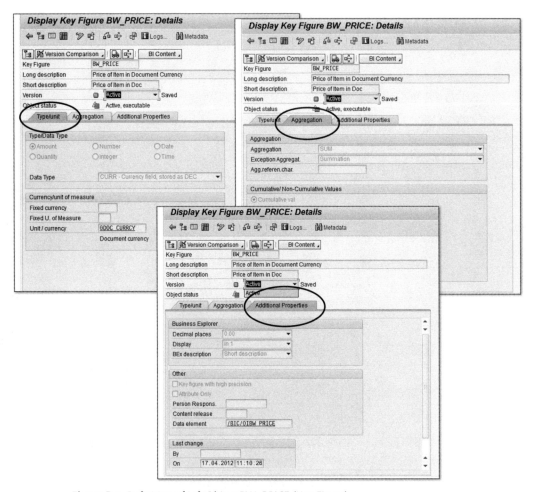

Figure B.4 Definition of InfoObject BW_PRICE (Key Figure)

C   Important Transaction Codes

SAP BW Overview

- Transaction /NEX: Close All Sessions and Exit Application
- Transaction RSA1: Data Warehousing Workbench

InfoObjects and Master Data

- Transaction RSA14: Data Warehousing Workbench (InfoObjects Tree)
- Transaction RSD1/RSD2/RSD3/RSD4: InfoObject Maintenance
- Transaction RSDIOBC: Edit InfoObject Catalog

DataStore Objects

- Transaction RSA11: Data Warehousing Workbench (InfoProviders Tree)
- Transaction RSDODS: Edit DataStore Object
- Transaction RSODSO_SETTINGS: Maintenance of Runtime Parameters for DSO

InfoCube

- Transaction LISTCUBE: List Viewer for InfoCubes
- Transaction LISTSCHEMA: Show InfoCube Schema
- Transaction RSDCUBE: Start: InfoCube Editing

InfoProviders

- Transaction RSDMPRO: Edit MultiProvider
- Transaction RSISET: Edit InfoSet

Extraction, Transformation, and Loading

- Transaction RSA2: DataSource Repository
- Transaction RSA5: Installation of DataSource from Business Content
- Transaction RSA12: Data Warehousing Workbench (InfoSource Tree)

▶ Transaction RSA13: Data Warehousing Workbench (Source System Tree)

▶ Transaction RSA15: Data Warehousing Workbench (DataSource Tree)

▶ Transaction RSDL: DB Connect: Check Program for the Connection

Extraction from SAP Systems

▶ Transaction LBWE: Logistics Cockpit Maintenance

▶ Transaction LBWG: Deletion of Setup Data

▶ Transaction RSA3: Test DataSource Extractor Checker

▶ Transaction RSA5: Installation of DataSource from Business Content

▶ Transaction RSA6: Maintain DataSources

▶ Transaction RSA7: BW Delta Queue Maintenance

▶ Transaction RSA8: DataSource Repository

▶ Transaction RSA9: Transfer Application Components

▶ Transaction RSO2: Create Generic DataSource

▶ Transaction SBIW: Display IMG (Settings for Data Transfer to BW)

Creating Queries, Reporting, and Analysis

▶ Transaction CMOD: Project Management for SAP Enhancements

▶ Transaction RRC1: Create Currency Conversion Type

▶ Transaction RRC2: Edit Currency Conversion Type

▶ Transaction RRC3: Display Currency Translation Type

▶ Transaction RRMX: Start BEx Analyzer

▶ Transaction RSBBS: Maintain Sender/Receiver Assignment (RRI)

▶ Transaction RSCRM_BAPI: Generation of Query Extracts

▶ Transaction RSRT: Query Monitor

▶ Transaction RSWSP: Edit Workspace

▶ Transaction RSWSPW: Mass Maintenance of Workspaces

▶ Transaction RSZC: Copying Queries Between InfoCubes

▶ Transaction RSZDELETE: Deletion of Query Objects

Integrated Planning

▸ Transaction RSPLAN: Modeling BI Integrated Planning

▸ Transaction RSPLF1: Start: Function Type Editing

▸ Transaction RSPLSE: BI Planning: Lock Management

Administration and Monitoring

▸ Transaction RSPC: Process Chain Maintenance

▸ Transaction RSPC1: Process Chain Display

▸ Transaction RSPC2: Process Chain via Process

▸ Transaction RSPCM: Monitor Daily Process Chains

▸ Transaction RSPC_RESTART: Restart Process Chain Run

▸ Transaction SE10: Transport Organizer

▸ Transaction SE11: ABAP Dictionary Maintenance

▸ Transaction SE16: Data Browser

▸ Transaction SE37: ABAP Function Modules

▸ Transaction SE38: ABAP Editor

▸ Transaction SE80: Object Navigator

▸ Transaction SM12: Display and Delete Locks

▸ Transaction SM21: Online System Log Analysis

▸ Transaction SM37: Overview of Job Selection

▸ Transaction SM50: Work Process Overview

▸ Transaction SM51: List of SAP Systems

▸ Transaction SM59: RFC Destinations (Display/Maintain)

▸ Transaction ST03N: Workload and Performance Statistics

▸ Transaction ST22: ABAP Dump Analysis

Customizing Settings

▸ Transaction RSCUSTA: Maintain BW Settings

▸ Transaction RSCUSTA2: ODS Settings

- Transaction RSCUSTV1: BW Customizing – View 1

- Transaction RSCUSTV2: BW Customizing – View 2

- Transaction RSCUSTV3: BW Customizing – View 3

- Transaction RSCUSTV4: BW Customizing – View 4

- Transaction RSCUSTV5: BW Customizing – View 5

- Transaction RSCUSTV6: BW Customizing – View 6

- Transaction RSCUSTV7: BW Customizing – View 7

- Transaction RSCUSTV8: BW Customizing – View 8

- Transaction RSCUSTV9: BW Customizing – View 9

- Transaction RSCUSTV10: BW Customizing – View 10

- Transaction RSCUSTV11: BW Customizing – View 11

- Transaction RSCUSTV12: Microsoft Analysis Services

- Transaction RSCUSTV13: RRI Settings for Web Reporting

- Transaction RSCUSTV14: OLAP: Cache Parameters

- Transaction RSCUSTV15: BW Customizing – View 15

- Transaction RSCUSTV16: BW Reporting

- Transaction RSCUSTV17: Settings: Currency Translation

- Transaction RSCUSTV18: DB Connect Settings

- Transaction RSCUSTV19: InfoSet Settings

- Transaction RSCUSTV21: BW Customizing – View 21

- Transaction RSCUSTV23: Analysis Authorization System

- Transaction RSCUSTV24: Quantity Conversion: Buffer Setting

- Transaction RSCUSTV25: Database Interface/Performance

- Transaction RSCUSTV26: Database Interface/Perf. (ORA)

- Transaction RSCUSTV27: Set Standard Web Templates

- Transaction RSCUSTV28: Determine Settings for Web Templates

- Transaction RSCUSTV29: Settings for Web Template

- Transaction RSCUSTV30: Load Distribution for Analys. Proc.

D   Important SAP Notes

SAP offers a number of online support applications, one of which is SAP Notes. SAP Notes help you avoid and correct errors in the SAP system. In this appendix, we have listed the SAP Notes that you will find the most relevant in the context of ABCD Corp. and SAP BW in general.

> **Caution**
>
> SAP is always updating and adding new SAP Notes based on recent product versions or to address newly found errors. You should therefore always refer to the latest version of any SAP Note that is available at *http://service.sap.com/notes*.

SAP Note Number	SAP Note Name
984229	F4 Modes for Input Help as of SAP NetWeaver 2004s BI
350024	BW-OLTP-APCO: Frequently Asked Questions (FAQ)
1013140	BI Frontend/BW Add-on: General Information and Limitations
1013201	Hardware and Software Requirement for BI Standalone Frontend
160317	Customer Namespace for Objects in the Business Warehouse
1646399	BI Content Activation Workbench: Additional Information
1056259	Collective Note: Performance of BI Planning
1009497	UD Connect: How to Update JDBC Driver
919694	UD Connect: JDBC Limitations and Performance
1050618	Problem Analysis When You Use a DTP to Load Master Data
130253	General Tips on Uploading Transaction Data to BW
928044	BI Lock Server
396647	FAQ: V3 Update: Questions and Answers
1607601	FAQ: Delta Errors
380078	FAQ: BW Delta Queue (RSA7): Questions and Answers
873694	Consulting: Delta Repeat and Status in Monitor/Data Target
1335058	BEx Analyzer: F4 Help, Read Mode Setting Value
121291	Tips and Tricks for the Use of Variables
1053310	Report-Report Interface: Application Rules
124662	Description of the Aggregation

SAP Note Number	SAP Note Name
152638	Aggregation Settings in Calculated Key Figures
460255	Information about Aggregation, Cumulation, Results Row
407260	FAQs: Compression of InfoCubes
903886	Hierarchy and Attribute Change Run
820183	New Authorization Concept in BI
846839	Types of Authorizations in BW
177875	Authorizations for Analyzing OLAP Problems
934848	Collective Note: (FAQ) BI Administration Cockpit
1025307	Composite Note for NW2004s Performance: Reporting
130696	Performance Trace in BW
309955	BW Statistics: Questions, Answers, and Errors
731682	Backup in BW and OLTP: Experiences, Risks, and Recommendations
1599602	FAQ: BW System Performance
751577	APD-FAQ: DataSource Query
1591837	How to Analyze Query Results
1709838	BW 7.3 on HANA: System Copy Using Backup and Recovery
1715048	BW 7.3 New Features for Installation or Migration

E   The Authors

Amol Palekar is director of Analytics and Service Delivery at TekLink International Inc. He leads the Application Management Services practice in TekLink, which focuses on global delivery engagements. Amol has led the SAP BI Architecture Council and SAP BI Center of Excellence at the companies where he has worked in the past. He has worked on BI programs for several Fortune 500 companies and has led BI project teams of various sizes for companies in the manufacturing, retail, CPG, automotive, and telecom industries. Amol is also a trainer and a regular speaker on the subject of BI, and he is recognized for his best-selling books on SAP BI and supply chain analytics.

Bharat Patel has almost 20 years of IT experience, which covers the entire lifecycle management of data warehousing solutions, from evaluation and identification to upgrade and retirement. He is a regular faculty member at SAP Partner Academy and SAP Labs in India, and he has published another book and many technical articles on SAP BW. He currently manages a large and complex SAP BW system at Bharat Petroleum Corp. Ltd., a Fortune 500 oil company.

Shreekant Shiralkar is a senior management professional with experience in leading and managing business functions, as well as technology consulting. In a career spanning more than 27 years, he established, developed, and diversified business units for Fortune 500 companies. He has mentored authors, published best-selling books and white papers on technology, and holds patents for technology and services. Shreekant is presently leading the SAP analytic practice globally for a leading technology company.

Index

N

O

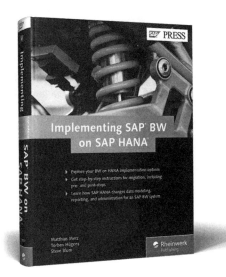

- ▶ Explore your SAP BW on SAP HANA implementation options
- ▶ Get step-by-step instructions for migration, including pre- and post-steps
- ▶ Learn how SAP HANA changes data modeling, reporting, and administration for an SAP BW system

Merz, Hügens, Blum

Implementing SAP BW on SAP HANA

If you're making the leap from SAP BW to SAP HANA, this book is your indispensable companion. Thanks to detailed pre-migration and post-migration steps, as well as a complete guide to the actual migration process, it's never been easier to HANA-ify your SAP BW system. Once your migration is complete, learn everything you need to know about data modeling, reporting, and administration. Are you ready for the next generation of SAP BW?

470 pages, 2015, $79.95/€79.95
ISBN 978-1-4932-1003-9
www.sap-press.com/3609

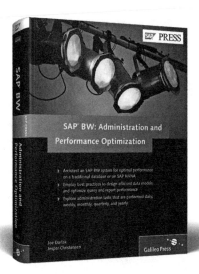

► Architect an SAP BW system for optimal performance on a traditional database or on SAP HANA

► Employ best practices to design efficient data models and optimize query and report performance

► Explore administration tasks that are performed daily, weekly, monthly, quarterly, and yearly

Joe Darlak, Jesper Christensen

SAP BW: Administration and Performance Optimization

This long-awaited resource offers the daily, weekly, monthly, quarterly, and yearly tasks that will make your SAP BW system shine. Walk through system setup and configuration to lay a sound foundation for effective data storage, and then employ performance tuning techniques to optimize system performance.

652 pages, 2014, $79.95/€79.95
ISBN 978-1-59229-853-2
www.sap-press.com/3341

- ▶ Get up to speed on the next generation of SAP business intelligence
- ▶ Learn how to model and visualize data to tell a story
- ▶ Find out about options for desktop, mobile, and cloud deployment

Christian Ah-Soon, Peter Snowdon

Getting Started with SAP Lumira

The Comprehensive Guide

What story does your data tell? See what SAP Lumira can do and how to identify trends and find hidden insights in your business data. Get the details on progressing from data acquisitions to data manipulation to data visualization so you can add some color to your data. See how SAP Lumira fits into existing BI landscapes and which administration options are best for each setup. This introduction to SAP Lumira will help make each picture—or chart—worth a thousand words.

540 pages, 2015, $69.95/€69.95
ISBN 978-1-4932-1033-6
www.sap-press.com/3645

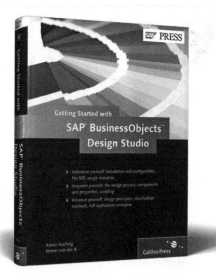

- ▶ Introduce yourself: installation and configuration, the IDE, usage scenarios

- ▶ Acquaint yourself: the design process, components and properties, scripting

- ▶ Advance yourself: design principles, visualization methods, full application examples

Xavier Hacking, Jeroen van der A

Getting Started with SAP BusinessObjects Design Studio

There's a new dashboard design kid on the block, and it's time you introduced yourself. How is Design Studio different from BEx WAD and Dashboards, and what can it do? This book will answer these questions, and will teach you how to use the tool to start building effective, interactive dashboards. What are you waiting for?

468 pages, 2014, $69.95/€69.95
ISBN 978-1-59229-895-2
www.sap-press.com/3410

Interested in reading more?

Please visit our website for all new
book and e-book releases from SAP PRESS.

www.sap-press.com